Praise for
A Documentary History of the United States

"Richard Heffner has assembled a portable canon of American documents that take us across the depth and breadth of our national experience. Here is fertile soil for exploring our past and imagining our future. Present crises notwithstanding, you cannot spend time within these pages and be skeptical of our capacity to overcome, survive, and thrive in the endless, vexing, and robust pursuit of a more perfect union."

—Bill Moyers

"For those who want the raw materials of American history, here is the invaluable source. An indispensable contribution to the understanding of our heritage."

—Robert A. Caro, author of the Pulitzer Prize–winning *The Power Broker* and the #1 *New York Times* bestseller *Master of the Senate*

"Whether you are a student of American history, a casual browser, or a speaker in need of a timely quote, you will benefit from having ready access to this excellent collection of important documents."

—Derek Bok, Emeritus President and the 300th Anniversary University Professor, Harvard University

"Words make history, and Richard Heffner has assembled the most important words that have defined America's journey from the Revolution to the present. Imaginatively selected and judiciously annotated, the documents in this collection capture the full range of the nation's colorful, consequential, and often contentious history. Simply the best such anthology available."

—David M. Kennedy, author of the Pulitzer Prize–winning *Freedom from Fear*

"A superb collection of documents, skillfully edited, with an edifying introduction to each chapter. An indispensable reference work for history buffs."

—Kenneth M. Stampp, author of *And the War Came*

continued . . .

"*A Documentary History of the United States* presents the vital documents of American history with incisive and informed commentary—an invaluable resource for the student, the teacher, and the history buff."

—Arthur M. Schlesinger, Jr., Pulitzer Prize and National Book award–winning author of *A Thousand Days* and *A Life in the 20th Century*

"Nothing compares to reading the word spoken or written at the great turning points. By compiling and introducing this collection of essential documents, Richard Heffner has done a wonderful service."

—Sylvia Nasar, author of *A Beautiful Mind*

"Not only a superb collection of notable documents but *history* in its most authentic form, as written by our greatest leaders, now creatively presented by a distinguished and discriminating historian."

—James MacGregor Burns, author of the Pulitzer Prize– and National Book Award–winning *Roosevelt: The Soldier of Freedom*

WORDS THAT MADE HISTORY

Here are the words of noted Americans in many of the major documents that have shaped and reflected American history—collected in one inexpensive volume, ideal for both student and general reader.

In addition to selecting and editing the actual texts of these speeches and other writings, historian Richard D. Heffner has written a series of brief interpolatory passages that explains the significance of these documents, together with their place in the events and developments of American history.

From these documents and commentaries, which range from the Declaration of Independence to the National Organization for Women's (NOW's) 1966 "Statement of Purpose," from Jefferson's First Inaugural Address to Obama's, from Walt Whitman's "Democratic Vistas" to Edward R. Murrow on television in American life, from Marbury v. Madison to Roe v. Wade, from major Lincoln and FDR speeches to Barack Obama's, the social, political, and intellectual patterns of American history through 9/11, the Bush/Cheney years, and the election of the first African-American as President of the United States emerge in sharp focus.

Both as a sourcebook of hard-to-find basic documents and as a stimulating guide to a fuller understanding of America's past and present, *A Documentary History of the United States* is an invaluable volume for every intelligent reader.

Richard D. Heffner received his A.B. and M.A. from Columbia University and has taught history and political science at the University of California, Sarah Lawrence College, the New School for Social Research, and NYU. University Professor of Communications and Public Policy at Rutgers since 1964, he also produces and moderates his prizewinning weekly public television series, *Richard Heffner's Open Mind*, which he began in 1956, and for twenty years was chairman of the motion picture industry's film-rating system. In addition to *A Documentary History of the United States*, Mr. Heffner has edited and introduced the Signet Classics edition of Alexis de Tocqueville's *Democracy in America*. Random House/Schocken Books published his *Conversations with Elie Wiesel*. Carroll & Graf published his *As they Saw It: A Conversational History of Modern America*. He is joined now by Harvard undergraduate and online journalist **Alexander Heffner**.

A DOCUMENTARY HISTORY OF THE UNITED STATES

RICHARD D. HEFFNER

WITH ALEXANDER HEFFNER

Expanded and Updated
Eighth Edition

A SIGNET BOOK

SIGNET
Published by New American Library, a division of
Penguin Group (USA) Inc., 375 Hudson Street,
New York, New York 10014, USA
Penguin Group (Canada), 90 Eglinton Avenue East, Suite 700, Toronto,
Ontario M4P 2Y3, Canada (a division of Pearson Penguin Canada Inc.)
Penguin Books Ltd., 80 Strand, London WC2R 0RL, England
Penguin Ireland, 25 St. Stephen's Green, Dublin 2,
Ireland (a division of Penguin Books Ltd.)
Penguin Group (Australia), 250 Camberwell Road, Camberwell, Victoria 3124,
Australia (a division of Pearson Australia Group Pty. Ltd.)
Penguin Books India Pvt. Ltd., 11 Community Centre, Panchsheel Park,
New Delhi – 110 017, India
Penguin Group (NZ), 67 Apollo Drive, Rosedale, North Shore 0632,
New Zealand (a division of Pearson New Zealand Ltd.)
Penguin Books (South Africa) (Pty.) Ltd., 24 Sturdee Avenue,
Rosebank, Johannesburg 2196, South Africa

Penguin Books Ltd., Registered Offices:
80 Strand, London WC2R 0RL, England

First published by Signet, an imprint of New American Library, a division of Penguin Group (USA) Inc. The seventh edition of this title was previously published in a Signet edition. The first six editions of this title were previously published in Mentor editions.

First Printing (Eighth Edition), October 2009
10 9 8 7 6 5 4 3 2

To my Mother and Father
with love, honor, and gratitude

—Richard D. Heffner, 1952

CONTENTS

FOREWORD

In this brief history of the United States many of the major sources of American political, economic, and intellectual life are presented essentially as they were written. For the sake of clarity, liberties have been taken with punctuation and spelling, and ellipses indicate that some passages have been omitted. But what in the broadest sense are many of the tangible and unquestioned raw materials of American history are objectively presented here for examination and evaluation, so that each reader becomes truly his own historian. On the other hand, the connective commentary which places the various documents in their historical context is necessarily subjective, for the past as "fact" is to be clearly distinguished from recorded history, which is largely "opinion." Thus the commentary, as the late Charles A. Beard characterized written history generally, is preeminently an "act of faith" which embodies not the past itself, but simply the author's own changeable understanding of the sequence, motivation, and conceptual meaning of certain events in the American past.

In innumerable ways *A Documentary History of the United States* is a joint venture, and I wish to express deepest appreciation to my many friends, students, colleagues, and teachers who aided so generously in its preparation. Special thanks to Edward McN. Burns and to Richard V. Chase, for their thoughtfulness, kindness, and thoroughness in reading and checking the original manuscript. Thanks also to Lawrence H. Chamberlain, Arthur W. Macmahon, Harry J. Carman, Allan Nevins, Eduard C. Lindeman, and Martin Levin for their criticisms and constant encouragement; to Marc Jaffe, my editor, for wisdom and patience beyond the call of duty; and always to Elaine, my wife, for everything.

—Richard D. Heffner

New York City
August 5, 1952

* * *

New documents have been added to the various editions of *A Documentary History of the United States.* Textual changes have also been made in the connective commentary to improve this edition and to bring it up to date. In all of these efforts I want to express my special gratitude to the indefatigable Daphne Doelger Dwyer, my longtime friend and associate, for her always insightful and generous assistance. My warmest thanks, too, to James Fabiano, Garrett Broad, Alex Rabinowitz, Sherine Aboelezz and Mary Sammons, who continue to find needles in haystacks, and to the many other students who for more than sixty years now have made teaching both a privilege and a joy.

I owe much to my friend and new editor, Tracy Bernstein, and to David Halpern of the Robbins Office, my first and only literary agent, whose wit, wisdom, and integrity I respect and admire more than I could possibly indicate.

Most important of all, of course, there is my profound hope that Dan and Beth, Andy and Carla, and particularly my wonderful grandchildren—Alexander, Jeremy, Zachary, and Sophia—all find here much to cherish and to preserve. It is for them to do so.

I would express my pleasure and pride, too, that time spent so well at Andover and Harvard with such ventures in online journalism as *Scoop08* and *Scoop44* have further led grandson Alexander to share my devotion to Clio, the Muse of History, and to join me here in helping revise what has become our newly Expanded and Updated Eighth Edition of *A Documentary History of the United States.* In time, if he chooses, this always rewarding task will become his alone.

Lastly, in the first edition of this book, I thanked Elaine, my wife, "for everything." Now, nearly six decades later, I feel blessed to be able to do so again.

—RICHARD D. HEFFNER

New York City
August 5, 2009

A DOCUMENTARY HISTORY OF THE UNITED STATES

Chapter 1

A NEW NATION

What then is the American, this new man? . . . He is an American, who leaving behind him all his ancient prejudices and manners, receives new ones from the new mode of life he has embraced, the new government he obeys, and the new rank he holds. He becomes an American by being received in the broad lap of our great Alma Mater. *Here individuals of all nations are melted into a new race of men, whose labours and posterity will one day cause great changes in the world. . . . The American is a new man, who acts upon new principles; he must therefore entertain new ideas, and form new opinions. From involuntary idleness, servile dependence, penury, and useless labour, he has passed to toils of a very different nature, rewarded by ample subsistence.—This is an American. . . .* HECTOR ST. JOHN DE CRÈVECŒUR, 1782.

Freed from the tyrannical economic, political, and ecclesiastical restraints of the Old World, and blessed with a bountiful environment whose rich and abundant resources, varied climate, and vast domain imbued in him an unquestioned faith in his own future, the American was in truth a "new man." Yet the roots of American society were firmly implanted in the great traditions of Western civilization, and ultimately American nationality was as heavily indebted to its European heritage of ideas and mode of life as it was to the new environment. Indeed, in its inception and its development, American colonial history was clearly a reflection of European experiences. The discovery of America resulted from the breakup of the feudal system, the rise of the nation-state, the revival of commerce, and the search for trade routes to the fabulous riches of the East. Later, the long process of English colonization of the New World was motivated both by the quest for free religious expression stemming largely from the Protestant Reformation of the sixteenth century, and by that desire for economic opportunity which had its origins in the middle-class business ethic peculiar to the modern Western world.

The final chapter of American colonial history was also written abroad, for the restrictive policies of British mercantilism provided an economic impetus to the American Revolution, just as the natural rights philosophy of the European Enlightenment set its ideological framework. Mercantilism, an economic arm of the rising nationalism of the seventeenth and eighteenth centuries, had as its major objectives national self-sufficiency and prosperity for the dominant merchant and banking class. A favorable balance of trade was particularly important to the mercantilist doctrine, for if more goods and services were sold abroad than were imported, gold and silver would come into the country and the nation's total economic strength would be augmented rather than depleted. Each nation desired a favorable balance of trade, however, and so the great mercantilist powers of Europe soon turned to overseas possessions as a source of economic strength. For these colonies existed solely to be exploited by the mother country—to produce essential raw materials cheaply, to provide an unlimited market for surplus manufactured goods, and to offer a minimum of economic competition.

British colonial policy amply demonstrated the mother country's intention of molding her American possessions into this mercantilist pattern. To free herself from dependence upon foreign nations for needed raw materials, the Navigation Acts of the seventeenth and eighteenth centuries listed various "enumerated commodities" (such as sugar, tobacco, indigo, and naval stores) which the colonials had to export to England alone. And in an effort to retain exclusive control of the rapidly growing American markets for British manufactured goods, all foreign commodities bound for the colonies were required to pass through England, where prohibitive export duties and freight and handling charges made transshipment intolerably expensive. Competition by the industrious colonists themselves was nearly eliminated through laws such as the Woolens Act (1699), the Hat Act (1732), and the Iron Act (1750), which prohibited or discouraged local efforts at manufacturing.

Though mercantilism benefited the colonists in certain respects—generous bounties, for instance, were paid for indigo and badly needed naval stores, and a monopoly of the English tobacco market was insured to the American producer—the economic well-being of the colonies was for the most part harshly subordinated to the needs of the mother country. Even the Southern settlements, whose staple crops—such as tobacco—well suited them for the colonial role, were hard pressed by the one-sided mercantilist system. And by the eve of the American Revolution Thomas Jefferson estimated that a persistently unfavorable colonial balance of trade had placed at least half of the tobacco planters of Maryland and Virginia hopelessly in debt to British creditors. At the same time the various Navigation and Trade Acts attempted to restrict severely the trading, shipping, manufacturing, and other economic activities of the settlements in the North, where climate and soil were not capable of supporting the large-scale cultivation of staple crops for the home market. Yet the colonies prospered, at least in the New England and Middle Atlantic regions. Smuggling and other evasions of mercantilist measures were prevalent, and for long decades before the conclusion of the French and Indian War in 1763, the British were too thoroughly immersed in a bitter imperial rivalry with France to enforce their restrictive legislation.

With the defeat of France, however, the British were able to bring to an end the era of "salutary neglect" and to turn their full attention once again to strict enforcement of colonial policy. Besides, Parliament now strongly reasserted its right to legislate for colonials who had long known virtual independence and self-rule and who were well versed in the liberal philosophy of the eighteenth-century Enlightenment. Political discontent was thus added to economic dislocation, and economic grievances soon found expression in the loftiest principles of political liberty. Royal (and even Parliamentary) efforts to enforce mercantilist policies were damned as contrary not only to the rights of Englishmen, but to the "natural rights of man" as well, while the colonists' fundamental antipathy to taxation of any kind achieved immortality in the idealistic slogan "no taxation without representation." The British were unmoved by these protests and in rapid succession the Sugar Act (1764), the Currency Act (1764), the Stamp Act (1765), the Townshend Duties (1767), the Tea Act (1773), and the Intolerable Acts (1774) taxed and regulated the colonial economy and imposed the severest restrictions upon colonial self-government.

The colonists were quick to reply. A Stamp Act Congress met in October, 1765, to denounce the hated tax on newspapers, magazines, commercial papers, and other documents, and an organization of patriots known as the Sons of Liberty directly forced the resignation of nearly all of the imperial stamp agents. American merchants agreed not to import British merchandise until the tax was repealed, and many persons stoutly refused to buy any stamps at all. Even though colonial pressures finally effected the repeal of the Stamp Tax, the tide of unrest continued to rise. Americans more and more frequently joined together to oppose imperial measures; and after British soldiers had fired into a jeering Boston mob (the "Boston Massacre" of March, 1770) popular resentment increased tremendously. Non-importation agreements, "Committees of Correspondence" (which Samuel Adams of Massachusetts organized to inform patriots throughout the colonies of current affairs), the "Boston Tea Party" of December, 1773, and finally the First Continental Congress that met in Philadelphia in September, 1774—all of these actions marked a growing sentiment for independence and separation from the mother country. And though there were many who still opposed the final break with England, the Revolution began in earnest in April, 1775, at Lexington and at Concord Bridge, where "embattled farmers stood and fired the shot heard round the world."

Tom Paine's enormously popular and influential pamphlet, "Common Sense," published anonymously in January, 1776, quickly helped solidify Americans' rebellious spirit. And in June, 1776, a resolution that "these United Colonies are, and of right ought to be, free and independent states" was offered before the Second Continental Congress by Richard Henry Lee of Virginia. Then on July 4 the Congress formally adopted (with modifications) Thomas Jefferson's draft of the Declaration of Independence. The Declaration expressed certain fundamental precepts: that all men are equally endowed with the self-evident natural rights of life, liberty, and the pursuit of happiness, that civil government is merely an instrument to guarantee these rights within the framework of social order, that when government becomes tyrannical the social compact is broken and it is the "right of the people to alter or to abolish it." These were precepts which clearly embodied the political tenets of the European Enlightenment. Thus for Americans whose intellectual heritage was largely European, and whose free environment as well was conducive to libertarian ideas, the Declaration (as Jefferson himself later wrote) expressed not "new ideas altogether," but rather the "common sense of the matter . . . the harmonizing sentiment of the day." Preeminently it was an eloquent "expression of the American mind," and to those who cherished the democratic faith of their fathers it was to remain for all times the fountainhead of American ideology.

"Common Sense," *Tom Paine, 1776*

. . . In the following pages I offer nothing more than simple facts, plain arguments, and common sense: and have no other preliminaries to settle with the reader, than that he will divest himself of prejudice and prepossession, and suffer his reason and his feelings to determine for themselves: that he will put on, or rather that he will not put off, the true character of a man, and generously enlarge his views beyond the present day.

Volumes have been written on the subject of the struggle between England and America. Men of all ranks have embarked in the controversy, from different motives, and with various designs; but all have been ineffectual, and the period of debate is closed. Arms as the last resource decide the contest; the appeal was the choice of the King, and the Continent has accepted the challenge. . . .

The Sun never shined on a cause of greater worth. 'Tis not the affair of a City, a County, a Province, or a Kingdom; but of a Continent—of at least one-eighth part of the habitable Globe. 'Tis not the concern of a day, a year, or an age; posterity are virtually involved in the contest, and will be more or less affected even to the end of time, by the proceedings now. Now is the seed-time of Continental union, faith and honour. The least fracture now will be like a name engraved with the point of a pin on the tender rind of a young oak; the wound would enlarge with the tree, and posterity read in it full grown characters. . . .

I have heard it asserted by some, that as America has flourished under her former connection with Great Britain, the same connection is necessary towards her future happiness, and will always have the same effect. Nothing can be more fallacious than this kind of argument. We may as well assert that because a child has thrived upon milk, that it is never to have meat, or that the first twenty years of our lives is to become a precedent for the next twenty. But even this is admitting more than is true; for I answer roundly that America would have flourished as much, and probably much more, had no European power taken any notice of her. The commerce by which she hath enriched herself are the necessaries of life, and will always have a market while eating is the custom of Europe.

But she has protected us, say some. That she hath engrossed us is true, and defended the Continent at our expense as well as her own, is admitted; and she would have defended Turkey from the same motive, *viz.* for the sake of trade and dominion.

Alas! we have been long led away by ancient prejudices and made large sacrifices to superstition. We have boasted the protection of Great Britain, without considering, that her motive was *interest* not *attachment;* and that she did not protect us from *our enemies* on *our account;* but from *her enemies* on *her own account,* from those who had no quarrel with us on any *other account,* and who will always be our enemies on the *same account.* Let Britain waive her pretentions to the Continent, or the Continent throw off the dependence, and we should be at peace with France and Spain, were they at war with Britain. . . .

But Britain is the parent country, say some. Then the more shame upon her conduct. Even brutes do not devour their young, nor savages make war upon their families. . . . Europe, and not England, is the parent country of America. . . .

I challenge the warmest advocate for reconciliation to show a single advantage that this Continent can reap by being connected with Great Britain. I repeat the challenge; not a single advantage is derived. Our corn will fetch its price in any market in Europe, and our imported goods must be paid for, buy them where we will.

But the injuries and disadvantages which we sustain by that connection, are without number; and our duty to mankind at large, as well as to ourselves, instructs us to renounce the alliance: because, any submission to, or dependence on, Great Britain, tends directly to involve this Continent in European wars and quarrels, and set us at variance with nations who would otherwise seek our friendship, and against whom we have neither anger nor complaint. As Europe is our market for trade, we ought to form no partial connection with any part of it. It is the true interest of America to steer clear of European contentions, which she never can do, while, by her dependence on Britain, she is made the makeweight in the scale of British politics. . . .

'Tis repugnant to reason, to the universal order of things, to all examples from former ages, to suppose that this Continent can long remain subject to any external power. The most sanguine in Britain doth not think so. The utmost stretch of human wisdom cannot, at this time, compass a plan, short of separation, which can promise the Continent even a year's security. Reconciliation is *now* a fallacious dream. Nature hath deserted the connection, and art cannot supply her place. For, as Milton wisely expresses, "never can true reconcilement grow where wounds of deadly hate have pierced so deep." . . .

To talk of friendship with those in whom our reason forbids us to have faith, and our affections wounded tho' a thousand pores instruct us to detest, is madness and folly. Every day wears out the little remains of kindred between us and them; and can there be any reason to hope, that as the relationship expires, the affection will encrease, or that we shall agree better when we have ten times more and greater concerns to quarrel over than ever?

Ye that tell us of harmony and reconciliation, can ye restore to us the time that is past? Can ye give to prostitution its former innocence? neither can ye reconcile Britain and America. The last cord now is broken, the people of England are presenting addresses against us. There are injuries which nature cannot forgive; she would cease to be nature if she did. As well can the lover forgive the ravisher of his mistress, as the Continent forgive the murders of Britain. . . .

O! ye that love mankind! Ye that dare oppose not only the tyranny but the tyrant, stand forth! Every spot of the old world is overrun with oppression. Freedom hath been hunted round the Globe. Asia and Africa have long expelled her. Europe regards her like a stranger, and England hath given her warning to depart. O! receive the fugitive, and prepare in time an asylum for mankind. . . .

The Declaration of Independence, *1776*

In Congress, July 4, 1776
The unanimous Declaration of the thirteen United States of America

When in the course of human events, it becomes necessary for one people to dissolve the political bands which have connected them with another, and to assume among the powers of the earth, the separate and equal station to which the Laws of Nature and of Nature's God entitle them, a decent respect to the opinions of mankind requires that they should declare the causes which impel them to the separation.

We hold these truths to be self-evident, that all men are created equal, that they are endowed by their Creator with certain unalienable rights, that among these are life, liberty and the pursuit of happiness. That to secure these rights, governments are instituted among men, deriving their just powers from the consent of the governed. That whenever any form of government becomes destructive of these ends, it is the right of the people to alter or to abolish it, and to institute new government, laying its foundation on such principles and organizing its powers in such form, as to them shall seem most likely to effect their safety and happiness. Prudence, indeed, will dictate that governments long established should not be changed for light and transient causes; and accordingly all experience hath shown, that mankind are more disposed to suffer, while evils are sufferable, than to right themselves by abolishing the forms to which they are accustomed. But when a long train of abuses and usurpations, pursuing invariably the same object evinces a design to reduce them under absolute despotism, it is their right, it is their duty, to throw off such government, and to provide new guards for their future security. Such has been the patient sufferance of these Colonies; and such is now the necessity which constrains them to alter their former systems of government. The history of the present King of Great Britain is a history of repeated injuries and usurpations, all having in direct object the establishment of an absolute tyranny over these States. To prove this, let facts be submitted to a candid world.

He has refused his assent to laws, the most wholesome and necessary for the public good.

He has forbidden his Governors to pass laws of immediate and pressing importance, unless suspended in their operation till his assent should be obtained; and when so suspended, he has utterly neglected to attend to them.

He has refused to pass other laws for the accommodation of large districts of people, unless those people would relinquish the right of representation in the Legislature, a right inestimable to them and formidable to tyrants only.

He has called together legislative bodies at places unusual, uncomfortable, and distant from the depository of their public records, for the sole purpose of fatiguing them into compliance with his measures.

He has dissolved representative houses repeatedly, for opposing with manly firmness his invasions on the rights of the people.

He has refused for a long time, after such dissolutions, to cause others to be elected; whereby the legislative powers, incapable of annihilation, have returned to the people at large for their exercise; the State remaining in the meantime exposed to all the dangers of invasion from without and convulsions within.

He has endeavoured to prevent the population of these States; for that purpose obstructing the laws of naturalization of foreigners; refusing to pass others to encourage their migration hither, and raising the conditions of new appropriations of lands.

He has obstructed the administration of justice, by refusing his assent to laws for establishing judiciary powers.

He has made judges dependent on his will alone, for the tenure of their offices, and the amount and payment of their salaries.

He has erected a multitude of new offices, and sent hither swarms of officers to harass our people, and eat out their substance.

He has kept among us, in times of peace, standing armies without the consent of our Legislatures.

He has affected to render the military independent of and superior to the civil power.

He has combined with others to subject us to a jurisdiction foreign to our constitution, and unacknowledged by our laws; giving his assent to their acts of pretended legislation:

For quartering large bodies of armed troops among us:

For protecting them, by a mock trial, from punishment for any murders which they should commit on the inhabitants of these States:

For cutting off our trade with all parts of the world:

For imposing taxes on us without our consent:

For depriving us, in many cases, of the benefits of trial by jury:

For transporting us beyond seas to be tried for pretended offences:

For abolishing the free system of English laws in a

neighbouring Province, establishing therein an arbitrary government, and enlarging its boundaries so as to render it at once an example and fit instrument for introducing the same absolute rule into these Colonies:

For taking away our Charters, abolishing our most valuable laws, and altering fundamentally the forms of our governments:

For suspending our own Legislatures, and declaring themselves invested with power to legislate for us in all cases whatsoever.

He has abdicated government here, by declaring us out of his protection and waging war against us.

He has plundered our seas, ravaged our coasts, burnt our towns, and destroyed the lives of our people.

He is at this time transporting large armies of foreign mercenaries to complete the works of death, desolation and tyranny, already begun with circumstances of cruelty and perfidy scarcely paralleled in the most barbarous ages, and totally unworthy the head of a civilized nation.

He has constrained our fellow citizens taken captive on the high seas to bear arms against their country, to become the executioners of their friends and brethren, or to fall themselves by their hands.

He has excited domestic insurrections amongst us, and has endeavoured to bring on the inhabitants of our frontiers, the merciless Indian savages, whose known rule of warfare, is an undistinguished destruction of all ages, sexes, and conditions.

In every stage of these oppressions we have petitioned for redress in the most humble terms: our repeated petitions have been answered only by repeated injury. A prince whose character is thus marked by every act which may define a tyrant is unfit to be the ruler of a free people.

Nor have we been wanting in attention to our British brethren. We have warned them from time to time of attempts by their Legislature to extend an unwarrantable jurisdiction over us. We have reminded them of the circumstances of our emigration and settlement here. We have appealed to their native justice and magnanimity, and we have conjured them by the ties of our common kindred to disavow these usurpations, which would inevitably interrupt our connections and correspondence. They too have been deaf to the voice of justice and of consanguinity. We must, therefore, acquiesce in the necessity, which denounces our separation, and hold them, as we hold the rest of mankind, enemies in war, in peace friends.

We, therefore, the Representatives of the United States of America, in General Congress assembled, appealing to the Supreme Judge of the world for the rectitude of our intentions, do, in the name, and by authority of the good people of these Colonies, solemnly publish and declare, That these United Colonies are, and of right ought to be Free and Independent States; that they are absolved from all allegiance to the British Crown, and that all political connection between them and the State of Great Britain, is and ought to be totally dissolved; and that as Free and Independent States, they have full power to levy war, conclude peace, contract alliances, establish commerce, and to do all other acts and things which Independent States may of right do. And for the support of this declaration, with a firm reliance on the protection of Divine Providence, we mutually pledge to each other our lives, our fortunes, and our sacred honor.

John Hancock.

New Hampshire
Josiah Bartlett,
Wm. Whipple,
Matthew Thornton.

Massachusetts Bay
Saml. Adams,
John Adams,
Robt. Treat Paine,
Elbridge Gerry.

Rhode Island
Step. Hopkins,
William Ellery.

Connecticut
Roger Sherman,
Sam'el Huntington,
Wm. Williams,
Oliver Wolcott.

Maryland
Samuel Chase,
Wm. Paca,
Thos. Stone,
Charles Carroll of Carrollton.

Virginia
George Wythe,
Richard Henry Lee,
Th. Jefferson,
Benja. Harrison,
Ths. Nelson, Jr.,
Francis Lightfoot Lee,
Carter Braxton.

New York
Wm. Floyd,
Phil. Livingston,
Frans. Lewis,
Lewis Morris.

Georgia
BUTTON GWINNETT,
LYMAN HALL,
GEO. WALTON.

Pennsylvania
ROBT. MORRIS,
BENJAMIN RUSH,
BENJA. FRANKLIN,
JOHN MORTON,
GEO. CLYMER,
JAS. SMITH,
GEO. TAYLOR,
JAMES WILSON,
GEO. ROSS.

Delaware
CAESAR RODNEY,
GEO. READ,
THO. M'KEAN.

North Carolina
WM. HOOPER,
JOSEPH HEWES,
JOHN PENN.

South Carolina
EDWARD RUTLEDGE,
THOS. HEYWARD, JUNR.,
THOMAS LYNCH, JUNR.,
ARTHUR MIDDLETON.

New Jersey
RICHD. STOCKTON,
JNO. WITHERSPOON,
FRAS. HOPKINSON,
JOHN HART,
ABRA. CLARK.

Chapter 2

THE LAW OF THE LAND

In 1783, the Treaty of Paris ended the Revolution and firmly secured American independence, but the enormously difficult problem of political reorganization remained to plague the erstwhile colonials. Though they had successfully swept away England's oppressive imperial rule, in its place they had yet to construct their own political system and to design a new equilibrium of liberty and order. The task of devising a constitution, formidable under the most favorable circumstances, proved particularly trying for the new nation. For beyond the single desire for independence there was little substantial agreement as to long-range political objectives amongst even the most fervid patriots.

Instead, a decided cleavage along class lines was evident throughout the Revolutionary crisis. A conservative group composed of wealthy Southern planters and Northern merchants, bankers, lawyers, and speculators sought independence to be free of British mercantilist restrictions and of an intolerable burden of debt to the mother country. But for the most part they wanted no fundamental social or economic change within the colonies themselves, and the status quo was to be maintained after independence was assured, with political power remaining in the possession of the well born, the educated, and the rich. On the other hand, the yeoman farmers, mechanics, artisans, and small businessmen who made up the radical patriots sought a *two-fold* revolution. Political ties to England were to be broken merely as a first step towards a revolution at home; and a new democratic government, based upon popular rule and responsive to the will of the people, was to destroy the social and economic privileges enjoyed by the colonial aristocracy.

Largely because Samuel Adams, Patrick Henry, and others of their leaders had played a prominent role in precipitating the final break with England, the radicals won important victories during and immediately after the war. Although conservatism was by no means completely routed, the radical viewpoint prevailed in many instances and there occurred a limited social revolution. Constitutions in the new states generally provided for more democracy than the colonial charters. Property qualifications for voting were lowered somewhat to permit a broader (though by no means universal) suffrage. Large estates were confiscated from loyalists, and though speculators secured much of these lands, a large quantity was made available to small farmers. The old feudal practices of entail—which kept huge land holdings intact by forbidding the division of an estate through inheritance—and primogeniture—which further fostered a landed aristocracy by making the first-born male heir to all land inheritances—were forbidden. In many states religious freedom received a considerable impetus from the separation of church and state. And generally the equalitarian principles of the Declaration of Independence were firmly impressed upon Americans who now sought to effect reforms in every aspect of national life.

The most significant radical victory, however, was the establishment of the Articles of Confederation. When independence was declared and the revolution begun, it was obvious that some form of permanent central authority must eventually supplant the Continental Congress. But the radicals well remembered British restraints upon democratic local self-government, and they were convinced that definitive political power must ultimately be concentrated in state legislatures susceptible to popular pressures rather than in a distant and less responsible strong central government. Thus the Articles of Confederation amply met the radicals' demands, for the common activities of the thirteen states were coordinated within a rather feeble "league of friendship" without significantly sacrificing local political control. Reflecting colonial experiences with tyrannical Royal governors, no provision was made for an independent executive department. Nor was a permanent federal judiciary created. Rather the sole organ of government was a one-house Congress in which each state retained its "sovereignty, freedom, and independence" and possessed but one vote. The agreement of nine states was necessary to pass legislation of importance, and a unanimous vote was required to amend the Articles. Besides, the powers granted to the government were severely limited. Congress might make war or peace, raise an army and navy by *requesting* quotas of men from the states, look after Indian affairs, borrow money, and administer a post office. But the government could not enforce its will or act directly upon the states or the people, and it totally lacked the essential powers to tax and to regulate commerce between the states.

Despite these severe limitations upon its power, the government under the Articles of Confederation did make lasting contributions to the national well-being, particularly in the creation of a permanent, democratic American colonial policy. In order to harmonize the various states' conflicting claims to Western lands, all of these territories were finally ceded to the central government (Maryland refused to ratify the Articles until 1781, when this decision was made). Then in the Ordinances of 1784 and 1785, and particularly in the famous Northwest Ordinance of 1787, provision was made for the organization of new lands into districts which were eventually to be admitted to the Union "on an equal footing with the original states in all respects whatsoever."

In all likelihood the majority of Americans were well satisfied with a government that had developed a liberal and farsighted land policy and had faithfully administered its responsibilities without at all encroaching upon the liberties of its citizens. But the less numerous, though more articulate and powerful conservative elements in American society were grievously outraged at what they considered the "failures" of the Articles of Confederation. Though it was inevitable that long years of war and the destruction of the old colonial system would produce depression and severe economic dislocation, conservatives blamed the confusions of the "Critical Period" after the Revolution entirely upon inherent weaknesses in the radical-inspired Articles. The answers to many of the nation's problems, they insisted, would be provided by the establishment of a powerful national government free to regulate interstate commerce, to tax, and to enforce its will directly upon the people. Such a government would necessarily strengthen the nation, for it would assure economic stability by bringing broad assistance to the conservative propertied groups. For the manufacturer, a high national tariff would protect his own goods from foreign competition and serve as a retaliation against other nations for their restrictions. For the shipper and trader, there would be naval protection for the nation's commerce, and favorable trade treaties with foreign lands that despised the weak Confederation. For domestic businessmen, there would be an end to the trade wars between the states, and the establishment of courts would enforce the obligation of contracts. For land speculators, there would be military protection against Indians whose ravages made Western settlement difficult and impaired land values. And for the creditor class generally, a uniform, controlled currency would put an end to the state legislatures' inflationary cheap money policies that devalued the dollar and made debts meaningless.

Fortunately for the conservative cause, the radical movement had been largely dissipated after its initial victory in the formulation of the weak Articles of Confederation. Now it was the conservatives' turn to organize political victory, and when in 1786 the Confederation government proved incapable of dealing with an agrarian insurrection in Western Massachusetts (Shays' Rebellion), they took bold steps towards counterrevolution. Leading conservatives had very early called for the revision of the Articles, and preliminary meetings had been held at Mount Vernon in 1785 and at Annapolis in 1786 to discuss ways and means of furthering state cooperation on trade and other matters. Then at the Annapolis Convention a resolution penned by Alexander Hamilton called for a new meeting "to render the constitution of the federal government adequate to the exigencies of the Union." And in February, 1787, the Congress invited all of the states to send delegates to a convention at Philadelphia in the spring of that year for the "sole and express purpose of revising the Articles of Confederation."

That the Constitutional Convention was predominantly conservatives goes without saying, for determined men of property within the various state legislatures had chosen representatives of their own social and economic persuasion. None of the old fiery radicals were present and of the fifty-five delegates who participated in the deliberations of the Convention most were substantial men of affairs personally interested in creating a strong central government. That the delegates wrote large areas of their conservative views into the Constitution was equally true, for the document which became the "supreme law of the land" fully met most of the propertied classes' objections to the weak and supposedly inadequate Articles of Confederation. Vast powers (including those to regulate interstate commerce and to tax) were conferred upon the national government, while the powers of the individual states were severely curtailed. And the entire national political structure was itself carefully guarded against an "excess of democracy" by an intricate set of checks and balances, the separation of powers, a difficult amending process, the indirect election of the President and of the Senate, the equal representation of large and small states in the Senate, and by the Presidential veto.

A bitter struggle remained, however, for the Constitution had yet to be approved by the necessary nine of the thirteen states. Now the radicals were thoroughly aroused as they studied the handiwork of the Convention whose instructions had been simply to revise the old Articles of Confederation. To a majority of Americans, the poorer classes generally, the consolidating character of the proposed federal Constitution smacked of despotism and class rule. But, with certain outstanding exceptions such as Patrick Henry and Richard Henry Lee of Virginia, the anti-Federalists were mostly inarticulate, and their strength in the state ratifying conventions was minimized by lack of systematic organization no less than by undemocratic restrictions upon voting. The Federalists, of course, were superbly organized, and they numbered amongst their most effective arguments for the Constitution a series of brilliant essays by Alexander Hamilton, James Madison, and John Jay. The *Federalist Papers* were read widely throughout the nation, and none more effectively defended the new government than Madison's Federalist Number Ten—a masterful statement of the founders' realistic appraisal of politics.

The skill and organization of the Federalists prevailed and the Constitution was ratified, but only after the first ten amendments, the "Bill of Rights," had been submitted to satisfy the demands of the majority of the people. Because of the radicals' fear of tyranny under the conservative constitution, bitter conflict between Federalists and anti-Federalists carried over into the early years of the Republic. Soon, however, popular victories at the polls proved these fears unfounded and demonstrated that the Founding Fathers had in fact possessed the vision and wisdom to create "a more perfect union" which did in time become truly a government "of the people, by the people, for the people."

The Constitution of the United States, *1787*

We the People of the United States, in order to form a more perfect union, establish justice, insure domestic tranquility, provide for the common defence, promote the general welfare, and secure the blessings of liberty to ourselves and our posterity, do ordain and establish this Constitution for the United States of America.

Article I

Sec. 1. All legislative powers herein granted shall be vested in a Congress of the United States, which shall consist of a Senate and House of Representatives.

Sec. 2. The House of Representatives shall be composed of members chosen every second year by the people of the several States, and the electors in each State shall have the qualifications requisite for electors of the most numerous branch of the State legislature.

No person shall be a Representative who shall not have attained to the age of twenty-five years, and been seven years a citizen of the United States, and who shall not, when elected, be an inhabitant of that State in which he shall be chosen.

Representatives and direct taxes shall be apportioned among the several States which may be included within this Union, according to their respective numbers, which shall be determined by adding to the whole number of free persons, including those bound to service for a term of years, and excluding Indians not taxed, three-fifths of all other persons. The actual enumeration shall be made within three years after the first meeting of the Congress of the United States, and within every subsequent term of ten years, in such manner as they shall by law direct. The number of Representatives shall not exceed one for every thirty thousand, but each State shall have at least one Representative; and until such enumeration shall be made, the State of New Hampshire shall be entitled to choose three, Massachusetts eight, Rhode Island and Providence Plantations one, Connecticut five, New York six, New Jersey four, Pennsylvania eight, Delaware one, Maryland six, Virginia ten, North Carolina five, South Carolina five, and Georgia three.

When vacancies happen in the representation from any State, the executive authority thereof shall issue writs of election to fill such vacancies.

The House of Representatives shall choose their

Speaker and other officers; and shall have the sole power of impeachment.

Sec. 3. The Senate of the United States shall be composed of two Senators from each State, chosen by the legislature thereof, for six years; and each Senator shall have one vote.

Immediately after they shall be assembled in consequence of the first election, they shall be divided as equally as may be into three classes. The seats of the Senators of the first class shall be vacated at the expiration of the second year, of the second class at the expiration of the fourth year, and of the third class at the expiration of the sixth year, so that one-third may be chosen every second year; and if vacancies happen by resignation, or otherwise, during the recess of the legislature of any State, the executive thereof may make temporary appointments until the next meeting of the legislature, which shall then fill such vacancies.

No person shall be a Senator who shall not have attained to the age of thirty years, and been nine years a citizen of the United States, and who shall not, when elected, be an inhabitant of that State for which he shall be chosen.

The Vice-President of the United States shall be President of the Senate, but shall have no vote, unless they be equally divided.

The Senate shall choose their other officers, and also a President pro tempore, in the absence of the Vice-President, or when he shall exercise the office of President of the United States.

The Senate shall have the sole power to try all impeachments. When sitting for that purpose, they shall be on oath or affirmation. When the President of the United States is tried, the Chief Justice shall preside: and no person shall be convicted without the concurrence of two-thirds of the members present.

Judgment in cases of impeachment shall not extend further than to removal from office, and disqualification to hold and enjoy any office of honor, trust or profit under the United States: but the party convicted shall nevertheless be liable and subject to indictment, trial, judgment, and punishment, according to law.

Sec. 4. The times, places and manner of holding elections for Senators and Representatives, shall be prescribed in each State by the legislature thereof; but the Congress may at any time by law make or alter such regulations, except as to the places of choosing Senators.

The Congress shall assemble at least once in every year, and such meeting shall be on the first Monday in December, unless they shall by law appoint a different day.

Sec. 5. Each house shall be the judge of the elections, returns and qualifications of its own members, and a majority of each shall constitute a quorum to do business; but a smaller number may adjourn from day to day, and may be authorized to compel the attendance of absent members, in such manner, and under such penalties as each House may provide.

Each house may determine the rules of its proceedings, punish its members for disorderly behaviour, and, with the concurrence of two-thirds, expel a member.

Each house shall keep a journal of its proceedings, and from time to time publish the same, excepting such parts as may in their judgment require secrecy; and the yeas and nays of the members of either house on any question shall, at the desire of one-fifth of those present, be entered on the journal.

Neither house, during the session of Congress, shall, without the consent of the other, adjourn for more than three days, nor to any other place than that in which the two houses shall be sitting.

Sec. 6. The Senators and Representatives shall receive a compensation for their services, to be ascertained by law, and paid out of the Treasury of the United States. They shall in all cases, except treason, felony and breach of the peace, be privileged from arrest during their attendance at the session of their respective houses, and in going to and returning from the same; and for any speech or debate in either house, they shall not be questioned in any other place.

No Senator or Representative shall, during the time for which he was elected, be appointed to any civil office under the authority of the United States which shall have been created, or the emoluments whereof shall have been increased during such time; and no person holding any office under the United States, shall be a member of either House during his continuance in office.

Sec. 7. All bills for raising revenue shall originate in the House of Representatives; but the Senate may propose or concur with amendments as on other bills.

Every bill which shall have passed the House of Representatives and the Senate, shall, before it become a law, be presented to the President of the United States; if he approve he shall sign it, but if not he shall return it, with his objections to that house in which it shall have originated, who shall enter the objections at large on their journal, and proceed to reconsider it. If after such reconsideration two-thirds of that house shall agree to pass the bill, it shall be sent, together with the objections, to the other house, by which it shall likewise be reconsidered, and if approved by two-thirds of that house, it shall become a law. But in all such cases the votes of both houses shall be determined by yeas and nays, and the names of the persons voting for and against the bill shall be entered on the journal of each house respectively. If any bill shall not be returned by the President within ten days (Sundays excepted) after it shall have been presented to him, the same shall be a law, in like manner as if he had signed it, unless the Congress by their adjournment prevent its return, in which case it shall not be a law.

Every order, resolution, or vote to which the concurrence of the Senate and House of Representatives may be necessary (except on a question of adjournment) shall be presented to the President of the United States; and before the same shall take effect, shall be approved by him, or being disapproved by him, shall be repassed by two-thirds of the Senate and House of Representatives, according to the rules and limitations prescribed in the case of a bill.

Sec. 8. The Congress shall have power to lay and collect taxes, duties, imposts, and excises, to pay the debts and provide for the common defence and general welfare of the United States; but all duties, imposts, and excises shall be uniform throughout the United States;

To borrow money on the credit of the United States;

To regulate commerce with foreign nations, and among the several States, and with the Indian tribes;

To establish a uniform rule of naturalization, and uniform laws on the subject of bankruptcies throughout the United States;

To coin money, regulate the value thereof, and of foreign coin, and fix the standard of weights and measures;

To provide for the punishment of counterfeiting the securities and current coin of the United States;

To establish post-offices and post-roads;

To promote the progress of science and useful arts, by securing for limited times to authors and inventors the exclusive right to their respective writings and discoveries;

To constitute tribunals inferior to the Supreme Court;

To define and punish piracies and felonies committed on the high seas, and offences against the law of nations;

To declare war, grant letters of marque and reprisal, and make rules concerning captures on land and water;

To raise and support armies, but no appropriation of money to that use shall be for a longer term than two years;

To provide and maintain a navy;

To make rules for the government and regulation of the land and naval forces;

To provide for calling forth the militia to execute the laws of the Union, suppress insurrections and repel invasions;

To provide for organizing, arming, and disciplining the militia, and for governing such part of them as may be employed in the service of the United States, reserving to the States respectively the appointment of the officers, and the authority of training the militia according to the discipline prescribed by Congress;

To exercise exclusive legislation in all cases whatsoever, over such district (not exceeding ten miles square) as may, by cession of particular States, and the acceptance of Congress, become the seat of the Government of the United States, and to exercise like authority over all places purchased by the consent of the legislature of the State in which the same shall be, for the erection of forts, magazines, arsenals, dockyards, and other needful buildings; and

To make all laws which shall be necessary and proper for carrying into execution the foregoing powers, and all other powers vested by this Constitution in the Government of the United States, or in any department or officer thereof.

Sec. 9. The migration or importation of such persons as any of the States now existing shall think proper to admit, shall not be prohibited by the Congress prior to the year one thousand eight hundred and eight, but a tax or duty may be imposed on such importation, not exceeding ten dollars for each person.

The privilege of the writ of habeas corpus shall not be suspended, unless when in cases of rebellion or invasion the public safety may require it.

No bill of attainder or ex post facto law shall be passed.

No capitation, or other direct, tax shall be laid, unless in proportion to the census or enumeration herein before directed to be taken.

No tax or duty shall be laid on articles exported from any State.

No preference shall be given by any regulation of commerce or revenue to the ports of one State over those of another: nor shall vessels bound to, or from, one State, be obliged to enter, clear, or pay duties in another.

No money shall be drawn from the Treasury but in consequence of appropriations made by law; and a regular statement and account of the receipts and expenditures of all public money shall be published from time to time.

No title of nobility shall be granted by the United States: and no person holding any office of profit or trust under them, shall, without the consent of the Congress, accept of any present, emolument, office, or title, of any kind whatever, from any king, prince or foreign State.

Sec. 10. No State shall enter into any treaty, alliance, or confederation; grant letters of marque and reprisal; coin money; emit bills of credit; make any thing but gold and silver coin a tender in payment of debts; pass any bill of attainder, ex post facto law, or law impairing the obligation of contracts, or grant any title of nobility.

No State shall, without the consent of the Congress, lay any imposts or duties on imports or exports, except what may be absolutely necessary for executing its inspection laws: and the net produce of all duties and imposts, laid by any State on imports or exports, shall be for the use of the Treasury of the United States; and all such laws shall be subject to the revision and control of the Congress.

No State shall, without the consent of Congress, lay any duty of tonnage, keep troops, or ships of war in time of peace, enter into any agreement or compact with another State, or with a foreign power, or engage in war, unless actually invaded, or in such imminent danger as will not admit of delay.

Article II

Sec. 1. The executive power shall be vested in a President of the United States of America. He shall hold his office during the term of four years, and, together with the Vice-President, chosen for the same term, be elected, as follows:

Each State shall appoint, in such manner as the legislature thereof may direct, a number of electors, equal to the whole number of Senators and Representatives to which the State may be entitled in the Congress: but no Senator or Representative, or person holding an office of trust or profit under the United States, shall be appointed an elector.

The electors shall meet in their respective States, and vote by ballot for two persons, of whom one at least shall not be an inhabitant of the same State with themselves. And they shall make a list of all the persons voted for, and of the number of votes for each; which list they shall sign and certify, and transmit sealed to the seat of the Government of the United States, directed to the President of the Senate. The President of the Senate shall, in the presence of the Senate and House of Representatives, open all the certificates, and the votes shall then be counted. The person having the greatest number of votes shall be the President, if such number be a majority of the whole number of electors appointed; and if there be more than one who have such majority, and have an equal number of votes, then the House of Representatives shall immediately choose by ballot one of them for President; and if no person have a majority, then from the five highest on the list the said house shall in like manner choose the President. But in choosing the President, the votes shall be taken by States, the representation from each State having one vote; a quorum for this purpose shall consist of a member or members from two-thirds of the States, and a majority of all the States shall be necessary to a choice. In every case, after the choice of the President, the person having the greatest number of votes of the electors shall be the Vice-President. But if there should remain two or more who have equal votes, the Senate shall choose from them by ballot the Vice-President.

The Congress may determine the time of choosing the electors, and the day on which they shall give their votes; which day shall be the same throughout the United States.

No person except a natural-born citizen, or a citizen of the United States, at the time of the adoption of this Constitution, shall be eligible to the office of President; neither shall any person be eligible to that office who shall not have attained to the age of thirty-five years, and been fourteen years a resident within the United States.

In case of the removal of the President from office, or of his death, resignation, or inability to discharge the powers and duties of the said office, the same shall devolve on the Vice-President, and the Congress may by law provide for the case of removal, death, resignation, or inability, both of the President and Vice-President, declaring what officer shall then act as President, and such officer shall act accordingly, until the disability be removed, or a President shall be elected.

The President shall, at stated times, receive for his services, a compensation, which shall neither be increased nor diminished during the period for which he shall have been elected, and he shall not receive within that period any other emolument from the United States, or any of them.

Before he enter on the execution of his office, he shall take the following oath or affirmation: "I do solemnly swear (or affirm) that I will faithfully execute the office of President of the United States, and will to the best of my ability, preserve, protect, and defend the Constitution of the United States."

Sec. 2. The President shall be Commander-in-Chief of the Army and Navy of the United States, and of the militia of the several States, when called into the actual service of the United States; he may require the opinion, in writing, of the principal officer in each of the executive departments, upon any subject relating to the duties of their respective offices, and he shall have power to grant reprieves and pardons for offences against the United States, except in cases of impeachment.

He shall have power, by and with the advice and consent of the Senate, to make treaties, provided two-thirds of the Senators present concur; and he shall nominate, and by and with the advice and consent of the Senate, shall appoint ambassadors, other public ministers and consuls, judges of the Supreme Court, and all other officers of the United States, whose appointments are not herein otherwise provided for, and which shall be established by law: but the Congress may by law vest the appointment of such inferior officers, as they think proper, in the President alone, in the courts of law, or in the heads of departments.

The President shall have power to fill up all vacancies that may happen during the recess of the Senate, by granting commissions which shall expire at the end of their next session.

Sec. 3. He shall from time to time give to the Congress information of the state of the Union, and recommend to their consideration such measures as he shall judge necessary and expedient; he may, on extraordinary occasions, convene both houses, or either of them, and in case of disagreement between them, with respect to the time of adjournment, he may adjourn them to such time as he shall think proper; he shall receive ambassadors and other public ministers; he shall take care that the laws be faithfully executed, and shall commission all the officers of the United States.

Sec. 4. The President, Vice-President and all civil officers of the United States, shall be removed from office on impeachment for, and conviction of, treason, bribery, or other high crimes and misdemeanors.

ARTICLE III

Sec. 1. The judicial power of the United States, shall be vested in one Supreme Court, and in such inferior courts as the Congress may from time to time ordain and establish. The judges, both of the supreme and inferior courts, shall hold their offices during good behaviour, and shall, at stated times, receive for their services, a compensation, which shall not be diminished during their continuance in office.

Sec. 2. The judicial power shall extend to all cases, in law and equity, arising under this Constitution, the laws of the United States, and treaties made, or which shall be made, under their authority; to all cases affecting ambassadors, other public ministers and consuls; to all cases of admiralty and maritime jurisdiction; to controversies to which the United States shall be a party; to controversies between two or more States; between a State and citizens of another State; between citizens of different States, between citizens of the same State claiming lands under grants of different States, and between a State, or the citizen thereof, and foreign States, citizens or subjects.

In all cases affecting ambassadors, other public ministers and consuls, and those in which a State shall be party, the Supreme Court shall have original jurisdiction. In all the other cases before mentioned, the Supreme Court shall have appellate jurisdiction, both as to law and fact, with such exceptions, and under such regulations as the Congress shall make.

The trial of all crimes, except in cases of impeachment, shall be by jury; and such trial shall be held in the State where the said crimes shall have been committed; but when not committed within any State, the trial shall be at such place or places as the Congress may by law have directed.

Sec. 3. Treason against the United States, shall consist only in levying war against them, or in adhering to their enemies, giving them aid and comfort. No person shall be convicted of treason unless on the testimony of two witnesses to the same overt act, or on confession in open court.

The Congress shall have power to declare the punishment of treason, but no attainder of treason shall work corruption of blood, or forfeiture except during the life of the person attainted.

Article IV

Sec. 1. Full faith and credit shall be given in each State to the public acts, records, and judicial proceedings of every other State. And the Congress may by general laws prescribe the manner in which such acts, records, and proceedings shall be provided, and the effect thereof.

Sec. 2. The citizens of each State shall be entitled to all privileges and immunities of citizens in the several States.

A person charged in any State with treason, felony, or other crime, who shall flee from justice, and be found in another State, shall on demand of the executive authority of the State from which he fled, be delivered up, to be removed to the State having jurisdiction of the crime.

No person held to service or labor in one State, under the laws thereof, escaping into another, shall, in consequence of any law or regulation therein, be discharged from such service or labor, but shall be delivered up on claim of the party to whom such service or labor may be due.

Sec. 3. New States may be admitted by the Congress into this Union; but no new States shall be formed or erected within the jurisdiction of any other State; nor any State be formed by the junction of two or more States; or parts of States, without the consent of the legislatures of the States concerned as well as of the Congress.

The Congress shall have power to dispose of and make all needful rules and regulations respecting the territory or other property belonging to the United States; and nothing in this Constitution shall be so construed as to prejudice any claims of the United States, or of any particular State.

Sec. 4. The United States shall guarantee to every State in this Union a republican form of government, and shall protect each of them against invasion; and on application of the legislature, or of the executive (when the legislature cannot be convened) against domestic violence.

ARTICLE V

The Congress, whenever two-thirds of both houses shall deem it necessary, shall propose amendments to this Constitution, or, on the application of the legislature of two-thirds of the several States, shall call a convention for proposing amendments, which, in either case, shall be valid to all intents and purposes, as part of this Constitution, when ratified by the legislatures of three-fourths of the several States, or by conventions in three-fourths thereof, as the one or the other mode of ratification may be proposed by the Congress; provided that no amendment which may be made prior to the year one thousand eight hundred and eight shall in any manner affect the first and fourth clauses in the ninth section of the first article; and that no State, without its consent, shall be deprived of its equal suffrage in the Senate.

ARTICLE VI

All debts contracted and engagements entered into, before the adoption of this Constitution, shall be as valid against the United States under this Constitution, as under the Confederation.

This Constitution, and the laws of the United States which shall be made in pursuance thereof; and all treaties made, or which shall be made, under the authority of the United States, shall be the supreme law of the land; and the judges in every State shall be bound thereby, anything in the Constitution or laws of any State to the contrary notwithstanding.

The Senators and Representatives before mentioned, and the members of the several State legislatures, and all executive and judicial officers, both of the United States and of the several States, shall be bound by oath or affirmation, to support this Constitution; but no religious test shall ever be required as a qualification to any office or public trust under the United States.

Article VII

The ratification of the conventions of nine States, shall be sufficient for the establishment of this Constitution between the States so ratifying the same.

Done in convention by the unanimous consent of the States present, the seventeenth day of September in the year of our Lord one thousand seven hundred and eighty-seven and of the independence of the United States of America the twelfth. In witness whereof, we have hereunto subscribed our names,

G^{o} WASHINGTON—Presid^{t} and deputy from Virginia

New Hampshire
John Langdon
Nicholas Gilman

Massachusetts
Nathaniel Gorham
Rufus King

Connecticut
W^{M} Sam^{L} Johnson
Roger Sherman

New York
Alexander Hamilton

New Jersey
Wil: Livingston
David Brearley
W^{M} Paterson

Delaware
Geo: Read
Gunning Bedford Jr.
John Dickinson
Richard Bassett
Jaco: Broom

Maryland
James McHenry
Dan of S^{T} Tho^{S} Jenifer
Dan^{L} Carroll

Virginia
John Blair
James Madison Jr.

North Carolina
W^{M} Blount

JONA: DAYTON
Pennsylvania
B. FRANKLIN
THOMAS MIFFLIN
ROB[T] MORRIS
GEO. CLYMER
THO[S] FITZSIMONS
JARED INGERSOLL
JAMES WILSON
GOUV MORRIS

RICH[D] DOBBS SPAIGHT
HU WILLIAMSON
South Carolina
J. RUTLEDGE
CHARLES COTESWORTH PINCKNEY
CHARLES PINCKNEY
PIERCE BUTLER
Georgia
WILLIAM FEW
ABR BALDWIN

AMENDMENTS TO THE CONSTITUTION

ARTICLES I–X Bill of Rights, *1791*

ARTICLE I

Congress shall make no law respecting an establishment of religion, or prohibiting the free exercise thereof; or abridging the freedom of speech, or of the press; or the right of the people peaceably to assemble, and to petition the government for a redress of grievances.

ARTICLE II

A well regulated militia, being necessary to the security of a free State, the right of the people to keep and bear arms, shall not be infringed.

ARTICLE III

No soldier shall, in time of peace be quartered in any house, without the consent of the owner, nor in time of war, but in a manner to be prescribed by law.

ARTICLE IV

The right of the people to be secure in their persons, houses, papers, and effects, against unreasonable searches and seizures, shall not be violated, and no warrants shall issue, but upon probable cause, supported by oath or affirmation, and particularly describing the place to be searched, and the persons or things to be seized.

Article V

No person shall be held to answer for a capital, or otherwise infamous crime, unless on a presentment or indictment of a grand jury, except in cases arising in the land or naval forces, or in the militia, when in actual service in time of war or public danger; nor shall any person be subject for the same offence to be twice put in jeopardy of life or limb; nor shall be compelled in any criminal case to be a witness against himself, nor be deprived of life, liberty, or property, without due process of law; nor shall private property be taken for public use, without just compensation.

Article VI

In all criminal prosecutions, the accused shall enjoy the right to a speedy and public trial, by an impartial jury of the State and district wherein the crime shall have been committed, which district shall have been previously ascertained by law, and to be informed of the nature and cause of the accusation; to be confronted with the witnesses against him; to have compulsory process for obtaining witnesses in his favor, and to have the assistance of counsel for his defence.

Article VII

In suits at common law, where the value in controversy shall exceed twenty dollars, the right of trial by jury shall be preserved, and no fact tried by a jury, shall be otherwise re-examined in any court of the United States, than according to the rules of the common law.

Article VIII

Excessive bail shall not be required, nor excessive fines imposed, nor cruel and unusual punishments inflicted.

ARTICLE IX

The enumeration in the Constitution, of certain rights, shall not be construed to deny or disparage others retained by the people.

ARTICLE X

The powers not delegated to the United States by the Constitution, nor prohibited by it to the States, are reserved to the States respectively, or to the people.

ARTICLE XI (1798)

The judicial power of the United States shall not be construed to extend to any suit in law or equity, commenced or prosecuted against one of the United States by citizens of another State, or by citizens or subjects of any foreign State.

ARTICLE XII (1804)

The electors shall meet in their respective states, and vote by ballot for President and Vice-President, one of whom, at least, shall not be an inhabitant of the same state with themselves; they shall name in their ballots the person voted for as President, and in distinct ballots the person voted for as Vice-President, and they shall make distinct lists of all persons voted for as President, and of all persons voted for as Vice-President, and of the number of votes for each, which lists they shall sign and certify, and transmit sealed to the seat of the Government of the United States, directed to the President of the Senate; The President of the Senate shall, in the presence of the Senate and House of Representatives, open all the certificates and the votes shall then be counted; The person having the greatest number of votes for President, shall be the President, if such number be a majority of the whole number of electors appointed; and if no person have such majority, then from the persons having the highest numbers not exceeding three on the list of those voted for as President, the House of Representatives shall choose immediately, by ballot, the President. But in choosing the President, the votes shall be taken by States, the representation from each State having one vote; a quorum for this purpose shall consist of a member or members from two-thirds of the States, and a majority of all the States shall be necessary to a choice. And if the House of Representatives shall not choose a President whenever the right of choice shall devolve upon them, before the fourth day of March next following, then the Vice-President shall act as President, as in the case of death or other constitutional disability of the President. The person having the greatest number of votes as Vice-President, shall be the Vice-President, if such number be a majority of the whole number of electors appointed, and if no person have a majority, then from the two highest numbers on the list, the Senate shall choose the Vice-President; a quorum for the purpose shall consist of two-thirds of the whole number of Senators, and a majority of the whole number shall be necessary to a choice. But no person constitutionally ineligible to the office of President shall be eligible to that of Vice-President of the United States.

Article XIII (1865)

Sec. 1. Neither slavery nor involuntary servitude, except as a punishment for crime whereof the party shall have been duly convicted, shall exist within the United States, or any place subject to their jurisdiction.

Sec. 2. Congress shall have power to enforce this article by appropriate legislation.

Article XIV (1868)

Sec. 1. All persons born or naturalized in the United States, and subject to the jurisdiction thereof, are citizens of the United States and of the State wherein they reside. No State shall make or enforce any law which shall abridge the privileges or immunities of citizens of the United States; nor shall any State deprive any person of life, liberty, or property, without due process of law; nor deny to any person within its jurisdiction the equal protection of the laws.

Sec. 2. Representatives shall be appointed among the several States according to their respective numbers, counting the whole number of persons in each State, excluding Indians not taxed. But when the right to vote at any election for the choice of electors for President and Vice-President of the United States, Representatives in Congress, the executive and judicial officer of any State, to support the Constitution of the United States, is denied to any of the male inhabitants of such State, being twenty-one years of age, and citizens of the United States, or in any way abridged, except for participation in rebellion, or other crime, the basis of representation therein shall be reduced in the proportion which the number of such male citizens shall bear to the whole number of male citizens twenty-one years of age in such State.

Sec. 3. No person shall be a Senator or Representative in Congress, or elector of President and Vice-President, or hold any office, civil or military, under the United States, or under any State, who, having previously taken an oath, as a member of Congress, or as an officer of the United States, or as a member of any State legislature, or as an executive or judicial officer of any State, to support the Constitution of the United States, shall have engaged in insurrection or rebellion against the same, or given aid or comfort to the enemies thereof. But Congress may by a vote of two-thirds of each house, remove such disability.

Sec. 4. The validity of the public debt of the United States, authorized by law, including debts incurred for payment of pensions and bounties for services in suppressing insurrection or rebellion, shall not be questioned. But neither the United States nor any State shall assume or pay any debt or obligation incurred in aid of insurrection or rebellion against the United States, or any claim for the loss or emancipation of any slave; but all such debts, obligations and claims shall be held illegal and void.

Sec. 5. The Congress shall have power to enforce, by appropriate legislation, the provisions of this article.

Article XV (1870)

Sec. 1. The right of citizens of the United States to vote shall not be denied or abridged by the United States or by any State on account of race, color, or previous condition of servitude.

Sec. 2. The Congress shall have power to enforce this article by appropriate legislation.

Article XVI (1913)

The Congress shall have power to lay and collect taxes on incomes, from whatever source derived, without apportionment among the several States and without regard to any census or enumeration.

Article XVII (1913)

The Senate of the United States shall be composed of two Senators from each State, elected by the people thereof, for six years, and each Senator shall have one vote. The electors in each State shall have the qualifications requisite for electors of the most numerous branch of the State legislature.

When vacancies happen in the representation of any State in the Senate, the executive authority of such State shall issue writs of election to fill such vacancies: *Provided,* That the legislature of any State may empower the executive thereof to make temporary appointments until the people fill the vacancies by election as the legislature may direct.

This amendment shall not be so construed as to affect the election or term of any Senator chosen before it becomes valid as part of the Constitution.

Article XVIII (1919)

After one year from the ratification of this article, the manufacture, sale, or transportation of intoxicating liquors within, the importation thereof into, or the exportation thereof from the United States and all territory subject to the jurisdiction thereof for beverage purposes is hereby prohibited.

The Congress and the several States shall have concurrent power to enforce this article by appropriate legislation.

This article shall be inoperative unless it shall have been ratified as an amendment to the Constitution by the legislatures of the several States, as provided in the Constitution, within seven years from the date of the submission hereof to the States by Congress.

ARTICLE XIX (1920)

The right of citizens of the United States to vote shall not be denied or abridged by the United States or by any State on account of sex.

The Congress shall have power to appropriate legislation to enforce the provisions of this article.

ARTICLE XX (1933)

Sec. 1. The terms of the President and Vice-President shall end at noon on the twentieth day of January, and the terms of Senators and Representatives at noon on the third day of January, of the years in which such terms would have ended if this article had not been ratified; and the terms of their successors shall then begin.

Sec. 2. The Congress shall assemble at least once in every year, and such meeting shall begin at noon on the third day of January, unless they shall by law appoint a different day.

Sec. 3. If, at the time fixed for the beginning of the term of the President, the President-elect shall have died, the Vice-President-elect shall become President. If a President shall not have been chosen before the time fixed for the beginning of his term, or if the President-elect shall have failed to qualify, then the Vice-President-elect shall act as President until a President shall have qualified; and the Congress may by law provide for the case wherein neither a President-elect nor a Vice-President-elect shall have qualified, declaring who shall then act as President, or the manner in which one who is to act shall be elected, and such person shall act accordingly until a president or vice-president shall have qualified.

Sec. 4. The Congress may by law provide for the case of the death of any of the persons from whom the House of Representatives may choose a President whenever the right of choice shall have devolved upon them, and for the case of the death of any of the persons from whom the Senate may choose a Vice-President whenever the right of choice shall have devolved upon them.

Sec. 5. Selections 1 and 2 shall take effect on the Fifteenth day of October following the ratification of this article.

Sec. 6. This article shall be inoperative unless it shall have been ratified as an amendment to the Constitution by the legislatures of three-fourths of the several States within seven years from the date of its submission.

Article XXI (1933)

Sec. 1. The eighteenth article of amendment to the Constitution of the United States is hereby repealed.
Sec. 2. The transportation or importation into any State, territory or possession of the United States for delivery or use therein of intoxicating liquors, in violation of the laws thereof, is hereby prohibited.
Sec. 3. This article shall be inoperative unless it shall have been ratified as an amendment to the Constitution by convention in the several States, as provided in the Constitution, within seven years from the date of the submission thereof to the States by the Congress.

Article XXII (1951)

Sec. 1. No person shall be elected to the office of the President more than twice, and no person who has held the office of President, or acted as President, for more than two years of a term to which some other person was elected President shall be elected to the office of the President more than once. But this Article shall not apply to any person holding the office of President when this Article was proposed by the Congress, and shall not prevent any person who may be holding the office of President or acting as President during the term within which this Article becomes operative, from holding the office of President, or acting as President, during the remainder of such term.

Sec. 2. This article shall be inoperative unless it shall have been ratified as an amendment to the Constitution by the legislatures of three-fourths of the several States within seven years from the date of its submission to the States by the Congress.

ARTICLE XXIII (1961)

Sec. 1. The District constituting the seat of Government of the United States shall appoint in such manner as the Congress may direct:

A number of electors of President and Vice-President equal to the whole number of Senators and Representatives in Congress to which the District would be entitled if it were a State, but in no event more than the least populous State; they shall be in addition to those appointed by the States, but they shall be considered, for the purposes of the election of President and Vice-President, to be electors appointed by a State; and they shall meet in the District and perform such duties as provided by the twelfth article of amendment.

Sec. 2. The Congress shall have power to enforce this article by appropriate legislation.

ARTICLE XXIV (1964)

Sec. 1. The right of citizens of the United States to vote in any primary or other election for President or Vice-President, for electors for President or Vice-President, or for Senator or Representative in Congress, shall not be denied or abridged by the United States or any State by reason of failure to pay any poll tax or other tax.

Sec. 2. The Congress shall have the power to enforce this article by appropriate legislation.

Article XXV (1967)

Sec. 1. In case of the removal of the President from office or of his death or resignation, the Vice-President shall become President.
Sec. 2. Whenever there is a vacancy in the office of the Vice-President, the President shall nominate a Vice-President who shall take office upon confirmation by a majority vote of both Houses of Congress.
Sec. 3. Whenever the President transmits to the President pro tempore of the Senate and the Speaker of the House of Representatives his written declaration that he is unable to discharge the powers and duties of his office, and until he transmits to them a written declaration to the contrary, such powers and duties shall be discharged by the Vice-President as Acting President.
Sec. 4. Whenever the Vice-President and a majority of either of the principal officers of the executive departments or of such other body as Congress may by law provide, transmit to the President pro tempore of the Senate and the Speaker of the House of Representatives their written declaration that the President is unable to discharge the powers and duties of his office, the Vice-President shall immediately assume the powers and duties of the office as Acting President.

Thereafter, when the President transmits to the President pro tempore of the Senate and the Speaker of the House of Representatives his written declaration that no inability exists, he shall resume the powers and duties of his office unless the Vice-President and a majority of either the principal officers of the executive department or of such other body as Congress may by law provide, transmit within four days to the President pro tempore of the Senate and the Speaker of the House of Representatives their written declaration that the President is unable to discharge the powers and duties of his office. Thereupon Congress shall decide the issue, assembling within forty-eight hours for that purpose if not in session. If the Congress, within twenty-one days after receipt of the latter written declaration, or, if Congress is not in session, within twenty-one days after Congress is required to assemble, determines by two-thirds vote of both houses that the President is unable to discharge the powers and duties of his office, the Vice-President shall continue to discharge the same as Acting President; otherwise, the President shall resume the powers and duties of his office.

ARTICLE XXVI (1971)

Sec. 1. The right of citizens of the United States, who are eighteen years of age or older, to vote shall not be denied or abridged by the United States or by any State on account of age.
Sec. 2. The Congress shall have power to enforce this article by appropriate legislation.

ARTICLE XXVII (1992)

No law, varying the compensation for the services of the Senators and Representatives, shall take effect, until an election of Representatives shall have intervened.

The Federalist Number Ten, *James Madison, 1787*

TO THE PEOPLE OF THE STATE OF NEW YORK: Among the numerous advantages promised by a well constructed Union, none deserves to be more accurately developed than its tendency to break and control the violence of faction. The friend of popular governments never finds himself so much alarmed for their character and fate, as when he contemplates their propensity to this dangerous vice. He will not fail, therefore, to set a due value on any plan which, without violating the principles to which he is attached, provides a proper cure for it. The instability, injustice, and confusion introduced into the public councils, have, in truth, been the mortal diseases under which popular governments have everywhere perished; as they continue to be the favorite and fruitful topics from which the adversaries to liberty derive their most specious declamations. The valuable improvements made by the American constitutions on the popular models, both ancient and modern, cannot certainly be too much admired; but it would be an unwarrantable partiality, to contend that they have as effectually obviated the danger on this side, as was wished and expected. Complaints are everywhere heard from our most considerate and virtuous citizens, equally the friends of public and private faiths, and of public and personal liberty, that our governments are too unstable, that the public good is disregarded in the conflicts of rival parties, and that measures are too often decided, not according to the rules of justice and the rights of the minor party, but by the superior force of an interested and overbearing majority. However anxiously we may wish that these complaints had no foundation, the evidence of known facts will not permit us to deny that they are in some degree true. It will be found, indeed, on a candid review of our situation, that some of the distresses under which we labor have been erroneously charged on the operation of our governments; but it will be found, at the same time, that other causes will not alone account for many of our heaviest misfortunes; and particularly, for that prevailing and increasing distrust of public engagements, and alarm for private rights, which are echoed from one end of the continent to the other. These must be chiefly, if not wholly, effects of the unsteadiness and injustice with which a factious spirit has tainted our public administrations.

By a faction, I understand a number of citizens, whether amounting to a majority or minority of the whole, who are united and actuated by some common impulse of passion, or of interest, adverse to the rights of other citizens, or to the permanent and aggregate interests of the community.

There are two methods of curing the mischiefs of faction: the one, by removing its causes; the other, by controlling its effects.

There are again two methods of removing the causes of faction: the one, by destroying the liberty which is essential to its existence; the other, by giving to every citizen the same opinions, the same passions, and the same interests.

It could never be more truly said than of the first remedy, that it was worse than the disease. Liberty is to faction what air is to fire, an ailment without which it instantly expires. But it could not be less folly to abolish liberty, which is essential to political life, because it nourishes faction, than it would be to wish the annihilation of air, which is essential to animal life, because it imparts to fire its destructive agency.

The second expedient is as impracticable as the first would be unwise. As long as the reason of man continues fallible, and he is at liberty to exercise it, different opinions will be formed. As long as the connection subsists between his reason and his self-love, his opinions and his passion will have a reciprocal influence on each other, and the former will be objects to which the latter will attach themselves. The diversity in the faculties of men, from which the rights of property originate, is not less an insuperable obstacle to a uniformity of interests. The protection of these faculties is the first object of government. From the protection of different and unequal faculties of acquiring property, the possession of different degrees and kinds of property immediately results; and from the influence of these on the sentiments and views of the respective proprietors, ensues a division of the society into different interests and parties.

The latent causes of faction are thus sown in the nature of man; and we see them everywhere brought into different degrees of activity, according to the different circumstances of civil society. A zeal for different opinions concerning religion, concerning government, and many other points, as well of speculation as of practise; an attachment to different leaders ambitiously contending for pre-eminence and power; or to persons of other descriptions whose fortunes have been interesting to the human passions, have, in turn, divided mankind into parties, inflamed them with mutual animosity, and rendered them much more disposed to vex and oppress each other than to co-operate for their common good. So strong is this propensity of mankind to fall into mutual animosities, that where no substantial occasion presents itself, the most frivolous and fanciful distinctions have been sufficient to kindle their unfriendly passions and excite their most violent conflicts. But the most common and durable source of factions has been the various and unequal distribution of property. Those who hold and those who are without property have ever formed distinct interests in society. Those who are creditors, and those who are debtors, fall under a like discrimination. A landed interest, a manufacturing interest, a mercantile interest, a moneyed interest, with many lesser interests, grow up of necessity in civilized nations, and divide them into different classes, actuated by different sentiments and views. The regulation of these various and interfering interests forms the principal task of modern legislation, and involves the spirit of party and faction in the necessary and ordinary operations of the government.

No man is allowed to be a judge in his own cause, because his interest would certainly bias his judgment, and, not improbably, corrupt his integrity. With equal, nay with greater reason, a body of men are unfit to be both judges and parties at the same time; yet what are many of the most important acts of legislation, but so many judicial determinations, not indeed concerning the rights of single persons, but concerning the rights of large bodies of citizens? And what are the different classes of legislators but advocates and parties to the causes which they determine? Is a law proposed concerning private debts? It is a question to which the creditors are parties on one side and the debtors on the other. Justice ought to hold the balance between them. Yet the parties are, and must be, themselves the judges; and the most numerous party, or, in other words, the most powerful faction, must be expected to prevail. Shall domestic manufactures be encouraged, and in what degree, by restrictions on foreign manufactures? These are questions which would be differently decided by the landed and the manufacturing classes, and probably by neither with a sole regard to justice and the public good. The apportionment of taxes on the various descriptions of property is an act which seems to require the most exact impartiality; yet there is, perhaps, no legislative act in which greater opportunity and temptation are given to a predominant party to trample on the rules of justice. Every shilling with which they overburden the inferior number, is a shilling saved to their own pockets.

It is in vain to say that enlightened statesmen will be able to adjust these clashing interests, and render them all subservient to the public good. Enlightened statesmen will not always be at the helm. Nor, in many cases, can such an adjustment be made at all without taking into view indirect and remote considerations, which will rarely prevail over the immediate interest which one party may find in disregarding the rights of another or the good of the whole.

The inference to which we are brought is, that the *causes* of faction cannot be removed, and that relief is only to be sought in the means of controlling its *effects*.

If a faction consists of less than a majority, relief is supplied by the republican principle, which enables the majority to defeat its sinister view by regular vote. It may clog the administration, it may convulse the society, but it will be unable to execute and mask its violence under the forms of the Constitution. When a majority is included in a faction, the form of popular government, on the other hand, enables it to sacrifice to its ruling passion or interest both the public good and the rights of other citizens. To secure the public good and private rights against the danger of such a faction, and at the same time to preserve the spirit and the form of popular government, is then the great object to which our inquiries are directed. Let me add that it is the great desideratum by which this form of government can be rescued from the opprobrium under which it has so long labored, and be recommended to the esteem and adoption of mankind.

By what means is this object attainable? Evidently by one of two only. Either the existence of the same passion or interest in a majority at the same time must be prevented, or the majority, having such coexistent passion or interest, must be rendered, by their number and local situation, unable to concert and carry into effect schemes of oppression. If the impulse and the opportunity be suffered to coincide, we well know that neither moral nor religious motives can be relied on as an adequate control. They are not found to be such on the injustice and violence of individuals, and lose their efficacy in proportion to the number combined together, that is, in proportion as their efficacy becomes needful.

From this view of the subject it may be concluded that a pure democracy, by which I mean a society consisting of a small number of citizens, who assemble and administer the government in person, can admit of no cure for the mischiefs of faction. A common passion or interest will, in almost every case, be felt by a majority of the whole; a communication and concert result from the form of government itself; and there is nothing to check the inducements to sacrifice the weaker party or an obnoxious individual. Hence it is that such democracies have ever been spectacles of turbulence and contention; have ever been found incompatible with personal security or the rights of property; and have in general been as short in their lives as they have been violent in their deaths. Theoretic politicians, who have patronized this species of government, have erroneously supposed that by reducing mankind to a perfect equality in their political rights, they would, at the same time, be perfectly equalized and assimilated in their possessions, their opinions, and their passions.

A republic, by which I mean a government in which the scheme of representation takes place, opens a different prospect, and promises the cure for which we are seeking. Let me examine the points in which it varies from pure democracy, and we shall comprehend both the nature of the cure and the efficacy which it must derive from the Union.

The two great points of difference between a democracy and a republic are: first, the delegation of the government, in the latter, to a small number of citizens, elected by the rest; secondly, the greater number of citizens, and greater sphere of country, over which the latter may be extended.

The effect of the first difference is, on the one hand, to refine and enlarge the public views, by passing them through the medium of a chosen body of citizens, whose wisdom may best discern the true interest of their country, and whose patriotism and love of justice will be least likely to sacrifice it to temporary or partial consideration. Under such a regulation, it may well happen that the public voice, pronounced by the representatives of the people, will be more consonant to the public good than if pronounced by the people themselves, convened for the purpose. On the other hand, the effect may be inverted. Men of factious tempers, of local prejudices, or of sinister designs, may, by intrigue, by corruption, or by other means, first obtain the suffrages, and then betray the interests, of the people. The question resulting is, whether small or extensive republics are more favorable to the election of proper guardians of the public weal; and it is clearly decided in favor of the latter by two obvious considerations:

In the first place, it is to be remarked that, however small the republic may be, the representatives must be raised to a certain number, in order to guard against the cabals of a few; and that, however large it may be, they must be limited to a certain number, in order to guard against the confusion of a multitude. Hence, the number of representatives in the two cases not being in proportion to that of the two constituents, and being proportionally greater in the small republic, it follows that, if the proportion of fit characters be not less in the large than in the small republic, the former will present a greater option, and consequently a greater probability of a fit choice.

In the next place, as each representative will be chosen by a greater number of citizens in the large than in the small republic, it will be more difficult for unworthy candidates to practice with success the vicious arts by which elections are too often carried; and the suffrages of the people being more free, will be more likely to centre in men who possess the most attractive merit and the most diffusive and established characters.

It must be confessed that in this, as in most other cases, there is a mean, on both sides of which inconveniences will be found to lie. By enlarging too much the number of electors, you render the representative too little acquainted with all their local circumstances and lesser interests; as by reducing it too much, you render him unduly attached to these, and too little fit to comprehend and pursue great and national objects. The federal Constitution forms a happy combination in this respect; the great and aggregate interests being referred to the national, the local and particular to the State legislatures.

The other point of difference is, the greater number of citizens and extent of territory which may be brought within the compass of republican than of democratic government; and it is this circumstance principally which renders factious combinations less to be dreaded in the former than in the latter. The smaller the society, the fewer probably will be the distinct parties and interests composing it; the fewer the distinct parties and interests, the more frequently will a majority be found of the same party; and the smaller the number of individuals composing a majority, and the smaller the compass within which they are placed, the more easily will they concert and execute their plans of oppression. Extend the sphere, and take in a greater variety of parties and interests; you make it less probable that a majority of the whole will have a common motive to invade the rights of other citizens; or if such a common motive exists, it will be more difficult for all who feel it to discover their own strength, and to act in unison with each other. Besides other impediments, it may be remarked that, where there is a consciousness of unjust or dishonorable purposes, communication is always checked by distrust in proportion to the number whose concurrence is necessary.

Hence, it clearly appears, that the same advantage which a republic has over a democracy, in controlling the effects of faction, is enjoyed by a large over a small republic—is enjoyed by the Union over the States composing it. Does the advantage consist in the substitution of representatives whose enlightened views and virtuous sentiments render them superior to local prejudices and to schemes of injustice? It will not be denied that the representation of the Union will be most likely to possess these requisite endowments. Does it consist in the greater security afforded by a greater variety of parties, against the event of any one party being able to outnumber and oppress the rest? In an equal degree does the increased variety of parties comprised within the Union, increase this security? Does it, in fine, consist in the greater obstacles opposed to the concert and accomplishment of the secret wishes of an unjust and interested majority? Here, again, the extent of the Union gives it the most palpable advantage.

The influence of factious leaders may kindle a flame within their particular States, but will be unable to spread a general conflagration through the other States. A religious sect may degenerate into a political faction in a part of the Confederacy; but the variety of sects dispersed over the entire face of it must secure the national councils against any danger from that source. A rage for paper money, for an abolition of debts, for an equal division of property, or for any other improper or wicked project, will be less apt to pervade the whole body of the Union than a particular member of it; in the same proportion as such a malady is more likely to taint a particular county or district, than an entire State.

In the extent and proper structure of the Union, therefore, we behold a republican remedy for the diseases most incident to republican government. And according to the degree of pleasure and pride we feel in being republicans, ought to be our zeal in cherishing the spirit and supporting the character of Federalists.

PUBLIUS

Chapter 3

FEDERALISTS VS. REPUBLICANS

Even when the Constitution had been ratified and George Washington unanimously chosen to preside over the destinies of the new republic, enormous difficulties faced those who sought to establish a "more perfect union." The Constitution provided merely a structural framework for the new government; the details of organization, procedure, and protocol had yet to be decided upon. Congress had to provide for its own organization, laws had to be passed to establish executive departments and a federal judiciary, and provision had to be made for an adequate revenue. Besides, precedents had to be set to answer those many questions on which the Constitution was silent: What was to be the relationship of the President to his department heads? In answer, Washington's practice of frequent consultation created the closely knit cabinet of advisers we know today. Was the "advice and consent" of the Senate to be sought before or after the President entered into treaty negotiations? The Senate's abrupt treatment when Washington came in person to seek prior advice on an Indian treaty convinced him—and his successors—that treaties should be submitted for ratification only after executive negotiations had been completed. In this fashion many of the extra-constitutional practices peculiar to American government today were derived from the experiences of Washington and his colleagues in the early years of the republic.

Final ratification of the Constitution and the establishment of the new government under Washington's leadership by no means resolved the severe conflict that had raged between Federalists and Anti-Federalists in the state ratifying conventions. Although the antagonists joined in support of Washington's efforts to set up the machinery of government, their intense struggle for control continued under the new Constitution, and soon political parties emerged to institutionalize old and deeply rooted antagonisms between classes and sections. Indeed, it was ironic that Washington, who sought so strenuously to avoid the dissensions of party, appointed as his chief cabinet officers the two distinguished Americans who were to be most closely identified with the rise of political factions. He chose as his Secretary of State the versatile and learned Thomas Jefferson, author of the Declaration of Independence, and as his Secretary of the Treasury the brilliant and dynamic Alexander Hamilton, who had so vigorously led the proponents of the Constitution. About these giants were to rage the party battles of the infant republic.

Hamilton's primary objective, as Secretary of the Treasury, was to make of the new government a powerful instrument for order and stability. He saw that "communities divide themselves into the few and the many. The first are the rich and well-born; the other the mass of the people." The masses are "turbulent and changing," but the "rich and well-born" seek order. Thus it was Hamilton's plan to secure for the federal government the active support not of the many—debtor farmers, artisans, and mechanics—but of the powerful few—merchants, bankers, and speculators who made up the creditor classes and formed the Federalist party. To assure that support to the new government, the Secretary very early submitted to Congress a series of brilliant Reports on the Public Credit. In rapid succession Hamilton's Reports called for the funding of the national debt and the assumption of state debts, measures that served not only to establish the nation's credit, but also to guarantee to speculating conservatives a new "interest" in the federal government; the passage of excise taxes, particularly a whiskey tax, harmless to the commercial East but so obnoxious to the agrarian West where bulky grain was converted into whiskey for easy transportation across the mountains; and the creation of a Bank of the United States, in whose stock the "rich and well-born" might invest most profitably. These measures were all quickly passed at Hamilton's insistence, but by a more and more angrily divided Congress. With them Hamilton achieved his immediate objectives, for they successfully wove an intricate net of profit that secured to the national government the enthusiastic support of wealthy Federalists. But even as his Reports were being written into law, Hamilton was arousing an opposition whose concern for popular interests would call forth widespread support which would finally drive the Federalist leader and his party from power.

Thomas Jefferson was no friend of anarchy or license—by birth, training, and temperament no fiery partisan of mobs. But neither did he share Hamilton's desperate fear of the people as a "great beast." To the thoughtful Virginian, government need not stand primarily as a symbol of order and stability; rather, the end of "legitimate government" was "freedom and the happiness of its citizens." A political philosophy so antithetical to Hamilton's quickly led the Secretary of State to assume the leadership of those groups organizing to defeat the Federalist program. As Federalists represented creditor mercantile and commercial interests, so the opposition, emerging as the Republican party, represented the debtor agrarian interests of a nation still predominantly agricultural. Under Jefferson and James Madison the new party bitterly opposed Hamilton's legislative proposals and eagerly awaited the time when the sacred name of Washington no longer would sanction and protect Federalist policy. In 1792 Washington again received a unanimous electoral vote as President, but party divisions were already so intense that his Federalist Vice-President, John Adams, received only 77 votes to 55 for the Republican George Clinton. Thus national political parties, neither provided for nor even foreseen by the framers of the Constitution, had early come to be the dominant fact of American political life.

When in February, 1791, Washington called upon Jefferson and Hamilton to submit their opinions on the constitutionality of legislation chartering a Bank of the United States, national political affiliations had already been well defined in terms of broad and basic interests. Though the letters they wrote in reply were couched in the language of the Constitution, the rival Secretaries wrote primarily as leaders of their respective parties. Fearful of extending the powers of an administration so deeply committed to the interests of Federalism, Jefferson spoke the mind of his party when he declared for a "strict" construction of the Constitution: his was a philosophy of limited government. Congress, he argued, had been delegated specifically enumerated powers; its further power "to make all laws necessary and proper" for carrying them into execution must not be loosely defined. "Necessary and proper," wrote Jefferson, mean "essential." A bank was not essential for carrying out the enumerated powers; therefore the Bank Bill was clearly unconstitutional.

For those whose interests were so well served by the ever more powerful Federalist-dominated central government, Hamilton as vigorously defended the Bank Bill. His was a "loose" or "broad" construction of the Constitution. Implied in the Constitution, wrote the conservative Secretary, was the power to pass even those measures that were "no more than needful, requisite, incidental, useful, or conducive to" carrying out the enumerated powers; the Bank Bill fell into this category and therefore was constitutional. Ultimately Washington accepted Hamilton's opinion and signed the bill. Since that time the doctrine of "implied powers" has been used to extend the functions of government to a point even Hamilton could not have foreseen.

But before long Federalists and Republicans were to reverse their political—and therefore their constitutional—positions. A decade after the famous letters on the Bank Bill a combination of agrarians and poorer urban groups had made Jefferson President, and the Federalists no longer controlled the central government. The victorious Republicans, now in office, spoke enthusiastically about a generously broad and nationalistic interpretation of the Constitution. And the defeated, disgruntled Federalists, now out of office, sought to return to the "true" principles of the Founding Fathers—principles of limited government so well defended, in 1791, by Thomas Jefferson!

On the Constitutionality of the Bank of the United States, *1791*

Jefferson to Washington:
I consider the foundation of the Constitution as laid on this ground: That "all powers not delegated to the United States, by the Constitution, nor prohibited by it to the States, are reserved to the States or to the people . . ." To take a single step beyond the boundaries thus specially drawn around the powers of Congress is to take possession of a boundless field of power, no longer susceptible of any definition.

The incorporation of a bank, and the powers assumed by this bill, have not, in my opinion, been delegated to the United States by the Constitution.

I. They are not among the powers specially enumerated: for these are: 1. A power to lay taxes for the purpose of paying the debts of the United States; but no debt is paid by this bill, nor any tax laid. Were it a bill to raise money, its origination in the Senate would condemn it by the Constitution.

2. "To borrow money." But this bill neither borrows money nor insures the borrowing it. The proprietors of the bank will be just as free as any other money-holders to lend or not to lend their money to the public. The operation proposed in the bill, first, to lend them two millions, and then to borrow them back again, cannot change the nature of the latter act, which will still be a payment, and not a loan, call it by what name you please.

3. To "regulate commerce with foreign nations, and among the states, and with the Indian tribes." To erect a bank, and to regulate commerce, are very different acts. He who erects a bank creates a subject of commerce in its bills; so does he who makes a bushel of wheat or digs a

dollar out of the mines; yet neither of these persons regulates commerce thereby. To make a thing which may be bought and sold is not to prescribe regulations for buying and selling. Besides, if this was an exercise of the power of regulating commerce, it would be void, as extending as much to the internal commerce of every State, as to its external. For the power given to Congress by the Constitution does not extend to the internal regulation of the commerce of a State (that is to say of the commerce between citizen and citizen), which remain exclusively with its own legislature; but to its external commerce only, that is to say, its commerce with another State, or with foreign nations, or with the Indian tribes. Accordingly the bill does not propose the measure as a regulation of trade, but as "productive of considerable advantages to trade." Still less are these powers covered by any other of the special enumerations.

II. Nor are they within either of the general phrases, which are the two following:

1. To lay taxes to provide for the general welfare of the United States, that is to say, "to lay taxes for the purpose of providing for the general welfare." For the laying of taxes is the power, and the general welfare the purpose for which the power is to be exercised. They are not to lay taxes *ad libitum* for any purpose they please but only to pay the debts or provide for the welfare of the Union. In like manner, they are not to do anything they please to provide for the general welfare but only to lay taxes for that purpose. To consider the latter phrase, not as describing the purpose of the first, but as giving a distinct and independent power to do any act they please, which might be for the good of the Union, would render all the preceding and subsequent enumerations of power completely useless.

It would reduce the whole instrument to a single phrase, that of instituting a Congress with power to do whatever would be for the good of the United States; and, as they would be the sole judges of the good or evil, it would be also a power to do whatever evil they please.

It is an established rule of construction where a phrase will bear either of two meanings to give it that which will allow some meaning to the other parts of the instrument and not that which would render all the others useless. Certainly no such universal power was meant to be given them. It was intended to lace them up straitly within the enumerated powers, and those without which, as means, these powers could not be carried into effect. It is known that the very power now proposed as a means was rejected as an end by the Convention which formed the Constitution. A proposition was made to them to authorize Congress to open canals, and an amendatory one to empower them to incorporate. But the whole was rejected, and one of the reasons for rejection urged in debate was that then they would have a power to erect a bank, which would render the great cities, where there were prejudices and jealousies on the subject, adverse to the reception of the Constitution.

2. The second general phrase is "to make all laws necessary and proper for carrying into execution the enumerated powers." But they can all be carried into execution without a bank. A bank therefore is not necessary and consequently not authorized by this phrase.

It has been urged that a bank will give great facility or convenience in the collection of taxes. Suppose this were true: yet the Constitution allows only the names which are "necessary," not those which are merely "convenient" for effecting the enumerated powers. If such a latitude of construction be allowed to this phrase as to give any nonenumerated power, it will go to every one, for there is not one which ingenuity may not torture into a convenience in some instance or other, to some one of so long a list of enumerated powers. It would swallow up all the delegated powers and reduce the whole to one power, as before observed. Therefore it was that the Constitution restrained them to the *necessary* means, that is to say, to those means without which the grant of power would be nugatory. . . .

Perhaps, indeed, bank bills may be a more convenient vehicle than treasury orders. But a little difference in the degree of convenience cannot constitute the necessity which the Constitution makes the ground for assuming any nonenumerated power. . . .

It may be said that a bank whose bills would have a

currency all over the States would be more convenient than one whose currency is limited to a single State. So it would be still more convenient that there should be a bank whose bills should have a currency all over the world. But it does not follow from this superior conveniency that there exists anywhere a power to establish such a bank or that the world may not get on very well without it.

Can it be thought that the Constitution intended that for a shade or two of convenience, more or less, Congress should be authorized to break down the most ancient and fundamental laws of the several States; such as those against mortmain, the laws of alienage, the rules of descent, the acts of distribution, the laws of escheat and forfeiture, the laws of monopoly? Nothing but a necessity invincible by any other means can justify such a prostitution of laws, which constitute the pillars of our whole system of jurisprudence. Will Congress be too straitlaced to carry the Constitution into honest effect, unless they may pass over the foundation laws of the State government for the slightest convenience of theirs?

The negative of the President is the shield provided by the Constitution to protect against the invasions of the legislature: 1. The right of the executive. 2. Of the judiciary. 3. Of the States and State legislatures. The present is the case of a right remaining exclusively with the States, and consequently one of those intended by the Constitution to be placed under its protection. . . .

*Hamilton to Washington:**

. . . Now it appears to the Secretary of the Treasury that this general principle is inherent in the very definition of government and essential to every step of the progress to be made by that of the United States, namely: That every power vested in a government is in its nature sovereign and includes, by force of the term, a right to employ all the means requisite and fairly applicable to the attainment of the ends of such power, and which are not precluded by restrictions and exceptions specified

* From *The Works of Alexander Hamilton* (Vol. III), edited by Henry Cabot Lodge. Used by permission of G. P. Putnam's Sons.

in the Constitution, or not immoral, or not contrary to the essential ends of political society. . . .

. . . The circumstance that the powers of sovereignty are in this country divided between the national and state governments does not afford the distinction required. It does not follow from this that each of the portion of powers delegated to the one or to the other is not sovereign with regard to its proper objects. It will only follow from it that each has sovereign power as to certain things and not as to other things. To deny that the Government of the United States has sovereign power, as to its declared purposes and trusts, because its power does not extend to all cases, would be equally to deny that the State governments have sovereign power in any case, because their power does not extend to every case. The tenth section of the first article of the Constitution exhibits a long list of very important things which they may not do. And thus the United States would furnish the singular spectacle of a political society without sovereignty, or of a people governed without government.

If it would be necessary to bring proof to a proposition so clear, as that which affirms that the powers of the Federal Government, as to its objects, were sovereign, there is a clause of its Constitution which would be decisive. It is that which declares that the Constitution, and the laws of the United States made in pursuance of it, and all treaties made, or which shall be made, under their authority, shall be the supreme law of the land. The power which can create the supreme law of the land in any case is doubtless sovereign as to such case.

This general and indisputable principle puts at once an end to the abstract question whether the United States have power to erect a corporation; that is to say, to give a legal or artificial capacity to one or more persons, distinct from the natural. For it is unquestionably incident to sovereign power to erect corporations, and consequently to that of the United States, in relation to the objects intrusted to the management of the Government. The difference is this: where the authority of the Government is general, it can create corporations in all cases; where it is confined to certain branches of legislation, it can create corporations only in those cases. . . .

. . . It is not denied that there are implied as well as express powers and that the former are as effectually delegated as the latter. And for the sake of accuracy it shall be mentioned that there is another class of powers which may be properly denominated resulting powers. It will not be doubted that, if the United States should make a conquest of any of the territories of its neighbors, they would possess sovereign jurisdiction over the conquered territory. This would be rather a result, from the whole mass of the powers of the Government, and from the nature of political society, than a consequence of either of the powers specially enumerated. . . .

. . . It is conceded that implied powers are to be considered as delegated equally with express ones. Then it follows that, as a power of erecting a corporation may as well be implied as any other thing, it may as well be employed as an instrument or means of carrying into execution any of the specified powers, as any other instrument or means whatever. The only question must be, in this, as in every other case, whether the means to be employed or, in this instance, the corporation to be erected, has a natural relation to any of the acknowledged objects or lawful ends of the Government. Thus a corporation may not be erected by Congress for superintending the police of the city of Philadelphia, because they are not authorized to regulate the police of that city. But one may be erected in relation to the collection of taxes, or to the trade with foreign countries, or to the trade between the States, or with the Indian tribes; because it is the province of the Federal Government to regulate those objects, and because it is incident to a general sovereign or legislative power to regulate a thing, to employ all the means which relate to its regulation to the best and greatest advantage. . . .

Through this mode of reasoning respecting the right of employing all the means requisite to the execution of the specified powers of the Government, it is objected that none but necessary and proper means are to be employed; and the Secretary of State maintains that no means are to be considered as necessary but those without which the grant of the power would be nugatory.

Nay, so far does he go in his restrictive interpretation of the word, as even to make the case of the necessity which shall warrant the constitutional exercise of the power to depend on casual and temporary circumstances; an idea which alone refutes the construction. The expediency of exercising a particular power, at a particular time, must, indeed, depend on circumstances; but the constitutional right of exercising it must be uniform and invariable, the same today as tomorrow.

All the arguments, therefore, against the constitutionality of the bill derived from the accidental existence of certain state banks—institutions which happen to exist today and, for aught that concerns the Government of the United States, may disappear tomorrow—must not only be rejected as fallacious but must be viewed as demonstrative that there is a radical source of error in the reasoning.

It is essential to the being of the national government that so erroneous a conception of the meaning of the word necessary should be exploded.

It is certain that neither the grammatical nor popular sense of the term requires that construction. According to both, necessary often means no more than needful, requisite, incidental, useful, or conducive to. It is a common mode of expression to say that it is necessary for a government or a person to do this or that thing, when nothing more is intended or understood than that the interests of the government or person require, or will be promoted by, the doing of this or that thing. The imagination can be at no loss for exemplifications of the use of the word in this sense. And it is the true one in which it is to be understood as used in the Constitution. The whole turn of the clause containing it indicates that it was the intent of the Convention, by that clause, to give a liberal latitude to the exercise of the specified powers. The expressions have peculiar comprehensiveness. They are, "to make all laws necessary and proper for carrying into execution the foregoing powers, and all other powers vested by the Constitution in the government of the United States, or in any department or officer thereof."

To understand the word as the Secretary of State does would be to depart from its obvious and popular sense and to give it a restrictive operation, an idea never before entertained. It would be to give it the same force as if the word absolutely or indispensably had been prefixed to it. . . .

The degree in which a measure is necessary can never be a test of the legal right to adopt it; that must be a matter of opinion and can only be a test of expediency. The relation between the measure and the end; between the nature of the means employed toward the execution of a power and the object of that power, must be the criterion of constitutionality, not the more or less of necessity or utility. . . .

This restrictive interpretation of the word necessary is also contrary to this sound maxim of construction; namely, that the powers contained in a constitution of government, especially those which concern the general administration of the affairs of a country, its finances, trade, defense, etc., ought to be construed liberally in advancement of the public good. This rule does not depend on the particular form of a government, or on the particular demarcation of the boundaries of its powers, but on the nature and objects of government itself. The means by which national exigencies are to be provided for, national inconveniences obviated, national prosperity promoted, are of such infinite variety, extent, and complexity, that there must of necessity be great latitude of discretion in the selection and application of those means. Hence, consequently, the necessity and propriety of exercising the authorities intrusted to a government on principles of liberal construction. . . .

But the doctrine which is contended for is not chargeable with the consequences imputed to it. It does not affirm that the national government is sovereign in all respects but that it is sovereign to a certain extent; that is, to the extent of the objects of its specified powers.

It leaves, therefore, a criterion of what is constitutional and of what is not so. This criterion is the end, to which the measure relates as a means. If the end be clearly comprehended within any of the specified powers, and if the measures have an obvious relation to that end, and is not forbidden by a particular provision of the Constitution, it may safely be deemed to come within the compass of the national authority. There is also this further criterion, which may materially assist the decision: Does the proposed measure abridge a pre-existing right of any State or of any individual? If it does not, there is a strong presumption in favor of its constitutionality, and slighter relations to any declared object of the Constitution may be permitted to turn the scale. . . .

It is presumed to have been satisfactorily shown in the course of the preceding observations:

1. That the power of the Government, as to the objects intrusted to its management, is, in its nature, sovereign.

2. That the right of erecting corporations is one inherent in, and inseparable from, the idea of sovereign power.

3. That the position that the Government of the United States can exercise no power but such as is delegated to it by its Constitution does not militate against this principle.

4. That the word necessary, in the general clause, can have no restrictive operation derogating from the force of this principle; indeed, that the degree in which a measure is or is not necessary cannot be a test of constitutional right but of expediency only.

5. That the power to erect corporations is not to be considered as an independent or substantive power but as an incidental and auxiliary one and was therefore more properly left to implication than expressly granted.

6. That the principle in question does not extend the power of the Government beyond the prescribed limits, because it only affirms a power to incorporate for purposes within the sphere of the specified powers.

And, lastly, that the right to exercise such a power in certain cases is unequivocally granted in the most positive and comprehensive terms. . . .

A hope is entertained that it has, by this time, been made to appear, to the satisfaction of the President, that a bank has a natural relation to the power of collecting taxes—to that of regulating trade—to that of providing for the common defense—and that, as the bill under consideration contemplates the Government in the light of a joint proprietor of the stock of the bank, it brings the case within the provision of the clause of the Constitution which immediately respects the property of the United States.

Under a conviction that such a relation subsists, the Secretary of the Treasury, with all deference, conceives, that it will result as a necessary consequence from the position, that all the specified powers of Government are sovereign, as to the proper objects; that the incorporation of a bank is a constitutional measure; and that the objections taken to the bill, in this respect, are ill founded. . . .

Chapter 4

NEUTRALITY AND NATIONAL GROWTH

The maintenance of American neutrality in the perilous early years of the Republic was a profound tribute to the wisdom and foresight of Washington and his colleagues. However great the difficulties peculiar to the establishment of the new government and the determination of national domestic policy, they were equaled, if not surpassed, by the difficulty of preserving peace. It was Washington's objective that the new nation should grow and thrive in peace until the strength of union was a reality and a just and powerful United States could assume its rightful position among the nations of the world. But peace was precarious, for war raged almost incessantly among the great powers of England, France and Spain. And Washington's dual task of preserving peace and affirming the integrity of the new government was made even more burdensome by bitter disagreements on foreign policy among party factions at home. Most of the great leaders concurred with Washington's strong feeling that peace was indispensable to the young nation's well-being. Beyond that, however, the area of their agreement was small indeed, and the political parties very early came to be identified with the foreign antagonists, the Republican as pro-French, the Federalist as pro-English. The overwhelming intensity of the partisan conflict over foreign policy was alarming.

Yet for nearly a quarter of a century of national progress under the new government, peace—if not absolute neutrality—was maintained, and time was secured to prove the experiment of American democracy successful. This, ultimately, was the supreme achievement of early American statesmanship.

When war broke out between England and France in 1793, the United States was forced to balance precariously between disastrous entanglements with the one or the other. Even before the war began, relations with the old mother country were marred by bad feelings. Antagonisms had been whipped up by England's refusal to abandon the Northwest forts and trading posts she had ceded at the end of the Revolutionary War. Americans were convinced that the English, intending to retain the posts permanently, were savagely encouraging the Indians to massacre oncoming settlers. Then, after war between England and France started, explosive fuel was added to a long-range fire when the English seized American vessels and cargoes—even those having only the slighest connection with the French trade—and began the unhappy practice of impressing American sailors into the Royal Navy. Popular hatred of England, matched only by a widespread enthusiasm for Revolutionary France, grew very quickly to proportions that seemed to augur war. Even the beloved Washington suffered outrageous abuse at the hands of inflamed Anglophobes when in 1795 he supported the treaty which Federalist Chief Justice John Jay had negotiated with the English. Washington himself deplored the tenor of the Jay Treaty; for though it provided for final abandonment of the Northwest posts, it seemed to concede more to the English than it gained from them. But Washington correctly estimated its real value to the nation: it provided a necessary breathing spell of peace. At his insistence, then, but by an extremely close vote, a reluctant Senate ratified the treaty and, at least for the immediate future, war with England was avoided.

Meanwhile relations with France were fast deteriorating. In 1793 the French Minister, blundering "Citizen" Genêt, though cheered wildly by a predominantly pro-French populace, had failed to win formal assistance from the American government for its warring sister republic. Arrogantly, Genêt then appealed for popular support over the President's head. Washington, however, with the concurrence of his entire cabinet, remained firm in the declaration of his recent Proclamation of Neutrality that the conduct of the United States should be "impartial towards the belligerents," and Genêt's mission remained a failure. Despairing of active assistance from the United States, France soon came to treat American neutral rights with the same studied disdain so long practiced by the English. Later, in John Adams' administration, French depredations threatened to turn the tide of popular feelings so completely as even to bring war with the former ally. In 1798, when three unnamed French officials (designated as X, Y, and Z) demanded bribes to receive a trio of American envoys, popular fury at the French knew no bounds and throughout the nation the angry cry echoed, "Millions for defense, but not one cent for tribute." Only John Adams' firm stand against this popular outcry saved the nation from plunging headlong into a full-fledged war with France. Again the new government was reprieved from a war that might have destroyed it.

Washington, and after him Adams, had struggled courageously to preserve peace, but not without suffering the vilest abuse from those whose personal or party interests opposed the statesmen's insistence upon impartial relations with all nations. Thus, when in 1796 Washington composed his valedictory, the memorable Farewell Address, he had long experienced the "baneful effects of the spirit of party" upon the nation's foreign as well as domestic affairs. Unwilling himself "to be longer buffeted in the public prints by a set of infamous scribblers," Washington here sought to establish principles of national behavior that were based upon unity rather than party factionalism. Drafted and revised in part by Madison, Jay, and particularly Hamilton, but always speaking the mind of the President, the Farewell Address embodied Washington's sage counsel to his fellow countrymen to "observe good faith and justice towards all nations" and to shun "permanent, inveterate antipathies against particular nations and passionate attachments for others." Of course, even as Washington bade farewell to the nation he had served so long and so well, pleading for the principles of unity, independence and good faith, opponents rejoiced that "the name of Washington ceases from this day to give currency to political iniquity and to legalize corruption." But if Washington's plea for an end to partisanship fell on deaf ears within both parties, nonetheless the Farewell Address stands as a profound tribute to his wisdom, sincerity, and statesmanship.

George Washington's Farewell Address, *1796*

FRIENDS AND FELLOW-CITIZENS: The period for a new election of a citizen, to administer the executive government of the United States, being not far distant, and the time actually arrived, when your thoughts must be employed in designating the person, who is to be clothed with that important trust, it appears to me proper, especially as it may conduce to a more distinct expression of the public voice, that I should now apprise you of the resolution I have formed, to decline being considered among the number of those out of whom a choice is to be made. . . .

I rejoice that the state of your concerns, external as well as internal, no longer renders the pursuit of inclination incompatible with the sentiment of duty or propriety; and am persuaded, whatever partiality may be retained for my services, that, in the present circumstances of our country, you will not disapprove my determination to retire.

The impressions, with which I first undertook the arduous trust, were explained on the proper occasion. In the discharge of this trust, I will only say, that I have, with good intentions, contributed toward the organization and administration of the Government, the best exertions of which a very fallible judgment was capable. Not unconscious, in the outset, of the inferiority of my qualifications, experience in my own eyes, perhaps still more in the eyes of others, has strengthened the motives to diffidence of myself; and every day the increasing weight of years admonishes me more and more, that the shade of retirement is as necessary to me as it will be welcome. Satisfied that if any circumstances have given peculiar value to my services, they were temporary, I have the consolation to believe, that while choice and prudence invite me to quit the political scene, patriotism does not forbid it.

. . . Solicitude for your welfare, which cannot end but with my life, and apprehension of danger, natural to that solicitude, urge me on an occasion like the present, to offer to your solemn contemplation, and to recommend to your frequent review, some sentiments; which are the result of much reflection, of no inconsiderable observation, and which appear to me all important to the permanency of your felicity as a people. These will be offered to you with the more freedom, as you can only see in them the disinterested warnings of a parting friend, who can possibly have no personal motive as his counsel. . . .

Interwoven as is the love of liberty with every ligament of your hearts, no recommendation of mine is necessary to fortify or confirm the attachment.

The unity of government which constitutes you one people is also now dear to you. It is justly so; for it is a main pillar in the edifice of your real independence, the support of your tranquility at home; your peace abroad; of your safety; of your prosperity; of that very liberty which you so highly prize. But as it is easy to foresee, that from different causes and from different quarters, much pains will be taken, many artifices employed, to weaken in your minds the conviction of this truth; as this is the point in your political fortress against which the batteries of internal and external enemies will be most constantly and actively (though often covertly and insidiously) directed, it is of infinite moment, that you should properly estimate the immense value of your national Union to your collective and individual happiness; that you should cherish a cordial, habitual and immoveable attachment to it; accustoming yourselves to think and speak of it as of the palladium of your political safety and prosperity; watching for its preservation with jealous anxiety; discountenancing whatever may suggest even a suspicion that it can in any event be abandoned, and indignantly frowning upon the first dawning of every attempt to alienate any portion of our country from the rest, or to enfeeble the sacred ties which now link together the various parts.

For this you have every inducement of sympathy and interest. Citizens by birth or choice, of a common country, that country has a right to concentrate your affections. The name of *American*, which belongs to you, in your national capacity, must always exalt the just pride of patriotism, more than any appellation derived from local discriminations. With slight shades of difference, you have the same religion, manners, habits and political principles. You have in a common cause fought and triumphed together. The independence and liberty you possess are the work of joint councils, and joint efforts; of common dangers, sufferings and successes.

But these considerations, however powerfully they address themselves to your sensibility are greatly outweighed by those which apply more immediately to your interest. Here every portion of our country finds the most commanding motives for carefully guarding and preserving the union of the whole.

The North, in an unrestrained intercourse with the South, protected by the equal laws of a common Government, finds in the productions of the latter, great additional resources of maritime and commercial enterprise and precious materials of manufacturing industry. The South in the same intercourse, benefitting by the agency of the North, sees its agriculture grow and its commerce expand. Turning partly into its own channels the seamen of the North, it finds its particular navigation envigorated; and while it contributes, in different ways, to nourish and increase the general mass of the national navigation, it looks forward to the protection of a maritime strength, to which itself is unequally adapted. The East, in a like intercourse with the West, already finds, and in the progressive improvement of interior communications, by land and water, will more and more find a valuable vent for the commodities which it brings from abroad, or manufactures at home. The West derives from the East supplies requisite to its growth and comfort, and what is perhaps of still greater consequence, it must of necessity owe the secure enjoyment of indispensable outlets for its own productions to the weight, influence, and the future maritime strength of the Atlantic side of the Union, directed by an indissoluble community of interest as one nation. Any other tenure by which the West can hold this essential advantage, whether derived from its own separate strength, or from an apostate and unnatural connection with any foreign power, must be intrinsically precarious.

While then every part of our country thus feels an immediate and particular interest in union, all the parts combined cannot fail to find in the united mass of means and efforts greater strength, greater resource, proportionably greater security from external danger, a less frequent interruption of their peace by foreign nations; and, what is of inestimable value, they must derive from union an exemption from those broils and wars between themselves, which so frequently afflict neighboring countries, not tied together by the same government; which their own rivalships alone would be sufficient to produce, but which opposite foreign alliances, attachments and intrigues would stimulate and imbitter. . . .

In contemplating the causes which may disturb our union, it occurs as a matter of serious concern, that any ground should have been furnished for characterizing parties by geographical discriminations: Northern and Southern; Atlantic and Western; whence designing men may endeavour to excite a belief that there is a real difference of local interests and views. One of the expedients of party to acquire influence, within particular districts, is to misrepresent the opinions and aims of other districts. You cannot shield yourselves too much against the jealousies and heart burnings which spring from these misrepresentations. . . .

To the efficacy and permanency of your union, a Government for the whole is indispensable. No alliances however strict between the parts can be an adequate substitute. They must inevitably experience the infractions and interruptions which all alliances in all times have experienced. Sensible of this momentous truth, you have improved upon your first essay, by the adoption of a Constitution of Government, better calculated than your former for an intimate union, and for the efficacious management of your common concerns. This Government, the offspring of your own choice uninfluenced and unawed, adopted upon full investigation and mature deliberation, completely free in its principles, in the distribution of its powers, uniting security with energy, and containing within itself a provision for its own amendment, has a just claim to your confidence and your support. Respect for its authority, compliance with its laws, acquiescence in its measures, are duties enjoined by the fundamental maxims of true liberty. . . .

Towards the preservation of your Government and the permanency of your present happy state, it is requisite, not only that you steadily discountenance irregular oppositions to its acknowledged authority, but also that you resist with care the spirit of innovation upon its principles however specious the pretexts. One method of assault may be to effect, in the forms of the Constitution, alterations which will impair the energy of the system, and thus to undermine what cannot be directly overthrown. In all the changes to which you may be invited, remember that time and habit are at least as necessary to fix the true character of governments, as of other human institutions; that experience is the surest standard, by which to test the real tendency of the existing Constitution of a country; that facility in changes upon the credit of mere hypothesis and opinion exposes to perpetual change, from the endless variety of hypothesis and opinion; and remember, especially, that for the efficient management of your common interests, in a country so extensive as ours, a government of as much vigor as is consistent with the perfect security of liberty is indispensable. Liberty itself will find in such a government, with powers properly distributed and adjusted, its surest guardian. . . .

I have already intimated to you the danger of parties in the State, with particular reference to the founding of them on geographical discriminations. Let me now take a more comprehensive view, and warn you in the most solemn manner against the baneful effects of the spirit of party, generally.

This spirit, unfortunately, is inseparable from our nature, having its root in the strongest passions of the human mind. It exists under different shapes in all governments, more or less stifled, controlled, or repressed; but, in those of the popular form it is seen in its greatest rankness and is truly their worst enemy. . . .

It serves always to distract the public councils and enfeeble the public administration. It agitates the community with ill-founded jealousies and false alarms, kindles the animosity of one part against another, foments occasionally riot and insurrection. It opens the door to foreign influence and corruption, which find a facilitated access to the government itself through the channels of party passions. Thus the policy and the will of one country, are subjected to the policy and will of another.

There is an opinion that parties in free countries are useful checks upon the administration of the Government and serve to keep alive the spirit of liberty. This within certain limits is probably true, and in governments of a monarchical cast, patriotism may look with indulgence, if not with favor, upon the spirit of party. But in those of the popular character, in governments purely elective, it is a spirit not to be encouraged. From their natural tendency, it is certain there will always be enough of that spirit for every salutary purpose. And there being constant danger of excess, the effort ought to be, by force of public opinion, to mitigate and assuage it. A fire not to be quenched, it demands a uniform vigilance to prevent its bursting into a flame, lest instead of warming it should consume. . . .

It is substantially true, that virtue or morality is a necessary spring of popular government. The rule indeed extends with more or less force to every species of free government. Who that is a sincere friend to it, can look with indifference upon attempts to shake the foundation of the fabric.

Promote then as an object of primary importance, institutions for the general diffusion of knowledge. In proportion as the structure of a government gives force to public opinion, it is essential that public opinion should be enlightened.

As a very important source of strength and security, cherish public credit. One method of preserving it is to use it as sparingly as possible; avoiding occasions of expense by cultivating peace, but remembering also that timely disbursements to prepare for danger frequently prevent much greater disbursements to repel it; avoiding likewise the accumulation of debt, not only by shunning occasions of expense, but by vigorous exertions in time of peace to discharge the debts which unavoidable wars may have occasioned, not ungenerously throwing upon posterity the burden which we ourselves ought to bear. . . .

Observe good faith and justice towards all nations; cultivate peace and harmony with all. Religion and morality enjoin this conduct; and can it be that good policy does not equally enjoin it? It will be worthy of a free, enlightened, and, at no distant period, a great nation, to give to mankind the magnanimous and too novel example of a people always guided by an exalted justice and benevolence. Who can doubt that in the course of time and things the fruits of such a plan would richly repay any temporary advantages which might be lost by a steady adherence to it? Can it be, that Providence has not connected the permanent felicity of a nation with its virtue? The experiment, at least, is recommended by every sentiment which ennobles human nature. Alas! is it rendered impossible by its vices?

In the execution of such a plan nothing is more essential than that permanent, inveterate antipathies against particular nations and passionate attachments for others should be excluded; and that in place of them just and amicable feelings towards all should be cultivated. The nation, which indulges towards another an habitual hatred, or an habitual fondness, is in some degree a slave. It is a slave to its animosity or to its affection, either of which is sufficient to lead it astray from its duty and its interest. Antipathy in one nation against another, disposes each more readily to offer insult and injury, to lay hold of slight causes of umbrage, and to be haughty and intractable, when accidental or trifling occasions of dispute occur. Hence frequent collisions, obstinate envenomed and bloody contests. . . .

So likewise, a passionate attachment of one nation for another produces a variety of evils. Sympathy for the favorite nation, facilitating the illusion of an imaginary common interest, in cases where no real common interest exists, and infusing into one the enmities of the other, betrays the former into a participation in the quarrels and wars of the latter, without adequate inducement or justification. It leads also to concessions to the favorite nation of privileges denied to others, which is apt doubly to injure the nation making the concessions; by unnecessarily parting with what ought to have been retained; and by exciting jealousy, ill-will, and a disposition to retaliate, in the parties from whom equal privileges are withheld. And it gives to ambitious, corrupted, or deluded citizens (who devote themselves to the favorite nation) facility to betray, or sacrifice the interests of their own country, without odium, sometimes even with popularity; gilding with the appearances of a virtuous sense of obligation, a commendable deference for public opinion, or a laudable zeal for public good, the base or foolish compliances of ambition, corruption or infatuation. . . .

Against the insidious wiles of foreign influence, (I conjure you to believe me fellow-citizens) the jealousy of a free people ought to be constantly awake; since history and experience prove that foreign influence is one of the most baneful foes of republican government. But that jealousy to be useful must be impartial; else it becomes the instrument of the very influence to be avoided, instead of a defence against it. Excessive partiality for one foreign nation and excessive dislike of another, cause those whom they actuate to see danger only on one side, and serve to veil and even second the arts of influence on the other. Real patriots, who may resist the intrigues of the favorite, are liable to become suspected and odious; while its tools and dupes usurp the applause and confidence of the people, to surrender their interests.

The great rule of conduct for us, in regard to foreign nations is in extending our commercial relations to have with them as little political connection as possible. So far as we have already formed engagements let them be fulfilled, with perfect good faith. Here let us stop.

Europe has a set of primary interests, which to us have none, or a very remote relation. Hence she must be engaged in frequent controversies, the causes of which are essentially foreign to our concerns. Hence therefore it must be unwise in us to implicate ourselves, by artificial ties, in the ordinary vicissitudes of her politics, or the ordinary combinations and collisions of her friendships, or enmities.

Our detached and distant situation invites and enables us to pursue a different course. If we remain one people, under an efficient government, the period is not far off, when we may defy material injury from external annoyance; when we may take such an attitude as will cause the neutrality we may at any time resolve upon to be scrupulously respected; when belligerent nations, under the impossibility of making acquisitions upon us, will not lightly hazard the giving us provocation; when we may choose peace or war, as our interest guided by our justice shall counsel.

Why forego the advantages of so peculiar a situation? Why quit our own to stand upon foreign ground? Why, by interweaving our destiny with that of any part of Europe, entangle our peace and prosperity in the toils of European ambition, rivalship, interest, humour, or caprice?

It is our true policy to steer clear of permanent alliances, with any portion of the foreign world. So far, I mean, as we are now at liberty to do it, for let me not be understood as capable of patronizing infidelity to existing engagements. I hold the maxim no less applicable to public than to private affairs, that honesty is always the best policy. I repeat it therefore, let those engagements be observed in their genuine sense. But in my opinion, it is unnecessary and would be unwise to extend them.

Taking care always to keep ourselves, by suitable establishments, on a respectably defensive posture, we may safely trust to temporary alliances for extraordinary emergencies.

Harmony, liberal intercourse with all nations, are recommended by policy, humanity and interest. But even our commercial policy should hold an equal and impartial hand; neither seeking nor granting exclusive favors or preferences; consulting the natural course of things; diffusing and diversifying by gentle means the streams of commerce, but forcing nothing; establishing with powers so disposed; in order to give to trade a stable course, to define the rights of our merchants, and to enable the Government to support them; conventional rules of intercourse, the best that present circumstances and mutual opinion will permit, but temporary, and liable to be from time to time abandoned or varied, as experience and circumstances shall dictate; constantly keeping in view, that it is folly in one nation to look for disinterested favors from another; that it must pay with a portion of its independence for whatever it may accept under that character; that by such acceptance, it may place itself in the condition of having given equivalents for nominal favors and yet of being reproached with ingratitude for not giving more. There can be no greater error than to expect, or calculate upon real favors from nation to nation. It is an illusion which experience must cure, which a just pride ought to discard. . . .

Though in reviewing the incidents of my administration, I am unconscious of intentional error, I am nevertheless too sensible of my defects not to think it probable that I may have committed many errors. Whatever they may be I fervently beseech the Almighty to avert or mitigate the evils to which they may tend. I shall also carry with me the hope that my country will never cease to view them with indulgence; and that after forty-five years of my life dedicated to its service, with an upright zeal, the faults of incompetent abilities will be consigned to oblivion, as myself must soon be to the mansions of rest. . . .

Chapter 5

THE JEFFERSONIAN REVOLUTION

In 1796 George Washington's refusal to seek a third term loosed a floodtide of partisanship that had been at least partially restrained during his administrations, and a bitterly contested Presidential campaign resulted in a narrow victory for the Federalist John Adams over the Republican Thomas Jefferson. Despite the narrowness of their victory, the Federalists made no effort in the next four years to relate their party's policy more closely to the will of the majority of Americans. Continuing to champion the wealthy commercial and mercantile creditor class, they ignored the needs and demands of the more numerous and less prosperous agrarians and urban workers and remained distinctly out of temper with the country at large. Yet they were determined to maintain political power and to that end employed oppression as an alternative to popular appeal. To undermine an increasingly powerful Republican party, the Federalist-dominated Congress in 1798 passed the infamous Alien and Sedition Acts. Aimed at foreigners who contributed much in numbers and leadership to the Republicans, the Alien Acts extended from five to fourteen years the naturalization period prior to citizenship (and the suffrage) and gave to the Federalist President extensive powers over aliens in peace as well as in war. The Sedition Act was intended to silence all opposition to the Federalists by providing fines and prison terms for "malicious" attacks on Congress or the President. These desperate acts threatened violent harm to the personal liberties essential to democracy, but in passing them the Federalists had signed their own death warrant, for each convicted Republican stood as a martyr to the cause of free speech, and the laws themselves were ample testimony to the undemocratic intentions of the party in power. In reply came the dramatic Kentucky and Virginia Resolutions, penned by Jefferson and James Madison. Arguing the right of the states to interpose their authority against an oppressive central government, they called upon their sister states to join in declaring unconstitutional the viciously discriminatory Federalist Acts. Later the constitutional question of states' rights would time and again be invoked by both parties to rationalize conflict with the immediate policies of the central government. More important immediately, however, was the effectiveness of the Resolutions in their original intent: to provide the Republicans a winning platform for the election of 1800. In that year Jefferson had merely to point to the Federalists' record in office to win the Presidency in a decisive Republican victory.

Late in life, Jefferson described the election of 1800 thus: "as real a revolution in the principles of our government as that of 1776 was in its form." But in his

Inaugural Address of March, 1801, the new President wisely sought to allay the bitter partisanship of recent years. To admirers gathered to witness the first Presidential Inauguration in the new capital city of Washington, Jefferson insisted that "We have called by different names brethren of the same principle. We are all Republicans—we are all Federalists." There was no hint of revolution, no threat of repudiation, in the conciliatory Inaugural; rather, Jefferson's address was a strong affirmation of faith in the young republic, although it had been dominated by Federalists since its inception. And to the dismay of many who had helped forge the victory of 1800, the new President's moderation was in act as well as word. National offices were not swept clean of Federalists appointed by Washington and Adams, for the notion that "to the victors belong the spoils" was peculiar to the later Jacksonian Democracy, not to Jeffersonianism. Fundamentally, the machinery of government bequeathed by the Federalists was kept intact. The fiscal system that Hamilton had contrived was not substantially altered—although the Treasury was no longer used to gain support for the government from the "rich and well-born"—and the public credit was as secure under Albert Gallatin, Jefferson's Secretary of the Treasury, as it had been under Hamilton. Besides, under a President who came to construe his powers so broadly as to allow him to purchase the vast expanse of the Louisiana Territory, the Hamiltonian-Federalist orientation towards a strong central government, though modified in many ways, was certainly not abandoned. Indeed, to many good Republicans it seemed that Jefferson had taken all too seriously his inaugural assertion that "We are all Republicans—we are all Federalists."

But if the structure and much of the content of government were not radically changed with Republican victory, and if, indeed, Hamilton's vision of a highly industrialized and centralized state was ultimately to prove more prophetic than Jefferson's early notions of limited government and an agrarian economy, still in the most fundamental terms Jefferson's election marked a real revolution. For it was a revolution in ideas—as Jefferson later wrote, "in the principles of government"—that saw the national government dedicated by the Jeffersonians to the principles of democracy and liberty, as Federalists had made of it a shrine to order and stability. No longer was the prime concern of government for the interests of the few, the wealthy business class, but rather for the freedom and happiness of all the people. Not that business interests were proscribed nor even so subordinated to agrarianism as to be severely damaged, for the nation's industrial growth continued under Jefferson and his Republican successors as it had before them. With the ascendancy of the Republicans, however, that growth was to continue without a strong control over government. Finally, Jefferson's great achievement and the real meaning of the "Revolution of 1800," was that he preserved the Federalists' tremendous steps toward national economic and political power while he infused into government the ideals of democracy and liberty. That the nation grew strong and became the great industrial power Hamilton had envisaged remains the most meaningful tribute to Jeffersonian Democracy; for it did so, not under the auspices of the oppressive plutocratic or aristocratic government Hamilton thought necessary, but rather within the context of a free, democratic government whose principles were Jeffersonian. And a nation that had repudiated the tyranny of a Federalist Sedition Act would long remember Jefferson's famous plea for freedom of thought and expression: "Even if there be any among us who would wish to dissolve this Union or to change its republican form, let them stand undisturbed as monuments of the safety with which error of opinion may be tolerated when reason is left free to combat it."

Alien and Sedition Acts

An Act Concerning Aliens, *June, 1798*

SECTION 1. Be it enacted by the Senate and House of Representatives of the United States of America in Congress assembled, That it shall be lawful for the President of the United States at any time during the continuance of this act to *order* all such *aliens* as he shall judge dangerous to the peace and safety of the United States, or shall have reasonable grounds to suspect are concerned in any treasonable or secret machinations against the government thereof, to depart out of the territory of the United States, within such time as shall be expressed in such order, which order shall be served on such alien by delivering him a copy thereof, or leaving the same at his usual abode, and returned to the office of the Secretary of State, by the marshal or other person to whom the same shall be directed. And in case any alien, so ordered to depart, shall be found at large within the United States after the time limited in such order for his departure, and not having obtained a *license* from the President to reside therein, or having obtained such *license* shall not have conformed thereto, every such alien shall, on conviction thereof, be imprisoned for a term not exceeding three years, and shall never after be admitted to become a citizen of the United States. . . .

SEC. 2. And be it further enacted, That it shall be lawful for the President of the United States, whenever he may deem it necessary for the public safety, to order to be removed out of the territory thereof, any alien who may or shall be in prison in pursuance of this act; and to cause to be arrested and sent out of the United States such of those aliens as shall have been ordered to depart therefrom and shall not have obtained a license as aforesaid, in all cases where, in the opinion of the President, the public safety requires a speedy removal. And if any alien so removed or sent out of the United States by the President shall voluntarily return thereto, unless by permission of the President of the United States, such alien, on conviction thereof, shall be imprisoned so long as, in the opinion of the President, the public safety may require. . . .

Sedition Act, *July, 1798*

SECTION 1. Be it enacted . . . That if any persons shall unlawfully combine or conspire together, with intent to oppose any measure or measures of the government of the United States, which are or shall be directed by proper authority, or to impede the operation of any law of the United States, or to intimidate or prevent any person holding a place or office in or under the government of the United States, from undertaking, performing, or executing his trust or duty; and if any person or persons, with intent as aforesaid, shall counsel, advise, or attempt to procure any insurrection, riot, unlawful assembly, or combination, whether such conspiracy, threatening, counsel, advice, or attempt shall have the proposed effect or not, he or they shall be deemed guilty of a high misdemeanor, and on conviction, before any court of the United States having jurisdiction thereof, shall be punished by a fine not exceeding five thousand dollars, and by imprisonment during a term not less than six months nor exceeding five years; and further, at the discretion of the court may be holden to find sureties for his good behavior in such sum, and for such time, as the said court may direct.

SEC. 2. And be it further enacted, That if any person shall write, print, utter, or publish, or shall cause or procure to be written, printed, uttered, or published, or shall knowingly and willingly assist or aid in writing, printing, uttering, or publishing any false, scandalous, and malicious writings or writings against the government of the United States, or either house of the Congress of the United States, or the President of the United States, with intent to defame the said government, or either house of the said Congress, or the said President, or to bring them, or either of them, into contempt or disrepute; or to excite against them, or either or any of them, the hatred of the good people of the United States, or to stir up sedition within the United States, or to excite any unlawful combinations therein, for opposing or resisting any law of the United States, or any act of the President of the United States, done in pursuance of any such law, or of the powers in him vested by the Constitution of the United States, or to resist, oppose, or defeat any such law or act, or to aid, encourage or abet any hostile designs of any foreign nation against the United States, their people or government, then such person, being thereof convicted before any court of the United States having jurisdiction thereof, shall be punished by a fine not exceeding two thousand dollars, and by imprisonment not exceeding two years.

SEC. 3. And be it further enacted and declared, That if any person shall be prosecuted under this act, for the writing or publishing any libel aforesaid, it shall be lawful for the defendant, upon the trial of the cause, to give in evidence in his defense, the truth of the matter contained in the publication charged as a libel. And the jury who shall try the cause shall have a right to determine the law and the fact, under the direction of the court, as in other cases. . . .

Kentucky and Virginia Resolutions

Kentucky Resolutions, *November, 1798*

I. *Resolved,* That the several states composing the United States of America are not united on the principle of unlimited submission to their general government; but that by compact under the style and title of a Constitution for the United States and of amendments thereto, they constituted a general government for special purposes, delegated to that government certain definite powers, reserving each state to itself, the residuary mass of right to their own self-government; and that, whensoever the general government assumes undelegated powers, its acts are unauthoritative, void, and of no force. That to this compact each state acceded as a state, and is an integral party, its co-states forming, as to itself, the other party: that the government created by this compact was not made the exclusive or final judge of the extent of the powers delegated to itself; since that would have made its discretion, and not the Constitution, the measure of its powers, but that, as in all other cases of compact among parties having no common judge, each party has an equal right to judge for itself, as well of infractions as of the mode and measure of redress. . . .

VII. *Resolved,* That the construction applied by the general government (as is evinced by sundry of their proceedings) to those parts of the Constitution of the United States which delegate to Congress a power to lay and collect taxes, duties, imposts, and excises; to pay the debts, and provide for the common defense, and general welfare of the United States, and to make all laws which shall be necessary and proper for carrying into execution the powers vested by the Constitution in the government of the United States, or any department thereof, goes to the destruction of all the limits prescribed to their power by the Constitution: that words meant by that instrument to be subsidiary only to the execution of the limited powers ought not to be so construed as themselves to give unlimited powers, nor a part so to be taken as to destroy the whole residue of the instrument: that the proceedings of the general government under color of these articles will be a fit and necessary subject for revisal and correction at a time of greater tranquility, while those specified in the preceding resolutions call for immediate redress.

VIII. *Resolved,* That the preceding Resolutions be transmitted to the senators and representatives in Congress from this Commonwealth, who are hereby enjoined to present the same to their respective Houses, and to use their best endeavors to procure, at the next session of Congress, a repeal of the aforesaid unconstitutional and obnoxious acts.

IX. *Resolved,* lastly, That the governor of this Commonwealth be, and is hereby authorized and requested to communicate the preceding Resolutions to the legislatures of the several states, to assure them that this Commonwealth considers Union for specified national purposes, and particularly for those specified in their late Federal Compact, to be friendly to the peace, happiness, and prosperity of all the states; that faithful to that compact according to the plain intent and meaning in which it was understood and acceded to by the several parties, it is sincerely anxious for its preservation; that it does also believe that, to take from the states all the powers of self-government, and transfer them to a general and consolidated government, without regard to the special delegations and reservations solemnly agreed to in that compact, is not for the peace, happiness, or prosperity of these states; and that, therefore, this Commonwealth is determined, as it doubts not its co-states are, tamely to submit to undelegated and consequently unlimited powers in no man or body of men on earth; that if the acts before specified should stand, these conclusions would flow from them; that the general government may place any act they think proper on the list of crimes and punish it themselves, whether enumerated or not enumerated by the Constitution as cognizable by them; that they may transfer its cognizance to the President or any other person, who may himself be the accuser, counsel, judge, and jury, whose suspicions may be the evidence, his order the sentence, his officer the executioner, and his breast the sole record of the transaction; that a very numerous and valuable description of the inhabitants of these states being by this precedent reduced as outlaws to the absolute dominion of one man, and the barrier of the Constitution thus swept away from us all, no rampart now remains against the passions and the powers of a majority of Congress, to protect from a like exportation or other more grievous punishment the minority of the same body, the legislature, judges, governors, and counselors of the states, nor their other peaceable inhabitants who may venture to reclaim the constitutional rights and liberties of the state and people, or who for other causes, good or bad, may be obnoxious to the views or marked by the suspicions of the President, or be thought dangerous to his or their elections or other interests, public or personal; that the friendless alien has indeed been selected as the safest subject of a first experiment, but the citizen will soon follow, or rather has already followed; for, already has a sedition act marked him as its prey; that these and successive acts of the same character, unless arrested on the threshold, may tend to drive these states into revolution and blood, and will furnish new calumnies against Republican governments, and new pretexts for those who wish it to be believed that man cannot be governed but by a rod of iron; that it would be a dangerous delusion were a confidence in the men of our choice to silence our fears for the safety of our rights; that confidence is everywhere the parent of despotism; free government is founded in jealousy and not in confidence; it is jealousy and not confidence which prescribes limited constitutions to bind down those whom we are obliged to trust with power; that our Constitution has accordingly fixed the limits to which and no further our confidence may go; and let the honest advocate of confidence read the Alien and Sedition Acts, and say if the Constitution has not been wise in fixing limits to the government it created, and whether we should be wise in destroying those limits; let him say what the government is if it be not a tyranny, which the men of our choice have conferred on the President, and the President of our choice has assented to and accepted over the friendly strangers, to whom the mild spirit of our country and its laws had pledged hospitality and protection; that the men of our choice have more respected the bare suspicions of the President than the solid rights of innocence, the claims of justification, the sacred force of truth, and the forms and substance of law and justice. In questions of power then let no more be heard of confidence in man, but bind him down from mischief by the claims of the Constitution. That this Commonwealth does therefore call on its co-states for an expression of their sentiments on the acts concerning aliens, and for the punishment of certain crimes herein before specified, plainly declaring whether these acts are or are not authorized by the Federal Compact. And it doubts not that their sense will be so announced as to prove their attachment unaltered to limited government, whether general or particular, and that the rights and liberties of their co-states will be exposed to no dangers by remaining embarked on a common bottom with their own; that they will concur with the Commonwealth in considering the said acts as so palpably against the Constitution as to amount to an undisguised declaration, that the compact is not meant to be the measure of the powers of the general government, but that it will proceed in the exercise over these states of all powers whatsoever; that they will view this as seizing the rights of the states and consolidating them in the hands of the general government with a power assumed to bind the states (not merely in cases made Federal) but in all cases whatsoever, by laws made, not with their consent, but by others against their consent; that this would be to surrender the form of government we have chosen, and to live under one deriving its powers from its own will, and not from our authority; and that the co-states, recurring to their natural right in cases not made Federal, will concur in declaring these acts void and of no force, and will each unite with this Commonwealth in requesting their repeal at the next session of Congress. . . .

Virginia Resolutions, *December, 1798*

Resolved, That the General Assembly of Virginia doth unequivocally express a firm resolution to maintain and defend the Constitution of the United States, and the Constitution of this state, against every aggression, either foreign or domestic; and that they will support the government of the United States in all measures warranted by the former.

That this Assembly most solemnly declares a warm attachment to the union of the states, to maintain which it pledges its powers; and that, for this end, it is their duty to watch over and oppose every infraction of those principles which constitute the only basis of that union, because a faithful observance of them can alone secure its existence and the public happiness.

That this Assembly doth explicitly and peremptorily declare that it views the powers of the federal government as resulting from the compact to which the states are parties, as limited by the plain sense and intention of the instrument constituting that compact, as no further valid than they are authorized by the grants enumerated in that compact; and that, in case of a deliberate, palpable, and dangerous exercise of other powers, not granted by the said compact, the states, who are parties thereto, have the right, and are in duty bound, to interpose, for arresting the progress of the evil, and for maintaining, within their respective limits, the authorities, rights, and liberties, appertaining to them.

That the General Assembly doth also express its deep regret that a spirit has, in sundry instances, been manifested by the federal government to enlarge its powers by forced constructions of the constitutional charter which defines them; and that indications have appeared of a design to expound certain general phrases (which, having been copied from the very limited grant of powers in the former Articles of Confederation, were the less liable to be misconstrued) so as to destroy the meaning and effect of the particular enumeration which necessarily explains and limits the general phrases, and so as to consolidate the states, by degrees, into one sovereignty, the obvious tendency and inevitable result of which would be to transform the present republican system of the United States into an absolute or, at best, a mixed monarchy.

That the General Assembly doth particularly PROTEST against the palpable and alarming infractions of the Constitution, in the two late cases of the "Alien and Sedition Acts," passed at the last session of Congress; the first of which exercises a power nowhere delegated to the federal government, and which, by uniting legislative and judicial powers to those of executive, subverts the general principles of free government, as well as the particular organization and positive provisions of the federal Constitution; and the other of which acts exercises, in like manner, a power not delegated by the Constitution, but, on the contrary, expressly and positively forbidden by one of the amendments thereto—a power which, more than any other, ought to produce universal alarm, because it is leveled against the right of freely examining public characters and measures, and of free communication among the people thereon, which has ever been justly deemed the only effectual guardian of every other right.

That this state having, by its Convention, which ratified the federal Constitution, expressly declared that, among other essential rights, "the liberty of conscience and the press cannot be canceled, abridged, restrained, or modified, by any authority of the United States," and from its extreme anxiety to guard these rights from every possible attack of sophistry and ambition, having, with other states, recommended an amendment for that purpose, which amendment was, in due time, annexed to the Constitution—it would mark a reproachful inconsistency, and criminal degeneracy, if an indifference were now shown to the most palpable violation of one of the rights thus declared and secured, and to the establishment of a precedent which may be fatal to the other.

That the good people of this commonwealth, having

ever felt, and continuing to feel, the most sincere affection for their brethren of the other states; the truest anxiety for establishing and perpetuating the union of all; and the most scrupulous fidelity to that Constitution, which is the pledge of mutual friendship, and the instrument of mutual happiness—the General Assembly doth solemnly appeal to the like dispositions in other states, in confidence that they will concur with this commonwealth in declaring, as it does hereby declare, that the acts aforesaid are unconstitutional; and that the necessary and proper measures will be taken *by each* for cooperating with this state, in maintaining unimpaired the authorities, rights and liberties, reserved to the states respectively, or to the people. . . .

Thomas Jefferson's First Inaugural Address, *1801*

FRIENDS AND FELLOW CITIZENS:—Called upon to undertake the duties of the first executive office of our country, I avail myself of the presence of that portion of my fellow citizens which is here assembled, to express my grateful thanks for the favor with which they have been pleased to look toward me, to declare a sincere consciousness that the task is above my talents, and that I approach it with those anxious and awful presentiments which the greatness of the charge and the weakness of my powers so justly inspire. A rising nation, spread over a wide and fruitful land, traversing all the seas with the rich productions of their industry, engaged in commerce with nations who feel power and forget right, advancing rapidly to destinies beyond the reach of mortal eye—when I contemplate these transcendent objects, and see the honor, the happiness, and the hopes of this beloved country committed to the issue and the auspices of this day, I shrink from the contemplation, and humble myself before the magnitude of the undertaking. Utterly indeed, should I despair, did not the presence of many whom I here see remind me, that in the other high authorities provided by our constitution, I shall find resources of wisdom, of virtue, and of zeal, on which to rely under all difficulties. To you, then, gentlemen, who are charged with the sovereign functions of legislation, and to those associated with you, I look with encouragement for that guidance and support which may enable us to steer with safety the vessel in which we are all embarked amid the conflicting elements of a troubled world.

During the contest of opinion through which we have passed, the animation of discussion and of exertions has sometimes worn an aspect which might impose on strangers unused to think freely and to speak and to write what they think; but this being now decided by the voice of the nation, announced according to the rules of the constitution, all will, of course, arrange themselves under the will of the law, and unite in common efforts for the common good. All, too, will bear in mind this sacred principle, that though the will of the majority is in all cases to prevail, that will, to be rightful, must be reasonable; that the minority possess their equal rights, which equal laws must protect, and to violate which would be oppression. Let us, then, fellow citizens, unite with one heart and one mind. Let us restore to social intercourse that harmony and affection without which liberty and even life itself are but dreary things. And let us reflect that having banished from our land that religious intolerance under which mankind so long bled and suffered, we have yet gained little if we countenance a political intolerance as despotic, as wicked, and capable of as bitter and bloody persecutions. During the throes and convulsions of the ancient world, during the agonizing spasms of infuriated man, seeking through blood and slaughter his long-lost liberty, it was not wonderful that the agitations of the billows should reach even this distant and peaceful shore; that this should be more felt and feared by some and less by others; that this should divide opinions as to measures of safety. But every difference of opinion is not a difference of principle. We have called by different names brethren of the same principle. We are all Republicans—we are all Federalists. If there be any among us who would wish to dissolve this Union or to change its republican form, let them stand undisturbed as monuments of the safety with which error of opinion may be tolerated where reason is left free to combat it. I know, indeed, that some honest men fear that a republican government cannot be strong; that this government is not strong enough. But would the honest patriot, in the full tide of successful experiment, abandon a government which has so far kept us free and firm, on the theoretic and visionary fear that this government, the world's best hope, may by possibility want energy to preserve itself? I trust not. I believe this, on the contrary, the strongest government on earth. I believe it is the only one where every man, at the call of the laws, would fly to the standard of the law, and would meet invasions of the public order as his own personal concern. Sometimes it is said that man cannot be trusted with the government of himself. Can he, then, be trusted with the government of others? Or have we found angels in the forms of kings to govern him? Let history answer this question.

Let us, then, with courage and confidence pursue our own federal and republican principles, our attachment to our union and representative government. Kindly separated by nature and a wide ocean from the exterminating havoc of one quarter of the globe; too high-minded to endure the degradations of the others; possessing a chosen country, with room enough for entertaining a due sense of our equal right to the use of our own faculties, to the acquisitions of our industry, to honor and confidence from our fellow citizens, resulting not from birth but from our actions and their sense of them; enlightened by a benign religion, professed, indeed, and practiced in various forms, yet all of them including honesty, truth, temperance, gratitude, and the love of man; acknowledging and adoring an overruling Providence, which by all its dispensations proves that it delights in the happiness of man here and his greater happiness hereafter; with all these blessings, what more is necessary to make us a happy and prosperous people? Still one thing more, fellow citizens—a wise and frugal government, which shall restrain men from injuring one another, which shall leave them otherwise free to regulate their own pursuits of industry and improvement, and shall not take from the mouth of labor the bread it has earned. This is the sum of good government, and this is necessary to close the circle of our felicities.

About to enter, fellow citizens, on the exercise of duties which comprehend everything dear and valuable to you, it is proper that you should understand what I deem the essential principles of our government, and consequently those which ought to shape its administration. I will compress them within the narrowest compass they will bear, stating the general principle, but not all its limitations. Equal and exact justice to all men, of whatever state or persuasion, religious or political; peace, commerce, and honest friendship, with all nations—entangling alliances with none; the support of the state governments in all their rights, as the most competent administrations for our domestic concerns and the surest bulwarks against anti-republican tendencies; the preservation of the general government in its whole constitutional vigor, as the sheet anchor of our peace at home and safety abroad; a jealous care of the right of election by the people—a mild and safe corrective of abuses which are lopped by the sword of the revolution where peaceable remedies are unprovided; absolute acquiescence in the decisions of the majority—the vital principle of republics, from which there is no appeal but to force, the vital principle and immediate parent of despotism; a well-disciplined militia—our best reliance in peace and for the first moments of war, till regulars may relieve them; the supremacy of the civil over the military authority; economy in the public expense, that labor may be lightly burdened; the honest payment of our debts and sacred preservation of the public faith; encouragement of agriculture, and of commerce as its handmaid; the diffusion of information and the arraignment of all abuses at the bar of public reason; freedom of religion; freedom of the press; freedom of person under the protection of the habeas corpus; and trial by juries impartially selected—these principles form the bright constellation which has gone before us, and guided our steps through an age of revolution and reformation. The wisdom of our sages and the blood of our heroes have been devoted to their attainment. They should be the creed of our political faith—the text of civil instruction—the touchstone by which to try the services of those we trust; and should we wander from them in moments of error or alarm, let us hasten to retrace our steps and to regain the road which alone leads to peace, liberty, and safety.

I repair, then, fellow citizens, to the post you have assigned me. With experience enough in subordinate offices to have seen the difficulties of this, the greatest of all, I have learned to expect that it will rarely fall to the lot of imperfect man to retire from this station with the reputation and the favor which bring him into it. Without pretensions to that high confidence reposed in our first and great revolutionary character, whose preeminent services had entitled him to the first place in his country's love, and destined for him the fairest page in the volume of faithful history, I ask so much confidence only as may give firmness and effect to the legal administration of your affairs. I shall often go wrong through defect of judgment. When right, I shall often be thought wrong by those whose positions will not command a view of the whole ground. I ask your indulgence for my own errors, which will never be intentional; and your support against the errors of others, who may condemn what they would not if seen in all its parts. The approbation implied by your suffrage is a consolation to me for the past; and my future solicitude will be to retain the good opinion of those who have bestowed it in advance, to conciliate that of others by doing them all the good in my power, and to be instrumental to the happiness and freedom of all.

Relying, then, on the patronage of your good will, I advance with obedience to the work, ready to retire from it whenever you become sensible how much better choice it is in your power to make. And may that Infinite Power which rules the destinies of the universe, lead our councils to what is best, and give them a favorable issue for your peace and prosperity.

Chapter 6

THE POWER OF THE COURT

For the Federalists, defeat in the election of 1800 was as decisive as it was bitter. Though they continued to intrigue against Jefferson's party, they would never again win national political power, and in 1815, after the ill-fated Hartford Convention, their party sank permanently into oblivion. At Hartford, desperate Federalists had abandoned their earlier nationalistic, loose interpretation of the Constitution, had protested the War of 1812 as "Madison's War," and in opposition to the war had espoused the very doctrines of states' rights and limited government they so vigorously opposed when in office. In 1815, however, most Americans were celebrating Jackson's bold victory in the Battle of New Orleans as the triumphant conclusion to the war with England, and their confidence in the now strongly nationalistic leadership of the Republican party was unbounded. Again, and for the last time, the Federalists had proved out of step with the majority of Americans. In the Presidential election of 1816 the nation overwhelmingly chose James Monroe, Madison's Secretary of State and the last of the distinguished Republican triumvirate of friends and neighbors which sarcastic Federalists had dubbed "the Virginia dynasty": Jefferson, Madison, and Monroe. Thus for more than two decades—until in the 1820's it would split into National Republicans under John Quincy Adams and Henry Clay and Democrats under Andrew Jackson—the Republican party dominated the nation's political life. So complete and long lasting was the political victory Jefferson had won in 1800!

To Jefferson's chagrin and intense anger, however, in at least one branch of government, the federal judiciary, defeated Federalists were able to limit the Republican triumph at the polls. For in the last weeks before Jefferson's inauguration in 1801, "lame duck" Federalists had reorganized, expanded, and "packed" the courts with conservative judges whose decisions might be counted upon to "check" somewhat the will of the new President and Congress. Foremost among John Adams' "midnight appointments" was that of Secretary of State John Marshall as Chief Justice of the Supreme Court. For thirty-four years this implacable Federalist was to dominate the highest court of the land, establishing judicial precedents that did much to determine the destinies of the young nation. Marshall immediately ranked high among Jefferson's Federalist antagonists, and between the two, fellow Virginians and kinsmen, raged the first of the many battles between Supreme Court and President that characterized American political and constitutional history.

The most significant of John Marshall's early achievements on the bench was his establishment of the doctrine of judicial review in the case of Marbury v. Madison. William Marbury, a Federalist, had been among Adams' last-minute appointments to the lower federal courts, but in the hectic final days of Adams' administration, Secretary of State John Marshall had neglected to give Marbury his commission. Later, the new Republican Secretary, James Madison, refused to do so. Marbury appealed to the Supreme Court—now presided over by Marshall—for a writ of mandamus ordering Madison to surrender the commission. The writ was to be issued under powers conferred upon the Court by the Judiciary Act of 1789. In 1803 Marshall delivered his famous decision, insisting first that in right and in law Marbury was entitled to his commission. Nevertheless the Chief Justice went on to deny Marbury's petition, asserting that the Court could not issue such writs of mandamus. The justices had reviewed the section of the Judiciary Act granting that power to the Court and had found it unconstitutional and void. Previously the Court had declared state laws unconstitutional and many of the Founding Fathers had taken for granted its power to pass upon the constitutionality of national laws. But nowhere did the Constitution *specifically* grant that power to the highest court. Though the Court would not again nullify an act of Congress until 1857 in the

Dred Scott case, Marshall's opinion in Marbury v. Madison thus set the most important of judicial precedents, that of judicial review of congressional legislation. Besides, the decision made brilliant strategy in the battle with the Republicans, for in declaring unconstitutional a law enacted by the Federalist Congress of 1789 and in rejecting the plea of a Federalist place-seeker, Marshall had cleverly removed from his decision the stigma of partisanship. Yet Jefferson fully appreciated the political significance of Marbury v. Madison and determined to attack the Court and particularly the Chief Justice, lest judicial review be employed to deny the will of the nation as expressed by its elected Republican legislators and Chief Executive. Jefferson's party even made efforts to remove the unfriendly justices. Justice Samuel Chase of the Supreme Court, an intemperately partisan Federalist, was actually impeached by the House of Representatives and only his acquittal by the Senate foiled the Republicans' plans to remove other obnoxious jurists and finally Marshall himself. But these schemes failed. Despite Jefferson's opposition, the Supreme Court under John Marshall had won its first important battle for judicial supremacy and had clearly emerged as a powerful factor in the American system of checks and balances.

For more than three decades after his famous decision in Marbury v. Madison, Marshall continued to lay the foundation of American constitutional law. Two of the most notable of his many opinions were delivered in 1819 in McCulloch v. Maryland and Dartmouth College v. Woodward. In question in the first case were the constitutionality of the Bank of the United States (Jefferson and Hamilton had debated the point in their famous letters to Washington in 1791) and the right of a state to tax the Bank. Maintaining his early nationalism—as other Federalists had not—Marshall fully accepted Hamilton's "loose" or "broad" construction of the Constitution to support federal powers that were "implied" rather than specifically enumerated in the Constitution. Sanctioning Hamilton's earlier opinion, Marshall wrote: "Let the end be legitimate, let it be within the scope of the constitution, and all means which are appropriate, which are plainly adapted to that end, which are not prohibited, but consist with the letter and spirit of the constitution, are constitutional. . . ." The Bank, then, though not provided for in the Constitution, was constitutional. Nor could Maryland tax the Bank, for "the power to tax involves the power to destroy" and a state could not be permitted to destroy the legitimate creature of what in Marshall's opinion was its superior, the national government.

At the same time, in Dartmouth College v. Woodward, the Chief Justice further limited state powers when he declared unconstitutional New Hampshire's efforts to revise Dartmouth's old colonial charter and place the college under state control. Charters were contracts, Marshall stated, and therefore inviolable by the states under the constitutional stricture against "impairing the obligation of contracts." Here, too, precedent set by the early Chief Justice proved profoundly important to the nation's later development. For Marshall's decision in the Dartmouth College case did much to promote and protect the business interests of the nation. Under it, particularly in the period of tremendous industrial expansion after the Civil War, state legislatures were frequently prevented from controlling corporations to which they had granted charters, even those whose business practices were most abusive.

Not only had Marshall struck powerful blows for the supremacy of the nation over the states, but in the best Hamiltonian-Federalist tradition, he had extended the protection of the Constitution to the propertied classes and had made of the Supreme Court a bulwark of economic conservatism.

Marbury v. Madison: Chief Justice John Marshall for the Supreme Court, *1803*

In the order in which the court has viewed this subject, the following questions have been considered and decided:

1. Has the applicant a right to the commission he demands?

2. If he has a right, and that right has been violated, do the laws of his country afford him a remedy?

3. If they do afford him a remedy, is it a mandamus issuing from this court? . . .

The first object of enquiry is,

Has the applicant a right to the commission he demands? . . .

It is therefore decidedly the opinion of the court, that when a commission has been signed by the President, the appointment is made; and that the commission is complete, when the seal of the United States has been affixed to it by the secretary of state. . . .

Mr. Marbury, then, since his commission was signed by the President, and sealed by the secretary of state, was appointed; and as the law creating the office, gave the officer a right to hold for five years, independent of the executive, the appointment was not revocable; but vested in the officer legal rights, which are protected by the laws of his country.

To withhold his commission, therefore, is an act deemed by the court not warranted by law, but violative of a vested legal right.

This brings us to the second enquiry: which is,

If he has a right, and that right has been violated, do the laws of his country afford him a remedy? . . .

The government of the United States has been emphatically termed a government of laws, and not of men. It will certainly cease to deserve this high appellation, if the laws furnish no remedy for the violation of a vested legal right.

By the Constitution of the United States, the President is invested with certain important political powers, in the exercise of which he is to use his own discretion, and is accountable only to his country in his political character, and to his own conscience. To aid him in the performance of these duties, he is authorized to appoint certain officers, who act by his authority and in conformity with his orders.

In such cases, their acts are his acts; and whatever opinion may be entertained of the manner in which executive discretion may be used, still there exists, and can exist, no power to control that discretion. . . .

The conclusion from this reasoning is, that where the heads of departments are the political or confidential agents of the executive, merely to execute the will of the

President, or rather to act in cases in which the executive possesses a constitutional or legal discretion, nothing can be more perfectly clear than that their acts are only politically examinable. But where a specific duty is assigned by law, and individual rights depend upon the performance of that duty, it seems equally clear that the individual who considers himself injured, has a right to resort to the laws of his country for a remedy. . . .

It is, then, the opinion of the court,

1. That by signing the commission of Mr. Marbury, the President of the United States appointed him a justice of peace, for the county of Washington, in the district of Columbia; and that the seal of the United States, affixed thereto by the secretary of state, is conclusive testimony of the verity of the signature, and of the completion of the appointment; and that the appointment conferred on him a legal right to the office for the space of five years.

2. That, having this legal title to the office, he has a consequent right to the commission; a refusal to deliver which, is a plain violation of that right, for which the laws of his country afford him a remedy. . . .

This, then, is a plain case for a mandamus, either to deliver the commission, or a copy of it from the record; and it only remains to be inquired whether it can issue from this court.

The act to establish the judicial courts of the United States authorizes the Supreme Court "to issue writs of mandamus, in cases warranted by the principles and usages of law, to any courts appointed, or persons holding office, under the authority of the United States."

The secretary of state, being a person holding an office under the authority of the United States, is precisely within the letter of the description; and if this court is not authorized to issue a writ of mandamus to such an officer, it must be because the law is unconstitutional and therefore absolutely incapable of conferring the authority and assigning the duties which its words purport to confer and assign.

The Constitution vests the whole judicial power of the United States in one supreme court and such inferior courts as Congress shall, from time to time, ordain and establish. This power is expressly extended to all cases arising under the laws of the United States and, consequently, in some form, may be exercised over the present case because the right claimed is given by a law of the United States.

In the distribution of this power it is declared that "the Supreme Court shall have original jurisdiction in all cases affecting ambassadors, other public ministers and consuls, and those in which a state shall be a party. In all other cases, the Supreme Court shall have appellate jurisdiction."

It has been insisted, at the bar, that as the original grant of jurisdiction, to the supreme and inferior courts, is general, and the clause, assigning original jurisdiction to the Supreme Court, contains no negative or restrictive words, the power remains to the legislature, to assign original jurisdiction to that court, in other cases than those specified in the article which has been recited, provided those cases belong to the judicial power of the United States.

If it had been intended to leave it in the discretion of the legislature to apportion the judicial power between the supreme and inferior courts according to the will of that body, it would certainly have been useless to have proceeded further than to have defined the judicial power and the tribunals in which it should be vested. The subsequent part of the section is mere surplusage—is entirely without meaning—if such is to be the construction. If Congress remains at liberty to give this court appellate jurisdiction, where the Constitution has declared their jurisdiction shall be original, and original jurisdiction where the Constitution has declared it shall be appellate, the distribution of jurisdiction, made in the Constitution, is form without substance.

Affirmative words are often, in their operation, negative of other objects than those affirmed; and in this case, a negative or exclusive sense must be given to them, or they have no operation at all.

It cannot be presumed that any clause in the Constitution is intended to be without effect; and, therefore, such a construction is inadmissible, unless the words require it. . . .

The authority, therefore, given to the Supreme Court

by the act establishing the judicial courts of the United States, to issue writs of mandamus to public officers, appears not to be warranted by the Constitution; and it becomes necessary to inquire whether a jurisdiction, so conferred, can be exercised.

The question whether an act, repugnant to the Constitution, can become the law of the land is a question deeply interesting to the United States but, happily, not of an intricacy proportioned to its interest. It seems only necessary to recognize certain principles, supposed to have been long and well established, to decide it.

That the people have an original right to establish, for their future government, such principles as, in their opinions, shall most conduce to their own happiness is the basis on which the whole American fabric has been erected. The exercise of this original right is a very great exertion; nor can it, nor ought it, to be frequently repeated. The principles, therefore, so established are deemed fundamental. And as the authority, from which they proceed, is supreme, and can seldom act, they are designed to be permanent.

This original and supreme will organizes the government and assigns to different departments their respective powers. It may either stop here or establish certain limits not to be transcended by those departments.

The government of the United States is of the latter description. The powers of the legislature are defined and limited; and that those limits may not be mistaken or forgotten, the Constitution is written. To what purpose are powers limited, and to what purpose is that limitation committed to writing, if these limits may, at any time, be passed by those intended to be restrained? The distinction between a government with limited and unlimited powers is abolished if those limits do not confine the persons on which they are imposed, and if acts prohibited and acts allowed are of equal obligation. It is a proposition too plain to be contested that the Constitution controls any legislative act repugnant to it or that the legislature may alter the Constitution by an ordinary act.

Between these alternatives there is no middle ground. The Constitution is either a superior paramount law, unchangeable by ordinary means, or it is on a level with ordinary legislative acts and, like other acts, is alterable when the legislature shall please to alter it.

If the former part of the alternative be true, then a legislative act contrary to the Constitution is not law; if the latter part be true, then written constitutions are absurd attempts, on the part of the people, to limit a power in its own nature illimitable.

Certainly, all those who have framed written constitutions contemplate them as forming the fundamental and paramount law of the nation, and, consequently, the theory of every such government must be, that an act of the legislature repugnant to the Constitution is void.

This theory is essentially attached to a written constitution and is, consequently, to be considered, by this court, as one of the fundamental principles of our society. It is not, therefore, to be lost sight of in the further consideration of this subject.

If an act of the legislature repugnant to the Constitution is void, does it, notwithstanding its invalidity, bind the courts and oblige them to give it effect? Or, in other words, though it be not law, does it constitute a rule as operative as if it was a law? This would be to overthrow, in fact, what was established in theory and would seem, at first view, an absurdity too gross to be insisted on. It shall, however, receive a more attentive consideration.

It is, emphatically, the province and duty of the judicial department to say what the law is. Those who apply the rule to particular cases must of necessity expound and interpret that rule. If two laws conflict with each other, the courts must decide on the operation of each.

So if a law be in opposition to the Constitution, if both the law and the Constitution apply to a particular case, so that the court must either decide that case conformably to the law, disregarding the Constitution, or conformably to the Constitution, disregarding the law, the court must determine which of these conflicting rules governs the case. This is of the very essence of judicial duty. If, then, the courts are to regard the Constitution, and the Constitution is superior to any ordinary act of the legislature, the Constitution, and not such ordinary act, must govern the case to which they both apply.

Those, then, who controvert the principle that the Constitution is to be considered, in court, as a paramount law are reduced to the necessity of maintaining that courts must close their eyes on the Constitution and see only the law.

This doctrine would subvert the very foundation of all written constitutions. It would declare that an act which, according to the principles and theory of our government, is entirely void, is yet, in practice, completely obligatory. It would declare that if the legislature shall do what is expressly forbidden, such act, nothwithstanding the express prohibition, is in reality effectual. It would be giving to the legislature a practical and real omnipotence, with the same breath which professes to restrict their powers within narrow limits. It is prescribing limits and declaring that those limits may be passed at pleasure.

That it thus reduces to nothing what we have deemed the greatest improvement on political institutions, a written constitution would of itself be sufficient, in America, where written constitutions have been viewed with so much reverence, for rejecting the construction. But the peculiar expressions of the Constitution of the United States furnish additional arguments in favor of its rejection.

The judicial power of the United States is extended to all cases arising under the Constitution. Could it be the intention of those who gave this power to say that, in using it, the Constitution should not be looked into? That a case arising under the Constitution should be decided without examining the instrument under which it arises?

This is too extravagant to be maintained.

In some cases, then, the Constitution must be looked into by the judges. And if they can open it at all, what part of it are they forbidden to read or to obey?

There are many other parts of the Constitution which serve to illustrate this subject. It is declared that "no tax or duty shall be laid on articles exported from any state." Suppose a duty on the export of cotton, or tobacco, or of flour; and a suit instituted to recover it.

Ought judgment to be rendered in such a case? Ought the judges to close their eyes on the Constitution and only see the law?

The Constitution declares that "no bill of attainder or *ex post facto* law shall be passed." If, however, such a bill should be passed and a person should be prosecuted under it, must the court condemn to death those victims whom the Constitution endeavors to preserve?

"No person," says the Constitution, "shall be convicted of treason, unless on the testimony of two witnesses to the same *overt* act, or on confession in open court." Here the language of the Constitution is addressed especially to the courts. It prescribes, directly for them, a rule of evidence not to be departed from. If the legislature should change that rule and declare one witness, or a confession out of court, sufficient for conviction, must the constitutional principle yield to the legislative act?

From these, and many other selections which might be made, it is apparent that the framers of the Constitution contemplated that instrument as a rule for the government of *courts* as well as of the legislature.

Why otherwise does it direct the judges to take an oath to support it? This oath certainly applies, in an especial manner, to their conduct in their official character. How immoral to impose it on them, if they were to be used as the instruments, and the knowing instruments, for violating what they swear to support!

The oath of office, too, imposed by the legislature is completely demonstrative of the legislative opinion on this subject. It is in these words: "I do solemnly swear that I will administer justice, without respect to persons, and do equal right to the poor and to the rich; and that I will faithfully and impartially discharge all the duties incumbent on me as, according to the best of my abilities and understanding, agreeably to the Constitution, and laws of the United States."

Why does a judge swear to discharge his duties agreeably to the Constitution of the United States if that Constitution forms no rule for his government? If it is closed upon him, and cannot be inspected by him? If such be the real state of things, this is worse than solemn mockery. To prescribe, or to take this oath, becomes equally a crime.

It is also not entirely unworthy of observation that, in declaring what shall be the supreme law of the land, the Constitution itself is first mentioned; and not the laws of the United States generally, but those only which shall be made in pursuance of the Constitution have that rank.

Thus, the particular phraseology of the Constitution of the United States confirms and strengthens the principle, supposed to be essential to all written constitutions, that a law repugnant to the Constitution is void and that courts, as well as other departments, are bound by that instrument.

The rule must be discharged.

Chapter 7

A BOLD FOREIGN POLICY

A dominant theme of American foreign policy in the early nineteenth century was a self-assertive and expansive nationalism. Earlier, under Washington and Adams, American statesmen had struggled to maintain neutrality for the infant republic. For the times their policy had been wise. In little more than a decade of peace the young nation had organized politically under the new Constitution, had consolidated its human and material resources, and had prospered considerably. But by the 1800's a strong sense of American nationality had arisen and confident nationalists were more concerned with expansion than with consolidation. The westward movement contributed much to this new nationalism, and with the rapid development of frontier regions (Kentucky became a state in 1792, Tennessee in 1796, Ohio in 1803) there came an ever increasing demand for further expansion: into Canada, into the Floridas, across the Mississippi River and into the lands beyond.

The greatest triumph of western expansionism, and one of the most important achievements of Jefferson's presidency, was the Louisiana Purchase of 1803. From the time of the first American settlements in the Ohio valley, Westerners who shipped farm produce down the Mississippi had depended upon Spain's permission to "deposit" their goods in New Orleans for transshipment to market. But Napoleon, whose purpose was to make France a power once again in the New World, in 1800 extorted Louisiana from a weak and compliant Spain. And in 1802 the Americans' "right of deposit" in New Orleans was suspended. Under pressure from furious Westerners who thought war not too strong a remedy for this attack upon their interests, Jefferson authorized James Monroe and Robert R. Livingston to purchase from Napoleon the city of New Orleans (and possibly West Florida) for no more than $10,000,000. Actually, Jefferson's envoys paid Napoleon $15,000,000, but for New Orleans and the whole territory of Louisiana! So vast an expanse was this—all or part of thirteen states would eventually be carved from it—that even Jefferson could not foresee its settlement "for a thousand years."

As the West grew in area and in population, so the section's political strength was enhanced and it came to play a determinate role in formulating American foreign policy. The War of 1812, traditionally associated with maritime New England as a struggle for the freedom of the seas, was in reality the West's war. Western "War Hawks" had demanded war, while New Englanders, fearing that their shipping interests would be more severely damaged by armed conflict with England than by her violation of their rights as neutrals, had actively opposed the war and at the Hartford Convention had threatened secession unless it were ended and the political power of the West curtailed. Nor were the bellicose Westerners disinterested, for they wanted much from the war with England: Canada to the north and Florida to the south. As John Randolph wrote, "Agrarian cupidity, not maritime right urges the war. . . . We have heard but one word—like the whippoorwill, but one eternal monotonous tone—Canada! Canada! Canada!" But British military successes, capped by the seizure of Washington, the nation's capital, frustrated these ambitions. And when in 1815 the Treaty of Ghent ended the indecisive war the West secured no spoils, not Canada nor Florida. Nevertheless, most Americans quickly erased from memory all save such splendid victories as Andrew Jackson's at the Battle of New Orleans, and at the close of the war they were more than ever convinced of America's invincible might. Not less convinced of their nation's destiny and right to round out its borders, in 1818 they wildly cheered the hero of New Orleans when in subduing the Seminole Indians he swept through Spanish Florida, deposed the Spanish Governor, and executed two British citizens. Finally, in 1821, Spain accepted the inevitable and formally surrendered Florida to the determined American expansionists.

Thus, faith in the nation's strength, and pride in its vast Western empire, had nourished a bold sense of national destiny. And the upsurge of flamboyant nationalism that characterized the years following the Treaty of Ghent, the "Era of Good Feelings," could not fail to be reflected in relations with the powerful nations of Europe. Soon the monarchs of the Old World were to learn that in determining the fate of any part of the Western Hemisphere the United States considered its will decisive. Although the Napoleonic invasion of Spain and the temporary collapse of the Spanish colonial system had given Latin Americans a taste of independence, with Napoleon's defeat, Spain's "legitimate" monarchy was restored and her old colonial empire reconstructed. Led by San Martín, Bolívar, and O'Higgins, the Latin Americans quickly rebelled against the mother country and, emulating their northern neighbor, established independent republics. With the ardent support of the great powers of Europe, whose "Holy Alliance" was dedicated to the suppression of revolution wherever it might occur, Spain sought to destroy these revolutionary governments. It was obvious to President Monroe and his Secretary of State, John Quincy Adams, that such an effort boded evil for the United States, whose interests were ever broadening. Were the European nations to succeed, they might well continue the colonization of the Americas; indeed they might soon establish new empires at the very borders of the United States. Determined to take a firm stand against European intervention in the Western Hemisphere, the United States formally recognized the new republics.

Adams had no intention of stopping there, for the European powers must specifically be warned against intervention in the New World. Ever concerned with the "balance of power" in Europe, and with her important commercial ties to the new Latin-American Republics, England was equally opposed to intervention by Spain and her allies. Canning, the English foreign secretary, suggested that the two nations issue a joint warning to the other powers. Monroe was amenable to this suggestion, as were his venerable advisers, former Presidents Jefferson and Madison, but Adams would not have the United States seem a mere "cock-boat in the wake of a British man-of-war" and the Secretary successfully insisted upon unilateral action. In December, 1823, in two widely separated passages in a message to Congress, the President enunciated the principles that have become famous as the Monroe Doctrine. The "American continents," Monroe insisted, were ". . . not to be considered subjects for future colonization by any European powers. . . ." Besides, the monarchies of Europe were far different from the republics of the Americas and "any attempt on their part to extend their system to any portion of this hemisphere" would be considered "as dangerous to our peace and safety." The United States was without the power to support these bold principles, however, and for many years Latin-American independence was protected more by the British Navy than by the presidential pronouncement. Yet, as Adams intended, the Monroe Doctrine has long stood as one of the most fundamental principles of American foreign policy.

The Monroe Doctrine, *James Monroe, 1823*

. . . At the proposal of the Russian Imperial Government, made through the minister of the Emperor residing here, a full power and instructions have been transmitted to the minister of the United States at St. Petersburg to arrange by amicable negotiation the respective rights and interests of the two nations on the northwest coast of this continent. A similar proposal had been made by His Imperial Majesty to the Government of Great Britain, which has likewise been acceded to. The Government of the United States has been desirous by this friendly proceeding of manifesting the great value which they have invariably attached to the friendship of the Emperor and their solicitude to cultivate the best understanding with his Government. In the discussions to which this interest has given rise and in the arrangements by which they may terminate the occasion has been judged proper for asserting, as a principle in which the rights and interests of the United States are involved, that the American continents, by the free and independent condition which they have assumed and maintain, are henceforth not to be considered as subjects for future colonization by any European powers. . . .

It was stated at the commencement of the last session that a great effort was then making in Spain and Portugal to improve the condition of the people of those countries, and that it appeared to be conducted with extraordinary moderation. It need scarcely be remarked that the result has been so far very different from what was then anticipated. Of events in that quarter of the globe, with which we have so much intercourse and from which we derive our origin, we have always been anxious and interested spectators. The citizens of the United States cherish sentiments the most friendly in favor of the liberty and happiness of their fellow-men on that side of the Atlantic. In the wars of the European powers in matters relating to themselves we have never taken any part, nor does it comport with our policy so to do. It is only when our rights are invaded or seriously menaced that we resent injuries or make preparation for our defense. With the movements in this hemisphere we are of necessity more immediately connected, and by causes which must be obvious to all enlightened and impartial observers. The political system of the allied powers is essentially different in this respect from that of America. This difference proceeds from that which exists in their respective Governments; and to the defense of our own, which has been achieved by the loss of so much blood and treasure, and matured by the wisdom of their most enlightened citizens, and under which we have enjoyed unexampled felicity, this whole nation is devoted. We owe it, therefore, to candor and to the amicable relations existing between the United States and those powers to declare that we should consider any attempt on their part to extend their system to any portion of this hemisphere as dangerous to our peace and safety. With the existing colonies or dependencies of any European power we have not interfered and shall not interfere. But with the Governments who have declared their independence and maintained it, and whose independence we have, on great consideration and on just principles, acknowledged, we could not view any interposition for the purpose of oppressing them, or controlling in any other manner their destiny, by any European power in any other light than as the manifestation of an unfriendly disposition toward the United States. In the war between those new Governments and Spain we declared our neutrality at the time of their recognition, and to this we have adhered, and shall continue to adhere, provided no change shall occur which, in the judgment of the competent authorities of this Government, shall make a corresponding change on the part of the United States indispensable to their security.

The late events in Spain and Portugal show that Europe is still unsettled. Of this important fact no stronger proof can be adduced than that the allied powers should have thought it proper, on any principle satisfactory to themselves, to have interposed by force in the internal concerns of Spain. To what extent such interposition may be carried, on the same principle, is a question in which all independent powers whose governments differ from theirs are interested, even those most remote, and surely none more so than the United States. Our policy in regard to Europe, which was adopted at an early stage of the wars which have so long agitated that quarter of the globe, nevertheless remains the same, which is, not to interfere in the internal concerns of any of its powers; to consider the government *de facto* as the legitimate government for us; to cultivate friendly relations with it, and to preserve those relations by a frank, firm, and manly policy, meeting in all instances the just claims of every power, submitting to injuries from none. But in regard to these continents circumstances are eminently and conspicuously different. It is impossible that the allied powers should extend their political system to any portion of either continent without endangering our peace and happiness; nor can anyone believe that our southern brethren, if left to themselves, would adopt it of their own accord. It is equally impossible, therefore, that we should behold such interposition in any form with indifference. If we look to the comparative strength and resources of Spain and those new Governments, and their distance from each other, it must be obvious that she can never subdue them. It is still the true policy of the United States to leave the parties to themselves, in the hope that other powers will pursue the same course.

Chapter 8

JACKSONIAN DEMOCRACY

Andrew Jackson's election in 1828—like Thomas Jefferson's in 1800 and Franklin D. Roosevelt's more than a century later—marked a significant change in American social and political thought, for Jackson thoroughly symbolized the widespread democratic impulse of the 1820's and 1830's. A half-century earlier Jefferson had declared as the philosophical basis of the Declaration of Independence the proposition that "all men are created equal"; and in the bloodless "Revolution of 1800" a crumbling Federalism had been laid low by the determined disciples of Jeffersonian Democracy. Yet the Jeffersonians were themselves essentially aristocratic in outlook and suspicious of popular rule. They believed in government *of* and *for* the people, but not necessarily *by* the people, as the classic, late-in-life exchange of letters on aristocracy between Jefferson and John Adams attested, and it was not until the Age of Jackson that equalitarianism became a pervasive theme of American life.

Now, however, political institutions underwent a profound transformation, and political control was rapidly transferred from an aristocracy of education, position, and wealth to the common man, the average American. Early in the republic's history each of the original states had imposed severe restrictions upon the suffrage, but the newly admitted Western states had enfranchised almost all of their adult white males and constitutional revisions soon brought the older states into line. Property qualifications for office were similarly abolished at the example of the West; terms of office were limited, as were the numbers of appointive or non-elective positions; and by the time of Jackson's first election each state, with the exception of Delaware and South Carolina, had provided that Presidential electors be chosen popularly rather than by the state legislatures. Important, too, was the widespread insistence that Presidential candidates be chosen by open party conventions instead of by tightly inbred legislative caucuses.

Jacksonian Democracy also brought a new equalitarian conception of public office: that all men were essentially of equal talents, that each American of normal intelligence was capable of holding any position in government, and that democracy required a rotation in office to prevent the development of an untouchable and undemocratic political bureaucracy. And though it was frequently abused by venal politicians for private gain, this notion that "to the victors belong the spoils" was a forthright expression of the simple democratic instinct for replacing office holders whose party had been repudiated with those who were more clearly "the people's choice." Leveling doctrines pervaded every area of social life as well, and there were some, like the French observer Alexis de Tocqueville in his classic "Democracy in America," who wondered whether Americans' liberties would long survive the nation's penchant for equality. For at times the tyranny of the majority proved even more oppressive than minority rule, and "King Numbers" seemed as despotic a sovereign as any in history.

Meanwhile Americans' democratic sympathies found ample expression in the myriad social and economic reform movements of the Jacksonian period. Determined to cleanse and purify the national life, they enthusiastically devoted their energies to such varied causes as free public education, women's rights, abolitionism, temperance, and the care of criminals and of the insane. With the steady growth of industry in the Northeast the labor movement also received an important impetus, for the squalor and impoverishment of the new urban working class were in striking contrast to contemporary ideals of equality and material well-being for all Americans.

Undoubtedly many of the new labor unions and workingmen's parties fervently supported the political ascendancy of Andrew Jackson. Yet the warrior-statesman's rough-and-tumble ways and his disdain for rank and ceremony identified him even more closely with the West, where a continuous frontier experience bred a firm faith in the capacity of the common man; and his hatred of privilege and monopoly made him equally the champion of the struggling entrepreneur. Thus in 1828 and again in 1832 Jackson, though a wealthy planter, was able to rally to his support the democratic forces of the nation—the workers, farmers and small businessmen—and to make the new Democratic party a symbol of the leveling spirit of the age.

Ultimately it was his spectacular war upon the second Bank of the United States that most clearly illustrated Jackson's libertarian instincts and his intolerance of monopoly. The charter of the first Bank of the United States (which Jefferson had emphatically opposed and Hamilton as firmly supported in their famous letters to Washington in 1791) had expired in 1811 and had not been immediately renewed. But in 1816, after the harsh fiscal experiences of the War of 1812, and in the midst of the nationalistic fervor that gripped the nation at the war's conclusion, Congress had enthusiastically chartered a second Bank, granting it important monopolies in the national banking business. By the 1820's, however, the "Era of Good Feelings" had been supplanted by a period of intense sectional and class conflict, and though conservative business leaders were well served by the Bank and by its aristocratic president, Nicholas Biddle, popular enthusiasm gave way to suspicion and distrust. Soon representatives of the underprivileged classes spoke of the Bank as a "financial octopus" and protested its vast power over the economic life of the nation.

Jackson fully shared this popular prejudice against the Bank, and like Jefferson before him he argued against its constitutionality. His real objections, however, were personal and political, for Biddle had used the Bank's resources to support anti-Jackson Congressmen and to defy the popular President. At the insistence of Henry Clay, Jackson's bitter rival in the West, Biddle actually precipitated the conflict himself. Jackson had early made known his hostility to the Bank, but there was no sure indication of his plans in regard to its recharter. Nevertheless in the early summer of 1832 Biddle forced a recharter bill through Congress. Since the old charter would not expire for four years, it was obvious that the Bank Bill had been timed to present Clay with a convenient campaign issue in the coming Presidential election, for the conservative National Republicans (soon to emerge as the new Whig party) erroneously believed that a Presidential veto would be extremely unpopular.

Instead, Jackson's forceful veto message gained him widespread support from all who feared the "concentration of power in the hands of a few men irresponsible to the people." Though his enemies denounced the Bank veto as "demagogic" and dictatorial and dubbed Jackson "King Andrew I," great numbers of "the humble members of society" saw in his veto message a clear expression of the era's growing democratic ideology. Once again they elected the hero of New Orleans to the highest office in the land.

On Aristocracy, Letters of John Adams and Thomas Jefferson

Adams to Jefferson

July, 1813

. . . I recollect, near thirty years ago, to have said carelessly to you that I wished I could find time and means to write something upon aristocracy. You seized upon the idea and encouraged me to do it with all that friendly warmth that is natural and habitual to you. I soon began and have been writing upon that subject ever since. I have been so unfortunate as never to be able to make myself understood. Your *"aristoi"* are the most difficult animals to manage of anything in the whole theory and practice of government. They will not suffer themselves to be governed. They not only exert all their subtilty, industry, and courage, but they employ the commonalty to knock to pieces every plan and model that the most honest architects in legislation can invent to keep them within bounds. Both patricians and plebeians are as furious as the workmen in England to demolish labor-saving machinery.

But who are these *"aristoi"*? Who shall judge? Who shall select these choice spirits from the rest of the congregation? Themselves? We must first find out and determine who themselves are. . . .

"Nobility in men is worth as much as it is in horses, asses, or rams; but the meanest-blooded puppy in the world, if he gets a little money, is as good a man as the best of them." Yet birth and wealth together have prevailed over virtue and talents in all ages. The many will acknowledge no other *"aristoi."* Your experience of this truth will not much differ from that of your old friend. . . .

Adams to Jefferson

August, 1813

. . . Has science, or morals, or philosophy, or criticism, or Christianity, advanced, or improved, or enlightened mankind upon this subject and shown them that the idea of the "well-born" is a prejudice, a phantom, a point-no-point, a Cape Fly-away, a dream?

I say it is the ordinance of God Almighty in the constitution of human nature and wrought into the fabric of the universe. Philosophers and politicians may nibble and quibble, but they never will get rid of it. Their only resource is to control it. Wealth is another monster to be subdued. Hercules could not subdue both or either. To subdue them by regular approaches, by a regular siege and strong fortifications, was my object in writing on aristocracy, as I proposed to you. . . .

If you deny any one of these positions, I will prove them to demonstration by examples drawn from your own Virginia, and from every other state in the Union, and from the history of every nation, civilized and savage, from all we know of the time of the creation of the world. . . .

We may call this sentiment a prejudice, because we can give what names we please to such things as we please; but in my opinion it is a part of the natural history of man, and politicians and philosophers may as well project to make the animal live without bones or blood as society can pretend to establish a free government without attention to it. . . .

Adams to Jefferson

September, 1813

. . . Now, my friend, who are the *"aristoi"*? Philosophers may answer, "The wise and good." But the world, mankind, have, by their practice, always answered, "The rich, the beautiful, and well-born." And philosophers themselves, in marrying their children, prefer the rich, the handsome, and the well-descended to the wise and good.

What chance have talents and virtues, in competition with wealth and birth? and beauty? . . .

> One truth is clear, by all the world confessed,
> Slow rises worth, by poverty oppressed.

The five pillars of aristocracy are beauty, wealth, birth, genius, and virtue. Any one of the three first can, at any time, overbear any one or both of the two last.

Let me ask again, what a wave of public opinion, in favor of birth, has been spread over the globe by Abraham, by Hercules, by Mahomet, by Guelphs, Ghibellines, Bourbons, and a miserable Scottish chief Stuart? By Zingis [Genghis Khan], by, by, by a million others. And what a wave will be spread by Napoleon and by Washington? Their remotest cousins will be sought and will be proud and will avail themselves of their descent. Call this principle prejudice, folly, ignorance, baseness, slavery, stupidity, adulation, superstition, or what you will, I will not contradict you. But the fact in natural, moral, political, and domestic history I cannot deny, or dispute, or question.

And is this great fact in the natural history of man, this unalterable principle of morals, philosophy, policy, domestic felicity, and daily experience from the Creation, to be overlooked, forgotten, neglected, or hypocritically waved out of sight by a legislator? By a professed writer upon civil government and upon constitution of civil government? . . .

Jefferson to Adams

October, 1813

. . . I agree with you that there is a natural aristocracy among men. The grounds of this are virtue and talents. Formerly, bodily powers gave place among the *aristoi*. But since the invention of gunpowder has armed the weak as well as the strong with missile death, bodily strength, like beauty, good humor, politeness, and other accomplishments, has become but an auxiliary ground of distinction.

There is also an artificial aristocracy, founded on wealth and birth, without either virtue or talents; for with these it would belong to the first class. The natural aristocracy I consider as the most precious gift of nature, for the instruction, the trusts, and government of society. And, indeed, it would have been inconsistent in Creation to have formed man for the social state and not to have provided virtue and wisdom enough to manage the concerns of the society. May we not even say that that form of government is the best which provides the most effectually for a pure selection of these natural *aristoi* into the offices of government? The artificial aristocracy is a mischievous ingredient in government, and provision should be made to prevent its ascendancy. On the question, What is the best provision? you and I differ; but we differ as rational friends, using the free exercise of our own reason and mutually indulging its errors. *You* think it best to put the *pseudo-aristoi* into a separate chamber of legislation, where they may be hindered from doing mischief by their co-ordinate branches, and where also they may be a protection to wealth against the agrarian and plundering enterprises of the majority of the people. I think that to give them power in order to prevent them from doing mischief is arming them for it and increasing instead of remedying the evil. For if the co-ordinate branches can arrest their action, so may they that of the co-ordinates. Mischief may be done negatively as well as positively. Of this, a cabal in the Senate of the United States has furnished many proofs. Nor do I believe them necessary to protect the wealthy; because enough of these will find their way into every branch of the legislation to protect themselves. From fifteen to twenty legislatures of our own, in action for thirty years past, have proved that no fears of an equalization of property are to be apprehended from them. *I* think the best remedy is exactly that provided by all our constitutions: to leave to the citizens the free election and separation of the *aristoi* from the *pseudo-aristoi,* of the wheat from the chaff. In general they will elect the real good and wise. In some instances, wealth may corrupt and birth blind them, but not in sufficient degree to endanger the society.

It is probable that our difference of opinion may, in some measure, be produced by a difference of character in those among whom we live. From what I have seen of Massachusetts and Connecticut myself, and still more from what I have heard, and the character given of the former by yourself, who know them so much better, there seems to be in those two states a traditionary reverence for certain families which has rendered the offices of the government nearly hereditary in those families. I presume that, from an early period of your history, members of those families happening to possess virtue and talents have honestly exercised them for the good of the people and by their services have endeared their names to them. . . .

With respect to aristocracy, we should further consider that, before the establishment of the American states, nothing was known to history but the man of the Old World, crowded within limits either small or overcharged and steeped in the vices which that situation generates. A government adapted to such men would be one thing; but a very different one, that for the man of these states. Here every one may have land to labor for himself, if he chooses; or, preferring the exercise of any other industry, may exact for it such compensation as not only to afford a comfortable subsistence but wherewith to provide for a cessation from labor in old age. Every one, by his property, or by his satisfactory situation, is interested in the support of law and order. And such men may safely and advantageously reserve to themselves a wholesome control over their public affairs, and a degree of freedom which, in the hands of the *canaille* of the cities of Europe, would be instantly perverted to the demolition and destruction of everything public and private. The history of the last twenty-five years of France, and of the last forty years in America, nay, of its last two hundred years, proves the truth of both parts of this observation.

But even in Europe a change has sensibly taken place in the mind of man. Science had liberated the ideas of those who read and reflect, and the American example had kindled feelings of right in the people. An insurrection has consequently begun, of science, talents, and courage, against rank and birth, which have fallen into contempt. It has failed in its first effort, because the mobs of the cities, the instrument used for its accomplishment, debased by ignorance, poverty, and vice, could not be restrained to rational action. But the world will recover from the panic of this first catastrophe. Science is progressive, and talents and enterprise on the alert. Resort may be had to the people of the country, a more governable power from their principles and subordination; and rank, and birth, and tinsel-aristocracy will finally shrink into insignificance even there. This, however, we have no right to meddle with. It suffices for us if the moral and physical condition of our own citizens qualifies them to select the able and good for the direction of their government with a recurrence of elections at such short periods as will enable them to displace an unfaithful servant before the mischief he meditates may be irremediable.

I have thus stated my opinion on a point on which we differ, not with a view to controversy, for we are both too old to change opinions which are the result of a long life of inquiry and reflection, but on the suggestions of a former letter of yours, that we ought not to die before we have explained ourselves to each other. We acted in perfect harmony, through a long and perilous contest for our liberty and independence. A constitution has been acquired, which, though neither of us thinks perfect, yet both consider as competent to render our fellow-citizens the happiest and the securest on whom the sun has ever shone. If we do not think exactly alike as to imperfections, it matters little to our country which, after devoting to it long lives of disinterested labor, we have delivered over to our successors in life, who will be able to take care of it and of themselves. . . .

Adams to Jefferson

November, 1813
. . . We are now explicitly agreed on one important point, viz., that "there is a natural aristocracy among men, the grounds of which are virtue and talents." You very justly indulge a little merriment upon this solemn subject of aristocracy. I often laugh at it too, for there is nothing in this laughable world more ridiculous than the management of it by almost all the nations of the earth; but while we smile, mankind have reason to say to us, as the frogs said to the boys, what is sport to you are wounds and death to us. When I consider the weakness, the folly, the pride, the vanity, the selfishness, the artifice, the low craft and mean cunning, the want of principle, the avarice, the unbounded ambition, the unfeeling cruelty of a majority of those (in all nations) who are allowed an aristocratical influence, and, on the other hand, the stupidity with which the more numerous multitude not only become their dupes, but even love to be taken in by their tricks, I feel a stronger disposition to weep at their destiny than to laugh at their folly.

But though we have agreed in one point, in words, it is not yet certain that we are perfectly agreed in sense. Fashion has introduced an indeterminate use of the word "talents." Education, wealth, strength, beauty, stature, birth, marriage, graceful attitudes and motions, gait, air, complexion, physiognomy, are talents, as well as genius, science, and learning. Any one of these talents that in fact commands or influences two votes in society gives to the man who possesses it the character of an aristocrat, in my sense of the word. Pick up the first hundred men you meet and make a republic. Every man will have an equal vote; but when deliberations and discussions are opened, it will be found that twenty-five, by their talents, virtues being equal, will be able to carry fifty votes. Every one of these twenty-five is an aristocrat in my sense of the word; whether he obtains his one vote in addition to his own, by his birth, fortune, figure, eloquence, science, learning, craft, cunning, or even his character for good fellowship, and a *bon vivant*. . . .

Your distinction between natural and artificial aristocracy does not appear to me founded. Birth and wealth are conferred on some men as imperiously by nature as genius, strength, or beauty. The heir to honors and riches and power has often no more merit in procuring these advantages than he has in obtaining a handsome face or an elegant figure. When aristocracies are established by human laws, and honor, wealth, and power are made hereditary by municipal laws and political institutions, then I acknowledge artificial aristocracy to commence; but this never commences till corruption in elections becomes dominant and uncontrollable. But this artificial aristocracy can never last. The everlasting envies, jealousies, rivalries, and quarrels among them; their cruel rapacities upon the poor ignorant people, their followers, compel these to set up Caesar, a demagogue, to be a monarch and master; *pour mettre chacun à sa place*. Here you have the origin of all artificial aristocracy, which is the origin of all monarchy. And both artificial aristocracy and monarchy, and civil, military, political, and hierarchical despotism, have all grown out of the natural aristocracy of "virtues and talents." . . .

Your distinction between the *aristoi* and *pseudo-aristoi* will not help the matter. I would trust one as soon as the other with unlimited power. . . .

You suppose a difference of opinion between you and me on the subject of aristocracy. I can find none. I dislike and detest hereditary honors, offices, emoluments established by law. So do you. I am for excluding legal hereditary distinctions from the United States as long as possible. So are you. I only say that mankind have not yet discovered any remedy against irresistible corruption in elections to offices of great power and profit, but making them hereditary. But will you say our elections are pure? Be it so, upon the whole. But do you recollect in history a more corrupt election than that of Aaron Burr to be President, or that of De Witt Clinton last year. By corruption here I mean a sacrifice of every national interest and honor to private and party objects. . . .

Where tends the mania of banks? At my table in Philadelphia, I once proposed to you to unite in endeavors to obtain an amendment of the Constitution, prohibiting to the separate states the power of creating banks; but giving Congress authority to establish one bank, with a branch in each state, the whole limited to ten millions of dollars. . . . But you spurned the proposition from you with disdain. This system of banks . . . I have always considered as a system of national injustice, a sacrifice of public and private interest to a few aristocratical friends and favorites. My scheme could have had no such effect. Verres plundered temples and robbed a few rich men; but he never made such ravages among private property in general nor swindled so much out of the pockets of the poor and the middle class of people as these banks have done! . . . What inequalities of talent have been introduced into this country by these aristocratical banks! Our Winthrops, Winslows, Bradfords, Saltonstalls, Quinceys, Chandlers, Leonards, Hutchinsons, Olivers, Sewalls, etc., are precisely in the situation of your Randolphs, Carters, and Burwells and Harrisons. Some of them unpopular for the part they took in the late Revolution, but all respected for their names and connections; and whenever they fall in with the popular sentiments, are preferred, *cæteris paribus*, to all others. . . .

Adams to Jefferson

December, 1813

. . . Aristocracy, like waterfowl, dives for ages and then rises with brighter plumage. It is a subtle venom that diffuses itself unseen over oceans and continents and triumphs over time. If I could prevent its deleterious influence, I would put it all into "the Hole" of Calcutta. But as this is impossible as it is a phoenix that rises again out of its own ashes, I know no better way than to chain it in a "hole by itself" and place a watchful sentinel on each side of it.

A hundred other foreign aristocracies have sown and are sowing their seeds in this country; and we have an abundance of them springing up in this country, not from virtues and talents, but from banks and land-jobbing. . . .

Veto of the Bank Renewal Bill, *Andrew Jackson, 1832*

The bill "to modify and continue" the act entitled "An act to incorporate the subscribers to the Bank of the United States" was presented to me on the 4th July instant. Having considered it with that solemn regard to the principles of the Constitution which the day was calculated to inspire, and come to the conclusion that it ought not to become a law, I herewith return it to the Senate, in which it originated, with my objections.

A bank of the United States is in many respects convenient for the Government and useful to the people. Entertaining this opinion, and deeply impressed with the belief that some of the powers and privileges possessed by the existing bank are unauthorized by the Constitution, subversive of the rights of the States, and dangerous to the liberties of the people, I felt it my duty at an early period of my Administration to call the attention of Congress to the practicability of organizing an institution combining all its advantages and obviating these objections. I sincerely regret that in the act before me I can perceive none of those modifications of the bank charter which are necessary, in my opinion, to make it compatible with justice, with sound policy, or with the Constitution of our country.

The present corporate body, denominated the president, directors, and company of the Bank of the United States, will have existed at the time this act is intended to take effect twenty years. It enjoys an exclusive privilege of banking under the authority of the General Government, a monopoly of its favor and support, and, as a necessary consequence, almost a monopoly of the foreign and domestic exchange. The powers, privileges, and favors bestowed upon it in the original charter, by increasing the value of the stock far above its par value, operated as a gratuity of many millions to the stockholders.

An apology may be found for the failure to guard against this result in the consideration that the effect of the original act of incorporation could not be certainly foreseen at the time of its passage. The act before me proposes another gratuity to the holders of the same stock, and in many cases to the same men, of at least seven millions more. This donation finds no apology in any uncertainty as to the effect of the act. On all hands it is conceded that its passage will increase at least 20 or 30 per cent more the market price of the stock, subject to the payment of the annuity of $200,000 per year secured by the act, thus adding in a moment one-fourth to its par value. It is not our own citizens only who are to receive the bounty of our Government. More than eight millions of the stock of this bank are held by foreigners. By this act the American Republic proposes virtually to make them a present of some millions of dollars. For these gratuities to foreigners, and to some of our own opulent citizens the act secures no equivalent whatever. They are the certain gains of the present stockholders under the operation of this act, after making full allowance for the payment of the bonus.

Every monopoly and all exclusive privileges are granted at the expense of the public, which ought to receive a fair equivalent. The many millions which this act proposes to bestow on the stockholders of the existing bank must come directly or indirectly out of the earnings of the American people. It is due to them, therefore, if their Government sell monopolies and exclusive privileges, that they should at least exact for them as much as they are worth in open market. The value of the monopoly in this case may be correctly ascertained. The twenty-eight millions of stock would probably be at an advance of 50 per cent, and command in market at least $42,000,000, subject to the payment of the present bonus. The present value of the monopoly, therefore, is $17,000,000, and this the act proposes to sell for three millions, payable in fifteen annual installments of $200,000 each.

It is not conceivable how the present stockholders can have any claim to the special favor of the Government. The present corporation has enjoyed its monopoly during the period stipulated in the original contract. If we must have such a corporation, why should not the Government sell out the whole stock and thus secure to the people the full market value of the privileges granted? Why should not Congress create and sell twenty-eight millions of stock, incorporating the purchases with all the powers and privileges secured in this act and putting the premium upon the sales into the Treasury?

But this act does not permit competition in the purchase of this monopoly. It seems to be predicated on the erroneous idea that the present stockholders have a prescriptive right not only to the favor but to the bounty of Government. It appears that more than a fourth part of the stock is held by foreigners and the residue is held by a few hundred of our own citizens, chiefly of the richest class. For their benefit does this act exclude the whole American people from competition in the purchase of this monopoly and dispose of it for many millions less than it is worth. This seems the less excusable because some of our citizens not now stockholders petitioned that the door of competition might be opened, and offered to take a charter on terms much more favorable to the Government and country.

But this proposition, although made by men whose aggregate wealth is believed to be equal to all the private stock in the existing bank, has been set aside, and the bounty of our Government is proposed to be again bestowed on the few who have been fortunate enough to secure the stock and at this moment wield the power of the existing institution. I can not perceive the justice or policy of this course. If our Government must sell monopolies, it would seem to be its duty to take nothing less than their full value, and if gratuities must be made once in fifteen or twenty years let them not be bestowed on the subjects of a foreign government nor upon a designated and favored class of men in our own country. It is but justice and good policy as far as the nature of the case will admit, to confine our favors to our own fellow-citizens, and let each in his turn enjoy an opportunity to profit by our bounty. In the bearings of the act before me upon these points I find ample reasons why it should not become a law.

It has been urged as an argument in favor of rechartering the present bank that the calling in its loans will produce great embarrassment and distress. The time allowed to close its concerns is ample, and if it has well managed its pressure will be light, and heavy only in case its management has been bad. If, therefore, it shall produce distress, the fault will be its own, and it would furnish a reason against renewing a power which has been so obviously abused. But will there ever be a time when this reason will be less powerful? To acknowledge its force is to admit that the bank ought to be perpetual, and as a consequence the present stockholders and those inheriting their rights as successors be established a privileged order, clothed both with great political power and enjoying immense pecuniary advantages from their connection with the Government.

The modifications of the existing charter proposed by this act are not such, in my view, as make it consistent with the rights of the States or the liberties of the people. The qualification of the right of the bank to hold real estate, the limitation of its power to establish branches, and the power reserved to Congress to forbid the circulation of small notes are restrictions comparatively of little value or importance. All the objectionable principles of the existing corporation, and most of its odious features, are retained without alleviation. . . .

In another of its bearings this provision is fraught with danger. Of the twenty-five directors of this bank five are chosen by the Government and twenty by the citizen stockholders. From all voice in these elections the foreign stockholders are excluded by the charter. In proportion, therefore, as the stock is transferred to foreign holders the extent of suffrage in the choice of directors is curtailed. Already is almost a third of the stock in foreign hands and not represented in elections. It is constantly passing out of the country, and this act will accelerate its departure. The entire control of the institution would necessarily fall into the hands of a few citizen stockholders, and the ease with which the object would be accomplished would be a temptation to designing men to secure that control in their own hands by monopolizing the remaining stock. There is danger that a president and directors would then be able to elect themselves from year to year, and without responsibility or control manage the whole concerns of the bank during the existence of its charter. It is easy to conceive that great evils to our country and its institutions might flow from such a concentration of power in the hands of a few men irresponsible to the people.

Is there no danger to our liberty and independence in a bank that in its nature has so little to bind it to our country? The president of the bank has told us that most of the State banks exist by its forbearance. Should its influence become concentered, as it may under the operation of such an act as this, in the hands of a self-elected directory whose interests are identified with those of the foreign stockholders, will there not be cause to tremble for the purity of our elections in peace and for the independence of our country in war? Their power would be great whenever they might choose to exert it; but if this monopoly were regularly renewed every fifteen or twenty years on terms proposed by themselves, they might seldom in peace put forth their strength to influence elections or control the affairs of the nation. But if any private citizen or public functionary should interpose to curtail its powers or prevent a renewal of its privileges, it can not be doubted that he would be made to feel its influence.

Should the stock of the bank principally pass into the hands of the subjects of a foreign country, and we should unfortunately become involved in a war with that country, what would be our condition? Of the course which would be pursued by a bank almost wholly owned by the subjects of a foreign power, and managed by those whose interests, if not affections, would run in the same direction there can be no doubt. All its operations within would be in aid of the hostile fleets and armies without. Controlling our currency, receiving our public moneys, and holding thousands of our citizens in dependence, it would be more formidable and dangerous than the naval and military power of the enemy.

If we must have a bank with private stockholders, every consideration of sound policy and every impulse of American feeling admonishes that it should be *purely*

American. Its stockholders should be composed exclusively of our own citizens, who at least ought to be friendly to our Government and willing to support it in times of difficulty and danger. So abundant is domestic capital that competition in subscribing for the stock of local banks has recently led almost to riots. To a bank exclusively of American stockholders, possessing the powers and privileges granted by this act, subscriptions for $200,000,000 could readily be obtained. Instead of sending abroad the stock of the bank in which the Government must deposit its funds and on which it must rely to sustain its credit in times of emergency, it would rather seem to be expedient to prohibit its sale to aliens under penalty of absolute forfeiture.

It is maintained by the advocates of the bank that its constitutionality in all its features ought to be considered as settled by precedent and by the decision of the Supreme Court. To this conclusion I can not assent. Mere precedent is a dangerous source of authority, and should not be regarded as deciding questions of constitutional power except where the acquiescence of the people and the States can be considered as well settled. So far from this being the case on this subject, an argument against the bank might be based on precedent. One Congress, in 1791, decided in favor of a bank; another, in 1811, decided against it. One Congress, in 1815, decided against a bank; another, in 1816, decided in its favor. Prior to the present Congress, therefore, the precedents drawn from that source were equal. If we resort to the States, the expressions of legislative, judicial, and executive opinions against the bank have been probably to those in its favor as 4 to 1. There is nothing in precedent, therefore, which, if its authority were admitted, ought to weigh in favor of the act before me.

If the opinion of the Supreme Court covered the whole ground of this act, it ought not to control the coordinate authorities of this Government. The Congress, the Executive, and the Court must each for itself be guided by its own opinion of the Constitution. Each public officer who takes an oath to support the Constitution swears that he will support it as he understands it, and not as it is understood by others. It is as much the duty of the House of Representatives, of the Senate, and of the President to decide upon the constitutionality of any bill or resolution which may be presented to them for passage or approval as it is of the supreme judges when it may be brought before them for judicial decision. The opinion of the judges has no more authority over Congress than one opinion of Congress has over the judges, and on that point the President is independent of both. The authority of the Supreme Court must not, therefore, be permitted to control the Congress or the Executive when acting in their legislative capacities, but to have only such influence as the force of their reasoning may deserve. . . .

The bank is professedly established as an agent of the executive branch of the Government, and its constitutionality is maintained on that ground. Neither upon the propriety of present action nor upon the provisions of this act was the Executive consulted. It has had no opportunity to say that it neither needs nor wants an agent clothed with such powers and favored by such exemptions. There is nothing in its legitimate functions which makes it necessary or proper. Whatever interest or influence, whether public or private, has given birth to this act, it can not be found either in the wishes or necessities of the executive department, by which present action is deemed premature, and the powers conferred upon its agent not only unnecessary, but dangerous to the Government and country.

It is to be regretted that the rich and powerful too often bend the acts of government to their selfish purposes. Distinctions in society will always exist under every just government. Equality of talents, of education, or of wealth can not be produced by human institutions. In the full enjoyment of the gifts of Heaven and the fruits of superior industry, economy, and virtue, every man is equally entitled to protection by law; but when the laws undertake to add to these natural and just advantages artificial distinctions, to grant titles, gratuities, and exclusive privileges, to make the rich richer and the potent more powerful, the humble members of society—the farmers, mechanics, and laborers—who have neither the time nor the means of securing like favors to themselves, have a right to complain of the injustice of their Government. There are no necessary evils in government. Its evils exist only in its abuses. If it would confine itself to equal protection, and, as Heaven does its rains, shower its favors alike on the high and the low, the rich and the poor, it would be an unqualified blessing. In the act before me there seems to be a wide and unnecessary departure from these just principles.

Nor is our Government to be maintained or our Union preserved by invasions of the rights and powers of the several States. In thus attempting to make our General Government strong we make it weak. Its true strength consists in leaving individuals and States as much as possible to themselves—in making itself felt, not in its power, but in its beneficence; not in its control, but in its protection; not in binding the States more closely to the center, but leaving each more unobstructed in its proper orbit.

Experience should teach us wisdom. Most of the difficulties our Government now encounters and most of the dangers which impend over our Union have sprung from an abandonment of the legitimate objects of Government by our national legislation, and the adoption of such principles as are embodied in this act. Many of our rich men have not been content with equal protection and equal benefits, but have besought us to make them richer by act of Congress. By attempting to gratify their desires we have in the results of our legislation arrayed section against section, interest against interest, and man against man, in a fearful commotion which threatens to shake the foundations of our Union. It is time to pause in our career to review our principles, and if possible revive that devoted patriotism and spirit of compromise which distinguished the sages of the Revolution and the fathers of our Union. If we can not at once, in justice to interests vested under improvident legislation, make our Government what it ought to be, we can at least take a stand against all new grants of monopolies and exclusive privileges, against any prostitution of our Government to the advancement of the few at the expense of the many, and in favor of compromise and gradual reform in our code of laws and system of political economy.

Chapter 9

LIBERTY OR UNION

Nationalism had been the keynote of the years immediately following the War of 1812—the period known as the "Era of Good Feelings"—for Americans seemed to be imbued with a profound sense of national identity that they had lacked before. Nowhere was this nationalism more completely expressed than in Congressional legislation sponsored by Republicans who had forsaken their earlier belief in states' rights and a severely limited national government. The permanent armed forces of the United States were strengthened; internal improvements, such as the construction of roads and canals, were authorized; a second Bank of the United States, which promised a stable and uniform national currency, was created; and, most significant for the future, high wartime tariffs were maintained and even increased to protect American industries that had sprung up during the war. Throughout the country there was widespread support for this impressive legislative program, and James Monroe's reelection to the Presidency in 1820 was a significant symbol of the period's vaunted political unity. For in that year Monroe received every electoral vote but one; lest another share with Washington the honor of a unanimous vote for President, one Republican elector had cast an opposing ballot.

Not far beneath this surface unity, however, there lay deeply rooted sectional antagonisms that within two generations were to erupt into civil war. And in 1820 an angry dispute over Missouri's admission to the Union gave Americans a foretaste of the conflict ahead. The country was torn by dissension when the South violently protested Northern efforts to prohibit the further introduction of slavery into Missouri as a condition for statehood. Though there were an equal number of slave and free states, with equal representation in the

United States Senate, the South had consistently been outstripped by the North in population growth. By 1820 it could claim only 89 members in the House of Representatives to the North's 123. For this reason the South considered it essential to its interests that slave and free states be numerically equal, guaranteeing a sectional balance at least in the Senate, and it bitterly resented the Northern proposals that would eventually make Missouri a free state. Besides, with the tremendous expansion of cotton cultivation that followed Eli Whitney's invention of the cotton gin in 1793, slavery had once again become an integral part of the Southern economy and the North's attempt to limit it was taken as a direct attack upon the South's well-being. But the scene had not yet been set for a prolonged open struggle between the sections, and the issue was soon settled by the Missouri Compromise. Missouri was admitted to the Union as a slave state without restrictions, and at the same time, to maintain the sectional balance, Maine was admitted as a free state. The historic Compromise further provided that with the exception of Missouri, slavery was to be prohibited permanently in all of the Louisiana Purchase territory above the 36° 30″ line and permitted below it. The nation rejoiced that the immediate problem had been resolved peacefully, but those whose insight into the dynamics of the sectional conflict was more profound saw that the Missouri question was only a prelude to a later, more fundamental—and possibly tragic—struggle.

Nevertheless both slavery itself and the burning question of a balance of political power between the sections were secondary and merely symptomatic of the more basic cleavage between the South's agrarian economy and the industrial economy of the North. After the War of 1812, Southern Congressmen like John C. Calhoun of South Carolina hoped to promote industrial development in their own section and supported nationalistic legislation such as high tariffs. Industrial failures and a tremendous increase in cotton production quickly disabused Southerners of this idea, however, and they returned to a defense of traditional agrarian ways. Indeed Calhoun and other Southern leaders soon came to champion states' rights and to oppose the nationalistic, industrial measures they so recently had advanced. Their conversion had its parallel in the North, where Calhoun's early arguments for a high tariff had been brilliantly countered by Daniel Webster, who at that time represented New England's mercantile and shipping interests in their opposition to industrialization. But by the 1820's the older mercantile interests were giving way to industrialism in the North, and the opportunistic Webster had shifted his allegiance to become the pro-industrial nationalist we remember today. Fundamentally Calhoun and Webster were at all times "sectionalists," each deeply committed to the immediate interests of his own section. Their respective metamorphoses—Calhoun's from nationalist to agrarian states' righter, and Webster's from mercantile states' righter to nationalist—provide us with the clearest possible picture of the realignment of their sections' economic interests. And later political struggles between the great leaders and their followers, whether over slavery or over the nature of the Union, were never more than ancillary to the basic sectional conflict between plantation agrarianism and industrialism.

One of the most memorable of these political struggles was the Webster-Hayne Debate of January, 1830. The immediate issue was an attempt by Senator Foot of Connecticut to limit Western land sales. Seizing upon the Foot Resolution as a vehicle for alienating the West from the North and winning support for Southern policies, Senator Hayne of South Carolina had launched a violent attack upon New England, questioning its patriotism and charging that section (particularly Massachusetts) with a selfish antipathy to the South and West alike. As presiding officer of the Senate, Vice-President Calhoun actually took no part in the debate. But it was evident to all that Hayne was Calhoun's spokesman as the younger Carolinian went on to espouse the superiority of the states over the national government and to insist that for the West no less than for the South nullification of national legislation by the "sovereign" states was a final answer to Northern tyranny. Then Webster rose in defense of his state, his section, and his new nationalism and delivered one of the most eloquent of American orations. The states had not created the Union, the Senator from Massachusetts proclaimed; rather it was the creature of all of the people, whose political organ (the national government) was superior to all others. Thus nullification could find no sanction in history and must be forsworn in favor of a firm devotion to the binding force of national authority. To those who cried "Liberty first and Union afterwards" the "Godlike Daniel" replied in a magnificent peroration with "that other sentiment, dear to every true American heart—Liberty *and* Union, now and forever, one and inseparable."

Three months later, at a dinner celebrating Jefferson's birthday, the West replied, through the greatest of its spokesmen, to the South's bid for political support. Andrew Jackson—his eyes fixed on Calhoun—rose dramatically to offer the Presidential toast: "Our Federal Union—it must be preserved!" The implications of Jackson's reply were unmistakable; the West, keenly national in its feelings and interests, had rejected the Southern lure of states' rights and sectionalism. Two years later North and West joined in support of Jackson's firm stand against the efforts of South Carolina to nullify the tariff of 1832. In his fiery appeal for patriotism and Union, Webster clearly had touched upon what Lincoln would later call the "mystic chords of memory"; he had spoken the heart no less than the mind of the nation.

Daniel Webster's Second Reply to Hayne, *1830*

. . . So, Sir, I understood the gentleman and am happy to find that I did not misunderstand him. What he contends for is that it is constitutional to interrupt the administration of the Constitution itself, in the hands of those who are chosen and sworn to administer it, by the direct interference, in form of law, of the states, in virtue of their sovereign capacity. The inherent right in the people to reform their government I do not deny; and they have another right, and that is to resist unconstitutional laws without overturning the government. It is no doctrine of mine that unconstitutional laws bind the people. The great question is: Whose prerogative is it to decide on the constitutionality or unconstitutionality of the laws? On that, the main debate hinges. The proposition that, in case of a supposed violation of the Constitution by Congress, the states have a constitutional right to interfere and annul the law of Congress is the proposition of the gentleman. I do not admit it. If the gentleman had intended no more than to assert the right of revolution for justifiable cause, he would have said only what all agree to. But I cannot conceive that there can be a middle course, between submission to the laws, when regularly pronounced constitutional, on the one hand, and open resistance, which is revolution or rebellion, on the other. I say the right of a state to annul a law of Congress cannot be maintained but on the ground of the inalienable right of man to resist oppression; that is to say, upon the ground of revolution. I admit that there is an ultimate violent remedy, above the Constitution and in defiance of the Constitution, which may be resorted to when a revolution is to be justified. But I do not admit that, under the Constitution and in conformity with it, there is any mode in which a state government, as a member of the Union, can interfere and stop the progress of the general government, by force of her own laws, under any circumstances whatever.

This leads us to inquire into the origin of this government and the source of its power. Whose agent is it? Is it the creature of the state legislatures or the creature of the people? If the government of the United States be the agent of the state governments, then they may control it, provided they can agree in the manner of controlling it; if it be the agent of the people, then the people alone can control it, restrain it, modify, or reform it. . . . It is, Sir, the people's Constitution, the people's government, made for the people, made by the people, and answerable to the people. The people of the United States have declared that this Constitution shall be the supreme law. We must either admit the proposition or dispute their authority. The states are, unquestionably, sovereign so far as their sovereignty is not affected by this supreme law. But the state legislatures, as political bodies, however sovereign, are yet not sovereign over the people. So far as the people have given power to the general government, so far the grant is unquestionably good, and the government holds of the people and not of the state governments. We are all agents of the same supreme power, the people. The general government and the state governments derive their authority from the same source. Neither can, in relation to the other, be called primary, though one is definite and restricted, and the other general and residuary. The national government possesses those powers which it can be shown the people have conferred on it, and no more. All the rest belongs to the state governments or to the people themselves. So far as the people have restrained state sovereignty, by the expression of their will, in the Constitution of the United States, so far, it must be admitted, state sovereignty is effectually controlled. I do not contend that it is, or ought to be, controlled further. The sentiment to which I have referred propounds that state sovereignty is only to be controlled by its own "feeling of justice"; that is to say, it is not to be controlled at all, for one who is to follow his own feelings is under no legal control. Now, however, men may think this ought to be, the fact is that the people of the United States have chosen to impose control on state sovereignties. There are those, doubtless, who wish they had been left without restraint; but the Constitution has ordered the matter differently. To make war, for instance, is an exercise of sovereignty; but the Constitution declares that no state shall make war. To coin money is another exercise of sovereign power; but no state is at liberty to coin money. Again, the Constitution says that no sovereign state shall be so sovereign as to make a treaty. These prohibitions, it must be confessed, are a control on the state sovereignty of South Carolina, as well as of the other states, which does not arise "from her own feelings of honorable justice." The opinion referred to, therefore, is in defiance of the plainest provisions of the Constitution.

. . . The Carolina doctrine, which the honorable member has now stood up on this floor to maintain . . . resolved that

> the tariff of 1828, and every other tariff designed to promote one branch of industry at the expense

> of others, is contrary to the meaning and intention of the federal compact; and such a dangerous, palpable, and deliberate usurpation of power, by a determined majority, wielding the general government beyond the limits of its delegated powers, as calls upon the states which compose the suffering minority, in their sovereign capacity, to exercise the powers which, as sovereigns, necessarily devolve upon them, when their compact is violated.

. . . This resolution holds the tariff of 1828, and every other tariff designed to promote one branch of industry at the expense of another, to be such a dangerous, palpable, and deliberate usurpation of power, as calls upon the states, in their sovereign capacity, to interfere by their own authority. . . . Let us suppose the state of South Carolina to express this same opinion by the voice of her legislature. That would be very imposing; but what then? Is the voice of one state conclusive? It so happens that, at the very moment when South Carolina resolves that the tariff laws are unconstitutional, Pennsylvania and Kentucky resolve exactly the reverse. *They* hold those laws to be both highly proper and strictly constitutional. . . .

In Carolina the tariff is a palpable, deliberate usurpation; Carolina, therefore, may nullify it and refuse to pay the duties. In Pennsylvania it is both clearly constitutional and highly expedient; and there the duties are to be paid. And yet we live under a government of uniform laws and under a Constitution too which contains an express provision, as it happens, that all duties shall be equal in all the states. Does not this approach absurdity?

If there be no power to settle such questions, independent of either of the states, is not the whole Union a rope of sand? Are we not thrown back again, precisely, upon the old Confederation?

It is too plain to be argued. Four-and-twenty interpreters of constitutional law, each with a power to decide for itself, and none with authority to bind anybody else, and this constitutional law the only bond of their union! What is such a state of things but a mere connection during pleasure or, to use the phraseology of the times, "during feeling"? And that feeling too, not the feeling of the people, who established the Constitution, but the feeling of the state governments. . . .

The people, then, Sir, erected this government. They gave it a Constitution, and in that Constitution they have enumerated the powers which they bestow on it. They have made it a limited government. They have defined its authority. They have restrained it to the exercise of such powers as are granted; and all others, they declare, are reserved to the states or the people. But, Sir, they have not stopped here. If they had, they would have accomplished but half their work. No definition can be so clear, as to avoid possibility of doubt; no limitation so precise, as to exclude all uncertainty. Who, then, shall construe this grant of the people? Who shall interpret their will, where it may be supposed they have left it doubtful? With whom do they repose this ultimate right of deciding on the powers of the government? Sir, they have settled all this in the fullest manner. They have left it with the government itself, in its appropriate branches. Sir, the very chief end, the main design, for which the whole Constitution was framed and adopted, was to establish a government that should not be obliged to act through state agency, or depend on state opinion and state discretion. The people had had quite enough of that kind of government under the Confederation. Under that system, the legal action, the application of law to individuals, belonged exclusively to the states. Congress could only recommend; their acts were not of binding force, till the states had adopted and sanctioned them. Are we in that condition still? Are we yet at the mercy of state discretion and state construction? Sir, if we are, then vain will be our attempt to maintain the Constitution under which we sit.

But, Sir, the people have wisely provided, in the Constitution itself, a proper, suitable mode and tribunal for settling questions of constitutional law. There are in the Constitution grants of powers to Congress and restrictions on these powers. There are, also, prohibitions on the states. Some authority must, therefore, necessarily exist having the ultimate jurisdiction to fix and ascertain the interpretation of these grants, restrictions, and prohibitions. The Constitution has itself pointed out, ordained, and established that authority. How has it accomplished this great and essential end? By declaring, Sir, that "the Constitution, and the laws of the United States made in pursuance thereof, shall be the supreme law of the land, anything in the constitution or laws of any state to the contrary notwithstanding."

This, Sir, was the first great step. By this the supremacy of the Constitution and laws of the United States is declared. The people so will it. No state law is to be valid which comes in conflict with the Constitution, or any law of the United States passed in pursuance of it. But who shall decide this question of interference? To whom lies the last appeal? This, Sir, the Constitution itself decides also, by declaring, that *"the judicial power shall extend to all cases arising under the Constitution and laws of the United States."* These two provisions cover the whole ground. They are, in truth, the keystone of the arch! With these it is a government; without them it is a confederation. In pursuance of these clear and express provisions, Congress established, at its very first session, in the judicial act, a mode for carrying them into full effect, and for bringing all questions of constitutional power to the final decision of the Supreme Court. It then, Sir, became a government. It then had the means of self-protection; and but for this, it would, in all probability, have been now among things which are past. Having constituted the government, and declared its powers, the people have further said that since somebody must decide on the extent of these powers, the government itself shall decide; subject, always, like other popular governments, to its responsibility to the people. And now, Sir, I repeat, how is it that a state legislature acquires any power to interfere? Who, or what, gives them the right to say to the people "We, who are your agents and servants for one purpose, will undertake to decide, that your other agents and servants, appointed by you for another purpose, have transcended the authority you gave them!" The reply would be, I think, not impertinent: "Who made you a judge over another's servants? To their own masters they stand or fall."

Sir, I deny this power of state legislatures altogether.

It cannot stand the test of examination. Gentlemen may say that, in an extreme case, a state government might protect the people from intolerable oppression. Sir, in such a case, the people might protect themselves, without the aid of the state governments. Such a case warrants revolution. It must make, when it comes, a law for itself. A nullifying act of a state legislature cannot alter the case, nor make resistance any more lawful. In maintaining these sentiments, Sir, I am but asserting the rights of the people. I state what they have declared and insist on their right to declare it. They have chosen to repose this power in the general government and I think it my duty to support it, like other constitutional powers.

. . . If, sir, the people in these respects had done otherwise than they have done, their Constitution could neither have been preserved, nor would it have been worth preserving. And if its plain provisions shall now be disregarded, and these new doctrines interpolated in it, it will become as feeble and helpless a being as its enemies, whether early or more recent, could possibly desire. It will exist in every State, but as a poor dependent on State permission. It must borrow leave to be, and will be no longer than State pleasure or State discretion sees fit to grant the indulgence and to prolong its poor existence.

But, sir, although there are fears, there are hopes also. The people have preserved this, their own chosen Constitution, for forty years, and have seen their happiness, prosperity, and renown grow with its growth and strengthen with its strength. They are now, generally, strongly attached to it. Overthrown by direct assault it cannot be; evaded, undermined, *nullified,* it will not be, if we and those who shall succeed us here as agents and representatives of the people shall conscientiously and vigilantly discharge the two great branches of our public trust—faithfully to preserve and wisely to administer it.

Mr. President, I have thus stated the reasons of my dissent to the doctrines which have been advanced and maintained. I am conscious of having detained you and the Senate much too long. I was drawn into the debate with no previous deliberation, such as is suited to the discussion of so grave and important a subject.

But it is a subject of which my heart is full, and I have not been willing to suppress the utterance of its spontaneous sentiments. I cannot, even now, persuade myself to relinquish it without expressing once more my deep conviction that, since it respects nothing less than the Union of the States, it is of most vital and essential importance to the public happiness. I profess, sir, in my career hitherto, to have kept steadily in view the prosperity and honor of the whole country and the preservation of our Federal Union. It is to that Union we owe our safety at home and our consideration and dignity abroad. It is to that Union that we are chiefly indebted for whatever makes us most proud of our country. That Union we reached only by the discipline of our virtues in the severe school of adversity. It had its origin in the necessities of disordered finance, prostrate commerce, and ruined credit. Under its benign influences these great interests immediately awoke as from the dead, and sprang forth with newness of life. Every year of its duration has teemed with fresh proofs of its utility and its blessings; and although our territory has stretched out wider and wider, and our population spread farther and farther, they have not outrun its protection or its benefits. It has been to us all a copious fountain of national, social, and personal happiness.

I have not allowed myself, sir, to look beyond the Union, to see what might lie hidden in the dark recess behind. I have not coolly weighed the chances of preserving liberty when the bonds that unite us together shall be broken asunder. I have not accustomed myself to hang over the precipice of disunion, to see whether, with my short sight, I can fathom the depth of the abyss below; nor could I regard him as a safe counselor in the affairs of this government whose thoughts should be mainly bent on considering, not how the Union may be best preserved, but how tolerable might be the condition of the people when it shall be broken up and destroyed. While the Union lasts, we have high, exciting, gratifying prospects spread out before us for us and our children. Beyond that I seek not to penetrate the veil. God grant that in my day, at least, that curtain may not rise! God grant that on my vision never may be opened what lies behind! When my eyes shall be turned to behold for the last time the sun in heaven, may I not see him shining on the broken and dishonored fragments of a once glorious Union; on States dissevered, discordant, belligerent; on a land rent with civil feuds, or drenched, it may be, in fraternal blood! Let their last feeble and lingering glance rather behold the gorgeous ensign of the republic, now known and honored throughout the earth, still full high advanced, its arms and trophies streaming in their original lustre, not a stripe erased or polluted nor a single star obscured, bearing for its motto no such miserable interrogatory as "What is all this worth?" nor those other words of delusion and folly, "Liberty first and Union afterwards"; but everywhere, spread all over in characters of living light, blazing on all its ample folds, as they float over the sea and over the land, and in every wind under the whole heavens, that other sentiment, dear to every true American heart—Liberty *and* Union, now and forever, one and inseparable!

Chapter 10

THE ABOLITIONIST CRUSADE

From the Missouri Compromise to the Civil War, the American political scene was almost continuously dominated by some aspect of the slavery question. But the sectional conflict was basically economic rather than political in nature, and in the final analysis even the ideological controversy over slavery was secondary to the struggle for national predominance between defensive adherents of Southern agrarianism and aggressive champions of Northern industrialism. For both sides, however, feelings could be raised more easily to the highest pitch and fiery partisans could be recruited with greatest dispatch if the issues were protested as moral rather than bluntly political or crassly economic. Besides, whatever its origins, for many Americans the slavery question had very early assumed the proportions of an intensely ideological contest—as the untiring and sometimes fanatical activities of both Southern apologists for slavery and Northern Abolitionists bear witness. During the four decades prior to the Civil War the sectional conflict most frequently took the form of a moral issue. And when finally the sections chose war to resolve their "irrepressible conflict," both were to make of it a great and holy crusade, for good against evil, for right against wrong.

Negro slavery had first been introduced into the American colonies in 1619 when a Dutch ship brought its cargo of human chattels to Virginia. Throughout the seventeenth and most of the eighteenth centuries, as the plantation system came to be an integral part of the Southern economy, slavery as the source of plantation labor seemed more and more closely identified with the South's economic well-being. Towards the end of the eighteenth century, however, depression struck at the plantation region, and Southern leaders lost confidence in their system of land and labor. After the American Revolution many Southerners, imbued with the ideals of liberty and equality expressed in the Declaration of Independence and disgruntled at what seemed the inadequacy of slave labor, urged at least the gradual abolition of slavery. One great Southern spokesman for liberty, Patrick Henry, openly proclaimed his guilt as a slaveholder: "Would anyone believe that I am Master of Slaves of my own purchase! I am drawn along by the general inconvenience of living without them; I will not, I cannot justify it." More and more frequently Southerners provided in their wills for the emancipation of their slaves, and in the years immediately after the Revolution the number of free Negroes increased considerably. An observer might have noted that slavery no longer played a vital role in the Southern economy; the barbaric institution seemed doomed.

Then in 1793 the Yankee Eli Whitney breathed new life into the plantation-slave system with his invention of the cotton gin. Previous laborious and expensive hand methods of separating the seed from the cotton had limited cotton production to the more easily separated long staple crop that could be grown only in the rich lowlands of the seacoast. But Whitney's remarkable machine for separating seed from cotton made possible the large-scale cultivation of the short staple crop that could be grown throughout almost the entire South. In 1790 Americans produced 4,000 bales of cotton; two decades later annual production was upwards of 175,000 bales; and by 1860 the figure had reached nearly 4,000,000 bales. This remarkable productive spurt marked a revitalization of the plantation system which in turn created a new demand for slave labor, and soon gradual emancipation was supplanted by a frantic search for an ever larger slave labor force. To a limited extent the planters' demands for more slaves were met—often by the disreputable practice of slave breeding and by the illegal slave trade—and the slave population increased from about one and a half million in 1820 to approximately four million in 1860. But with the tremendous westward expansion of "King Cotton" the demand for slaves constantly outstripped the supply, and a prime field hand who cost five to seven hundred dollars in 1820 brought over eighteen hundred dollars in 1860. In 1790 slavery had appeared moribund, but by the 1820's to many wealthy Southerners human bondage seemed the foundation of their prosperity.

As their human chattels once again came to play a vital role in the plantation economy, the Southerners felt pressed to translate the slaves' new function into moral terms. Earlier apologies for slavery as a "necessary evil" were manifestly unsuitable for this period of expansion; now Negro slavery was proclaimed altogether righteous, moral, and even beneficial to the slave himself. Slavery was no longer merely defended; rather it was defiantly pronounced a "positive good," and soon Southerners formulated an elaborate pro-slavery argument that found sanction for slavery in selections from Scripture, in historical references to slavery among ancient peoples, and in "scientific" theories of the slaves' "biological inferiority."

There were numbers of Americans, however, who remained unconvinced by the slaveholders' rationalizations and who abhorred the South's "peculiar institution" as vicious, brutalizing, and immoral. Many of them joined the numerous Northern societies dedicated to the abolition of slavery, and the sincere, though sometimes unreasoning, intensity of purpose of the Abolitionists offered proof of the moral, if not the numerical, strength of the anti-slavery cause.

Closely identified with the Abolition movement was the aggressive and fearless William Lloyd Garrison, a New England journalist who had lent his pen and energies to the cause of many other contemporary reform movements, such as temperance, pacifism and women's rights. On January 1, 1831, even before he organized the powerful New England Anti-Slavery Society, Garrison gave voice to America's conscience when he dedicated his new journal, *The Liberator*, to abolitionism. Recanting his earlier acceptance of the "popular but pernicious doctrine of *gradual* abolition," Garrison demanded the immediate emancipation and enfranchisement of the slaves. "On this subject I do not wish to think, or speak, or write, with moderation," he wrote. "I am in earnest—I will not equivocate—I will not excuse—I will not retreat a single inch—AND I WILL BE HEARD."

Throughout the length and breadth of the land Garrison and his followers were heard, but they met the angry opposition of most Northerners as well as Southerners. Before the Civil War the Abolitionists were seldom truly representative of Northern thought, for they had too closely identified themselves with radicalism generally. Above the Mason-Dixon line they were ridiculed as fanatics, ostracized from polite society, and sometimes violently assaulted for their activities. In 1835 a frenzied mob attacked Garrison, tied a rope around his neck, and dragged him through the streets of Boston; two years later an Illinois mob killed the Abolitionist editor Elijah P. Lovejoy. As the "irrepressible conflict" approached the proportions of war, however, the Abolitionists were making more and more converts to their cause. Most important, through constant vilification of the slaveholders they were creating in Northern minds an image of Southern life that did much to aggravate sectional antagonisms. Then, when compromise was finally abandoned and the war came, Northern leaders more easily made of it a holy crusade against a "slaveocracy" that had already been stereotyped as cruel, godless and immoral. Though they had by no means created it, the Abolitionists had done much to intensify the sectional conflict and to foster disillusionment with a government that tolerated human slavery, as some years later Henry David Thoreau would proclaim in his widely influential "Essay on Civil Disobedience."

The First Issue of *The Liberator, 1831*

In the month of August, I issued proposals for publishing *The Liberator* in Washington city; but the enterprise, though hailed in different sections of the country, was palsied by public indifference. Since that time, the removal of the *Genius of Universal Emancipation* to the Seat of Government has rendered less imperious the establishment of a similar periodical in that quarter.

During my recent tour for the purpose of exciting the minds of the people by a series of discourses on the subject of slavery, every place that I visited gave fresh evidence of the fact, that a greater revolution in public sentiment was to be effected in the free states—*and particularly in New England*—than at the south. I found contempt more bitter, opposition more active, detraction more relentless, prejudice more stubborn, and apathy more frozen, than among slave owners themselves. Of course, there were individual exceptions to the contrary. This state of things afflicted, but did not dishearten me. I determined, at every hazard, to lift up the standard of emancipation in the eyes of the nation, *within sight of Bunker Hill and in the birth place of liberty.* That standard is now unfurled; and long may it float, unhurt by the spoliations of time or the missiles of a desperate foe—yea, till every chain be broken, and every bondman set free! Let Southern oppressors tremble—let their secret abettors tremble—let their Northern apologists tremble—let all the enemies of the persecuted blacks tremble.

I deem the publication of my original Prospectus unnecessary, as it has obtained a wide circulation. The principles therein inculcated will be steadily pursued in this paper, excepting that I shall not array myself as the political partisan of any man. In defending the great cause of human rights, I wish to derive the assistance of all religions and of all parties.

Assenting to the "self-evident truth" maintained in the American Declaration of Independence, "that all men are created equal, that they are endowed by their Creator with certain unalienable rights, that among these are life, liberty and the pursuit of happiness," I shall strenuously contend for the immediate enfranchisement of our slave population. In Park Street Church, on the Fourth of July, 1829, in an address on slavery, I unreflectingly assented to the popular but pernicious doctrine of *gradual* abolition. I seize this opportunity to make a full and unequivocal recantation, and thus publicly to ask pardon of my God, of my country, and of my brethren the poor slaves, for having uttered a sentiment so full of timidity, injustice, and absurdity. A similar recantation, from my pen, was published in the *Genius of Universal Emancipation* at Baltimore, in September, 1829. My conscience is now satisfied.

I am aware, that many object to the severity of my language; but is there not cause for severity? I *will be* as harsh as truth, and as uncompromising as justice. On this subject, I do not wish to think, or speak, or write, with moderation. No! no! Tell a man whose house is on fire, to give a moderate alarm; tell him to moderately rescue his wife from the hands of the ravisher; tell the mother to gradually extricate her babe from the fire into which it has fallen;—but urge me not to use moderation in a cause like the present. I am in earnest—I will not equivocate—I will not excuse—I will not retreat a single inch—AND I WILL BE HEARD. The apathy of the people is enough to make every statue leap from its pedestal, and to hasten the resurrection of the dead.

It is pretended, that I am retarding the cause of emancipation by the coarseness of my invective and the precipitancy of my measures. *The charge is not true.* On this question my influence,—humble as it is,—is felt at this moment to be a considerable extent, and shall be felt in coming years—not perniciously, but beneficially—not as a curse, but as a blessing; and posterity will bear testimony that I was right. I desire to thank God, that he enables me to disregard "the fear of man which bringeth a snare," and to speak his truth in its simplicity and power.

And here I close with this fresh dedication:

> "Oppression! I have seen thee, face to face,
> And met thy cruel eye and cloudy brow;
> But thy soul-withering glance I fear not now—
> For dread to prouder feelings doth give place
> Of deep abhorrence! Scorning the disgrace
> Of slavish knees that at thy footstool bow,
> I also kneel—but with far other bow
> Do hail thee and thy herd of hirelings base:—
> I swear, while life-blood warms my throbbing
> veins,
> Still to oppose and thwart, with heart and hand,
> Thy brutalizing sway—till Afric's chains
> Are burst, and Freedom rules the rescued land,—
> Tramping Oppression and his iron rod:
> *Such is the vow I take*—SO HELP ME GOD!"

Chapter 11

THE SECTIONAL CONFLICT

As an articulate minority the South had no greater spokesman than John C. Calhoun. Indeed of all Southerners it was the coldly logical South Carolinian who had most systematically analyzed the dynamics of the South's position in the Union. Calhoun had clearly perceived that the rapidly industrializing, creditor North was relegating the agrarian, debtor South to a minor role in the nation's economy. He saw realistically that political subjugation would follow, and that as the South became more and more of an economic and political minority within the nation, its whole social structure would be jeopardized by the aggressive and numerically superior North. Besides, even within the South the ruling, slave-owning planter class which Calhoun represented was threatened by the specter of majority rule, since the owners of many slaves and large plantations were few in number. Out of a total Southern white population of 8,000,000 in 1860 there were only 384,000 who actually owned any slaves, while more than three-fourths of the white population had no direct interest in the plantation-slave system at all. Of the slave-owning group, 300,000 owned fewer than 10 slaves each, while only 2,500 owned more than 100 slaves and could be considered members of the dominant planter aristocracy. Here, too, the South's rulers were a small minority and feared majority rule. But an artfully contrived pro-slavery argument prevailed among most other Southerners. Expressed best perhaps in "Sociology for the South," George Fitzhugh's aggressive defense of slavery in contrast to the North's exploitation of wage labor, and in William J. Grayson's parallel epic poem, "The Hireling and the Slave," this argument seemed to make even poor Southern whites loath to surrender the "superiority" that color alone provided them. They seemed more concerned with keeping the legal bonds of slavery between themselves and the Negroes than in disrupting a slave economy that served the purposes of the wealthy planters alone. Therefore, though acutely conscious of the class as well as sectional status of the planting aristocracy, Calhoun first addressed himself to the more immediate sectional conflict and formulated a philosophy of minority rights that was designed, through constitutional checks, to prevent a Northern controlled majority from imposing its will upon the South. At the same time his affirmation of the South's rights within the nation helped to maintain unbroken the power of the minority planting class within the South itself.

Ultimately Calhoun's theorizing led to the repudiation of majority rule and to the doctrines of nullification and secession. In 1832 South Carolina actually proclaimed the tariff of that year null and void within her borders and warned that any attempt to enforce the national law would be met with armed resistance. At length the crisis was met by compromise: the ordinance of nullification was withdrawn and the tariff was lowered. More important, however, was the fact that Carolina planters had found a way of denying the nation's will, and nearly three decades later they would lead ten other Southern states in embracing secession as the logical conclusion to Calhoun's arguments for minority rights. It was ironic that Calhoun should contrive this philosophic framework of a sectionalism that eventually would be the rationale for dismemberment of the

Union, for he had begun his career as the staunchest of nationalists. Yet his metamorphosis from nationalist to sectionalist was in keeping with his recognition of basic economic changes within the nation. The nationalism he had espoused in the early decades of the nineteenth century had then been consistent with the economic interests of the South, but Calhoun saw that the new high-tariff nationalism of the 1830's and 1840's was geared solely to the interests of the industrial North. It was to this later nationalism that he objected so strongly and in answer to which he changed from ardent nationalist to redoubtable sectionalist.

In 1850, at the very end of Calhoun's life, North and South joined in battle once more on what seemed to the philosopher of sectionalism the most crucial question of all: should slavery be permitted to expand freely, with the full protection of the national government, into the new lands acquired in 1848 at the end of the Mexican War? Again Calhoun looked to political realities. If the Southern "slave power" were to be denied free and protected access to the nation's new Territories, the North would people these regions, would organize them politically, and eventually would bring them into the union under its own aegis. Then, with its new allies, the North would so completely overwhelm the Southern minority in Congress that slavery and eventually all of the South's interests and institutions would be destroyed by the tyrannical majority. If this were not ultimately to be her lot, Calhoun insisted, the South must accept nothing less than an unconditional guarantee of slavery in all of the Territories. And when the "Great Compromiser," Henry Clay, offered his famous Compromise of 1850—providing for the organization of lands ceded by Mexico without such a guarantee, though conceding to the South its long desired stringent Fugitive Slave Law—Calhoun prepared to raise an angry if enfeebled voice against it.

Unaware that for ten years the sectional conflict would increase in intensity and bitterness until finally the last bonds of union would be severed by cannon fire, the giants of America's past and of her future were gathered in the Congress that on March 4, 1850, heard Calhoun's last and most famous speech on the slavery question.

Clay, Webster, and Benton—they were from the past. Seward, Chase, Douglas, and Jefferson Davis—they were of the future. It was to these leaders that Calhoun made his final plea for what he considered the rights of his beloved South. As if prophetic of the fate of his section's cause, Calhoun's words, immediately directed against the Compromise of 1850, were his dying words. As the courageous but aged statesman was helped into the Senate Chamber, the galleries were jammed with those who came to hear the great spokesman of the Old South for the last time. But Calhoun, who would live but four weeks more, was too weak to deliver his address and begged leave for Senator Mason of Virginia to read it for him.

It was obvious on all sides, Calhoun maintained, that the Union was breaking up; the great political parties were sectional rather than national, and even the churches were being divided into Northern and Southern branches. It was actually the North that had disrupted the Union by destroying the earlier equilibrium between sections and interests. The North had grown many times more rapidly than the South in resources and population and had in consequence seized political and economic control of the nation. The North had imposed tariffs upon an unwilling but helpless South, had monopolized offices in the national government, had prohibited Southerners from equal access to the nation's territories, and had viciously and unremittingly attacked the South's domestic institutions. As matters stood the South could not with honor and safety remain within the Union. If the Union were to be preserved in its original intent, the North must enforce the fugitive slave laws, must end its anti-slavery agitation, must grant the South equal rights in the Territories, and must accept constitutional changes designed to restore equality between the sections. Primarily these constitutional changes were based upon the concept of "concurrent majorities"—a majority of each section must concur in enacting national legislation. And, as he revealed elsewhere, Calhoun would provide for a dual Presidency: one President to represent the South and the other to represent the North, each with an independent veto power. Thus the South, though numerically a distinct minority, would have a voice in the national government equal to that of the rapidly expanding North. Thus minority rights would become minority rule, or at least minority control.

The alternative to such concessions by the North, Calhoun warned, would be disunion. But the Compromise of 1850, which was warmly supported by Daniel Webster in his famous "Seventh of March" speech, was accepted by the nation despite the violent opposition of extremists in both sections. Ten years later the nation well remembered Calhoun's somber prophecy as his native South Carolina led her sister states in secession from the Union.

John C. Calhoun on the Slavery Question, *1850*

I have, Senators, believed from the first that the agitation of the subject of slavery would, if not prevented by some timely and effective measure, end in disunion. Entertaining this opinion, I have, on all proper occasions, endeavored to call the attention of both the two great parties which divide the country to adopt some measure to prevent so great a disaster, but without success. The agitation has been permitted to proceed, with almost no attempt to resist it, until it has reached a point when it can no longer be disguised or denied that the Union is in danger. You have thus had forced upon you the greatest and the gravest question that can ever come under your consideration: How can the Union be preserved?

To give a satisfactory answer to this mighty question, it is indispensable to have an accurate and thorough knowledge of the nature and the character of the cause by which the Union is endangered. Without such knowledge it is impossible to pronounce, with any certainty, by what measure it can be saved; just as it would be impossible for a physician to pronounce, in the case of some dangerous disease, with any certainty, by what remedy the patient could be saved, without similar knowledge of the nature and character of the cause which produced it. The first question, then, presented for consideration, in the investigation I propose to make, in order to obtain such knowledge, is, What is it that has endangered the Union?

To this question there can be but one answer: that the immediate cause is the almost universal discontent which pervades all the States composing the Southern section of the Union. This widely extended discontent is not of recent origin. It commenced with the agitation of the slavery question, and has been increasing ever since. The next question, going one step further back, is—What has caused this widely diffused and almost universal discontent?

It is a great mistake to suppose, as is by some, that it originated with demagogues, who excited the discontent with the intention of aiding their personal advancement, or with the disappointed ambition of certain politicians, who resorted to it as the means of retrieving their fortunes. On the contrary, all the great political influences of the section were arrayed against excitement, and exerted to the utmost to keep the people quiet. The great mass of the people of the South were divided, as in the other section, into Whigs and Democrats. The leaders and the presses of both parties in the South were very solicitous to prevent excitement and to preserve quiet; because it was seen that the effects of the former would necessarily tend to weaken, if not destroy, the political ties which united them with their respective parties in the other section. Those who know the strength of party ties will readily appreciate the immense force which this cause exerted against agitation, and in favor of preserving quiet. But, great as it was, it was not sufficient to prevent the widespread discontent which now pervades the section. No; some cause, far deeper and more powerful than the one supposed, must exist, to account for discontent so wide and deep. The question then recurs, What is the cause of this discontent? It will be found in the belief of the people of the Southern States, as prevalent as the discontent itself, that they cannot remain, as things now are, consistently with honor and safety, in the Union. The next question to be considered is, What has caused this belief?

One of the causes is, undoubtedly, to be traced to the long-continued agitation of the slave question on the part of the North, and the many aggressions which they have made on the rights of the South during the time. . . .

There is another lying back of it, with which this is intimately connected, that may be regarded as the great and primary cause. This is to be found in the fact that the equilibrium between the two sections, in the Government as it stood when the constitution was ratified and the Government put in action, has been destroyed. At that time there was nearly a perfect equilibrium between the two, which afforded ample means to each to protect itself against the aggression of the other; but, as it now stands, one section has the exclusive power of controlling the Government, which leaves the other without any adequate means of protecting itself against its encroachment and oppression. To place this subject distinctly before you, I have, Senators, prepared a brief statistical statement, showing the relative weight of the two sections in the Government under the first census of 1790 and the last census of 1840.

According to the former, the population of the United States, including Vermont, Kentucky, and Tennessee, which then were in their incipient condition of becoming States, but were not actually admitted, amounted to 3,929,827. Of this number the Northern States had 1,997,899, and the Southern 1,952,072, making the difference of only 45,827 in favor of the former States. The number of States, including Vermont, Kentucky, and Tennessee, were sixteen; of which eight, including Vermont, belonged to the Northern section, and eight, including Kentucky and Tennessee, to the Southern—making an equal division of the States between the two sections under the first census. There was a small preponderance in the House of Representatives, and in the Electoral College, in favor of the Northern, owing to the fact that, according to the provisions of the constitution, in estimating federal numbers five slaves count but three; but it was too small to affect sensibly the perfect equilibrium which, with that exception, existed at the time. Such was the equality of the two sections when the States composing them agreed to enter into a Federal Union. Since then the equilibrium between them has been greatly disturbed.

According to the last census the aggregate population of the United States amounted to 17,063,357, of which the Northern section contained 9,728,920, and the Southern 7,334,437, making a difference in round numbers, of 2,400,000. The number of States has increased from sixteen to twenty-six, making an addition of ten States. In the meantime the position of Delaware had become doubtful as to which section she properly belonged. Considering her as neutral, the Northern States will have thirteen and the Southern States twelve, making a difference in the Senate of two Senators in favor of the former. According to the apportionment under the census of 1840, there were two hundred and twenty-three members of the House of Representatives, of which the Northern States had one hundred and thirty-five, and the Southern States (considering Delaware as neutral) eighty-seven, making a difference in favor of the former in the House of Representatives of forty-eight. The difference in the Senate of two members, added to this, gives to the North in the electoral college, a majority of fifty. Since the census of 1840, four States have been added to the Union—Iowa, Wisconsin, Florida, and Texas. They leave the difference in the Senate as it stood when the census was taken; but add two to the side of the North in the House, making the present majority in the House in its favor fifty, and in the Electoral College fifty-two.

The result of the whole is to give the Northern section a predominance in every department of the Government, and thereby concentrate in the two elements which constitute the Federal Government—majority of States, and a majority of their population, estimated in federal numbers. Whatever section concentrates the two in itself possesses the control of the entire Government.

But we are just at the close of the sixth decade, and the commencement of the seventh. The census is to be taken this year, which must add greatly to the decided preponderance of the North in the House of Representatives and in the electoral college. The prospect is, also, that a great increase will be added to its present preponderance in the Senate, during the period of the decade, by the addition of new States. Two territories, Oregon and Minnesota, are already in progress, and strenuous efforts are making to bring in three additional States from the territory recently conquered from Mexico;

which, if successful, will add three other States in a short time to the Northern section, making five States; and increasing the present number of its States from fifteen to twenty, and of its Senators from thirty to forty. On the contrary, there is not a single territory in progress in the Southern section, and no certainty that any additional State will be added to it during the decade. The prospect then is that the two sections in the Senate, should the efforts now made to exclude the South from the newly acquired territories succeed, will stand, before the end of the decade, twenty Northern States to fourteen Southern (considering Delaware as neutral), and forty Northern Senators to twenty-eight Southern. This great increase of Senators, added to the great increase of members of the House of Representatives and the Electoral College on the part of the North, which must take place under the next decade, will effectually and irretrievably destroy the equilibrium which existed when the Government commenced.

Had this destruction been the operation of time, without the interference of the government, the South would have had no reason to complain; but such was not the fact. It was caused by the legislation of this Government, which was appointed, as the common agent of all, and charged with the protection of the interests and security of all. The legislation by which it has been effected, may be classed under three heads. The first, is that series of acts by which the South has been excluded from the common territory belonging to all the States as members of the Federal Union—which have had the effect of extending vastly the portion allotted to the Northern section, and restricting within narrow limits the portion left the South. The next consists in adopting a system of revenue and disbursements, by which an undue proportion of the burden of taxation has been imposed upon the South, and an undue proportion of its proceeds appropriated to the North; and the last is a system of political measures, by which the original character of the Government has been radically changed. I propose to bestow upon each of these, in the order they stand, a few remarks, with the view of showing that it is owing to the action of this Government, that the equilibrium between the two sections has been destroyed, and the whole powers of the system centered in a sectional majority. . . .

The result of the whole of these causes combined is, that the North has acquired a decided ascendency over every department of this Government, and through it a control over all the powers of the system. A single section governed by the will of the numerical majority, has now, in fact, the control of the Government and the entire powers of the system. . . .

As, then, the North has the absolute control over the Government, it is manifest, that on all questions between it and the South, where there is a diversity of interests, the interest of the latter will be sacrificed to the former, however oppressive the effects may be; as the South possesses no means by which it can resist, through the action of the Government. But if there was no question of vital importance to the South, in reference to which there was a diversity of views between the two sections, this state of things might be endured, without the hazard of destruction to the South. But such is not the fact. There is a question of vital importance to the Southern section, in reference to which the views and feelings of the two sections are as opposite and hostile as they can possibly be.

I refer to the relation between the two races in the Southern section, which constitutes a vital portion of her social organization. Every portion of the North entertains views and feelings more or less hostile to it. Those most opposed and hostile, regard it as a sin, and consider themselves under the most sacred obligation to use every effort to destroy it. Indeed, to the extent that they conceive that they have power, they regard themselves as implicated in the sin, and responsible for not suppressing it by the use of all and every means. Those less opposed and hostile, regard it as a crime—an offence against humanity, as they call it; and although not so fanatical, feel themselves bound to use all efforts to effect the same object; while those who are least opposed and hostile, regard it as a blot and a stain on the character of which they call the Nation, and feel themselves accordingly bound to give it no countenance or support. On the contrary, the Southern section regards the relation as one which cannot be destroyed without subjecting the two races to the greatest calamity; and the section to poverty, desolation, and wretchedness; and accordingly they feel bound, by every consideration of interest and safety, to defend it.

This hostile feeling on the part of the North towards the social organization of the South long lay dormant, but it only required some cause to act on those who felt most intensely that they were responsible for its continuance, to call it into action. The increasing power of this Government, and of the control of the Northern section over all its departments, furnished the cause. It was this which made an impression on the minds of many, that there was little or no restraint to prevent the Government from doing whatever it might choose to do. This was sufficient of itself to put the most fanatical portion of the North in action, for the purpose of destroying the existing relation between the two races in the South.

The first organized movement towards it commenced in 1835. Then, for the first time, societies were organized, presses established, lecturers sent forth to excite the people of the North, and incendiary publications scattered over the whole South through the mail. The South was thoroughly aroused. Meetings were held everywhere, and resolutions adopted, calling upon the North to apply a remedy to arrest the threatened evil, and pledging themselves to adopt measures for their own protection, if it was not arrested. . . .

As for myself, I believed at that early period . . . that agitation would follow, and that it would in the end, if not arrested, destroy the Union. I then so expressed myself in debate . . . but in vain. Had my voice been heeded . . . the agitation which followed would have been prevented, and the fanatical zeal . . . which has brought us to our present perilous condition, would have become extinguished, from the want of fuel to feed the flame. That was the time for the North to have shown her devotion to the Union; but, unfortunately, both of the great parties of that section were so intent on obtaining or retaining party ascendency, that all other considerations were overlooked or forgotten.

What has since followed are but natural consequences. With the success of their first movement, this small fanatical party began to acquire strength; and with that, to become an object of courtship to both the great parties. The necessary consequence was, a further increase of power, and a gradual tainting of the opinions of both of the other parties with their doctrines, until the infection has extended over both; and the great mass of the population of the North, who, whatever may be their opinion of the original abolition party, which still preserves its distinctive organization, hardly ever fail, when it comes to acting, to co-operate in carrying out their measures. . . .

Such is a brief history of the agitation, as far as it has yet advanced. Now I ask, Senators, what is there to prevent its further progress, until it fulfills the ultimate end proposed, unless some decisive measure should be adopted to prevent it? Has any one of the causes, which has added to its increase from its original small and contemptible beginning until it has attained its present magnitude, diminished in force? Is the original cause of the movement—that slavery is a sin, and ought to be suppressed—weaker now than at the commencement? Or is the abolition party less numerous or influential, or have they less influence with, or control over the two great parties of the North in elections? Or has the South greater means of influencing or controlling the movements of this Government now, than it had when the agitation commenced? To all these questions but one answer can be given: No, no, no. The very reverse is true. Instead of being weaker, all the elements in favor of agitation are stronger now than they were in 1835, when it first commenced, while all the elements of influence on the part of the South are weaker. Unless something decisive is done, I again ask what is to stop this agitation, before the great and final object at which it aims—the abolition of slavery in the States—is consummated? Is it, then, not certain, that if something is not done to arrest it, the South will be forced to choose between abolition and secession? Indeed, as events are now moving, it will not require the South to secede, in order to dissolve the Union. Agitation will of itself effect it, of which its past history furnishes abundant proof—as I shall next proceed to show.

It is a great mistake to suppose that disunion can be

effected by a single blow. The cords which bound these States together in one common Union, are far too numerous and powerful than that. Disunion must be the work of time. It is only through a long process, and successively, that the cords can be snapped, until the whole fabric falls asunder. Already the agitation of the slavery question has snapped some of the most important, and has greatly weakened all the others, as I shall proceed to show.

The cords that bind the States together are not only many, but various in character. Some are spiritual or ecclesiastical; some political; other social. Some appertain to the benefit conferred by the Union, and others to the feeling of duty and obligation.

The strongest of those of a spiritual and ecclesiastical nature, consisted in the unity of the great religious denominations, all of which originally embraced the whole Union. All these denominations, with the exception, perhaps, of the Catholics were organized very much upon the principle of our political institutions. Beginning with smaller meetings, corresponding with the political divisions of the country, their organization terminated in one great central assemblage, corresponding very much with the character of Congress. At these meetings the principal clergymen and lay members of the respective denominations, from all parts of the Union, met to transact business relating to their common concerns. It was not confined to what appertained to the doctrines and discipline of the respective denominations, but extended to plans for disseminating the Bible, establishing missions, distributing tracts, and of establishing presses for the publications of tracts, newspapers, and periodicals, with a view of diffusing religious information, and for the support of their respective doctrines and creeds. All this combined contributed greatly to strengthen the bonds of the Union. The ties which held each denomination together formed a strong cord to hold the whole Union together; but, powerful as they were, they have not been able to resist the explosive effect of slavery agitation. . . .

The strongest cord, of a political character, consists of the many and powerful ties that have held together the two great parties which have, with some modifications, existed from the beginning of the Government. They both extended to every portion of the Union, and strongly contributed to hold all its parts together. But this powerful cord has fared no better than the spiritual. It resisted, for a long time, the explosive tendency of the agitation, but has finally snapped under its force—if not entirely, in a great measure. Nor is there one of the remaining cords which has not been greatly weakened. To this extent the Union has already been destroyed by agitation, in the only way it can be, sundering and weakening the cords which bind it together.

If the agitation goes on, the same force, acting with increased intensity, as has been shown, will finally snap every cord, when nothing will be left to hold the States together except force. But surely, that can, with no propriety of language, be called a Union, when the only means by which the weaker is held connected with the stronger portion is force. It may, indeed, keep them connected; but the connection will partake much more of the character of subjugation, on the part of the weaker to the stronger, than the union of free, independent, and sovereign States, in one confederation as they stood in the early stages of the Government, and which only is worthy of the sacred name of Union.

Having now, Senators, explained what is that endangers the Union, and traced it to its cause, and explained its nature and character, the question again recurs, How can the Union be saved? To this I answer: There is but one way by which it can be, and that is, by adopting such measures as will satisfy the States belonging to the Southern section, that they can remain in the Union consistently with their honor and their safety. There is, again, only one way by which this can be effected, and that is by removing the causes by which this belief has been produced. Do this, and discontent will cease, harmony and kind feelings between the sections be restored, and every apprehension of danger to the Union removed. The question then is, How can this be done? But, before I undertake to answer this question, I propose to show by what the Union cannot be saved.

It cannot, then, be saved by eulogies on the Union, however splendid or numerous. The cry of "Union, Union, the glorious Union!" can no more prevent disunion than the cry of "Health, health, glorious health!" on the part of the physician, can save a patient lying dangerously ill. So long as the Union, instead of being regarded as a protector, is regarded in the opposite character, by not much less than a majority of the States, it will be in vain to attempt to conciliate them by pronouncing eulogies on it.

Besides, this cry of Union comes commonly from those whom we cannot believe to be sincere. It usually comes from our assailants. But we cannot believe them to be sincere; for, if they loved the Union, they would necessarily be devoted to the constitution. It made the Union, and to destroy the constitution would be to destroy the Union. But the only reliable and certain evidence of devotion to the constitution is, to abstain, on the one hand, from violating it, and to repel, on the other, all attempts to violate it. It is only by faithfully performing these high duties that the constitution can be preserved, and with it the Union.

But how stands the profession of devotion to the Union by our assailants, when brought to this test? Have they abstained from violating the constitution? Let the many Acts passed by the Northern States to set aside and annul the clause of the Constitution providing for the delivery up of fugitive slaves answer. I cite this, not that it is the only instance (for there are many others), but because the violation in this particular is too notorious and palpable to be denied. Again, have they stood forth faithfully to repel violations of the constitution? Let their course in reference to the agitation of the slavery question, which was commenced and has been carried on for fifteen years, avowedly for the purpose of abolishing slavery in the States—an object all acknowledged to be unconstitutional—answer. Let them show a single instance, during this long period, in which they have denounced the agitators or their attempts to effect what is admitted to be unconstitutional, or a single measure which they have brought forward for that purpose. How can we, with all these facts before us, believe that they are sincere in their profession of devotion to the Union, or avoid believing their profession is but intended to increase the vigor of their assaults and to weaken the force of our resistance?

Nor can we regard the profession of devotion to the Union, on the part of those who are not our assailants, as sincere, when they pronounce eulogies upon the Union, evidently with the intent of charging us with disunion, without uttering one word of denunciation against our assailants. If friends of the Union, their course should be to unite with us in repelling these assaults, and denouncing the authors as enemies of the Union. Why they avoid this, and pursue the course they do, it is for them to explain.

Nor can the Union be saved by invoking the name of the illustrious Southerner whose mortal remains repose on the western bank of the Potomac. He was one of us—a slaveholder and a planter. We have studied his history, and find nothing in it to justify submission to wrong. On the contrary, his great fame rests on the solid foundation, that, while he was careful to avoid doing wrong to others, he was prompt and decided in repelling wrong. I trust that, in this respect, we profited by his example.

Nor can we find any thing in his history to deter us from seceding from the Union, should it fail to fulfill the objects for which it was instituted, by being permanently and hopelessly converted into the means of oppressing instead of protecting us. On the contrary, we find much in his example to encourage us, should we be forced to the extremity of deciding between submission and disunion. . . .

Having now shown what cannot save the Union, I return to the question with which I commenced. How can the Union be saved? There is but one way by which it can with any certainty; and that is, by a full and final settlement, on the principle of justice, of all the questions at issue between the two sections. The South asks for justice, simple justice, and less she ought not to take. She has no compromise to offer, but the Constitution; and no concession or surrender to make. She has already surrendered so much that she has little left to surrender. Such a settlement would go to the root of the evil, and remove all cause of discontent, by satisfying the South, that she could remain honorably and safely in the Union, and thereby restore the harmony and fraternal feeling between the sections, which existed anterior to the Missouri agitation. Nothing else can, with any certainty, finally and for ever settle the questions at issue, terminate agitation, and save the Union.

But can this be done? Yes, easily; not by the weaker party, for it can of itself do nothing, not even protect itself, but by the stronger. The North has only to will it to accomplish it, to do justice by conceding to the South an equal right in the acquired territory, and to do her duty by causing the stipulations relative to fugitive slaves to be faithfully fulfilled, to cease the agitation of the slave question, and to provide for the insertion of a provision in the Constitution, by an amendment, which will restore to the South, in substance, the power she possessed of protecting herself, before the equilibrium between the sections was destroyed by the action of this Government. There will be no difficulty in devising such a provision, one that will protect the South, and which, at the same time, will improve and strengthen the Government, instead of impairing and weakening it.

But will the North agree to this? It is for her to answer the question. But, I will say, she cannot refuse, if she has half the love of the Union which she professes to have, or without justly exposing herself to the charge that her love of power and aggrandizement is far greater than her love of the Union. At all events, the responsibility of saving the Union rests on the North, and not on the South. The South cannot save it by any act of hers, and the North may save it without any sacrifice whatever, unless to do justice, and to perform her duties under the Constitution, should be regarded by her as a sacrifice.

It is time, Senators, that there should be an open and manly avowal on all sides, as to what is intended to be done. If the question is not now settled, it is uncertain whether it ever can hereafter be; and we, the representatives of the States of this Union, regarded as governments, should come to a distinct understanding as to our respective views, in order to ascertain whether the great questions at issue can be settled or not. If you, who represent the stronger portion, cannot agree to settle them on the broad principle of justice and duty, say so; and let the States we both represent agree to separate and part in peace. If you are unwilling we should part in peace, tell us so; and we shall know what to do, when you reduce the question to submission or resistance. If you remain silent, you will compel us to infer by your acts what you intend. In that case, California will become the test question. If you admit her, under all the difficulties that oppose her admission, you compel us to infer that you intend to exclude us from the whole of the acquired territories, with the intention of destroying, irretrievably, the equilibrium between the two sections. We would be blind not to perceive in that case, that your real objects are power and aggrandizement, and infatuated not to act accordingly.

I have now, Senators, done my duty in expressing my opinions fully, freely, and candidly, on this solemn occasion. In doing so, I have been governed by the motives which have governed me in all the stages of the agitation of the slavery question since its commencement. I have exerted myself, during the whole period, to attest it, with the intention of saving the Union, if it could be done; and if it could not, save the section where it has pleased Providence to cast my lot, and which I sincerely believe has justice and the Constitution on its side. Having faithfully done my duty to the best of my ability, both to the Union and my section, throughout this agitation, I shall have the consolation, let what will come, that I am free from all responsibility.

"The Hireling and the Slave,"
William J. Grayson, 1854

How small the choice, from cradle to the grave,
Between the lot of Hireling and of Slave!
To each alike applies the stern decree,
That man shall labour; whether bond or free,
For all that toil, the recompense we claim—
Food, fire, a home and clothing—is the same.
The manumitted serfs of Europe find
Unchanged this sad estate of all mankind;
What blessing to the churls has freedom proved,
What want supplied, what task or toil removed?
Hard work and scanty wages still their lot,
In youth o'erlaboured, and in age forgot,

The mocking boon of freedom they deplore,
In wants, cares, labours never known before.
    Free but in name—the slaves of endless toil,
In Britain still they turn the stubborn soil,
Spread on each sea her sails for every mart,
Ply in her cities every useful art;
But vainly may the Peasant toil and groan,
To speed the plough in furrows not his own;
In vain the art is plied, the sail is spread,
The daily work secures no daily bread;
With hopeless eye, the pauper Hireling sees
The homeward sail swell proudly to the breeze,
Rich fabrics, wrought by his unequalled hand,
Borne by each breeze to every distant land;
Unbounded wealth, propitious seasons yield,
And bounteous harvests crown the smiling field;
The streams of wealth that foster pomp and pride,
No food nor shelter for his wants provide,
He fails to win, by toil intensely hard,
The bare subsistence—labour's least reward.
    In squalid hut—a kennel for the poor,
Or noisome cellar, stretched upon the floor,
His clothing rags, of filthy straw his bed,
With offal from the gutter daily fed,
Thrust out from Nature's board, the Hireling lies—
No place for him that common board supplies,
No neighbor helps, no charity attends,
No philanthropic sympathy befriends;
None heed the needy wretch's dying groan,
He starves unsuccor'd, perishes unknown.
    These are the miseries, such the wants, the cares,
The bliss that freedom for the serf prepares;
Vain in his skill in each familiar task,
Capricious Fashion shifts her Protean mask,
His ancient craft gives work and bread no more,
And want and death sit scowling at his door.
    Close by the hovel, with benignant air,
To lordly halls illustrious crowds repair—
The Levite tribes of Christian love that show
No care nor pity for a neighbor's woe;
Who meet, each distant evil to deplore,
But not to clothe or feed their country's poor;
They waste no thought on common wants or pains,

On misery hid in filthy courts and lanes,
On alms that ask no witnesses but Heaven,
By pious hands to secret suffering given;
Theirs the bright sunshine of the public eye,
The pomp and circumstance of charity,
The crowded meeting, the repeated cheer,
The sweet applause of prelate, prince or peer,
The long report of pious trophies won
Beyond the rising of the setting sun,
The mutual smile, the self-complacent air,
The laboured speech and Pharisaic prayer,
Thanksgivings for their purer hearts and hands,
Scorn for the publicans of other lands,
And soft addresses—Sutherland's delight,
That gentle dames at pious parties write—
These are the cheats that vanity prepares,
The soft deceits of her seductive fairs,
When Exeter expands her portals wide,
And England's saintly coteries decide
The proper nostrum for each evil known
In every land on earth, except their own,
But never heed the sufferings, wants, or sins,
At home, where all true charity begins.
    There, unconcerned, the philanthropic eye
Beholds each phase of human misery;
Sees the worn child compelled in mines to slave
Through narrow seams of coal, a living grave,
Driven from the breezy hill, the sunny glade,
By ruthless hearts, the drudge of labour made,
Unknown the boyish sport, the hour of play,
Stript of the common boon, the light of day,
Harnessed like brutes, like brutes to tug and strain
And drag, on hands and knees, the loaded wain:
There crammed in huts, in reeking masses thrown,
All moral sense and decency unknown,
With no restraint, but what the felon knows,
With the sole joy, that beer or gin bestows,
To gross excess and brutalizing strife,
The drunken Hireling dedicates his life:
There women prostitute themselves for bread,
Mothers rejoice to find their infants dead,
Childhood bestows no childish sports or toys,
Age, neither reverence nor repose enjoys,

Labour, with hunger, wages ceaseless strife,
And want and suffering only end with life;
In crowded huts, contagious ills assail,
Insidious typhus and its plagues prevail;
Gaunt famine prowls around his pauper prey,
And daily sweeps his ghastly hosts away;
Unburied corpses taint the summer air,
And crime and outrage revel with despair.
Or—from their humble homes and native land
Forced by a landlord's pitiless command,
Far, in ungenial climes, condemned to roam,
That sheep may batten in the peasant's home—
The pauper exiles, from the hill that yields
One parting look on their abandoned fields,
Behold with tears, no manhood can restrain,
Their ancient hamlet level'd with the plain:
They go, a squalid band, unhoused, unfed,
The sky their only roof, the ditch their bed,
In crowded ships, new miseries to find,
More hideous still than those they left behind;
Grim Chol'ra thins their ranks, ship fevers sweep
Their livid tythes of victims to the deep;
The sad survivors, on a foreign shore,
The double loss of homes and friends deplore,
And beg a stranger's bounty to supply
The food and shelter that their homes deny.
Yet homebred misery, such as this, imparts
Nor grief, nor care, to philanthropic hearts;
The tear of sympathy forever flows,
Though not for Saxon or for Celtic woes;
The hireling white, without a pitying eye,
Or helping hand, at home may starve and die;
But that the distant black may softlier fare,
Eat, sleep and play, exempt from toil and care,
All England's meek philanthropists unite,
With frantic eagerness, harangue and write,
By purchased tools, diffuse distrust and hate,
Sow factions strife, in each dependent State,
Cheat with delusive lies the public mind,
Invent the cruelties, they fail to find,
Slander, in pious garb, with prayer and hymn,
And blast a people's fortune for a whim.
Cursed by these factious arts, that take the guise

Of charity, to cheat the good and wise,
The bright Antilles see, from year to year,
Their harvests fail, their fortunes disappear;
The cane no more its golden treasure yields;
Unsightly weeds deform the fertile fields;
The negro freeman—thrifty while a slave,
Becomes a helpless drone or crafty knave,
Each effort to improve his nature foils;
Begs, steals, or sleeps and starves, but never toils,
For savage sloth, mistakes the freedom won,
And ends, the mere barbarian he begun.
Taught by the Master's efforts, by his care,
Fed, clothed, protected, many a patient year,
From trivial numbers now to millions grown,
With all the white man's useful arts their own,
Industrious, docile, skilled in wood and field,
To guide the plough, the sturdy axe to wield,
The Negroes schooled by Slavery embrace
The highest portion of the Negro race;
And none the savage native will compare,
Of barbarous Guinea, with its offspring here.
    If bound to daily labour while he lives,
His is the daily bread that labour gives;
Guarded from want, from beggary secure,
He never feels what Hireling crowds endure,
Nor knows, like them, in hopeless want to crave,
For wife and child, the comforts of the slave,
Or the sad thought that, when about to die,
He leaves them to the world's cold charity,
And sees them forced to seek the poor-house door—
The last, sad, hated refuge of the poor.
    Still Europe's pious coteries sigh and groan
Note our defects, yet never see their own,
Grieve that the Slave is never taught to write,
And reads no better than the Hireling White;
Do their own ploughmen no instruction lack,
Have whiter clowns more knowledge than the Black?
Has the French peasant, or the German boor,
Of learning's treasure any larger store;
Have Ireland's millions, flying from the rule
Of those who censure, ever known a school?
A thousand years, and Europe's wealth impart
No means to mend the Hireling's head or heart;

They build no schools to teach the pauper White,
Their toiling millions neither read nor write;
Whence then the idle clamour when they rave
For schools and teachers for the distant Slave?
And why the soft regret, the coarse attack,
If Justice punish the offending Black?
Are Whites not punished?—When Utopian times
Shall drive from Earth all miseries and crimes,
And teach the World the art to do without
The cat, the gauntlet, and the brutal knout,
Banish the halter, galley, jails and chains,
And strip the law of penalties and pains;
Here too, offence and wrong they may prevent,
And Slaves, with Hirelings, need no punishment:
'Till then, what lash of Slavery will compare
With the dread scourge that British soldiers bear?
What gentle rule, in Britain's Isle, prevails,
How rare her use of gibbets, stocks and jails!
How much humaner, than a master's whip,
Her penal colony and convict ship!
Whose code of law can darker pages show,
Where blood for smaller misdemeanors flow?
The trifling theft or trespass that demands,
For slaves, light penance from a master's hands,
Where Europe's milder punishments are known,
Incur the penalty of death alone.
And yet the Master's lighter rule ensures
More order than the sternest code secures;
No mobs of factious workmen gather here,
No strikes we dread, no lawless riots fear;
Nuns, from their convent driven, at midnight fly,
Churches, in flames, ask vengeance from the sky,
Seditious schemes in bloody tumults end,
Parsons incite, and Senators defend,
But not where Slaves their easy labours ply,
Safe from the snare, beneath a Master's eye;
In useful tasks engaged, employed their time,
Untempted by the demagogue to crime,
Secure they toil, uncursed their peaceful life,
With freedom's hungry broils and wasteful strife,
No want to goad, no faction to deplore,
The Slave escapes the perils of the poor.

* * *

And yet the life, so unassailed by care,
So blest with moderate work, with ample fare,
With all the good the pauper Hireling needs,
The happier Slave on each plantation leads;
Safe from harassing doubts and annual fears,
He dreads no famine, in unfruitful years;
If harvest fail from inauspicious skies,
The Master's providence his food supplies;
No paupers perish here for want of bread,
Or lingering live, by foreign bounty fed;
No exiled trains of homeless peasants go,
In distant climes, to tell their tales of woe;
Far other fortune, free from care and strife,
For work, or bread, attends the Negro's life,
And Christian Slaves may challenge as their own,
The blessings claimed in fabled states alone—
The cabin home, not comfortless, though rude,
Light daily labour, and abundant food,
The sturdy health, that temperate habits yield,
The cheerful song, that rings in every field,
The long, loud laugh, that freemen seldom share,
Heaven's boon to bosoms unapproached by care,
And boisterous jest and humour unrefined,
That leave, though rough, no painful sting behind;
While, nestling near, to bless their humble lot,
Warm social joys surround the Negro's cot,
The evening dance its merriment imparts,
Love, with his rapture, fills their youthful hearts,
And placid age, the task of labour done,
Enjoys the summer shade, the winter's sun,
And, as through life no pauper want he knows,
Laments no poorhouse penance at its close.

His too the Christian privilege to share
The weekly festival of praise and prayer;
For him the Sabbath shines with holier light,
The air is balmier, and the sky more bright;
Winter's brief suns with warmer radiance glow,
With softer breath the gales of autumn blow,
Spring with new flowers more richly strews the ground,
And summer spreads a fresher verdure round;
The early shower is past; the joyous breeze
Shakes patt'ring rain drops from the rustling trees,

And with the sun, the fragrant offerings rise,
From Nature's censers to the bounteous skies;
With cheerful aspect, in his best array,
To the far forest church he takes his way;
With kind salute the passing neighbor meets,
With awkward grace the morning traveller greets,
And joined by crowds, that gather as he goes,
Seeks the calm joy the Sabbath morn bestows.

Chapter 12

THE FATEFUL DECADE

The dramatic gold rush of the Forty-Niners, the phenomenal growth of a vast railroad network joining distant regions of the country, the conquest of the oceans by Yankee clipper ships, the rapid transformation of the upper Mississippi Valley into the nation's most important agricultural region, and a tremendous boom in industry and commerce—all of these made the 1850's years of prosperity and plenty. Reform as well was very much in the air at mid-century, as particularly evidenced by the Woman's Rights movement formally promulgated at the 1848 Seneca Falls convention. These were also fitful, angry, and divisive years, in which tempers grew shorter and more heated, in which the personal ties of kinship and friendship were often broken by the deep emotionalism that marked the persistent debate over the morality of slavery. And when in 1858 Abraham Lincoln warned that "A house divided against itself cannot stand," there were already many Americans who feared that the bitterness of the ideological conflict was evidence that the house was in truth divided.

Throughout this fateful decade before secession or war the most intensely emotional area of conflict between the sections concerned the fugitive slaves. Though the number of Negroes who escaped the brutal regimen of slavery was small, Southerners were particularly infuriated at the assistance rendered their chattels by the Northern "Underground Railroad," a carefully guarded route of farm houses from which Abolitionists sped the fortunate fugitives northward to freedom. Frequently, however, the slaveholder had his revenge when long-suffering fugitives were seized by federal officers and returned to bondage under the stringent Fugitive Slave Act of 1850. But thoughtful Southerners may have tempered their immediate satisfaction with fearful concern for the future when in 1854 they beheld the spectacle of usually staid Boston roused to fury by the apprehension of a fugitive slave, one Anthony Burns. Burns was surrendered to his master, but in the face of an angry mob that was restrained from freeing him only by the presence of four platoons of marines, United States artillery, cavalry units, and the police, one thousand men strong. That it cost up to \$100,000 to return this one fugitive was far less significant than that Northern attitudes towards slavery were visibly changing—two decades before, another Boston mob had savagely attacked the arch-Abolitionist, William Lloyd Garrison. The new Northern temper boded ill for the slaveholders.

The North's enthusiastic reception of Harriet Beecher Stowe's *Uncle Tom's Cabin* was further testimony to the increasingly bad feelings between the sections. This classic indictment of slavery made innumerable friends for the anti-slavery cause as Little Eva, Topsy, Uncle Tom, and Simon Legree called forth compassion for the oppressed slaves and hatred for the oppressors. Three hundred thousand copies of the novel were sold in the first year after publication, and some years later, when the sections were already joined in mortal combat, it is reported that President Lincoln remarked to Mrs. Stowe: "So you're the little woman who wrote the book that made this great war!" But constantly mounting emotions found their outlet in bloodshed long before the war came. Even within the halls of Congress sectional tempers had led to violence and Congressmen who were outspoken on the slavery question frequently carried a brace of pistols or a bowie knife in self-defense.

Essentially human slavery was no more pleasing to Southerners than to Northerners; rather the South had rationalized its "peculiar institution" as just and altogether righteous only when slave labor had come to seem essential to the plantation system and thus to the section's prosperity. Slavery was the focus of attention, but the basic conflict was between Northern industrialism and Southern plantation agrarianism, and it was to find its most immediate expression in the fiercely debated political question of the expansion of slavery into the Territories. If slavery were permitted to expand into the new Territories, these areas would be settled and organized politically by Southerners; if the expansion of slavery were prohibited, the new Territories would be politically controlled by Northerners. And when statehood was achieved the Territories would provide the one section or the other with important new Congressional power to enact or reject the economic program of high tariffs, subsidies, and internal improvements that the industrial North demanded and the agrarian South bitterly opposed. By the 1850's, confronted by an already numerically—and thus politically—superior North, desperate Southerners were insisting that they would remain within the Union only as long as slavery was unconditionally *guaranteed* in the Territories. They damned the Compromise of 1850, which provided for "squatter sovereignty," the right of the settlers themselves to determine whether slavery should be permitted or prohibited. But in 1854, the Southerners applauded the Kansas-Nebraska Act that again provided for "popular sovereignty," this time because the Act at least opened to the possibility of slavery territory from which it had previously been prohibited by the Missouri Compromise of 1820. And soon the nation was appalled at the spectacle of "Bleeding Kansas," as Northerners and Southerners opened battle to determine which section should organize the Territory, whether Kansas would ultimately bring additional political power to the free or to the slave states.

Actually, it was in the Supreme Court, not in Congress, that the pro-slavery forces won their most decisive victory. In March, 1857, speaking for a court that was predominately Southern, Chief Justice Roger B. Taney delivered his famous decision in Dred Scott v. Sanford. Scott, a Missouri Negro, was suing his master, arguing that he had automatically attained his freedom when taken to Illinois, a free state, and then to Minnesota Territory, where slavery had specifically been forbidden by the Missouri Compromise. The case had long been before the Court, and the nation had anxiously awaited its decision; now the momentous importance of Taney's words was obvious to all. Taney first declared that Scott, as a Negro, was not a citizen and therefore could not sue in the Federal courts. The Chief Justice might have stopped there and simply dismissed Scott's petition for freedom, but he went on to delight the Southern expansionists by insisting—and this was the crucial part of the opinion—that Scott could not possibly have been freed by his stay in Minnesota Territory, because Minnesota was not free territory! In fact, Congress had no power to create a free Territory! Thus the Missouri Compromise had been unconstitutional, for, contrary to the Fifth Amendment, it had deprived Southerners of their slave property without due process of law. Under the new decision slavery could not be forbidden in the Territories.

Southerners were overjoyed at the decision. The question of the expansion of slavery seemed to have been settled for all time: now it might spread freely through all of the Territories with the sanction of a Court that had read Southern extremism into the Constitution. But that the Court had by no means effectually disposed of the issue was evident in the North's vehement opposition to Taney's decision. There were increasingly large numbers of Northerners who now would agree with one prominent Republican that "There is a higher law than the Constitution." And soon many of them would fight to uphold that "higher law."

Seneca Falls Declaration of Sentiments and Resolutions, *1848*

DECLARATION OF SENTIMENTS

When, in the course of human events, it becomes necessary for one portion of the family of man to assume among the people of the earth a position different from that which they have hitherto occupied, but one to which the laws of nature and of nature's God entitle them, a decent respect to the opinions of mankind requires that they should declare the causes that impel them to such a course.

We hold these truths to be self-evident: that all men and women are created equal; that they are endowed by their Creator with certain inalienable rights; that among these are life, liberty, and the pursuit of happiness; that to secure these rights governments are instituted, deriving their just powers from the consent of the governed. Whenever any form of government becomes destructive of these ends, it is the right of those who suffer from it to refuse allegiance to it, and to insist upon the institution of a new government, laying its foundation on such principles, and organizing its powers in such form, as to them shall seem most likely to effect their safety and happiness. Prudence, indeed, will dictate that governments long established should not be changed for light and transient causes; and accordingly all experience hath shown that mankind are more disposed to suffer while evils are sufferable, than to right themselves by abolishing the forms to which they are accustomed. But when a long train of abuses and usurpations, pursuing invariably the same object, evinces a design to reduce them under absolute despotism, it is their duty to throw off such government, and to provide new guards for their future security. Such has been the patient sufferance of the women under this government, and such is now the necessity which constrains them to demand the equal station to which they are entitled.

The history of mankind is a history of repeated injuries and usurpations on the part of man toward woman, having in direct object the establishment of an absolute tyranny over her. To prove this, let facts be submitted to a candid world.

He has never permitted her to exercise her inalienable right to the elective franchise.

He has compelled her to submit to laws, in the formation of which she had no voice.

He has withheld from her rights which are given to the most ignorant and degraded men—both natives and foreigners.

Having deprived her of this first right of a citizen, the elective franchise, thereby leaving her without representation in the halls of legislation, he has oppressed her on all sides.

He has made her, if married, in the eye of the law, civilly dead.

He has taken from her all right in property, even to the wages she earns.

He has made her, morally, an irresponsible being, as she can commit many crimes with impunity, provided they be done in the presence of her husband. In the covenant of marriage, she is compelled to promise obedience to her husband, he becoming to all intents and purposes, her master—the law giving him power to deprive her of her liberty, and to administer chastisement.

He has so framed the laws of divorce, as to what shall be the proper causes, and in case of separation, to whom the guardianship of the children shall be given, as to be wholly regardless of the happiness of women—the law, in all cases, going upon a false supposition of the supremacy of man, and giving all power into his hands.

After depriving her of all rights as a married woman, if single, and the owner of property, he has taxed her to support a government which recognizes her only when her property can be made profitable to it.

He has monopolized nearly all the profitable employments, and from those she is permitted to follow, she receives but a scanty remuneration. He closes against her all the avenues to wealth and distinction which he considers most honorable to himself. As a teacher of theology, medicine, or law, she is not known.

He has denied her the facilities for obtaining a thorough education, all colleges being closed against her.

He allows her in Church, as well as State, but a subordinate position, claiming Apostolic authority for her exclusion from the ministry, and, with some exceptions, from any public participation in the affairs of the Church.

He has created a false public sentiment by giving to the world a different code of morals for men and women, by which moral delinquencies which exclude women from society, are not only tolerated, but deemed of little account in man.

He has usurped the prerogative of Jehovah himself, claiming it as his right to assign for her a sphere of action, when that belongs to her conscience and to her God.

He has endeavored, in every way that he could, to destroy her confidence in her own powers, to lessen her self-respect and to make her willing to lead a dependent and abject life.

Now, in view of this entire disfranchisement of one-half the people of this country, their social and religious degradation—in view of the unjust laws above mentioned, and because women do feel themselves aggrieved, oppressed, and fraudulently deprived of their most sacred rights, we insist that they have immediate admission to all the rights and privileges which belong to them as citizens of the United States.

In entering upon the great work before us, we anticipate no small amount of misconception, misrepresentation, and ridicule; but we shall use every instrumentality within our power to effect our object. We shall employ agents, circulate tracts, petition the State and National legislatures, and endeavor to enlist the pulpit and the press on our behalf. We hope this Convention will be followed by a series of Conventions embracing every part of the country.

RESOLUTIONS

WHEREAS, The great precept of nature is conceded to be, that, "man shall pursue his own true and substantial happiness." Blackstone in his Commentaries remarks, that this law of Nature being coeval with mankind, and dictated by God himself, is of course superior in obligation to any other. It is binding over all the globe, in all countries and at all times; no human laws are of any validity if contrary to this, and such of them as are valid, derive all their force, and all their validity, and all their authority, mediately and immediately, from this original; therefore,

Resolved, That all laws which prevent woman from occupying such a station in society as her conscience shall dictate, or which place her in a position inferior to that of man, are contrary to the great precept of nature, and therefore of no force or authority.

Resolved, That woman is man's equal—was intended to be so by the Creator, and the highest good of the race demands that she should be recognized as such.

Resolved, That the women of this country ought to be enlightened in regard to the laws under which they live, that they may no longer publish their degradation by declaring themselves satisfied with their present position, nor their ignorance, by asserting that they have all the rights they want.

Resolved, That inasmuch as man, while claiming for himself intellectual superiority, does accord to woman moral superiority, it is pre-eminently his duty to encourage her to speak and teach, as she has an opportunity, in all religious assemblies.

Resolved, That the same amount of virtue, delicacy, and refinement of behavior that is required of woman in the social state, should also be required of man, and the same transgressions should be visited with equal severity on both man and woman.

Resolved, That the objection of indelicacy and impropriety, which is so often brought against woman when she addresses a public audience, comes with a very ill-grace from those who encourage, by their attendance, her appearance on the stage, in the concert, or in feats of the circus.

Resolved, That woman has too long rested satisfied in the circumscribed limits which corrupt customs and a perverted application of the Scriptures have marked out for her, and that it is time she should move in the enlarged sphere which her great Creator has assigned her.

Resolved, That it is the duty of the women of this country to secure to themselves their sacred right to the elective franchise.

Resolved, That the equality of human rights results necessarily from the fact of the identity of the race in capabilities and responsibilities.

Resolved, That the speedy success of our cause depends upon the zealous and untiring efforts of both men and women, for the overthrow of the monopoly of the pulpit, and for the securing to women an equal participation with men in the various trades, professions, and commerce.

Resolved, therefore, That, being invested by the

Creator with the same capabilities, and the same consciousness of responsibility for their exercise, it is demonstrably the right and duty of woman, equally with man, to promote every righteous cause by every righteous means; and especially in regard to the great subjects of morals and religion, it is self-evidently her right to participate with her brother in teaching them, both in private and in public, by writing and by speaking, by any instrumentalities proper to be used, and in any assemblies proper to be held; and this being a self-evident truth growing out of the divinely implanted principles of human nature, any custom or authority adverse to it, whether modern or wearing the hoary sanction of antiquity, is to be regarded as self-evident falsehood, and at war with mankind.

Dred Scott v. Sanford: Chief Justice Roger B. Taney for the Supreme Court, *1857*

. . . There are two leading questions presented by the record:

1. Had the Circuit Court of the United States jurisdiction to hear and determine the case between these parties? And,

2. If it had jurisdiction, is the judgment it has given erroneous or not?

The plaintiff in error was, with his wife and children, held as slaves by the defendant, in the State of Missouri, and he brought this action in the Circuit Court of the United States for that district, to assert the title of himself and his family to freedom.

The declaration is . . . that he and the defendant are citizens of different States; that is, that he is a citizen of Missouri, and the defendant a citizen of New York.

The defendant pleaded in abatement to the jurisdiction of the court, that the plaintiff was not a citizen of the State of Missouri, as alleged in his declaration, being a Negro of African descent whose ancestors were pure African blood, and who were brought into this country and sold as slaves . . .

Before we speak of the pleas in bar, it will be proper to

dispose of the questions which have arisen on the plea in abatement.

That plea denies the right of the plaintiff to sue in a court of the United States, for the reasons therein stated.

If the question raised by it is legally before us, and the court should be of opinion that the facts stated in it disqualify the plaintiff from becoming a citizen, in the sense in which that word is used in the Constitution of the United States, then the judgment of the Circuit Court is erroneous, and must be reversed. . . .

The question to be decided is, whether the plaintiff is not entitled to sue as a citizen in a court of the United States. . . .

The question is simply this: Can a Negro, whose ancestors were imported into this country, and sold as slaves, become a member of the political community formed and brought into existence by the Constitution of the United States, and as such become entitled to all the rights, and privileges, and immunities, guaranteed by that instrument to the citizen? One of which rights is the privilege of suing in a court of the United States in the cases specified in the Constitution.

It will be observed, that the plea applies to that class of persons only whose ancestors were Negroes of the African race, and imported into this country, and sold and held as slaves. The only matter in issue before the court, therefore, is whether the descendants of such slaves, when they shall be emancipated, or who are born of parents who had become free before their birth, are citizens of a State, in the sense in which the word citizen is used in the Constitution of the United States. . . .

The words "people of the United States" and "citizens" are synonymous terms, and mean the same thing. They both describe the political body who, according to our republican institutions, form the sovereignty, and who hold the power and conduct the government through their representatives. They are what we familiarly call the "sovereign people," and every citizen is one of this people, and a constituent member of this sovereignty. The question before us is, whether the class of persons described in the plea in abatement compose a portion of this people, and are constituent members of this sovereignty? We think they are not, and that they are not included, and were not intended to be included, under the word "citizens" in the Constitution, and can, therefore, claim none of the rights and privileges which that instrument provides for and secures to citizens of the United States. On the contrary, they were at that time considered as a subordinate and inferior class of beings, who had been subjugated by the dominant race, and whether emancipated or not, yet remained subject to their authority, and had no rights or privileges but such as those who held the power and the government might choose to grant them. . . .

In discussing this question, we must not confound the rights of citizenship which a State may confer within its own limits, and the rights of citizenship as a member of the Union. It does not by any means follow, because he has all the rights and privileges of a citizen of a State, that he must be a citizen of the United States. He may have all of the rights and privileges of the citizen of a State, and yet not be entitled to the rights and privileges of a citizen in any other State. For, previous to the adoption of the Constitution of the United States, every State had the undoubted right to confer on whomsoever it pleased the character of a citizen, and to endow him with all its rights. But this character, of course, was confined to the boundaries of the State, and gave him no rights or privileges in other States beyond those secured to him by the laws of nations and the comity of States. Nor have the several States surrendered the power of conferring these rights and privileges by adopting the Constitution of the United States. Each State may still confer them upon an alien, or any one it thinks proper, or upon any class or description of persons; yet he would not be a citizen in the sense in which that word is used in the Constitution of the United States, nor entitled to sue as such in one of its courts, nor to the privileges and immunities of a citizen in the other States. The rights which he would acquire would be restricted to the State which gave them. . . .

It is very clear, therefore, that no State can, by any Act or law of its own, passed since the adoption of the Constitution, introduce a new member into the political community created by the Constitution of the

United States. It cannot make him a member of this community by making him a member of its own. And for the same reason it cannot introduce any person, or description of persons, who were not intended to be embraced in this new political family, which the Constitution brought into existence, but were intended to be excluded from it.

The question then arises, whether the provisions of the Constitution, in relation to the personal rights and privileges to which the citizen of a State should be entitled, embraced the Negro African race, at that time in this country, or who might afterwards be imported, who had then or should afterwards be made free in any State; and to put it in the power of a single State to make him a citizen of the United States, and endue him with the full rights of citizenship in every other State without their consent. Does the Constitution of the United States act upon him whenever he shall be made free under the laws of a State, and raised there to the rank of a citizen, and immediately clothe him with all the privileges of a citizen in every other State, and in its own courts?

The court think the affirmative of these propositions cannot be maintained. And if it cannot, the plaintiff in error could not be a citizen of the State of Missouri, within the meaning of the Constitution of the United States, and, consequently, was not entitled to sue in its courts.

It is true, every person, and every class and description of persons, who were at the time of the adoption of the Constitution recognized as citizens in the several States, became also citizens of this new political body; but none other; it was formed by them, and for them and their posterity, but for no one else. And the personal rights and privileges guaranteed to citizens of this new sovereignty were intended to embrace those only who were then members of the several state communities, or who should afterwards, by birthright or otherwise, become members, according to the provisions of the Constitution and the principles on which it was founded. . . .

It becomes necessary, therefore, to determine who were citizens of the several States when the Constitution was adopted. And in order to do this, we must recur to the governments and institutions of the thirteen Colonies, when they separated from Great Britain and formed new sovereignties. . . . We must inquire who, at that time, were recognized as the people or citizens of a State. . . .

In the opinion of the court, the legislation and histories of the times, and the language used in the Declaration of Independence, show, that neither the class of persons who had been imported as slaves, nor their descendants, whether they had become free or not, were then acknowledged as a part of the people, nor intended to be included in the general words used in that memorable instrument.

It is difficult at this day to realize the state of public opinion in relation to that unfortunate race, which prevailed in the civilized and enlightened portions of the world at the time of the Declaration of Independence, and when the Constitution of the United States was framed and adopted. . . .

They had for more than a century before been regarded as beings of an inferior order and altogether unfit to associate with the white race, either in social or political relations; and so far inferior that they had no rights which the white man was bound to respect; and that the Negro might justly and lawfully be reduced to slavery for his benefit. He was bought and sold and treated as an ordinary article of merchandise and traffic whenever a profit could be made by it. This opinion was at that time fixed and universal in the civilized portion of the white race. It was regarded as an axiom in morals as well as in politics, which no one thought of disputing, or supposed to be open to dispute; and men in every grade and position in society daily and habitually acted upon it in their private pursuits, as well as in matters of public concern, without doubting for a moment the correctness of this opinion.

. . . A Negro of the African race was regarded . . . as an article of property and held and bought and sold as such in every one of the thirteen Colonies which united in the Declaration of Independence and afterward formed the Constitution of the United States. The slaves were more or less numerous in the different Colonies, as slave labor was found more or less profitable. But no one seems to have doubted the correctness of the prevailing opinion of the time.

The legislation of the different Colonies furnished positive and indisputable proof of this fact. . . .

The language of the Declaration of Independence is equally conclusive:

It begins by declaring that "When, in the course of human events, it becomes necessary for one people to dissolve the political bands which have connected them with another, and to assume, among the powers of the earth the separate and equal station to which the laws of nature and nature's God entitle them, a decent respect for the opinions of mankind requires that they should declare the causes which impel them to the separation."

It then proceeds to say: "We hold these truths to be self-evident: that all men are created equal; that they are endowed by their Creator with certain inalienable rights; that among these are life, liberty, and the pursuit of happiness; that to secure these rights, governments are instituted, deriving their just powers from the consent of the governed."

The general words above quoted would seem to embrace the whole human family, and if they were used in a similar instrument at this day would be so understood. But it is too clear for dispute that the enslaved African race were not intended to be included and formed no part of the people who framed and adopted this declaration; for if the language, as understood in that day, would embrace them, the conduct of the distinguished men who framed the Declaration of Independence would have been utterly and flagrantly inconsistent with the principles they asserted; and instead of the sympathy of mankind, to which they so confidently appealed, they would have deserved and received universal rebuke and reprobation.

Yet the men who framed this declaration were great men—high in literary acquirements—high in their sense of honor, and incapable of asserting principles inconsistent with those on which they were acting. They perfectly understood the meaning of the language they used and how it would be understood by others; and they knew that it would not in any part of the civilized world be supposed to embrace the Negro race, which, by common consent, had been excluded from civilized governments and the family of nations and doomed to slavery. They spoke and acted according to the then established doctrine and principles and in the ordinary language of the day, and no one misunderstood them. The unhappy black race were separated from the white by indelible marks, and laws long before established, and were never thought of or spoken of except as property and when the claims of the owner or the profit of the trader were supposed to need protection.

This state of public opinion had undergone no change when the Constitution was adopted, as is equally evident from its provisions and language.

The brief preamble sets forth by whom it was formed, for what purposes, and for whose benefit and protection. It declares that it is formed by the *people* of the United States; that is to say, by those who were members of the different political communities in the several states; and its great object is declared to be to secure the blessing of liberty to themselves and their posterity. It speaks in general terms of the *people* of the United States, and of *citizens* of the several states, when it is providing for the exercise of the powers granted or the privileges secured to the citizen. It does not define what description of persons are intended to be included under these terms, or who shall be regarded as a citizen and one of the people. It uses them as terms so well understood that no further description or definition was necessary. . . .

But there are two clauses in the Constitution which point directly and specifically to the Negro race as a separate class of persons, and show clearly that they were not regarded as a portion of the people or citizens of the Government then formed.

One of these clauses reserves to each of the thirteen States the right to import slaves until the year 1808, if it thinks it proper. And the importation which it thus sanctions was unquestionably of persons of the race of which we are speaking, as the traffic in slaves in the United States had always been confined to them. And by the other provision the States pledge themselves to each other to maintain the right of property of the master, by delivering up to him any slave who may have escaped from his service, and be found within their respective territories. . . . And these two provisions show, conclusively, that neither the description of persons therein referred to, nor their descendants, were embraced in any of the other provisions of the Constitution; for certainly these two clauses were not intended to confer on them or their posterity the blessings of liberty, or any of the personal rights so carefully provided for the citizen. . . .

Indeed, when we look to the condition of this race in the several States at the time, it is impossible to believe that these rights and privileges were intended to be extended to them. . . .

The legislation of the States therefore shows, in a manner not to be mistaken, the inferior and subject condition of that race at the time the Constitution was adopted, and long afterwards, throughout the thirteen States by which that instrument was framed; and it is hardly consistent with the respect due to these States, to suppose that they regarded at that time, as fellow-citizens and members of the sovereignty, a class of beings whom they had thus stigmatized. . . . More especially, it cannot be believed that the large slave-holding States regarded them as included in the word "citizens," or would have consented to a constitution which might compel them to receive them in that character from another State. For if they were so received, and entitled to the privileges and immunities of citizens, it would exempt them from the operation of the special laws and from the police regulations which they considered to be necessary for their own safety. . . . And all of this would be done in the face of the subject race of the same color, both free and slaves, inevitably producing discontent and insubordination among them, and endangering the peace and safety of the State. . . .

. . . Upon a full and careful consideration of the subject, the court is of opinion that, upon the facts stated in the plea in abatement, Dred Scott was not a citizen of Missouri within the meaning of the Constitution of the United States, and not entitled as such to sue in its courts; and, consequently, that the Circuit Court had no jurisdiction of the case, and that the judgment on the plea in abatement is erroneous. . . .

We proceed, therefore, to inquire whether the facts relied on by the plaintiff entitled him to his freedom. . . .

In considering this part of the controversy, two questions arise: 1. Was he, together with his family, free in Missouri by reason of the stay in the territory of the United States hereinbefore mentioned? 2. If they were not, is Scott himself free by reason of his removal to Rock Island, in the State of Illinois, as stated in the above admissions?

We proceed to examine the first question.

The Act of Congress, upon which the plaintiff relies, declares that slavery and involuntary servitude, except as a punishment for crime, shall be forever prohibited in all that part of the territory ceded by France, under the name of Louisiana, which lies north of thirty-six degrees thirty minutes north latitude, and not included within the limits of Missouri. And the difficulty which meets us at the threshold of this part of the inquiry is, whether Congress was authorized to pass this law under any of the powers granted to it by the Constitution; for if the authority is not given by that instrument, it is the duty of this court to declare it void and inoperative, and incapable of conferring freedom upon any one who is held as a slave under the laws of any one of the States.

The counsel for the plaintiff has laid much stress upon that article in the Constitution which confers on Congress the power "to dispose of and make all needful rules and regulations respecting the territory or other property belonging to the United States"; but, in the judgment of the court, that provision has no bearing on the present controversy, and the power there given, whatever it may be, is confined, and was intended to be confined, to the territory which at that time belonged to, or was claimed by, the United States, and was within their boundaries as settled by the treaty with Great Britain, and can have no influence upon a territory afterwards acquired from a foreign Government. It was a special provision for a known and particular territory, and to meet a present emergency, and nothing more. . . .

If this clause is construed to extend to territory acquired by the present Government from a foreign nation, outside of the limits of any charter from the British

Government to a colony, it would be difficult to say, why it was deemed necessary to give the Government the power to sell any vacant lands belonging to the sovereignty which might be found within it; and if this was necessary, why the grant of this power should precede the power to legislate over it and establish a Government there; and still more difficult to say, why it was deemed necessary so specially and particularly to grant the power to make needful rules and regulations in relation to any personal or movable property it might acquire there. For the words, *other property* necessarily, by every known rule of interpretation, must mean property of a different description from territory or land. And the difficulty would perhaps be insurmountable in endeavoring to account for the last member of the sentence, which provides that "nothing in this Constitution shall be so construed as to prejudice any claims of the United States or any particular State," or to say how any particular State could have claims in or to a territory ceded by a foreign Government, or to account for associating this provision with the preceding provisions of the clause, with which it would appear to have no connection. . . .

But the power of Congress over the person or property of a citizen can never be a mere discretionary power under our Constitution and form of Government. The powers of the Government and the rights and privileges of the citizen are regulated and plainly defined by the Constitution itself. And when the Territory becomes a part of the United States, the Federal Government enters into possession in the character impressed upon it by those who created it. It enters upon it with its powers over the citizen strictly defined, and limited by the Constitution, from which it derives its own existence, and by virtue of which alone it continues to exist and act as a government and sovereignty. It has no power of any kind beyond it; and it cannot, when it enters a Territory of the United States, put off its character, and assume discretionary or despotic powers which the Constitution has denied to it. It cannot create for itself a new character separated from the citizens of the United States, and the duties it owes them under the provisions of the Constitution. The Territory being a part of the United States, the Government and the citizen both enter it under the authority of the Constitution, with their respective rights defined and marked out; and the Federal Government can exercise no power over his person or property, beyond what that instrument confers, nor lawfully deny any right which it has reserved. . . .

The rights of private property have been guarded with equal care. Thus the rights of property are united with the rights of person, and placed on the same ground by the fifth amendment to the Constitution. . . . An Act of Congress which deprives a person of the United States of his liberty or property merely because he came himself or brought his property into a particular Territory of the United States, and who had committed no offense against the laws, could hardly be dignified with the name of due process of law. . . .

And this prohibition is not confined to the States, but the words are general, and extend to the whole territory over which the Constitution gives it power to legislate, including those portions of it remaining under territorial government, as well as that covered by States. It is a total absence of power everywhere within the dominion of the United States, and places the citizens of a territory, so far as these rights are concerned, on the same footing with citizens of the States, and guards them as firmly and plainly against any inroads which the general government might attempt, under the plea of implied or incidental powers. And if Congress itself cannot do this—if it is beyond the powers conferred on the Federal Government—it will be admitted, we presume, that it could not authorize a territorial government to exercise them. It could confer no power on any local government, established by its authority, to violate the provisions of the Constitution.

It seems, however, to be supposed, that there is a difference between property in a slave and other property, and that different rules may be applied to it in expounding the Constitution of the United States.

But . . . if the Constitution recognizes the right of property of the master in a slave, and makes no distinction between that description of property and other property owned by a citizen, no tribunal, acting under the authority of the United States, whether it be legislative, executive, or judicial, has a right to draw such a distinction, or deny to it the benefit of the provisions and guarantees which have been provided for the protection of private property against the encroachments of the Government.

Now . . . the right of property in a slave is distinctly and expressly affirmed in the Constitution. The right to traffic in it, like an ordinary article of merchandise and property, was guaranteed to the citizens of the United States, in every State that might desire it, for twenty years. And the Government in express terms is pledged to protect it in all future time, if the slave escapes from his owner. . . . And no word can be found in the Constitution which gives Congress a greater power over slave property, or which entitles property of that kind to less protection than property of any other description. The only power conferred is the power coupled with the duty of guarding and protecting the owner in his rights.

Upon these considerations, it is the opinion of the court that the Act of Congress which prohibited a citizen from holding and owning property of this kind in the territory of the United States north of the line therein mentioned, is not warranted by the Constitution, and is therefore void; and that neither Dred Scott himself, nor any of his family, were made free by being carried into this territory; even if they had been carried there by the owner, with the intention of becoming a permanent resident. . . .

Upon the whole, therefore, it is the judgment of this court, that it appears by the record before us that the plaintiff in error is not a citizen of Missouri, in the sense in which that word is used in the Constitution; and that the Circuit Court of the United States, for that reason, had no jurisdiction in the case, and could give no judgment in it.

Its judgment for the defendant must, consequently, be reversed, and a mandate issued directing the suit to be dismissed for want of jurisdiction.

Chapter 13

WAR!

Even as Abraham Lincoln took his solemn oath on March 4, 1861, to "preserve, protect and defend" the government of all the states, secession was a reality and the Union, to many, was a meaningless and anachronistic misnomer. The election of 1860, a final political battle within the Union between sections long joined in bitter conflict, had resulted in an impressive victory for a Republican party that had been founded only six years earlier and that was completely and wholeheartedly Northern in its orientation. Opposed by the Northern Democrat Stephen A. Douglas and two other candidates, Lincoln had received only 40 per cent of the popular vote and was therefore a minority President; but he had won a substantial majority in the Electoral College despite the fact that not a single Southern or Border state voted for him. To the South this victory of an avowed Northern party in a national election completed the political imbalance between the sections that her statesmen had long feared and deplored. Besides, in their steadfast opposition to the further expansion of slavery, Republicans could prevent the South from ever redressing that imbalance, for now slaveholders might not organize and bring into the Union new slave states to bolster their section's waning political power. Republicans disclaimed any intentions of interfering with slavery in the states; indeed, even after Lincoln's election and with his full approval they proposed an amendment to the Constitution that would guarantee slavery forever within the South. But they were determined above all else to set aside the Dred Scott decision that protected slavery in the nation's new Territories. And many Southerners were certain that Lincoln's sectional victory prophesied as well the eventual writing into law of the whole Republican platform with its demand for economic measures (such as high tariffs, free land for Western settlers, and internal improvements) so opposed to what the South considered its necessary and legitimate plantation-economy interests. Thus in anger and disgust, with South Carolina once again in the vanguard, the disaffected Southern states began their long threatened secession from the Union. When Lincoln became the sixteenth President of the United States, seven states had already seceded, more were in the process, and Jefferson Davis and Alexander H. Stephens had been selected President and Vice-President under a provisional constitution of the Confederate States of America.

The interregnum between Lincoln's election and his inauguration was filled with excitement, bewilderment, and tension in the North as well as the South. Many Northerners had voted for Lincoln without fully realizing that his election might finally result in secession. Now the die had been cast and, as President Buchanan struggled desperately to maintain peace and the Union, all the North, indeed all the world, awaited Lincoln's Inaugural Address as a pronouncement of the new administration's policy in the secession crisis. During these fateful months Lincoln suffered much abuse at the hands of those who saw him only as a political unknown, an awkward and incompetent party wheel-horse to whom they referred variously as a "Simple Susan," an "Ape," or a "Baboon." All were quick with advice; from all sides, from high places and low, Lincoln received demands that he meet the crisis in this way or that. Some wanted to let the South secede in peace; others wanted immediate military coercion of the secessionists; still others hoped for peaceful reconciliation after concessions by Lincoln on the vital question of the expansion of slavery into the Territories. Lincoln listened patiently to all but remained the master of his own house, and in his Inaugural Address maintained the same moderate but determined position he had long espoused.

Ironically, the venerable Chief Justice of the Supreme Court, Roger B. Taney, whose Dred Scott decision Lincoln had so derided, administered the oath of office on this fine, brisk March day. And it is reported that Stephen A. Douglas, recently Lincoln's bitter opponent, reached forward, took, and held on his lap Lincoln's immense stove-pipe hat when the new President could find no place for it during the ceremonies. These acts were symbolic, for the address was conciliatory in tone. The President saw no need for secession; he and his party had "no purpose, directly or indirectly, to interfere with the institution of slavery in the States where it exists." Besides, disunion was impossible, Lincoln insisted, for the Union was perpetual; ordinances of secession were meaningless, and the Union remained unbroken. No person or state would be coerced by the national Government; there would be no invasion of the South; no use of force—but the laws would be enforced. Would the Southerners obey them? For there would be no war unless the South were to violate the laws of the nation. The "momentous issue of civil war" was not, Lincoln maintained, in his hands, but in those of his "dissatisfied fellow-countrymen." This was superb political strategy on Lincoln's part, for he had deliberately maneuvered the South into a position of responsibility for war or peace.

Thus, the war did not come because of ineptitude; Lincoln's generation did not blunder into war. Nor was the Civil War "inevitable," an "irrepressible conflict." Bitterness, antagonism, and conflict between societies whose economic, political, and cultural patterns were so opposed—these were irrepressible, but war was not. Rather conciliation failed in this last crisis because both sections had determined what their basic interests were and, when they were at stake, refused to make those compromises necessary to prevent war. Six weeks after Lincoln's inauguration Southern batteries fired on Fort Sumter, and the war came.

Abraham Lincoln's First Inaugural Address, *1861*

Fellow-Citizens of the United States: In compliance with a custom as old as the government itself, I appear before you to address you briefly, and to take in your presence the oath prescribed by the Constitution of the United States to be taken by the President "before he enters on the execution of his office."

I do not consider it necessary at present for me to discuss those matters of administration about which there is no special anxiety or excitement.

Apprehension seems to exist among the people of the Southern States that by the accession of a Republican administration their property and their peace and personal security are to be endangered. There has never been any reasonable cause for such apprehension. Indeed, the most ample evidence to the contrary has all the while existed and been open to their inspection. It is found in nearly all the published speeches of him who now addresses you. I do but quote from one of those speeches when I declare that "I have no purpose, directly or indirectly, to interfere with the institution of slavery in the States where it exists. I believe I have no lawful right to do so, and I have no inclination to do so." Those who nominated and elected me did so with full knowledge that I had made this and many similar declarations, and had never recanted them.

And, more than this, they placed in the platform for my acceptance, and as a law to themselves and to me, the clear and emphatic resolution which I now read:

> RESOLVED, That the maintenance inviolate of the rights of the States, and especially the right of each State to order and control its own domestic institutions according to its own judgment exclusively, is essential to that balance of power on which the perfection and endurance of our political fabric depend, and we denounce the lawless invasion by armed force of the soil of any State or Territory, no matter under what pretext, as among the gravest of crimes.

I now reiterate these sentiments; and, in doing so, I only press upon the public attention the most conclusive evidence of which the case is susceptible, that the property, peace, and security of no section are to be in any wise endangered by the now incoming administration. I add, too, that all the protection which, consistently with the Constitution and the laws, can be given, will be cheerfully given to all the States when lawfully demanded, for whatever cause—as cheerfully to one section as to another.

There is much controversy about the delivering up of fugitives from service or labor. The clause I now read is as plainly written in the Constitution as any other of its provisions:

> No person held to service or labor in one State, under the laws thereof, escaping into another, shall in consequence of any law or regulation therein be discharged from such service or labor, but shall be delivered up on claim to the party to whom such service or labor may be due.

It is scarcely questioned that this provision was intended by those who made it for the reclaiming of what we call fugitive slaves; and the intention of the lawgiver is the law. All members of Congress swear their support to the whole Constitution—to this provision as much as to any other. To the proposition then, that slaves whose cases come within the terms of this clause "shall be delivered up," their oaths are unanimous. Now, if they would make the effort in good temper, could they not with nearly equal unanimity frame and pass a law by means of which to keep good that unanimous oath?

There is some difference of opinion whether this clause should be enforced by national or by State authority; but surely that difference is not a very material one. If the slave is to be surrendered, it can be of little consequence to him or to others by which authority is done. And should any one in any case be content that his oath shall go unkept on a merely unsubstantial controversy as to how it shall be kept?

Again, in any law upon this subject, ought not all the safeguards of liberty known in civilized and humane jurisprudence to be introduced, so that a free man be not, in any case, surrendered as a slave? And might it not be well at the same time to provide by law for the enforcement of that clause in the Constitution which guarantees that "the citizens of each State shall be entitled to all privileges and immunities of citizens in the several States"?

I take the official oath today with no mental reservations, and with no purpose to construe the Constitution or laws by any hypercritical rules. And while I do not choose now to specify particular acts of Congress as proper to be enforced, I do suggest that it will be much safer for all, both in official and private stations, to conform to and abide by all those acts which stand unrepealed, than to violate any of them, trusting to find impunity in having them held to be unconstitutional.

It is seventy-two years since the first inauguration of a President under our National Constitution. During that period fifteen different and greatly distinguished citizens have, in succession, administered the executive branch of the government. They have conducted it through many perils, and generally with great success. Yet, with all this scope of precedent, I now enter upon the same task for the brief constitutional term of four years under great and peculiar difficulty. A disruption of the Federal Union, heretofore only menaced, is now formidably attempted.

I hold that, in contemplation of universal law and of the Constitution, the Union of these States is perpetual. Perpetuity is implied, if not expressed, in the fundamental law of all national governments. It is safe to assert that no government proper ever had a provision in its organic law for its own termination.

Continue to execute all the express provisions of our National Constitution, and the Union will endure forever—it being impossible to destroy it except by some action not provided for in the instrument itself.

Again, if the United States be not a government proper, but an association of States in the nature of contract merely, can it, as a contract, be peaceably unmade by less than all the parties who made it? One party to a contract may violate it—break it, so to speak; but does it not require all to lawfully rescind it?

Descending from these general principles, we find the proposition that, in legal contemplation, the Union is perpetually confirmed by the history of the Union itself. The Union is much older than the Constitution. It was formed, in fact, by the Articles of Association in 1774. It was matured and continued by the Declaration of Independence in 1776. It was further matured, and the faith of all the then thirteen States expressly plighted and engaged that it should be perpetual, by the Articles of Confederation in 1778. And, finally, in 1787 one of the declared objects for ordaining and establishing the Constitution was "to form a more perfect Union."

But if the destruction of the Union by one or by a party only of the States be lawfully possible, the Union is less perfect than before the Constitution, having lost the vital element of perpetuity.

It follows from these views that no State upon its own mere motion can lawfully get out of the Union; that resolves and ordinances to that effect are legally void; and that acts of violence, within any State or States, against the authority of the United States, the insurrectionary or revolutionary, according to circumstances.

I therefore consider that, in view of the Constitution and the laws, the Union is unbroken; and to the extent of my ability I shall take care, as the Constitution itself expressly enjoins upon me, that the laws of the Union be faithfully executed in all the States. Doing this I deem to be only a simple duty on my part; and I shall perform it so far as practicable, unless my rightful masters, the American people, shall withhold the requisite means, or in some authoritative manner direct the contrary. I trust this will not be regarded as a menace, but only as the declared purpose of the union that it will constitutionally defend and maintain itself.

In doing this there needs to be no bloodshed or violence; and there shall be none, unless it be forced upon the national authority. The power confided to me will be used to hold, occupy, and possess the property and places belonging to the Government, and to collect the duties and imposts; but beyond what may be necessary for these objects, there will be no invasion, no using of force against or among the people anywhere. Where hostility to the United States, in any interior locality, shall be so great and universal as to prevent competent resident citizens from holding the Federal offices, there will be no attempt to force obnoxious strangers among the people for that object. While the strict legal right may exist in the Government to enforce the exercise of these offices, the attempt to do so would be so irritating, and so nearly impracticable withal, that I deem it better to forego for the time the uses of such offices.

The mails, unless repelled, will continue to be furnished in all parts of the Union. So far as possible, the people everywhere shall have that sense of perfect security which is most favorable to calm thought and reflection. The course here indicated will be followed unless current events and experience shall show a modification or change to be proper, and in every case and exigency my best discretion will be exercised according to circumstances actually existing, and with a view and a hope of a peaceful solution of the national troubles and the restoration of fraternal sympathies and affections.

That there are persons in one section or another who seek to destroy the Union at all events, and are glad of any pretext to do it, I will neither affirm nor deny; but if there be such, I need address no word to them. To those, however, who really love the Union may I not speak?

Before entering upon so grave a matter as the destruction of our national fabric, with all its benefits, its memories, and its hopes, would it not be wise to ascertain precisely why we do it? Will you hazard so desperate a step while there is any possibility that any portion of the ills you fly from have no real existence? Will you, while the certain ills you fly to are greater than all the real ones you fly from—will you risk the commission of so fearful a mistake?

All profess to be content in the Union if all constitutional rights can be maintained. Is it true, then, that any right, plainly written in the Constitution, has been denied? I think not. Happily the human mind is so constituted that no party can reach to the audacity of doing this. Think, if you can, of a single instance in which a plainly written provision of the Constitution has ever been denied. If by the mere force of numbers a majority should deprive a minority of any clearly written constitutional right, it might, in a moral point of view, justify revolution—certainly would if such a right were a vital one. But such is not our case. All the vital rights of minorities and of individuals are so plainly assured to them by affirmations and negations, guarantees and prohibitions, in the Constitution, that controversies never arise concerning them. But no organic law can ever be framed with a provision specifically applicable to every question which may occur in practical administration. No foresight can anticipate, nor any document of reasonable length contain, express provisions for all possible questions. Shall fugitives from labor be surrendered by national or by State authority? The Constitution does not expressly say. *May* Congress prohibit slavery in the Territories? The Constitution does not expressly say. *Must* Congress protect slavery in the Territories? The Constitution does not expressly say.

From questions of this class spring all our constitutional controversies, and we divide upon them into majorities and minorities. If the minority will not acquiesce, the majority must, or the Government must cease. There is no other alternative; for continuing the Government is acquiescence on one side or the other.

If a minority in such case will secede rather than acquiesce, they make a precedent which in turn will divide and ruin them; for a minority of their own will secede from them whenever a majority refuses to be controlled by such minority. For instance, why may not any portion of a new confederacy a year or two hence arbitrarily secede again, precisely as portions of the present Union now claim to secede from it? All who cherish disunion sentiments are now being educated to the exact temper of doing this.

Is there such perfect identity of interests among the States to compose a new Union, as to produce harmony only, and prevent renewed secession?

Plainly, the central idea of secession is the essence of anarchy. A majority held in restraint by constitutional checks and limitations, and always changing easily with deliberate changes of popular opinions and sentiments, is the only true sovereign of a free people. Whoever rejects it does, of necessity, fly to anarchy or to despotism. Unanimity is impossible; the rule of a minority, as a permanent arrangement, is wholly inadmissible; so that, rejecting the majority principle, anarchy or despotism in some form is all that is left.

I do not forget the position, assumed by some, that constitutional questions are to be decided by the Supreme Court; nor do I deny that such decision must be binding, in any case, upon the parties to a suit, as to the object of that suit, while they are also entitled to very high respect and consideration in all parallel cases by all other departments of the government. And while it is obviously possible that such decision may be erroneous in any given case, still the evil effect following it, being limited to that particular case, with the chance that it may be overruled and never become a precedent for other cases, can better be borne than could the evils of a different practice.

At the same time, the candid citizen must confess that if the policy of the Government, upon vital questions affecting the whole people, is to be irrevocably fixed by decisions of the Supreme Court, the instant they are made, in ordinary litigation between parties in personal actions, the people will have ceased to be their own rulers, having to that extent practically resigned their government into the hands of that eminent tribunal. Nor is there in this view any assault upon the court or the judges. It is a duty from which they may not shrink to decide cases properly brought before them, and it is no fault of theirs if others seek to turn their decisions to political purposes.

One section of our country believes slavery is right, and ought to be extended, while the other believes it is wrong, and ought not to be extended. This is the only substantial dispute. The fugitive slave clause of the Constitution, and the law for the suppression of the foreign slave trade, are each as well enforced, perhaps, as any law can ever be in a community where the moral sense of the people imperfectly supports the law itself. The great body of the people abide by the dry legal obligation in both cases, and a few break over in each. This, I think, cannot be perfectly cured; and it would be worse in both cases after the separation of the sections than before. The foreign slave trade, now imperfectly suppressed, would be ultimately revived, without restriction, in one section, while fugitive slaves, now only partially surrendered, would not be surrendered at all by the other.

Physically speaking, we cannot separate. We cannot remove our respective sections from each other, nor build an impassable wall between them. A husband and wife may be divorced, and go out of the presence and beyond the reach of each other; but the different parts of our country cannot do this. They cannot but remain face to face, and intercourse, either amicable or hostile, must continue between them. Is it possible, then, to make that intercourse more advantageous or more satisfactory after separation than before? Can aliens make treaties easier than friends can make laws? Can treaties be more faithfully enforced between aliens than laws can among friends? Suppose you go to war, you cannot fight always; and when, after much loss on both sides, and no gain on either, you cease fighting, the identical old questions as to terms of intercourse are again upon you.

This country, with its institutions, belongs to the people who inhabit it. Whenever they shall grow weary of the existing Government, they can exercise their constitutional right of amending it, or their revolutionary right to dismember or overthrow it. I cannot be ignorant of the fact that many worthy and patriotic citizens are desirous of having the National Constitution amended. While I make no recommendation of amendments, I fully recognize the rightful authority of the people over the whole subject, to be exercised in either of the modes prescribed in the instrument itself; and I should, under existing circumstances, favor rather than oppose a fair opportunity being afforded the people to act upon it. I will venture to add that to me the convention mode seems preferable, in that it allows amendments to originate with the people themselves, instead of only permitting them to take or reject propositions originated by others not specially chosen for the purpose, and which might not be precisely such as they would wish to either accept or refuse. I understand a proposed amendment to the Constitution—which amendment, however, I have not seen—has passed Congress, to the effect that the Federal Government shall never interfere with the domestic institutions of the States, including that of persons held to service. To avoid misconstruction of what I have said I depart from my purpose not to speak of particular amendments so far as to say that, holding such a provision to now be implied constitutional law, I have no objection to its being made express and irrevocable.

The chief magistrate derives all his authority from the

people, and they have conferred none upon him to fix terms for the separation of the States. The people themselves can do this also if they choose; but the executive, as such, has nothing to do with it. His duty is to administer the present Government, as it came to his hands, and to transmit it, unimpaired by him, to his successor.

Why should there not be a patient confidence in the ultimate justice of the people? Is there any better or equal hope in the world? In our present differences is either party without faith of being in the right? If the Almighty Ruler of Nations, with his eternal truth and justice, be on your side of the North, or on yours of the South, that truth and that justice will surely prevail by the judgment of this great tribunal of the American people.

By the frame of the Government under which we live, this same people have wisely given their public servants but little power for mischief; and have, with equal wisdom, provided for the return of that little to their own hands at very short intervals. While the people retain their virtue and vigilance, no administration, by any extreme of wickedness or folly, can very seriously injure the Government in the short space of four years.

My countrymen, one and all, think calmly and well upon this whole subject. Nothing valuable can be lost by taking time. If there be an object to hurry any of you in hot haste to a step which you would never take deliberately, that object will be frustrated by taking time; but no good object can be frustrated by it. Such of you as are now dissatisfied, still have the old Constitution unimpaired, and, on the sensitive point, the laws of your own framing under it; while the new administration will have no immediate power, if it would, to change either. If it were admitted that you who are dissatisfied hold the right side in the dispute, there still is no single good reason for precipitate action. Intelligence, patriotism, Christianity, and a firm reliance on Him who has never yet forsaken this favored land, are still competent to adjust in the best way all our present difficulty.

In your hands, my dissatisfied fellow-countrymen, and not in mine, is the momentous issue of civil war. The Government will not assail you. You can have no conflict without being yourselves the aggressors. You have no oath registered in heaven to destroy the Government, while I shall have the most solemn one to "preserve, protect, and defend it."

I am loathe to close. We are not enemies, but friends. We must not be enemies. Though passion may have strained, it must not break our bonds of affection. The mystic chords of memory, stretching from every battlefield and patriot grave to every living heart and hearthstone all over this broad land, will yet swell the chorus of the Union when again touched, as surely they will be, by the better angels of our nature.

Chapter 14

THE PROPHET OF DEMOCRACY

Though Abraham Lincoln's election in 1860 was followed by secession, the formation of a Southern Confederacy, and ultimately by civil war, it did not resolve—even in the North—the ever perplexing slavery question. The Abolitionist Crusade had made innumerable converts to the anti-slavery cause since the 1830's. But many, if not most, Northerners continued to espouse the cause of Union even more fervently than that of the Negro slave, and throughout the entire war Northern politics reflected a bitter conflict between anti-slavery and Unionist sentiments. If the war were to be won, the administration must be assured the political support of both groups; thus Lincoln's supreme wartime task was to strike a balance between Radicals who would first free the slaves, and Conservatives who would first preserve the Union.

Traditionally, of course, the Emancipation Proclamation has identified Lincoln most closely with the anti-slavery cause, and he remains enshrined in the hearts of free men the world over as the "Great Emancipator." Lincoln *did* thoroughly despise slavery; he thought it a vicious, brutalizing anachronism. "As I would not be a slave," Lincoln wrote, "so I would not be a master." Yet his opposition to slavery was based less on humanitarian grounds than on his acute realization that human bondage was corruptive of the very principles that had made the nation great. To Lincoln, America was democracy, and if slavery were to expand, it would destroy democracy. Again and again Lincoln warned his fellow countrymen that America's democratic tradition, based on "our ancient faith" that all men are created equal, could not long survive the extension of slavery. If Americans were further to deny their forefathers' faith in liberty and equality they would eventually lose their own freedom:

> Destroy this spirit and you have planted the seeds of despotism at your own doors. Familiarize yourselves with the chains of bondage and you prepare your own limbs to wear them. Accustomed to trample on the rights of others, you . . . become the fit subjects of the first cunning tyrant who rises among you.

Thus it was to preserve democracy in America and ultimately to foster its principles throughout the world that Lincoln was uncompromisingly opposed to the further spread of slavery.

But Lincoln was no friend of the Abolitionists. He decried their radical demand for immediate emancipation and proposed instead gradual emancipation, compensation for the owners and, perhaps, colonization abroad for the freedmen. Besides, though he would not permit slavery to expand, Lincoln had denied neither the Southerners' constitutional right to hold chattels within the Southern states nor the Northerners' obligation to return fugitive slaves.

Even limited to the Southern states slavery was oppressively an evil, but Lincoln would accept it where it already existed to avoid the still greater evil of secession and disunion. For to Lincoln the American Union was a magnificent experiment in democracy, the "last, best hope of earth." Still, the Union was sacred only as it remained an expression of freedom and democracy, and when in 1860–1861 the price of union was the further expansion of slavery, Lincoln chose disunion and war.

But when the war came Lincoln resisted the Radicals' demand that he proclaim it a moral crusade against slavery. Thus he risked their enmity and angry opposition by revoking a military order that would free the slaves of rebellious citizens in Missouri and by severely rebuking the popular General John C. Frémont for this unauthorized action. In the summer of 1862 Lincoln clearly set forth his position on the slavery question. On August 19, in his widely read and extremely influential *New York Tribune,* Horace Greeley published a "Prayer of Twenty Millions." Addressed to the President, Greeley's famous "Prayer" demanded that the Federal Government make emancipation its announced policy. To this radical proposal Lincoln replied in a widely reprinted letter:

> If there be those who would not save the Union unless they could at the same time *save* slavery, I do not agree with them. If there be those who would not save the Union unless they could at the same time *destroy* slavery, I do not agree with them. My paramount object in this struggle *is* to save the Union, and is *not* either to save or destroy slavery. If I could save the Union without freeing *any* slave, I would do it; if I could save it by freeing *all* the slaves, I would do it; and if I could do it by freeing some and leaving others alone, I would also do that. What I do about slavery and the colored race, I do because I believe it helps to save this Union; and what I forbear, I forbear because I do *not* believe it would help to save the Union. I shall do *less* whenever I shall believe what I am doing hurts the cause, and I shall do *more* whenever I believe doing more will help the cause. I shall try to correct errors when shown to be errors; and I shall adopt new views so fast as they shall appear to be true views.

Actually, Lincoln almost immediately adopted "new views," but only because he had re-assayed the pressures of Northern politics and the need for foreign support. He now concluded that he could no longer dare Radical opposition without seriously endangering the Union cause. Well organized and determined, the Radicals were possessed of political power disproportionate to their actual numbers, and it had become evident to the war President that the Confederacy could be defeated only with their ungrudging support. Besides, at a time when European powers had yet to be impressed by Northern military prowess, Lincoln saw that a statement of lofty war aims would go far to gain their respect and moral support. Thus on September 22, after Confederate troops under Robert E. Lee had been defeated at Antietam (it had been Secretary of State Seward's wise suggestion that the bold proclamation be postponed until military victory should make it meaningful), Lincoln issued his preliminary Emancipation Proclamation. Southerners were called upon to end their rebellion by January 1, 1863. Were they to surrender within the remaining 100 days, their slaves, as well as those of the loyal slaveholders, would be protected; but on that date "all persons held as slaves within any State or designated part of a State the people whereof shall then be in rebellion . . . shall be then, thenceforward, and forever free." And on the first day of 1863, that the Union might more surely be preserved, Abraham Lincoln issued his final Emancipation Proclamation and the Civil War became a crusade for freedom.

Lincoln is remembered as the "Great Emancipator" and remains universally a symbol of Union. Yet the martyred President might more appropriately and consistently be honored first as America's prophet of democracy. For it was on the great battlefield at Gettysburg, on November 19, 1863, that this giant amongst men taught that he had struck the chains of bondage from the slaves and had preserved his beloved Union, only to the end that "government of the people, by the people, for the people, shall not perish from the earth."

The Emancipation Proclamation, *Abraham Lincoln, 1863*

WHEREAS on the twenty-second day of September, in the year of our Lord one thousand eight hundred and sixty-two, a proclamation was issued by the President of the United States, containing, among other things, the following, to wit:

> That on the first day of January, in the year of our Lord one thousand eight hundred and sixty-three, all persons held as slaves within any State, or designated part of a State, the people whereof shall then be in rebellion against the United States, shall be then, thenceforward, and forever free; and the Executive Government of the United States, including the military and naval authority thereof, will recognize and maintain the freedom of such persons, and will do no act or acts to repress such persons, or any of them, in any efforts they may make for their actual freedom.
>
> That the Executive will, on the first day of January aforesaid, by proclamation, designate the States and parts of States, if any, in which the people thereof respectively shall then be in rebellion against the United States; and the fact that any State, or the people thereof, shall on that day be in good faith represented in the Congress of the United States by members chosen thereto at elections wherein a majority of the qualified voters of such State shall have participated, shall in the absence of strong countervailing testimony be deemed conclusive evidence that such State and the people thereof are not then in rebellion against the United States.

Now, therefore, I, Abraham Lincoln, President of the United States, by virtue of the power in me vested as Commander-in-Chief of the Army and Navy of the United States, in time of actual armed rebellion against the authority and government of the United States, and as a fit and necessary war measure for suppressing said rebellion, do, on this first day of January, in the year of our Lord one thousand eight hundred and sixty-three, and in accordance with my purpose so to do, publicly proclaimed for the full period of 100 days from the day first above mentioned, order and designate as the States and parts of States wherein the people thereof, respectively, are this day in rebellion against the United States, the following, to wit:

> Arkansas, Texas, Louisiana (except the parishes of St. Bernard, Plaquemines, Jefferson, St. John, St. Charles, St. James, Ascension, Assumption, Terre Bonne, Lafourche, St. Mary, St. Martin, and Orleans, including the city of New Orleans), Mississippi, Alabama, Florida, Georgia, South Carolina, North Carolina, and Virginia (except the forty-eight counties designated as West Virginia, and also the counties of Berkeley, Accomac, Northampton, Elizabeth City, York, Princess Anne, and Norfolk, including the cities of Norfolk and Portsmouth), and which excepted parts are for the present left precisely as if this proclamation were not issued.

And by virtue of the power and for the purpose aforesaid, I do order and declare that all persons held as slaves within said designated States and parts of States are, and henceforward shall be, free; and that the Executive Government of the United States, including the military and naval authorities thereof, shall recognize and maintain the freedom of said persons.

And I hereby enjoin upon the people so declared to be free to abstain from all violence, unless in necessary self-defense; and I recommend to them that, in all cases where allowed, they labor faithfully for reasonable wages.

And I further declare and make known that such persons of suitable condition will be received into the armed service of the United States to garrison forts, positions, stations, and other places, and to man vessels of all sorts in said service.

And upon this act, sincerely believed to be an act of justice, warranted by the Constitution upon military necessity, I invoke the considerate judgment of mankind and the gracious favor of Almighty God.

In witness whereof, I have hereunto set my hand and caused the seal of the United States to be affixed.

Done at the city of Washington, the first day of January, in the year of our Lord one thousand eight hundred and sixty-three, and of the independence of the United States of America the eighty-seventh.

By the President: ABRAHAM LINCOLN

WILLIAM H. SEWARD, Secretary of State.

The Gettysburg Address, *Abraham Lincoln, 1863*

Fourscore and seven years ago our fathers brought forth on this continent a new nation, conceived in liberty, and dedicated to the proposition that all men are created equal.

Now we are engaged in a great civil war, testing whether that nation, or any nation so conceived and so dedicated, can long endure. We are met on a great battlefield of that war. We have come to dedicate a portion of that field as a final resting-place for those who here gave their lives that that nation might live. It is altogether fitting and proper that we should do this.

But, in a larger sense, we cannot dedicate—we cannot consecrate—we cannot hallow—this ground. The brave men, living and dead, who struggled here, have consecrated it far above our poor power to add or detract. The world will little note nor long remember what we say here, but it can never forget what they did here. It is for us, the living, rather, to be dedicated here to the unfinished work which they who fought here have thus far so nobly advanced. It is rather for us to be here dedicated to the great task remaining before us—that from these honored dead we take increased devotion to that cause for which they gave the last full measure of devotion; that we here highly resolve that these dead shall not have died in vain; that this nation, under God, shall have a new birth of freedom; and that government of the people, by the people, for the people, shall not perish from the earth.

Chapter 15

THE CONFLICT OVER RECONSTRUCTION

On April 9, 1865, in the town of Appomattox Court House in Virginia, the gallant Robert E. Lee surrendered his armies—and the Southern cause—to General Ulysses S. Grant. The war was over; the Union had been preserved. And eight months later, in the Thirteenth Amendment to the Constitution, a reunited nation proclaimed that "Neither slavery nor involuntary servitude . . . shall exist within the United States, or any place subject to their jurisdiction." Finally and unequivocally, slavery was destroyed and four million freedmen became a living monument to the more than six hundred thousand young men who had laid down their lives in the great conflict. But in its ultimate meaning for the nation the final legacy of the four long and tragic years of civil war was even more far reaching than emancipation. For the war had wrought such profound changes in American life that Appomattox as much symbolized the transformation of an old and familiar America into a new nation as it marked the destruction of the Old South.

Of all the revolutionary changes that heralded the emergence of modern America, none was more fundamental nor more dramatic than the triumph of industrial capitalism. During the bitter years of sectional controversy that preceded secession and war, Southern agrarians had steadfastly opposed Northern industrialists. Yet, ironically enough, it was the South's very act of secession that guaranteed the final defeat of agrarianism and the rise to power of the new industrial class. For only in disunion and in the absence of the South's large Congressional delegation, could the Republican party, as the political agent of this dynamic new group, muster enough power to push its desired legislation through Congress. The war years saw the passage of innumerable bills—raising tariffs, granting subsidies, and establishing national fiscal agencies—whose effect, and probably whose design, was not only to rally the nation's economic power to meet the needs of war, but also thoroughly and irrevocably to entrench in power the aggressively self-seeking industrial group. And when the war ended the agrarian South had been defeated even more decisively in the Halls of Congress than on the battlefields. By the time of Appomattox the United States, her destinies now firmly in the hands of Northern businessmen and those who would do their political bidding, was rapidly abandoning her traditional agrarian ways and becoming a predominantly industrial nation.

It was, in large part, to protect the fruits of this economic revolution, not to defend the freedman's new rights nor even to wreak vengeance upon the defeated Southerners, that Radical Republicans imposed military and political control on the South in the tragic era of Reconstruction that followed the war. The earlier, humanitarian Radicals, the fiery Abolitionists to whom the Republican party served only as a means for attaining emancipation, had been supplanted in party councils by new Radicals whose concern was material rather than humanitarian. To these new Radicals emancipation and Negro suffrage were themselves merely means; the end was consolidation of the enormous gains made in wartime by the triumphant industrial class. But consolidation could be achieved only through continued Republican control of Congress, and this control would be completely upset were the South to send back to the national legislature the same anti-industrialist representatives who had so persistently opposed Republican measures before the war. Throughout Reconstruction, therefore, the objective of the Radical Republicans was to translate emancipation into a political weapon and to impose Negro suffrage upon a violently protesting South, not in consideration of the freedman's undeniable rights, but out of concern for Republican strength. Negro votes were Republican votes, and as long as they were needed no measure, not even rigorous military reorganization of the South, was too harsh to guarantee the Negroes' political and civil rights under the Fourteenth and Fifteenth Amendments to the Constitution. But later, when Negro suffrage no longer served Republican ends, zeal for the Negroes' rights disappeared.

Radical Reconstruction was not, of course, totally unopposed. Unsympathetic to the Radicals' motives, Abraham Lincoln had rejected as a pernicious abstraction their purposefully vindictive theory that seceded Southern states had "committed suicide" and as "conquered territories" were under the jurisdiction and the mercy of the Republican Congress. Lincoln had very early presented his own moderate plan of presidential reconstruction, but the Radicals bitterly resented it as unwarranted presidential interference. Similarly, they scorned the fervent plea of his Second Inaugural Address, delivered shortly before Appomattox, that the nation strive toward reunion "With malice toward none, with charity for all." Six weeks later, on April 14, 1865, when the great war leader was struck down by an assassin's bullet, Radical Republicans exclaimed that it was "God's will." And even as the nation mourned the tragic death of "Father Abraham," Radical Republicans rejoiced, singing the praises of the new President, Andrew Johnson of Tennessee, for his violent denunciations of wealthy and aristocratic Southern secessionists. But in their expectation that Johnson would approve Radical Reconstruction, the Republicans had clearly misjudged him. He was, in truth, bitterly opposed to the great slaveowning planters, but only as he was representative of poor white farmers who had no interest in slavery. Johnson was still a Southerner and, more important, an agrarian who equally disliked the Northern industrial plutocracy and the Southern plantation aristocracy. Like Lincoln before him, but without his predecessor's shrewdness and political adeptness, Johnson soon openly opposed the Radicals' program. Immediately the vindictive Republican leaders turned upon him in fury. In 1868 Radicals in the House of Representatives impeached the President for "high crimes and misdemeanors," and in the Senate they failed by only one vote to secure the necessary two-thirds for conviction of these charges. Johnson was acquitted, but his enemies had shown their strength. Radicalism was undeniably

King, and the harshest of Reconstruction governments had been imposed by military force upon the Southern states.

Largely dominated by uneducated and inexperienced Negroes, sympathetic local whites known as "scalawags," and opportunistic Northern "carpetbaggers," these Radical state governments were frequently extravagant and corrupt. Nevertheless, the Ku Klux Klan and other instruments designed by the Southern whites to terrorize Negroes who supported the "carpetbag" governments expressed far more than a simple mass reaction to political corruption. Misconduct in high office, after all, was by no means peculiar to the South during Reconstruction, for public morals were deplorably low throughout the nation. Actually, in adopting their violently oppressive tactics Southern whites were indicating their basic hostility to *any* free and equal participation in the political process by the Negroes whom they had so recently, and so unwillingly, emancipated. Besides, in the debate over corruption, the great liberal and humanitarian accomplishments of the Reconstruction governments were often lost sight of: they had granted social and economic, as well as political rights to the freedmen; they had established much-needed schools and welfare agencies for Negroes and whites alike; and they had made important efforts at reforming the archaic and undemocratic practices of Southern state governments.

Protected by Federal troops, these governments could remain in power only at the pleasure of Northern Republicans. And by the mid-1870's the Republicans were sufficiently disturbed at growing Western and laborite opposition to their conservative economic policies to seek less precarious Southern cooperation. The disputed presidential election of 1876, in which both the Republican Hayes and the Democratic Tilden claimed victory, provided the setting for a compromise between the conservative elements among both Southern Democrats and Northern Republicans. Immediately, Southerners would help make Hayes President and grateful Republicans would withdraw the remaining Federal troops from the South. Of far greater significance, the supposed antagonists recognized a common interest in the maintenance of the new economic order and its profitable expansion into the South. Conservative Southerners were to share in the fruits of industrial capitalism, and the South was to become a great prop to the new order it had once opposed. Thus, as the supreme economic result of the Civil War was the triumph of industrial capitalism, its great political achievement was the emergence of a tacit but nonetheless effective coalition of conservatives North and South. And it was to secure this alliance that the North abandoned the Negro and brought Radical Reconstruction to an end.

Had Lincoln lived, the course of Reconstruction might possibly have been far different. For the magnificent statesman's only concern had been "to bind up the nation's wounds . . . to do all which may achieve and cherish a just and lasting peace." Besides, Lincoln was the master politician where Johnson was inept. Yet, such virulent economic and political forces dominated this "tragic era," that individual men counted for little. Had the wartime leader continued to oppose Radical Reconstruction he probably would not have been spared the vindictiveness with which the Radicals in Congress attacked the powers and prerogatives of the Chief Executive. And there were those who gave thanks that Lincoln had fallen early in victory rather than later in defeat.

Abraham Lincoln's Second Inaugural Address, *1865*

Fellow-Countrymen: At this second appearing to take the oath of the Presidential office, there is less occasion for an extended address than there was at the first. Then a statement, somewhat in detail, of a course to be pursued, seemed fitting and proper. Now, at the expiration of four years, during which public declarations have been constantly called forth on every point and phase of the great contest which still absorbs the attention and engrosses the energies of the nation, little that is new could be presented. The progress of our arms, upon which all else chiefly depends, is as well known to the public as to myself; and it is, I trust, reasonably satisfactory and encouraging to all. With high hope for the future, no prediction in regard to it is ventured.

On the occasion corresponding to this four years ago, all thoughts were anxiously directed to an impending civil war. All dreaded it—all sought to avert it. While the inaugural address was being delivered from this place, devoted altogether to saving the Union without war, insurgent agents were in the city seeking to destroy it without war—seeking to dissolve the Union, and divide effects, by negotiation. Both parties deprecated war; but one of them would make war rather than let the nation survive; and the other would accept war rather than let it perish. And the war came.

One-eighth of the whole population were colored slaves, not distributed generally over the Union, but localized in the Southern part of it. These slaves constituted a peculiar and powerful interest. All knew that this interest was, somehow, the cause of the war. To strengthen, perpetuate, and extend this interest was the object for which the insurgents would rend the Union, even by war; while the government claimed no right to do more than to restrict the territorial enlargement of it.

Neither party expected for the war the magnitude or the duration which it has already attained. Neither anticipated that the cause of the conflict might cease with, or even before, the conflict itself should cease. Each looked for an easier triumph, and a result less fundamental and astounding. Both read the same Bible, and pray to the same God; and each invokes His aid against the other. It may seem strange that any men should dare to ask a just God's assistance in wringing their bread from the sweat of other men's faces; but let us judge not, that we be not judged. The prayers of both could not be answered. That of neither has been answered fully. The Almighty has His own purposes. "Woe unto the world because of offenses! for it must needs be that offenses come; but woe to that man by whom the offense cometh." If we shall suppose that American slavery is one of those offenses which, in the providence of God, must needs come, but which, having continued through His appointed time, He now wills to remove, and that He gives to both North and South this terrible war, as the woe due to those by whom the offense came, shall we discern therein any departure from those divine attributes which the believers in a living God always ascribe to Him? Fondly do we hope, fervently do we pray, that this mighty scourge of war may speedily pass away. Yet, if God wills that it continue until all the wealth piled by the bondsman's two hundred and fifty years of unrequited toil shall be sunk, and until every drop of blood drawn with the lash shall be paid by another drawn with the sword, as was said three thousand years ago, so still it must be said, "The judgments of the Lord are true and righteous altogether."

With malice toward none, with charity for all, with firmness in the right, as God gives us to see the right, let us strive on to finish the work we are in, to bind up the nation's wounds, to care for him who shall have borne the battle, and for his widow, and his orphan—to do all which may achieve and cherish a just and lasting peace among ourselves and with all nations.

Chapter 16

THE GILDED AGE

Industrial expansion—ruthless, audacious, and unrelenting—was undeniably a major theme of American life in the decades from Appomattox to the end of the nineteenth century. Characterized by industry's rapid exploitation of the nation's vast human and material resources, and by the feverish accumulation of huge personal and corporate fortunes, this was America's great Age of Enterprise. But it was also America's Gilded Age, an age of aggressiveness, of unbridled acquisitiveness, of coarseness and vulgarity, when concern for the traditional principles of public and private morality had been supplanted by the worship of Mammon. By 1900 American businessmen had guided the nation to such heights of material success that she entered the new century a stridently powerful industrial giant. But to some thoughtful Americans it seemed that the high human values of an earlier America had been tragically sacrificed in the process.

By the end of the Civil War the scene had been well set for the phenomenal growth of business and for the ideological as well as physical conquest of America by her mighty captains of industry. Investment capital was readily available, for numbers of entrepreneurs had made large profits in the war years. Incredibly rich natural resources in timber, fertile lands, metals, coal, iron, and oil were at the disposal of business. A practically unlimited supply of cheap labor, increased yearly by an ever-growing stream of immigrants from distant shores, waited to serve the industrial colossus. An enormous continent guaranteed a profitable and seemingly insatiable domestic market, and a rapidly developing railroad network provided an extensive transportation system to bring together these abundant resources. But the triumph of business enterprise cannot be accounted for in these terms alone. Three other factors played a particularly decisive role: the personalities and genius of American business leaders, the constant assistance rendered business by a friendly national government, and the nation's acceptance of an ethic that transformed its social order into a business civilization.

In the harsh competitiveness of an industrial age, business leaders rose rapidly to positions of prestige and power: Andrew Carnegie in steel, John D. Rockefeller in oil, Philip D. Armour in meatpacking, J. Pierpont Morgan in finance, and James J. Hill, Leland Stanford, and Edward H. Harriman in railroads. These were the leaders of a new American aristocracy, the giants who controlled the nation's industries, its wealth, and, some maintained, its very destinies. Family, education, and gentility were not, however, the usual adornments of America's new overlords. Most often they were of humble origin, without education or training. Yet almost to a man they possessed aggressive personal traits and an unlimited capacity for business affairs that went far to secure them treasure in a brutally piratical age. They were hardheaded, and hardworking, enterprising, domineering, and imaginative men. Their extravagant visions of personal gain were seldom beclouded with concern for the welfare of their laborers or the many weaker competitors whom they frequently destroyed by fair means or foul. They combined shrewdness in the manipulation of men and materials with a genius for organization to create fabulous industrial empires that astounded the world. And the business elite's thorough mastery of the art of monopolization was clearly evidenced in Rockefeller's consolidation of the nation's oil industry into the Standard Oil trust and Carnegie's domination of almost the entire steel industry.

To these lords of industry and their admirers, the boldness and the enormity of their accomplishments, the development of the continent's natural riches, the construction of an immense national productive plant, and the creation of unheard-of wealth, raised them to heroic stature. But to the critics of the Gilded Age they were simply Robber Barons whose arts were those of the rapacious, though often romantic, highwayman. The magnitude of their achievements could not be gainsaid, yet the cost seemed truly appalling. And their critics argued cogently that to admire the Robber Barons was not only to condone trickery, cruelty, and frequently robbery, but also to applaud men whose very fortunes proved them most adept at these practices.

Those who criticized and would restrain the venal spirit of the age were to find no effective recourse in the political arena, however, for there the cunning of the entrepreneur found its counterpart in the chicanery of the politician. Like her *nouveaux riches,* America's politicos were fiercely dedicated to private profit and unconcerned with the public good. Throughout the period unscrupulous national and state legislators were openly bought and sold by the highest bidders, and during Ulysses S. Grant's administrations (1869–1877) a large segment of the Executive branch of the national government was viciously corrupt. The disgraceful Credit Mobilier railroad scandal—involving among others two Vice-Presidents of the United States, Schuyler Colfax and Henry Wilson, as well as a future President, James A. Garfield—proved to be truly symptomatic of the times. American political life, with many of its practitioners engaged in an orgy of thievery that permeated every level of government activity, was at its lowest ebb.

Though businessmen spent large sums to purchase vulnerable politicians, their investments in political power paid lush dividends in governmental assistance to industry's unrestrained expansion. Railroad interests alone received from friendly Federal and state governments land grants and subsidies that attained staggering proportions. These land grants equaled in size the state of Texas, and their value, together with direct money grants made to the railroads, totaled almost three-quarters of a billion dollars! Meanwhile the industrial community at large profited enormously from steep tariff walls erected against foreign competitors. And government assistance was by no means limited only to such positive forms. For government again served industry well in maintaining a consistently negative, hands-off attitude toward steadily mushrooming trusts and monopolies that trampled indifferently over all who stood in the path to profit. And when, under the pressures of an aroused and angry citizenry, some state legislatures did actually pass regulatory acts, these acts were swept aside as unconstitutional by a conservative Supreme Court that later emerged as industry's most ardent champion. Supported by the highest court in the land, the alliance between business and government seemed truly impregnable.

These economic and political developments were greatly facilitated by equally significant changes in the whole course of American thought. Embracing the ideological and ethical assumptions that underlay the Gilded Age, Americans generally viewed with enthusiasm the triumphant emergence of a business civilization whose most appropriate symbol was the dollar sign. And the coarse standards of the business community were clearly reflected in almost every aspect of American behavior. Yet men like E. L. Godkin, the caustic editor of the *Nation,* Henry Adams, grandson and great-grandson of Presidents, the poet James Russell Lowell, and others of their circle who composed America's older, declining intellectual aristocracy, inveighed bitterly against what Godkin termed a "chromo civilization."

Even Walt Whitman, the poet who once had sung most exuberantly of America's democratic virtues, strength, and cultural creativeness, now pondered whether his nation's rampant, materialistic postwar individualism hadn't bequeathed her a "hollowness of heart" that in the Gilded Age was manifest everywhere in deceit, faithlessness, cruelty, corruption. Whitman's "Democratic Vistas," published in 1871, lacked the broad optimism of *Leaves of Grass* and his other early affirmations of faith in democracy. Now Whitman felt that "vulgarians" dominated America and that the democratic individualism which a generation before seemed to have promised great national poetry, art, creativeness, had actually degenerated into petty and depraved self-seeking. Not that Whitman had lost all faith in democracy—which for him, as for Lincoln, was synonymous with America—but now he saw its promise and true grandeur in the future only, its materialistic failures in the "chromo civilization" around him.

Despite these criticisms, however, the very materialistic "values" that Whitman and the others deplored were widely accepted. And most Americans, though separated from the rising plutocracy by a vast gulf of riches, came fervently to share its material standards of success. Thus, when the multi-millionaire steel magnate, Andrew Carnegie, propounded an elaborate rationalization of the new highly competitive economic order, he faithfully reflected the temper of contemporary America.

Though concerned in large part with the philanthropic duties of the man of wealth as the "mere agent and trustee for his poorer brethren," Carnegie's essay "Wealth" was significantly couched in the language of Darwinian evolutionary ideas that had already made a deep impression upon American thought. In his *Origin of Species,* the English scientist Charles Darwin had explained the evolution from low to higher living forms in terms of Nature's inexorable struggle for existence and the consequent survival of the fittest. Immediately industry's apologists seized upon these ideas in self-justification, seeking to translate Darwin's observations of natural phenomena into laws of social behavior. As a major spokesman for the Social Darwinists, Carnegie wrote that though competitiveness "may be sometimes hard for the individual, it is best for the race, because it insures the survival of the fittest in every department." We must accept "great inequality of environment, the concentration of business . . . in the hands of a few, and the law of competition between these as being not only beneficial, but essential for the future progress of the race." Thus the cutthroat competition of the Age of Enterprise was equated with Nature's own struggle for existence and sanctioned as natural and right. The giants who survived the struggle, the economic masters of the nation, were judged the "fittest" of the race; and even the most brutal business practices were esteemed as tools of survival and human progress.

Yet the Social Darwinists were not wholly consistent. They demanded for themselves positive assistance from government in the form of tariffs, land grants, and subsidies. At the same time they condemned regulatory or social legislation as unwarranted interference with the law of the jungle, fraught with the most dire consequences for the "future progress of the race." Despite these inconsistencies, however, until the advent of Progressivism at the end of the century, large numbers of Americans remained imbued with the ideas of the Social Darwinists.

"Democratic Vistas," *Walt Whitman, 1871*

. . . America, filling the present with greatest deeds and problems, cheerfully accepting the past, including feudalism (as, indeed, the present is but the legitimate birth of the past, including feudalism), counts, as I reckon, for her justification and success, (for who, as yet, dare claim success?) almost entirely on the future. Nor is that hope unwarranted. To-day, ahead, though dimly yet, we see, in vistas, a copious, sane, gigantic offspring. For our New World I consider far less important for what it has done, or what it is, than for results to come. Sole among nationalities, these States have assumed the task to put in forms of lasting power and practicality, on areas of amplitude rivaling the operations of the physical kosmos, the moral political speculations of ages, long, long deferr'd, the democratic republican principle, and the theory of development and perfection by voluntary standards and self-reliance. Who else, indeed, except the United States, in history, so far, have accepted in unwitting faith, and, as we now see, stand, act upon, and go security for, these things?

But preluding no longer, let me strike the key-note of the following strain. First premising that, though the passages of it have been written at widely different times, (it is, in fact, a collection of memoranda, perhaps for future designers, comprehenders,) and though it may be open to the charge of one part contradicting another—for there are opposite sides to the great question of democracy, as to every great question—I feel the parts harmoniously blended in my own realization and convictions, and present them to be read only in such oneness, each page and each claim and assertion modified and temper'd by the others. Bear in mind, too, that they are not the result of studying up in political economy, but of the ordinary sense, observing, wandering among men, these States, these stirring years of war and peace. I will not gloss over the appalling dangers of universal suffrage in the United States. In fact, it is to admit and face these dangers I am writing. To him or her within whose thought rages the battle, advancing, retreating, between democracy's convictions, aspirations, and the people's crudeness, vice, caprices, I mainly write this essay. I shall use the words America and democracy as convertible terms. Not an ordinary one is the issue. The United States are destined either to surmount the gorgeous history of feudalism, or else prove the most tremendous failure of time. Not the least doubtful am I on any prospects of their material success. . . .

Admitting all this, with the priceless value of our political institutions, general suffrage, (and fully acknowledging the latest, widest opening of the doors,) I say that, far deeper than these, what finally and only is to make of our western world a nationality superior to any hither known, and outtopping the past, must be vigorous, yet unsuspected Literatures, perfect personalities, and sociologies, original transcendental, and expressing (what, in highest sense, are not yet express'd at all,) democracy and the modern. With these, and out of these, I promulge new races of Teachers, and of perfect Women, indispensable to endow the birth-stock of a New World. For feudalism, caste, the ecclesiastic traditions, though palpably retreating from political institutions, still hold essentially, by their spirit, even in this country, entire possession of more important fields, indeed the very subsoil, of education, and of social standards and literature.

I say that democracy can never prove itself beyond cavil, until it founds and luxuriantly grows its own forms of art, poems, schools, theology, displacing all that exists, or that has been produced anywhere in the past, under opposite influences. . . . Our fundamental want to-day in the United States, with closest, amplest reference to present conditions, and to the future, is of a class, and the clear idea of a class, of native authors, literatuses, far different, far higher in grade than any yet known, sacerdotal, modern, fit to cope with our occasions, lands, permeating the whole mass of American mentality, taste, belief, breathing into it a new breath of life, giving it decision, affecting politics far more than the popular superficial suffrage, with results inside and underneath the elections of Presidents or Congresses—radiating, begetting appropriate teachers, schools, manners, and, as its grandest result, accomplishing, (what neither the schools nor the churches and their clergy have hitherto accomplish'd, and without which this nation will no more stand, permanently, soundly, than a house will stand without a substratum,) a religious and moral character beneath the political and productive and intellectual bases of the States. . . .

I say we had best look our times and lands searchingly in the face, like a physician diagnosing some deep disease. Never was there, perhaps, more hollowness at heart than at present, and here in the United States. Genuine belief seems to have left us. The underlying principles of the States are not honestly believ'd in, (for all this hectic glow, and these melodramatic screamings,) nor is humanity itself believ'd in. What penetrating eye does not everywhere see through the mask? The spectacle is appalling. We live in an atmosphere of hypocrisy throughout. The men believe not in the women, nor the women in the men. A scornful superciliousness rules in literature. The aim of all the *littérateurs* is to find something to make fun of. A lot of churches, sects, &c., the most dismal phantasms I know, usurp the name of religion. Conversation is a mass of badinage. From deceit in the spirit, the mother of all false deeds, the offspring is already incalculable. . . . The depravity of the business classes of our country is not less than has been supposed, but infinitely greater. The official services of America, national, state, and municipal, in all their branches and departments, except the judiciary, are saturated in corruption, bribery, falsehood, maladministration; and the judiciary is tainted. The great cities reek with respectable as much as non-respectable robbery and scoundrelism. In fashionable life, flippancy, tepid amours, weak infidelism, small aims, or no aims at all, only to kill time. In business, (this all-devouring modern word, business,) the one sole object is, by any means, pecuniary gain. The magician's serpent in the fable ate up all the other serpents; and moneymaking is our magician's serpent, remaining today sole master of the field. The best class we show, is but a mob of fashionably dress'd speculators and vulgarians. True, indeed, behind this fantastic farce, enacted on the visible stage of society, solid things and stupendous labors are to be discover'd, existing crudely and going on in the background, to advance and tell themselves in time. Yet the truths are none the less terrible. I say that our New World democracy, however great a success in uplifting the masses out of their sloughs, in materialistic development, products, and in a certain highly-deceptive superficial popular intellectuality, is, so far, an almost complete failure in its social aspects, and in really grand religious, moral, literary, and esthetic results. . . .

Then still the thought returns, (like the thread-passage in overtures,) giving the key and echo to these pages. When I pass to and fro, different latitudes, different seasons, beholding the crowds of the great cities, New York, Boston, Philadelphia, Cincinnati, Chicago, St. Louis, San Francisco, New Orleans, Baltimore—when I mix with these interminable swarms of alert, turbulent, good-natured, independent citizens, mechanics, clerks, young persons—at the idea of this mass of men, so fresh and free, so loving and so proud, a singular awe falls upon me. I feel, with dejection and amazement, that among our geniuses and talented writers or speakers, few or none have yet really spoken to this people, created a single image-making work for them, or absorb'd the central spirit and the idiosyncrasies which are theirs—and which, thus, in highest ranges, so far remain entirely uncelebrated, unexpress'd.

Dominion strong is the body's; dominion stronger is the mind's. What has fill'd, and fills to-day our intellect, our fancy, furnishing the standards therein, is yet foreign. The great poems, Shakspere included, are poisonous to the idea of the pride and dignity of the common people, the lifeblood of democracy. The models of our literature, as we get it from other lands, ultra-marine, have had their birth in courts, and bask'd and grown in castle sunshine; all smells of princes' favors. Of workers of a certain sort, we have, indeed, plenty, contributing after their kind; many elegant, many learn'd, all complacent. But touch'd by the national test, or tried by the standards of democratic personality, they wither to ashes. I say I have not seen a single writer, artist, lecturer, or what not, that has confronted the voiceless but ever erect and active, pervading, underlying will and typic aspiration of the land, in a spirit kindred to itself. Do you call those genteel little creatures American poets? Do you term that perpetual, pistareen, paste-pot work, American art, American drama, taste, verse? I think I hear, echoed as from some mountaintop afar in the west, the scornful laugh of the Genius of these States. . . .

America has yet morally and artistically originated nothing. She seems singularly unaware that the models of persons, books, manners, &c., appropriate for former conditions and for European lands, are but exiles and exotics here. No current of her life, as shown on the surfaces of what is authoritatively called her society, accepts or runs into social or esthetic democracy; but all the currents set squarely against it. Never, in the Old World, was thoroughly upholster'd exterior appearance and show, mental and other, built entirely on the idea of caste, and on the sufficiency of mere outside acquisition—never were glibness, verbal intellect, more the test, the emulation—more loftily elevated as head and sample—than they are on the surface of our republican States this day. The writers of a time hint the mottoes of its gods. The word of the modern, say these voices, is the word Culture.

We find ourselves abruptly in close quarters with the enemy. This word Culture, or what it has come to represent, involves, by contrast, our whole theme, and has been, indeed, the spur, urging us to engagement. Certain questions arise. As now taught, accepted and carried out, are not the processes of culture rapidly creating a class of supercilious infidels, who believe in nothing? Shall a man lose himself in countless masses of adjustments, and be so shaped with reference to this, that, and the other, that the simply good and healthy and brave parts of him are reduced and clipped away, like the bordering of box in a garden? You can cultivate corn and roses and orchards—but who shall cultivate the mountain peaks, the ocean, and the tumbling gorgeousness of the clouds? Lastly—is the readily-given reply that culture only seeks to help, systematize, and put in attitude, the elements of fertility and power, a conclusive reply?

I do not so much object to the name, or word, but I should certainly insist, for the purposes of these States, on a radical change of category, in the distribution of precedence. I should demand a programme of culture, drawn out, not for a single class alone, or for the parlors or lecture-rooms, but with an eye to practical life, the west, the working-men, the facts of farms and jack-planes and engineers, and of the broad range of the women also of the middle and working strata, and with reference to the perfect equality of women, and of a grand and powerful motherhood. I should demand of this programme or theory a scope generous enough to include the widest human area. It must have for its spinal meaning the formation of a typical personality of character, eligible to the uses of the high average of men—and *not* restricted by conditions ineligible to the masses. The best culture will always be that of the manly and courageous instincts, and loving perceptions, and of self-respect—aiming to form, over this continent, an idiocrasy of universalism, which, true child of America, will bring joy to its mother, returning to her in her own spirit, recruiting myriads of offspring, able, natural, perceptive, tolerant, devout believers in her, America, and with some definite instinct why and for what she has arisen, most vast, most formidable of historic births, and is, now and here, with wonderful step, journeying through Time. . . .

"Wealth," *Andrew Carnegie, 1889*

The problem of our age is the proper administration of wealth, so that the ties of brotherhood may still bind together the rich and poor in harmonious relationship. The conditions of human life have not only been changed, but revolutionized within the past few hundred years. In former days there was little difference between the dwelling, dress, food, and environment of the chief and those of his retainers. The Indians are today where civilized man then was. When visiting the Sioux I was led to the wigwam of the chief. It was just like the others in external appearance, and even within the difference was trifling between it and those of the poorest of his braves. The contrast between the palace of the millionaire and the cottage of the laborer with us today measures the change which has come with civilization.

This change, however, is not to be deplored, but welcomed as highly beneficial. It is well, nay, essential for the progress of the race, that the houses of some should be homes for all that is highest and best in literature and the arts, and for all the refinements of civilization, rather than that none should be so. Much better this great irregularity than universal squalor. Without wealth there can be no Maecenas. The "good old times" were not good old times. Neither master nor servant was as well situated then as today. A relapse to old conditions would be disastrous to both—not the least so to him who serves—and would sweep away civilization with it. But whether the change be for good or ill, it is upon us, beyond our power to alter, and therefore to be accepted and made the best of. It is a waste of time to criticise the inevitable.

It is easy to see how the change has come. One illustration will serve for almost every phase of the cause. In the manufacture of products we have the whole story. It applies to all combinations of human industry, as stimulated and enlarged by the inventions of this scientific age. Formerly articles were manufactured at the domestic hearth or in small shops which formed part of the household. The master and his apprentices worked side by side, the latter living with the master, and therefore subject to the same conditions. When these apprentices rose to be masters, there was little or no change in their mode of life, and they, in turn, educated in the same routine succeeding apprentices. There was, substantially, social equality, and even political equality, for those engaged in industrial pursuits had then little or no political voice in the State.

But the inevitable result of such a mode of manufacture was crude articles at high prices. Today the world obtains commodities of excellent quality at prices which even the generation preceding this would have deemed incredible. In the commercial world similar causes have produced similar results, and the race is benefited thereby. The poor enjoy what the rich could not before afford. What were the luxuries have become the necessities of life. The laborer has now more comforts than the farmer had a few generations ago. The farmer has more luxuries than the landlord had, and is more richly clad and better housed. The landlord has books and pictures rarer, and appointments more artistic, than the King could then obtain.

The price we pay for this salutary change is, no doubt, great. We assemble thousands of operatives in the factory, in the mine, and in the counting-house, of whom the employer can know little or nothing, and to whom the employer is little better than a myth. All intercourse between them is at an end. Rigid castes are formed, and, as usual, mutual ignorance breeds mutual distrust. Each caste is without sympathy for the other, and ready to credit anything disparaging in regard to it. Under the law of competition, the employer of thousands is forced into the strictest economies, among which the rates paid to labor figure prominently, and often there is friction between the employer and the employed, between capital and labor, between rich and poor. Human society loses homogeneity.

The price which society pays for the law of competition, like the price it pays for cheap comforts and luxuries, is also great; but the advantages of this law are also greater still, for it is to this law that we owe our wonderful material development, which brings improved conditions in its train. But, whether the law be benign or not, we must say of it, as we say of the change in the conditions of men to which we have referred: It is here; we cannot evade it; no substitutes for it have been found; and while the law may be sometimes hard for the individual, it is best for the race, because it insures the survival of the fittest in every department. We accept and welcome, therefore, as conditions to which we must accommodate ourselves, great inequality of environment, the concentration of business, industrial and commercial, in the hands of a few, and the law of competition between these, as being not only beneficial, but essential for the future progress of the race. Having accepted these, it follows that there must be great scope for the exercise of special ability in the merchant and in the manufacturer who has to conduct affairs upon a great scale. That this talent for organization and management is rare among men is proved by the fact that it invariably secures for its possessor enormous rewards, no matter where or under what laws or conditions. The experienced in affairs always rate the *man* whose services can be obtained as a partner as not only the first consideration, but such as to render the question of his capital scarcely worth considering, for such men soon create capital; while, without the special talent required, capital soon takes wings. Such men become interested in firms or corporations using millions; and estimating only simple interest to be made upon the capital invested, it is inevitable that their income must exceed their expenditures, and that they must accumulate wealth. Nor is there any middle ground which such men can occupy, because the great manufacturing or commercial concern which does not earn at least interest upon its capital soon becomes bankrupt. It must either go forward or fall behind: to stand still is impossible. It is a condition essential for its successful operation that it should be thus far profitable, and even that, in addition to interest on capital, it should make profit. It is a law, as certain as any of the others named, that men possessed of this peculiar talent for affairs, under the free play of economic forces, must, of necessity, soon be in receipt of more revenue than can be judiciously expended upon themselves; and this law is as beneficial for the race as the others.

Objections to the foundations upon which society is based are not in order, because the condition of the race is better with these than it has been with any others which have been tried. Of the effect of any new substitutes proposed we cannot be sure. The socialist or anarchist who seeks to overturn present conditions is to be regarded as attacking the foundation upon which civilization itself rests, for civilization took its start from the day that the capable, industrious workman said to his incompetent and lazy fellow, "If thou dost not sow, thou shalt not reap," and thus ended primitive communism by separating the drones from the bees. One who studies this subject will soon be brought face to face with the conclusion that upon the sacredness of property civilization itself depends—the right of the laborer to his hundred dollars in the savings bank, and equally the legal right of the millionaire to his millions. To those who propose to substitute communism for this intense individualism the answer, therefore, is: The race has tried that. All progress from that barbarous day to the present time has resulted from its displacement. Not evil, but good, has come to the race from the accumulation of wealth by those who have the ability and energy that produce it. But even if we admit for a moment that it might be better for the race to discard its present foundation, individualism—that it is a nobler ideal that man should labor, not for himself alone, but in and for a brotherhood of his fellows, and share with them all in common, realizing Swedenborg's idea of Heaven, where, as he says, the angels derive their happiness, not from laboring for self, but for each other—even admit all this, and a sufficient answer is: This is not evolution, but revolution. It necessitates the changing of human nature itself—a work of aeons, even if it were good to change it, which we cannot know. It is not practicable in our day or in our age. Even if desirable theoretically, it belongs to another and long-succeeding sociological stratum. Our duty is with what is practicable now; with the next step possible in our day and generation. It is criminal to waste our energies in endeavoring to uproot, when all we can profitably or possibly accomplish is to bend the universal tree of humanity a little in the direction most favorable to the production of good fruit under existing circumstances. We might as well urge the destruction of the highest existing type of man because he failed to reach our ideal as to favor the destruction of Individualism, Private Property, the Law of Accumulation of Wealth, and the Law of Competition; for these are the highest results of human experience, the soil in which society so far has produced the best fruit. Unequally or unjustly, perhaps, as these laws sometimes operate, and imperfect as they appear to the Idealist, they are, nevertheless, like the highest type of man, the best and most valuable of all that humanity has yet accomplished.

We start, then, with a condition of affairs under which the best interests of the race are promoted, but which inevitably gives wealth to the few. Thus far, accepting conditions as they exist, the situation can be surveyed and pronounced good. The question then arises—and, if the foregoing be correct, it is the only question with which we have to deal: What is the proper mode of administering wealth after the laws upon which civilization is founded have thrown it into the hands of the few? And it is of this great question that I believe I offer the true solution. . . .

There are but three modes in which surplus wealth can be disposed of. It can be left to the families of the decedents; or it can be bequeathed for public purposes; or finally, it can be administered during their lives by its possessors. Under the first and second modes most of the wealth of the world that has reached the few has hitherto been applied. Let us in turn consider each of these modes. The first is the most injudicious. In monarchical countries, the estates and the greatest portion of the wealth are left to the first son, that the vanity of the parent may be gratified by the thought that his name and title are to descend to succeeding generations unimpaired. The condition of this class in Europe today teaches the futility of such hopes or ambitions. The successors have become impoverished through their follies or from the fall in the value of land. Even in Great Britain the strict law of entail has been found inadequate to maintain the status of an hereditary class. Its soil is rapidly passing into the hands of the stranger. Under republican institutions the division of property among the children is much fairer, but the question which forces itself upon thoughtful men in all lands is: Why should men leave great fortunes to their children? If this is done from affection, is it not misguided affection? Observation teaches that, generally speaking, it is not well for the children that they should be so burdened. Neither is it well for the state. Beyond providing for the wife and daughters moderate sources of income, and very moderate allowances indeed, if any, for the sons, men may well hesitate, for it is no longer questionable that great sums bequeathed oftener work more for the injury than for the good of the recipients. . . .

As to the second mode, that of leaving wealth at death for public uses, it may be said that this is only a means for the disposal of wealth, provided a man is content to wait until he is dead before it becomes of much good in the world. Knowledge of the results of legacies bequeathed is not calculated to inspire the brightest hopes of much posthumous good being accomplished. The cases are not few in which the real object sought by the testator is not attained, nor are they few in which his real wishes are thwarted. In many cases the bequests are so used as to become only monuments of his folly. It is well to remember that it requires the exercise of not less ability than that which acquired the wealth to use it so as to be really beneficial to the community. Besides this, it may fairly be said that no man is to be extolled for doing what he cannot help doing, nor is he to be thanked by the community to which he only leaves wealth at death. Men who leave vast sums in this way may fairly be thought men who would not have left it at all, had they been able to take it with them. . . .

The growing disposition to tax more and more heavily large estates left at death is a cheering indication of the growth of a salutary change in public opinion. The State of Pennsylvania now takes—subject to some exceptions—one-tenth of the property left by its citizens. The budget presented in the British Parliament the other day proposes to increase the death duties; and, most significant of all, the new tax is to be a graduated one. Of all forms of taxation, this seems the wisest.

Men who continue hoarding great sums all their lives, the proper use of which for public ends would work good to the community, should be made to feel that the community, in the form of the state, cannot thus be deprived of its proper share. By taxing estates heavily at death the state marks its condemnation of the selfish millionaire's unworthy life. . . . This policy would work powerfully to induce the rich man to attend to the administration of wealth during his life, which is the end that society should always have in view as being that by far most fruitful for the people. Nor need it be feared that this policy would sap the root of enterprise and render men less anxious to accumulate, for to the class whose ambition it is to leave great fortunes and be talked about after their death, it will attract even more attention, and, indeed, be a somewhat nobler ambition to have enormous sums paid over to the state from their fortunes.

There remains, then, only one mode of using great fortunes; but in this we have the true antidote for the temporary unequal distribution of wealth, the reconciliation of the rich and the poor—a reign of harmony—another ideal, differing, indeed, from that of the communist in requiring only the further evolution of existing conditions, not the total overthrow of our civilization. It is founded upon the present most intense individualism, and the race is prepared to put it in practice by degrees whenever it pleases. Under its sway we shall have an ideal state, in which the surplus wealth of the few will become, in the best sense, the property of the many, because administered for the common good, and this wealth, passing through the hands of the few, can be made a much more potent force for the elevation of our race than if it had been distributed in small sums to the people themselves. Even the poorest can be made to see this, and to agree that great sums gathered by some of their fellow-citizens and spent for public purposes, from which the masses reap the principal benefit, are more valuable to them than if scattered among themselves in trifling amounts through the course of many years. . . .

This, then, is held to be the duty of the man of wealth: First, to set an example of modest, unostentatious living, shunning display or extravagance; to provide moderately for the legitimate wants of those dependent upon him; and after doing so to consider all surplus revenues which come to him simply as trust funds, which he is called upon to administer, and strictly bound as a matter of duty to administer in the manner which, in his judgment, is best calculated to produce the most beneficial results for the community—the man of wealth thus becoming the mere agent and trustee for his poorer brethren, bringing to their service his superior wisdom, experience, and ability to administer, doing for them better than they would or could do for themselves. . . .

The best uses to which surplus wealth can be put have already been indicated. Those who would administer wisely must, indeed, be wise, for one of the serious obstacles to the improvement of our race is indiscriminate charity. It were better for mankind that the millions of the rich were thrown into the sea than so spent as to encourage the slothful, the drunken, the unworthy. Of every thousand dollars spent in so-called charity today, it is probable that $950 is unwisely spent; so spent, indeed, as to produce the very evils which it proposes to mitigate or cure. A well-known writer of philosophic books admitted the other day that he had given a quarter of a dollar to a man who approached him as he was coming to visit the house of his friend. He knew nothing of the habits of this beggar; knew not the use that would be made of this money, although he had every reason to suspect that it would be spent improperly. This man professed to be a disciple of Herbert Spencer; yet the quarter-dollar given that night will probably work more injury than all the money which its thoughtless donor will ever be able to give in true charity will do good. He only gratified his own feelings, saved himself from annoyance—and this was probably one of the most selfish and very worst actions of his life, for in all respects he is most worthy.

In bestowing charity, the main consideration should be to help those who will help themselves; to provide part of the means by which those who desire to improve may do so; to give those who desire to rise the aids by which they may rise; to assist, but rarely or never to do all. Neither the individual nor the race is improved by alms-giving. Those worthy of assistance, except in rare cases, seldom require assistance. The really valuable men of the race never do, except in cases of accident or sudden change. . . . The best means of benefiting the community is to place within its reach the ladders upon which the aspiring can rise—parks, and means of recreation, by which men are helped in body and mind; works of art, certain to give pleasure and improve the public taste, and public institutions of various kinds, which will improve the general condition of the people—in this manner returning their surplus wealth to the mass of their fellows in the forms best calculated to do them lasting good.

Thus is the problem of rich and poor to be solved. The laws of accumulation will be left free; the laws of distribution free. Individualism will continue, but the millionaire will be but a trustee of the poor; intrusted for a season with a great part of the increased wealth of the community, but administering it for the community far better than it could or would have done for itself. The best minds will thus have reached a stage in the development of the race in which it is clearly seen that there is no mode of disposing of surplus wealth creditable to thoughtful and earnest men into whose hands it flows save by using it year by year for the general good. This day already dawns. But a little while, and although, without incurring the pity of their fellows, men may die sharers in great business enterprises from which their capital cannot be or has not been withdrawn, and is left chiefly at death for public uses, yet the man who dies leaving behind him millions of available wealth, which was his to administer during life, will pass away "unwept, unhonored, and unsung," no matter to what uses he leaves the dross which he cannot take with him. Of such as these the public verdict will then be: "The man who dies thus rich dies disgraced."

Such, in my opinion, is the true Gospel concerning Wealth, obedience to which is destined some day to solve the problem of the Rich and the Poor, and to bring "Peace on earth, among men Good Will."

Chapter 17

FROM FRONTIER TO FACTORY

From the earliest English settlements at Jamestown in 1607 to the end of the nineteenth century the westward movement provided succeeding generations of Americans with a common frontier experience. First the farther reaches of the low country along the Atlantic seaboard, then the Allegheny Mountains, the Mississippi River, the Missouri River, the Great Plains, and finally the Rocky Mountains: these were the great frontier lines between virgin wilderness and an ever-expanding American civilization. At all times there were new frontiers to explore, new lands to conquer. And the seeming boundlessness of the West called forth a buoyant American optimism that Jefferson expressed in his vision of ample room within the public domain for the free and unlimited settlement of "our descendants to the hundredth and thousandth generation."

This characteristic optimism proved unfounded. Less than a century after Jefferson purchased the extensive Louisiana Territory in 1803, America's free Western lands were largely exhausted and the frontier had become less reality than myth or memory. The reasons were clear, for at midcentury the discovery of gold in California had inaugurated some four decades of unparalleled westward expansion. Boisterous forty-niners were followed by tens and then hundreds of thousands of native pioneers who made the long trek westward in search of free or cheap land under the generous Homestead Act of 1862. And the great transcontinental railroads, seeking first a supply of cheap labor and then settled Western communities to serve, encouraged millions of oppressed Europeans to migrate to the New World, where land was plentiful and the streets were supposedly "paved with gold." As natives and immigrants alike poured into the West the burdens of settlement were immeasurably lightened by the effective, though brutal, elimination of hostile Indian tribes. Meanwhile a booming cattle industry and continuing discoveries of rich gold and silver deposits throughout the Far West lured others who sought fortune. Only the frenzied rise of industry surpassed the sweeping intensity of this last thrust westward. But finally, and inevitably, the West was devoured by its settlers, and early in the 1890's the superintendent of the census announced the passing of the frontier. Land was still available in many parts of the nation, but the Great West—familiar to Americans of all generations—had been exhausted.

Few Americans were aware of the census report or of its meaning. But Frederick Jackson Turner, a brilliant young scholar at the University of Wisconsin, saw the passing of the frontier as an event of great national importance. And in 1893 he read before the American Historical Association a perceptive and challenging paper on "The Significance of the Frontier in American History." Rejecting historians' traditional view of American civilization as a simple continuation of European beginnings, Turner stated his own frontier thesis briefly but effectively: "The existence of an area of free land, its continuous recession, and the advance of American settlement westward explain American development." To Turner, American ideals and institutions were not the legacy of the Old World. Rather they were the creatures of the psychological and material demands of a uniquely American frontier. It was to the West, then, not to the East or to Europe, that Americans were indebted for their sense of nationality, their instinct for democracy, and particularly their characteristic independence and individualism.

In the 1890's Turner's frontier thesis seemed immediately appropriate. The western frontier had been pushed to its farthest limits. Yet Turner saw traditional American values as largely western in origin. What would be their fate now that the West was gone? In answer there were already unmistakable signs of change in the whole tenor of American life. As the nation soberly turned its energies from the exploitation to the consolidation and conservation of its human and material resources, the boom psychology that had earlier marked the westward movement was gradually supplanted by a more responsible sense of group or social values. And a subtle shift in emphasis from an exuberant and excessive individualism to unfamiliar patterns of collective thought and action was particularly evident. To some these fundamental changes in the American climate of opinion seemed to bear out Turner's thesis. Yet it remains difficult to determine whether the relationship of these changes to the passing of the frontier was causal or coincidental. Indeed, to a considerable extent industrialization and urbanization, which had begun three decades before, when westward expansion was at its highest peak, were responsible for this new orientation. For the rapid development of industrial capitalism and the mass movement from rural to urban areas had been accompanied by complex social and economic problems that defied solution within the ideological framework of an older, individualistic agrarianism.

Bitter conflict between capital and labor was the gravest of these problems. Industrialization had already brought great riches to a number of rising businessmen, and ultimately it would bring material well-being to the nation at large. But immediately the wealth of the entrepreneur had been matched only by the growing impoverishment and insecurity of the workingman. Business profits and dividends had increased prodigiously, but wages remained pitifully low; large industrial combinations had limited competition to make capital investments secure, but workers continuously faced unemployment incidental to technological improvement and to depression; industry had enjoyed the generous favors of government, but Federal and state troops frequently deprived workers of their one weapon against capital, the strike. In short, as the lot of the laborer grew increasingly harsh, progress and poverty seemed inextricably bound together. Still, during this early phase of industrialization the availability of free Western land had served somewhat as a psychological safety valve for the frustrations of factory life, though only an occasional discontented laborer had actually been able to pull up stakes and make his way westward. Now, however, the disappearance of the open frontier shattered even the illusion of choice, compounding labor's difficulties and kindling class conflict, and the 1890's proved to be a nervous and turbulent decade, deeply scarred by unrelenting economic warfare between capital and labor.

Earlier, of course, there had been important, though generally confused and inadequate, efforts to organize the growing armies of labor on a national scale. Solidarity amongst workingmen had not been achieved, but these first union experiences and failures provided the later labor movement important lessons. In 1866, under the impetus of rising prices and lagging wages, the National Labor Union had consolidated various national trade unions into one great federation designed to promote social and political reform. Large numbers of workers were attracted at first; the delegates to the 1868 convention represented 600,000 members. But its loose organization and vague, general efforts at reform did not meet the immediate needs of overworked and underpaid laborers. And in 1872 the National Labor Union formally deserted its trade-union orientation when its leaders formed the National Labor Reform party and entered national politics. For the next decade and a half American labor was represented by the Noble Order of the Knights of Labor. Highly centralized, emphasizing industrial rather than trade unionism, and embracing all members of the working class in one big union, the new organization grew rapidly, and in 1886 membership totaled 700,000. For a number of years the Knights proved to be a powerful force in American life, particularly as an articulate pressure group. Ultimately, however, overcentralization, confusion between immediate economic objectives and utopian reforms, and conflicting interests between skilled and unskilled workers led to the Knights' downfall. But in the late 1880's the American Federation of Labor stood ready to carry on labor's battles. Learning bitter lessons from its forerunners, the new union maintained organizational authority and responsibility without overcentralization, confined its membership generally to skilled workers, eschewed politics except to reward its friends and punish its enemies, and concentrated on immediate objectives such as higher wages, shorter hours, and better working conditions. Steadily and consistently doing battle to win for the workingman a larger and fairer share of industrial America's vast wealth, under the energetic leadership of Samuel Gompers the Federation quickly emerged as labor's leading champion.

By the 1890's American labor had yet to win its major battles. Bringing to bear every weapon at its disposal—the lockout, the "yellow-dog" contract, the blacklist, strike-breaking troops or armed thugs, the injunction—industry still bitterly fought labor's right to bargain collectively and to strike. In the bloody Homestead strike against the Carnegie Steel Company in 1892, when management used Pinkerton detectives to break the grip of the union, and in the Pullman strike in 1894, when, despite Gompers' protest in his much noted "Letter on Labor in Industrial Society," injunctions and Federal troops destroyed the valiant efforts of Eugene V. Debs' American Railway Union, labor lost its most violent encounters with organized capital. Yet industry's victories proved futile—or worse. For they not only spurred labor on to greater organizational efforts, but they also impressed fair-minded and frightened Americans with the need for collective social action to redress the growing imbalance between capital and labor, between rich and poor, and, as Booker T. Washington pointed out, between Whites and Blacks who would make their way up from slavery. Whether fundamentally the cause was to be found in the passing of the frontier and the Great West, or in the development of industry and the rise of the city, it was obvious that the free economic opportunities of an earlier America were fast disappearing. Now most middle-class Americans seemed determined to recapture economic democracy and secure social justice for all, though to do so they had to abandon older ideas of individual self-help and look to government for direction and even control. By the turn of the new century the nation was obviously preparing to commit itself as enthusiastically to new conceptions of social responsibility and general welfare as earlier it had espoused the principles of laissez-faire.

"The Significance of the Frontier in American History,"* *Frederick Jackson Turner, 1893*

In a recent bulletin of the Superintendent of the Census for 1890 appear these significant words: "Up to and including 1880 the country had a frontier of settlement, but at present the unsettled area has been so broken into by isolated bodies of settlement that there can hardly be said to be a frontier line. In the discussion of its extent, its westward movement, etc., it can not, therefore, any longer have a place in the census reports." This brief official statement marks the closing of a great historic movement. Up to our own day American history has been in a large degree the history of the colonization of the Great West. The existence of an area of free land, its continuous recession, and the advance of American settlement westward, explain American development.

Behind institutions, behind constitutional forms and modifications, lie the vital forces that call these organs into life and shape them to meet changing conditions. The peculiarity of American institutions is the fact that they have been compelled to adapt themselves to the changes of an expanding people—to the changes involved in crossing a continent, in winning a wilderness, and in developing at each area of this progress out of the primitive economic and political conditions of the frontier into the complexity of city life. Said Calhoun in 1817, "We are great, and rapidly—I was about to say fearfully—growing!" So saying, he touched the distinguishing feature of American life. All peoples show development; the germ theory of politics has been sufficiently emphasized. In the case of most nations, however, the development has occurred in a limited area; and if the nation has expanded, it has met other growing peoples whom it has conquered. But in the case of the United States we have a different phenomenon. Limiting our attention to the Atlantic coast, we have the familiar phenomenon of the evolution of institu-

*From *The Frontier in American History* by Frederick Jackson Turner. Copyright, 1920, by Frederick J. Turner. Copyright, 1948, by Caroline Mae S. Turner. Used by permission of Henry Holt and Company.

tions in a limited area, such as the rise of representative government; the differentiation of simple colonial governments into complex organs; the progress from primitive industrial society, without division of labor, up to manufacturing civilization. But we have in addition to this a recurrence of the process of evolution in each western area reached in the process of expansion. Thus American development has exhibited not merely advance along a single line, but a return to primitive conditions on a continually advancing frontier line, and a new development for that area. American social development has been continually beginning over again on the frontier. This perennial rebirth, this fluidity of American life, this expansion westward with its new opportunities, its continuous touch with the simplicity of primitive society, furnish the forces dominating American character. The true point of view in the history of this nation is not the Atlantic coast, it is the Great West. Even the slavery struggle . . . occupies its important place in American history because of its relation to westward expansion.

In this advance, the frontier is the outer edge of the wave, the meeting point between savagery and civilization. Much has been written about the frontier from the point of view of border warfare and the chase, but as a field for the serious study of the economist and the historian it has been neglected.

The American frontier is sharply distinguished from the European frontier, a fortified boundary line running through dense populations. The most significant thing about the American frontier is, that it lies at the hither edge of free land. In the census reports it is treated as the margin of that settlement which has a density of two or more to the square mile. The term is an elastic one, and for our purposes does not need sharp definition. We shall consider the whole frontier belt, including the Indian country and the outer margin of the "settled area" of the census reports. This paper will make no attempt to treat the subject exhaustively; its aim is simply to call attention to the frontier as a fertile field for investigation, and to suggest some of the problems which arise in connection with it.

In the settlement of America we have to observe how

European life entered the continent, and how America modified and developed that life and reacted on Europe. Our early history is the study of European germs developing in an American environment. Too exclusive attention has been paid by institutional students to the Germanic origins, too little to the American factors. The frontier is the line of most rapid and effective Americanization. The wilderness masters the colonist . . . at the frontier the environment is at first too strong for the man. He must accept the conditions which it furnishes, or perish, and so he fits himself into the Indian clearings and follows the Indian trails. Little by little he transforms the wilderness, but the outcome is not the old Europe, not simply the development of Germanic germs. . . . The fact is, that here is a new product that is American. At first, the frontier was the Atlantic coast. It was the frontier of Europe in a very real sense. Moving westward, the frontier became more and more American. As successive terminal moraines result from successive glaciations, so each frontier leaves its traces behind it, and when it becomes a settled area the region still partakes of the frontier characteristics. Thus the advance of the frontier has meant a steady movement away from the influence of Europe, a steady growth of independence on American lines. And to study this advance, the men who grow up under these conditions, and the political, economic, and social results of it, is to study the really American part of our history. . . .

In these successive frontiers we find natural boundary lines which have served to mark and to affect the characteristics of the frontiers, namely: the "fall line"; the Allegheny Mountains; the Mississippi; the Missouri where its direction approximates north and south; the line of the arid lands, approximately the ninety-ninth meridian; and the Rocky Mountains. The fall line marked the frontier of the seventeenth century; the Alleghenies that of the eighteenth; the Mississippi that of the first quarter of the nineteenth; the Missouri that of the middle of this century (omitting the California movement); and the belt of the Rocky Mountains and the arid tract, the present frontier. Each was won by a series of Indian wars.

At the Atlantic frontier one can study the germs of

processes repeated at each successive frontier. We have the complex European life sharply precipitated by the wilderness into the simplicity of primitive conditions. The first frontier had to meet its Indian question, its question of the disposition of the public domain, of the means of intercourse with older settlements, of the extension of political organization, of religious and educational activity. And the settlement of these and similar questions for one frontier served as a guide for the next. The American student needs not to go to the "prim little townships of Sleswick" for illustrations of the law of continuity and development. For example, he may study the origin of our land policies in the colonial land policy; he may see how the system grew by adapting the statutes to the customs of the successive frontiers. He may see how the mining experience in the lead regions of Wisconsin, Illinois, and Iowa was applied to the mining laws of the Sierras, and how our Indian policy has been a series of experimentations on successive frontiers. Each tier of new States has found in the older ones material for its constitutions. Each frontier has made similar contributions to American characters. . . .

But with all these similarities there are essential differences, due to the place element and the time element. . . .

It would be a work worth the historian's labors to mark these various frontiers and in detail compare one with another. Not only would there result a more adequate conception of American development and characteristics, but invaluable additions would be made to the history of society.

Loria, the Italian economist, has urged the study of colonial life as an aid in understanding the stages of European development, affirming that colonial settlement is for economic science what the mountain is for geology, bringing to light primitive stratifications. "America," he says, "has the key to the historical enigma which Europe has sought for centuries in vain, and the land which has no history reveals luminously the course of universal history." There is much truth in this. The United States lies like a huge page in the history of society. Line by line as we read this continental page from West to East we find the record of social evolution. It begins with the Indian and the hunter; it goes on to tell of the disintegration of savagery by the entrance of the trader, the pathfinder of civilization; we read the annals of the pastoral stage in ranch life; the exploitation of the soil by the raising of unrotated crops of corn and wheat in sparsely settled farming communities; the intensive culture of the denser farm settlement; and finally the manufacturing organization with city and factory system. This page is familiar to the student of census statistics, but how little of it has been used by our historians. Particularly in eastern States this page is a palimpsest. What is now a manufacturing State was in an earlier decade an area of intensive farming. Earlier yet it had been a wheat area, and still earlier the "range" had attracted the cattle-herder. Thus Wisconsin, now developing manufacture, is a State with varied agricultural interests. But earlier it was given over to almost exclusive grain-raising, like North Dakota at the present time.

. . . Having now roughly outlined the various kinds of frontiers, . . . we may next inquire what were the influences on the East and on the Old World. . . .

First, we note that the frontier promoted the formation of a composite nationality for the American people. The coast was preponderantly English, but the later tides of continental immigration flowed across to the free lands. This was the case from the early colonial days. The Scotch-Irish and the Palatine Germans, or "Pennsylvania Dutch," furnished the dominant element in the stock of the colonial frontier. With these peoples were also the freed indented servants, or redemptioners, who at the expiration of their time of service passed to the frontier. . . . Very generally these redemptioners were of non-English stock. In the crucible of the frontier the immigrants were Americanized, liberated, and fused into a mixed race, English in neither nationality nor characteristics. The process has gone on from the early days to our own. Burke and other writers in the middle of the eighteenth century believed that Pennsylvania was "threatened with the danger of being wholly foreign in language, manners and perhaps even inclinations." The German and Scotch-Irish elements in the frontier of the South were only less great. In the middle of the present century the German element in Wisconsin was already so considerable that leading publicists looked to the creation of a German state out of the commonwealth by concentrating their colonization. Such examples teach us to beware of misinterpreting the fact that there is a common English speech in America into a belief that the stock is also English.

In another way the advance of the frontier decreased our dependence on England. The coast, particularly of the South, lacked diversified industries, and was dependent on England for the bulk of its supplies. In the South there was even a dependence on the Northern colonies for articles of food. . . . Before long the frontier created a demand for merchants. As it retreated from the coast it became less and less possible for England to bring her supplies directly to the consumer's wharfs, and carry away staple crops, and staple crops began to give way to diversified agriculture for a time. The effect of this phase of the frontier upon the northern section is perceived when we realize how the advance of the frontier aroused seaboard cities like Boston, New York, and Baltimore to engage in rivalry for what Washington called "the extensive and valuable trade of a rising empire."

The legislation which most developed the powers of the national government, and played the largest part in its activity, was conditioned on the frontier. Writers have discussed the subjects of tariff, land, and internal improvement, as subsidiary to the slavery question. . . . This is a wrong perspective. The pioneer needed the goods of the coast, and so the grand series of internal improvement and railroad legislation began, with potent nationalizing effects. Over internal improvements occurred great debates, in which grave constitutional questions were discussed. Sectional groupings appear in the votes, profoundly significant for the historian. Loose construction increased as the nation marched westward. But the West was not content with bringing the farm to the factory. Under the lead of Clay—"Harry of the West"—protective tariffs were passed, with the cry of bringing the factory to the farm. The disposition of the public lands was a third important subject of national legislation influenced by the frontier. . . .

It is safe to say that the legislation with regard to land, tariff, and internal improvements—the American system of the nationalizing Whig party—was conditioned on frontier ideas and needs. But it was not merely in legislative action that the frontier worked against the sectionalism of the coast. The economic and social characteristics of the frontier worked against sectionalism. The men of the frontier had closer resemblances to the Middle region than to either of the other sections. Pennsylvania had been the seed-plot of frontier emigration, and, although she passed on her settlers along the Great Valley into the west of Virginia and the Carolinas, yet the industrial society of these Southern frontiersmen was always more like that of the Middle region than like that of the tide water portion of the South, which later came to spread its industrial type throughout the South.

The Middle region, entered by New York harbor, was an open door to all Europe. The tide water part of the South represented typical Englishmen, modified by a warm climate and servile labor, and living in baronial fashion on great plantations; New England stood for a special English movement, Puritanism. The Middle region was less English than the other sections. It had a wide mixture of nationalities, a varied society, the mixed town and county system of local government, a varied economic life, many religious sects. In short, it was a region mediating between New England and the South, and the East and the West. It represented that composite nationality which the contemporary United States exhibits, that juxtaposition of non-English groups, occupying a valley or a little settlement, and presenting reflections of the map of Europe in their variety. It was democratic and non-sectional, if not national; "easy, tolerant, and contented"; rooted strongly in material prosperity. It was typical of the modern United States. It was least sectional, not only because it lay between North and South, but also because with no barriers to shut out its frontiers from its settled region, and with a system of connecting waterways, the Middle region mediated between East and West as well as between North and South. Thus it became the typically American region. Even the New Englander, who was shut out from the frontier by the Middle region, tarrying in New York or

Pennsylvania on his westward march, lost the acuteness of his sectionalism on the way.

. . . This nationalizing tendency . . . transformed the democracy of Jefferson into the national republicanism of Monroe and the democracy of Andrew Jackson. The West of the War of 1812, the West of Clay, and Benton and Harrison, and Andrew Jackson, shut off by the Middle States and the mountains from the coast sections, had a solidarity of its own with national tendencies. On the tide of the Father of Waters, North and South met and mingled into a nation. Interstate migration went steadily on—a process of cross-fertilization of ideas and institutions. The fierce struggle of the sections over slavery on the western frontier does not diminish the truth of this statement; it proves the truth of it. Slavery was a sectional trait that would not down, but in the West it could not remain sectional. It was the greatest of frontiersmen who declared: "I believe this Government can not endure permanently half slave and half free. It will become all of one thing or all of the other." Nothing works for nationalism like intercourse within the nation. Mobility of population is death to localism, and the western frontier worked irresistibly in unsettling population. The effect reached back from the frontier and affected profoundly the Atlantic coast and even the Old World.

But the most important effect of the frontier has been in the promotion of democracy here and in Europe. As has been indicated, the frontier is productive of individualism. Complex society is precipitated by the wilderness into a kind of primitive organization based on the family. The tendency is anti-social. It produces antipathy to control, and particularly to any direct control. The tax-gatherer is viewed as a representative of oppression. . . . Frontier conditions prevalent in the colonies are important factors in the explanation of the American Revolution, where individual liberty was sometimes confused with absence of all effective government. The same conditions aid in explaining the difficulty of instituting a strong government in the period of the confederacy. The frontier individualism has from the beginning promoted democracy.

The frontier States that came into the Union in the

first quarter of a century of its existence came in with democratic suffrage provisions, and had reactive effects of the highest importance upon the older States whose peoples were being attracted there. An extension of the franchise became essential. It was *western* New York that forced an extension of suffrage in the constitutional convention of that State in 1821; and it was *western* Virginia that compelled the tide water region to put a more liberal suffrage provision in the constitution framed in 1830, and to give to the frontier region a more nearly proportionate representation with the tide water aristocracy. The rise of democracy as an effective force in the nation came in with western preponderance under Jackson and William Henry Harrison, and it meant the triumph of the frontier—with all of its good and with all of its evil elements. . . .

So long as free land exists, the opportunity for a competency exists, and economic power secures political power. But the democracy born of free land, strong in selfishness and individualism, intolerant of administrative experience and education, and pressing individual liberty beyond its proper bounds, has its dangers as well as its benefits. Individualism in America has allowed a laxity in regard to governmental affairs which has rendered possible the spoils system and all the manifest evils that follow from the lack of a highly developed civic spirit. In this connection may be noted also the influence of frontier conditions in permitting lax business honor, inflated paper currency and wild-cat banking. The colonial and revolutionary frontier was the region whence emanated many of the worst forms of an evil currency. The West in the War of 1812 repeated the phenomenon on the frontier of that day, while the speculation and wild-cat banking of the period of the crisis of 1837 occurred on the new frontier belt of the next tier of States. Thus each one of the periods of lax financial integrity coincides with a period when a new set of frontier communities had arisen, and coincides in area with these successive frontiers, for the most part. The recent Populist agitation is a case in point. Many a State that now declines any connection with the tenets of the Populists, itself adhered to such ideas in an earlier stage of the development of the State. A primitive society can hardly be expected to show the intelligent appreciation of the complexity of business interests in a developed society. The continual recurrence of these areas of paper money agitation is another evidence that the frontier can be isolated and studied as a factor in American history of the highest importance. . . .

From the conditions of frontier life came intellectual traits of profound importance. The works of travelers along each frontier from colonial days onward describe certain common traits, and these traits have, while softening down, still persisted as survivals in the place of their origin, even when a higher social organization succeeded. The result is that to the frontier the American intellect owes its striking characteristics. That coarseness and strength combined with acuteness and inquisitiveness; that practical, inventive turn of mind, quick to find expedients; that masterful grasp of material things, lacking in the artistic but powerful to effect great ends; that restless, nervous energy; that dominant individualism, working for good and for evil, and withal that buoyancy and exuberance which comes with freedom—these are traits of the frontier, or traits called out elsewhere because of the existence of the frontier. Since the days when the fleet of Columbus sailed into the waters of the New World, America has been another name for opportunity, and the people of the United States have taken their tone from the incessant expansion which has not only been open but has even been forced upon them. He would be a rash prophet who would assert that the expansive character of American life has now entirely ceased. Movement has been its dominant fact, and, unless this training has no effect upon a people, the American energy will continually demand a wider field for its exercise. But never again will such gifts of free land offer themselves. For a moment, at the frontier, the bonds of custom are broken and unrestraint is triumphant. There is no *tabula rasa*. The stubborn American environment is there with its imperious summons to accept its conditions; the inherited ways of doing things are also there; and yet, in spite of environment, and in spite of custom, each frontier did indeed furnish a new field of opportunity, a gate of escape from the bondage of the past; and freshness, and confidence, and scorn of older society, impatience of its restraints and its ideas, and indifference to its lessons, have accompanied the frontier. What the Mediterranean Sea was to the Greeks, breaking the bond of custom, offering new experiences, calling out new institutions and activities, that, and more, the ever retreating frontier has been to the United States directly, and to the nations of Europe more remotely. And now, four centuries from the discovery of America, at the end of a hundred years of life under the Constitution, the frontier has gone, and with its going has closed the first period of American history.

Letter on Labor in Industrial Society, *Samuel Gompers, 1894*

You say that as you stated in your charge to the Grand Jury, you believe in labor organizations within such lawful and reasonable limits as will make them a service to the laboring man, and not a menace to the lawful institutions of the country.

I have had the pleasure of reading your charge to the Grand Jury, and have only partially been able to discover how far you believe in labor organizations. You would certainly have no objection officially or personally to workingmen organizing, and in their meetings discuss perhaps "the origin of man," benignly smiling upon each other, and declaring that all existing things are right, going to their wretched homes to find some freedom in sleep from gnawing hunger. You would have them extol the virtues of monopolists and wreckers of the people's welfare. You would not have them consider seriously the fact that more than two millions of their fellows are unemployed, and though willing and able, cannot find the opportunity to work, in order that they may sustain themselves, their wives and their children. You would not have them consider seriously the fact that Pullman who has grown so rich from the toil of his workingmen, that he can riot in luxury, while he heartlessly turns these very workmen out of their tenements into the streets and leave to the tender mercies of corporate greed. Nor would you have them ponder upon the hundreds of other Pullmans of different names.

You know, or ought to know, that the introduction of machinery is turning into idleness thousands, faster than new industries are founded, and yet, machinery certainly should not be either destroyed or hampered in its full development. The laborer is a man, he is made warm by the same sun and made cold—yes, colder—by the same winter as you are. He has a heart and brain, and feels and knows the human and paternal instinct for those depending upon him as keenly as do you.

What shall the workers do? Sit idly by and see the vast resources of nature and the human mind be utilized and monopolized for the benefit of the comparative few? No. The laborers must learn to think and act, and soon, too, that only by the power of organization, and common concert of action, can either their manhood be maintained, their rights to life (work to sustain it) be recognized, and liberty and rights secured.

Since you say that you favor labor organizations within certain limits, will you kindly give to thousands of your anxious fellow citizens what you believe the workers could and should do in their organizations to solve this great problem? Not what they should not do. You have told us that.

I am not one of those who regards the entire past as a failure. I recognize the progress made and the improved conditions of which nearly the entire civilized world are the beneficiaries. I ask you to explain, however, that if the wealth of the whole world is, as you say, "pre-eminently and beneficially the nation's wealth," how is it that thousands of able-bodied, willing, earnest men and women are suffering the pangs of hunger? We may boast of our wealth and civilization, but to the hungry man and woman and child our progress is a hollow mockery, our civilization a sham, and our "national wealth" a chimera.

You recognize that the industrial forces set in motion by steam and electricity have materially changed the structure of our civilization. You also admit that a system has grown up where the accumulations of the individual have passed from his control into that of representative combinations and trusts, and that the tendency in this direction is on the increase. How, then, can you consistently criticize the workingmen for recognizing that as individuals they can have no influence in deciding what the wages, hours of toil and conditions of employment shall be?

You evidently have observed the growth of corporate wealth and influence. You recognize that wealth, in order to become more highly productive, is concentrated into fewer hands, and controlled by representatives and directors, and yet you sing the old siren song that the workingman should depend entirely upon his own "individual effort."

The school of *laissez faire*, of which you seem to be a pronounced advocate, has produced great men in advocating the theory of each for himself, and his Satanic Majesty taking the hindermost, but the most pronounced advocates of your school of thought in economics have, when practically put to the test, been compelled to admit that combination and organization of the toiling masses are essential both to prevent the deterioration and to secure an improvement in the condition of the wage earners.

If, as you say, the success of commercial society depends upon the full play of competition, why do not you and your confreres turn your attention and direct the shafts of your attacks against the trusts and corporations, business wreckers and manipulators in the food products—the necessities of the people. Why garland your thoughts in beautiful phrase when speaking of these modern vampires, and steep your pen in gall when writing of the laborers' efforts to secure some of the advantages accruing from the concentrated thought and genius of the ages? . . .

One becomes enraptured in reading the beauty of your description of modern progress. Could you have had in mind the miners of Spring Valley or Pennsylvania, or the clothing workers of the sweat shops of New York or Chicago when you grandiloquently dilate, "Who is not rich to-day when compared with his ancestors of a century ago? The steamboat and the railroad bring to his breakfast table the coffees of Java and Brazil, the fruits from Florida and California, and the steaks from the plains. The loom arrays him in garments and the factories furnish him with a dwelling that the richest contemporaries of his grandfather would have envied. With health and industry he is a prince."

Probably you have not read within the past year of babies dying of starvation at their mothers' breasts. More than likely the thousands of men lying upon the bare stones night after night in the City Hall of Chicago last winter escaped your notice. You may not have heard of the cry for bread that was sounded through this land of plenty by thousands of honest men and women. But should these and many other painful incidents have passed you by unnoticed, I am fearful that you may learn of them with keener thoughts with the coming sleets and blasts of winter.

You say that "labor cannot afford to attack capital." Let me remind you that labor has no quarrel with capital, as such. It is merely the possessors of capital who refuse to accord to labor the recognition, the right, the justice which is the laborers' due, with whom we contend.

See what is implied by your contemptuous reference to the laborer when you ask, "Will the conqueror destroy his trophy?" Who ever heard of a conqueror marching unitedly with his *trophy,* as you would have them? But if by your comparison you mean that the conqueror is the corporation, the trust, the capitalist class, and ask then whether they would destroy their *trophy,* I would have you ask the widows and orphans of the thousands of men killed annually through the avarice of railroad corporations refusing to avail themselves of modern appliances in coupling and other improvements on their railroads.

Inquire from the thousands of women and children whose husbands or fathers were suffocated or crushed in the mines through the rapacious greed of stockholders clamoring for more dividends. Investigate the sweating dens of the large cities. Go to the mills, factories, through the country. Visit the modern tenement houses or hovels in which thousands of workers are compelled to eke out an existence. Ask these whether the conqueror (monopoly) cares whether his trophy (the laborers) is destroyed or preserved. Ascertain from employers whether the laborer is not regarded the same as a machine, thrown out as soon as all the work possible has been squeezed out of him.

Are you aware that all the legislation ever secured for the ventilation or safety of mines, factory or workshop is the result of the efforts of organized labor? Do you know that the trade unions were the shield for the seven-year-old children from being the conqueror's trophy until they become somewhat older? And that the reformatory laws now on the statute books, protecting or defending the trophies of both sexes, young and old, from the fond care of the conquerors, were wrested from Congresses, legislatures and parliaments despite the Pullmans, the Jeffries, the Ricks, the Tafts, the Williams, the Woods, or the Grosscups.

By what right, sir, do you assume that the labor organizations do not conduct their affairs within lawful limits, or that they are a menace to the lawful institutions of the country? Is it because some thoughtless or overzealous member at a time of great excitement and smarting under a wrong may violate under a law or commit an improper act? Would you apply the same rule to the churches, the other moral agencies and organizations that you do to the organizations of labor? If you did, the greatest moral force of life to-day, the trade unions, would certainly stand out the clearest, brightest and purest. Because a certain class (for which you and a number of your colleagues on the bench seem to be the special pleaders) have a monopoly in their lines of trade, I submit that this is no good reason for their claim to have a monopoly on true patriotism or respect for the lawful institutions of the country. . . .

Year by year man's liberties are trampled under foot at the bidding of corporations and trusts, rights are invaded and law perverted. In all ages wherever a tyrant has shown himself he has always found some willing judge to clothe that tyranny in the robes of legality, and modern capitalism has proven no exception to the rule.

You may not know that the labor movement as represented by the trades unions, stands for right, for justice, for liberty. You may not imagine that the issuance of an injunction depriving men of a legal as well as a natural right to protect themselves, their wives and little ones, must fail of its purpose. Repression or oppression never yet succeeded in crushing the truth or redressing a wrong.

In conclusion let me assure you that labor will organize and more compactly than ever and upon practical lines, and despite relentless antagonism, achieve for humanity a nobler manhood, a more beautiful womanhood and a happier childhood.

Atlanta Exposition Address, *Booker T. Washington, 1893*

One-third of the population of the South is of the Negro race. No enterprise seeking the material, civil, or moral welfare of this section can disregard this element of our population and reach the highest success. I but convey to you, Mr. President and Directors, the sentiment of the masses of my race when I say that in no way have the value and manhood of the American Negro been more fittingly and generously recognized than by the managers of this magnificent Exposition at every stage of its progress. It is a recognition that will do more to cement the friendship of the two races than any occurrence since the dawn of our freedom.

Not only this, but the opportunity here afforded will awaken among us a new era of industrial progress. Ignorant and inexperienced, it is not strange that in the first years of our new life we began at the top instead of at the bottom; that a seat in Congress or the state legislature was more sought than real estate or industrial skill; that the political convention or stump speaking had more attractions than starting a dairy farm or truck garden.

A ship lost at sea for many days suddenly sighted a friendly vessel. From the mast of the unfortunate vessel was seen a signal, "Water, water; we die of thirst!" The answer from the friendly vessel at once came back, "Cast down your bucket where you are." And a third and fourth signal for water was answered, "Cast down your bucket where you are." The captain of the distressed vessel, at last heeding the injunction, cast down his bucket, and it came up full of fresh, sparkling water from the mouth of the Amazon River. To those of my race who depend on bettering their condition in a foreign land or who underestimate the importance of cultivating friendly relations with the Southern white man, who is their next-door neighbour, I would say: "Cast down your bucket where you are"—cast it down in making friends in every manly way of the people of all races by whom we are surrounded.

Cast it down in agriculture, mechanics, in commerce, in domestic service, and in the professions. And in this connection it is well to bear in mind that whatever other sins the South may be called to bear, when it comes to business, pure and simple, it is in the South that the Negro is given a man's chance in the commercial world, and in nothing is this Exposition more eloquent than in emphasizing this chance. Our greatest danger is that in the great leap from slavery to freedom we may overlook the fact that the masses of us are to live by the productions of our hands, and fail to keep in mind that we shall prosper in proportion as we learn to dignify and glorify common labour and put brains and skill into the common occupations of life; shall prosper in proportion as we learn to draw the line between the superficial and the substantial, the ornamental gewgaws of life and the useful. No race can prosper till it learns that there is as much dignity in tilling a field as in writing a poem. It is at the bottom of life we must begin, and not at the top. Nor should we permit our grievances to overshadow our opportunities.

To those of the white race who look to the incoming of those of foreign birth and strange tongue and habits for the prosperity of the South, were I permitted I would repeat what I say to my own race, "Cast down your bucket where you are." Cast it down among the eight millions of Negroes whose habits you know, whose fidelity and love you have tested in days when to have proved treacherous meant the ruin of your firesides. Cast down your bucket among these people who have, without strikes and labour wars, tilled your fields, cleared your forests, builded your railroads and cities, and brought forth treasures from the bowels of the earth, and helped make possible this magnificent representation of the progress of the South. Casting down your bucket among my people, helping and encouraging them as you are doing on these grounds, and to education of head, hand, and heart, you will find that they will buy your surplus land, make blossom the waste places in your fields, and run your factories. While doing this, you can be sure in the future, as in the past, that you and your families will be surrounded by the most patient, faithful, law-abiding, and un-resentful people that the world has seen. As we have proved our loyalty to you in the past, in nursing your children, watching by the sick-bed of your mothers and fathers, and often following them with tear-dimmed eyes to their graves, so in the future, in our humble way, we shall stand by you with a devotion that no foreigner can approach, ready to lay down our lives, if need be, in defence of yours, interlacing our industrial, commercial, civil, and religious life with yours in a way that shall make the interests of both races one. In all things that are purely social we can be as separate as the fingers, yet one as the hand in all things essential to mutual progress.

There is no defence or security for any of us except in the highest intelligence and development of all. If anywhere there are efforts tending to curtail the fullest growth of the Negro, let these efforts be turned into stimulating, encouraging, and making him the most useful and intelligent citizen. Effort or means so invested will pay a thousand per cent interest. These efforts will be twice blessed—"blessing him that gives and him that takes."

There is no escape through law of man or God from the inevitable:—

> The laws of changeless justice bind
> Oppressor with oppressed;
> And close as sin and suffering joined
> We march to fate abreast.

Nearly sixteen millions of hands will aid you in pulling the load upward, or they will pull against you the load downward. We shall constitute one-third and more of the ignorance and crime of the South, or one-third its intelligence and progress; we shall contribute one-third to the business and industrial prosperity of the South, or we shall prove a veritable body of death, stagnating, depressing, retarding every effort to advance the body politic.

Gentlemen of the Exposition, as we present to you our humble effort at an exhibition of our progress, you must not expect overmuch. Starting thirty years ago with ownership here and there in a few quilts and pumpkins and chickens (gathered from miscellaneous sources), remember the path that has led from these to the inventions and production of agricultural implements, buggies, steam-engines, newspapers, books, statuary, carving, paintings, the management of drugstores and banks, has not been trodden without contact with thorns and thistles. While we take pride in what we exhibit as a result of our independent efforts, we do not for a moment forget that our part in this exhibition would fall far short of your expectations but for the constant help that has come to our educational life, not only from the Southern states, but especially from Northern philanthropists, who have made their gifts a constant stream of blessing and encouragement.

The wisest among my race understand that the agitation of questions of social equality is the extremest folly, and that progress in the enjoyment of all the privileges that will come to us must be the result of severe and constant struggle rather than of artificial forcing. No race that has anything to contribute to the markets of the world is long in any degree ostracized. It is important and right that all privileges of the law be ours, but it is vastly more important that we be prepared for the exercises of these privileges. The opportunity to earn a dollar in a factory just now is worth infinitely more than the opportunity to spend a dollar in an opera-house.

In conclusion, may I repeat that nothing in thirty years has given us more hope and encouragement, and drawn us so near to you of the white race, as this opportunity offered by the Exposition; and here bending, as it were, over the altar that represents the results of the struggles of your race and mine, both starting practically empty-handed three decades ago, I pledge that in your effort to work out the great and intricate problem which God has laid at the doors of the South, you shall have at all times the patient, sympathetic help of my race; only let this be constantly in mind, that, while from representations in these buildings of the product of field, of forest, of mine, of factory, letters, and art, much good will come, yet far above and beyond material benefits will be that higher good, that, let us pray God, will come, in a blotting out of sectional differences and racial animosities and suspicions, in a determination to administer absolute justice, in a willing obedience among all classes to the mandates of law. This, this, coupled with our material prosperity, will bring into our beloved South a new heaven and a new earth.

Chapter 18

GRASSROOTS REBELLION

Although industrial capitalism and its laissez-faire business ethic largely dominated American life and thought throughout the last half of the nineteenth century, protest and nonconformity were not unknown. Indeed, America had hardly embarked upon her great Age of Enterprise when reformers and militant protesters emerged to challenge her formidable new overlords, the mighty captains of industry and their political henchmen. But protest was amorphous and ill-defined, and as the political and economic abuses that accompanied industrialization became more pronounced, Americans were confronted with a bewildering array of reform movements that in principle and practice differed radically among themselves. At one extreme, under the leadership of E. L. Godkin of the *Nation* and George William Curtis of *Harper's Weekly*, a small group of aristocratic eastern intellectuals devoted themselves almost entirely to immediate political reform, proposing simply an extensive civil service and high public morals to redress the rank corruption that permeated every level of American government. Though appalled at the abject materialism of America's new business civilization, these good-government leaders (contemptuous politicos dubbed them "goo-goos") seemed totally unaware of the close connection between political corruption and the abusive business practices of unfettered, competitive industrialism, and they inveterately shunned any suggestion of governmental interference in the economic life of the nation. At the opposite extreme were groups of radical reformers who as consistently refused to work within the existing framework of laissez-faire industrial capitalism. Thus Marxian Socialists, Single-Taxers who championed the confiscatory single tax on unearned land values that Henry George urged in his widely read *Progress and Poverty,* and Nationalists who were inspired by Edward Bellamy's popular novel of utopian totalitarianism, *Looking Backward,* all proposed basic economic reforms that would utilize the full coercive power of the State to root out the poverty, inequality, and insecurity that had been fostered by America's economic revolution.

But the most significant and widespread area of discontent and protest in the post-Civil War period was agrarian in origin and orientation, and the American farmer seemed determined to steer a middle course between "goo-goos" and radicals. Like the civil service reformer, the farmer avoided long-range considerations of social planning and control, and he had no direct purpose to abandon free enterprise capitalism. Like his radical contemporaries, however, he was fully prepared to attain immediate objectives through State action, and throughout the period his angry cries for governmental intervention to secure economic and political reform seriously threatened and frightened the industrial ruling class.

Nor were the farmer's demands for reform without cause. Constantly subjected to the vicissitudes of drought and storm—and market—the farm population was in many ways even more deprived than the propertyless workers who crowded into the city. For as the farmer continued his barren, isolated, and culturally impoverished life, rural areas lagged far behind in the enjoyment of a higher standard of living, and the benefits of the industrial revolution seemed largely confined to the rapidly growing cities. Agriculture suffered a particularly severe depression during the thirty years before 1897, and the farmer's economic situation had grown increasingly more desperate as his costs mounted and prices for farm products tumbled. Cotton that cost 6 or 7 cents per pound to produce sold for 4 or 5 cents, while wheat that had brought $1.45 per bushel at the end of the Civil War brought 49 cents thirty years later, and corn that sold for 75 cents in 1869 fell to 28 cents in 1889. Crushed between minimal farm prices and the intolerable burden of debts assumed in prosperous, expansive years, it was the oppressed and disgruntled farmer who spearheaded America's crusade for reform.

Fundamentally, declining farm prices and income were due to a vastly increased competition of farm products on the world market and to the overexpansion of agriculture that had taken place during the Civil War. In assaying his plight, however, the farmer almost invariably attributed hard times to an inadequate money supply and to the immediate, tangible abuses he suffered at the hands of his economic masters, the railroads and the banks. Against the railroads his grievances were real enough. The carriers not only charged the farmer exorbitant rates that frequently took the value of one bushel of wheat or corn to pay the freight on another, but through rebates and other secret agreements they viciously discriminated against him in favor of larger and wealthier shippers. The bankers, too, as money became scarcer, as interest rates on loans and mortgages soared, and as foreclosures multiplied, seemed the farmer's mortal enemies. As one Nebraska farm editor lamented, "We have three crops—corn, freight rates, and interest. The farmers farm the land, and the businessmen farm the farmers."

These, then, were the embattled farmer's "devils," and the Granger laws of the 1870's and 1880's represented his early attempts to wield the power of government against their evil practices. Commonly known as the Grange, the Patrons of Husbandry had been founded in 1867 primarily as a social organization. But by the 1870's, when its members numbered one and a half million, agrarian distress and discontent had been so intensified that inevitably the Granger movement assumed political proportions. Rousing themselves to enormous political activity, in many Western states the Grangers elected large delegations of farm representatives to state legislatures that now for the first time subjected the railroads to stringent public control.

Typically the Granger laws established state railroad commissions to set fair rates and to abolish discrimination between small and large shippers, and for some years—in 1876 the Supreme Court upheld their validity in Munn v. Illinois—they encountered no insurmountable constitutional barriers. But in the famous Wabash case of 1886 the Supreme Court reversed its earlier position and initiated a series of judicial decisions that for all practical purposes ended effective state regulation. Holding that the railroads were interstate enterprises beyond state control, and that state regulatory acts violated the "due process" clause of the 14th Amendment ("No State shall . . . deprive any person of life, liberty, or property, without due process of law"), in case after case the judges declared against the constitutionality of Granger legislation. By the 1890's, then, through severe limitations on the states' "police" powers, the high court had effectually nullified two decades of agrarian efforts to secure economic democracy.

Rebuffed by a conservative judiciary in these first steps towards relief and reform, the embattled farmer turned next to the national government. In response to a great wave of indignation that followed the Wabash case, Congress passed the Interstate Commerce Act of 1887, outlawing such railroad abuses as rebates, preferential rates, and pooling agreements that eliminated effective competition among the carriers. At the same time an Interstate Commerce Commission was created to investigate and prosecute violations of the new law. Then in 1890, in part as a further concession to farmers who attributed their higher living costs to monopolies and trusts, the Sherman Antitrust Act declared illegal "every contract, combination . . . or conspiracy in restraint of trade." Superficially the farmers seemed to have accomplished a great deal, for Congress had at least filled the legislative void left by the Court's denial of state powers and had taken an important initial step towards Federal regulation of industry. Yet, because of continued judicial opposition and legislative as well as administrative indifference, both of these acts proved ineffectual. Not only did Congress fail to grant to the Interstate Commerce Commission the essential power to fix rates, but consistently adverse judicial interpretations of the law tended to restrict whatever statutory power the Commission did possess. Similarly, enforcement of the Sherman Act was hampered by a hostile judiciary—in 1895 the Supreme Court ruled that the Sugar Trust's control of ninety-five percent of the nation's sugar refining did *not* constitute a violation of the anti-trust law—and particularly by the lack of any real enthusiasm on the part of Democratic and Republican politicians alike for a vigorous campaign against the trusts.

Essentially the leaders of both major parties were unsympathetic to agrarian needs and demands, and the farmer quickly concluded that little was to be accomplished within the framework of a do-nothing two-party system. Quadrennially the parties performed their traditional political rituals: "ins" solemnly met to "point with pride" at their record in office, while "outs" noisily assembled to "view with alarm" the same four years. But basic issues were only occasionally debated and even the personalities around whom the heated campaigns raged were generally undistinguished and lacking in important political principle. Thus the stage seemed set for a party of revolt, and for some years before the decisive election of 1896 angry Western and Southern farmers rallied together under the banner of Populism to "raise less corn and more Hell." Earlier third-party movements, such as the Greenback party, had failed to make any appreciable impression on American political life, but these first local Populist groups achieved considerable success in the state and Congressional elections of 1890. And on July 4, 1892, their representatives met at Omaha, Nebraska, to organize a national People's party and to formulate the decisive Omaha platform that, appropriate to the date, was to serve as the farmer's Declaration of Independence.

Polling more than a million popular votes, and obtaining 22 votes in the electoral college for General James B. Weaver of Iowa, the Populist party made a spectacular showing in the Presidential election of 1892. In the off-year elections of 1894, when a widespread depression that followed the Panic of 1893 had convinced even greater numbers of dissatisfied farmers and laborers to desert the conservative older parties, the Populists repeated these astounding triumphs. Obviously the Populist Revolt had attained serious proportions, and the nation anxiously awaited the Presidential election of 1896, when Democrats and Republicans must either succumb to agrarian and labor demands for reform or battle to preserve the *status quo*. The issue was clear-cut, for protest had already been largely focused on the money question. Since the Civil War, debtor farmers had persistently advocated an expanded money supply as an inflationary measure to raise farm prices and relieve farm distress. Now the farmer almost entirely subordinated his other demands to the cry for "free silver": currency expansion through the free and unlimited coinage of silver as well as gold.

Thoroughly dominated by conservative "hard-money" men, in 1896 the Republicans nominated Governor William McKinley of Ohio for the Presidency, and adopted a platform that defiantly took up the Populist challenge, declaring unequivocally for the Gold Standard and for the entire economic and political structure to which agrarian and labor dissenters took such violent exception. The Democrats, too, had their share of conservative "Gold Bugs," among whom they numbered the incumbent President, Grover Cleveland. But when the party met to choose a platform and a Presidential candidate, it was controlled instead by reform groups who repudiated Cleveland, adopted much of the Populist platform of 1892, and rallied around the magnificent William Jennings Bryan, whose stirring "Cross of Gold" speech helped win the party to the cause of silver and the Democratic nomination for the "Boy Orator." Later the Populists also nominated Bryan as their candidate and the choice before the American people was clear: McKinley, the "advance agent of prosperity," was the candidate of business and conservatism, while Bryan spoke for the farmer, the laborer, and the underprivileged classes generally in their efforts to put the Government of the United States once again at the service of all of the American people.

Supported by most of the nation's great industries under the generalship of the fabulous Mark ("Dollar Mark") Hanna, McKinley won in an exceedingly bitter campaign that was marred by vicious attacks upon Bryan and his followers as "fanatics," "communists," and "revolutionaries." Of course Populism was not "revolutionary" in Marxian terms, for the farmer had no intention of destroying fundamental American political and economic institutions. Indeed, within a few decades both major parties had adopted a substantial portion of the Populist demands and the threat of a formidable third party disappeared altogether. Yet in 1896 a successful Bryan would have made strenuous efforts to alter the tone and orientation of the national government from an industrial to an agrarian bias. Besides, the Populist insistence that government extend its authority to protect the interests of all the people had a strong influence on the development of contemporary conceptions of the proper role of the State. And, although farm agitation diminished after 1897 with the return of prosperity and the rise of farm prices, ultimately the real significance of the Populist Revolt can best be measured in terms of the important inroads the social, economic, and political reforms of the twentieth century have made upon the abuses against which the farmer battled so desperately in the last decades of the nineteenth century.

The Populist Party Platform, *1892*

Assembled upon the 116th anniversary of the Declaration of Independence, the People's Party of America, in their first national convention, invoking upon their action the blessing of Almighty God, put forth in the name and on behalf of the people of this country, the following preamble and declaration of principles:

Preamble

The conditions which surround us best justify our cooperation; we meet in the midst of a nation brought to the verge of moral, political, and material ruin. Corruption dominates the ballot-box, the legislatures, the Congress, and touches even the ermine of the bench. The people are demoralized; most of the States have been compelled to isolate the voters at the polling places to prevent universal intimidation and bribery. The newspapers are largely subsidized or muzzled, public opinion silenced, business prostrated, homes covered with mortgages, labor impoverished, and the land concentrated in the hands of capitalists. The urban workmen are denied the right to organize for self-protection, imported pauperized labor beats down their wages, a hireling standing army, unrecognized by our laws, is established to shoot them down, and they are rapidly degenerating into European conditions. The fruits of the toil of millions are boldly stolen to build up colossal fortunes for a few, unprecedented in the history of mankind; and the possessors of those, in turn, despise the Republic and endanger liberty. From the same prolific womb of governmental injustice we breed the two great classes—tramps and millionaires.

The national power to create money is appropriated to enrich bondholders; a vast public debt payable in legal tender currency has been funded into gold-bearing bonds, thereby adding millions to the burdens of the people.

Silver, which has been accepted as coin since the dawn of history, has been demonetized to add to the purchasing power of gold by decreasing the value of all forms of property as well as human labor, and the supply of currency is purposely abridged to fatten usurers, bankrupt enterprise, and enslave industry. A vast conspiracy against mankind has been organized on two continents, and it is rapidly taking possession of the world. If not met and overthrown at once it forebodes terrible social convulsions, the destruction of civilization, or the establishment of an absolute despotism.

We have witnessed for more than a quarter of a century the struggles of the two great political parties for power and plunder, while grievous wrongs have been inflicted upon the suffering people. We charge that the controlling influences dominating both these parties have permitted the existing dreadful conditions to develop without serious effort to prevent or restrain them. Neither do they now promise us any substantial reform. They have agreed together to ignore, in the coming campaign, every issue but one. They propose to drown the outcries of a plundered people with the uproar of a sham battle over the tariff, so that capitalists, corporations, national banks, rings, trusts, watered stock, the demonetization of silver and the oppressions of the usurers may all be lost sight of. They propose to sacrifice our homes, lives, and children on the altar of mammon; to destroy the multitude in order to secure corruption funds from the millionaires.

Assembled on the anniversary of the birthday of the nation, and filled with the spirit of the grand general and chief who established our independence, we seek to restore the government of the Republic to the hands of "the plain people," with which class it originated. We assert our purposes to be identical with the purposes of the National Constitution; to form a more perfect union and establish justice, insure domestic tranquillity, provide for the common defence, promote the general welfare, and secure the blessings of liberty for ourselves and our posterity.

We declare that this Republic can only endure as a free government while built upon the love of the whole people for each other and for the nation; that it cannot be pinned together by bayonets; that the Civil War is over, and that every passion and resentment which grew out of it must die with it, and that we must be in fact, as we are in name, one united brotherhood of free men.

Our country finds itself confronted by conditions for which there is no precedent in the history of the world; our annual agricultural productions amount to billions of dollars in value, which must, within a few weeks or months, be exchanged for billions of dollars' worth of commodities consumed in their production; the existing currency supply is wholly inadequate to make this exchange; the results are falling prices, the formation of combines and rings, the impoverishment of the producing class. We pledge ourselves that if given power we will labor to correct these evils by wise and reasonable legislation, in accordance with the terms of our platform.

We believe that the power of government—in other words, of the people—should be expanded (as in the case of the postal service) as rapidly and as far as the good sense of an intelligent people and the teachings of experience shall justify, to the end that oppression, injustice, and poverty shall eventually cease in the land.

While our sympathies as a party of reform are naturally upon the side of every proposition which will tend to make men intelligent, virtuous, and temperate, we nevertheless regard these questions, important as they are, as secondary to the great issues now pressing for solution, and upon which not only our individual prosperity but the very existence of free institutions depend; and we ask all men to first help us to determine whether we are to have a republic to administer before we differ as to the conditions upon which it is to be administered, believing that the forces of reform this day organized will never cease to move forward until every wrong is remedied and equal rights and equal privileges securely established for all the men and women of this country.

PLATFORM

We declare, therefore:

First.—That the union of the labor forces of the United States this day consummated shall be permanent and perpetual; may its spirit enter into all hearts for the salvation of the Republic and the uplifting of mankind.

Second.—Wealth belongs to him who creates it, and every dollar taken from industry without an equivalent is robbery. "If any will not work, neither shall he eat." The interests of rural and civic labor are the same; their enemies are identical.

Third.—We believe that the time has come when the railroad corporations will either own the people or the people must own the railroads, and should the Government enter upon the work of owning and managing all railroads, we should favor an amendment to the Constitution by which all persons engaged in the Government service shall be placed under a civil service regulation of the most rigid character, so as to prevent the increase of the power of the national administration by the use of such additional Government employees.

Finance.—We demand a national currency, safe, sound, and flexible, issued by the general Government only, a full legal tender for all debts, public and private, and that without the use of banking corporations, a just, equitable, and efficient means of distribution direct to the people, at a tax not to exceed 2 per cent per annum, to be provided as set forth in the sub-treasury plan of the Farmers' Alliance, or a better system; also by payments in discharge of its obligations for public improvements.

1. We demand free and unlimited coinage of silver and gold at the present legal ratio of 16 to 1.

2. We demand that the amount of circulating medium be speedily increased to not less than $50 per capita.

3. We demand a graduated income tax.

4. We believe that the money of the country should be kept as much as possible in the hands of the people, and hence we demand that all State and national revenues shall be limited to the necessary expenses of the Government, economically and honestly administered.

5. We demand that postal savings banks be established by the Government for the safe deposit of the earnings of the people and to facilitate exchange.

Transportation.—Transportation being a means of exchange and a public necessity, the Government should own and operate the railroads in the interest of the people. The telegraph, telephone, like the post-office system, being a necessity for the transmission of news, should be owned and operated by the Government in the interest of the people.

Land.—The land, including all the natural resources of wealth, is the heritage of the people, and should not be monopolized for speculative purposes, and alien ownership of land should be prohibited. All land now held by railroads and other corporations in excess of their actual needs, and all lands now owned by aliens should be reclaimed by the Government and held for actual settlers only.

Expression of Sentiments

Your Committee on Platform and Resolutions beg leave unanimously to report the following:

Whereas, Other questions have been presented for our consideration, we hereby submit the following, not as a part of the Platform of the People's Party, but as resolutions expressive of the sentiment of this Convention:

1. *Resolved,* That we demand a free ballot and a fair count in all elections, and pledge ourselves to secure

it to every legal voter without Federal intervention, through the adoption by the States of the unperverted Australian or secret ballot system.

2. *Resolved,* That the revenue derived from a graduated income tax should be applied to the reduction of the burden of taxation now levied upon the domestic industries of this country.

3. *Resolved,* That we pledge our support to fair and liberal pensions to ex-Union soldiers and sailors.

4. *Resolved,* That we condemn the fallacy of protecting American labor under the present system, which opens our ports to the pauper and criminal classes of the world and crowds out our wage-earners; and we denounce the present ineffective laws against contract labor, and demand the further restriction of undesirable emigration.

5. *Resolved,* That we cordially sympathize with the efforts of organized workingmen to shorten the hours of labor, and demand a rigid enforcement of the existing eight-hour law on Government work, and ask that a penalty clause be added to the said law.

6. *Resolved,* That we regard the maintenance of a large standing army of mercenaries, known as the Pinkerton system, as a menace to our liberties, and we demand its abolition; and we condemn the recent invasion of the Territory of Wyoming by the hired assassins of plutocracy, assisted by Federal officers.

7. *Resolved,* That we commend to the favorable consideration of the people and the reform press the legislative system known as the initiative and referendum.

8. *Resolved,* That we favor a constitutional provision limiting the office of President and Vice-President to one term, and providing for the election of Senators of the United States by a direct vote of the people.

9. *Resolved,* That we oppose any subsidy or national aid to any private corporation for any purpose.

10. *Resolved,* That this convention sympathizes with the Knights of Labor and their righteous contest with the tyrannical combine of clothing manufacturers of Rochester, and declare it to be the duty of all who hate tyranny and oppression to refuse to purchase the goods made by the said manufacturers, or to patronize any merchants who sell such goods.

"Cross of Gold" Speech,*
William Jennings Bryan, 1896

I would be presumptuous, indeed, to present myself against the distinguished gentlemen to whom you have listened if this were a mere measuring of abilities; but this is not a contest between persons. The humblest citizen in all the land, when clad in the armor of a righteous cause, is stronger than all the hosts of error. I come to speak to you in defense of a cause as holy as the cause of liberty—the cause of humanity.

When this debate is concluded, a motion will be made to lay upon the table the resolution offered in commendation of the administration, and also the resolution offered in condemnation of the administration. We object to bringing this question down to the level of persons. The individual is but an atom; he is born, he acts, he dies; but principles are eternal; and this has been a contest over a principle.

Never before in the history of this country has there been witnessed such a contest as that through which we have just passed. Never before in the history of American politics has a great issue been fought out as this issue has been, by the voters of a great party. On the fourth of March 1895 a few Democrats, most of them members of Congress, issued an address to the Democrats of the nation, asserting that the money question was the paramount issue of the hour; declaring that a majority of the Democratic party had the right to control the action of the party on this paramount issue; and concluding with the request that the believers in the free coinage of silver in the Democratic party should organize, take charge of, and control the policy of the Democratic party. Three months later, at Memphis, an organization was perfected, and the silver Democrats went forth openly and courageously proclaiming their belief, and declaring that, if successful, they would crystallize into a platform the declaration which they had made. Then began the conflict. With a zeal approaching the zeal which inspired the crusaders who followed

*Reprinted from *Speeches of William Jennings Bryan*. Copyright 1909. Used by permission of Funk & Wagnalls Company.

Peter the Hermit, our silver Democrats went forth from victory unto victory until they are now assembled, not to discuss, not to debate, but to enter up the judgment already rendered by the plain people of this country. In this contest brother has been arrayed against brother, father against son. The warmest ties of love, acquaintance and association have been disregarded; old leaders have been cast aside when they have refused to give expression to the sentiments of those whom they would lead, and new leaders have sprung up to give direction to this cause of truth. Thus has the contest been waged, and we have assembled here under as binding and solemn instructions as were ever imposed upon representatives of the people.

We do not come as individuals. As individuals we might have been glad to compliment the gentleman from New York, but we know that the people for whom we speak would never be willing to put him in a position where he could thwart the will of the Democratic party. I say it was not a question of persons; it was a question of principle, and it is not with gladness, my friends, that we find ourselves brought into conflict with those who are now arrayed on the other side.

The gentleman who preceded me spoke of the State of Massachusetts; let me assure him that not one present in all this convention entertains the least hostility to the people of the State of Massachusetts, but we stand here representing people who are the equals, before the law, of the greatest citizens in the State of Massachusetts. When you come before us and tell us that we are about to disturb your business interests, we reply that you have disturbed our business interests by your course.

We say to you that you have made the definition of a business man too limited in its application. The man who is employed for wages is as much a business man as his employer, the attorney in a country town is as much a business man as the corporation counsel in a great metropolis; the merchant at the cross-roads store is as much a business man as the merchant of New York; the farmer who goes forth in the morning and toils all day—who begins in the spring and toils all summer—and who by the application of brain and muscle to the natural resources of the country creates wealth, is as much a business man as the man who goes upon the board of trade and bets upon the price of grain; the miners who go down a thousand feet into the earth, or climb two thousand feet upon the cliffs, and bring forth from their hiding places the precious metals to be poured into the channels of trade are as much business men as the few financial magnates who, in a back room, corner the money of the world. We come to speak for this broader class of business men.

Ah, my friends, we say not one word against those who live upon the Atlantic coast, but the hardy pioneers who have braved all the dangers of the wilderness, who have made the desert to blossom as the rose—the pioneers away out there [pointing to the West], who rear their children near to Nature's heart, where they can mingle their voices with the voices of the birds—out there where they have erected schoolhouses for the education of their young, churches where they praise their Creator, and cemeteries where rest the ashes of their dead—these people, we say, are as deserving of the consideration of our party as any people in this country. It is for these that we speak. We do not come as aggressors. Our war is not a war of conquest; we are fighting in the defense of our homes, our families, and posterity. We have petitioned, and our petitions have been scorned; we have entreated, and our entreaties have been disregarded; we have begged, and they have mocked when our calamity came. We beg no longer; we entreat no more; we petition no more. We defy them.

The gentleman from Wisconsin has said that he fears a Robespierre. My friends, in this land of the free you need not fear that a tyrant will spring up from among the people. What we need is an Andrew Jackson to stand, as Jackson stood, against the encroachments of organized wealth.

They tell us that this platform was made to catch votes. We reply to them that changing conditions make new issues; that the principles upon which Democracy rests are as everlasting as the hills, but that they must be applied to new conditions as they arise. Conditions have arisen, and we are here to meet these conditions. They tell us that the income tax ought not to be brought in here; that it is a new idea. They criticize us for our criticism of the Supreme Court of the United States. My friends, we have not criticized; we have simply called attention to what you already know. If you want criticisms, read the dissenting opinions of the court. There you will find criticisms. They say that we passed an unconstitutional law; we deny it. The income tax law was not unconstitutional when it was passed; it was not unconstitutional when it went before the Supreme Court for the first time; it did not become unconstitutional until one of the judges changed his mind, and we cannot be expected to know when a judge will change his mind. The income tax is just. It simply intends to put the burdens of government justly upon the backs of the people. I am in favor of an income tax. When I find a man who is not willing to bear his share of the burdens of the government which protects him, I find a man who is unworthy to enjoy the blessings of a government like ours.

They say that we are opposing national bank currency; it is true. If you will read what Thomas Benton said, you will find he said that, in searching history, he could find but one parallel to Andrew Jackson; that was Cicero, who destroyed the conspiracy of Cataline and saved Rome. Benton said that Cicero only did for Rome what Jackson did for us when he destroyed the bank conspiracy and saved America. We say in our platform that we believe that the right to coin and issue money is a function of government. We believe it. We believe that it is a part of sovereignty, and can no more with safety be delegated to private individuals than we could afford to delegate to private individuals the power to make penal statutes or levy taxes. Mr. Jefferson, who was once regarded as good Democratic authority, seems to have differed in opinion from the gentleman who has addressed us on the part of the minority. Those who are opposed to this proposition tell us that the issue of paper money is a function of the bank, and that the Government ought to go out of the banking business. I stand with Jefferson rather than with them, and tell them, as he did, that the issue of money is a function of government, and that the banks ought to go out of the governing business.

They complain about the plank which declares against

life tenure in office. They have tried to strain it to mean that which it does not mean. What we oppose by that plank is the life tenure which is being built up in Washington, and which excludes from participation in official benefits the humbler members of society.

Let me call your attention to two or three important things. The gentleman from New York says that he will propose an amendment to the platform providing that the proposed change in our monetary system shall not affect contracts already made. Let me remind you that there is no intention of affecting those contracts which according to present laws are made payable in gold; but if he means to say that we cannot change our monetary system without protecting those who have loaned money before the change was made, I desire to ask him where, in law or in morals, he can find justification for not protecting the debtors when the act of 1873 was passed, if he now insists that we must protect the creditors.

He says he will also propose an amendment which will provide for the suspension of free coinage if we fail to maintain the parity within a year. We reply that when we advocate a policy which we believe will be successful, we are not compelled to raise a doubt as to our own sincerity by suggesting what we shall do if we fail. I ask him, if he would apply his logic to us, why he does not apply it to himself. He says he wants this country to try to secure an international agreement. Why does he not tell us what he is going to do if he fails to secure an international agreement? There is more reason for him to do that than there is for us to provide against the failure to maintain the parity. Our opponents have tried for twenty years to secure an international agreement, and those are waiting for it most patiently who do not want it at all.

And now, my friends, let me come to the paramount issue. If they ask us why it is that we say more on the money question than we say upon the tariff question, I reply that, if protection has slain its thousands, the gold standard has slain its tens of thousands. If they ask us why we do not embody in our platform all the things that we believe in, we reply that when we have restored the money of the Constitution all other necessary reforms will be possible; but that until this is done there is no other reform that can be accomplished.

Why is it that within three months such a change has come over the country? Three months ago, when it was confidently asserted that those who believe in the gold standard would frame our platform and nominate our candidates, even the advocates of the gold standard did not think that we could elect a President. And they had good reason for their doubt, because there is scarcely a State here today asking for the gold standard which is not in the absolute control of the Republican party. But note the change. Mr. McKinley was nominated at St. Louis upon a platform which declared for the maintenance of the gold standard until it can be changed into bimetalism by international agreement. Mr. McKinley was the most popular man among the Republicans, and three months ago everybody in the Republican party prophesied his election. How is it today? Why, the man who was once pleased to think that he looked like Napoleon, that man shudders today when he remembers that he was nominated on the anniversary of the battle of Waterloo. Not only that, but as he listens he can hear with ever-increasing distinctness the sound of the waves as they beat upon the lonely shores of St. Helena.

Why this change? Ah, my friends, is not the reason for the change evident to any one who will look at the matter? No private character, however pure, no personal popularity, however great, can protect from the avenging wrath of an indignant people a man who will declare that he is in favor of fastening the gold standard upon this country, or who is willing to surrender the right of self-government and place the legislative control of our affairs in the hands of foreign potentates and powers.

We go forth confident that we shall win. Why? Because upon the paramount issue of this campaign there is not a spot of ground upon which the enemy will dare to challenge battle. If they tell us that the gold standard is a good thing, we shall point to their platform and tell them that their platform pledges the party to get rid of the gold standard and substitute bimetalism. If the gold standard is a good thing, why try to get rid of it? I call your attention to the fact that some of the very people who are in this convention today and who tell us that we ought to declare in favor of international bimetalism—thereby declaring that the gold standard is wrong and that the principle of bimetalism is better—these very people four months ago were open and avowed advocates of the gold standard, and were then telling us that we could not legislate two metals together, even with the aid of all the world. If the gold standard is a good thing, we ought to declare in favor of its retention and not in favor of abandoning it; and if the gold standard is a bad thing why should we wait until other nations are willing to help us to let go? Here is the line of battle, and we care not upon which issue they force the fight; we are prepared to meet them on either issue or on both. If they tell us that the gold standard is the standard of civilization, we reply to them that this, the most enlightened of all the nations of the earth, has never declared for a gold standard and that both the great parties this year are declaring against it. If the gold standard is the standard of civilization, why, my friends, should we not have it? If they come to meet us on that issue we can present the history of our nation. More than that; we can tell them that they will search the pages of history in vain to find a single instance where the common people of any land have ever declared themselves in favor of the gold standard. They can find where the holders of fixed investments have declared for a gold standard, but not where the masses have.

Mr. Carlisle said in 1878 that this was a struggle between "the idle holders of idle capital" and "the struggling masses, who produce the wealth and pay the taxes of the country"; and, my friends, the question we are to decide is: Upon which side will the Democratic party fight; upon the side of "the idle holders of idle capital" or upon the side of "the struggling masses"? That is the question which the party must answer first, and then it must be answered by each individual hereafter. The sympathies of the Democratic party, as shown by the platform, are on the side of the struggling masses who have ever been the foundation of the Democratic party. There are two ideas of government. There are those who believe that, if you will only legislate to make the well-to-do prosperous, their prosperity will leak through on those below. The Democratic idea, however, has been that if you legislate to make the masses prosperous, their prosperity will find its way up through every class which rests upon them.

You come to us and tell us that the great cities are in favor of the gold standard; we reply that the great cities rest upon our broad and fertile prairies. Burn down your cities and leave our farms, and your cities will spring up again as if by magic; but destroy our farms and the grass will grow in the streets of every city in the country.

My friends, we declare that this nation is able to legislate for its own people on every question, without waiting for the aid or consent of any other nation on earth; and upon that issue we expect to carry every State in the Union. I shall not slander the inhabitants of the fair State of Massachusetts nor the inhabitants of the State of New York by saying that, when they are confronted with the proposition, they will declare that this nation is not able to attend to its own business. It is the issue of 1776 over again. Our ancestors, when but three millions in number, had the courage to declare their political independence of every other nation; shall we, their descendants, when we have grown to seventy millions, declare that we are less independent than our forefathers? No, my friends, that will never be the verdict of our people. Therefore, we care not upon what lines the battle is fought. If they say bimetalism is good, but that we cannot have it until other nations help us, we reply that, instead of having a gold standard because England has, we will restore bimetalism, and then let England have bimetalism because the United States has it. If they dare to come out in the open field and defend the gold standard as a good thing, we will fight them to the uttermost. Having behind us the producing masses of this nation and the world, supported by the commercial interests, the laboring interests, and the toilers everywhere, we will answer their demand for a gold standard by saying to them: You shall not press down upon the brow of labor this crown of thorns, you shall not crucify mankind upon a cross of gold.

Chapter 19

IMPERIAL AMERICA

America's late-nineteenth-century venture in imperialism marked a decisive turning point in the nation's history. A vigorous and rather flamboyant expansionism had long characterized American foreign policy, but with the major exception of Alaska (purchased in 1867) this earlier expansion had been into contiguous rather than outlying territories, and new lands had all eventually been admitted to the Union with rights and privileges equal to those of older states. Besides, these coveted regions were generally sparsely populated and presented neither the serious problem of assimilation of native cultures nor the need for a burdensome bureaucracy to administer the affairs of subject colonial peoples. To the expansionists of the 1890's, however, the vision of America's "Manifest Destiny" was not limited to continental shores alone. As the passing of the frontier and the rounding out of the nation's furthermost boundaries signaled the final conquest of the continent, many Americans eagerly turned their eyes outward to champion a "large policy" for the republic. On every hand they were urged to recognize the "Mission of America" to carry the benefits and blessings of an advanced civilization to their numerous less fortunate brethren in the backward areas of the world, particularly the Far East and the Caribbean. Such plans for overseas expansion had been put before the American public before, but not until this last decade of the nineteenth century were most Americans convinced that their nation's destiny was inextricably bound up in securing, civilizing, humanizing, "sanitizing," Christianizing, and maintaining overseas possessions. In short, in the nineties Americans were finally to assume what Rudyard Kipling had called "the white man's burden"—and incidentally to acquire a vast colonial empire.

America's new willingness, or need, to assert herself imperially was probably connected very closely with the rapid development of industrial capitalism. For thirty years since the end of the Civil War an expanding, dynamic capitalism had safely and profitably engaged the nation in domestic projects of imperial proportions. A widespread network of railroads had spanned the continent; the Trans-Mississippi West had been thoroughly explored and colonized; the nation's vast natural resources, the raw materials of a factory civilization, had been thoroughly exploited; and great industrial empires had been created to serve an ever-expanding domestic market. But by the 1890's American industry was producing a surplus over what the domestic market, with purchasing power at the prevailing low level, could absorb; manufacturers were seeking supplies of certain raw materials that were not produced domestically; and business leaders generally were complaining that internal investment in an already well developed nation no longer provided the fantastic opportunities for profit of earlier decades. Now the business community turned its attention and energies to investments abroad, and American capital poured first into Hawaii and Cuba, and then at the turn of the century into other distant, underdeveloped areas of the world. Inevitably the flag followed the dollar, and foreign trade and investments brought extensive overseas possessions and protectorates in their wake. Then a large navy was deemed necessary to protect new possessions or "spheres of influence," and more island bases were sought to service this far-flung navy; and so the imperial circle went, ever widening. Nor was the imperialist pattern unfamiliar. For England, France, Germany, and several lesser nations had long since joined in bitter rivalry for the raw materials, the markets, and the investment potentials of the "uncivilized" world. America was merely a belated participant in the scramble for empire.

These overseas ventures were not, however, motivated by economic drives alone, and the expansionism of the nineties is to be explained less in terms of economic interests forcing a pliant government's hand than of intellectual and particularly emotional forces that gripped the entire nation. Indeed, the most blatant example of

American aggressiveness, the Spanish-American War of 1898, was emphatically popular in origin and was waged despite the vehement objections of the larger portion of the business community. At the end of the brief war, when the spoils were well in hand and popular enthusiasm had already carried America well along the path to empire, businessmen were quick to make the nation's new possessions economically advantageous, and in the twentieth century their concern for profit considerably influenced America's imperial plans. But business had for the most part opposed the coming of war at the very moment that "jingoes" and the "yellow press" were making much of the nation's psychological readiness for aggression to whip up explosive feelings against Spanish misrule in Cuba.

Thus the tempo of acquisition quickened for reasons more deeply rooted in popular feeling than in private greed, and every bellicose act of national self-assertion was widely cheered. But Americans' aggressiveness did not stem from genuine feelings of security and self-esteem. Instead their boastful sense of "mission," their racism, and their nativism stemmed largely from fear rather than faith. For this was no "age of confidence"; rather it was an age of internal chaos and turbulence, when depression, farm revolt, labor strife, the specter of monopolization, and continuous conflict between older agrarian values and the material symbols of a new industrial urbanism beset middle-class Americans with overwhelming confusion and anxiety. The nervous energies that popular leaders channeled into a wild enthusiasm for expansion were less the product of a real feeling for mastery and world domination than an expression of immaturity, insecurity, and fear.

Foremost among the "jingoes" who advocated a "large policy" for the United States was Theodore Roosevelt, an aristocratic and Harvard-bred young historian, reformer, and politician whose early association with the Dakota badlands had given him the frontiersman's generally belligerent outlook and a taste for the "strenuous life." These were characteristics that thoroughly endeared him to a public ripe for aggressive self-reliance. Responding to popular acclaim, the inflammatory Roosevelt vigorously preached the expansionist doctrines of the eminent naval historian and philosopher of imperialism, Captain Alfred T. Mahan, whose volumes on the influence of sea power in history had made a profound impression on educated Americans. Affirming America's destiny to "look outward" beyond national borders, Mahan argued that the nation's honor and prestige, as well as her defense and trade, depended upon the acquisition of numerous overseas naval bases, the control of the Caribbean and trade routes to the Far East, and the creation of an insurpassable naval force. There were some Americans, of course, who took violent exception to Mahan's doctrines and to the bombastic, flag-waving jingoism of Roosevelt and his followers. But the anti-imperialists were hopelessly out of temper with their times, and when in 1897 Assistant Secretary of the Navy Roosevelt delivered his famous Naval War College speech on preparedness ("Washington's Forgotten Maxim"), he met with widespread approval throughout the country. In this classic expression of naval expansionism Roosevelt asked for "a great navy . . . an armament fit for the nation's needs, not primarily to fight, but to avert fighting." Roosevelt declared that "preparation for war is the surest guaranty for peace," and he extolled the "soldierly virtues" as the "most valuable of all qualities." One year later the "glorious little war" with Spain secured an empire for America and swept the indomitable Colonel of the "Rough Riders" into the Governorship of New York. From there he rose rapidly to the Vice-Presidency, and then, in 1901, to the Presidency of the United States.

Fantastically energetic and ebullient—John Morley once described the President as "an interesting combination of St. Vitus and St. Paul"—Roosevelt played a particularly vital role in sparking and directing America's expansionist drive. But Roosevelt's greatest significance in this period was as a folk hero, as a living, fighting symbol of the nervous energies that dominated America. Earlier statesmen of a very different turn of mind and character had at times surrendered to the expansionist demands of an anxiety-ridden public. In 1893 the anti-imperialist Grover Cleveland had successfully opposed the annexation of Hawaii when American sugar planters, without regard for the native majority, staged a revolution in an attempt to protect their own extensive investments in the islands and sought admission to the Union. Nevertheless two years later even the courageous Cleveland submitted to the jingoist fervor in an act of national self-assertion that momentarily endeared him to the most violent expansionists. For in the Olney Doctrine of 1895 Cleveland peremptorily ordered the British to arbitrate a disturbing boundary dispute with Venezuela, claiming that "Today the United States is practically sovereign on this continent, and its fiat is law upon the subjects to which it confines its interposition." Ultimately England succumbed to Cleveland's bellicose demands, and the President was wildly applauded for twisting the lion's tail so ferociously. The unwarlike McKinley, too, had surrendered to the tide of popular feeling when he took the nation to war with Spain and presided over the acquisition of Guam, Puerto Rico and the Philippines, the annexation of the Hawaiian Islands, and the establishment of a protectorate over Cuba. Thus Cleveland and McKinley had contributed largely to America's emergence as a great imperial power. But they had done so halfheartedly and under intense pressure from an aroused public, while Roosevelt so thoroughly embodied the national temper that his every thought and act, however childlike or warlike, unhesitatingly bespoke the swashbuckling spirit of adolescent America.

Anti-imperialists violently denounced the colonial bequest of the war with Spain, but most Americans retorted with cries of "Don't haul down the flag" and turned to Theodore Roosevelt to half-lead, half-follow them into the expansive years of the early twentieth century. The keystone of Roosevelt's foreign policy was his injunction that the nation "speak softly and carry a big stick." But Americans seldom spoke softly in those feverish years. In 1899–1900 Secretary of State John Hay had demanded an "Open Door" policy in China, insisting that American traders be treated equally with the nationals of those countries that had forcibly extorted trade concessions from the defenseless Chinese. Then in 1903 Roosevelt actively interfered in the internal affairs of Colombia, aiding and abetting a revolution in that Latin-American republic that left Panama free to negotiate an isthmian canal route with the impatient "Colossus of the North." And in his Annual Messages of 1904–5 the "Roosevelt Corollary" to the Monroe Doctrine warned our Latin neighbors that "Chronic wrong-doing, or an impotence which results in a general loosening of the ties of civilized society . . . may force the United States, however reluctantly . . . to the exercise of an international police power." This bold enlargement of American prerogatives throughout the Western hemisphere was frequently invoked in the following two decades to justify armed interference in the domestic as well as foreign affairs of the republics to the South. But by the late 1920's and early 1930's America's youthful aggressiveness had been largely dissipated by the tremendous burdens of world power. Under the guidance of Herbert Hoover and Franklin D. Roosevelt the nation's attitude toward the sovereign powers of the Western hemisphere underwent profound change, and a genuine sense of mutual respect and responsibility among equals—the "Good Neighbor" policy—was substituted for the "Big Stick" and "Dollar Diplomacy." America had finally come of age.

"The United States Looking Outward"*
Alfred T. Mahan, 1890

Indications are not wanting of an approaching change in the thoughts and policy of Americans as to their relations with the world outside their own borders. For the past quarter of a century, the predominant idea, which has asserted itself successfully at the polls and shaped the course of the Government, has been to preserve the home market for the home industries. The employer and the workman alike have been taught to look at the various economical measures proposed from this point of view, to regard with hostility any step favoring the intrusion of the foreign producer upon their own domain, and rather to demand increasingly rigorous measures of exclusion than to acquiesce in any loosening of the chain

*From *The Interest of America in Sea Power,* Alfred T. Mahan; Little Brown & Co., 1897.

that binds the consumer to them. The inevitable consequence has followed, as in all cases when the mind or the eye is exclusively fixed in one direction, that the danger of loss or the prospect of advantage in another quarter has been overlooked; and although the abounding resources of the country have maintained the exports at a high figure, this flattering result has been due more to the superabundant bounty of nature than to the demand of other nations for our protected manufacturers.

For nearly the lifetime of a generation, therefore, American industries have been thus protected, until the practice has assumed the force of a tradition, and is clothed in the mail of conservatism. In their mutual relations, these industries resemble the activities of a modern ironclad that has heavy armor, but inferior engines and guns; mighty for defense, weak for offense. Within, the home market is secured; but outside, beyond the broad seas, there are the markets of the world, that can be entered and controlled only by a vigorous contest, to which the habit of trusting to protection by statute does not conduce.

At bottom, however, the temperament of the American people is essentially alien to such a sluggish attitude. Independently of all bias for or against protection, it is safe to predict that, when the opportunities for gain abroad are understood, the course of American enterprise will cleave a channel by which to reach them. . . .

The interesting and significant feature of this changing attitude is the turning of the eyes outward, instead of inward only, to seek the welfare of the country. To affirm the importance of distant markets, and the relation to them of our own immense powers of production, implies logically the recognition of the link that joins the products and the markets—that is, the carrying trade; the three together constituting that chain of maritime power to which Great Britain owes her wealth and greatness. Further, is it too much to say that, as two of these links, the shipping and the markets, are exterior to our own borders, the acknowledgment of them carries with it a view of the relations of the United States to the world radically distinct from the simple idea of self-sufficingness? We shall not follow far this line of thought before there will dawn the realization of America's unique position, facing the older worlds of the East and West, her shores washed by the oceans which touch the one or the other, but which are common to her alone.

Coincident with these signs of change in our own policy there is restlessness in the world at large which is deeply significant, if not ominous. It is beside our purpose to dwell upon the internal state of Europe, whence, if disturbances arise, the effect upon us may be but partial and indirect. But the great seaboard powers there do not stand on guard against their continental rivals only; they cherish also aspirations for commercial extension, for colonies, and for influence in distant regions, which may bring, and, even under our present contracted policy, already have brought them into collision with ourselves. The incident of the Samoa Islands, trivial apparently, was nevertheless eminently suggestive of European ambitions. America then roused from sleep as to interests closely concerning her future. At this moment internal troubles are imminent in the Sandwich Islands, where it should be our fixed determination to allow no foreign influence to equal our own. All over the world German commercial and colonial push is coming into collision with other nations: witness the affair of the Caroline Islands with Spain; the partition of New Guinea with England; the yet more recent negotiation between these two powers concerning their share in Africa viewed with deep distrust and jealousy by France; the Samoa affair; the conflict between German control and American interests in the islands of the western Pacific; and the alleged progress of German influence in Central and South America. . . .

There is no sound reason for believing that the world has passed into a period of assured peace outside the limits of Europe. Unsettled political conditions, such as exist in Haiti, Central America, and many of the Pacific Islands, especially the Hawaiian group, when combined with great military or commercial importance as is the case with most of these positions, involve, now as always, dangerous germs of quarrel, against which it is prudent at least to be prepared. Undoubtedly, the general temper of nations is more averse from war than it was of old. If no less selfish and grasping than our predecessors, we feel more dislike to the discomforts and sufferings attendant upon a breach of peace; but to retain that highly valued repose and the undisturbed enjoyment of the returns of commerce, it is necessary to argue upon somewhat equal terms of strength with an adversary. It is the preparedness of the enemy, and not acquiescence in the existing state of things, that now holds back the armies of Europe.

On the other hand, neither the sanctions of international law nor the justice of a cause can be depended upon for a fair settlement of differences, when they come into conflict with a strong political necessity on the one side opposed to comparative weakness on the other. In our still pending dispute over the seal-fishing of Bering Sea, whatever may be thought of the strength of our argument, in view of generally admitted principles of international law, it is beyond doubt that our contention is reasonable, just, and in the interest of the world at large. But in the attempt to enforce it we have come into collision not only with national susceptibilities as to the honor of the flag, which we ourselves very strongly share, but also with a state governed by a powerful necessity, and exceedingly strong where we are particularly weak and exposed. Not only has Great Britain a mighty navy and we a long defenseless seacoast, but it is a great commercial and political advantage to her that her larger colonies, and above all Canada, should feel that the power of the mother country is something which they need, and upon which they can count. . . . Whatever arrangement of this question is finally reached, the fruit of Lord Salisbury's attitude scarcely can fail to be a strengthening of the sentiments of attachment to, and reliance upon, the mother country, not only in Canada, but in the other great colonies. These feelings of attachment and mutual dependence supply the living spirit, without which the nascent schemes for imperial federation are but dead mechanical contrivances; nor are they without influence upon such generally unsentimental considerations as those of buying and selling, and the course of trade.

This dispute, seemingly paltry yet really serious, sudden in its appearance and dependent for its issue upon other considerations than its own merits, may serve to convince us of many latent and yet unforeseen dangers to the peace of the western hemisphere, attendant upon the opening of a canal through the Central American Isthmus. In a general way, it is evident enough that this canal, by modifying the direction of trade routes, will induce a great increase of commercial activity and carrying trade throughout the Caribbean Sea; and that this now comparatively deserted nook of the ocean will become, like the Red Sea, a great thoroughfare of shipping, and will attract, as never before in our day, the interest and ambition of maritime nations. Every position in that sea will have enhanced commercial and military value, and the canal itself will become a strategic centre of the most vital importance. Like the Canadian Pacific Railroad, it will be a link between the two oceans; but, unlike it, the use, unless most carefully guarded by treaties, will belong wholly to the belligerent which controls the sea by its naval power. In case of war, the United States will unquestionably command the Canadian Railroad, despite the deterrent force of operations by the hostile navy upon our seaboard; but no less unquestionably will she be impotent, as against any of the great maritime powers, to control the Central American canal. Militarily speaking, and having reference to European complications only, the piercing of the Isthmus is nothing but a disaster to the United States, in the present state of her military and naval preparation. It is especially dangerous to the Pacific coast; but the increased exposure of one part of our seaboard reacts unfavorably upon the whole military situation.

Despite a certain great original superiority conferred by our geographical nearness and immense resources—due, in other words, to our natural advantages, and not to our intelligent preparations—the United States is woefully unready, not only in fact but in purpose to assert in the Caribbean and Central America a weight of influence proportioned to the extent of her interests. We have not the navy, and, what is worse, we are not willing to have the navy, that will weigh seriously in any disputes with those nations whose interests will conflict there with our own. We have not, and we are not anxious to provide, the defense of the seaboard which will leave the navy free for its work at sea. We have not, but many other powers have, positions, either within or on the borders of the Caribbean which not only possess great natural advantages for the control of that sea, but have received and are receiving that artificial strength of fortification and armament which will make them practically inexpungnable. On the contrary, we have not on the Gulf of Mexico even the beginning of a navy yard which could serve as the base of our operations. Let me not be misunderstood. I am not regretting that we have not the means to meet on terms of equality the great navies of the Old World. I recognize, what few at least say, that despite its great surplus revenue, this country is poor in proportion to its length of seaboard and its exposed points. That which I deplore, and which is a sober, just, and reasonable cause of deep national concern is that the nation neither has nor cares to have its sea frontier so defended, and its navy of such power, as shall suffice, with the advantages of our position, to weigh seriously when inevitable discussions arise—such as we have recently had about Samoa and Bering Sea, and which may at any moment come up about the Caribbean Sea or the canal. Is the United States, for instance, prepared to allow Germany to acquire the Dutch stronghold of Curaçao, fronting the Atlantic outlet of both the proposed canals of Panama and Nicaragua? Is she prepared to acquiesce in any foreign power purchasing from Haiti a naval station on the Windward Passage, through which pass our steamer routes to the Isthmus? Would she acquiesce in a foreign protectorate over the Sandwich Islands, that great central station of the Pacific, equidistant from San Francisco, Samoa, and the Marquesas, and an important post on our lines of communication with both Australia and China? Or will it be maintained that any one of these questions, supposing it to arise, is so exclusively one-sided, the arguments of policy and right so exclusively with us, that the other party will at once yield his eager wish, and gracefully withdraw? Was it so at Samoa? Is it so as regards the Bering Sea? The motto seen on so many ancient cannon, *Ultima ratio regum,* is not without its message to republics.

It is perfectly reasonable and legitimate, in estimating our needs of military preparation, to take into account the remoteness of the chief naval and military nations from our shores, and the consequent difficulty of maintaining operations at such a distance. It is equally proper, in framing our policy, to consider the jealousies of the European family of states, and their consequent unwillingness to incur the enmity of a people so strong as ourselves; their dread of our revenge in the future, as well as their inability to detach more than a certain part of their forces to our shores without losing much of their own weight in the councils of Europe. In truth, a careful determination of the force that Great Britain or France could probably spare for operations against our coasts, if the latter were suitably defended, without weakening their European position or unduly exposing their colonies and commerce, is the starting-point from which to calculate the strength of our own navy. . . .

While, therefore, the advantages of our own position in the western hemisphere, and the disadvantages under which the operations of a European state would labor, are undeniable and just elements in the calculations of the statesman, it is folly to look upon them as sufficient alone for our security. Much more needs to be cast into the scale that it may incline in favor of our strength. They are mere defensive factors, and partial at that. Though distant, our shores can be reached; being defenseless, they can detain but a short time a force sent against them. With a probability of three months' peace in Europe, no maritime power would fear to support its demands by a number of ships with which it would be loath indeed to part for a year.

Yet, were our sea frontier as strong as it now is weak, passive self-defense, whether in trade or war, would be but a poor policy, so long as this world continues to be one of struggle and vicissitude. All around us now is strife; "the struggle of life," "the race of life," are phrases so familiar that we do not feel their significance till we stop to think about them. Everywhere nation is arrayed against nation; our own no less than others. What is our protective system but an organized warfare? In carrying it on, it is true, we have only to use certain procedures which all states now concede to be a legal exercise of the national power, even though injurious to themselves. It is lawful, they say, to do what we will with our own.

Are our people, however, so unaggressive that they are likely not to want their own way in matters where their interests turn on points of disputed right, or so little sensitive as to submit quietly to encroachment by others in quarters where they long have considered their own influence should prevail?

Our self-imposed isolation in the matter of markets, and the decline of our shipping interest in the last thirty years, have coincided singularly with an actual remoteness of this continent from the life of the rest of the world. . . .

When the Isthmus is pierced, this isolation will pass away, and with it the indifference of foreign nations. From wheresoever they come and whithersoever they afterward go, all ships that use the canal will pass through the Caribbean. Whatever the effect produced upon the prosperity of the adjacent continent and islands by the thousand wants attendant upon maritime activity, around such a focus of trade will centre large commercial and political interests. To protect and develop its own, each nation will seek points of support and means of influence in a quarter where the United States always has been jealously sensitive to the intrusion of European powers. The precise value of the Monroe Doctrine is understood very loosely by most Americans, but the effect of the familiar phrase has been to develop a national sensitiveness, which is a more frequent cause of war than material interests; and over disputes caused by such feelings there will preside none of the calming influence due to the moral authority of international law, with its recognized principles, for the points in dispute will be of policy, of interest, not of conceded right. Already France and Great Britain are giving to ports held by them a degree of artificial strength uncalled for by their present importance. They look to the near future. Among the islands and on the mainland there are many positions of great importance, held now by weak or unstable states. Is the United States willing to see them sold to a powerful rival? But what right will she invoke against the transfer? She can allege but one, that of her reasonable policy supported by her might.

Whether they will or no, Americans must now begin to look outward. . . .

Corollary to the Monroe Doctrine, *Theodore Roosevelt, 1904, 1905*

1904

. . . It is not true that the United States feels any land hunger or entertains any projects as regards the other nations of the Western Hemisphere save such as are for their welfare. All that this country desires is to see the neighboring countries stable, orderly, and prosperous. Any country whose people conduct themselves well can count upon our hearty friendship. If a nation shows that it knows how to act with reasonable efficiency and decency in social and political matters, if it keeps order and pays its obligations, it need fear no interference from the United States. Chronic wrongdoing, or an impotence which results in a general loosening of the ties of civilized society, may in America, as elsewhere, ultimately require intervention by some civilized nation, and in the Western Hemisphere the adherence of the United States to the Monroe Doctrine may force the United States, however reluctantly, in flagrant cases of such wrongdoing or impotence, to the exercise of an international police power. If every country washed by the Caribbean Sea would show the progress in stable and just civilization which with the aid of the Platt amendment Cuba has shown since our troops left the island, and which so many of the republics in both Americas are constantly and brilliantly showing, all question of interference by this Nation with their affairs would be at an end. Our interests and those of our southern neighbors are in reality identical. They have great natural riches, and if within their borders the reign of law and justice obtains, prosperity is sure to come to them. While they thus obey the primary laws of civilized society they may rest assured that they will be treated by us in a spirit of cordial and helpful sympathy. We would interfere with them only in the last resort, and then only if it became evident that their inability or unwillingness to do justice at home and abroad had violated the rights of the United States or had invited foreign aggression to the detriment of the entire body of American nations. It is a mere truism to say that every nation, whether in America or anywhere else, which desires to maintain its freedom, its independence, must ultimately realize that the right of such independence can not be separated from the responsibility of making good use of it.

In asserting the Monroe Doctrine, in taking such steps as we have taken in regard to Cuba, Venezuela, and Panama, and in endeavoring to circumscribe the theater of war in the Far East, and to secure the open door in China, we have acted in our own interest as well as in the interest of humanity at large. There are, however, cases in which, while our own interests are not greatly involved, strong appeal is made to our sympathies. . . . But in extreme cases action may be justifiable and proper. What form the action shall take must depend upon the circumstances of the case; that is, upon the degree of the atrocity and upon our power to remedy it. The cases in which we could interfere by force of arms as we interfered to put a stop to intolerable conditions in Cuba are necessarily very few.

1905

. . . It must be understood that under no circumstances will the United States use the Monroe Doctrine as a cloak for territorial aggression. We desire peace with all the world, but perhaps most of all with the other peoples of the American Continent. There are, of course, limits to the wrongs which any self-respecting nation can endure. It is always possible that wrong actions toward this Nation, or toward citizens of this Nation, in some State unable to keep order among its own people, unable to secure justice from outsiders, and unwilling to do justice to those outsiders who treat it well, may result in our having to take action to protect our rights; but such action will not be taken with a view to territorial aggression, and it will be taken at all only with extreme reluctance and when it has become evident that every other resource has been exhausted.

Moreover, we must make it evident that we do not intend to permit the Monroe Doctrine to be used by any nation on this Continent as a shield to protect it from the consequences of its own misdeeds against foreign nations. If a republic to the south of us commits a tort against a foreign nation, such as an outrage against a citizen of that nation, then the Monroe Doctrine does not force us to interfere to prevent punishment of the tort, save to see that the punishment does not assume the form of territorial occupation in any shape. The case is more difficult when it refers to a contractual obligation. Our own Government has always refused to enforce such contractual obligations on behalf of its citizens by an appeal to arms. It is much to be wished that all foreign governments would take the same view. But they do not; and in consequence we are liable at any time to be brought face to face with disagreeable alternatives. On the one hand, this country would certainly decline to go to war to prevent a foreign government from collecting a just debt; on the other hand, it is very inadvisable to permit any foreign power to take possession, even temporarily, of the custom houses of an American Republic in order to enforce the payment of its obligations; for such temporary occupation might turn into a permanent occupation. The only escape from these alternatives may at any time be that we must ourselves undertake to bring about some arrangement by which so much as possible of a just obligation shall be paid. It is far better that this country should put through such an arrangement, rather than allow any foreign country to undertake it. To do so insures the defaulting republic from having to pay debt of an improper character under duress, while it also insures honest creditors of the republic from being passed by in the interest of dishonest or grasping creditors. Moreover, for the United States to take such a position offers the only possible way of insuring us against a clash with some foreign power. The position is, therefore, in the interest of peace as well as in the interest of justice. It is of benefit to our people; it is of benefit to foreign peoples; and most of all it is really of benefit to the people of the country concerned. . . .

Chapter 20

THE PROGRESSIVE FERMENT

Seldom in the nation's history has the impulse for reform been more pervasive or more intense than in the Progressive Era at the turn of the twentieth century. For this was truly the Golden Age of Reform, when the fears and anxieties of middle-class Americans hard pressed between corporate power from above and the laboring masses from below had been channeled not only into an aggressive, boastful expansionism, but into a humanitarian, collectivist Progressivism as well. The task of the Progressives lay clear before them. With speed and consummate skill America's mighty Captains of Industry had created a magnificent productive plant and had presided over the rapid proliferation of national wealth. But with boundless riches came incredible poverty of purpose and spirit. If unfettered industrial capitalism had achieved for the nation vast material strength that placed her among the great powers of the world, it had also at least momentarily overridden Americans' sense of justice and fair play. Personal acquisitiveness had been substituted for social conscience, the Gospel of Wealth for the Social Gospel. Now the Progressives had to recapture the rich human values of an earlier age, adapt them to the realities of collective economic power, and lead the nation in its quest for social justice.

From 1900 to the beginning of the First World War much of the energy of Progressivism was devoted to the formulation of new social philosophies and ideologies for a nation whose physical power had grown more rapidly than its understanding. And the seminal works of John Dewey, Thorstein Veblen, Charles A. Beard, Herbert Croly, and Walter Lippmann were powerful instruments in the ultimate reorientation of American thought. But the Progressive challenge was as pressing as it was formidable, and the overwhelming economic, social, and political problems that beset the nation demanded immediate attention and action. On every hand huge combinations of capital had emerged in the form of trusts and monopolies that dwarfed the small independent businessman and threatened the economic basis of individualistic, middle-class democracy in America. For example, in 1901 the gigantic United States Steel Corporation was organized by J. P. Morgan & Company with a capitalization that reached the staggering sum of almost one and a half billion dollars. Such industrial empires produced tremendous wealth, but while the privileged few were enriched, impoverishment was the lot of the many. Thus great fortunes and unspeakable poverty grew side by side in a nation fascinated by the spectacle of material production though little concerned with the problems of distribution. And by 1896 it was estimated that one-eighth of the population owned ninety percent of the nation's property, while increasingly large numbers of Americans were propertyless altogether.

At the same time that unequal distribution of wealth created widely separated and deeply antagonistic economic classes, the rise of the city similarly brought social problems of unparalleled proportions. Some Americans chose to attribute the evils of urban life to the great numbers of "new" immigrants from Eastern and Southern Europe who settled in the cities. Actually, in intelligence, character, and ambition there was little to distinguish the "new" immigrant from the "old" immigrant who had come from the British Isles or Western and Northern Europe. It was America that was "new," not the immigrant. An earlier, agrarian America had offered its immigrants ample free land for settlement, but by the 1890's industrial capitalism had subdued the continent, conquered its free lands and last frontiers, and firmly established a business civilization that seemed to provide room for urban factory workers only. The newcomer from foreign shores had little choice; he must settle in the cities to earn a living. For this reason alone the "new" immigrant was identified with the poverty, slums, disease, crime, and vice peculiar to the entire movement from rural to urban areas that marked America's industrial revolution.

The systematic extension of governmental power to

eliminate these evils was a major theme of the Progressive movement. In the late nineteenth century the disciples of Henry George and Edward Bellamy, two of the most thoroughgoing philosophers of social control, had consistently been more vocal than numerous, while angry agrarians who precipitated the Populist Revolt of the 1890's had found their enthusiasm for collective social action waning with the rise of farm prices and the return of farm prosperity. Nevertheless, these early demands for State action to provide for the general welfare had made considerable inroads upon Americans' traditional adherence to laissez-faire. In the 1900's large numbers of middle-class Americans were wary of the predatory power of concentrated wealth, fearful of impending conflict between big business and the underprivileged classes generally, and profoundly disturbed by the social dislocations that accompanied urbanization. They rallied to the support of Progressive measures that called for considerable State interference in the social and economic life of the nation. And within a comparatively few years Federal and state governments alike had begun a widespread campaign to regulate those industries which vitally affected the public interest, to curb somewhat the extensive power of the trusts, to encourage fairer labor practices, and to help preserve and protect the nation's human resources through widely expanded social services.

While these first efforts at social and economic legislation laid the groundwork for the Welfare State of a later generation, Progressive leaders were equally concerned with the details of political reform. With a vast increase in its powers and responsibilities, it was imperative that government be made more responsive to the popular will and that new standards of honesty and administrative efficiency be widely adopted. Progressivism therefore stimulated an intense public interest in reform measures that promised to insure the direct and competent administration of the processes of democracy. Within the states the initiative and referendum permitted a small percentage of the electorate to petition the submission of laws directly to the general public for acceptance or rejection. The recall provided a means by which dishonest or unpopular public officials might be removed from office by majority vote before the expiration of their regular terms. And the direct primary somewhat reduced the power of political machines by giving the voters an opportunity to name party nominees as well as to choose between the final candidates for office. In the field of local government experiments were made to supplant the frequently corrupt mayoralty system with a "commission" form of government in which all municipal functions were entrusted to a small group of commissioners responsible for their respective departments. And the "city manager" plan attempted to emulate business techniques, granting all nonpolitical functions to a managerial expert who conducted municipal affairs as he would a giant business establishment. Besides these accomplishments on the state and local levels, two reforms within the national government were of exceptional importance. Throughout the period of industrial supremacy that followed the Civil War, the Constitutional provision for the election of United States Senators by the various state legislatures had permitted a corrupt alliance between corporate wealth and purchasable state politicians to make of the national upper house a "millionaires' club" dominated by the representatives of "vested interests." But in 1913 the Seventeenth Amendment to the Constitution was ratified, providing for the direct election of Senators, and the heavy hand of privilege was somewhat lifted. Then in 1920, long after various Western states had granted the ballot to women, another Progressive demand finally met with national success when the Nineteenth Amendment was ratified and women's suffrage became a reality in every state of the Union.

Principle and plan, however, seldom contributed as importantly to the achievement of these liberal measures as did the aggressive apostles of reform who dominated the Progressive Era. Such indefatigable crusaders as "Fighting Bob" LaFollette, Governor of Wisconsin and later United States Senator, and "Golden Rule" Jones, the Mayor of Toledo, Ohio, continuously dramatized the effectiveness of honesty, intelligence, and training in the administration of public affairs. In the widely read public journals Lincoln Steffens, Ida Tarbell, Ray Stannard Baker, Upton Sinclair, David Graham Phillips, and numerous others, "muckrakers" excitingly exposed the evils of business and politics. But by far the most influential of the many stimulating personalities who lent color and character to Progressivism were the incomparably dynamic and dramatic Theodore Roosevelt and the highly intellectual, highly idealistic Woodrow Wilson. Both men were determined and inspiring leaders who considerably enhanced the power and prestige of the Presidency; both were broadly liberal in their political orientation; both advocated far-reaching changes in the national structure that later contributed importantly to the New Deal and the Fair Deal. And in 1912, when they faced each other in a bitter three-cornered race for the Presidency (with Roosevelt the third-party Bull Moose or Progressive candidate, Wilson the Democratic candidate, and William Howard Taft the standard-bearer of the Old Guard in the Republican party), their respective cries for a "New Nationalism" and a "New Freedom" seemed very much alike. Actually, however, on the issue of the trusts there existed a fundamental conflict between the two men and their respective philosophies of government that symbolized a deep confusion in Progressive thinking.

Roosevelt's sure sense of the popular—a contemporary attributed to "Teddy" the "psychology of the mutt"—made him truly the era's prophet. Nevertheless impatient critics charged that as President his bold verbal attacks upon the "malefactors of great wealth," his fiery threats to "bust the trusts," and his exhilarating promises of a Square Deal for all Americans were thoroughly out of keeping with his actual achievements. The "aggressive" Roosevelt, LaFollette insisted, had meekly and unnecessarily knuckled under to unfriendly Congressional demands that Progressive legislation be shorn of much of its potential strength. And others later pointed out that even the cautious and avowedly conservative Taft prosecuted twice as many trusts in his four years as President (1909–1913) as had the much vaunted "trust-buster" Roosevelt during nearly eight years in office (1901–1909). Yet Roosevelt had not enjoyed a free hand as President and the frequent disparity between his word and his deed was largely due to the fact that throughout his administration the Republican

Square Dealer was continuously forced to seek concessions from an unsympathetic Congress dominated by ultraconservative members of his own party. And Roosevelt *did* make numerous substantial contributions to the Progressive cause. He confounded the previously untouchable business community by invoking the long dormant Sherman Anti-Trust Act against the Northern Securities Company, an enormous consolidation of railroad interests that involved such masters of capital as E. H. Harriman and J. P. Morgan; he pushed and cajoled through Congress the Pure Food and Drug Act and various laws designed to conserve the nation's depleted natural resources; through compromise and concession he secured essential, if not thoroughly adequate, regulatory railroad legislation; and, most significantly, he led the American people in the all-important *first* steps towards meaningful national reform.

Fate, not popular choice, had taken Roosevelt from the Vice-Presidency to the highest office in the land in 1901 when an assassin's bullets ended President McKinley's life. In 1904, therefore, Roosevelt was particularly delighted to be decisively elected in his own right, and in the enthusiasm of the moment pledged himself not to seek reelection four years hence. He did choose his successor, however, and for a while there was hope that the genial and devoted Taft might competently carry on a Progressive administration. But this hope proved illusory, for Taft, conservative at heart and singularly lacking in Roosevelt's penchant for compromise, was incapable of reconciling the interests of Progressives within the Republican Party with those of the conservative standpatters who dominated party councils. This fundamental schism quickly widened and in 1910, aided by the Democratic minority, insurgent Republicans in the House of Representatives struck a vital blow at the party's conservative hierarchy by stripping "Uncle Joe" Cannon, the autocratic Speaker of the House, of much of the power he had wielded to block Progressive legislation. Yet the revolt against "Cannonism" was only a first step, and the insurgents were determined either to capture control of the Republican Party or to create an independent party that would nominate a Progressive in 1912.

Meanwhile Roosevelt returned from big-game hunting in the wilds of Africa equally convinced that a genuine Progressive, preferably himself, must be nominated. The former President had already abandoned the older formulas of economic reform he so loudly advocated a decade earlier, since "trust-busting" had proved singularly ineffective. Prosecution under the antitrust laws dissolved monopolistic interests in a technical sense only, and effective reintegration of legally separated units (through an informal "community of interests") was not uncommon. Combination seemed truly basic to the nature of modern American business, and the "New Nationalism" that Roosevelt now espoused not only embraced most of the political and social reforms of the moment, but also accepted as both "inevitable and necessary" the concentration of extensive economic power in large corporations. Were these mammoth economic units to prove abusive, Roosevelt would regulate rather than dissolve them, maintaining instead of destroying their effective contributions to America's material wealth. In this way "big business" would be matched by "big government." This was in essence the program that Roosevelt presented to the nation in his famous speech at Osawatomie, Kansas, in August 1910. With this program he captured the presidential nomination of an independent Progressive Party in 1912, and with it he suffered defeat at the hands of Woodrow Wilson's "New Freedom."

Trained as an historian and political scientist, Woodrow Wilson had early distinguished himself academically, rising to the presidency of Princeton University in 1902, a year after Theodore Roosevelt entered the White House. Then in 1910 Wilson abandoned academic life to become Governor of New Jersey, and two years later, on the basis of a brilliant reform record, he captured the Democratic nomination for President of the United States. Thus Wilson entered the political arena at the very height of the movement towards monopolization and the concentration of economic power. Like Roosevelt, he saw very clearly the tremendous transformation this new power had wrought in American life generally. The "Old Order Changeth," wrote the scholar in politics. "We have changed our economic conditions, absolutely, from top to bottom; and, with our economic society, the organization of our life." Both Progressive leaders, then, were aware of the collective nature of twentieth-century industrial development and of its impact upon the nation's traditionally individualistic social structure. But where Roosevelt thoroughly accepted the "new order of society," Wilson firmly rejected it, dedicating himself to restoring the economic realities of an earlier century. Indeed, the keynote of Wilson's first Inaugural Address was his assertion that "our work is a work of restoration."

Like Hamilton a century before, Theodore Roosevelt was vitally impressed by vast aggregates of power, and his "New Nationalism" sought social justice by extending the powers of the central government, particularly those of the Chief Executive, whom he regarded as peculiarly the "steward of the public welfare." "Big business" must be good or suffer regulation by "big government." Wilson, on the other hand, was essentially Jeffersonian in his orientation, and his "New Freedom" feared all bigness, whether economic or political, as potentially destructive of democracy. When he announced that the "old political formulas do not fit the present problems; they read now like documents taken out of a forgotten age," Wilson was referring primarily to the boldest type of nineteenth-century laissez-faire. An absolute "hands-off" attitude on the part of the national government would permit big business to strangle altogether the middle-class small businessman whose strength and survival Wilson regarded as vital to the nation's well-being. Therefore, government must abandon its "old formulas"; it must interfere in the economic life of the nation not only to destroy privilege but also to preserve economic competition and prevent the "men on the make" from being squeezed out of existence by the giant corporation, the trust, and the monopoly. Yet government must not expand its own power until it, too, became a threat to the individual.

In the 1912 campaign Wilson persistently attacked the plan of the "New Nationalism" merely to regulate the monopolies. If permitted to grow, Wilson insisted, big business would soon control the government itself, and governmental regulation of business would be truly a farce. Roosevelt in turn thought the advocates of the "New Freedom" were agrarian reactionaries, because they were basically out of sympathy with the growth of those giant economic units whose untrammeled productivity he considered the promise of American democracy. In theory, of course, the "New Freedom" *did* stand for the simple antitrust policies of discontented nineteenth-century agrarians. Ironically, however, Woodrow Wilson won the election of 1912 only to preside over the extraordinary growth of business and government alike. The Underwood-Simmons Tariff Act of 1913 did revise the tariff downward to deprive monopolistic business of the usual protection of Republican trade laws; the Federal Reserve Act of 1913, by decentralizing the nation's credit resources, did attack the "money trust" that the Pujo Committee of the House of Representatives claimed was controlled by a few New York banking houses; and the Clayton Act of 1914 did give added strength to the government's antitrust activities. Yet all of these measures, together with many other efforts towards social justice, meant the broad extension of government authority over the nation and its citizens. Thus Wilson ultimately created the "big government" Roosevelt had urged, and in 1917–1918 a wartime demand for unlimited production gave a tremendous impetus to "big business" as well. Wilson had to a large degree met the Progressive challenge, but in doing so he had sacrificed much of his basic antipathy to the subordination of the individual to power of any kind, whether in business or in government.

The New Nationalism, *Theodore Roosevelt, 1910*

We come here today to commemorate one of the epoch-making events of the long struggle for the rights of man, the long struggle for the uplift of humanity. Our country—this great republic—means nothing unless it means the triumph of a real democracy, the triumph of popular government, and, in the long run, of an economic system under which each man shall be guaranteed the opportunity to show the best that there is in him. That is why the history of America is now the central feature of the history of the world; for the world has set its face hopefully toward our democracy; and, O my fellow citizens, each one of you carries on your shoulders not only the burden of doing well for the sake of your own country, but the burden of doing well and seeing that this nation does well for the sake of mankind. . . .

At many stages in the advance of humanity, conflict between the men who possess more than they have earned and the men who have earned more than they possess is the central condition of progress. In our day it appears as the struggle of free men to gain and hold the right of self-government as against the special interests, who twist the methods of free government into machinery for defeating the popular will. At every stage, and under all circumstances, the essence of the struggle is to equalize opportunity, destroy privilege, and give to the life and citizenship of every individual the highest possible value both to himself and to the commonwealth. . . .

Practical equality of opportunity for all citizens, when we achieve it, will have two great results. First, every man will have a fair chance to make of himself all that in him lies; to reach the highest point to which his capacities, unassisted by special privilege of his own and unhampered by the special privileges of others, can carry him, and to get for himself and his family substantially what he has earned. Second, equality of opportunity means that the commonwealth will get from every citizen the highest service of which he is capable. No man who carries the burden of the special privileges of another can give to the commonwealth that service to which it is fairly entitled.

I stand for the square deal. But when I say that I am for the square deal, I mean not merely that I stand for fair play under the present rules of the game, but that I stand for having those rules changed so as to work for a more substantial equality of opportunity and of reward for equally good service. . . .

When I say I want a square deal for the poor man, I do not mean that I want a square deal for the man who remains poor because he has not got the energy to work for himself. If a man who has had a chance will not make good, then he has got to quit. . . .

Now, this means that our government, national and State, must be freed from the sinister influence or control of special interests. Exactly as the special interests of cotton and slavery threatened our political integrity before the Civil War, so now the great special business interests too often control and corrupt the men and methods of government for their own profit. We must drive the special interests out of politics. . . .

The true friend of property, the true conservative, is he who insists that property shall be the servant and not the master of the commonwealth; who insists that the creature of man's making shall be the servant and not the master of the man who made it. The citizens of the United States must effectively control the mighty commercial forces which they have themselves called into being.

There can be no effective control of corporation while their political activity remains. To put an end to it will be neither a short nor an easy task, but it can be done.

We must have complete and effective publicity of corporate affairs, so that the people may know beyond peradventure whether the corporations obey the law and whether their management entitles them to the confidence of the public. It is necessary that laws should be passed to prohibit the use of corporate funds directly or indirectly for political purposes; it is still more necessary that such laws should be thoroughly enforced. Corporate expenditures for political purposes, and especially such expenditures by public service corporations, have supplied one of the principal sources of corruption in our political affairs.

It has become entirely clear that we must have government supervision of the capitalization, not only of public service corporations, including, particularly, railways, but of all corporations doing an interstate business. I do not wish to see the nation forced into the ownership of the railways if it can possibly be avoided, and the only alternative is thoroughgoing and effective regulation, which shall be based on a full knowledge of all the facts, including a physical valuation of property.

This physical valuation is not needed, or, at least, is very rarely needed, for fixing rates; but it is needed as the basis of honest capitalization.

We have come to recognize that franchises should never be granted except for a limited time, and never without proper provision for compensation to the public. It is my personal belief that the same kind and degree of control and supervision which should be exercised over public service corporations should be extended also to combinations which control necessaries of life, such as meat, oil, and coal, or which deal in them on an important scale. I have no doubt that the ordinary man who has control of them is much like ourselves. I have no doubt he would like to do well, but I want to have enough supervision to help him realize that desire to do well.

I believe that the officers, and, especially, the directors, of corporations should be held personally responsible when any corporation breaks the law.

Combinations in industry are the result of an imperative economic law which cannot be repealed by political legislation. The effort at prohibiting all combination has substantially failed. The way out lies, not in attempting to prevent such combinations, but in completely controlling them in the interest of the public welfare. . . .

No man should receive a dollar unless that dollar has been fairly earned. Every dollar received should represent a dollar's worth of service rendered—not gambling in stocks, but service rendered. The really big fortune, the swollen fortune, by the mere fact of its size acquires qualities which differentiate it in kind as well as in degree from what is possessed by men of relatively small means. Therefore, I believe in a graduated income tax on big fortunes, and in another tax which is far more easily collected and far more effective—a graduated inheritance tax on big fortunes, properly safe-guarded against evasion and increasing rapidly in amount with the size of the estate.

The people of the United States suffer from periodical financial panics to a degree substantially unknown among the other nations which approach us in financial strength. There is no reason why we should suffer what they escape. It is of profound importance that our financial system should be promptly investigated, and so thoroughly and effectively revised as to make it certain that hereafter our currency will no longer fail at critical times to meet our needs. . . .

Of conservation I shall speak more at length elsewhere. Conservation means development as much as it does protection. I recognize the right and duty of this generation to develop and use the natural resources of our land; but I do not recognize the right to waste them, or to rob, by wasteful use, the generations that come after us. I ask nothing of the nation except that it so behave as each farmer here behaves with reference to his own children. That farmer is a poor creature who skins the land and leaves it worthless to his children. The farmer is a good farmer who, having enabled the land to support himself and to provide for the education of his children, leaves it to them a little better than he found it himself. I believe the same thing of a nation. . . .

Nothing is more true than that excess of every kind is followed by reaction; a fact which should be pondered by reformer and reactionary alike. We are face to face with new conceptions of the relations of property to human welfare, chiefly because certain advocates of the rights of property as against the rights of men have been pushing their claims too far. The man who wrongly holds that every human right is secondary to his profit must now give way to the advocate of human welfare, who rightly maintains that every man holds his property subject to the general right of the community to regulate its use to whatever degree the public welfare may require it. . . .

National efficiency has many factors. It is a necessary result of the principle of conservation widely applied. In the end it will determine our failure or success as a Nation. National efficiency has to do, not only with natural resources and with men, but it is equally concerned with institutions. The State must be made efficient for the work which concerns only the people of the State; and the Nation for that which concerns all the people. There must remain no neutral ground to serve as a refuge for lawbreakers, and especially for lawbreakers of great wealth, who can hire the vulpine legal cunning which will teach them how to avoid both jurisdictions.

It is a misfortune when the national legislature fails to do its duty in providing a national remedy, so that the only national activity is the purely negative activity of the judiciary in forbidding the state to exercise power in the premises.

I do not ask for overcentralization; but I do ask that we work in a spirit of broad and far-reaching nationalism when we work for what concerns our people as a whole. We are all Americans. Our common interests are as broad as the continent. . . . The national Government belongs to the whole American people, and where the whole American people are interested, that interest can be guarded effectively only by the national Government. The betterment which we seek must be accomplished, I believe, mainly through the national Government.

The American people are right in demanding that New Nationalism, without which we cannot hope to deal with new problems. The New Nationalism puts the national need before sectional or personal advantage. It is impatient of the utter confusion that results from local legislatures attempting to treat national issues as local issues. It is still more impatient of the impotence which springs from overdivision of governmental powers, the impotence which makes it possible for local selfishness or for legal cunning, hired by wealthy special interests, to bring national activities to a deadlock. This New Nationalism regards the executive power as the steward of the public welfare. It demands of the judiciary that it shall be interested primarily in human welfare rather than in property, just as it demands that the representative body shall represent all the people rather than any one class or section of the people.

I believe in shaping the ends of government to protect property as well as human welfare. Normally, and in the long run, the ends are the same; but whenever the alternative must be faced, I am for men and not for property. . . .

I am far from underestimating the importance of dividends; but I rank dividends below human character. Again, I do not have any sympathy with the reformer who says he does not care for dividends. Of course, economic welfare is necessary, for a man must pull his own weight and be able to support his family. I know well that the reformers must not bring upon the people economic ruin, or the reforms themselves will go down in the ruin. But we must be ready to face temporary disaster, whether or not brought on by those who will war against us to the knife. Those who oppose all reform will do well to remember that ruin in its worst form is inevitable if our national life brings us nothing better than swollen fortunes for the few and the triumph in both politics and business of a sordid and selfish materialism.

If our political institutions were perfect, they would absolutely prevent the political domination of money in any part of our affairs. We need to make our political representatives more quickly and sensitively responsive to the people whose servants they are. More direct action by the people in their own affairs under proper safeguards is vitally necessary. The direct primary is a step in this direction, if it is associated with a corrupt practices act effective to prevent the advantage of the man willing recklessly and unscrupulously to spend money over his more honest competitor. It is particularly important that all money received or expended for campaign purposes should be publicly accounted for, not only after election, but before election as well. Political action must be made simpler, easier, and freer from confusion for every citizen. I believe that the prompt removal of unfaithful or incompetent public servants should be made easy and sure in whatever way experience shall show to be most expedient in any given class of cases.

One of the fundamental necessities in a representative government such as ours is to make certain that the men to whom the people delegate their power shall serve the people by whom they are elected, and not the special interests. I believe that every national officer, elected or appointed, should be forbidden to perform any service or receive any compensation, directly or indirectly, from interstate corporations; and a similar provision could not fail to be useful within the states.

The object of government is the welfare of the people. The material progress and prosperity of a nation are desirable chiefly so far as they lead to the moral and material welfare of all citizens. Just in proportion as the average man and woman are honest, capable of sound judgement and high ideals, active in public affairs—

but, first of all, sound in their home life, and the father and mother of healthy children whom they bring up well—just so far, and no further, we may count our civilization a success. We must have—I believe we have already—a genuine and permanent moral awakening, without which no wisdom of legislation or administration really means anything; and, on the other hand, we must try to secure the social and economic legislation without which any improvement due to purely moral agitation is necessarily evanescent. . . . No matter how honest and decent we are in our private lives, if we do not have the right kind of law and the right kind of administration of the law, we cannot go forward as a nation. That is imperative; but it must be an addition to, and not a substitution for, the qualities that make up good citizens. In the last analysis, the most important element in any man's career must be the sum of those qualities which, in the aggregate, we speak of as character. If he has not got it, then no law that the wit of man can devise, no administration of the law by the boldest and strongest executive, will avail to help him. We must have the right kind of character—character that makes a good husband—that makes a man a good neighbor. You must have that, and, then, in addition, you must have the kind of law and the kind of administration of the law which will give to those qualities in the private citizen the best possible chance for development. The prime problem of our nation is to get the right type of good citizenship, and, to get it, we must have progress, and our public men must be genuinely progressive.

The Old Order Changeth,* *Woodrow Wilson, 1912*

There is one great basic fact which underlies all the questions that are discussed on the political platform at the present moment. That singular fact is that nothing is done in this country as it was done twenty years ago.

We are in the presence of a new organization of society. Our life has broken away from the past. The life of

*From *The New Freedom* by Woodrow Wilson. Copyright 1913 by Doubleday & Company, Inc.

America is not the life that it was twenty years ago; it is not the life that it was ten years ago. We have changed our economic conditions, absolutely, from top to bottom; and, with our economic society, the organization of our life. The old political formulas do not fit the present problems; they read now like documents taken out of a forgotten age. The older cries sound as if they belonged to a past age which men have almost forgotten.

Things which used to be put into the party platforms of ten years ago would sound antiquated if put into a platform now. We are facing the necessity of fitting a new social organization, as we did once fit the old organization, to the happiness and prosperity of the great body of citizens; for we are conscious that the new order of society has not been made to fit and provide the convenience or prosperity of the average man. The life of the nation has grown infinitely varied. It does not center now upon questions of governmental structure or of the distribution of governmental powers. It centers upon questions of the very structure and operation of society itself, of which government is only the instrument. Our development has run so fast and so far along the lines sketched in the earlier day of constitutional definition, has so crossed and interlaced those lines, has piled upon them such novel structures of trust and combination, has elaborated within them a life so manifold, so full of forces which transcend the boundaries of the country itself and fill the eyes of the world, that a new nation seems to have been created which the old formulas do not fit or afford a vital interpretation of.

We have come upon a very different age from any that preceded us. We have come upon an age when we do not do business in the way in which we used to do business—when we do not carry on any of the operations of manufacture, sale, transportation, or communication as men used to carry them on. There is a sense in which in our day the individual has been submerged. In most parts of our country men work, not for themselves, not as partners in the old way in which they used to work, but generally as employees—in a higher or lower grade—of great corporations. There was a time when corporations played a very minor part in our business affairs, but now they play the chief part, and most men are the servants of corporations.

You know what happens when you are the servant of a corporation. You have in no instance access to the men who are really determining the policy of the corporation. If the corporation is doing the things that it ought not to do, you really have no voice in the matter and must obey the orders, and you have oftentimes with deep mortification to cooperate in the doing of things which you know are against the public interest. Your individuality is swallowed up in the individuality and purpose of a great organization.

It is true that, while most men are thus submerged in the corporation, a few, a very few, are exalted to a power which as individuals they could never have wielded. Through the great organizations of which they are the heads, a few are enabled to play a part unprecedented by anything in history in the control of the business operations of the country and in the determination of the happiness of great numbers of people.

Yesterday, and ever since history began, men were related to one another as individuals. To be sure there were the family, the Church, and the State, institutions which associated men in certain wide circles of relationship. But in the ordinary concerns of life, in the ordinary work, in the daily round, men dealt freely and directly with one another. Today, the everyday relationships of men are largely with great impersonal concerns, with organizations, not with other individual men.

Now this is nothing short of a new social age, a new era of human relationship, a new stage-setting for the drama of life.

In this new age we find, for instance, that our laws with regard to the relations of employer and employee are in many respects wholly antiquated and impossible. They were framed for another age, which nobody now living remembers, which is, indeed, so remote from our life that it would be difficult for many of us to understand it if it were described to us. The employer is now generally a corporation or a huge company of some kind; the employee is one of hundreds or of thousands brought together, not by individual masters whom they know and with whom they have personal relations, but by agents of one sort or another. Workingmen are marshaled in great numbers for the performance of a multitude of particular tasks under a common discipline. They generally use dangerous and powerful machinery, over whose repair and renewal they have no control. New rules must be devised with regard to their obligations and their rights, their obligations to their employers and their responsibilities to one another. Rules must be devised for their protection, for their compensation when injured, for their support when disabled.

There is something very new and very big and very complex about these new relations of capital and labor. A new economic society has sprung up, and we must effect a new set of adjustments. We must not pit power against weakness. The employer is generally, in our day, as I have said, not an individual, but a powerful group; and yet the workingman when dealing with his employer is still, under our existing law, an individual. . . .

What we have to discuss is, not wrongs which individuals intentionally do—I do not believe there are a great many of those—but the wrongs of a system. I want to record my protest against any discussion of this matter which would seem to indicate that there are bodies of our fellow-citizens who are trying to grind us down and do us injustice. There are some men of that sort. I don't know how they sleep o'nights, but there are men of that kind. Thank God, they are not numerous. The truth is, we are all caught in a great economic system which is heartless. The modern corporation is not engaged in business as an individual. When we deal with it, we deal with an impersonal element, an immaterial piece of society. . . .

And do our laws take note of this curious state of things? Do they even attempt to distinguish between a man's act as a corporation director and as an individual? They do not. Our laws still deal with us on the basis of the old system. The law is still living in the dead past which we have left behind. . . .

Since I entered politics, I have chiefly had men's views confided to me privately. Some of the biggest men in the United States, in the field of commerce and manufacture, are afraid of somebody, are afraid of something. They know that there is a power somewhere so organized, so subtle, so watchful, so interlocked, so complete, so pervasive, that they had better not speak above their breath when they speak in condemnation of it.

They know that America is not a place of which it can be said, as it used to be, that a man may choose his own calling and pursue it just as far as his abilities enable him to pursue it; because today, if he enters certain fields, there are organizations which will use means against him that will prevent his building up a business which they do not want to have built up; organizations that will see to it that the ground is cut from under him and the markets shut against him. For if he begins to sell to certain retail dealers, to any retail dealers, the monopoly will refuse to sell to those dealers, and those dealers, afraid, will not buy the new man's wares.

And this is the country which has lifted to the admiration of the world its ideals of absolutely free opportunity, where no man is supposed to be under any limitation except the limitations of his character and of his mind; where there is supposed to be no distinction of class, no distinction of blood, no distinction of social status, but where men win or lose on their merits.

American industry is not free, as once it was free; American enterprise is not free; the man with only a little capital is finding it harder to get into the field, more and more impossible to compete with the big fellow. Why? Because the laws of this country do not prevent the strong from crushing the weak. That is the reason, and because the strong have crushed the weak the strong dominate the industry and the economic life of this country. No man can deny that the lines of endeavor have more and more narrowed and stiffened; no man who knows anything about the development of industry in this country can have failed to observe that the larger kinds of credit are more and more difficult to obtain, unless you obtain them under the terms of uniting your efforts with those who already control the industries of the country; and nobody can fail to observe that any man who tries to set himself up in competition with any process of manufacture which has been taken under the control of large combinations of capital will presently find himself either squeezed out or obliged to sell and allow himself to be absorbed.

There is a great deal that needs reconstruction in the United States. . . .

The present organization of business was meant for the big fellows and was not meant for the little fellows; it was meant for those who are at the top and was meant to exclude those who are at the bottom; it was meant to shut out beginners, to prevent new entries in the race, to prevent the building up of competitive enterprises that would interfere with the monopolies which the great trusts have built up.

What this country needs above everything else is a body of laws which will look after the men who are on the make rather than the men who are already made. Because the men who are already made are not going to live indefinitely, and they are not always kind enough to leave sons as able and as honest as they are.

The originative part of America, the part of America that makes new enterprises, the part into which the ambitious and gifted workingman makes his way up, the class that saves, that plans, that organizes, that presently spreads its enterprises until they have a national scope and character—that middle class is being more and more squeezed out by the processes which we have been taught to call processes of prosperity. Its members are sharing prosperity, no doubt; but what alarms me is that they are not *originating* prosperity. No country can afford to have its prosperity originated by a small controlling class. The treasury of America does not lie in the brains of the small body of men now in control of the great enterprises that have been concentrated under the direction of a very small number of persons. The treasury of America lies in those ambitions, those energies, that cannot be restricted to a special favored class. It depends upon the inventions of unknown men, upon the originations of unknown men, upon the ambitions of unknown men. Every country is renewed out of the ranks of the unknown, not out of the ranks of those already famous and powerful and in control.

There has come over the land that un-American set of conditions which enables a small number of men who control the Government to get favors from the Government; by those favors to exclude their fellows from equal business opportunity; by those favors to extend a network of control that will presently dominate every industry in the country, and so make men forget the ancient time when America lay in every hamlet, when America was to be seen in every fair valley, when America displayed her great forces on the broad prairies, ran her fine fires of enterprise up over the mountain sides and down into the bowels of the earth, and eager men were everywhere captains of industry, not employees; not looking to a distant city to find out what they might do, but looking about among their neighbors, finding credit according to their character, not according to their connections, finding credit in proportion to what was known to be in them and behind them, not in proportion to the securities they held that were approved where they were not known. In order to start an enterprise now, you have to be authenticated, in a perfectly impersonal way, not according to yourself, but according to what you own that somebody else approves of your owning. You cannot begin such an enterprise as those that have made America until you are so authenticated, until you have succeeded in obtaining the goodwill of large allied capitalists. Is that freedom? That is dependence, not freedom.

We used to think in the old-fashioned days when life was very simple that all that government had to do was to put on a policeman's uniform, and say, "Now don't anybody hurt anybody else." We used to say that the ideal of government was for every man to be left alone and not interfered with, except when he interfered with somebody else; and that the best government was the government that did as little governing as possible. That was the idea that obtained in Jefferson's time. But we are coming now to realize that life is so complicated that we are not dealing with the old conditions, and that the law has to step in and create new conditions under which we may live, the conditions which will make it tolerable for us to live. . . .

Why are we in the presence, why are we at the threshold, of a revolution? Because we are profoundly disturbed by the influences which we see reigning in the determination of our public life and our public policy. There was a time when America was blithe with self-confidence. She boasted that she, and she alone, knew the processes of popular government; but now she sees her sky overcast; she sees that there are at work forces which she did not dream of in her hopeful youth.

Don't you know that some man with eloquent tongue, without conscience, who did not care for the nation, could put this whole country into a flame? Don't you know that this country from one end to the other believes that something is wrong? What an opportunity it would be for some man without conscience to spring up and say: "This is the way. Follow me!"—and lead in paths of destruction!

The old order changeth—changeth under our very eyes, not quietly and equably, but swiftly and with the noise and heat and tumult of reconstruction.

I suppose that all struggle for law has been conscious, that very little of it has been blind or merely instinctive. It is the fashion to say, as if with superior knowledge of affairs and of human weakness that every age has been an age of transition, and that no age is more full of change than another; yet in very few ages of the world can the struggle for change have been so widespread, so deliberate, or upon so great a scale as in this in which we are taking part.

The transition we are witnessing is no equable transition of growth and normal alteration; no silent, unconscious unfolding of one age into another, its natural heir and successor. Society is looking itself over, in our day, from top to bottom; is making fresh and critical analysis of its very elements; is questioning its oldest practices as freely as its newest, scrutinizing every arrangement and motive of its life; and it stands ready to attempt nothing less than a radical reconstruction, which only frank and honest counsels and the forces of generous co-operation can hold back from becoming a revolution. We are in a temper to reconstruct economic society, as we were once in a temper to reconstruct a political society, and political society may itself undergo a radical modification in the process. I doubt if any age was ever more conscious of its task or more unanimously desirous of radical and extended changes in its economic and political practice.

We stand in the presence of a revolution—not a bloody revolution; America is not given to the spilling of blood—but a silent revolution, whereby America will insist upon recovering in practice those ideals which she has always professed, upon securing a government devoted to the general interest and not to special interests.

We are upon the eve of a great reconstruction. It calls for creative statesmanship as no age has done since that great age in which we set up the government under which we live, that government which was the admiration of the world until it suffered wrongs to grow up under it which have made many of our own compatriots question the freedom of our institutions and preach revolution against them. I do not fear revolution. I have unshaken faith in the power of America to keep its self-possession. Revolution will come in peaceful guise, as it came when we put aside the crude government of the Confederation and created the great Federal Union which governs individuals, not States, and which has been these hundred and thirty years our vehicle of progress. Some radical changes we must make in our law and practice. Some reconstructions we must push forward, which a new age and new circumstances impose upon us. But we can do it all in calm and sober fashion, like statesmen and patriots.

I do not speak of these things in apprehension, because all is open and above-board. This is not a day in which great forces rally in secret. The whole stupendous program must be publicly planned and canvassed. Good temper, the wisdom that comes of sober counsel, the energy of thoughtful and unselfish men, the habit of co-operation and compromise which has been bred in us by long years of free government, in which reason rather than passion has been made to prevail by the sheer virtue of candid and universal debate, will enable us to win through to still another great age without violence.

Chapter 21

THE GREAT CRUSADE AND AFTER

When on March 4, 1913, Woodrow Wilson became President of the United States, the American mind was far from thoughts of war and peace. Though for two decades Americans had enjoyed both the material and the emotional satisfactions of imperialist expansion, they had not yet fully accepted the limitations and responsibilities that accompany predominance in world affairs. The acquisition of a colonial empire had marked the formal abandonment of isolationism, but few were aware that now the nation's destiny might be determined in the chancelleries of the world. Most Americans were still provincial enough to believe that they could assume and divest themselves of the burden of world leadership at will, and in the heat of the 1912 Presidential campaign national energies were once again directed toward domestic issues to the exclusion of any real concern for international interests and commitments. Indeed, while Wilson's Inaugural Address solemnly pointed the way to national reconstruction, it contained not a single reference to America's relations with foreign nations or to the seething troubles of the world at large.

Nevertheless, foreign affairs became a major concern of Wilson's administration. From his first days in office there raged a bitter quarrel with Mexico's revolutionary leaders which frequently threatened to erupt into war. And the vulnerability of America's new position of power was strikingly demonstrated by her inability to remain aloof from the world conflict precipitated in the summer of 1914 by the assassination of Archduke Ferdinand, heir apparent to the Austro-Hungarian throne. Wilson immediately issued a Proclamation of Neutrality, and at first the European conflagration seemed of small concern to a distant people intent upon domestic reform. Eventually, however, America's involvement in the stakes of world diplomacy proved stronger than the illusion of isolation, and in April 1917, after several years of vacillation and confusion, she entered the war on the side of the Allies.

No single factor of itself "caused" America to fight, though British propaganda, American economic ties to the Allies, and unrestricted German submarine warfare all played significant roles in leading the nation on the road to war. And in molding American opinion even the outstanding success of British propaganda depended largely upon Americans' latent sympathy with the Allied cause. Numbers of German-Americans supported the Fatherland, and many citizens of Irish extraction bitterly and continuously denounced the British, but from the very beginning of the war public opinion was for the most part decidedly pro-Ally. The subtle bonds of language, custom, and a common literary and political heritage tied America more closely to England in war than ever before in peace; while traditional attachment to the French was fostered by recollections of France's gallant contributions to the American Revolution. The stage was set, then, for a widespread propaganda campaign designed to maneuver a cautious but sympathetic public into war. Throughout the nation British-inspired articles, speeches, lectures, debates, and films argued the case against Germany. From college presidents to practicing journalists influential persons in every profession were enlisted to add an aura of validity to even the most outrageously false atrocity stories of German brutality. And Americans were assured on every hand that Germany alone was responsible for a war which ostensibly was a struggle between democracy and civilization on the one side and autocracy and barbarism on the other. Besides, Germany's feeble propaganda effort proved highly ineffective. It was handicapped both by an inability to grasp American modes of thought and by the bald facts that the Kaiser's troops *did* openly violate Belgian neutrality, that a German U-boat *did* torpedo the *Lusitania* with the loss of hundreds of lives, and that German espionage agents *did* attempt sabotage in American munitions plants. Thus the efficient British propaganda machine impressed upon the American mind stereotypes of German motives and ambitions that went far to prepare the nation psychologically for war against the aggressive "Hun."

Extensive business and financial ties to the Allies further jeopardized American neutrality, for they made the prospect of a German victory materially as well as ideologically unpalatable. When the war began, it had been clear to Wilson and to William Jennings Bryan, his Secretary of State, that economic involvement with either of the belligerents might compromise the nation's neutral status and lead to war. At first, therefore, the government refused to sanction loans by American bankers to the warring powers. But the President vigorously opposed an embargo that would have cut off altogether shipments abroad, and cash or credit purchases, whether of contraband or noncontraband, could still be made. Though forced to liquidate a large part of their assets in the United States to pay for these goods, the Allies alone benefited from Wilson's open policy, for control of the seas enabled them to transport foodstuffs and munitions to their own forces and to prevent neutral and enemy vessels alike from reaching Germany with American cargoes. Soon, however, Allied assets and credits in the United States were exhausted by tremendous expenditures, and Wilson was faced with an unhappy choice. If he reversed his earlier position and now approved of large-scale private loans to the Allies to finance continued purchases of American goods, he would skirt the edge of belligerency and endanger American neutrality. Yet if he refused to permit these loans, not only would the Allied cause be seriously endangered, but the national economy, largely geared to war demands, would suffer serious dislocation and depression. Under intense pressure from a frightened business community and from Allied sympathizers among his advisers (the pacific and impartial Bryan had already resigned from the Cabinet), Wilson finally made his fateful choice to withdraw the government's opposition to private loans for the belligerents. And by the spring of 1917, when the United States formally entered the World War, Americans had already loaned approximately two billion dollars to the Allies (though only $27 million to Germany) and had made their economy even more dependent upon Allied purchases of war material. The nation's economic stake in an Allied victory had grown enormously; with this huge investment, though not necessarily because of it, had come war.

Still, whatever the underlying causes of America's ultimate readiness to join forces with the Allies, it was the German U-boat that immediately plunged the nation into war. Mistress of the seas, England had again and again taken liberties with American neutral rights in her efforts to blockade the Central Powers; she had arbitrarily declared the North Sea a military zone, making that vital trade area largely inaccessible to neutral shipping; she had forced countless American ships to distant ports for visit and search; and under a vastly extended contraband list she had seized American cargoes bound directly or indirectly (through other neutral countries) for Germany. Yet British depredations had not taken American lives; American shippers had been generously compensated for their property losses; and though the State Department went through the formality of protesting these high-handed practices, the emotional and economic ties between the two countries were far too close to permit even the threat of retaliation.

On the other hand, German violations of American rights were received very differently, for here there was no reservoir of friendship and interest to temper national indignation. Early in 1915 Germany proclaimed a submarine war zone around the British Isles in order to counter the Allied blockade, warning that enemy ships would be torpedoed on sight. But now the American government refused to acquiesce as timidly as it had with the British earlier. Instead it continued to permit its citizens unlimited travel aboard Allied ships in the restricted zone, ominously declaring that Germany alone would be held to "strict accountability" if American lives or property were lost.

Submarine warfare very quickly took its toll. On May 7, 1915, a British liner, the *Lusitania,* was torpedoed and sunk without warning, with the loss of nearly 1,200 persons, over 100 of whom were Americans. Other American lives and ships were lost during the year that followed, and though Wilson himself insisted that "There is such a thing as a man being too proud to fight," the bitterness and seeming finality of American protests led the Germans, on May 4, 1916, to pledge that unresisting merchantmen would not be sunk without warning and adequate provision for passengers and crew. But eight months later, in January 1917, Germany announced that unrestricted submarine warfare would resume immediately and that U-boats would torpedo all ships, whether neutral or belligerent, found in the war zone. The logic behind this new position was clear, though mistaken. The German High Command had recognized that such a policy would be followed by war with the great Western power, but it was equally convinced that in the near future America could not aid the Allies any more as an active belligerent than she had as a "benevolent" neutral, for now German U-boats would be totally unrestricted in their efforts to send American cargoes to the bottom of the sea. Then on April 2, 1917, after several more American ships had been torpedoed, Woodrow Wilson appeared before the Congress to take up the German challenge. "Property can be paid for," said the President in his memorable war message, but "the lives of peaceful and innocent people cannot be. The present German submarine warfare against commerce is a warfare against mankind." Four days later the Congress acceded to the President's request, and war was declared against Germany.

Wilson's own role in molding America's final decision to enter the war is difficult to evaluate, for at no time was the austere reformer free from tormenting conflict on the grave issue before him. As an historian, Wilson was familiar enough with the ways of international power politics to see through many of the Allied propaganda claims, and when the war began in Europe he called upon the American people to be "impartial in thought as well as in action" so that the nation might maintain absolute neutrality between the belligerents. Even as late as the presidential election of 1916, when the Republican Charles Evans Hughes opposed Wilson, the Democrats were able to make effective use of the slogan "He kept us out of war." But official proclamations could not change, nor even disguise, Wilson's own deep involvement with the Allied cause. His broad sympathy for the English and his intense feeling that the Allies were fighting "our fight" far outweighed his dim and merely intellectual awareness of the war's imperialist origins. Yet even these fervid sympathies did not permit him fully and satisfactorily to resolve his personal inner conflict between the choices of war and peace, for the controlled and puritanical President was not capable of lightly brushing aside his understanding and totally succumbing to his feelings. At length, of course, he chose war, but not without the gravest of misgivings engendered both by his somewhat reluctant recognition of the essentially nonideological nature of the world struggle and by his basic antipathy to war itself. To a less scrupulous, less self-demanding statesman such misgivings would have brought balance and humility; but to the perfectionist Wilson they brought only confusion and a tortured sense of guilt which convinced him that the war must be a holy crusade to "make the world safe for democracy."

Earlier Wilson had called for a "peace without victory"; now he placed America's physical and moral might behind his famous Fourteen Points for a just and lasting peace. Wilson's Fourteenth Point, providing for a "general association of nations . . . for the purpose of affording mutual guarantees of political independence and territorial integrity to great and small states alike," was the cornerstone of his plans for international order. And when the Treaty of Versailles was drawn up at the end of the war Wilson made several concessions in his other idealistic demands in order to assure the creation of a meaningful League of Nations. These concessions to Clemenceau of France, Lloyd George of England, and Orlando of Italy were to no avail, however, for it was the Republican leaders of the United States Senate, not the nationalist statesmen of Europe, who fought most bitterly against Wilson's League and who contributed to its ultimate defeat by refusing American participation.

Doubtlessly partisanship played a decisive role in formulating Congressional opposition to the League. Those "irreconcilable" isolationists who bitterly opposed American participation in *any* formal international organization were alone too few to prevent the two-thirds Senate vote necessary for ratification of the Treaty of Versailles, into which was written the Covenant of the League of Nations. Indeed, Wilson's leading

Republican opponent, Senator Henry Cabot Lodge, Chairman of the powerful Committee on Foreign Relations, had only a few years earlier heartily endorsed a league to enforce peace. But the Treaty before the Senate was exclusively Wilsonian and Democratic, and the Massachusetts Republican was determined either to defeat Wilson's creation or, preferably, to make it over into a Republican document through extensive reservations and amendments. Wilson was equally determined to have the treaty as it stood or not at all. Neither man was willing to give way to the other. In November, 1919, and again in March 1920, moderate Republicans joined with the hard core of Senate isolationists to defeat the Treaty *without* the Lodge reservations. And Wilson Democrats, obeying their intransigent chief's wishes, joined with these same isolationists to defeat the Treaty *with* the Lodge reservations.

Thus Wilson must share with Lodge and his followers much of the responsibility for the defeat of the Treaty and the League in the Senate. Sincerely convinced that only a totally unqualified League could justify and atone for the death and destruction brought by the holocaust to which he had himself committed the nation, Wilson had lost all sense of political necessity. Late in 1918, on the very eve of victory, he had made a foolishly partisan appeal to the country to elect a Democratic Congress, implying that only the party in power might successfully end the war and make peace secure; and the nation had replied by electing a Republican House and a Republican Senate. When he went to Europe later that year Wilson took only one Republican adviser, and not a single Senator, to the Versailles Peace Conference, thereby antagonizing not only an already highly aroused opposition party, but also the legislative body that must ultimately accept or reject whatever treaty he might bring home. Finally, in the summer of 1919 Wilson took his case to the country in an exhausting round of speeches, of which the most moving was his address at Pueblo, Colorado, where he finally succumbed to physical exhaustion and suffered a near-fatal stroke. But the President had unfortunately forgotten the role of compromise in the democratic process, and his efforts were in vain. The irony of Wilson's Presidency was that the domestic reformer should have been so completely caught up in the embroilments of world affairs. Its supreme tragedy was that his own single-minded devotion to the establishment of the machinery of international cooperation—exactly as he had conceived it, without reservation or amendment—should have helped destroy the lasting peace for which he had fought so valiantly and which he considered a personal as much as a national imperative.

War Message to Congress, *Woodrow Wilson, 1917*

Gentlemen of the Congress: I have called the Congress into extraordinary session because there are serious, very serious, choices of policy to be made, and made immediately, which it was neither right nor constitutionally permissible that I should assume the responsibility of making.

On the third of February last I officially laid before you the extraordinary announcement of the Imperial German Government that on and after the first day of February it was its purpose to put aside all restraints of law or of humanity and use its submarines to sink every vessel that sought to approach either the ports of Great Britain and Ireland or the western coasts of Europe or any of the ports controlled by the enemies of Germany within the Mediterranean. That had seemed to be the object of the German submarine warfare earlier in the war, but since April of last year the Imperialist Government had somewhat restrained the commanders of its undersea craft in conformity with its promise then given to us that passenger boats should not be sunk and that due warning would be given to all other vessels which its submarines might seek to destroy, when no resistance was offered or escape attempted, and care taken that their crews were given at least a fair chance to save their lives in their open boats. The precautions taken were meagre and haphazard enough, as was proved in distressing instance after instance in the progress of the cruel and unmanly business, but a certain degree of restraint was observed. The new policy has swept every restriction aside. Vessels of every kind, whatever their flag, their character, their cargo, their destination, their errand, have been ruthlessly sent to the bottom without warning and without thought of help or mercy for those on board, the vessels of friendly neutrals along with those of belligerents. Even hospital ships and ships carrying relief to the sorely bereaved and stricken people of Belgium, though the latter were provided with safe conduct through the proscribed areas by the German Government itself and were distinguished by unmistakable marks of identity, have been sunk with the same reckless lack of compassion or of principle.

I was for a little while unable to believe that such things would in fact be done by any government that had hitherto subscribed to the humane practices of civilized nations. International law had its origin in the attempt to set up some law which would be respected and observed upon the seas, where no nation had right of dominion and where lay the free highways of the world. By painful stage after stage has that law been built up, with meagre enough results, indeed, after all was accomplished that could be accomplished, but always with a clear view, at least, of what the heart and conscience of mankind demanded. This minimum of right the German Government has swept aside under the plea of retaliation and necessity and because it had no weapons which it could use at sea except these which it is impossible to employ as it is employing them without throwing to the winds all scruples of humanity or of respect for the understandings that were supposed to underlie the intercourse of the world. I am not now thinking of the loss of property involved, immense and serious as that is, but only of the wanton and wholesale destruction of the lives of non-combatants, men, women, and children, engaged in pursuits which have always, even in the darkest periods of modern history, been deemed innocent and legitimate. Property can be paid for; the lives of peaceful and innocent people cannot be. The present German submarine warfare against commerce is a warfare against mankind. . . .

When I addressed the Congress on the twenty-sixth of February last I thought that it would suffice to assert our neutral rights with arms, our right to use the seas against unlawful interference, our right to keep our people safe against unlawful violence. But armed neutrality, it now appears, is impracticable. Because submarines are in effect outlaws when used as the German submarines have been used against merchant shipping, it is impossible to defend ships against their attacks as the law of nations has assumed that merchantmen would defend themselves against privateers or cruisers, visible craft giving chase upon the open sea. It is common prudence in such circumstances, grim necessity indeed, to endeavour to destroy them before they have shown their own intention. They must be dealt with upon sight, if dealt with at all. The German Government denies the right of neutrals to use arms at all within the areas of the sea which it has proscribed, even in the defense of rights which no modern publicist has ever before questioned their right to defend. The intimation is conveyed that the armed guards which we have placed on our merchant ships will be treated as beyond the pale of law and subject to be dealt with as pirates would be. Armed neutrality is ineffectual enough at best; in such circumstances and in the face of such pretensions it is worse than ineffectual: it is likely only to produce what it was meant to prevent; it is practically certain to draw us into the war without either the rights or the effectiveness of belligerents. There is one choice we cannot make, we are incapable of making: we will not choose the path of submission and suffer the most sacred rights of our nation and our people to be ignored or violated. The wrongs against which we now array ourselves are no common wrongs; they cut to the very roots of human life.

With a profound sense of the solemn and even tragical character of the step I am taking and of the grave responsibilities which it involves, but in unhesitating obedience to what I deem my constitutional duty, I advise that the Congress declare the recent course of the Imperial German Government to be in fact nothing less than war against the Government and people of the United States; that it formally accept the status of belligerent which has thus been thrust upon it; and that it take immediate steps not only to put the country in a more thorough state of defense but also to exert all its power and employ all its resources to bring the

Government of the German Empire to terms and end the war. . . .

While we do these things, these deeply momentous things, let us be very clear, and make very clear to all the world what our motives and our objects are. My own thought has not been driven from its habitual and normal course by the unhappy events of the last two months, and I do not believe that the thought of the nation has been altered or clouded by them. I have exactly the same things in mind now that I had in mind when I addressed the Senate on the twenty-second of January last; the same that I had in mind when I addressed the Congress on the third of February and on the twenty-sixth of February. Our object now, as then, is to vindicate the principles of peace and justice in the life of the world as against selfish and autocratic power and to set up amongst the really free and self-governed peoples of the world such a concert of purpose and of action as will henceforth ensure the observance of those principles. Neutrality is no longer feasible or desirable where the peace of the world is involved and the freedom of its peoples, and the menace to that peace and freedom lies in the existence of autocratic governments backed by organized force which is controlled wholly by their will, not by the will of their people. We have seen the last of neutrality in such circumstances. We are at the beginning of an age in which it will be insisted that the same standards of conduct and of responsibility for wrong done shall be observed among nations and their governments that are observed among the individual citizens of civilized states.

We have no quarrel with the German people. We have no feeling towards them but one of sympathy and friendship. It was not upon their impulse that their government acted in entering the war. It was not with their previous knowledge or approval. It was a war determined upon as wars used to be determined upon in the old, unhappy days when peoples were nowhere consulted by their rulers and wars were provoked and waged in the interest of dynasties or of little groups of ambitious men who were accustomed to use their fellow men as pawns and tools. Self-governed nations do not fill their neighbour states with spies or set the course of intrigue to bring about some critical posture of affairs which will give them an opportunity to strike and make conquest. Such designs can be successfully worked out only under cover and where no one has the right to ask questions. Cunningly contrived plans of deception or aggression, carried, it may be, from generation to generation, can be worked out and kept from the light only within the privacy of courts or behind the carefully guarded confidences of a narrow and privileged class. They are happily impossible where public opinion commands and insists upon full information concerning all the nation's affairs.

A steadfast concert for peace can never be maintained except by a partnership of democratic nations. No autocratic government could be trusted to keep faith within it or observe its covenants. It must be a league of honour, a partnership of opinion. Intrigue would eat its vitals away; the plottings of inner circles who could plan what they would and render account to no one would be a corruption seated at its very heart. Only free peoples can hold their purpose and their honour steady to a common end and prefer the interests of mankind to any narrow interest of their own. . . .

We are accepting this challenge of hostile purpose because we know that in such a government, following such methods, we can never have a friend; and that in the presence of its organized power, always lying in wait to accomplish we know not what purpose, there can be no assured security for the democratic governments of the world. We are now about to accept gauge of battle with this natural foe to liberty and shall, if necessary, spend the whole force of the nation to check and nullify its pretensions and its power. We are glad, now that we see the facts with no veil of false pretence about them, to fight thus for the ultimate peace of the world and for the liberation of its peoples, the German peoples included: for the rights of nations great and small and the privilege of men everywhere to choose their way of life and of obedience. The world must be made safe for democracy. Its peace must be planted upon the tested foundations of political liberty. We have no selfish ends to serve. We desire no conquest, no dominion. We seek no indemnities for ourselves, no material compensation for the sacrifices we shall freely make. We are but one of the champions of the rights of mankind. We shall be satisfied when those rights have been made as secure as the faith and the freedom of nations can make them.

Just because we fight without rancour and without selfish object, seeking nothing for ourselves but what we shall wish to share with all free peoples, we shall, I feel confident, conduct our operations as belligerents without passion and ourselves observe with proud punctilio the principles of right and of fair play we profess to be fighting for. . . .

It will be all the easier for us to conduct ourselves as belligerents in a high spirit of right and fairness because we act without animus, not in enmity towards a people or with the desire to bring any injury or disadvantage upon them, but only in armed opposition to an irresponsible government which has thrown aside all considerations of humanity and of right and is running amuck. We are, let me say again, the sincere friends of the German people, and shall desire nothing so much as the early re-establishment of intimate relations of mutual advantage between us—however hard it may be for them, for the time being, to believe that this is spoken from our hearts. We have borne with their present government through all these bitter months because of that friendship—exercising a patience and forbearance which would otherwise have been impossible. We shall, happily, still have an opportunity to prove that friendship in our daily attitude and actions towards the millions of men and women of German birth and native sympathy who live amongst us and share our life, and we shall be proud to prove it towards all who are in fact loyal to their neighbours and to the Government in the hour of test. They are, most of them, as true and loyal Americans as if they had never known any other fealty or allegiance. They will be prompt to stand with us in rebuking and restraining the few who may be of a different mind and purpose. If there should be disloyalty, it will be dealt with with a firm hand of stern repression; but, if it lifts its head at all, it will lift it only here and there and without countenance except from a lawless and malignant few.

It is a distressing and oppressive duty, Gentlemen of

the Congress, which I have performed in thus addressing you. There are, it may be, many months of fiery trial and sacrifice ahead of us. It is a fearful thing to lead this great peaceful people into war, into the most terrible and disastrous of all wars, civilization itself seeming to be in the balance. But the right is more precious than peace, and we shall fight for the things which we have always carried nearest our hearts—for democracy, for the right of those who submit to authority to have a voice in their own governments, for the rights and liberties of small nations, for a universal dominion of right by such a concert of free people as shall bring peace and safety to all nations and make the world itself at last free. To such a task we can dedicate our lives and our fortunes, everything that we are and everything that we have, with the pride of those who know that the day has come when America is privileged to spend her blood and her might for the principles that gave her birth and happiness and the peace which she has treasured. God helping her, she can do no other.

Fourteen Points
Woodrow Wilson, 1918

Gentlemen of the Congress:

. . . It will be our wish and purpose that the processes of peace, when they are begun, shall be absolutely open and that they shall involve and permit henceforth no secret understandings of any kind. The day of conquest and aggrandizement is gone by; so is also the day of secret covenants entered into in the interest of particular governments and likely at some unlooked-for moment to upset the peace of the world. It is this happy fact, now clear to the view of every public man whose thoughts do not still linger in an age that is dead and gone, which makes it possible for every nation whose purposes are consistent with justice and the peace of the world to avow now or at any other time the objects it has in view.

We entered this war because violations of right had occurred which touched us to the quick and made the life of our own people impossible unless they were corrected and the world secured once for all against their recurrence. What we demand in this war, therefore, is nothing peculiar to ourselves. It is that the world be made fit and safe to live in; and particularly that it be made safe for every peace-loving nation which, like our own, wishes to live its own life, determine its own institutions, be assured of justice and fair dealing by the other peoples of the world as against force and selfish aggression. All the peoples of the world are in effect partners in this interest, and for our own part we see very clearly that unless justice be done to others it will not be done to us. The program of the world's peace, therefore, is our program; and that program, the only possible program, as we see it is this:

I. Open covenants of peace, openly arrived at, after which there shall be no private international understandings of any kind but diplomacy shall proceed always frankly and in the public view.

II. Absolute freedom of navigation upon the seas, outside territorial waters, alike in peace and in war, except as the seas may be closed in whole or in part by international action for the enforcement of international covenants.

III. The removal, so far as possible, of all economic barriers and the establishment of an equality of trade conditions among all the nations consenting to the peace and associating themselves for its maintenance.

IV. Adequate guarantees given and taken that national armaments will be reduced to the lowest point consistent with domestic safety.

V. A free, open-minded, and absolutely impartial adjustment of all colonial claims, based upon a strict observance of the principle that in determining all such questions of sovereignty the interests of the populations concerned must have equal weight with the equitable claims of the government whose title is to be determined.

VI. The evacuation of all Russian territory and such a settlement of all questions affecting Russia as will secure the best and freest coöperation of the other nations of the world in obtaining for her an unhampered and unembarrassed opportunity for the independent determination of her own political development and national policy and assure her of a sincere welcome into the society of free nations under institutions of her own choosing; and, more than a welcome, assistance also of every kind that she may need and may herself desire. The treatment accorded Russia by her sister nations in the months to come will be the acid test of their good will, of their comprehension of her needs as distinguished from their own interests, and of their intelligent and unselfish sympathy.

VII. Belgium, the whole world will agree, must be evacuated and restored, without any attempt to limit the sovereignty which she enjoys in common with all other free nations. No other single act will serve as this will serve to restore confidence among the nations in the laws which they have themselves set and determined for the government of their relations with one another. Without this healing act the whole structure and validity of international law is forever impaired.

VIII. All French territory should be freed and the invaded portions restored, and the wrong done to France by Prussia in 1871 in the matter of Alsace-Lorraine, which has unsettled the peace of the world for nearly fifty years, should be righted, in order that peace may once more be made secure in the interest of all.

IX. A readjustment of the frontiers of Italy should be effected along clearly recognizable lines of nationality.

X. The peoples of Austria-Hungary, whose place among the nations we wish to see safe-guarded and assured, should be accorded the freest opportunity of autonomous development.

XI. Rumania, Serbia, and Montenegro should be evacuated; occupied territories restored; Serbia accorded free and secure access to the sea; and the relations of the several Balkan states to one another determined by friendly counsel along historically established lines of allegiance and nationality; and international guarantees of the political and economic independence and territorial integrity of the several Balkan states should be entered into.

XII. The Turkish portions of the present Ottoman Empire should be assured a secure sovereignty, but the other nationalities which are now under Turkish rule should be assured an undoubted security of life and an absolutely unmolested opportunity of autonomous development, and the Dardanelles should be permanently opened as a free passage to the ships and commerce of all nations under international guarantees.

XIII. An independent Polish state should be erected which should include the territories inhabited by indisputably Polish populations, which should be assured a free and secure access to the sea, and whose political and economic independence and territorial integrity should be guaranteed by international covenant.

XIV. A general association of nations must be formed under specific covenants for the purpose of affording mutual guarantees of political independence and territorial integrity to great and small states alike.

In regard to these essential rectifications of wrong and assertions of right we feel ourselves to be intimate partners of all the governments and peoples associated together against the Imperialists. We cannot be separated in interest or divided in purpose. We stand together until the end.

For such arrangements and covenants we are willing to fight and to continue to fight until they are achieved; but only because we wish the right to prevail and desire a just and stable peace such as can be secured only by removing the chief provocations to war, which this program does not remove. We have no jealousy of German greatness, and there is nothing in this program that impairs it. We grudge her no achievement or distinction of learning or of pacific enterprise such as have made her record very bright and very enviable. We do not wish to injure her or to block in any way her legitimate influence or power. We do not wish to fight her either with arms or with hostile arrangements of trade if she is willing to associate herself with us and the other peace-loving nations of the world in covenants of justice and law and fair dealing. We wish her only to accept a place of equality among the peoples of the world,—the new world in which we now live,—instead of a place of mastery.

Neither do we presume to suggest to her any alteration or modification of her institutions. But it is necessary, we must frankly say, and necessary as a preliminary to any intelligent dealings with her on our part, that we should know whom her spokesmen speak for when they speak to us, whether for the Reichstag majority or for the military party and the men whose creed is imperial domination.

We have spoken now, surely, in terms too concrete to admit of any further doubt or question. An evident principle runs through the whole program I have outlined. It is the principle of justice to all peoples and nationalities, and their right to live on equal terms of liberty and safety with one another, whether they be strong or weak. Unless this principle be made its foundation no part of the structure of international justice can stand. The people of the United States could act upon no other principle; and to the vindication of this principle they are ready to devote their lives, their honor, and everything that they possess. The moral climax of this the culminating and final war for human liberty has come, and they are ready to put their own strength, their own highest purpose, their own integrity and devotion to the test.

The Pueblo Speech on the League of Nations
Woodrow Wilson, 1919

. . . There have been unpleasant impressions as well as pleasant impressions, my fellow citizens, as I have crossed the continent. I have perceived more and more that men have been busy creating an absolutely false impression of what the treaty of peace and the covenant of the League of Nations contain and mean. . . . Therefore, in order to clear away the mists, in order to remove the impressions, in order to check the falsehoods that have clustered around this great subject, I want to tell you a few simple things about the treaty and the covenant.

. . . It is a people's treaty, that accomplishes by a great sweep of practical justice the liberation of men who never could have liberated themselves, and the power of the most powerful nations has been devoted not to their aggrandizement but to the liberation of people whom they could have put under their control if they had chosen to do so. Not one foot of territory is demanded by the conquerors, not one single item of submission to their authority is demanded by them. The men who sat around that table in Paris knew that the time had come when the people were no longer going to consent to live under masters, but were going to live the lives that they chose themselves, to live under such governments as they chose themselves to erect. That is the fundamental principle of this great settlement. . . .

At the front of this great treaty is put the covenant of the League of Nations. . . . Unless you get the united, concerted purpose and power of the great Governments of the world behind this settlement, it will fall down like a house of cards. There is only one power to put behind the liberation of mankind, and that is the power of mankind. It is the power of the united moral forces of the world, and in the covenant of the League of Nations the moral forces of the world are mobilized. . . . They enter into a solemn promise to one another that they will never use their power against one another for aggression; that they never will impair the territorial integrity of a neighbor; that they never will interfere with the political independence of a neighbor; that they will abide by the principle that great populations are entitled to determine their own destiny and that they will not interfere with that destiny; and that no matter what differences arise amongst them they will never resort to war without first having . . . either submitted the matter of controversy to arbitration, in which case they agree to abide by the result without question or submitted it to the consideration of the Council of the League of Nations . . . agreeing that there shall be six months allowed for the mature consideration of . . . the Council, and agreeing that at the expiration of the six months, even if they are not then ready to accept the advice of the Council with regard to the settlement of the dispute, they will still not go to war for another three months. In other words, they consent, no matter what happens, to submit every matter of difference between them to the judgment of mankind, and just so certainly as they do that, . . . war will be pushed out of the foreground of terror in which it has kept the world for generation after generation, and men will know that there will be a calm time of deliberate counsel. The most dangerous thing for a bad cause is to expose it to the opinion of the world. The most certain way that you can prove that a man is mistaken is by letting all his neighbors know what he thinks, by letting all his neighbors discuss what he thinks, and if he is in the wrong you will notice that he will stay at home, he will not walk on the street. He will be afraid of the eyes of his neighbors. He will be afraid of their judgment of his character. He will know that his cause is lost unless he can sustain it by the arguments of right and of justice. The same law that applies to individuals applies to nations. . . .

When you come to the heart of the covenant, my fellow citizens, you will find . . . there is something in article 10 that you ought to realize and ought to accept or reject. Article 10 is the heart of the whole matter. . . . Article 10 provides that every member of the League covenants to respect and preserve the territorial integrity and existing political independence of every other member of the League as against external aggression. Not against internal disturbance. There was not a man at that table who did not admit the sacredness of the right of self-determination, the sacredness of the right of any body of people to say that they would not continue to live under the Government they were then living under, and under article 11 of the covenant they are given a place to say whether they will live under it or not. For following article 10 is article 11, which makes it the right of any member of the League at any time to call attention to anything, anywhere, that is likely to disturb the peace of the world or the good understanding between nations upon which the peace of the world depends. . . . Now, read articles 10 and 11. You will see that international law is revolutionized by putting morals into it. Article 10 says that no member of the League, and that includes all these nations that have demanded these things unjustly of China, shall impair the territorial integrity or the political independence of any other member of the League. China is going to be a member of the League. Article 11 says that any member of the League can call attention to anything that is likely to disturb the peace of the world or the good understanding between nations, and China is for the first time in the history of mankind afforded a standing before the jury of the world. I, for my part, have a profound sympathy for China, and I am proud to have taken part in an arrangement which promises the protection of the world to the rights of China. The whole atmosphere of the world is changed by a thing like that, my fellow citizens. The whole international practice of the world is revolutionized.

But you will say, "what is the second sentence of article 10? That is what gives very disturbing thoughts." The second sentence is that the Council of the League shall advise what steps, if any, are necessary to carry out the guaranty of the first sentence, namely, that the members will respect and preserve the territorial integrity and political independence of the other members. I do not know any other meaning for the word "advise" except "advise." The Council advises, and it can not advise without the vote of the United States. Why gentlemen should fear that the Congress of the United States would be advised to do something that it did not want to do I frankly can not imagine, because they can not even be advised to do anything unless their own representative has participated in the advice. It may be that that will impair somewhat the vigor of the League, but, nevertheless, the fact is so, that we are not obliged to take any advice except our own, which to any man who wants to go his own course is a very satisfactory state of affairs. Every man regards his own advice as best, and I dare say every man mixes his own advice with some thought of his own interest. Whether we use it wisely or unwisely, we can use the vote of the United States to make impossible drawing the United States into any enterprise that she does not care to be drawn into.

Yet article 10 strikes at the taproot of war. Article 10 is a statement that the very things that have always been sought in imperialistic wars are henceforth forgone by every ambitious nation in the world. I would have felt very lonely, my fellow countrymen, and I would have felt very much disturbed if, sitting at the peace table in Paris, I had supposed that I was expounding my own ideas. Whether you believe it or not, I know the relative size of my own ideas; I know how they stand related in bulk and proportion to the moral judgments of my fellow countrymen, and I purposed nothing whatever at the peace table at Paris that I had not sufficiently certain knowledge embodied the moral judgment of the citizens of the United States. I had gone over there with, so to say, explicit instructions. Don't you remember that we laid down fourteen points which should contain the principles of the settlement? They were not my points. In every one of them I was conscientiously trying to read the thought of the people of the United States, and after I uttered those points I had every assurance given me that could be given me that they did speak the moral judgment of the United States and not my single judgment. . . .

I am dwelling upon these points, my fellow citizens, in spite of the fact that I dare say to most of you they are perfectly well known, because in order to meet the present situation we have got to know what we are dealing with. We are not dealing with the kind of document which this is represented by some gentlemen to be; and inasmuch as we are dealing with a document simon-pure in respect of the very principles we have professed and lived up to, we have got to do one or other of two things—we have got to adopt it or reject it. There is no middle course. You can not go in on a special-privilege basis of your own. I take it that you are too proud to ask to be exempted from responsibilities which the other members of the League will carry. We go in upon equal terms or we do not go in at all; and if we do not go in, my fellow citizens, think of the tragedy of that result—the only sufficient guaranty to the peace of the world withheld! Ourselves drawn apart with that dangerous pride which means that we shall be ready to take care of ourselves, and that means that we shall maintain great standing armies and an irresistible navy; that means we shall have the organization of a military nation; that means we shall have a general staff, with the kind of power that the general staff of Germany had, to mobilize this great manhood of the Nation when it pleases, all the energy of our young men drawn into the thought and preparation for war. What of our pledges to the men that lie dead in France? We said that they went over there, not to prove the prowess of America or her readiness for another war but to see to it that there never was such a war again. It always seems to make it difficult for me to say anything, my fellow citizens, when I think of my clients in this case. My clients are the children; my clients are the next generation. They do not know what promise and bonds I undertook when I ordered the armies of the United States to the soil of France, but I know, and I intend to redeem my pledges to the children; they shall not be sent upon a similar errand.

Again and again, my fellow citizens, mothers who lost their sons in France have come to me and, taking my hand, have shed tears upon it not only, but they had added, "God bless you, Mr. President!" Why, my fellow citizens, should they pray God to bless me? I advised the Congress of the United States to create the situation that led to the death of their sons. I ordered their sons overseas. I consented to their sons being put in the most difficult parts of the battle line, where death was certain, as in the impenetrable difficulties of the forest of Argonne. Why should they weep upon my hand and call down the blessings of God upon me? Because they believe that their boys died for something that vastly transcends any of the immediate and palpable objects of the war. They believe, and they rightly believe, that their sons saved the liberty of the world. They believe that wrapped up with the liberty of the world is the continuous protection of that liberty by the concerted powers of all civilized people. They believe that this sacrifice was made in order that other sons should not be called upon for a similar gift—the gift of life, the gift of all that died—and if we did not see this thing through, if we fulfilled the dearest present wish of Germany and now dissociated ourselves from those alongside whom we fought in the war, would not something of the halo go away from the gun over the mantelpiece, or the sword? Would not the old uniform lose something of its significance? These men were crusaders. They were not going forth to prove the might of the United States. They were going forth to prove the might of justice and right, and all the world accepted them as crusaders, and their transcendent achievement has made all the world believe in America as it believes in no other nation organized in the modern world. There seems to me to stand between us and the rejection or qualification of this treaty the serried ranks of those boys in khaki, not only these boys who came home, but those dear ghosts that still deploy upon the fields of France.

My friends, on last Decoration Day I went to a beautiful hillside near Paris, where was located the cemetery of Suresnes, a cemetery given over to the burial of the American dead. Behind me on the slopes was rank upon rank of living American soldiers, and lying before me upon the levels of the plain was rank upon rank of departed American soldiers. Right by the side of the stand where I spoke there was a little group of French women who had adopted those graves, had made themselves mothers of those dear ghosts by putting flowers every day upon those graves, taking them as their own sons, their own beloved, because they had died in the same cause—France was free and the world was free because America had come! I wish some men in public life who are now opposing the settlement for which these men died could visit such a spot as that. I wish that the thought that comes out of those graves could penetrate their consciousness. I wish that they could feel the moral obligation that rests upon us not to go back on those boys, but to see the thing through, to see it through to the end and make good their redemption of the world. For nothing less depends upon this decision, nothing less than the liberation and salvation of the world. . . .

Chapter 22

BOOM AND BUST

In the Presidential election of 1920, a war-weary and disillusioned America formally abandoned the enlightened Progressivism it had embraced in the early years of the century and embarked upon a decade-long quest for "normalcy." Though plans for domestic reform had been set aside and liberalism generally had been subordinated to oppressive demands for wartime conformity, the energies of Progressivism had not been entirely dissipated during the World War, for Woodrow Wilson had successfully channeled them into commanding aspirations for international understanding and world peace.

But when the war to "make the world safe for democracy" was over, when the peace had been won—and then lost—and the lofty visions of Wilsonian idealism had been largely dispelled, then Americans shed the burdens both of internationalism and of social experimentation. Despairing of crusades and crusaders, they sent to the White House a handsome, genial mediocrity who promised "not heroics, but healing; not nostrums, but normalcy; not revolution, but restoration; not experimentation, but equipoise." Warren Gameliel Harding was surely not a great leader, but his "folksiness," his small town ways, his easy identification with the average citizen, and particularly his conviction that America's salvation lay in a return to the simple formulas of McKinley Republicanism thoroughly endeared the Ohio politician to a tired and rather indifferent nation that eschewed reform and longed for nothing more strenuous than "equipoise" and "normalcy."

"Normalcy" itself was a complex phenomenon that defied analysis if not description, and two of its major themes, license and intolerance, were patently self-contradictory. War had wrought absolute havoc with the Victorian moral code that long dominated American life, and the boisterous, roaring twenties were marked with a widespread moral laxity undreamed of only a few years before. Now movies, magazines, and books designed for mass consumption dealt frankly and rather heatedly with sex; taboos against vulgarity were flagrantly disregarded, even in public; brazen flappers cut and bobbed their hair, rouged and lipsticked their faces, and immodestly wore their skirts higher and higher above the ankle; and a defiant younger generation loudly proclaimed that its newfound freedom was the only thing it would take at all seriously. Meanwhile the Eighteenth Amendment to the Constitution had brought Prohibition with the speakeasy, the hip flask, the rumrunner, and the beginnings of organized crime. And on a political level a series of outrageous scandals high up in the Harding administration reflected an unmistakable breakdown in public as well as private morals.

But if lawlessness and a profound revolt in manners and morals characterized the postwar era, Americans more than compensated for this liberal self-indulgence with a political conservatism that bred fear and intolerance. For most middle-class Americans these were golden years of plenty and they thoroughly despised the unorthodox few whose attacks upon the established order threatened to undermine the nation's prosperity and material well-being. In an atmosphere charged with suspicion and bigotry, criticism was soon equated with disloyalty; vigilante groups sprang up all over the country to brand as "un-American" those who dared question the political and economic status quo; and the imposition of loyalty oaths, the arrest and deportation of alien agitators, and the purging of radicals from their seats in various state legislatures heralded an official crusade against the bogeys of "Bolshevism" and the "Red Menace." Besides, in a nation where mass production and mass communication had standardized nearly every aspect of daily living (Americans everywhere wore the same factory-made clothes, saw the same movies, listened to the same radio programs, drove the same cars, and read the same advertisements and canned editorials in chain newspapers) an enormous premium was placed upon conformity, while unorthodoxy and innovation were regarded with distrust. And though the revival of the Ku Klux Klan was a particularly extreme example of the national temper, it was undeniably true that Negroes, Jews, Catholics, and members of other minorities that stood outside the carefully molded and guarded pattern of one hundred percent White Protestant Americanism suffered frequent discrimination or attack.

Still, not even the hysterical intolerance of the twenties could destroy entirely the American tradition of liberal protest, and though far less successful than H. L. Mencken, Ernest Hemingway, John Dos Passos and other writers who attacked traditionalism in literature, there were many who dared challenge traditionalism in politics. Laborers and farmers who failed to enjoy a much vaunted Republican prosperity were particularly aware of the necessity for political action to stem the tide of conservatism, and in 1924 various farm and labor groups banded together to form an independent Progressive Party with Senator Robert M. LaFollette of Wisconsin as its candidate for President. For the first time in its history the American Federation of Labor officially endorsed a Presidential candidate and the Progressive ticket polled an impressive 5,000,000 votes. Yet it was clear that a complacent nation had overwhelmingly heeded the Republican admonition that its choice was "Coolidge or Chaos," and the new third party was quickly abandoned when a final tabulation revealed that its candidate had run far behind the 8,000,000 votes for conservative Democrat John W. Davis and the nearly 16,000,000 votes for Calvin Coolidge, an extremely conservative Republican who had succeeded to the Presidency upon Harding's death in 1923. Liberal agitation did not end with Coolidge's triumph, however, and a vociferous Farm Bloc in Congress continued to press for legislation to aid underprivileged and hard-pressed agrarians who were caught between soaring costs and a rapidly declining farm income. Nevertheless Coolidge was convinced that "the business of America is business," not agriculture nor even the welfare of all citizens, and the President twice vetoed the McNary-Haugen Bill that was designed, through government support, to keep an exportable agriculture surplus from depressing farm prices by glutting the domestic market. Other efforts at relief for the farmer and the worker were equally unsuccessful.

But the chief prophet and high priest of Republican prosperity and conservatism was neither Harding (who longed for a time when there would be "less government in business and more business in government") nor the dour Coolidge. Rather it was Herbert Clark Hoover, who had served under both men as Secretary of Commerce and who was himself the Republican standard-bearer in the Presidential election of 1928. In that year the liberal, urban element in the Democratic party had asserted itself once again, forcing the nomination of Alfred E. Smith. Smith's Catholicism was undoubtedly an important factor in his defeat, for even in the traditionally Solid South, Democrats passed over their party's candidate to vote for the Protestant Hoover. But Smith's record of progressive social reform as Governor of New York compelled Hoover to express the political philosophy that was to dominate Republican thinking in the harsh depression years of his own administration

(1929–1933) no less than it had in the era of prosperity presided over by Harding and Coolidge. And Hoover's speech on "Rugged Individualism," delivered at the very end of the 1928 campaign, ranks with Carnegie's defense of the Gospel of Wealth as a classic statement of American conservatism.

Answering those who called upon government to assume a greater and more positive responsibility for the general welfare, Hoover argued that the "American system of rugged individualism" had brought untold prosperity and strength to the nation. On the other hand, the "doctrines of paternalism and state socialism" would mean "the destruction of self-government through centralization of government" and "the undermining of the individual initiative and enterprise through which our people have grown to unparalleled greatness." Implying that government interference in economic activities must necessarily lead to socialism, Hoover insisted that its ultimate effect would be to "impair the very basis of liberty and freedom," for "You cannot extend the mastery of the Government over the daily working life of a people without at the same time making it the master of the people's souls and thoughts."

To his critics it seemed ironic that Hoover should argue so vehemently against government intervention in the economic life of the nation. For as chief architect of the Republican business program of the twenties Hoover had approved government aid to *business* that took not only the negative forms of stringent economies (usually in social services), huge tax reductions, the elimination of government competition with private industry, and the practical suspension of the antitrust laws, but also the very positive form of subsidies and incredibly high tariffs. Besides, as Secretary of Commerce, Hoover had enthusiastically given official sanction and encouragement to large-scale private investment abroad and to the creation of vast domestic business and trade associations designed primarily to increase industrial efficiency and profit. Possibly these blatant examples of government assistance to the business community were uppermost in Hoover's mind when he spoke of "ordered liberty" and denied that his was a "system of laissez-faire" or that the "United States is free-for-all and devil-take-the-hindmost." For surely there was little else in Hoover's philosophy of "Rugged Individualism" to distinguish it in theory or in practice, from the rampant Social Darwinism of the late nineteenth century.

Though "Rugged Individualism" was doubtless in the mainstream of an American ideology which had at least temporarily rejected Progressive notions of reform and social control, Hoover was in office less than a year before his philosophy of government was tested and found tragically inadequate. In October 1929, the bottom literally dropped out of a bullish, speculative stock market and a decade of unparalleled prosperity came abruptly to an end. A nation which only a few months before had complacently assumed that it had reached the high "permanent plateau of prosperity" found itself in the doldrums of depression, and desperate years of unemployment, poverty, and insecurity soon provided a grim contrast to the feverish, booming twenties. Yet Hoover's conception of the role of the State remained fundamentally unchanged; just as earlier the administration had denied any responsibility to temper the fantastic orgy of speculation which finally precipitated the 1929 Crash, so now Hoover and his followers steadfastly refused to summon the full resources of government to succor the needy and provide relief for the homeless and jobless. Eventually, of course, an aroused public opinion forced Hoover to combat the Great Depression with more than the futile assurances of the day that "Prosperity is just around the corner," and the Republican statesman actually departed considerably from the traditional practice of permitting panic and depression simply to run their course. But even his rather grudging efforts at government intervention were consistent with an immovably conservative orientation, for though the President favored a Reconstruction Finance Corporation to bolster failing *industries* with Federal funds, he firmly opposed government assistance to *individuals.* Some had assumed that the exigencies of depression would necessarily make important inroads upon Hoover's devotion to "Rugged Individualism." Actually, however, neither this nineteenth-century ideal nor its practitioners were flexible enough to adapt to the shock of depression or to meet the pressing need for an appropriate new understanding of the relationship between the State and the individual in twentieth-century industrial America. And early in the thirties the American people rejected those whom they regarded as the false prophets of conservatism and turned with renewed faith and hope to the Progressivism of Theodore Roosevelt, Robert M. LaFollette, Woodrow Wilson, and now Franklin D. Roosevelt.

"Rugged Individualism,"*
Herbert C. Hoover, 1928

This campaign now draws to a close. The platforms of the two parties defining principles and offering solutions of various national problems have been presented and are being earnestly considered by our people. . . .

In my acceptance speech I endeavored to outline the spirit and ideals by which I would be guided in carrying that platform into administration. Tonight, I will not deal with the multitude of issues which have been already well canvassed. I intend rather to discuss some of those more fundamental principles and ideals upon which I believe the Government of the United States should be conducted. . . .

But in addition to this great record of contributions of the Republican Party to progress, there has been a further fundamental contribution—a contribution underlying and sustaining all the others—and that is the resistance of the Republican Party to every attempt to inject the Government into business in competition with its citizens.

After the war, when the Republican Party assumed administration of the country, we were faced with the problem of determination of the very nature of our national life. During 150 years we have builded up a form of self-government and a social system which is peculiarly our own. It differs essentially from all others in the world. It is the American system. It is just as definite and positive a political and social system as has ever been

*Reprinted from *The New Day* by Herbert Hoover by permission of the author and of the publishers, Stanford University Press.

developed on earth. It is founded upon a particular conception of self-government in which decentralized local responsibility is the very base. Further than this, it is founded upon the conception that only through ordered liberty, freedom, and equal opportunity to the individual will his initiative and enterprise spur on the march of progress. And in our insistence upon equality of opportunity has our system advanced beyond all the world.

During the war we necessarily turned to the Government to solve every difficult economic problem. The Government having absorbed every energy of our people for war, there was no other solution. For the preservation of the State the Federal Government became a centralized despotism which undertook unprecedented responsibilities, assumed autocratic powers, and took over the business of citizens. To a large degree we regimented our whole people temporarily into a socialistic state. However justified in time of war, if continued in peace time it would destroy not only our American system but with it our progress and freedom as well.

When the war closed, the most vital of all issues both in our own country and throughout the world was whether Governments should continue their wartime ownership and operation of many instrumentalities of production and distribution. We were challenged with a peace-time choice between the American system of rugged individualism and a European philosophy of diametrically opposed doctrines—doctrines of paternalism and state socialism. The acceptance of these ideas would have meant the destruction of self-government through centralization of government. It would have meant the undermining of the individual initiative and enterprise through which our people have grown to unparalleled greatness.

The Republican Party from the beginning resolutely turned its face away from these ideas and these war practices. A Republican Congress cooperated with the Democratic Administration to demobilize many of our war activities. At that time the two parties were in accord upon that point. When the Republican Party came into full power it went at once resolutely back to our fundamental conception of the State and the rights and responsibilities of the individual. Thereby it restored confidence and hope in the American people, it freed and stimulated enterprise, it restored the Government to its position as an umpire instead of a player in the economic game. For these reasons the American people have gone forward in progress while the rest of the world has halted, and some countries have even gone backward. If any one will study the causes of retarded recuperation in Europe, he will find much of it due to the stifling of private initiative on one hand, and overloading of the Government with business on the other.

There has been revived in this campaign, however, a series of proposals which, if adopted, would be a long step toward the abandonment of our American system and a surrender to the destructive operation of governmental conduct of commercial business. Because the country is faced with difficulty and doubt over certain national problems—that is, prohibition, farm relief and electrical power—our opponents propose that we must thrust government a long way into the businesses which give rise to these problems. In effect, they abandon the tenets of their own party and turn to State socialism as a solution for the difficulties presented by all three. It is proposed that we shall change from prohibition to the State purchase and sale of liquor. If their agricultural relief program means anything, it means that the Government shall directly or indirectly buy and sell and fix prices of agricultural products. And we are to go into the hydro-electric power business. In other words, we are confronted with a huge program of government in business.

There is, therefore, submitted to the American people a question of fundamental principle. That is, shall we depart from the principles of our American political and economic system, upon which we have advanced beyond all the rest of the world, in order to adopt methods based on principles destructive of its very foundations? And I wish to emphasize the seriousness of these proposals. I wish to make my position clear; for this goes to the very roots of American life and progress.

I should like to state to you the effect that this projection of government in business would have upon our system of self-government and our economic system.

That effect would reach to the daily life of every man and woman. It would impair the very basis of liberty and freedom not only for those left outside the fold of expanded bureaucracy but for those embraced within it.

Let us first see the effect upon self-government. When the Federal Government undertakes to go into commercial business it must at once set up the organization and administration of that business, and it immediately finds itself in a labyrinth, every alley of which leads to the destruction of self-government.

Commercial business requires a concentration of responsibility. Self-government requires decentralization and many checks and balances to safeguard liberty. Our Government to succeed in business would need become in effect a despotism. There at once begins the destruction of self-government.

The first problem of the Government about to adventure in commercial business is to determine a method of administration. It must secure leadership and direction. Shall this leadership be chosen by political agencies or shall we make it elective? The hard practical fact is that leadership in business must come through the sheer rise in ability and character. That rise can only take place in the free atmosphere of competition. Competition is closed by bureaucracy. Political agencies are feeble channels through which to select able leaders to conduct commercial business.

Government, in order to avoid the possible incompetence, corruption, and tyranny of too great authority in individuals entrusted with commercial business, inevitably turns to boards and commissions. To make sure that there are checks and balances, each member of such boards and commissions must have equal authority. Each has his separate responsibility to the public, and at once we have the conflict of ideas and the lack of decision which would ruin any commercial business. It has contributed greatly to the demoralization of our shipping business. Moreover, these commissions must be representative of different sections and different political parties, so that at once we have an entire blight upon coordinated action within their ranks which destroys any possibility of effective administration.

Moreover, our legislative bodies cannot in fact delegate their full authority to commissions or to individuals for the conduct of matters vital to the American people; for if we would preserve government by the people we must preserve the authority of our legislators in the activities of our Government.

Thus every time the Federal Government foes into a commercial business, five hundred and thirty-one Senators and Congressmen become the actual board of directors of that business. Every time a State government goes into business one or two hundred state Senators and Legislators become the actual directors of that business. Even if they were supermen and if there were no politics in the United States, no body of such numbers could competently direct commercial activities; for that requires initiative, instant decision, and action. It took Congress six years of constant discussion to even decide what the method of administration of Muscle Shoals should be.

When the Federal Government undertakes to go into business, the State governments are at once deprived of control and taxation of that business; when a State government undertakes to go into business, it at once deprives the municipalities of taxation and control of that business. Municipalities, being local and close to the people, can, at times, succeed in business where Federal and State Governments must fail. We have trouble enough with log-rolling in legislative bodies today. It originates naturally from desires of citizens to advance their particular section or to secure some necessary service. It would be multiplied a thousandfold were the Federal and State Governments in these businesses.

The effect upon our economic progress would be even worse. Business progressiveness is dependent on competition. New methods and new ideas are the outgrowth of the spirit of adventure, of individual initiative, and of individual enterprise. Without adventure there is no progress. No Government administration can rightly take chances with taxpayers' money. . . .

The Government in commercial business does not tolerate amongst its customers the freedom of competitive reprisals to which private business is subject. Bureaucracy does not tolerate the spirit of independence;

it spreads the spirit of submission into our daily life and penetrates the temper of our people not with the habit of powerful resistance to wrong but with the habit of timid acceptance of irrestible might.

Bureaucracy is ever desirous of spreading its influence and its power. You cannot extend the mastery of the Government over the daily working life of a people without at the same time making it the master of the people's souls and thoughts. Every expansion of Government in business means that Government in order to protect itself from the political consequences of its errors and wrongs is driven irresistibly without peace to greater and greater control of the nation's press and platform. Free speech does not live many hours after free industry and free commerce die.

It is a false liberalism that interprets itself into the Government operation of commercial business. Every step of bureaucratizing of the business of our country poisons the very roots of liberalism—that is, political equality, free speech, free assembly, free press, and equality of opportunity. It is the road not to more liberty but to less liberty. Liberalism should be found not striving to spread bureaucracy but striving to set bounds to it. True liberalism seeks all legitimate freedom, first in the confident belief that without such freedom the pursuit of all other blessings and benefits is vain. That belief is the foundation of all American progress, political as well as economic.

Liberalism is a force truly of the spirit, a force proceeding from the deep realization that economic freedom cannot be sacrificed if political freedom is to be preserved. Even if governmental conduct of business could give us more efficiency instead of less efficiency, the fundamental objection to it would remain unaltered and unabated. It would destroy political equality. It would increase rather than decrease abuse and corruption. It would stifle initiative and invention. It would undermine the development of leadership. It would cramp and cripple the mental and spiritual energies of our people. It would extinguish equality and opportunity. It would dry up the spirit of liberty and progress. For these reasons primarily it must be resisted. For a hundred and fifty years liberalism has found its true spirit in the American system, not in the European systems.

I do not wish to be misunderstood in this statement. I am defining a general policy. It does not mean that our Government is to part with one iota of its national resources without complete protection to the public interest. I have already stated that where the Government is engaged in public works for purposes of flood control, of navigation, of irrigation, of scientific research or national defense, or in pioneering a new art, it will at times necessarily produce power or commodities as a by-product. But they must be a by-product of the major purpose, not the major purpose itself.

Nor do I wish to be misinterpreted as believing that the United States is free-for-all and devil-take-the-hindmost. The very essence of equality of opportunity and of American individualism is that there shall be no domination by any group or combination in this Republic, whether it be business or political. On the contrary, it demands economic justice as well as political and social justice. It is no system of laissez-faire.

I feel deeply on this subject because during the war I had some practical experience with governmental operation and control. I have witnessed not only at home but abroad the many failures of Government in business. I have seen its tyrannies, its injustices, its destructions of self-government, its undermining of the very instinct which carry our people forward to progress. I have witnessed the lack of advance, the lowered standards of living, the depressed spirits of people working under such a system. My objection is based not upon theory or upon a failure to recognize wrong or abuse, but I know the adoption of such methods would strike at the very roots of American life and would destroy the very basis of American progress.

Our people have the right to know whether we can continue to solve our great problems without abandonment of our American system. I know we can. We have demonstrated that our system is responsive enough to meet any new and intricate development in our economic and business life. We have demonstrated that we can meet any economic problem and still maintain our democracy as master in its own house and that we can at the same time preserve equality of opportunity and individual freedom. . . .

And what have been the results of our American system? Our country has become the land of opportunity to those born without inheritance, not merely because of the wealth of its resources and industry, but because of this freedom of initiative and enterprise. Russia has natural resources equal to ours. Her people are equally industrious, but she has not had the blessings of one hundred and fifty years of our form of government and of our social system.

By adherence to the principles of decentralized self-government, ordered liberty, equal opportunity, and freedom to the individual our American experiment in human welfare has yielded a degree fo well-being unparalleled in all the world. It has come nearer to the abolition of poverty, to the abolition of fear of want, than humanity has ever reached before. Progress of the past seven years is the proof of it. This alone furnishes the answer to our opponents who ask us to introduce destructive elements into the system by which this has been accomplished.

Let us see what this system has done for us in our recent years of difficult and trying reconstruction and let us then solemnly ask ourselves if we now wish to abandon it.

As a nation we came out of the war with great losses. We made no profits from it. The apparent increases in wages were at that time fictitious. We were poorer as a nation when we emerged from the war. Yet during these last eight years we have recovered from these losses and increased our national income by over one-third, even if we discount the inflation of the dollar. That there has been a wide diffusion of our gain in wealth and income is marked by a hundred proofs. I know of no better test of the improved conditions of the average family than the combined increase in assets of life and industrial insurance, building and loan associations, and savings deposits. These are the savings banks of the average man. These agencies alone have in seven years increased by nearly 100 per cent to the gigantic sum of over fifty billions of dollars, or nearly one-sixth of our whole national wealth. We have increased in home ownership, we have expanded the investments of the average man.

. . . We have in this short period decreased the fear of poverty, the fear of unemployment, the fear of old age; and these are fears that are the greatest calamities of human kind. . . .

In bringing this address to a conclusion I should like to restate to you some of the fundamental things I have endeavored to bring out.

The foundations of progress and prosperity are dependent as never before upon the wise policies of government, for government now touches at a thousand points the intricate web of economic and social life.

Under administration by the Republican Party in the last seven and one-half years our country as a whole has made unparalleled progress and this has been in generous part reflected to this great city. Prosperity is no idle expression. It is a job for every worker; it is the safety and the safeguard of every business and every home. A continuation of the policies of the Republican Party is fundamentally necessary to the further building up of this prosperity.

I have dwelt at some length on the principles of relationship between the Government and business. I make no apologies for dealing with this subject. The first necessity of any nation is the smooth functioning of the vast business machinery for employment, feeding, clothing, housing, and providing luxuries and comforts to a people. Unless these basic elements are properly organized and function, there can be no progress in business, in education, literature, music, or art. There can be no advance in the fundamental ideas of a people. A people cannot make progress in poverty.

I have endeavored to present to you that the greatness of America has grown out of a political and social system and a method of control of economic forces distinctly its own—our American system—which has carried this great experiment in human welfare further than ever before in all history. We are nearer today to the ideal of the abolition of poverty and fear from the lives of men and women that ever before in any land. And I again repeat that the departure from our American system by injecting principles destructive to it which our opponents propose will jeopardize the very liberty and freedom of our people, will destroy equality of opportunity, not alone to ourselves but to our children. . . .

Chapter 23

THE ROOSEVELT REVOLUTION

The triumphant election in 1932 of Franklin D. Roosevelt, the liberal Democratic Governor of New York, was in the largest sense a profound reaffirmation of America's continuing faith in the essential capacity of democracy to survive the crises of depression and economic instability. A generation devoted to the quest for security had witnessed the rise of Communist, Fascist, and Nazi dictatorships in other nations. And in the United States the Great Depression, with its long years of poverty and acute distress, its breadlines, its soup kitchens, and its ever-mounting unemployment rolls, led many Americans to question seriously the efficacy of the democratic process. Indeed, had the depression grown worse, and had the national government continued to deny its responsibility to provide for those of our citizens who had been overcome by disaster, then the counsel of extremists might have been heeded and democracy abandoned in despair. But Americans turned instead to a liberal statesman whose purpose was to strengthen rather than to destroy traditional American values and institutions, and who pledged himself to devote unstintingly the full resources of democratic government to the rehabilitation of the depression-worn nation.

Ultimately it was the reforms of the New Deal that preserved American democracy from immediate collapse and protected it against the threatened inroads of totalitarianism of both the Left and Right. Not only did the New Deal seek to maintain the essential fabric of America's free economy, but its widely debated techniques of government regulation were entirely within the framework of a long-established American tradition of social control. Over a half century earlier state

Granger laws had attempted rigorous control of railroad abuses; and the Interstate Commerce Act of 1887 and the Sherman Antitrust Act of 1890 had committed the national government as well to a real, if rather limited, role in the regulation of industry. The Populists of the 1890's had demanded specific reforms which predated much of the Roosevelt farm program. And the extensive governmental activities of Theodore Roosevelt's Square Deal, his proposed New Nationalism, and Woodrow Wilson's New Freedom provided ample precedent for many of the New Deal's experiments in liberal reform. Even Herbert Hoover's minimal efforts at government intervention anticipated somewhat the substance, if not the spirit, of his successor's bold acts.

Nevertheless the New Deal did reflect a significant change in the nation's concept of the proper relationship between the State and the individual, and to many Americans it seemed that the election of 1932, as Jefferson had written of his own election in 1800, was "as real a revolution in the principles of our government as that of 1776 was in its form." Government participation in the economic life of the country could no longer be considered an entirely novel response to national crisis, but in the Roosevelt administration such activity became the *dominant* pattern and government assumed a broad and continuous new responsibility for the social and economic well-being of all the people. In a 1932 campaign address to the Commonwealth Club of San Francisco, Roosevelt had stated very clearly his belief that the economic basis of the nineteenth century's expansive, laissez-faire individualism had disappeared with the end of the last frontier and the completion of "our industrial plant" and that "our task now is not discovery or exploitation of natural resources, or necessarily producing more goods." The times called for a "reappraisal of values." Now government must play a major role in "the soberer, less dramatic business of administering resources and plants already in hand, of seeking to re-establish foreign markets for our surplus production, of meeting the problem of underconsumption, of adjusting production to consumption, of distributing wealth and products more equitably, of adapting existing economic organizations to the service of the people." Leftist critics scored the New Deal as disorganized and haphazard, totally without plan or philosophy, but this new orientation towards the State as the active, permanent guardian of the general welfare actually formed the persistent central theme of the "Roosevelt Revolution."

Yet the essence of the New Deal was as much in its spirit as in its ideology, for Roosevelt shrewdly sensed that a distressed and disheartened people needed most of all the strong moral conviction of his famous First Inaugural Address: "This great Nation will endure as it has endured, will revive and will prosper. . . . The only thing we have to fear is fear itself—nameless, unreasoning, unjustified terror which paralyzes needed efforts to convert retreat into advance." Graced with a warm and winning personality, Roosevelt again and again employed the masterful device of radio "fireside chats" to report directly to an anxious national audience, and his calm assurance did much to restore Americans' confidence in themselves and in their government. But brave words were not enough, and the exciting first hundred days of the Roosevelt Era saw an effective leadership translate the President's Inaugural assertion that "we must act, and act quickly" into a rapid succession of dramatic measures. To avert the total collapse of an already badly shaken banking system, the President proclaimed a national "bank holiday," closing the banks until steps might be taken to protect the savings of vast numbers of small depositors. A Federal Emergency Relief Administration (FERA) was created to make direct and immediate contributions to the states for relief purposes. A Civilian Conservation Corps (CCC) quickly put over a quarter of a million idle young men to the constructive task of preserving the nation's natural resources. A Works Progress Administration (WPA) restored the self-respect of millions of older unemployed by taking them from the relief rolls and employing their talents on public projects of permanent value—whether they were unskilled laborers or writers, artists, historians or musicians. Like many of the alphabetical agencies created during the depression emergency, these work-relief projects were temporary and frankly experimental, but they thoroughly vindicated the New Deal's assumption that needy Americans wanted work, not the dole, and they amply demonstrated the government's new and continuing determination to provide for the underprivileged "forgotten man."

Relief measures of necessity received highest priority in the grim early years of the Roosevelt administration, but recovery and reform ranked importantly too. The long-range objective of the New Deal was to place the American economy back on its feet, in good working order and with adequate safeguards against the inequities and maladjustments responsible for the tragic boom and bust of the twenties. Here again the Congress followed strong Executive leadership, adopting almost in its entirety each of the legislative proposals made by the President and his remarkable group of advisers known collectively—and sometimes derisively—as the "Brain Trust." An expanded and "democratized" Reconstruction Finance Corporation (RFC) was authorized to lend enormous sums of Federal monies not only to the largest financial institutions—as it had under Hoover—but to smaller faltering industries as well. And a Public Works Administration (PWA) was created to "prime" the "pump" of national economic activity through an extensive program of government spending. The New Dealers were convinced that Hoover's technique (as Roosevelt described it) of helping "only those at the top, in the pious hope that the few at the top would in their benevolence or generosity pass that help on" was inadequate to the times and that the key to recovery lay instead in increased consumer purchasing power. To this end an Agricultural Adjustment Administration (AAA) brought about a program of crop curtailment and government-supported price levels, and a National Recovery Administration (NRA) attempted the same for the urban industrial worker.

It was, of course, in the realm of labor relations that the New Deal accomplished its most sweeping economic reforms. Formal guarantees of labor's right to organize and to bargain collectively were written into Section 7(a) of the act which created the NRA and later into the National Labor Relations Act. And in 1938 the Fair Labor Standards Act established a legal floor under wages and a ceiling over working hours for employees engaged in interstate commerce. These measures and the administration's obvious eagerness to deal with labor as industry's equal gave a tremendous impetus to the growth of organized labor. But labor's gains were quickly challenged by management, and the mid-thirties were marred by a long series of sit-down strikes, boycotts, and lockouts that frequently were accompanied by violence and bloodshed. Besides, all was not well within labor's own house. A long-standing conflict between the respective advocates of trade and industrial unionism had resulted in a schism within the venerable and rather conservative American Federation of Labor and in the creation of a rival Congress of Industrial Organizations. Inter-union struggles were particularly bitter and continuous jurisdictional disputes seriously threatened labor's recent strides forward. But under the dynamic leadership of John L. Lewis the CIO proved remarkably successful in recruiting large armies of unorganized industrial workers, and by the end of the decade each of the giant labor organizations could claim a membership of 4,000,000.

Important reforms were enacted in other areas as well. The nation's antitrust laws were enforced with renewed vigor in a concerted effort to control the trend towards monopoly and the concentration of wealth that was so clearly revealed in the reports of the Temporary National Economic Committee (TNEC). A Securities and Exchange Commission (SEC) was created to guard against a recurrence of the fraudulent and speculative stock market practices that had contributed so much to the 1929 Crash. A generously conceived Social Security Act inaugurated a program of old-age insurance, unemployment insurance, and financial assistance for dependent children, the crippled, and the blind. And a Tennessee Valley Authority (TVA) that was empowered not only to generate and to sell cheap electricity, but also to conduct flood-control, reforestation, community organization and educational programs for the impoverished people of the Valley, provided a daring experiment in social planning.

All of these measures for relief, recovery and reform were designed to insure a free, democratic society against the ravages of poverty and insecurity, for Roosevelt was firmly convinced that the "liberty of a democracy is not safe if its business system does not provide employment and produce and distribute goods in such a way as to sustain an acceptable standard of living." To critics who vigorously opposed the New Deal in the name of a Jeffersonian tradition of limited government, the President cogently replied that in twentieth-century industrial America the real threat to individual freedom lay not in the expanding services of democratic government, but rather in the irresponsible power of concentrated wealth. Now Americans' liberties were seriously endangered by privileged, monopolistic economic power, and a limited Welfare State must supplant the Laissez-Faire State of the nineteenth century, not to hamper individualism, but to protect it.

Though there were some who accused the President of creating a vast Federal bureaucracy merely to foster his own political ambitions, and though the cry of "dictator" was heard over and over again, most Americans heartily approved of the New Deal. In the Congressional elections of 1934 an already sizable Democratic legislative majority was substantially increased; and in the Presidential election of 1936 Roosevelt soundly defeated Alfred M. Landon, the "Kansas Coolidge," who carried only Maine and Vermont for the Republican Party. But these handsome victories at the polls made no impression at all upon the judicial branch of the national Government, and it was in the rarified, though hardly unprejudicial atmosphere of a conservative and largely hostile Supreme Court that Roosevelt, as Jefferson before him, encountered his most formidable opposition. Here a majority of the "nine old men"—whose tenure had begun long before the "Roosevelt Revolution"—interpreted the Constitution in such a manner as to invalidate vital portions of the New Deal's liberal legislative program. The Court had long been a bulwark of conservatism, but seldom before had the Justices so flagrantly flouted the will of the popularly chosen Congress and Chief Executive or so consistently read into the Constitution what Justice (later Chief Justice) Harlan F. Stone described as their own "personal economic predilections." And when the NRA, the AAA, the Municipal Bankruptcy Act, the Farm Mortgage Act, and the Guffey Coal Act were all declared unconstitutional, then the President realized that the entire New Deal would suffer judicial emasculation if drastic action were not quickly taken. Thus, early in 1937 the administration proposed legislation which permitted Justices of the high court to retire on full pay at the age of seventy and which empowered the President to appoint an additional Justice—until the Supreme Court numbered fifteen—for each of the judges who remained on the bench after the retirement age. Roosevelt argued that his plan would "save our National Constitution from hardening of the judicial arteries," but his opponents joined in attacking it as a "court-packing" measure, and when the Congress defeated the court reform bill the administration suffered a major political setback.

The Court was not unimpressed by this attack upon its prerogatives, however, and even as the controversial bill was being debated and defeated in Congress the Justices conceded that an aroused public might someday impose even more stringent limitations upon judicial review were the popular will further denied. Bowing to expediency, the Court very quickly became more receptive to social legislation, and in 1937 the New Deal was upheld in several particularly important decision. In N.L.R.B. v. Jones & Laughlin Steel Corporation the Court sustained the National Labor Relations Act, despite the fact that distinguished lawyers who had studied the Court's earlier decisions on related matters had strongly advised their clients that the law was unconstitutional. In Helvering v. Davis the Court sustained the Social Security Act in a decision which liberally construed Congressional power to tax for the general welfare. In West Coast Hotel Co. v. Parrish the Court upheld the right of the State of Washington to pass minimum wage legislation, though less than a year before a similar law in New York had been invalidated, and though in 1923 a Federal minimum wage act for the District of Columbia had been set aside in Adkins v. Children's Hospital.

The Supreme Court's voluntary about-face was historic—some called it "the switch in time that saved nine." But within a few years death and resignation permitted Roosevelt to remake the membership himself.

Soon conservatives such as McReynolds, Sutherland, and Van Devanter were replaced by the liberals Hugo Black, Felix Frankfurter, William O. Douglas, Frank Murphy, and Robert Jackson, and the Court withdrew farther and farther from the realm of law-making. Besides, by the end of the decade comparatively few Americans entirely rejected the New Deal philosophy of social control. There were many who continued bitterly to criticize the President as incompetent or dictatorial, and even less partisan observers seriously questioned both the desirability of extreme centralization of power in the Federal government at Washington and the essential wisdom of continuously strengthening the power of the Chief Executive at the expense of the power and prestige of the Congress and the Supreme Court. But for the most part the "Roosevelt Revolution" had made its permanent impression upon national life and it seemed as if Americans would never again enjoy—or regret—an era of laissez-faire.

[NOTE: This last, perhaps wishful reading of the Roosevelt legacy further illumines Charles A. Beard's earlier cited characterization of all recorded history as preeminently an "act of faith," embodying largely an author's own changeable understanding of the past.

Written first at midtwentieth century, this historical judgment may now seem even further documented by the addition here of FDR's profoundly egalitarian 1936 "Rendezvous with Destiny" speech ("Necessitous men are not free men" . . . "Liberty requires opportunity to make a living . . . which gives man not only enough to live by, but something to live for"). But this "act of faith" in a *permanent* Roosevelt Revolution was actually misplaced and deserved to be severely questioned by the time of the Reagan/Bush 41/Gingrich mantra of "deregulation," "supply-side economics," "government is the problem, not the solution" in the 1980's and 1990's; and it surely ought to have been revised by the turn of the twenty-first century and its openly laissez-faire, antiregulation, "primacy of the marketplace" Bush 43/Cheney years of boom and bust, so reminiscent of America in the

Roaring Twenties and the economic panic and Depression that followed.

There is no permanence to historical interpretation, as changing opinions about Barack Obama's presidency may themselves in time demonstrate, and as Pulitzer Prize-winning historian Arthur M. Schlesinger, Jr., pointed out so wisely in "Folly's Antidote," his insightful Century Association-*New York Times* Op-Ed comments on history newly included in this book. Nor should there be.

RDH, 2009]

Franklin D. Roosevelt's First Inaugural Address, *1933*

President Hoover, Mr. Chief Justice, my friends:

This is a day of national consecration, and I am certain that my fellow-Americans expect that on my induction into the Presidency I will address them with a candor and a decision which the present situation of our nation impels.

This is pre-eminently the time to speak the truth, the whole truth, frankly and boldly. Nor need we shrink from honestly facing conditions in our country today. This great nation will endure as it has endured, will revive and will prosper.

So first of all let me assert my firm belief that the only thing we have to fear is fear itself—nameless, unreasoning, unjustified terror which paralyzes needed efforts to convert retreat into advance.

In every dark hour of our national life a leadership of frankness and vigor has met with that understanding and support of the people themselves which is essential to victory. I am convinced that you will again give that support to leadership in these critical days.

In such a spirit on my part and on yours we face our common difficulties. They concern, thank God, only material things. Values have shrunken to fantastic levels; taxes have risen; our ability to pay has fallen, government of all kinds is faced by serious curtailment of income; the means of exchange are frozen in the currents of trade; the withered leaves of industrial enterprise lie on every side; farmers find no markets for their produce; the savings of many years in thousands of families are gone.

More important, a host of unemployed citizens face the grim problem of existence, and an equally great number toil with little return. Only a foolish optimist can deny the dark realities of the moment.

Yet our distress comes from no failure of substance. We are stricken by no plague of locusts. Compared with the perils which our forefathers conquered because they believed and were not afraid, we have still much to be thankful for. Nature still offers her bounty and human efforts have multiplied it. Plenty is at our doorstep, but a generous use of it languishes in the very sight of the supply.

Primarily, this is because the rulers of the exchange of mankind's goods have failed through their own stubbornness and their own incompetence, have admitted that failure and abdicated. Practices of the unscrupulous money changers stand indicted in the court of public opinion, rejected by the hearts and minds of men.

True, they have tried, but their efforts have been cast in the pattern of an outworn tradition. Faced by failure of credit, they have proposed only the lending of more money.

Stripped of the lure of profit by which to induce our people to follow their false leadership, they have resorted to exhortations, pleading tearfully for restored confidence. They know only the rules of a generation of self-seekers.

They have no vision, and when there is no vision the people perish.

The money changers have fled from their high seats in the temple of our civilization. We may now restore that temple to the ancient truths.

The measure of the restoration lies in the extent to which we apply social values more noble than mere monetary profit.

Happiness lies not in the mere possession of money; it lies in the joy of achievement, in the thrill of creative effort.

The joy and moral stimulation of work no longer must be forgotten in the mad chase of evanescent profits. These dark days will be worth all they cost us if they teach us that our true destiny is not to be ministered unto but to minister to ourselves and to our fellow-men.

Recognition of the falsity of material wealth as the standard of success goes hand in hand with the abandonment of the false belief that public office and high political position are to be valued only by the standards of pride of place and personal profit; and there must be an end to a conduct in banking and in business which too often has given to a sacred trust the likeness of callous and selfish wrongdoing.

Small wonder that confidence languishes, for it thrives only on honesty, on honor, on the sacredness of obligations, on faithful protection, on unselfish performance. Without them it cannot live.

Restoration calls, however, not for changes in ethics alone. This nation asks for action, and action now.

Our greatest primary task is to put people to work. This is no unsolvable problem if we face it wisely and courageously.

It can be accomplished in part by direct recruiting by the government itself, treating the task as we would treat the emergency of a war, but at the same time, through this employment, accomplishing greatly needed projects to stimulate the use of our natural resources.

Hand in hand with this, we must frankly recognize the overbalance of population in our industrial centers and, by engaging on a national scale in the redistribution, endeavor to provide a better use of the land for those best fitted for the land.

The task can be helped by definite efforts to raise the values of agricultural products and with this the power to purchase the output of our cities.

It can be helped by preventing realistically the tragedy of the growing loss, through foreclosure, of our small homes and our farms.

It can be helped by insistence that the Federal, State and local governments act forthwith on the demand that their cost be drastically reduced.

It can be helped by the unifying of relief activities which today are often scattered, uneconomical and unequal. It can be helped by national planning for and supervision of all forms of transportation and of communications and other utilities which have a definitely public character.

There are many ways in which it can be helped, but it can never be helped merely by talking about it. We must act, and act quickly.

Finally, in our progress toward a resumption of work we require two safeguards against a return to the evils of the old order; there must be a strict supervision of all banking and credits and investments; there must be an end to speculation with other people's money, and there must be provision for an adequate but sound currency.

These are the lines of attack. I shall presently urge upon a new Congress in special session detailed measures for their fulfillment, and I shall seek the immediate assistance of the several States.

Through this program of action we address ourselves to putting our own national house in order and making income balance outgo.

Our international trade relations, though vastly important, are in point of time and necessity, secondary to the establishment of a sound national economy.

I favor as a practical policy the putting of first things first. I shall spare no effort to restore world trade by international economic readjustment, but the emergency at home cannot wait on the accomplishment.

The basic thought that guides these specific means of national recovery is not narrowly nationalistic.

It is the insistence, as a first consideration, upon the interdependence of the various elements in, and parts of, the United States—a recognition of the old and permanently important manifestation of the American spirit of the pioneer.

It is the way to recovery. It is the immediate way. It is the strongest assurance that the recovery will endure.

In the field of world policy I would dedicate this nation to the policy of the good neighbor—the neighbor who resolutely respects himself and, because he does so, respects the rights of others—the neighbor who respects his obligations and respects the sanctity of his agreements in and with a world of neighbors.

If I read the temper of our people correctly, we now

realize as we have never before, our interdependence on each other; that we cannot merely take, but we must give as well; that if we are to go forward we must move as a trained and loyal army willing to sacrifice for the good of a common discipline, because, without such discipline, no progress is made, no leadership becomes effective.

We are, I know, ready and willing to submit our lives and property to such discipline because it makes possible a leadership which aims at a larger good.

This I propose to offer, pledging that the larger purposes will bind upon us all as a sacred obligation with a unity of duty hitherto evoked only in time of armed strife.

With this pledge taken, I assume unhesitatingly the leadership of this great army of our people, dedicated to a disciplined attack upon our common problems.

Action in this image and to this end is feasible under the form of government which we have inherited from our ancestors.

Our Constitution is so simple and practical that it is possible always to meet extraordinary needs by changes in emphasis and arrangement without loss of essential form.

That is why our constitutional system has proved itself the most superbly enduring political mechanism the modern world has produced. It has met every stress of vast expansion of territory, of foreign wars, of bitter internal strife, of world relations.

It is to be hoped that the normal balance of executive and legislative authority may be wholly adequate to meet the unprecedented task before us. But it may be that an unprecedented demand and need for undelayed action may call for temporary departure from that normal balance of public procedure.

I am prepared under my constitutional duty to recommend the measures that a stricken nation in the midst of a stricken world may require.

The measures, or such other measures as the Congress may build out of its experience and wisdom, I shall seek, within my constitutional authority, to bring to speedy adoption.

But in the event that the Congress shall fail to take

one of these two courses, and in the event that the national emergency is still critical, I shall not evade the clear course of duty that will then confront me.

I shall ask Congress for the one remaining instrument to meet the crisis—broad executive power to wage a war against the emergency as great as the power that would be given me if we were in fact invaded by a foreign foe.

For the trust reposed in me I will return the courage and the devotion that befit the time. I can do no less.

We face the arduous days that lie before us in the warm courage of national unity; with the clear consciousness of seeking old and precious moral values; with the clean satisfaction that comes from the stern performance of duty by old and young alike.

We aim at the assurance of a rounded and permanent national life.

We do not distrust the future of essential democracy. The people of the United States have not failed. In their need they have registered a mandate that they want direct, vigorous action.

They have asked for discipline and direction under leadership. They have made me the present instrument of their wishes. In the spirit of the gift I take it.

In this dedication of a nation we humbly ask the blessing of God. May He protect each and every one of us! May He guide me in the days to come!

"A Rendezvous with Destiny"
Franklin D. Roosevelt, 1936

Members of the Democratic Convention, my friends: Here, and in every community throughout the land, we are met at a time of great moment to the future of the Nation. It is an occasion to be dedicated to the simple and sincere expression of an attitude toward problems, the determination of which will profoundly affect America. I come not only as a leader of a party, not only as a candidate for high office, but as one upon whom many critical hours have imposed and still impose a grave responsibility.

For the sympathy, help and confidence with which Americans have sustained me in my task, I am grateful.

For their loyalty I salute the members of our great party, in and out of political life in every part of the Union. I salute those of other parties, especially those in the Congress of the United States who on so many occasions have put partisanship aside. I thank the Governors of the several States, their Legislatures, their State and local officials who participated unselfishly and regardless of party in our efforts to achieve recovery and destroy abuses. Above all I thank the millions of Americans who have borne disaster bravely and have dared to smile through the storm. America will not forget these recent years, will not forget that the rescue was not a mere party task. It was the concern of all of us. In our strength we rose together, rallied our energies together, applied the old rules of common sense, and together survived. In those days we feared fear. That was why we fought fear. And today, my friends, we have won against the most dangerous of our foes. We have conquered fear.

But I cannot, with candor, tell you that all is well with the world. Clouds of suspicion, tides of ill will and intolerance gather darkly in many places. In our own land we enjoy indeed a fullness of life greater than that of most Nations. But the rush of modern civilization itself has raised for us new difficulties, new problems which must be solved if we are to preserve to the United States the political and economic freedom for which Washington and Jefferson planned and fought. Philadelphia is a good city in which to write American history. This is fitting ground on which to reaffirm the faith of our fathers; to pledge ourselves to restore to the people a wider freedom; to give to 1936 as the founders gave to 1776—an American way of life.

That very word "freedom," in itself and of necessity, suggests freedom from some restraining power. In 1776 we sought freedom from the tyranny of a political autocracy—from the eighteenth-century royalists who held special privileges from the crown. It was to perpetuate their privilege that they governed without the consent of the governed; that they denied the right of free assembly and free speech; that they restricted the worship of God; that they put the average man's property and the average man's life in pawn to the mercenaries of dynastic power; that they regimented the people. And so it was to win freedom from the tyranny of political autocracy that the American Revolution was fought. That victory gave the business of governing into the hands of the average man, who won the right with his neighbors to make and order his own destiny through his own Government. Political tyranny was wiped out at Philadelphia on July 4, 1776.

Since that struggle, however, man's inventive genius released new forces in our land which reordered the lives of our people. The age of machinery, of railroads; of steam and electricity; the telegraph and the radio; mass production, mass distribution—all of these combined to bring forward a new civilization and with it a new problem for those who sought to remain free. For out of this modern civilization, economic royalists carved new dynasties. New kingdoms were built upon concentration of control over material things. Through new uses of corporations, banks and securities, new machinery of industry and agriculture, of labor and capital—all undreamed-of by the fathers—the whole structure of modern life was impressed into this royal service.

There was no place among this royalty for our many thousands of small-business men and merchants who sought to make a worthy use of the American system of initiative and profit. They were no more free than the worker or the farmer. Even honest and progressive-minded men of wealth, aware of their obligation to their generation, could never know just where they fitted into this dynastic scheme of things. It was natural and perhaps human that the privileged princes of these new economic dynasties, thirsting for power, reached out for control over Government itself. They created a new despotism and wrapped it in the robes of legal sanction. In its service new mercenaries sought to regiment the people, their labor, and their property. And as a result the average man once more confronts the problem that faced the Minute Man. The hours men and women worked, the wages they received, the conditions of their labor—these had passed beyond the control of the people, and were imposed by this new industrial dictatorship. The savings of the average family, the capital of the small-business man, the investments set aside for old age—other people's money—these were tools which the new economic royalty used to dig itself in. Those who tilled the soil no longer reaped the rewards which were their right. The small measure of their gains was decreed by men in distant cities. Throughout the Nation, opportunity was limited by monopoly. Individual initiative was crushed in the cogs of a great machine. The field open for free business was more and more restricted. Private enterprise, indeed, became too private. It became privileged enterprise, not free enterprise.

An old English judge once said: "Necessitous men are not free men." Liberty requires opportunity to make a living—a living decent according to the standard of the time, a living which gives man not only enough to live by, but something to live for. For too many of us the political equality we once had won was meaningless in the face of economic inequality. A small group had concentrated into their own hands an almost complete control over other people's property, other people's money, other people's labor—other people's lives. For too many of us life was no longer free; liberty no longer real; men could no longer follow the pursuit of happiness. Against economic tyranny such as this, the American citizen could appeal only to the organized power of Government. The collapse of 1929 showed up the despotism for what it was. The election of 1932 was the people's mandate to end it. Under that mandate, it is being ended. The royalists of the economic order have conceded that political freedom was the business of the Government, but they have maintained that economic slavery was nobody's business. They granted that the Government could protect the citizen in his right to vote, but they denied that the Government could do anything to protect the citizen in his right to work and his right to live.

Today we stand committed to the proposition that freedom is no half-and-half affair. If the average citizen is guaranteed equal opportunity in the polling place, he must have equal opportunity in the market place.

These economic royalists complain that we seek to overthrow the institutions of America. What they really complain of is that we seek to take away their power. Our allegiance to American institutions requires the overthrow of this kind of power. In vain they seek to hide behind the Flag and the Constitution. In their blindness they forget what the Flag and the Constitution stand for. Now, as always, they stand for democracy, not tyranny; for freedom, not subjection; and against a dictatorship by mob rule and the overprivileged alike.

The brave and clear platform adopted by this Convention, to which I heartily subscribe, sets forth that Government in a modern civilization has certain inescapable obligations to its citizens, among which are protection of the family and the home, the establishment of a democracy of opportunity, and aid to those overtaken by disaster. But the resolute enemy within our gates is ever ready to beat down our words unless in greater courage we will fight for them. For more than three years, we have fought for them. This Convention, in every word and deed, has pledged that that fight will go on.

The defeats and victories of these years have given to us as a people a new understanding of our Government and of ourselves. Never since the early days of the New England town meeting have the affairs of Government been so widely discussed and so clearly appreciated. It has been brought home to us that the only effective guide for the safety of this most worldly of worlds, the greatest guide of all, is moral principle.

We do not see faith, hope and charity as unattainable ideals, but we use them as stout supports of a Nation fighting the fight for freedom in a modern civilization. Faith—in the soundness of democracy in the midst of dictatorships. Hope—renewed because we know so well the progress we have made. Charity—in the true spirit of that grand old word. For charity literally translated from the original means love, the love that understands, that does not merely share the wealth of the giver, but in true sympathy and wisdom helps men to help themselves.

We seek not merely to make Government a mechanical implement, but to give it the vibrant personal character that is the very embodiment of human charity. We are poor indeed if this Nation cannot afford to lift from every recess of American life the dread fear of the unemployed that they are not needed in the world. We cannot afford to accumulate a deficit in the books of human fortitude. In the place of the palace of privilege, we seek to build a temple out of faith and hope and charity.

It is a sobering thing, my friends, to be a servant of this great cause. We try in our daily work to remember that the cause belongs not to us, but to the people. The standard is not in the hands of you and me alone. It is carried by America. We seek daily to profit from experience, to learn to do better as our task proceeds.

Governments can err, Presidents do make mistakes, but the immortal Dante tells us that divine justice weighs the sins of the cold-blooded and the sins of the warmhearted in different scales. Better the occasional faults of a Government that lives in a spirit of charity than the consistent omissions of a Government frozen in the ice of its own indifference.

There is a mysterious cycle in human events. To some generations much is given. Of other generations much is expected. This generation of Americans has a rendezvous with destiny.

In this world of ours in other lands, there are some people who, in times past, have lived and fought for freedom, and seem to have grown too weary to carry on the fight. They have sold their heritage of freedom for the illusion of a living. They have yielded their democracy. I believe in my heart that only our success can stir their ancient hope. They begin to know that here in America we are waging a great and successful war. It is not alone a war against want and destitution and economic demoralization. It is more than that; it is a war for the survival of democracy. We are fighting to save a great and previous form of government for ourselves and for the world.

I accept the commission you have tendered me. I join with you. I am enlisted for the duration of the war.

N.L.R.B. v. Jones & Laughlin Steel Corporation, *1937*

In a proceeding under the National Labor Relations Act of 1935, the National Labor Relations Board found that the petitioner, Jones & Laughlin Steel Corporation, had violated the Act by engaging in unfair labor practices affecting commerce. . . . The unfair labor practices charged were that the corporation was discriminating against members of the union with regard to hire and tenure of employment, and was coercing and intimidating its employees in order to interfere with their self-organization. The discriminatory and coercive action alleged was the discharge of certain employees. . . .

Contesting the ruling of the Board, the respondent argues (1) that the Act is in reality a regulation of labor relations and not of interstate commerce; (2) that the Act can have no application to the respondent's relations with its production employees because they are not subject to regulation by the Federal Government; and (3) that the provisions of the Act violate Section 2 of Article III and the Fifth and Seventh Amendments of the Constitution of the United States. . .

Respondent says that whatever may be said of employees engaged in interstate commerce, the industrial relations and activities in the manufacturing department of respondent's enterprise are not subject to federal regulations. The argument rests upon the proposition that manufacturing in itself is not commerce. . . .

The Government distinguishes these cases. The various parts of respondent's enterprise are described as interdependent and as thus involving "a great movement of iron ore, coal and limestone along well-defined paths to the steel mills, thence through them, and thence in the form of steel products into the consuming centers of the country—a definite and well-understood course of business." It is urged that these activities constitute a "stream" or "flow" of commerce, of which the Aliquippa manufacturing plant is the focal point, and that industrial strife at that point would cripple the entire movement. Reference is made to our decision sustaining the Packers and Stockyards Act. The Court found that the stockyards were but a "throat" through which the current of commerce flowed and the transactions which there occurred could not be separated from that movement. . . .

We do not find it necessary to determine whether these features of defendant's business dispose of the asserted analogy to the "stream of commerce" cases. The congressional authority to protect interstate commerce from burdens and obstructions is not limited to transactions which can be deemed to be an essential part of a "flow" of interstate or foreign commerce. Burdens and obstructions may be due to injurious action springing from other sources. The fundamental principle is that the power to regulate commerce is the power to enact "all appropriate legislation" for "its protection and advancement"; to adopt measures "to promote its growth and insure its safety"; "to foster, protect, control and restrain." That power is plenary and may be exerted to protect interstate commerce "no matter what the source of the dangers which threaten it." Although activities may be intrastate in character when separately considered, if they have such a close and substantial relation to interstate commerce that their control is essential or appropriate to protect that commerce from burdens and obstructions, Congress cannot be denied the power to exercise that control. Undoubtedly the scope of this power must be considered in the light of our dual system of government and may not be extended so as to embrace effects upon interstate commerce so indirect and remote that to embrace them, in view of our complex society, would effectually obliterate the distinction between what is national and what is local and create a completely centralized government. The question is necessarily one of degree. . . .

It is thus apparent that the fact that the employees here concerned were engaged in production is not determinative. The question remains as to the effect upon interstate commerce of the labor practice involved. . . .

Giving full weight to respondent's contention with respect to a break in the complete continuity of the "stream of commerce" by reason of respondent's manufacturing operations, the fact remains that the stoppage of these operations by industrial strife would have a most serious effect upon interstate commerce. In view of respondent's far-flung activities, it is idle to say that the effect would be indirect or remote. It is obvious that it would be immediate and might be catastrophic. We are asked to shut our eyes to the plainest facts of our national life and to deal with the question of direct and indirect effects in an intellectual vacuum. Because there may be but indirect and remote effects upon interstate commerce in connection with a host of local enterprises throughout the country, it does not follow that other industrial activities do not have such a close and intimate relation to interstate commerce as to make the presence of industrial strife a matter of the most urgent national concern. When industries organize themselves on a national scale, making their relation to interstate commerce the dominant factor in their activities, how can it be maintained that their industrial labor relations constitute a forbidden field into which Congress may not enter when it is necessary to protect interstate commerce from the paralyzing consequences of industrial war? We have often said that interstate commerce itself is a practical conception. It is equally true that interferences with that commerce must be appraised by a judgement that does not ignore actual experience.

Experience has abundantly demonstrated that the recognition of the right of employees to self-organization and to have representatives of their own choosing for the purpose of collective bargaining is often an essential condition of industrial peace. Refusal to confer and negotiate has been one of the most prolific causes of strife. This is such an outstanding fact in the history of labor disturbances that it is a proper subject of judicial notice and requires no citation of instances. But with respect to the appropriateness of the recognition of self-organization and representation in the promotion of peace, the question is not essentially different in the case of employees in industries of such a character that interstate commerce is put in jeopardy from the case of employees of transportation companies. And of what avail is it to protect the facility of transportation, if interstate commerce is throttled with respect to the commodities to be transported!

These questions have frequently engaged the attention of Congress and have been the subject of many inquiries. The steel industry is one of the great basic industries of the United States, with ramifying activities affecting interstate commerce at every point. The Government aptly refers to the steel strike of 1919–1920 with its far-reaching consequences. The fact that there appears to have been no major disturbance in that industry in the more recent period did not dispose of the possibilities of future and like dangers to interstate commerce which Congress was entitled to foresee and to exercise its protective power to forestall. It is not necessary again to detail the facts as to respondent's enterprise. Instead of being beyond the pale, we think that it presents in a most striking way the close and intimate relation which a manufacturing industry may have to interstate commerce and we have no doubt that Congress had constitutional authority to safeguard the right of respondent's employees to self-organization and freedom in the choice of representatives for collective bargaining. . . .

Our conclusion is that the order of the Board was within its competency and that the Act is valid. . . .

Helvering et al. v. Davis, *1937*

The Social Security Act is challenged once again. . . .

The purge of nation-wide calamity that began in 1929 has taught us many lessons. Not the least is the solidarity of interests that may once have seemed to be divided. Unemployment spreads from state to state, the hinterland now settled that in pioneer days gave an avenue of escape. Spreading from state to state, unemployment is an ill not particular but general, which may be checked, if Congress so determines, by the resources of the Nation. . . .

But the ill is all one or at least not greatly different whether men are thrown out of work because there is no longer work to do or because the disabilities of age make them incapable of doing it. Rescue becomes necessary irrespective of the cause. The hope behind this statute is to save men and women from the rigors of the poor house as well as from the haunting fear that such a lot awaits them when journey's end is near. . . .

A recent study of the Social Security Board informs us that "one-fifth of the aged in the United Sates were receiving old-age assistance, emergency relief, institutional care, employment under the works program, or some other form of aid from public or private funds; two-fifths to one-half were dependent on friends and relatives; one-eighth had some income from earnings; and possibly one-sixth had some savings or property. Approximately three out of four persons 65 or over were probably dependent wholly or partially on others for support." We summarize in the margin the results of other studies by state and national commissions. They point the same way.

The problem is plainly national in area and dimensions. Moreover, laws of the separate states cannot deal with it effectively. Congress, at least, had a basis for that belief. States and local governments are often lacking in the resources that are necessary to finance an adequate program of security for the aged. This is brought out with a wealth of illustration in recent studies of the problem. Apart from the failure of resources, states and local governments are at times reluctant to increase so heavily the burden of taxation to be borne by their residents for fear of placing themselves in a position of economic disadvantage as compared with neighbors or competitors. . . .

A system of old age pensions has special dangers of its own, if put in force in one state and rejected in another. The existence of such a system is a bait to the needy and dependent elsewhere, encouraging them to migrate and seek a haven of repose. Only a power that is national can serve the interests of all.

Whether wisdom or unwisdom resides in the scheme of benefits it is not for us to say. The answer to such inquiries must come from Congress, not the courts. Our concern here as often is with power, not with wisdom. Counsel for respondent has recalled to us the virtues of self-reliance and frugality. There is a possibility, he says, that aid from a paternal government may sap those sturdy virtues and breed a race of weaklings. If Massachusetts so believes and shapes her laws in that conviction, must her breed of sons be changed, he asks, because some other philosophy of government finds favor in the halls of Congress? But the answer is not doubtful. One might ask with equal reason whether the system of protective tariffs is to be set aside at will in one state or another whenever local policy prefers the rule of *laissez faire*. The issue is a closed one. It was fought out long ago. When money is spent to promote the general welfare, the concept of welfare or the opposite is shaped by Congress, not the states. So the concept be not arbitrary, the locality must yield. Constitution, Art. VI, Par. 2.

Ordered Accordingly.

West Coast Hotel Co. v. Parrish, *1937*

This case presents the question of the constitutional validity of the minimum wage law of the State of Washington.

The Act, entitled, "minimum Wages for Women," authorizes the fixing of minimum wages for women and minors. . . .

The appellant conducts a hotel. The appellee Elsie Parrish was employed as a chambermaid and (with her husband) brought this suit to recover the difference between the wages paid her and the minimum wage fixed pursuant to the state law. The minimum wage was $14.50 per week of 48 hours. The appellant challenged the act as repugnant to the due process clause of the Fourteenth Amendment of the Constitution of the United States. The Supreme Court of the State, reversing the trial court, sustained the statute and directed judgment for the plaintiff. . . .

The case is here on appeal.

The appellant relies upon the decision of this Court in *Adkins v. Children's Hospital*, which has held invalid the District of Columbia Minimum Wage Act which was attacked under the due process clause of the Fifth Amendment. . . .

The Supreme Court of Washington has upheld the minimum wage statute of this State. It has decided that the statute is a reasonable exercise of the police power of the State. In reaching that conclusion the State court has invoked principles long established by this Court in the application of the Fourteenth Amendment. The State court has refused to regard the decision in the *Adkins* case as determinative and has pointed to our decisions both before and since that case as justifying its position. We are of the opinion that this ruling of the State court demands on our part a re-examination of the *Adkins* case. The importance of the question, in which many States having similar laws are concerned, the close division by which the decision in the *Adkins* case was reached, and the economic conditions which have supervened, and in the light of which the reasonableness of the exercise of the protective power of the State must be considered, make it not only appropriate, but we think imperative, that in deciding the present case the subject should receive fresh consideration. . . .

The principle which must control our decision is not in doubt. The constitutional provision invoked is the due process clause of the Fourteenth Amendment governing the States, as the due process clause invoked in the *Adkins* case governed Congress. In each case the violation alleged by those attacking minimum wage regulation for women is deprivation of freedom of contract. What is this freedom? The Constitution does not speak of freedom of contract. It speaks of liberty and prohibits the deprivation of liberty without due process of law. In prohibiting that deprivation the Constitution does not recognize an absolute and uncontrollable liberty. Liberty in each of its phases has its history and connotation. But the liberty safeguarded is liberty in a social organization which requires the protection of law against the evils which menace the health, safety, morals and welfare of the people. Liberty under the Constitution is thus necessarily subject to the restraints of due process, and regulation which is reasonable in relation to its subject and is adopted in the interests of the community is due process. . . .

The minimum wage to be paid under the Washington statute is fixed after full consideration by representatives of employers, employees and the public. It may be assumed that the minimum wage is fixed in consideration of the services that are performed in the particular occupations under normal conditions. Provision is made for special licenses at less wages in the case of women who are incapable of full service. The statement of Mr. Justice Holmes in the *Adkins* case is pertinent:

This statute does not compel anybody to pay anything. It simply forbids employment at rates below those fixed as the minimum requirement of health and right living. It is safe to assume that women will not be employed at even the lowest wages allowed unless they earn them, or unless the employer's business can sustain the burden. In short the law in its character and operation is like hundreds of so-called police laws that have been upheld. . . .

What can be closer to the public interest than the health of women and their protection from unscrupulous and overreaching employers? And if the protection of women is a legitimate end of the exercise of state power, how can it be said that the requirement of the payment of a minimum wage fairly fixed in order to meet the very necessities of existence is not an admissible means to that end? The legislature of the State was clearly entitled to consider the situation of women in employment, the fact that they are in the class receiving the least pay, that their bargaining power is relatively weak, and that they are the ready victims of those who would take advantage of their necessitous circumstances. The legislature was entitled to adopt measures to reduce the evils of the "sweating system," the exploiting of workers at wages so low as to be insufficient to meet the bare cost of living, thus making their very helplessness the occasion of a most injurious competition. The legislature had the right to consider that its minimum wage requirements would be an important aid in carrying out its policy of protection. The adoption of similar requirements by many States evidences a deepseated conviction both as to the presence of the evil and as to the means adopted to check it. Legislative response to that conviction cannot be regarded as arbitrary or capricious and that is all we have to decide. Even if the wisdom of the policy be regarded as debatable and its effects uncertain, still the legislature is entitled to its judgment.

There is an additional and compelling consideration which recent economic experience has brought into a strong light. The exploitation of a class of workers who are in an unequal position with respect to bargaining power and are thus relatively defenceless against the denial of a living wage is not only detrimental to their health and well being but casts a direct burden for their support upon the community. What these workers lose in wages the taxpayers are called upon to pay. The bare cost of living must be met. We may take judicial notice of the unparalleled demands for relief which arose during the recent period of depression and still continue to an alarming extent despite the degree of economic recovery which has been achieved. It is unnecessary to cite official statistics to establish what is of common knowledge through the length and breadth of the land. While in the instant case no factual brief has been presented, there is no reason to doubt that the State of Washington has encountered the same social problem that is present elsewhere. The community is not bound to provide what is in effect a subsidy for unconscionable employers. The community may direct its law-making power to correct the abuse which springs from their selfish disregard of the public interest. . . .

Our conclusion is that the case of *Adkins v. Children's Hospital, supra* should be, and is overruled. The judgment of the Supreme Court of the State of Washington is affirmed.

Chapter 24

THE END OF ISOLATION

However far-reaching the social and economic reforms that constituted the "Roosevelt Revolution," it was as war leader rather than as domestic reformer that Franklin D. Roosevelt made his most profound impression upon the course of American life. Under his bold leadership American foreign policy ultimately underwent a transformation even more revolutionary than that in political thought, and by the time of the President's death in April 1945, the nation seemed permanently to have abandoned isolationism and accepted its full responsibilities as a great world power. Yet like Woodrow Wilson before him, Roosevelt entered the Presidency with a minor concern for foreign affairs, and during the early thirties America's relations with the world around her were generally conducted on a rather narrow, nationalistic basis which offered little suggestion of the broadly conceived program of international cooperation of Roosevelt's second and third administrations.

In only two areas did Roosevelt immediately indicate an attitude which differed importantly from the provincial nationalism long characteristic of American foreign policy. Convinced that economic reform depended largely upon the removal of the barriers to international trade, he heartily endorsed the reciprocal trade program of Secretary of State Cordell Hull. The prohibitive Hawley-Smoot Tariff, which Hoover signed in 1930 over the strenuous objections of 1,000 professional economists, had brought extensive foreign retaliation against American goods. But the Trade Agreements Act of 1934 authorized the reduction of tariff rates by as much as fifty percent in return for similar concessions from other nations, and within a few years reciprocal agreements had brought a vastly increased foreign trade.

Meanwhile Roosevelt abandoned the threatening "Big Stick" policy in Latin-American relations and adopted instead "the policy of the good neighbor—the neighbor who resolutely respects himself and, because he does so, respects the rights of others—the neighbor who respects his obligations and respects the sanctity of his agreements in and with a world of neighbors." The United States ended its protectorate over Cuba, pledging nonintervention in the internal affairs of her sister republics to the South; the last American marines were withdrawn from Haiti; and the Monroe Doctrine was reinterpreted as an expression of multilateral Pan-American policy rather than merely the unilateral pronouncement of the United States. It would take many years before the once aggressively self-assertive "Colossus of the North" could entirely dispel the fears of her Latin-American neighbors, but the Good Neighbor Policy proved a wise and eminently successful first step in that direction.

Aside from these departures from tradition, however, in the early days of the New Deal there were few indications of the outstanding leadership Franklin D. Roosevelt was eventually to offer the democratic world in its fight for freedom. Setting the nation's own house in order demanded the President's full attention and energies and seemed to leave little time for concern with the world at large. Besides, in the thirties American public opinion was firmly set against embroilment in foreign affairs. To the general disillusionment which followed World War I had been added intense chagrin at the failure of former Allies to pay their war debts. Then, when the Nye Committee of the Senate revealed that munitions makers had enjoyed huge earnings from 1914 to 1918, a great many Americans cynically concluded that the war had been fought merely for the profit of a greedy few. From 1935 to 1937 these feelings all found expression in a series of Neutrality Acts which were designed to keep America out of future wars by placing an embargo upon the export of arms to belligerent nations, by prohibiting the extension of loans and credits to belligerents, by forbidding Americans to travel on belligerent vessels, and by preventing the arming of American merchant ships.

Yet war clouds were rapidly gathering throughout the world, and neutrality was hardly possible for a democracy surrounded by totalitarian aggressors. In 1931 Imperial Japan seized Manchuria from China, and in 1937 she launched another vicious and unprovoked attack upon that near-defenseless nation in an effort to establish a Japanese dominated "New Order" in the Far East. In 1935 Benito Mussolini, the "sawdust Caesar" of Fascist Italy, began an imperialist war against Ethiopia. And in 1936, after Japanese and Italian aggressions had indicated very clearly the collapse of collective security and the ineffectiveness of the League of Nations, Nazi Germany remilitarized the Rhineland as a prelude to Adolf Hitler's mad quest for world domination.

Most Americans thoroughly deplored the rise of totalitarianism and their sympathies were sincerely extended to persecuted minorities within the dictator nations and to the hapless victims of totalitarian aggression. But the national temper was still largely isolationist, and there seemed little likelihood that popular opinion would tolerate active intervention abroad. Thus Roosevelt's course was all the more difficult. Though at first he had been somewhat indifferent to world politics, he actually had come much sooner than most of his countrymen to a real understanding of the formidable threat that aggressive dictatorship anywhere in the world posed to the United States and to democracy everywhere. It was clearly the President's task to educate the nation to the imminent danger to its security, and in his famous "Quarantine" speech of 1937 he warned that there is a "solidarity and interdependence about the modern world, both technically and morally, which makes it impossible for any nation completely to isolate itself from economic and political upheavals in the rest of the world. . . ." "The epidemic of world lawlessness is spreading. . ." he argued, and America must join the free world in quarantining aggressors as she would quarantine those who suffer from physical disease. "Let no one imagine that America will escape, that it may expect mercy, that this Western Hemisphere will not be attacked, and that it will continue tranquilly and peacefully to carry on the ethics and the arts of civilization."

Internationalists cheered the "Quarantine" speech as an unequivocal statement of America's stake in collective security, but most Americans were less farsighted, and the President's grim lecture on the realities of international politics was greeted with widespread public apathy or hostility. Yet the dictator nations themselves soon provided the basis for Roosevelt's eloquent and increasingly frequent lessons in world diplomacy. Interventionist sentiment was immeasurably strengthened by further Japanese assaults upon China; by Hitler's demand that democratic Czechoslovakia surrender the Sudetenland to Germany or face total war; by appeasement at Munich, where England and France deserted that small republic to guarantee what British Prime Minister Neville Chamberlain naïvely called "peace in our time"; by Hitler's armed march into what remained of Czechoslovakia after the Munich betrayal; and by Mussolini's rape of Albania. Then in August 1939, the signature of a nonaggression pact between Nazi Germany and Communist Russia further shocked Americans from their complacency. Now protected against war on two fronts, Hitler ordered his armies to march into Poland, and when England and France finally resisted the Nazi aggressor, World War II began.

Even after England and France had taken up Hitler's

challenge to peace and to democracy, America was largely opposed to direct involvement in war. Though there was little pro-German sentiment within the nation, and though most Americans fervently prayed for an Allied victory over totalitarian aggression, American assistance in 1939 was limited to repealing the arms embargo of the Neutrality Acts and permitting "cash and carry" sales of war supplies to the belligerents. In the Spring of 1940, however, when Denmark, Norway, Belgium, Holland, Luxembourg, and finally France all fell in rapid order before Hitler's onrushing armies, Americans finally awoke to the menace to their own safety and freedom and embraced more enthusiastically the realistic leadership of Franklin D. Roosevelt. There remained those who deemed the President as a "warmonger" and the isolationist "America First Committee" proved a powerful antidote to the interventionist Committee to Defend America by Aiding the Allies. But there was a general approval of the government's intensive preparedness program for "total defense," and in September 1940, Congress enacted the nation's first peacetime conscription law.

By 1940 most Americans had come to agree with this President that "we must make America the arsenal of democracy" and in September they warmly applauded the transfer—by Executive Order—of fifty overage destroyers to the hard-pressed British. Though generally a fervent supporter of the Allied cause, Wendell Willkie, the popular Republican candidate for President in the election of 1940, roundly denounced the destroyer deal as a "dictatorial action" and rebuked the President for not seeking prior Congressional approval. But Roosevelt easily overrode these criticisms and was reelected despite bitter partisan opposition and traditional objections to a third term for any President. His foreign aid program continued unabated. Early in 1941 he submitted to the Congress a plan which would permit the government to lend or lease or otherwise transfer military supplies to any nation whose defense was essential to American security. Then in his "Four Freedoms" speech the President summoned the full moral strength of America in support of the Lend-Lease Bill, announcing to the world—as Wilson had in his Fourteen Points—

that America's goal was a postwar world which would enjoy freedom of speech, freedom of religion, freedom from want, and freedom from fear. In the Summer of 1941 Roosevelt and British Prime Minister Winston Churchill held a secret shipboard rendezvous in the Atlantic, where the senior statesmen of the free world drew up an "Atlantic Charter" to state precisely the ideological nature of the war against totalitarianism.

Even at this point Americans spoke hopefully of all-out aid to the Allies *short of war*, but the Rome-Berlin-Tokyo Axis soon determined the nation's fate otherwise. On December 7, 1941—"a day that will live in infamy"—the Japanese launched a disastrous surprise attack upon Pearl Harbor and other American outposts in the Pacific. Within a week the United States was officially at war with the Axis powers. Americans fought because they had been attacked; yet it was also true that the attack would not have come had they been willing to appease the dictators as England and France had done so furtively at Munich, had they been willing to sacrifice their ideals, to abandon their fellow democracies to total destruction, and to postpone the day when they would ultimately stand alone against a hostile, Axis-dominated world. Thus the nation was not forced or tricked into war; rather out of enlightened self-interest she had deliberately chosen what Winston Churchill so dramatically described as the path of "blood, toil, tears, and sweat."

"Quarantine" Speech, *Franklin D. Roosevelt, 1937*

I am glad to come once again to Chicago and especially to have the opportunity of taking part in the dedication of this important project of civic betterment.

On my trip across the continent and back I have been shown many evidences of the results of common sense cooperation between municipalities and the Federal Government, and I have been greeted by tens of thousands of Americans who have told me in every look and word that their material and spiritual well-being has made great strides forward in the past few years.

And yet, as I have seen with my own eyes, the prosperous farms, the thriving factories and the busy railroads, as I have seen the happiness and security and peace which covers our wide land, almost inevitably I have been compelled to contrast our peace with very different scenes being enacted in other parts of the world.

It is because the people of the United States under modern conditions must, for the sake of their own future, give thought to the rest of the world, that I, as the responsible executive head of the Nation, have chosen this great inland city and this gala occasion to speak to you on a subject of definite national importance.

The political situation in the world, which of late has been growing progressively worse, is such as to cause grave concern and anxiety to all the peoples and nations who wish to live in peace and amity with their neighbors.

Some fifteen years ago the hopes of mankind for a continuing era of international peace were raised to great heights when more than sixty nations solemnly pledged themselves not to resort to arms in furtherance of their national aims and policies. The high aspirations expressed in the Briand-Kellog Peace Pact and the hopes for peace thus raised have of late given way to a haunting fear of calamity. The present reign of terror and international lawlessness began a few years ago.

It began through unjustified interference in the internal affairs of other nations or the invasion of alien territory in violation of treaties; and has now reached a stage where the very foundations of civilization are seriously threatened. The landmarks and traditions which have marked the progress of civilization toward a condition of law, order and justice are being wiped away.

Without a declaration of war and without warning or justification of any kind, civilians, including vast numbers of women and children, are being ruthlessly murdered with bombs from the air. In times of so-called peace, ships are being attacked and sunk by submarines without cause or notice. Nations are fomenting and taking sides in civil warfare in nations that have never done them any harm. Nations claiming freedom for themselves deny it to others.

Innocent peoples, innocent nations, are being cruelly sacrificed to a greed for power and supremacy which is devoid of all sense of justice and humane considerations.

To paraphrase a recent author, "perhaps we foresee a time when men, exultant in the technique of homicide, will rage so hotly over the world that every precious thing will be in danger, every book and picture and harmony, every treasure garnered through two millenniums, the small, the delicate, the defenseless—all will be lost or wrecked or utterly destroyed."

If those things come to pass in other parts of the world, let no one imagine that America will escape, that America may expect mercy, that this Western Hemisphere will not be attacked and that it will continue tranquilly and peacefully to carry on the ethics and the arts of civilization.

If those days come, "there will be no safety by arms, no help from authority, no answer in science. The storm will rage till every flower of culture is trampled and all human beings are leveled in a vast chaos."

If those days are not to come to pass—if we are to have a world in which we can breathe freely and live in amity without fear—the peace-loving nations must make a concerted effort to uphold laws and principles on which alone peace can rest secure.

The peace-loving nations must make a concerted effort in opposition to those violations of treaties and those ignorings of humane instincts which today are creating a state of international anarchy and instability from which there is no escape through mere isolation or neutrality.

Those who cherish their freedom and recognize and respect the equal right of their neighbors to be free and live in peace must work together for the triumph of law and moral principles in order that peace, justice and confidence may prevail in the world. There must be a return to a belief in the pledged word, in the value of a signed treaty. There must be recognition of the fact that national morality is as vital as private morality.

A bishop wrote me the other day: "It seems to me that something greatly needs to be said in behalf of ordinary humanity against the present practice of carrying the horrors of war to helpless civilians, especially women and children. It may be that such a protest might be regarded by many, who claim to be realists, as futile, but may it not be that the heart of mankind is so filled with horror at the present heedless suffering that that force could be mobilized in sufficient volume to lessen such cruelty in the days ahead. Even though it may take twenty years, which God forbid, for civilization to make effective its corporate protest against this barbarism, surely strong voices may hasten the day."

There is a solidarity and interdependence about the modern world, both technically and morally, which makes it impossible for any nation completely to isolate itself from economic and political upheavals in the rest of the world, especially when such upheavals appear to be spreading and not declining. There can be no stability or peace either within nations or between nations except under laws and moral standards adhered to by all. International anarchy destroys every foundation for peace. It jeopardizes either the immediate or the future security of every nation, large or small. It is, therefore, a matter of vital interest and concern to the people of the United States that the sanctity of international treaties and the maintenance of international morality be restored.

The overwhelming majority of the peoples and nations of the world today want to live in peace. They seek the removal of barriers against trade. They want to exert themselves in industry, in agriculture and in business, that they may increase their wealth through the production of wealth-producing goods rather than striving to produce military planes and bombs and machine guns and cannon for the destruction of human lives and useful property.

In those nations of the world which seem to be piling armament on armament for purposes of aggression, and those other nations which fear acts of aggression against them and their security, a very high proportion of their national income is being spent directly for armaments. It runs from thirty to as high as fifty percent. We are fortunate. The proportion that we in the United States spend is far less—eleven or twelve percent.

How happy we are that the circumstances of the moment permit us to put our money into bridges and boulevards, dams and reforestation, the conservation of our soil and many other kinds of useful works rather than in to huge standing armies and vast supplies of implements of war.

I am compelled and you are compelled, nevertheless, to look ahead. The peace, the freedom and the security of ninety percent of the population of the world is being jeopardized by the remaining ten percent who are threatening a breakdown of all international order and law. Surely the ninety percent who want to live in peace under law and in accordance with moral standards that have received almost universal acceptance through the centuries can and must find some way to make their will prevail.

The situation is definitely of universal concern. The questions involved relate not merely to violations of specific provisions of particular treaties; they are questions of war and of peace, of international law and especially of principles of humanity. It is true that they involve definite violations of agreements, and especially of the Covenant of the League of Nations, the Briand-Kellog Pact and the Nine Power Treaty. But they also involve problems of world economy, world security and world humanity.

It is true that the moral consciousness of the world must recognize the importance of removing injustices and well-founded grievances; but at the same time it must be aroused to the cardinal necessity of honoring sanctity of treaties, of respecting the rights and liberties of others and of putting an end to acts of international aggression.

It seems to be unfortunately true that the epidemic of world lawlessness is spreading.

When an epidemic of physical disease starts to spread, the community approves and joins in a quarantine of the patients in order to protect the health of the community against the spread of the disease.

It is my determination to pursue a policy of peace. It is my determination to adopt every practicable measure to avoid involvement in war. It ought to be inconceivable that in this modern era, and in the face of experience, any nation could be so foolish and ruthless as to run the risk of plunging the whole world into war by invading and violating, in contravention of solemn treaties, the territory of other nations that have done them no real harm and are too weak to protect themselves adequately. Yet the peace of the world and the welfare and security of every nation, including our own, is today being threatened by that very thing.

No nation which refuses to exercise forbearance and to respect the freedom and rights of others can long remain strong and retain the confidence and respect of other nations. No nation ever loses its dignity or its good standing by conciliating its differences, and by exercising great patience with, and consideration for, the rights of other nations.

War is a contagion, whether it be declared or undeclared. It can engulf states and peoples remote from the original scene of hostilities. We are determined to keep out of war, yet we cannot insure ourselves against the disastrous effects of war and the dangers of involvement. We are adopting such measures as will minimize our risk of involvement, but we cannot have complete protection in a world of disorder in which confidence and security have broken down.

If civilization is to survive, the principles of the Prince of Peace must be restored. Trust between nations must be revived.

Most important of all, the will for peace on the part of peace-loving nations must express itself to the end that nations that may be tempted to violate their agreements and the rights of others will desist from such a course. There must be positive endeavors to preserve peace.

America hates war. America hopes for peace. Therefore, America actively engages in the search for peace.

"Four Freedoms" Speech, *Franklin D. Roosevelt, 1941*

I address you, the Members of the Seventy-seventh Congress, at a moment unprecedented in the history of the Union. I use the word "unprecedented," because at no previous time has American security been as seriously threatened from without as it is today.

Since the permanent formation of our Government under the Constitution, in 1789, most of the periods of crisis in our history have related to our domestic affairs. Fortunately, only one of these—the four-year War between the States—ever threatened our national unity. Today, thank God, one hundred and thirty million Americans, in forty-eight states, have forgotten points of the compass in our national unity.

It is true that prior to 1914 the United States often had been disturbed by events in other Continents. We had even engaged in two wars with European nations and in a number of undeclared wars in the West Indies, in the Mediterranean and in the Pacific for the maintenance of American rights and for the principles of peaceful commerce. But in no case had a serious threat been raised against our national safety or our continued independence.

What I seek to convey is the historic truth that the United States as a nation has at all times maintained clear, definite opposition to any attempt to lock us in behind an ancient Chinese wall while the procession of civilization went past. Today, thinking of our children and of their children, we oppose enforced isolation for ourselves or for any other part of the Americas.

That determination of ours, extending over all these years, was proved, for example, during the quarter century of wars following the French Revolution.

While the Napoleonic struggles did threaten interests of the United States because of the French foothold in the West Indies and in Louisiana, and while we engaged in the War of 1812 to vindicate our right to peaceful trade, it is nevertheless clear that neither France nor Great Britain, nor any other nation, was aiming at domination of the whole world.

In like fashion, from 1815 to 1914—ninety-nine years—no single war in Europe or in Asia constituted a real threat against our future or against the future of any other American nation.

Except in the Maximilian interlude in Mexico, no foreign power sought to establish itself in this Hemisphere; and the strength of the British fleet in the Atlantic has been a friendly strength. It is still a friendly strength.

Even when World War broke out in 1914, it seemed to contain only small threat of danger to our own American future. But, as time went on, the American people began to visualize what the downfall of democratic nations might mean to our own democracy.

We need not overemphasize imperfections in the Peace of Versailles. We need not harp on failure of the democracies to deal with problems of world reconstruction. We should remember that the Peace of 1919 was far less unjust than the kind of "pacification" which began even before Munich, and which is being carried on under the new order of tyranny that seeks to spread over every continent today. The American people have unalterably set their faces against that tyranny.

Every realist knows that the democratic way of life is at this moment being directly assailed in every part of the world—assailed either by arms, or by secret spreading of poisonous propaganda by those who seek to destroy unity and promote discord in nations that are still at peace.

During sixteen long months this assault has blotted out the whole pattern of democratic life in an appalling number of independent nations, great and small. The assailants are still on the march, threatening other nations, great and small.

Therefore, as your President, performing my constitutional duty to "give to the Congress information of the state of the Union," I find it, unhappily, necessary to report that the future and the safety of our country and of our democracy are overwhelmingly involved in events far beyond our borders.

Armed defense of democratic existence is now being gallantly waged in four continents. If that defense fails, all the population and all the resources of Europe, Asia, Africa and Australia will be dominated by the conquerors. Let us remember that the total of those populations and their resources in those four continents greatly exceeds the sum total of the population and the resources of the whole of the Western Hemisphere many times over.

In times like these it is immature——and incidentally, untrue—for anybody to brag that an unprepared America, single-handed, and with one hand tied behind its back, can hold off the whole world.

No realistic American can expect from a dictator's peace international generosity, or return of true independence, or world disarmament, or freedom of expression, or freedom of religion, or even good business.

Such a peace would bring no security for us or for our neighbors. "Those, who would give up essential liberty to purchase a little temporary safety, deserve neither liberty nor safety."

As a nation, we may take pride in the fact that we are soft-hearted; but we cannot afford to be soft-headed.

We must always be wary of those who with sounding brass and a tinkling cymbal preach the "ism" of appeasement.

We must especially beware of that small group of selfish men who would clip the wings of the American eagle in order to feather their own nests.

I have recently pointed out how quickly the tempo of modern warfare could bring into our very midst the physical attack which we must eventually expect if the dictator nations win this war.

There is much loose talk of our immunity for immediate and direct invasion from across the seas. Obviously, as long as the British Navy retains its power, no such danger exists. Even if there were no British Navy, it is not probable that any enemy would be stupid enough to attack us by landing troops in the United States from across thousands of miles of ocean, until it had acquired strategic bases from which to operate.

But we learn much from the lessons of the past years in Europe—particularly the lesson of Norway, whose essential seaports were captured by treachery and surprise built up over a series of years.

The first phase of the invasion of this Hemisphere would not be the landing of regular troops. The necessary strategic points would be occupied by secret agents and their dupes, and great numbers of them are already here, and in Latin America.

As long as the aggressor nations maintain the offensive, they—not we—will choose the time and the place and the method of their attack.

That is why the future of all the American Republics is today in serious danger.

That is why this Annual Message to the Congress is unique in our history.

That is why every member of the Executive Branch

of the Government and every member of the Congress faces great responsibility and great accountability.

The need of the moment is that our actions and our policy should be devoted primarily—almost exclusively—to meeting this foreign peril. For all our domestic problems are now a part of the great emergency.

Just as our national policy in internal affairs has been based upon a decent respect for the rights and the dignity of all our fellow men within our gates, so our national policy in foreign affairs has been based on a decent respect for the rights and dignity of all nations, large and small. And the justice of morality must and will win in the end.

Our national policy is this:

First, by an impressive expression of the public will and without regard to partisanship, we are committed to all-inclusive national defense.

Second, by an impressive expression of the public will and without regard to partisanship, we are committed to full support of all those resolute peoples, everywhere, who are resisting aggression and are thereby keeping war away from our Hemisphere. By this support, we express our determination that the democratic cause shall prevail; and we strengthen the defense and the security of our own nation.

Third, by an impressive expression of the public will and without regard to partisanship, we are committed to the proposition that principles of morality and considerations for our own security will never permit us to acquiesce in a peace dictated by aggressors and sponsored by appeasers. We know that enduring peace cannot be bought at the cost of other people's freedom.

In the recent national election there was no substantial difference between the two great parties in respect to that national policy. No issue was fought out on this line before the American electorate. Today it is abundantly evident that American citizens everywhere are demanding and supporting speedy and complete action in recognition of obvious danger.

Therefore, the immediate need is a swift and driving increase in our armament production. . . .

New circumstances are constantly begetting new needs for our safety. I shall ask this Congress for greatly increased new appropriations and authorizations to carry on what we have begun.

I also ask this Congress for authority and for funds sufficient to manufacture additional munitions and war supplies of many kinds, to be turned over to those nations which are now in actual war with aggressor nations.

Our most useful and immediate role is to act as an arsenal for them as well as for ourselves. They do not need man power, but they do need billions of dollars worth of the weapons of defense.

The time is near when they will not be able to pay for them all in ready cash. We cannot, and we will not, tell them that they must surrender, merely because of inability to pay for the weapons which we know they must have.

I do not recommend that we make them a loan of dollars with which to pay for these weapons—a loan to be repaid in dollars.

I recommend that we make it possible for those nations to continue to obtain war materials in the United States, fitting their orders into our own program. Nearly all their matériel would, if the time ever came, be useful for our own defense.

Taking counsel of expert military and naval authorities, considering what is best for our own security, we are free to decide how much should be kept here and how much should be sent abroad to our friends who by their determined and heroic resistance are giving us time in which to make ready our own defense.

For what we send abroad, we shall be repaid within a reasonable time following the close of hostilities, in similar materials, or, at our option, in other goods of many kinds, which they can produce and which we need.

Let us say to the democracies: "We Americans are vitally concerned in your defense of freedom. We are putting forth our energies, our resources and our organizing powers to give you the strength to regain and maintain a free world. We shall send you, in ever-increasing numbers, ships, planes, tanks, guns. This is our purpose and our pledge."

In fulfillment of this purpose we will not be intimidated by the threats of dictators that they will regard as a breach of international law or as an act of war our aid to the democracies which dare to resist their aggression. Such aid is not an act of war, even if a dictator should unilaterally proclaim it so to be.

When the dictators, if the dictators, are ready to make war upon us, they will not wait for an act of war on our part. They did not wait for Norway or Belgium or the Netherlands to commit an act of war.

Their only interest is in a new one-way international law, which lacks mutuality in its observance, and, therefore, becomes an instrument of oppression.

The happiness of future generations of Americans may well depend upon how effective and how immediate we can make our aid felt. No one can tell the exact character of the emergency situations that we may be called upon to meet. The Nation's hands must not be tied when the Nation's life is in danger.

We must all prepare to make the sacrifices that the emergency—almost as serious as war itself—demands. Whatever stands in the way of speed and efficiency in defense preparations must give way to the national need.

A free nation has the right to expect full cooperation from all groups. A free nation has the right to look to the leaders of business, of labor, and of agriculture to take the lead in stimulating effort, not among other groups but within their own groups.

The best way of dealing with the few slackers or trouble makers in our midst is, first, to shame them by patriotic example, and, if that fails, to use the sovereignty of Government to save Government.

As men do not live by bread alone, they do not fight by armaments alone. Those who man our defenses, and those behind them who build our defenses, must have the stamina and the courage which come from unshakeable belief in the manner of life which they are defending. The mighty action that we are calling for cannot be based on a disregard of all things worth fighting for.

The Nation takes great satisfaction and much strength from the things which have been done to make its people conscious of their individual stake in the preservation of democratic life in America. Those things have toughened the fibre of our people, have renewed their faith and strengthened their devotion to the institutions we make ready to protect.

Certainly this is no time for any of us to stop thinking about the social and economic problems which are the root cause of the social revolution which is today a supreme factor in the world.

For there is nothing mysterious about the foundations of a healthy and strong democracy. The basic things expected by our people of their political and economic systems are simple. They are:

Equality of opportunity for youth and for others.

Jobs for those who can work.

Security for those who need it.

The ending of special privilege for the few.

The preservation of civil liberties for all.

The enjoyment of the fruits of scientific progress in a wider and constantly rising standard of living.

These are the simple, basic things that must never be lost sight of in the turmoil and unbelievable complexity of our modern world. The inner and abiding strength of our economic and political systems is dependent upon the degree to which they fulfill these expectations.

Many subjects connected with our social economy call for immediate improvement.

As examples:

We should bring more citizens under the coverage of old-age pensions and unemployment insurance.

We should widen the opportunities for adequate medical care.

We should plan a better system by which persons deserving or needing gainful employment may obtain it.

I have called for personal sacrifice. I am assured of the willingness of almost all Americans to respond to that call.

A part of the sacrifice means the payment of more money in taxes. In my Budget Message I shall recommend that a greater portion of this great defense program be paid for from taxation than we are paying today. No person should try, or be allowed, to get rich out of this program; and the principle of tax payments in accordance with ability to pay should be constantly before our eyes to guide our legislation.

If the Congress maintains these principles, the voters,

putting patriotism ahead of pocketbooks, will give you their applause.

In the future days, which we seek to make secure, we look forward to a world founded upon four essential human freedoms.

The first is freedom of speech and expression—everywhere in the world.

The second is freedom of every person to worship God in his own way—everywhere in the world.

The third is freedom from want—which, translated into world terms, means economic understandings which will secure to every nation a healthy peacetime life for its inhabitants—everywhere in the world.

The fourth is freedom from fear—which, translated into world terms means a world-wide reduction of armaments to such a point and in such a thorough fashion that no nation will be in a position to commit an act of physical aggression against any neighbor—anywhere in the world.

That is no vision of a distant millennium. It is a definite basis for a kind of world attainable in our own time and generation. That kind of world is the very antithesis of the so-called new order of tyranny which the dictators seek to create with the crash of a bomb.

To that new order we oppose the greater conception—the moral order. A good society is able to face schemes of world domination and foreign revolutions alike without fear.

Since the beginning of our American history, we have been engaged in change—in a perpetual peaceful revolution—a revolution which goes on steadily, quietly adjusting itself to changing conditions—without the concentration camp or the quick-lime in the ditch. The world order which we seek is the cooperation of free countries, working together in a friendly, civilized society.

This nation has placed its destiny in the hands and heads and hearts of its millions of free men and women; and its faith in freedom under the guidance of God. Freedom means the supremacy of human rights everywhere. Our support goes to those who struggle to gain those rights or keep them. Our strength is our unity of purpose.

To that high concept there can be no end save victory.

The Atlantic Charter, *1941*

Joint declaration of the President of the United States of America and the Prime Minister, Mr. Churchill, representing His Majesty's Government in the United Kingdom, being met together, deem it right to make known certain common principles in the national policies of their respective countries on which they base their hopes for a better future of the world.

First, their countries seek no aggrandizement, territorial or other;

Second, they desire to see no territorial changes that do not accord with the freely expressed wishes of the peoples concerned;

Third, they respect the right of all peoples to choose the form of government under which they will live; and they wish to see sovereign rights and self-government restored to those who have been forcibly deprived of them;

Fourth, they will endeavor, with due respect for their existing obligations, to further the enjoyment by all states, great or small, victor or vanquished, of access on equal terms, to the trade and to the raw materials of the world which are needed for their economic prosperity;

Fifth, they desire to bring about the fullest collaboration between all nations in the economic field with the object of securing, for all, improved labor standards, economic advancement, and social security;

Sixth, after the final destruction of the Nazi tyranny, they hope to see established a peace which will afford to all nations the means of dwelling in safety within their own boundaries, and which will afford assurance that all the men in all the lands may live out their lives in freedom from fear and want;

Seventh, such a peace should enable all men to traverse the high seas and oceans without hindrance;

Eighth, they believe that all of the nations of the world, for realistic as well as spiritual reasons, must come to the abandonment of the use of force. Since no future peace can be maintained if land, sea, or air armaments continue to be employed by nations which threaten, or may threaten, aggression outside of their frontiers, they believe, pending the establishment of a wider and permanent system of general security, that the disarmament of such nations is essential. They will likewise aid and encourage all other practicable measures which will lighten for peace-loving peoples the crushing burden of armaments.

Chapter 25

THE COLD WAR

On January 1, 1942, less than a month after Pearl Harbor, twenty-six nations at war with the Axis powers signed the historic Declaration of the United Nations, thus binding themselves to full and unstinting efforts against the common enemy and unifying themselves in the struggle against totalitarian aggression. Equally significant in the development of collective security were the frequent international conferences—at Quebec, Casablanca, Cairo, Teheran, and Yalta—which marked continuous, close cooperation on military and diplomatic matters among the major Allied powers, particularly England, Russia, and the United States. When this wartime harmony and singleness of purpose culminated in the defeat of the Axis powers and in creation of the United Nations world organization at the San Francisco Conference in April 1945, it seemed to hopeful men everywhere that global war must soon give way to a new world founded upon the principles of law and order.

The United States was now fully prepared to abandon the disastrous isolationism of the post-Versailles generation. Diehards remained who opposed American involvement in any scheme for international cooperation, but war had taught the overwhelming majority of Americans that world interdependence was an inescapable reality, and the United Nations was enthusiastically cheered throughout the country. Besides, Franklin D.

Roosevelt had proved too skillful a politician to repeat Wilson's tragic blunder of making world organization both a party and a personal issue. Instead the President had shrewdly identified the administration's war and peace policies with such outstanding Republican statesmen as Wendell L. Willkie, Henry L. Stimson, Frank Knox, and Senator Arthur H. Vandenburg (a former isolationist and ranking minority member of the important Senate Foreign Relations Committee). Bipartisanship worked well, for even in the election of 1944, when Roosevelt defeated Thomas E. Dewey to win a precedent-shattering fourth term, conflict over foreign policy was at a minimum. At the San Francisco Conference and for some time thereafter the leaders of both major parties assumed the responsibility of assuring official American support for the United Nations.

Nazi Germany collapsed in May 1945, under the combined pressures of Western forces led by General Dwight D. Eisenhower and of Russian forces from the east. Four months later, after the cities of Hiroshima and Nagasaki had been almost totally destroyed by America's newly developed, incredibly powerful atom bomb, the Japanese surrendered, and the war was over. But peace and security were not to be long enjoyed by a war-weary world, for disunity among the former allies was apparent almost as soon as the war ended. A bitter "cold war" broke out between the East and the West, and the United Nations very quickly became the scene of continuous disagreements between the Soviet Union and the United States.

Then in March 1947, when the American government believed that the independence of Greece and Turkey was being seriously threatened by Soviet imperial ambitions, President Harry S Truman (who had succeeded to the Presidency after Roosevelt's untimely death in April 1945) appeared before Congress to announce a revolutionary change in American foreign policy:

> At the present moment in world history nearly every nation must choose between alternative ways of life. The choice is too often not a free one. One way of life is based upon the will of the ma-

> jority. . . . The second way of life is based upon the will of the minority forcibly imposed upon the majority. It relies upon terror and oppression, a controlled press and radio, fixed elections, and the suppression of personal freedoms. I believe that it must be the policy of the United States to support free peoples who are resisting attempted subjugation by armed minorities or by outside pressures. . . .

Then the President further urged financial support for the administration's new plan to "contain" Communist power through economic and military assistance abroad.

Congress quickly approved the Truman Doctrine and granted the President's initial request for $400,000,000. Yet it was clear that the war-devastated nations of Western Europe could not long survive an extensive cold war with the East unless their economies were reconstructed and strengthened, for Communism fed upon poverty and chaos. Thus in a speech at Harvard University in June 1947, Secretary of State George C. Marshall announced that if Europe were to indicate a willingness to work hard at its own recovery, then the United States would make large sums of money available for economic reconstruction. The Russians bitterly denounced the Marshall Plan, and within the United States itself the administration encountered considerable resistance from former isolationists who once again argued for American withdrawal from foreign commitments. A European Recovery Program was enacted in April 1948, and an Economic Cooperation Administration was established under the direction of Paul G. Hoffman, a Republican industrialist, to administer multi-billion-dollar American grants to bolster resistance to Soviet aggression.

The Marshall Plan proved immediately effective in Western Europe, and Americans hoped that economic rehabilitation would prove an insurmountable barrier to further Communist penetration. That this faith in mutual aid and cooperation was justified was indicated in 1948–1949 when the strengthened free nations of Europe supported America's successful efforts to break a Russian blockade of Berlin, and again in the spring of 1949 when they joined with the United States and Canada to form the North Atlantic Alliance. But continuing tension and conflict, following so soon worldwide holocaust and the unleashing of what seemed ultimate atomic weaponry, terrified thoughtful persons everywhere with the further specter of mutual annihilation. And it remained for American novelist William Faulkner, as he received the 1949 Nobel Prize for Literature, most sensitively to sum up mankind's best hope for survival: the triumph of the human spirit, even as nations locked in cold war appeared unceasingly to denigrate it. But it was foreign service officer George F. Kennan's harsh 1947 article (attributed only to "X") on the sources of Soviet conduct that was most widely hailed as providing the appropriately tough-minded theoretical basis for America's new policy of containment.

The Marshall Plan, *George C. Marshall, 1947*

I need not tell you, gentlemen, that the world situation is very serious. That must be apparent to all intelligent people. I think one difficulty is that the problem is one of such enormous complexity that the very mass of facts presented to the public by press and radio make it exceedingly difficult for the man in the street to reach a clear appraisement of the situation. Furthermore, the people of this country are distant from the troubled areas of the earth and it is hard for them to comprehend the plight and consequent reactions of the long-suffering peoples, and the effect of those reactions on their governments in connection with our efforts to promote peace in the world.

In considering the requirements for the rehabilitation of Europe, the physical loss of life, the visible destruction of cities, factories, mines and railroads was correctly estimated, but it has become obvious during recent months that this visible destruction was probably less serious than the dislocation of the entire fabric of European economy. For the past ten years conditions have been highly abnormal.

The feverish preparation for war and the more feverish maintenance of the war effort engulfed all aspects of national economies. Machinery has fallen into disrepair or is entirely obsolete. Under the arbitrary and destructive Nazi rule, virtually every possible enterprise was geared into the German war machine. Long-standing commercial ties, private institutions, banks, insurance companies and shipping companies disappeared, through loss of capital, absorption through nationalization or by simple destruction.

In many countries, confidence in the local currency has been severely shaken. The breakdown of the business structure of Europe during the war was complete. Recovery has been seriously retarded by the fact that two years after the close of hostilities a peace settlement with Germany and Austria has not been agreed upon. But even given a more prompt solution of these difficult problems, the rehabilitation of the economic structure of Europe quite evidently will require a much longer time and greater effort than had been foreseen.

There is a phase of this matter which is both interesting and serious. The farmer has always produced the foodstuffs to exchange with the city dweller for the other necessities of life. This division of labor is the basis of modern civilization. At the present time it is threatened with breakdown. The town and city industries are not producing adequate goods to exchange with the food-producing farmer. Raw materials and fuel are in short supply. Machinery is lacking or worn out.

The farmer or the peasant cannot find the goods for sale which he desires to purchase. So the sale of his farm produce for money which he cannot use, seems to him an unprofitable transaction. He, therefore, has withdrawn many fields from crop cultivation and is using them for grazing. He feeds more grain to stock and finds for himself and his family an ample supply of food, however, short he may be on clothing and the other ordinary gadgets of civilization. Meanwhile, people in the cities are short of food and fuel. So the governments are forced to use their foreign money and credits to procure these necessities abroad. This process exhausts funds which are urgently needed for reconstruction. Thus a very serious situation is rapidly developing which bodes no good for the world. The modern system of the division of labor upon which the exchange of products is based is in danger of breaking down.

The truth of the matter is that Europe's requirements for the next three or four years of foreign food and other essential products—principally from America—are so much greater than her present ability to pay that she must have substantial additional help, or face economic, social and political deterioration of a very grave character.

The remedy lies in breaking the vicious circle and restoring the confidence of the European people in the economic future of their own countries and of Europe as a whole. The manufacturer and the farmer throughout wide areas must be able and willing to exchange their products for currencies, the continuing value of which is not open to question.

Aside from the demoralizing effect on the world at large and the possibilities of disturbances arising as a result of the desperation of the people concerned, the consequences to the economy of the United States should be apparent to all. It is logical that the United States should do whatever it is able to do to assist in the return of normal economic health in the world, without which there can be no political stability and no assured peace.

Our policy is directed not against any country or doctrine but against hunger, poverty, desperation and chaos. Its purpose should be the revival of a working economy in the world so as to permit the emergence of political and social conditions in which free institutions can exist. Such assistance, I am convinced, must not be on a piecemeal basis as various crises develop. Any assistance that this Government may render in the future should provide a cure rather than a mere palliative.

Any government that is willing to assist in the task of recovery will find full cooperation, I am sure, on the part of the United States Government. Any government which maneuvers to block the recovery of other countries cannot expect help from us. Furthermore, governments, political parties or groups which seek to perpetuate human misery in order to profit therefrom politically or otherwise will encounter the opposition of the United States.

It is already evident that, before the United States Government can proceed much further in its efforts to alleviate the situation and help start the European world on its way to recovery, there must be some agreement among the countries of Europe as to the requirements of the situation and the part those countries themselves will take in order to give proper effect to whatever action might be undertaken by this Government. It would be neither fitting nor efficacious for this Government to undertake to draw up unilaterally a program designed to place Europe on its feet economically. This is the business of the Europeans. The initiative, I think, must come from Europe. The role of this country should consist of friendly aid in the drafting of a European program and of later support of such a program so far as it may be practical for us to do so. The program should be a joint one, agreed to by a number, if not all European nations.

An essential part of any successful action on the part of the United States is an understanding on the part of the people of America of the character of the problem and the remedies to be applied. Political passion and prejudice should have no part. With foresight, and a willingness on the part of our people to face up to the vast responsibility which history has clearly placed upon our country, the difficulties I have outlined can and will be overcome.

"Sources of Soviet Conduct," *George F. Kennan ("X"), 1947*

. . . Of the original ideology, nothing has been officially junked. Belief is maintained in the basic badness of capitalism, in the inevitability of its destruction, in the obligation of the proletariat to assist in that destruction and to take power into its own hands. But stress has come to be laid primarily on those concepts which relate most specifically to the Soviet régime itself: to its position as the sole truly Socialist régime in a dark and misguided world, and to the relationships of power within it.

The first of these concepts is that of the innate antagonism between capitalism and Socialism. We have seen how deeply that concept has become imbedded in foundations of Soviet power. It has profound implications for Russia's conduct as a member of international society. It means that there can never be on Moscow's side any sincere assumption of a community of aims between the Soviet Union and powers which are regarded as capitalist. It must invariably be assumed in Moscow that the aims of the capitalist world are antagonistic to the Soviet régime, and therefore to the interests of the peoples it controls. If the Soviet Government occasionally sets its signature to documents which would indicate the contrary, this is to be regarded as a tactical manoeuvre permissible in dealing with the enemy (who is without honor) and should be taken in the spirit of *caveat emptor.* Basically, the antagonism remains. It is postulated. And from it flow many of the phenomena which we find disturbing in the Kremlin's conduct of foreign policy: the secretiveness, the lack of frankness, the duplicity, the wary suspiciousness, and the basic unfriendliness of purpose. These phenomena are there to stay, for the foreseeable future. There can be variations of degree and of emphasis. When there is something the Russians want from us, one or the other of these features of their policy may be thrust temporarily into the background; and when that happens there will always be Americans who will leap forward with gleeful announcements that "the Russians have changed," and some who will even try to take credit for having brought about such "changes." But we should not be misled by tactical manoeuvres. These characteristics of Soviet policy, like the postulate from which they flow, are basic to the internal nature of Soviet power, and will be with us, whether in the foreground or the background, until the internal nature of Soviet power is changed.

This means that we are going to continue for a long time to find the Russians difficult to deal with. It does not mean that they should be considered as embarked upon a do-or-die program to overthrow our society by a given date. The theory of the inevitability of the eventual fall of capitalism has the fortunate connotation that there is no hurry about it. The forces of progress can take their time in preparing the final *coup de grâce.* Meanwhile, what is vital is that the "Socialist fatherland"—that oasis of power which has been already won for Socialism in the person of the Soviet Union—should be cherished and defended by all good Communists at home and abroad, its fortunes promoted, its enemies badgered and confounded. The promotion of premature, "adventuristic" revolutionary projects abroad which might embarrass Soviet power in any way would be an inexcusable, even a counter-revolutionary act. The cause of Socialism is the support and promotion of Soviet power, as defined in Moscow.

This brings us to the second of the concepts important to contemporary Soviet outlook. That is the infallibility of the Kremlin. The Soviet concept of power, which permits no focal points of organization outside the Party itself, requires that the Party leadership remain in theory the sole repository of truth. For if truth were to be found elsewhere, there would be justification for its expression in organized activity. But it is precisely that which the Kremlin cannot and will not permit.

The leadership of the Communist Party is therefore always right, and has been always right ever since in 1929 Stalin formalized his personal power by announcing that decisions of the Politburo were being taken unanimously.

On the principle of infallibility there rests the iron discipline of the Communist Party. In fact, the two concepts are mutually self-supporting. Perfect discipline requires recognition of infallibility. Infallibility requires the observance of discipline. And the two together go far to determine the behaviorism of the entire Soviet apparatus of power. But their effect cannot be understood unless a third factor be taken into account: namely, the fact that the leadership is at liberty to put forward for tactical purposes any particular thesis which it finds useful to the cause at any particular moment and to require the faithful and unquestioning acceptance of that thesis by the members of the movement as a whole. This means that truth is not a constant but is actually created, for all intents and purposes, by the Soviet leaders themselves. It may vary from week to week, from month to month. It is nothing absolute and immutable—nothing which flows from objective reality. It is only the most recent manifestation of the wisdom of those in whom the ultimate wisdom is supposed to reside, because they represent the logic of history. The accumulative effect of these factors is to give to the whole subordinate apparatus of Soviet power an unshakeable stubbornness and steadfastness in its orientation. This orientation can be changed at will by the Kremlin but by no other power. Once a given party line has been laid down on a given issue of current policy, the whole Soviet governmental machine, including the mechanism of diplomacy, moves inexorably along the prescribed path, like a persistent toy automobile wound up and headed in a given direction, stopping only when it meets with some unanswerable force. The individuals who are the components of this machine are unamenable to argument or reason which comes to them from outside sources. Their whole training has taught them to mistrust and discount the glib persuasiveness of the outside world. Like the white dog before the phonograph, they hear only the "master's voice." And if they are to be called off from the purposes last dictated to them, it is the master who must call them off. Thus the foreign representative cannot hope that his words will make any impression on them. The most that he can hope is that they will be transmitted to those at the top, who are capable of changing the party line. But even those are not likely to be swayed by any normal logic in the words of the bourgeois representative. Since there can be no appeal to common purposes, there can be no appeal to common mental approaches. For this reason, facts speak louder than words to the ears of the Kremlin; and words carry the greatest weight when they have the ring of reflecting, or being backed up by, facts of unchallengeable validity.

But we have seen that the Kremlin is under no ideological compulsion to accomplish its purposes in a hurry. Like the Church, it is dealing in ideological concepts which are of long-term validity, and it can afford to be patient. It has no right to risk the existing achievements of the revolution for the sake of vain baubles of the future. The very teachings of Lenin himself require great caution and flexibility in the pursuit of Communist purposes. Again, these precepts are fortified by the lessons of Russian history: of centuries of obscure battles between nomadic forces over the stretches of a vast unfortified plain. Here caution, circumspection, flexibility and deception are the valuable qualities; and their value finds natural appreciation in the Russian or the oriental mind. Thus the Kremlin has no compunction about retreating in the face of superior force. And being under the compulsion of no timetable, it does not get panicky under the necessity for such retreat. Its political action is a fluid stream which moves constantly, wherever it is permitted to move, toward a given goal. Its main concern is to make sure that it has filled every nook and cranny available to it in the basin of world power. But if it finds unassailable barriers in its path, it accepts these philosophically and accommodates itself to them. The main thing is that there should always be pressure, unceasing constant pressure, toward the desired goal. There is no trace of any feeling in Soviet psychology that that goal must be reached at any given time.

These considerations make Soviet diplomacy at once easier and more difficult to deal with than the diplomacy of individual aggressive leaders like Napoleon and Hitler. On the one hand it is more sensitive to contrary force, more ready to yield on individual sectors of the diplomatic front when that force is felt to be too strong, and thus more rational in the logic and rhetoric of power. On the other hand it cannot be easily defeated or discouraged by a single victory on the part of its opponents. And the patient persistence by which it is animated means that it can be effectively countered not by sporadic acts which represent the momentary whims of democratic opinion but only by intelligent long-range policies on the part of Russia's adversaries—policies no less steady in their purpose, and no less variegated and resourceful in their application, than those of the Soviet Union itself.

In these circumstances it is clear that the main element of any United States policy toward the Soviet Union must be that of a long-term, patient but firm and vigilant containment of Russian expansive tendencies. It is important to note, however, that such a policy has nothing to do with outward histrionics: with threats or blustering or superfluous gestures of outward "toughness." While the Kremlin is basically flexible in its reaction to political realities, it is by no means unamenable to considerations of prestige. Like almost any other government, it can be placed by tactless and threatening gestures in a position where it cannot afford to yield even though this might be dictated by its sense of realism. The Russian leaders are keen judges of human psychology, and as such they are highly conscious that loss of temper and of self-control is never a source of strength in political affairs. They are quick to exploit such evidences of weakness. For these reasons, it is a *sine qua non* of successful dealing with Russia that the foreign government in question should remain at all times cool and collected and that its demands on Russian policy should be put forward in such a manner as to leave the way open for a compliance not too detrimental to Russian prestige.

In the light of the above, it will be clearly seen that the Soviet pressure against the free institutions of the western world is something that can be contained by the adroit and vigilant application of counter-force at a series of constantly shifting geographical and political points, corresponding to the shifts and manoeuvres of Soviet policy, but which cannot be charmed or talked out of existence. The Russians look forward to a duel of infinite duration, and they see that already they have scored great successes. It must be borne in mind that there was a time when the Communist Party represented far more of a minority in the sphere of Russian national life than Soviet power today represents in the world community.

But if ideology convinces the rulers of Russia that truth is on their side and that they can therefore afford to wait, those of us on whom that ideology has no claim are free to examine objectively the validity of that premise. The Soviet thesis not only implies complete lack of control by the west over its own economic destiny, it likewise assumes Russian unity, discipline and patience over an infinite period. Let us bring this apocalyptic vision down to earth, and suppose that the western world finds the strength and resourcefulness to contain Soviet power over a period of ten to fifteen years. What does that spell for Russia itself?

The Soviet leaders, taking advantage of the contributions of modern technique to the arts of despotism, have solved the question of obedience within the confines of their power. Few challenge their authority; and even those who do are unable to make that challenge valid as against the organs of suppression of the state.

The Kremlin has also proved able to accomplish its purpose of building up in Russia, regardless of the interests of the inhabitants, an industrial foundation of heavy metallurgy, which is, to be sure, not yet complete but which is nevertheless continuing to grow and is approaching those of the other major industrial countries. All of this, however, both the maintenance of internal political security and the building of heavy industry, has been carried out at a terrible cost in human life and in human hopes and energies. It has necessitated the use of forced labor on a scale unprecedented in modern times under conditions of peace. It has involved the neglect or abuse of other phases of Soviet economic life, particularly agriculture, consumers' goods production, housing and transportation.

To all that, the war has added its tremendous toll of destruction, death and human exhaustion. In consequence of this, we have in Russia today a population which is physically and spiritually tired. The mass of the people are disillusioned, skeptical and no longer as accessible as they once were to the magical attraction which Soviet power still radiates to its followers abroad. The avidity with which people seized upon the slight respite accorded to the Church for tactical reasons during the war was eloquent testimony to the fact that their capacity for faith and devotion found little expression in the purposes of the régime.

In these circumstances, there are limits to the physical and nervous strength of people themselves. These limits are absolute ones, and are binding even for the cruelest dictatorship, because beyond them people cannot be driven. The forced labor camps and the other agencies of constraint provide temporary means of compelling people to work longer hours than their own volition or mere economic pressure would dictate; but if people survive them at all they become old before their time and must be considered as human casualties to the demands of dictatorship. In either case their best powers are no longer available to society and can no longer be enlisted in the service of the state.

Here only the younger generation can help. The younger generation, despite all vicissitudes and sufferings, is numerous and vigorous; and the Russians are a talented people. But it still remains to be seen what will be the effects on mature performance of the abnormal emotional strains of childhood which Soviet dictatorship created and which were enormously increased by the war. Such things as normal security and placidity of home environment have practically ceased to exist in the Soviet Union outside of the most remote farms and villages. And observers are not yet sure whether that is not going to leave its mark on the over-all capacity of the generation now coming into maturity.

In addition to this, we have the fact that Soviet economic development, while it can list certain formidable achievements, has been precariously spotty and uneven. Russian Communists who speak of the "uneven development of capitalism" should blush at the contemplation of their own national economy. Here certain branches of economic life, such as the metallurgical and machine industries, have been pushed out of all proportion to other sectors of economy. Here is a nation striving to become in a short period one of the great industrial nations of the world while it still has no highway network worthy of the name and only a relatively primitive network of railways. Much has been done to increase efficiency of labor and to teach primitive peasants something about the operation of machines. But maintenance is still a crying deficiency of all Soviet economy. Construction is hasty and poor in quality. Depreciation must be enormous. And in vast sectors of economic life it has not yet been possible to instill into labor anything like that general culture of production and technical self-respect which characterizes the skilled worker of the west.

It is difficult to see how these deficiencies can be corrected at an early date by a tired and dispirited population working largely under the shadow of fear and compulsion. And as long as they are not overcome, Russia will remain economically a vulnerable, and in a certain sense an impotent, nation, capable of exporting its enthusiasms and of radiating the strange charm of its primitive political vitality but unable to back up those articles of export by the real evidences of material power and prosperity.

Meanwhile, a great uncertainty hangs over the political life of the Soviet Union. That is the uncertainty involved in the transfer of power from one individual or group of individuals to others.

This is, of course, outstandingly the problem of the personal position of Stalin. We must remember that his succession to Lenin's pinnacle of preëminence in the Communist movement was the only such transfer of individual authority which the Soviet Union has experienced. That transfer took twelve years to consolidate. It cost the lives of millions of people and shook the state to its foundations. The attendant tremors were felt all through the international revolutionary movement, to the disadvantage of the Kremlin itself.

It is always possible that another transfer of preëminent power may take place quietly and inconspicuously, with no repercussions anywhere. But again, it is possible that the questions involved may unleash, to use some of Lenin's words, one of those "incredibly swift transitions" from "delicate deceit" to "wild violence" which characterize Russian history, and may shake Soviet power to its foundations.

But this is not only a question of Stalin himself. There has been, since 1938, a dangerous congealment of political life in the higher circles of Soviet power. . . .

Who can say whether, in these circumstances, the eventual rejuvenation of the higher spheres of authority (which can only be a matter of time) can take place smoothly and peacefully, or whether rivals in the quest for higher power will not eventually reach down into these politically immature and inexperienced masses in order to find support for their respective claims? If this were ever to happen, strange consequences could flow for the Communist Party: for the membership at large has been exercised only in the practices of iron discipline and obedience and not in the arts of compromise and accommodation. And if disunity were ever to seize and paralyze the Party, the chaos and weakness of Russian society would be revealed in forms beyond description. For we have seen that Soviet power is only a crust concealing an amorphous mass of human beings among whom no independent organizational structure is tolerated. In Russia there is not even such a thing as local government. The present generation of Russians have never known spontaneity of collective action. If, consequently, anything were ever to occur to disrupt the unity and efficacy of the Party as a political instrument, Soviet Russia might be changed overnight from one of the strongest to one of the weakest and most pitiable of national societies.

Thus the future of Soviet power may not be by any means as secure as Russian capacity for self-delusion would make it appear to the men in the Kremlin. That they can keep power themselves, they have demonstrated. That they can quietly and easily turn it over to others remains to be proved. Meanwhile, the hardships of their rule and the vicissitudes of international life have taken a heavy toll of the strength and hopes of the great people on whom their power rests. It is curious to note that the ideological power of Soviet authority is strongest today in areas beyond the frontiers of Russia, beyond the reach of its police power. This phenomenon brings to mind a comparison used by Thomas Mann in his great novel "Buddenbrooks." Observing that human institutions often show the greatest outward brilliance at a moment when inner decay is in reality farthest advanced, he compared the Buddenbrook family, in the days of its greatest glamour, to one of those stars whose light shines most brightly on this world when in reality it has long since ceased to exist. And who can say with assurance that the strong light still cast by the Kremlin on the dissatisfied peoples of the western world is not the powerful afterglow of a constellation which is in actuality on the wane? This cannot be proved. And it cannot be disproved. But the possibility remains (and in the opinion of this writer it is a strong one) that Soviet power, like the capitalist world of its conception, bears within it the seeds of its own decay, and that the sprouting of these seeds is well advanced.

* * *

It is clear that the United States cannot expect in the foreseeable future to enjoy political intimacy with the Soviet régime. It must continue to regard the Soviet Union as a rival, not a partner, in the political arena. It must continue to expect that Soviet policies will reflect no abstract love of peace and stability, no real faith in the possibility of a permanent happy coexistence of the Socialist and capitalist worlds, but rather a cautious, persistent pressure toward the disruption and weakening of all rival influence and rival power.

Balanced against this are the facts that Russia, as opposed to the western world in general, is still by far the weaker party, that Soviet policy is highly flexible, and that Soviet society may well contain deficiencies which will eventually weaken its own total potential. This would of itself warrant the United States entering with reasonable confidence upon a policy of firm containment, designed to confront the Russians with unalterable counter-force at every point where they show signs of encroaching upon the interests of a peaceful and stable world.

But in actuality the possibilities for American policy are by no means limited to holding the line and hoping for the best. It is entirely possible for the United States to influence by its actions the internal developments, both within Russia and throughout the international Communist movement, by which Russian policy is largely determined. This is not only a question of the modest measure of informational activity which this government can conduct in the Soviet Union and elsewhere, although that, too, is important. It is rather a question of the degree to which the United States can create among the peoples of the world generally the impression of a country which knows what it wants, which is coping successfully with the problems of its internal life and with the responsibilities of a World Power, and which has a spiritual vitality capable of holding its own among the major ideological currents of the time. To the extent that such an impression can be created and maintained, the aims of Russian Communism must appear sterile and quixotic, the hopes and enthusiasm of Moscow's supporters must wane, and added strain must be imposed on the Kremlin's foreign policies. For the palsied decrepitude of the capitalist world is the keystone of Communist philosophy. Even the failure of the United States to experience the early economic depression which the ravens of the Red Square have been predicting with such complacent confidence since hostilities ceased would have deep and important repercussions throughout the Communist world.

By the same token, exhibitions of indecision, disunity and internal disintegration within this country have an exhilarating effect on the whole Communist movement. At each evidence of these tendencies, a thrill of hope and excitement goes through the Communist world; a new jauntiness can be noted in the Moscow tread; new groups of foreign supporters climb on to what they can only view as the band wagon of international politics; and Russian pressure increases all along the line in international affairs.

It would be an exaggeration to say that American behavior unassisted and alone could exercise a power of life and death over the Communist movement and bring about the early fall of Soviet power in Russia. But the United States has it in its power to increase enormously the strains under which Soviet policy must operate, to force upon the Kremlin a far greater degree of moderation and circumspection than it has had to observe in recent years, and in this way to promote tendencies which must eventually find their outlet in either the break-up or the gradual mellowing of Soviet power. For no mystical, Messianic movement—and particularly not that of the Kremlin—can face frustration indefinitely without eventually adjusting itself in one way or another to the logic of that state of affairs.

Thus the decision will really fall in large measure in this country itself. The issue of Soviet-American relations is in essence a test of the over-all worth of the United States as a nation among nations. To avoid destruction the United States need only measure up to its own best traditions and prove itself worthy of preservation as a great nation.

Surely, there was never a fairer test of national quality than this. In the light of these circumstances, the thoughtful observer of Russian-American relations will find no cause for complaint in the Kremlin's challenge to American society. He will rather experience a certain gratitude to a Providence which, by providing the American people with this implacable challenge, has made their entire security as a nation dependent on their pulling themselves together and accepting the responsibilities of moral and political leadership that history plainly intended them to bear.

Acceptance Speech for the Nobel Prize for Literature, *William Faulkner, 1949*

I feel that this award was not made to me as a man, but to my work—a life's work in the agony and sweat of the human spirit, not for glory and least of all for profit, but to create out of the materials of the human spirit something which did not exist before. So this award is only mine in trust. It will not be difficult to find a dedication for the money part of it commensurate with the purpose and significance of its origin. But I would like to do the same with the acclaim too, by using this moment as a pinnacle from which I might be listened to by the young men and women already dedicated to the same anguish and travail, among whom is already that one who will some day stand here where I am standing.

Our tragedy today is a general and universal physical fear so long sustained by now that we can even bear it. There are no longer problems of the spirit. There is only the question: When will I be blown up? Because of this, the young man or woman writing today has forgotten the problem of the human heart in conflict with itself which alone can make good writing because only that is worth writing about, worth the agony and the sweat.

He must learn them again. He must teach himself that the basest of all things is to be afraid; and, teaching himself that, forget it forever, leaving no room in his workshop for anything but the old verities and truths of the heart, the old universal truths lacking which any story is ephemeral and doomed—love and honor and pity and pride and compassion and sacrifice. Until he does so, he labors under a curse. He writes not of love but of lust, of defeats in which nobody loses anything of value, and of victories without hope and, worst of all, without pity or compassion. His griefs grieve on no universal bones, leaving no scars. He writes not of the heart but of the glands.

Until he relearns these things, he will write as though he stood among and watched the end of man. I decline to accept the end of man. It is easy enough to say that man is immortal simply because he will endure: that when the last dingdong of doom has clanged and faded from the last worthless rock hanging tideless in the last red and dying evening, that even then there will still be one more sound: that of his puny inexhaustible voice, still talking. I refuse to accept this. I believe that man will not merely endure: he will prevail. He is immortal, not because he alone among creatures has an inexhaustible voice, but because he has a soul, a spirit capable of compassion and sacrifice and endurance. The poet's, the writer's, duty is to write about these things. It is his privilege to help man endure by lifting his heart, by reminding him of the courage and honor and hope and pride and compassion and pity and sacrifice which have been the glory of his past. The poet's voice need not merely be the record of man, it can be one of the props, the pillars to help him endure and prevail.

Chapter 26

AMERICA AT MIDCENTURY

Just as in the field of foreign affairs post–World War II America had no real intention of giving up its new sense of international responsibility and returning to prewar isolationism, so in domestic affairs it showed no overwhelming desire to return to "normalcy," to forsake outright the liberalism and social progress of the 1930's for the more conservative political formulas of the distant past. To be sure, there no longer seemed to be any great sense of urgency about domestic reform, and possibly the extension and liberalization of Social Security benefits marked the only major step toward such reform, while housing, health, and education proposals languished. Yet essentially this was a period when the social experiments, and to a considerable extent even the very ideology of the New Deal, were being ever more thoroughly institutionalized and consolidated within the fabric of American life.

Despite President Harry S Truman's warnings, conservative elements in Congress forced the end of price controls soon after the war, much to the acute dismay of the "little man" (no longer Franklin D. Roosevelt's "forgotten man"), for inflation took over and the cost of living soared to distressing heights. Also, the Taft-Hartley Act of 1947, passed over President Truman's vigorous veto, threatened to curb unions somewhat. But ever-rising incomes within the booming American economy offset high living costs; and the Taft-Hartley "slave labor law," as it was labeled, surely failed to cripple the labor movement, as both the A.F. of L. and the C.I.O. grew and flourished until their merger into one giant labor organization in 1955.

Besides, the Presidential election of 1948 also indicated few particularly conservative tendencies in the United States. On the much-favored Republican ticket, both Presidential nominee Thomas E. Dewey and Vice-Presidential nominee Earl Warren represented the liberal wing of their party and promised a continuation of basic New Deal measures. Ex-Vice-President Henry A. Wallace ran on a left-wing Progressive Party ticket. And underdog Harry S Truman, who conducted the most dynamic campaign Americans had seen in a good many years, barnstormed on an unabashedly liberal platform to win the Presidency in an astonishing upset victory. Pollsters, prophets, and politicians had all picked Republican Dewey as the sure winner. But aside from a widespread admiration for Democrat Truman's "guts" in running against overwhelming odds, one deciding factor in the electoral upset probably was the President's promise of continued high price supports for the farmer. Rising costs and the end of a wartime agricultural boom had left the American farmer in desperate straits, ever more dependent upon government subsidies, and thus upon political promises. Nor was this situation remedied—or even importantly relieved—in the following decades.

But still another factor in the 1948 Democratic victory, and a domestic theme that more than any other dominated postwar America, was the civil rights issue. President Truman had taken a firm stand against the concept of second-class citizenship, and he had urged strong national legislation to guarantee full civil rights for America's black population. This had caused Southern "Dixiecrats" to bolt the 1948 Democratic Convention and to nominate for President South Carolina's Governor J. Strom Thurmond on a States' Rights Party ticket. Thus, in the face of this Democratic split, Truman's ultimate victory was all the more miraculous, and it served all the more dramatically to point up America's new willingness to go farther and farther towards guaranteeing equal rights to all, towards justifying in practice the nation's older heritage of Jeffersonian democratic beliefs.

In 1952, of course, the United States finally experienced a change in national political power, when in the Presidential election of that year Republican Dwight D. Eisenhower defeated Democrat Adlai E. Stevenson, to end twenty years of Democratic rule. There continued to be partisan differences of opinion over such issues as high prices, unemployment, taxes, farm subsidies, public power, reductions in our armed forces and the proper techniques of insuring both internal security and individual liberties. And, until he was finally censured by his colleagues in the Senate, Republican Senator Joseph R. McCarthy of Wisconsin dominated the nation's headlines with violent attacks on what he called Democratic "softness" towards Communism. (Ultimately in his much publicized hunt for Communists in government McCarthy would attack the Republican Eisenhower Administration, which had not rejected him, but with which he disagreed on many issues almost as fiercely as the Democratic Truman Administration before it.)

Generally, however, the new Republican "team" made few fundamental changes in the domestic policies set down by Democratic Presidents Roosevelt and Truman. And on one point at least—with the singular exception of the South—there seemed to be widespread national and partisan agreement: that on May 17, 1954,

Chief Justice Earl Warren, recently appointed by President Eisenhower, had struck a most dramatic blow for America's historic principles of democracy and equality. On that date, speaking for a unanimous Supreme Court, the Chief Justice of the United States declared that segregation of black and white children in our public schools is unconstitutional (Brown v. Board of Education). This was a radical reversal of the Court's earlier finding (in Plessy v. Ferguson, 1896) in favor of the "separate but equal" doctrine that segregation generally is permissible when equal facilities are provided for black and white. In 1896 Justice John Marshall Harlan had dissented vigorously from the majority decision, arguing that "our Constitution is colorblind, and neither knows nor tolerates classes among citizens." And this was the position the Court unanimously came to in 1954, speaking through Chief Justice Warren. There were some who felt that the Warren opinion was based more on ethics and sociology than on history and law, but one thing was certain: it was thoroughly and vigorously consistent with the spirit of the American heritage.

Recognizing the pressures of custom and precedent within the South itself, and sympathizing with that region's enormous task in revamping its entire educational structure, the Court permitted desegregation to progress at a moderate tempo, "with all deliberate speed." But moderation was not to be a substitute for action, and the Court continued to strike down the barriers to equality for all Americans raised by those who would not accept the inevitable triumph of democracy.

The Warren decision was a significant milestone in America's domestic development; even more than that, however, it was also a profound contribution to our foreign policy. It added true moral substance to what President Eisenhower had said in his Inaugural Address of January 20, 1953: ". . . destiny has laid upon our country the responsibility of the free world's leadership." And, indeed, President Eisenhower's efforts during his years in office were to be mainly concerned with America's posture in relation to foreign affairs. Even as the United States grew to fifty states with the admission in 1959 first of Alaska and then of Hawaii, the world itself appeared to shrink, and its many danger points seemed ever closer to home. The technological advances that took place with incredible rapidity in the 1950's and 1960's increased speeds, shortened distances, and made it ever more necessary that men learn to live together in peace.

The Space Age officially began in October 1957, when Russia announced the successful launching of Sputnik I, the first man-made satellite. The Russian achievement drastically spurred American space-science efforts, and within a few years both nations had orbited astronaut-manned vehicles many times around the earth, were vying to see which would first land a man on the moon, and were otherwise venturing more and more boldly into outer space.

Meanwhile, on earth, conflict between East and West still preoccupied men concerned with human survival. Behind an impenetrable "Iron Curtain," Russian-inspired puppet governments continued to dominate European "satellite" states, while Soviet propaganda and Soviet pressures in other parts of the world promised no easy resolution of the Cold War. In response, determined to build up its military power, the West had created the North Atlantic Treaty Organization (NATO) to take major steps toward unity and collective strength in the face of aggression.

Actually, it was in the Far East that collective security was put to its most severe test. For in June 1950, Soviet-trained and -equipped North Korean troops had launched a large-scale invasion of South Korea. The United Nations Security Council immediately called upon member nations to help repel the invaders, and President Harry S Truman boldly dispatched American armed forces to support the UN "police action." The Communist invaders were finally halted, and this new determination to stand firm against aggression anywhere seemed to be a decisive move in the struggle between two worlds. But the fighting in Korea was long and bitter; it stirred up unrest at home that was partially responsible for the Democratic defeat in 1952, and it wasn't until July 1953, that the new Eisenhower Administration arranged an armistice that in truth was no more a total victory than it was a total defeat. Besides, Communist-led forces intensified their drive to control Southeast Asia, and it seemed clear that the Far East would long remain a source of international conflict.

Conflict had begun to assume somewhat different dimensions, however, when in March 1953 the Kremlin announced that Joseph Stalin was dead. The Soviet Union gradually adopted a so-called new look and began a "peace offensive," which some people thought resulted only from the Communists' realization that ultimate possession by both Russia and the United States of all-destructive thermonuclear weapons had made war intolerable. Under Nikita Khrushchev the Iron Curtain was raised somewhat; there were more and more frequent exchanges of visits between East and West, and Russia's top leaders made goodwill trips far beyond their country's borders.

But in the Western world cautious and experienced observers remained thoroughly skeptical of the Soviet Union's real intentions. In the midst of continued thermonuclear weapon testing and Russian rejection of meaningful disarmament proposals, they argued convincingly that the West must remain strong in military, industrial, and scientific areas. And yet others argued as cogently that to a democracy nurtured in peace there may also be danger inherent in the continuing buildup of such strengths. After eight years as President of mid-twentieth-century America, Dwight D. Eisenhower in his extraordinary Farewell Address of January 17, 1961, warned his fellow countrymen to be ever strong, but also to guard against both "the acquisition of unwarranted influence" over American life by "the military-industrial complex" and the Cold War danger that "public policy could itself become the captive of a scientific-technological elite." These words Americans carried with them as they looked to the long future.

Brown v. Board of Education:
Chief Justice Earl Warren for the Supreme Court, 1954

These cases come to us from the States of Kansas, South Carolina, Virginia, and Delaware. They are premised on different facts and different local conditions, but a common legal question justifies their consideration together in this consolidated opinion.

In each of the cases, minors of the Negro race, through their legal representatives, seek the aid of the courts in obtaining admission to the public schools of their community on a nonsegregated basis. In each instance, they had been denied admission to schools attended by white children under laws requiring or permitting segregation according to race.

This segregation was alleged to deprive the plaintiffs of the equal protection of the laws under the Fourteenth Amendment. In each of the cases other than the Delaware case, a three-judge Federal District Court denied relief to the plaintiffs on the so-called "separate but equal" doctrine announced by this court in Plessy v. Ferguson.

Under that doctrine, equality of treatment is accorded when the races are provided substantially equal facilities, even though these facilities be separate. In the Delaware case, the Supreme Court of Delaware adhered to that doctrine, but ordered that the plaintiffs be admitted to the white schools because of their superiority to the Negro schools.

The plaintiffs contend that segregated public schools are not "equal" and cannot be made "equal" and that, hence, they are deprived of the equal protection of the laws. Because of the obvious importance of the question presented, the Court took jurisdiction. Argument was heard in the 1952 term, and reargument was heard this term on certain questions propounded by the Court.

Reargument was largely devoted to the circumstances surrounding the adoption of the Fourteenth Amendment in 1868. It covered, exhaustively, consideration of the Amendment in Congress, ratification by the states, then existing practices in racial segregation, and the views of proponents and opponents of the Amendment.

This discussion and our own investigation convince us that although these sources cast some light, it is not enough to resolve the problem with which we are faced.

At best, they are inconclusive. The most avid proponents of the postwar Amendments undoubtedly intended them to remove all legal distinctions among "all persons born or naturalized in the United States."

Their opponents, just as certainly, were antagonistic to both the letter and the spirit of the Amendments and wished them to have the most limited effect. What others in Congress and the State Legislature had in mind cannot be determined with any degree of certainty.

An additional reason for the inclusive nature of the Amendment's history, with respect to segregated schools, is the status of public education at that time. In the South, the movement toward free common schools, supported by general taxation, had not yet taken hold. Education of white children was largely in the hands of private groups. Education of Negroes was almost nonexistent, and practically all of the race was illiterate. In fact, any education of Negroes was forbidden by law in some states.

Today, in contrast, many Negroes have achieved outstanding success in the arts and sciences as well as in the business and professional world. It is true that public education has already advanced further in the North, but the effect of the Amendment on Northern States was generally ignored in the Congressional debates.

Even in the North, the conditions of public education did not approximate those existing today. The curriculum was usually rudimentary; ungraded schools were common in rural areas; the school term was but three months a year in many states; and compulsory school attendance was virtually unknown.

As a consequence, it is not surprising that there should be so little in the history of the Fourteenth Amendment relating to its intended effect on public education.

In the first cases in this court construing the Fourteenth Amendment, decided shortly after its adoption, the court interpreted it as proscribing all state-imposed discriminations against the Negro race.

The doctrine of "Separate but Equal" did not make its appearance in this court until 1896 in the case of Plessy v. Ferguson, supra, involving not education but transportation.

American courts have since labored with the doctrine for over half a century. In this court, there have been six cases involving the "separate but equal" doctrine in the field of public education.

In Cumming v. County Board of Education, and Gong Lum v. Rice, the validity of the doctrine itself was not challenged. In most recent cases, all on the graduate school level, inequality was found in that specific benefits enjoyed by white students were denied to Negro students of the same educational qualifications. Missouri ex rel. Gaines v. Canada, 305 U.S. 337; Sipuel v. Oklahoma, 332 U.S. 331; Sweatt v. Painter, 339 U.S. 629; McLaurin v. Oklahoma State Regents, 339 U.S. 637.

In nine of these cases it was necessary to re-examine the doctrine to grant relief to the Negro plaintiff. And in Sweatt v. Painter, supra, the court expressly reserved decision on the question whether Plessy v. Ferguson should be held inapplicable to public education.

In the instant cases, that question is directly presented. Here, unlike Sweatt v. Painter, there are findings below that the Negro and white schools involved have been equalized or are being equalized, with respect to buildings, curricula, qualifications and salaries of teachers, and other "tangible" factors.

Our decision, therefore, cannot turn on merely a comparison of these tangible factors in the Negro and white schools involved in each of the cases. We must look instead to the effect of segregation itself on public education.

In approaching this problem, we cannot turn the clock back to 1868, when the Amendment was adopted, or even to 1896, when Plessy v. Ferguson was written. We must consider public education in the light of its full development and its present place in American life throughout the nation. Only in this way can it be determined if segregation in public schools deprives these plaintiffs of the equal protection of the laws.

Today, education is perhaps the most important function of state and local governments. Compulsory school attendance laws and the great expenditures for education both demonstrate our recognition of the importance of education to our democratic society. It is required in the performance of our most basic public responsibilities, even service in the armed forces. It is the very foundation of good citizenship.

Today, it is a principal instrument in awakening the child to cultural values, in preparing him for later professional training, and in helping him to adjust normally to his environment.

In these days, it is doubtful that any child may reasonably be expected to succeed in life if he is denied the opportunity of an education. Such an opportunity, where the state has undertaken to provide it, is a right which must be made available to all on equal terms.

We come then to the question presented: Does segregation of children in public schools solely on the basis of race, even though the physical facilities and other "tangible" factors may be equal, deprive the children of the minority group of equal educational opportunities? We believe that it does.

In Sweatt v. Painter, supra, in finding that a segregated law school for Negroes could not provide them equal educational opportunities, this court relied in large part on "those qualities which are incapable of objective measurement but which make for greatness in a law school."

In McLaurin v. Oklahoma State Regents, supra, the court, in requiring that a Negro admitted to a white graduate school be treated like all other students, again resorted to intangible considerations: "*** his ability to study, engage in discussions and exchange views with other students, and, in general, to learn his profession."

Such considerations apply with added force to children in grade and high schools. To separate them from others of similar age and qualifications solely because of their race generates a feeling of inferiority as to their status in the community that may affect their hearts and minds in a way unlikely ever to be undone.

The effect of this separation on their education opportunities was well stated by a finding in the Kansas case by a court which, nevertheless felt compelled to rule against the Negro plaintiffs:

> Segregation of white and colored children in public schools has a detrimental effect upon the colored children. The impact is greater when it has the sanction of the law; for the policy of separating the races is usually interpreted as denoting the inferiority of the Negro group. . . .
>
> A sense of inferiority affects the motivation of a child to learn. Segregation with the sanction of law, therefore, has a tendency to retard the educational and mental development of Negro children and to deprive them of some of the benefits they would receive in a racially integrated school system.

Whatever may have been the extent of psychological knowledge at the time of Plessy v. Ferguson, this finding is amply supported by modern authority. Any language in Plessy v. Ferguson contrary to this finding is rejected.

We conclude that in the field of public education the doctrine of "separate but equal" has no place. Separate educational facilities are inherently unequal. Therefore, we hold that the plaintiffs and others similarly situated for whom the actions have been brought are, by reason of the segregation complained of, deprived of the equal protection of the laws guaranteed by the Fourteenth Amendment. This disposition makes unnecessary any discussion whether such segregation also violates the Due Process Clause of the Fourteenth Amendment.

Because these are class actions, because of the wide applicability of this decision, and because of the great variety of local conditions, the formulation of decrees in these cases presents problems of considerable complexity. On reargument, the consideration of appropriate relief was necessarily subordinated to the primary question—the constitutionality of segregation in public education.

We have now announced that such segregation is a denial of the equal protection of the laws. In order that we may have the full assistance of the parties in formulating decrees, the cases will be restored to the docket, and the parties are requested to present further argument. . . .

The Attorney General of the United States is again invited to participate. The Attorneys General of the states requiring or permitting segregation in public education will also be permitted to appear as amici curiae upon request to do so. . . .

IT IS SO ORDERED.

Dwight D. Eisenhower's Farewell Address, *1961*

Good evening, my fellow Americans. . . .

Three days from now, after half a century in the service of our country, I shall lay down the responsibilities of office as, in traditional and solemn ceremony, the authority of the Presidency is vested in my successor.

This evening I come to you with a message of leave-taking and farewell, and to share a few final thoughts with you, my countrymen. . . .

I wish the new President, and all who will labor with him, Godspeed. I pray that the coming years will be blessed with peace and prosperity for all. . . .

We now stand ten years past the midpoint of a century that has witnessed four major wars among great nations—three of these involved our own country.

Despite these holocausts America is today the strongest, the most influential and most productive nation in the world. Understandably proud of this preeminence, we yet realize that America's leadership and prestige depend, not merely upon our unmatched material progress, riches and military strength, but on how we use our power in the interests of world peace and human betterment.

Throughout America's adventure in free government, our basic purposes have been to keep the peace;

to foster progress in human achievement; and to enhance liberty, dignity and integrity among peoples and among nations.

To strive for less would be unworthy of a free and religious people.

Any failure traceable to arrogance or our lack of comprehension or readiness to sacrifice would inflict upon us grievous hurt, both at home and abroad.

Progress toward these noble goals is persistently threatened by the conflict now engulfing the world. It commands our whole attention, absorbs our very beings. . . .

Threats, new in kind or degree, constantly arise. Of these, I mention two only.

A vital element in keeping the peace is our military establishment. Our arms must be mighty, ready for instant action, so that no potential aggressor may be tempted to risk his own destruction.

Our military organization today bears little relation to that known of any of my predecessors in peacetime—or, indeed, by the fighting men of World War II or Korea.

Until the latest of our world conflicts, the United States had no armaments industry. American makers of plowshares could, with time and as required, make swords as well.

But we can no longer risk emergency improvisation of national defense. We have been compelled to create a permanent armaments industry of vast proportions. Added to this, three and a half million men and women are directly engaged in the defense establishment. We annually spend on military security alone more than the net income of all United States corporations.

Now this conjunction of an immense military establishment and a large arms industry is new in the American experience. The total influence—economic, political, even spiritual—is felt in every city, every statehouse, every office of the Federal Government. We recognize the imperative need for this development. Yet we must not fail to comprehend its grave implications. Our toil, resources and livelihood are all involved; so is the very structure of our society.

In the councils of Government, we must guard against the acquisition of unwarranted influence, whether sought or unsought, by the military-industrial complex. The potential for the disastrous rise of misplaced power exists and will persist.

We must never let the weight of this combination endanger our liberties or democratic processes. We should take nothing for granted. Only an alert and knowledgeable citizenry can compel the proper meshing of the huge industrial and military machinery of defense with our peaceful methods and goals, so that security and liberty may prosper together.

Akin to, and largely responsible for the sweeping changes in our industrial-military posture has been the technological revolution during recent decades.

In this revolution research has become central. It also becomes more formalized, complex and costly. A steadily increasing share is conducted for, by, or at the direction of the Federal Government.

Today the solitary inventor, tinkering in his shop, has been overshadowed by task forces of scientists, in laboratories and testing fields. In the same fashion, the free university, historically the fountainhead of free ideas and scientific discovery, has experienced a revolution in the conduct of research. Partly because of the huge costs involved, a Government contract becomes virtually a substitute for intellectual curiosity.

For every old blackboard there are now hundreds of new electronic computers.

The prospect of domination of the nation's scholars by Federal employment, project allocations and the power of money is ever present, and is gravely to be regarded.

Yet, in holding scientific research and discovery in respect, as we should, we must also be alert to the equal and opposite danger that public policy could itself become the captive of a scientific-technological elite.

It is the task of statesmanship to mold, to balance, and to integrate these and other forces, new and old, within the principles of our democratic system ever aiming toward the supreme goals of our free society. . . .

Disarmament, with mutual honor and confidence, is a continuing imperative. Together we must learn how to compose differences—not with arms, but with intellect and decent purpose. Because this need is so sharp and apparent, I confess that I lay down my official responsibilities in this field with a definite sense of disappointment. As one who has witnessed the horror and the lingering sadness of war, as one who knows that another war could utterly destroy this civilization which has been so slowly and painfully built over thousands of years, I wish I could say tonight that a lasting peace is in sight.

Happily, I can say that war has been avoided. Steady progress toward our ultimate goal has been made. But so much remains to be done. . . .

To all the peoples of the world, I once more give expression to America's prayerful and continuing aspiration:

We pray that peoples of all faiths, all races, all nations, may have their great human needs satisfied; that those now denied opportunity shall come to enjoy it to the full; that all who yearn for freedom may experience its spiritual blessings, those who have freedom will understand, also, its heavy responsibility; that all who are insensitive to the needs of others will learn charity, and that the sources—scourges of poverty, disease and ignorance will be made to disappear from the earth; and that in the goodness of time, all peoples will come to live together in a peace guaranteed by the binding force of mutual respect and love. . . .

Thank you, and good night.

Chapter 27

FROM THE NEW FRONTIER TO THE GREAT SOCIETY

"So let us begin anew." With these Inaugural words, on January 20, 1961, John Fitzgerald Kennedy set his country upon the thousand extraordinary days of national self-renewal that were given to his Presidency. And ultimately those words—and his deeds—would be judged less by the traditional criterion of legislative enactment than within the larger, more meaningful context of national enrichment: of America's rededication to justice and to the life of reason, to a renewed movement forward, to the dynamic, underlying principles of the American heritage that the vigorous and courageous leader seemed somehow to sum up in his very person.

The youngest man ever to be elected President, Democrat Kennedy at forty-three succeeded Republican Eisenhower—at seventy the oldest man to preside over this nation's destiny. And to many the change was both profound and symbolic; the bold, articulate New Englander—intellectual, politician, historian, war hero, with a style and grace and vigor that inspired to self-sacrifice so many young Americans—proclaimed in his Inaugural Address "to friend and foe alike, that the torch has been passed to a new generation of Americans—born in this century, tempered by war, disciplined by a hard and bitter peace, proud of our ancient heritage."

John F. Kennedy had by no means been thrust into the Presidency by an overwhelming national consensus. Indeed, in November, 1960, out of a total vote of almost 69,000,000, his popular lead over Republican Vice President Richard M. Nixon was only slightly more than 100,000 votes. Presumably even that bare margin of victory had been attained only because the unprecedented nationwide series of Nixon-Kennedy face-to-face television and radio debates had brought both candidates into the homes of some 70,000,000 Americans, showing the handsome, less well-known junior Senator from Massachusetts to be knowledgeable, cool, serious, and purposeful beyond his years and reputation, and perhaps modifying the political liability that if elected he would be the first Roman Catholic in the White House.

Thus, as he assumed the Presidency, John F. Kennedy was acutely aware of being handicapped by having far less than a popular mandate. From the White House he eschewed undue executive pressure upon House and Senate when legislative independence ran high and when wisdom and reason commanded otherwise—much to the undisguised despair of those liberals whose concept of Presidential leadership was limited by their passion for counting Administration bills passed by the Congress. But even while the more astute President bided his legislative time, the New Frontier for which he had campaigned so strenuously was made real by the tone his Administration set, by the healthy, hopeful readiness with which he actively sought out new approaches to the monumental domestic and international problems before the country, and by the infectious enthusiasm and penchant for excellence that enabled him to attract to the nation's service dedicated men and women of high standards and intellect whose absence and aloofness from the world of public affairs had too long been noted.

To many the Peace Corps seemed best and most dramatically to symbolize President Kennedy's capacity to help America—particularly her younger citizens—to recognize and then to realize the nation's highest and most honorable instincts. Mobilizing skilled manpower in teaching, child care, agriculture, public health, and many other fields of service as it trained young Americans to assist less fortunate peoples around the world, the Peace Corps also mobilized the nation's deep idealism, providing a bright cornerstone to the Administration's efforts to utilize America's potential for achievement and leadership both at home and abroad.

Indeed, in an age of science, when America's astronauts were performing incredible feats of courage and daring, constantly pushing back even the newest frontiers of man's knowledge of the physical world, such leadership was most appropriate. Nor was it less so when attention was turned to the myriad social and economic problems that still plagued the nation. Inroads were made upon the ever-destructive scourge of unemployment; efforts were made to encourage business and general economic activity, to increase the nation's productivity, and to extend the material benefits of a more and more affluent society to those who shared in it to only the smallest degree. These actions necessarily took place on a national level, but the states could not avoid their responsibilities either. And as it became abundantly clear that the complexities of industrialized urban and suburban American life called for drastically modernized state governments, the Supreme Court handed down major decisions requiring the reappointment of state legislatures that were historically but undemocratically weighted in favor of rural areas, on the more equitable basis of one man, one vote, in order to make them more representative and presumably better equipped to deal with contemporary challenges.

Even more important in this period of domestic upheaval, however, was a basic decision made in June, 1963, in the White House itself: that in the strife-torn area of civil rights the appropriate and politically feasible time had finally come for the President of the United States to exercise the decisive leadership that alone could set America's moral house in order. Before, the time had not been right; now it was. Before, the national climate of opinion would not have tolerated, would not in its response have made effective and meaningful, the full exercise of Presidential leadership in civil rights. But now public opinion was receptive. The nation had finally been roused by continued violence against the American Negro as well as by the Negroes' own newly militant and forthright demands for a final realization of the concern for human rights that is so deeply rooted in the American heritage. And as no President before him had done, John F. Kennedy, on June 11, 1963, in a dramatic and emotion-laden television address appealed to what Lincoln had once called "the better angels of our nature" to help set right the relationship of American to American, asking the Congress to quicken the long process of providing adequate national legislative guarantees of the rights of all men. That year, too, having written from a Birmingham jail his extraordinary "unwise and untimely" response to criticism of civil disobedience, Dr. Martin Luther King would lead a massive civil rights March on Kennedy's Washington, and "have a dream" of

> that day when all of God's children, black men and white men, Jews and Gentiles, Protestants and Catholics, will be able to join hands and sing in the words of the old Negro spiritual, "Free at last, Free at last, Great God a-mighty, We are free at last."

It was, of course, in the realm of world affairs that the short-lived Kennedy Administration made its most obvious contributions—despite the early Bay of Pigs fiasco, which the new President blundered into by half-heartedly endorsing a plan, launched during the previous Administration, to support an abortive attempt by Cuban refugees to "invade" Cuba and to overthrow Communist dictator Fidel Castro.

No such mistake was made again. When Russia's Khrushchev threatened the President at a 1961 summit meeting and later built the infamous Berlin Wall, the United States stood firm, held its temper and its ground. And in the fall of 1962, when threatening Russian missile bases in Cuba brought civilization to the very brink of nuclear holocaust, John F. Kennedy's cool firmness and decisiveness forced the Soviet Union to back down before what clearly would be American retaliation, and, more important, forced the entire world, particularly the prime antagonists, to realize how vital it was to accommodate national differences before another such confrontation might—even accidentally—take us all over the brink.

For as important as President Kennedy's posture of strength and firmness, so was his famous Inaugural plea: "Let us never negotiate out of fear. But let us never fear to negotiate." Nor was this an idle thought, for the President—knowing as no man else could the enormous danger in continuing and escalating the nuclear arms race—was determined to take important and realistic first steps toward a ban on the nuclear testing that for generations to come could poison our atmosphere and then toward bilateral disarmament itself. To Kennedy, man's fate depended wholly upon a lessening of tensions, upon accommodation rather than war between East and West. Thus, in the summer of 1963 the Soviet Union and the United States agreed upon a "hot line" to facilitate instant communications and to minimize the danger of critical, fatal misunderstanding between Moscow and Washington. And in June, 1963, President Kennedy delivered his historic "Strategy of Peace" address at American University, urging the two great powers, under the assumption that peace is possible and war not inevitable, to reexamine areas of conflict between themselves and their basic attitudes toward each other. Asserting that the United States would refrain from nuclear testing in the atmosphere so long as others did so too, President Kennedy proposed a "strategy of peace" to lead the United States and the Soviet Union out of the "vicious and dangerous cycle" of cold war. Less than two months later men of goodwill everywhere applauded as the United States, Great Britain, and the Soviet Union signed a formal test ban treaty that would considerably diminish the further contamination of the atmosphere shared by East and West and would at least to some degree begin to thaw relations between them. With this stunning diplomatic achievement, John F. Kennedy's major place in man's history was assured.

And not too soon. For on November 22, 1963, the youthful President was dead, murdered by an assassin's bullets. America's splendid rendezvous with uncommon greatness was over.

"Let us continue" was Lyndon B. Johnson's singular plea to his countrymen as he succeeded to the Presidency. Long experienced as a Congressman, then a Senator from Texas, and under Kennedy a most active and responsible Vice President, Johnson took up the reins of government with a calmness and command that gave the shaken nation both renewed confidence in its future and, once again, deep appreciation for its cherished principle of continuity in high office. Picking up precisely where the fallen leader had been stopped, the skilled new Chief Executive brought all of his legislative experience to bear upon making a reality of Kennedy's promised program. Seemingly with a national consensus—built perhaps upon sadness and grief—that Kennedy had not achieved in 1960, President Johnson broke through the long-standing Congressional logjam that had so plagued his predecessor, even achieving the strong Civil Rights bill for which John F. Kennedy had pleaded. In a May, 1964, landmark speech at the University of Michigan, the President gave stirring expression to his vision of a Great Society not only resting on "abundance and liberty for all" but challenged also to use its great wealth and resources "to enrich and elevate our national life, and to advance the quality of our American civilization." Translating his aspirations into action at almost every level of government, he initiated a wide range of innovative social and economic programs that appeared vastly to enhance his popularity. And in November, 1964, Lyndon Johnson was elected President in his own right, defeating Arizona's Republican Senator Barry M. Goldwater in an unprecedented landslide victory that gave him over 61 percent of the total popular vote.

Nor did the world outside stand still. By this time Khrushchev had been removed from office in Russia without this signaling an end to a seemingly decisive ideological split between Communist leaders in China and the Soviet Union; the Chinese had exploded their first nuclear bomb; conflict in Vietnam worsened; and the many international problems that beset the new President grew ever more horrendous. But there were now new opportunities, too, largely because on the world stage a great man had come and played his brief role; in the long future John Fitzgerald Kennedy would not be forgotten.

John F. Kennedy's Inaugural Address, *1961*

We observe today not a victory of party but a celebration of freedom—symbolizing an end as well as a beginning—signifying renewal as well as change. For I have sworn before you and Almighty God the same solemn oath our forebears prescribed nearly a century and three-quarters ago.

The world is very different now. For man holds in his mortal hands the power to abolish all forms of human poverty and all forms of human life. And yet the same revolutionary beliefs for which our forebears fought are still at issue around the globe—the belief that the rights of man come not from the generosity of the state but from the hand of God.

We dare not forget today that we are the heirs of that first revolution. Let the word go forth from this time and place, to friend and foe alike, that the torch has been passed to a new generation of Americans—born in this century, tempered by war, disciplined by a hard and bitter peace, proud of our ancient heritage—and unwilling to witness to or permit the slow undoing of those human rights to which this nation has always been committed, and to which we are committed today at home and around the world.

Let every nation know, whether it wishes us well or ill, that we shall pay any price, bear any burden, meet any hardship, support any friend, oppose any foe to assure the survival and the success of liberty.

This much we pledge—and more.

To those old allies whose cultural and spiritual origins we share, we pledge the loyalty of faithful friends. United, there is little we cannot do in a host of new cooperative ventures. Divided, there is little we can do—for we dare not meet a powerful challenge at odds and split asunder.

To those new states whom we welcome to the ranks of the free, we pledge our word that one form of colonial control shall not have passed away merely to be replaced by a far more iron tyranny. We shall not always expect to find them supporting our view. But we shall always hope to find them strongly supporting their own freedom—and to remember that, in the past, those who foolishly sought power by riding the back of the tiger ended up inside.

To those people in the huts and villages of half the globe struggling to break the bonds of mass misery, we pledge our best efforts to help them help themselves, for whatever period is required—not because the Communists may be doing it, not because we seek their votes, but because it is right. If a free society cannot help the many who are poor, it cannot save the few who are rich.

To our sister republics south of our border, we offer a special pledge—to convert our good words into good deeds—in a new alliance for progress—to assist free men and free governments in casting off the chains of poverty. But this peaceful revolution of hope cannot become the prey of hostile powers. Let all our neighbors know that we shall join with them to oppose aggression or subversion anywhere in the Americas. And let every other power know that this hemisphere intends to remain the master of its own house.

To that world assembly of sovereign states, the United Nations, our last best hope in an age where the instruments of war have far outpaced the instruments of peace, we renew our pledge of support—to prevent it from becoming merely a forum for invective—to strengthen its shield of the new and the weak—and to enlarge the area in which its writ may run.

Finally, to those nations who would make themselves our adversary, we offer not a pledge but a request: that both sides begin anew the quest for peace, before the dark powers of destruction unleashed by science engulf all humanity in planned or accidental self-destruction.

We dare not tempt them with weakness. For only when our arms are sufficient beyond doubt can we be certain beyond doubt that they will never be employed.

But neither can two great and powerful groups of nations take comfort from our present course—both sides overburdened by the cost of modern weapons, both rightly alarmed by the steady spread of the deadly atom, yet both racing to alter that uncertain balance of terror that stays the hand of mankind's final war.

So let us begin anew—remembering on both sides that civility is not a sign of weakness, and sincerity is always subject to proof. Let us never negotiate out of fear. But let us never fear to negotiate.

Let both sides explore what problems unite us instead of belaboring those problems which divide us.

Let both sides, for the first time, formulate serious and precise proposals for the inspection and control of arms—and bring the absolute power to destroy other nations under the absolute control of all nations.

Let both sides seek to invoke the wonders of science instead of its terrors. Together let us explore the stars, conquer the deserts, eradicate disease, tap the ocean depths and encourage the arts and commerce.

Let both sides unite to heed in all corners of the earth the command of Isaiah—to "undo the heavy burdens . . . [and] let the oppressed go free."

And if a beachhead of cooperation may push back the jungles of suspicion, let both sides join in creating a new endeavor—not a new balance of power, but a new world of law, where the strong are just and the weak secure and the peace preserved.

All this will not be finished in the first 100 days. Nor will it be finished in the first 1,000 days, nor in the life of this Administration, nor even perhaps in our lifetime on this planet. But let us begin.

In your hands, my fellow citizens, more than mine, will rest the final success or failure of our course. Since this country was founded, each generation of Americans has been summoned to give testimony to its national loyalty. The graves of young Americans who answered the call to service surround the globe.

Now the trumpet summons us again—not as a call to bear arms, though arms we need—not as a call to battle, though embattled we are—but a call to bear the burden of a long twilight struggle year in and year out, "rejoicing in hope, patient in tribulation"—a struggle against the common enemies of man: tyranny, poverty, disease and war itself.

Can we forge against these enemies a grand and global alliance, north and south, east and west, that can assure a more fruitful life for all mankind? Will you join in that historic effort?

In the long history of the world, only a few generations have been granted the role of defending freedom in its hour of maximum danger. I do not shrink from this responsibility—I welcome it. I do not believe that any of us would exchange places with any other people or any other generation. The energy, the faith, the devotion which we bring to this endeavor will light our country and all who serve it—and the glow from that fire can truly light the world.

And so, my fellow Americans: ask not what your country can do for you—ask what you can do for your country.

My fellow citizens of the world: ask not what America will do for you, but what together we can do for the freedom of man.

Finally, whether you are citizens of America or citizens of the world, ask of us here the same high standards of strength and sacrifice which we ask of you. With a good conscience our only sure reward, with history the final judge of our deeds, let us go forth to lead the land we love, asking His blessing and His help, but knowing that here on earth God's work must truly be our own.

The American University "Strategy of Peace" Speech, *John F. Kennedy, 1963*

. . . I have, therefore, chosen this time and place to discuss a topic on which ignorance too often abounds and the truth is too rarely perceived—and that is the most important topic on earth: peace.

What kind of peace do I mean and what kind of peace do we seek? Not a Pax Americana enforced on the world by American weapons of war. Not the peace of the grave or the security of the slave. I am talking about genuine peace—the kind of peace that makes life on earth worth living—and the kind that enables men and nations to grow and to hope and build a better life for their children—not merely peace for Americans but peace for all men and women—not merely peace in our time but peace in all time.

I speak of peace because of the new face of war. Total war makes no sense in an age where great powers can maintain large and relatively invulnerable nuclear forces and refuse to surrender without resort to those forces. It makes no sense in an age when a single nuclear weapon contains almost ten times the explosive force delivered by all the Allied air forces in the second world war. It makes no sense in an age when the deadly poisons produced by a nuclear exchange would be carried by wind and water and soil and seed to the far corners of the globe and to generations yet unborn.

Today the expenditure of billions of dollars every year on weapons acquired for the purpose of making sure we never need them is essential to the keeping of peace. But surely the acquisition of such idle stockpiles—which can only destroy and can never create—is not the only, much less the most efficient, means of assuring peace.

I speak of peace, therefore, as the necessary rational end of rational men. I realize the pursuit of peace is not as dramatic as the pursuit of war—and frequently the words of the pursuer fall on deaf ears. But we have no more urgent task.

Some say that it is useless to speak of peace or world law or world disarmament—and that it will be useless until the leaders of the Soviet Union adopt a more enlightened attitude. I hope they do. I believe we can help them do it.

But I also believe that we must re-examine our own attitudes—as individuals and as a nation—for our attitude is as essential as theirs. And every graduate of this school, every thoughtful citizen who despairs of war and wishes to bring peace, should begin by looking inward—by examining his own attitude toward the course of the cold war and toward freedom and peace here at home.

First: Examine our attitude toward peace itself. Too many of us think it is impossible. Too many think it is unreal. But that is a dangerous, defeatist belief. It leads to the conclusion that war is inevitable—that mankind is doomed—that we are gripped by forces we cannot control.

We need not accept that view. Our problems are man-made. Therefore, they can be solved by man. And man can be as big as he wants. No problem of human destiny is beyond human beings. Man's reason and spirit have often solved the seemingly unsolvable—and we believe they can do it again.

I am not referring to the absolute, infinite concepts of universal peace and goodwill of which some fantasies and fanatics dream. I do not deny the value of hopes and dreams but we merely invite discouragement and incredulity by making that our only and immediate goal.

Let us focus instead on a more practical, more attainable peace—based not on a sudden revolution in human nature but on a gradual evolution in human institutions—on a series of concrete actions and effective agreement which are in the interests of all concerned.

There is no single, simple key to this peace—no grand or magic formula to be adopted by one or two powers. Genuine peace must be the product of many nations, the sum of many acts. It must be dynamic, not static, changing to meet the challenge of each new generation. For peace is a process—a way of solving problems.

With such a peace, there will still be quarrels and conflicting interests, as there are within families and nations. World peace, like community peace, does not require that each man love his neighbor—it requires only that they live together with mutual tolerance, submitting their disputes to a just and peaceful settlement.

And history teaches us that enmities between nations, as between individuals, do not last forever. However fixed our likes and dislikes may seem, the tide of time and events will often bring surprising changes in the relations between nations and neighbors.

So let us persevere. Peace need not be impracticable—and war need not be inevitable. By defining our goal more clearly—by making it seem more manageable and less remote—we can help all people to see it, to draw hope from it, and to move irresistibly towards it.

And second: Let us reexamine our attitude towards the Soviet Union. It is discouraging to think that their leaders may actually believe what their propagandists write.

It is discouraging to read a recent authoritative Soviet text on military strategy and find, on page after page, wholly baseless and incredible claims—such as the allegation that "American imperialist circles are preparing to unleash different types of war . . . that there is a very real threat of a preventative war being unleashed by American imperialists against the Soviet Union . . . (and that) the political aims" and I quote, "of the American imperialists are to enslave economically and politically the European and other capitalist countries . . . (and) to achieve world domination . . . by means of aggressive war."

Truly, as it was written long ago: "The wicked flee when no man pursueth." Yet it is sad to read these Soviet statements—to realize the extent of the gulf between us. But it is also a warning—a warning to the American people not to fall into the same trap as the Soviets, not to see only a distorted and desperate view of the other side, not to see conflict as inevitable, accommodation as impossible and communication as nothing more than an exchange of threats.

No government or social system is so evil that its people must be considered as lacking in virtue. As Americans, we find Communism profoundly repugnant as a negation of personal freedom and dignity. But we can still hail the Russian people for their many achievements—in science and space, in economic and industrial growth, in culture, in acts of courage.

Among the many traits the peoples of our two countries have in common, none is stronger than our mutual abhorrence of war. Almost unique among the major world powers, we have never been at war with each other. And no nation in the history of battle ever suffered more than the Soviet Union in the second world war. At least 20,000,000 lost their lives. Countless millions of homes and families were burned or sacked. A third of the nation's territory, including two-thirds of its industrial base, was turned into a wasteland—a loss equivalent to the destruction of this country east of Chicago.

Today, should total war ever break out again—no matter how—our two countries will be the primary targets. It is an ironic but accurate fact that the two strongest powers are the two in the most danger of devastation. All we have built, all we have worked for, would be destroyed in the first 24 hours. And even in the cold war—which brings burdens and dangers to so many countries, including this nation's closest allies—our two countries bear the heaviest burdens. For we are both devoting massive sums of money to weapons that could be better devoted to combat ignorance, poverty and disease.

We are both caught up in a vicious and dangerous cycle with suspicion on one side breeding suspicion on the other, and new weapons begetting counter-weapons.

In short, both the United States and its allies, and the Soviet Union and its allies, have a mutually deep interest in a just and genuine peace and in halting the arms race. Agreements to this end are in the interests of the Soviet Union as well as ours—and even the most hostile nations can be relied upon to accept and keep those treaty obligations and only those treaty obligations, which are in their own interest.

So, let us not be blind in our differences—but let us also direct attention to our common interests and the means by which those differences can be resolved. And if we cannot end now our differences, at least we can help make the world safe for diversity. For, in the final analysis, our most basic common link is that we all inhabit this small planet. We all breathe the same air. We all cherish our children's future. And we are all mortal.

Third: Let us re-examine our attitude towards the

cold war, remembering we are not engaged in a debate, seeking to pile up debating points. We are not here distributing blame or pointing the finger of judgment. We must deal with the world as it is, and not as it might have been had the history of the last eighteen years been different.

We must, therefore, persevere in the search for peace in the hope that constructive changes within the Communist bloc might bring within reach solutions which now seem beyond us. We must conduct our affairs in such a way that it becomes in the Communists' interest to agree on a genuine peace. And above all, while defending our own vital interests, nuclear powers must avert those confrontations which bring an adversary to a choice of either a humiliating retreat or a nuclear war. To adopt that kind of course in the nuclear age would be evidence only of the bankruptcy of our policy—or of a collective death-wish for the world.

To secure these ends, America's weapons are non-provocative, carefully controlled, designed to deter and capable of selective use. Our military forces are committed to peace and disciplined in self-restraint. Our diplomats are instructed to avoid unnecessary irritants and purely rhetorical hostility.

For we can seek a relaxation of tensions without relaxing our guard. And, for our part, we do not need to use threats to prove that we are resolute. We do not need to jam foreign broadcasts out of fear our faith will be eroded. We are unwilling to impose our system on any unwilling people—but we are willing and able to engage in peaceful competition with any people on earth.

Meanwhile, we seek to strengthen the United Nations, to help solve its financial problems, to make it a more effective instrument for peace, to develop it into a genuine world security system—a system capable of resolving disputes on the basis of law, of insuring the security of the large and the small, and of creating conditions under which arms can finally be abolished.

At the same time we seek to keep peace inside the non-Communist world, where many nations, all of them our friends, are divided over issues which weaken Western unity, which invite Communist intervention, or which threaten to erupt into war.

Our efforts in West New Guinea, in the Congo, in the Middle East and the Indian subcontinent have been persistent and patient despite criticism from both sides. We have also tried to set an example for others—by seeking to adjust small but significant differences with our own closest neighbors in Mexico and Canada.

Speaking of other nations, I wish to make one point clear. We are bound to many nations by alliances. These alliances exist because our concern and theirs substantially overlap. Our commitment to defend Western Europe and West Berlin, for example, stands undiminished because of the identity of our vital interests. The United States will make no deal with the Soviet Union at the expense of other nations and other peoples, not merely because they are our partners, but also because their interests and ours converge.

Our interests converge, however, not only in defending the frontiers of freedom, but in pursuing the paths of peace.

It is our hope—and the purpose of allied policies—to convince the Soviet Union that she, too, should let each nation choose its own future, so long as that choice does not interfere with the choices of others. The communist drive to impose their political and economic system on others is the primary cause of world tension today. For there can be no doubt that, if all nations could refrain from interfering in the self-determination of others, the peace would be much more assured.

This will require a new effort to achieve world law—a new context for world discussions. It will require increased understanding between the Soviets and ourselves. And increased understanding will require increased contact and communication.

One step in this direction is the proposed arrangement for a direct line between Moscow and Washington, to avoid on each side the dangerous delays, misunderstanding, and misreadings of the other's actions which might occur in a time of crisis.

We have also been talking in Geneva about other first-step measures of arms control, designed to limit the intensity of the arms race and reduce the risks of accidental war.

Our primary long-range interest in Geneva, however,

is general and complete disarmament—designed to take place by stages, permitting parallel political developments to build the new institutions of peace which would take the place of arms. The pursuit of disarmament has been an effort of this Government since the 1920's. It has been urgently sought by the past three Administrations. And however dim the prospects are today, we intend to continue this effort—to continue it in order that all countries, including our own, can better grasp what the problems and the possibilities of disarmament are.

The only major area of these negotiations where the end is in sight—yet where a fresh start is badly needed—is in a treaty to outlaw nuclear tests. The conclusion of such a treaty—so near and yet so far—would check the spiraling arms race in one of the most dangerous areas. It would place the nuclear powers in a position to deal more effectively with one of the greatest hazards which man faces in 1963—the further spread of nuclear weapons. It would increase our security—it would decrease the prospects of war.

Surely this goal is sufficiently important to require our steady pursuit, yielding neither to the temptation to give up the whole effort nor the temptation to give up our insistence on vital and responsible safeguards.

I am taking this opportunity, therefore, to announce two important decisions in this regard:

First: Chairman Khrushchev, Prime Minister Macmillan and I have agreed that high-level discussions will shortly begin in Moscow towards early agreement on a comprehensive test ban treaty. Our hopes must be tempered with the caution of history—but with our hopes go the hopes of all mankind.

Second: To make clear our good faith and solemn convictions on the matter, I now declare that the United States does not propose to conduct nuclear tests in the atmosphere so long as other states do not do so. We will not be the first to resume. Such a declaration is no substitute for a formal binding treaty—but I hope it will help us achieve one. Nor would such a treaty be a substitute for disarmament—but I hope it will help us achieve it.

Finally, my fellow Americans, let us examine our attitude towards peace and freedom here at home. The quality and spirit of our own society must justify and support our efforts abroad. We must show it in the dedication of our own lives—as many of you who are graduating today will have an opportunity to do, by serving without pay in the Peace Corps abroad or in the proposed National Service Corps here at home.

But wherever we are, we must all, in our daily lives, live up to the age-old faith that peace and freedom walk together. In too many of our cities today, the peace is not secure because freedom is incomplete.

It is the responsibility of the executive branch at all levels of government—local, state and national—to provide and protect that freedom for all of our citizens by all means within our authority. It is the responsibility of the legislative branch at all levels, wherever the authority is not now adequate, to make it adequate. And it is the responsibility of all citizens in all sections of this country to respect the rights of others and respect the law of the land.

All this is not unrelated to world peace. "When a man's ways please the Lord," the Scriptures tell us, "he maketh even his enemies to be at peace with him." And is not peace, in the last analysis, basically a matter of human rights—the right to live out our lives without fear of devastation—the right to breathe air as nature provided it—the right of future generations to a healthy existence?

While we proceed to safeguard our national interests, let us also safeguard human interests. And the elimination of war and arms is clearly in the interest of both.

No treaty, however much it may be to the advantage of all, however tightly it may be worded, can provide absolute security against the risks of deception and evasion. But it can—if it is sufficiently effective in its enforcement and it is sufficiently in the interests of its signers—offer far more security and far fewer risks than an unabated, uncontrolled, unpredictable arms race.

The United States, as the world knows, will never start a war. We do not want a war. We do not now expect a war. This generation of Americans has already had enough—more than enough—of war and hate and oppression. We shall be prepared if others wish it. We shall be alert to try to stop it. But we shall also do our part to build a world of peace where the weak are safe and the strong are just.

We are not helpless before that task or hopeless of its success. Confident and unafraid, we labor on—not toward a strategy of annihilation but toward a strategy of peace. Thank you.

Civil Rights Speech, *John F. Kennedy, 1963*

Good evening, my fellow citizens.

This afternoon, following a series of threats and defiant statements, the presence of Alabama National Guardsmen was required on the University of Alabama to carry out the final and unequivocal order of the United States District Court of the Northern District of Alabama.

That order called for the admission of two clearly qualified young Alabama residents who happened to have been born Negro.

That they were admitted peacefully on the campus is due in good measure to the conduct of the students of the University of Alabama who met their responsibilities in a constructive way.

I hope that every American, regardless of where he lives, will stop and examine his conscience about this and other related incidents.

This nation was founded by men of many nations and backgrounds. It was founded on the principle that all men are created equal, and that the rights of every man are diminished when the rights of one man are threatened.

Today we are committed to a worldwide struggle to promote and protect the rights of all who wish to be free. And when Americans are sent to Vietnam or West Berlin we do not ask for whites only.

It ought to be possible, therefore, for American students of any color to attend any public institution they select without having to be backed up by troops. It ought to be possible for American consumers of any color to receive equal service in places of public accommodation, such as hotels and restaurants, and theaters and retail stores without being forced to resort to demonstrations in the street.

And it ought to be possible for American citizens of any color to register and to vote in a free election without interference or fear of reprisal.

It ought to be possible, in short, for every American to enjoy the privileges of being American without regard to his race or his color.

In short, every American ought to have the right to be treated as he would wish to be treated, as one would wish his children to be treated. But this is not the case.

The Negro baby born in America today, regardless of the section or the state in which he is born, has about one-half as much chance of completing a high school as a white baby, born in the same place, on the same day; one-third as much chance of becoming a professional man; twice as much chance of becoming unemployed; about one-seventh as much chance of earning $10,000 a year; a life expectancy which is seven years shorter and the prospects of earning only half as much.

This is not a sectional issue. Difficulties over segregation and discrimination exist in every city, in every state of the Union, producing in many cities a rising tide of discontent that threatens the public safety.

Nor is this a partisan issue. In a time of domestic crisis, men of goodwill and generosity should be able to unite regardless of party or politics.

This is not even a legal or legislative issue alone. It is better to settle these matters in the courts than on the streets, and new laws are needed at every level. But law alone cannot make men see right.

We are confronted primarily with a moral issue. It is as old as the Scriptures and is as clear as the American Constitution. The heart of the question is whether all Americans are to be afforded equal rights and equal opportunities; whether we are going to treat our fellow Americans as we want to be treated.

If an American, because his skin is dark, cannot eat lunch in a restaurant open to the public; if he cannot send his children to the best public school available; if he cannot vote for the public officials who represent him; if, in short, he cannot enjoy the full and free life which all of us want, then who among us would be content to have the color of his skin changed and stand in his place?

Who among us would then be content with the counsels of patience and delay? One hundred years of delay have passed since President Lincoln freed the slaves, yet their heirs, their grandsons, are not fully free. They are not yet freed from the bonds of injustice; they are not yet freed from social and economic oppression.

And this nation, for all its hopes and all its boasts, will not be fully free until all its citizens are free.

We preach freedom around the world, and we mean it. And we cherish our freedom here at home. But are we to say to the world—and much more importantly to each other—that this is the land of the free, except for the Negroes; that we have no second-class citizens, except Negroes; that we have no class or caste system, no ghettos, no master race, except with respect to Negroes?

Now the time has come for this nation to fulfill its promise. The events in Birmingham and elsewhere have so increased the cries for equality that no city or state or legislative body can prudently choose to ignore them.

The fires of frustration and discord are burning in every city, North and South. Where legal remedies are not at hand, redress is sought in the streets in demonstrations, parades and protests, which create tensions and threaten violence—and threaten lives.

We face, therefore, a moral crisis as a country and a people. It cannot be met by repressive police action. It cannot be left to increased demonstrations in the streets. It cannot be quieted by token moves or talk. It is a time to act in the Congress, in your state and local legislative body, and, above all, in all of our daily lives.

It is not enough to pin the blame on others, to say this is a problem of one section of the country or another, or deplore the facts that we face. A great change is at hand, and our task, our obligation is to make that revolution, that change peaceful and constructive for all.

Those who do nothing are inviting shame as well as violence. Those who act boldly are recognizing right as well as reality.

Next week I shall ask the Congress of the United States to act, to make a commitment it has not fully made in this century to the proposition that race has no place in American life or law.

The Federal judiciary has upheld that proposition in a series of forthright cases. The Executive Branch has adopted that proposition in the conduct of its affairs, including the employment of Federal personnel, and the use of Federal facilities, and the sale of Federally financed housing.

But there are other necessary measures which only the Congress can provide, and they must be provided at this session.

The old code of equity law under which we live commands for every wrong a remedy. But in too many communities, in too many parts of the country wrongs are inflicted on Negro citizens and there are no remedies in law.

Unless the Congress acts their only remedy is the street.

I am, therefore, asking the Congress to enact legislation giving all Americans the right to be served in facilities which are open to the public—hotels, restaurants and theaters, retail stores and similar establishments. This seems to me to be an elementary right.

Its denial is an arbitrary indignity that no American in 1963 should have to endure, but many do.

I have recently met with scores of business leaders, urging them to take voluntary action to end this discrimination. And I've been encouraged by their response. And in the last two weeks over 75 cities have seen progress made in desegregating these kinds of facilities.

But many are unwilling to act alone. And for this reason nationwide legislation is needed, if we are to move this problem from the streets to the courts.

I'm also asking Congress to authorize the Federal Government to participate more fully in lawsuits designed to end segregation in public education. We have succeeded in persuading many districts to desegregate voluntarily. Dozens have admitted Negroes without violence.

Today a Negro is attending a state-supported institution in every one of our 50 states. But the pace is very slow.

Too many Negro children entering segregated grade schools at the time of the Supreme Court's decision nine years ago will enter segregated high schools this fall, having suffered a loss which can never be restored.

The lack of an adequate education denies the Negro a chance to get a decent job. The orderly implementation of the Supreme Court decision, therefore, cannot be left solely to those who may not have the economic resources to carry their legal action or who may be subject to harassment.

Other features will be also requested, including greater protection for the right to vote.

But legislation, I repeat, cannot solve this problem alone. It must be solved in the homes of every American in every community across our country.

In this respect, I want to pay tribute to those citizens, North and South, who've been working in their communities to make life better for all.

They are acting not out of a sense of legal duty but out of a sense of human decency. Like our soldiers and sailors in all parts of the world, they are meeting freedom's challenge on the firing line and I salute them for their honor—their courage.

My fellow Americans, this is a problem which faces us all, in every city of the North as well as the South.

Today there are Negroes unemployed—two or three times as many compared to whites—moving into the large cities, unable to find work; young people particularly out of work, without hope, denied equal rights, denied the opportunity to eat at a restaurant or a lunch counter, or go to a movie theater; denied the right to a decent education; denied, almost today, the right to attend a state university even though qualified.

It seems to me that these are matters which concern us all—not merely Presidents, or Congressmen, or Governors, but every citizen of the United States.

This is one country. It has become one country because all of us and all the people who came here had an equal chance to develop their talents.

We cannot say to 10 per cent of the population that "you can't have that right. Your children can't have the chance to develop whatever talents they have, that the only way that they're going to get their rights is to go in the street and demonstrate."

I think we owe them and we owe ourselves a better country than that.

Therefore, I'm asking for your help in making it easier for us to move ahead and provide the kind of equality of treatment which we would want ourselves—to give a chance for every child to be educated to the limit of his talent.

As I've said before, not every child has an equal talent or an equal ability or equal motivation. But they should have the equal right to develop their talent and their ability and their motivation to make something of themselves.

We have a right to expect that the Negro community will be responsible, will uphold the law. But they have a right to expect the law will be fair, that the Constitution will be color blind, as Justice Harlan said at the turn of the century.

This is what we're talking about. This is a matter which concerns this country and what it stands for, and in meeting it I ask the support of all of our citizens.

Thank you very much.

The Birmingham City Jail "Unwise and Untimely" Letter, *Martin Luther King, Jr., 1963*

My dear Fellow Clergymen,
While confined here in the Birmingham City Jail, I came across your recent statement calling our present activities "unwise and untimely" . . . since I feel that you are men of genuine goodwill and your criticisms are sincerely set forth, I would like to answer your statement in what I hope will be patient and reasonable terms.

I think I should give the reason for my being in Birmingham, since you have been influenced by the argument of "outsiders coming in" . . . Several months ago our local affiliate here in Birmingham invited us to be on call to engage in a nonviolent direct action program if such were deemed necessary. . . . So I am here, along with several members of my staff, because we were invited here. I am here because I have basic organizational ties here.

Beyond this, I am in Birmingham because injustice is here. Just as the eighth-century prophets left their little villages and carried their "thus saith the Lord" far beyond the boundaries of their home towns; and just as the Apostle Paul left his little village of Tarsus and carried the gospel of Jesus Christ to practically every hamlet and city of the Graeco-Roman world, I too am compelled to carry the gospel of freedom beyond my particular home town. Like Paul, I must constantly respond to the Macedonian call for aid.

Moreover, I am cognizant of the interrelatedness of all communities and states. I cannot sit idly by in Atlanta and not be concerned about what happens in Birmingham. Injustice anywhere is a threat to justice everywhere. We are caught in an inescapable network of mutuality, tied in a single garment of destiny. Whatever affects one directly affects all indirectly. Never again can we afford to live with the narrow, provincial "outside agitator" idea. Anyone who lives inside the United States can never be considered an outsider anywhere in this country.

You deplore the demonstrations that are presently taking place in Birmingham. But I am sorry that your statement did not express a similar concern for the conditions that brought the demonstrations into being. I am sure that each of you would want to go beyond the superficial social analyst who looks merely at effects, and does not grapple with underlying causes. I would not hesitate to say that it is unfortunate that so-called demonstrations are taking place in Birmingham at this time, but I would say in more emphatic terms that it is even more unfortunate that the white power-structure of this city left the Negro community with no other alternative . . .

Birmingham is probably the most thoroughly segregated city in the United States. Its ugly record of police brutality is known in every section of this country. Its unjust treatment of Negroes in the courts is a notorious reality. There have been more unsolved bombings of Negro homes and churches in Birmingham than in any city in this nation. These are the hard, brutal, and unbelievable facts. On the basis of these conditions Negro leaders sought to negotiate with the city fathers. But the political leaders consistently refused to engage in good-faith negotiation. . . .

You may well ask, "Why direct action? Why sit-ins, marches, etc.? Isn't negotiation a better path?" You are exactly right in your call for negotiation. Indeed, this is the purpose of direct action. Nonviolent direct action seeks to create such a crisis and establish such creative tension that a community that has constantly refused to negotiate is forced to confront the issue. It seeks so to dramatize the issue that it can no longer be ignored. I just referred to the creation of tension as a part of the work of the nonviolent resister. This may sound rather shocking. But I must confess that I am not afraid of the word tension. I have earnestly worked and preached against violent tension, but there is a type of constructive nonviolent tension that is necessary for growth. Just as Socrates felt that it was necessary to create a tension in the mind so that individuals could rise from the bondage of myths and half-truths to the unfettered realm of creative analysis and objective appraisal, we must see the need of having nonviolent gadflies to create the kind of tension in society that will help men to rise from the dark depths of prejudice and racism to the majestic heights of understanding and brotherhood. So the purpose of the direct action is to create a situation so crisis-packed that it will inevitably open the door to negotiation. We, therefore, concur with you in your call for negotiation. Too long has our beloved Southland been bogged down in the tragic attempt to live in monologue rather than dialogue. . . .

My friends, I must say to you that we have not made a single gain in civil rights without determined legal and nonviolent pressure. History is the long and tragic story of the fact that privileged groups seldom give up their privileges voluntarily. Individuals may see the moral fight and voluntarily give up their unjust posture; but as Reinhold Niebuhr has reminded us, groups are more immoral than individuals.

We know through painful experience that freedom is never voluntarily given by the oppressor; it must be demanded by the oppressed. Frankly, I have never yet engaged in a direct-action movement that was "well timed," according to the timetable of those who have not suffered unduly from the disease of segregation. For years now I have heard the word "Wait!" It rings in the ear of every Negro with a piercing familiarity. This "wait" has almost always meant "never." It has been a tranquilizing thalidomide, relieving the emotional stress for a moment, only to give birth to an ill-formed infant of frustration. We must come to see with the distinguished jurist of yesterday that "justice too long delayed is justice denied." We have waited for more than three hundred and forty years for our constitutional and God-given rights. The nations of Asia and Africa are moving with jetlike speed toward the goal of political independence, and we still creep at horse and buggy pace toward the gaining of a cup of coffee at a lunch counter. I guess it is easy for those who have never felt the stinging darts of segregation to say, "Wait." But when you have seen vicious mobs lynch your mothers and fathers at will and drown your sisters and brothers at whim; when you have seen hate-filled policemen curse, kick, brutalize, and even kill your black brothers and sisters with impunity; when you see the vast majority of your twenty million Negro brothers smothering in an airtight cage of poverty in the midst of an affluent society; when you suddenly find your tongue twisted and your speech stammering as you seek to explain to your six-year-old daughter why she can't go to the public amusement park that has just been advertised on television, and see tears welling up in her little eyes when she is told that Funtown is closed to colored children, and see the depressing clouds of inferiority begin to form in her little mental sky, and see her begin to distort her little personality by unconsciously developing a bitterness toward white people; when you have to concoct an answer for a five-year-old son asking in agonizing pathos: "Daddy, who do white people treat colored people so mean?"; when you take a cross-country drive and find it necessary to sleep night after night in the uncomfortable corners of your automobile because no motel will accept you; when you are humiliated day in and day out by nagging signs reading "white" and "colored"; when your first name becomes "nigger" and your middle name becomes "boy" (however old you are) and your last name becomes "John," and when your wife and mother are never given the respected title "Mrs."; when you are harried by day and haunted at night by the fact that you are a Negro, living constantly at tip-toe stance never quite knowing what to expect next, and plagued with inner fears and outer resentments; when you are forever fighting a degenerating sense of "nobodiness"; then you will understand why we find it difficult to wait. There comes a time when the cup of endurance runs over, and men are no longer willing to be plunged into an abyss of injustice where they experience the blackness of corroding despair. I hope, sirs, you can understand our legitimate and unavoidable impatience.

You express a great deal of anxiety over our willingness to break laws. This is certainly a legitimate concern. Since we so diligently urge people to obey the Supreme Court's decision of 1954 outlawing segregation in the public schools, it is rather strange and paradoxical to find us consciously breaking laws. One may well ask, "How can you advocate breaking some laws and obeying others?" The answer is found in the fact that there are two types of laws: There are *just* and there are *unjust* laws. I would agree with Saint Augustine that "an unjust law is no law at all."

Now what is the difference between the two? How does one determine when a law is just or unjust? A just law is a man-made code that squares with the moral law or the law of God. An unjust law is a code that is out of harmony with the moral law. To put it in the terms of Saint Thomas Aquinas, an unjust law is a human law that is not rooted in eternal and natural law. Any law that uplifts human personality is just. Any law that degrades human personality is unjust. All segregation statutes are unjust because segregation distorts the soul and damages the personality. It gives the segregator a false sense of superiority, and the segregated a false sense of inferiority. To use the words of Martin Buber, the great Jewish philosopher, segregation substitutes an "I-it" relationship for the "I-thou" relationship, and ends up relegating persons to the status of things. So segregation is not only politically wrong but sinful. Paul Tillich has said that sin is separation. Isn't segregation an existential expression of man's tragic separation, an expression of his awful estrangement, his terrible sinfulness? So I can urge men to disobey segregation ordinances because they are morally wrong. . . .

There are some instances when a law is just on its face and unjust in its application. For instance, I was arrested Friday on a charge of parading without a permit. Now there is nothing wrong with an ordinance which requires a permit for a parade, but when the ordinance is used to preserve segregation and to deny citizens the First Amendment privilege of peaceful assembly and peaceful protest, then it becomes unjust.

I hope you can see the distinction I am trying to point out. In no sense do I advocate evading or defying the law as the rabid segregationist would do. This would lead to anarchy. One who breaks an unjust law must do it *openly, lovingly* (not hatefully as the white mothers did in New Orleans when they were seen on television screaming "nigger, nigger, nigger"), and with a willingness to accept the penalty. I submit that an individual who breaks a law that conscience tells him is unjust, and willingly accepts the penalty by staying in jail to arouse the conscience of the community over its injustice, is in reality expressing the very highest respect for law.

Of course, there is nothing new about this kind of civil disobedience. It was seen sublimely in the refusal of Shadrach, Meshach, and Abednego to obey the laws of Nebuchadnezzar because a higher moral law was involved. It was practiced superbly by the early Christians who were willing to face hungry lions and the excruciating pain of chopping blocks, before submitting to certain unjust laws of the Roman empire. To a degree academic freedom is a reality today because Socrates practiced civil disobedience.

We can never forget that everything Hitler did in German was "legal" and everything the Hungarian freedom fighters did in Hungary was "illegal." It was "illegal" to aid and comfort a Jew in Hitler's Germany. But I am sure that if I had lived in Germany during that time, I would have aided and comforted my Jewish brothers even though it was illegal. If I lived in a Communist country today, where certain principles dear to the Christian faith are suppressed, I believe I would openly advocate disobeying these anti-religious laws. I must make two honest confessions to you, my Christian and Jewish brothers. First I must confess that over the last few years I have been gravely disappointed with the white moderate. I have almost reached the regrettable conclusion that the Negro's great stumbling block in the stride toward freedom is not the White Citizen's Council-er or the Ku Klux Klanner, but the white moderate who is more devoted to "order" than to justice; who prefers a negative peace which is the absence of tension to a positive peace which is the presence of justice; who constantly says "I agree with you in the goal you seek, but I can't agree with your methods of direct action"; who paternalistically feels that he can set the timetable for another man's freedom; who lives by the myth of time and who constantly advises the Negro to wait until a "more convenient season." Shallow understanding from people of goodwill is more frustrating than absolute misunderstanding from people of ill will. Lukewarm acceptance is much more bewildering than outright rejection.

I had hoped that the white moderate would understand that law and order exist for the purpose of establishing justice, and that when they fail to do this they become dangerously structured dams that block the flow of social progress. I had hoped that the white moderate would understand that the present tension in the South is merely a necessary phase of the transition from an obnoxious negative peace, where the Negro passively accepted his unjust plight, to a substance-filled positive peace, where all men will respect the dignity and worth of human personality. Actually, we who engage in nonviolent direct action are not the creators of tension. We merely bring to the surface the hidden tension that is already alive. We bring it out in the open where it can be seen and dealt with. Like a boil that can never be cured as long as it is covered up but must be opened with all its pus-flowing ugliness to the natural medicines of air and light, injustice must likewise be exposed, with all of the tension its exposing creates, to the light of human conscience and the air of national opinion before it can be cured.

In your statement you asserted that our actions, even

though peaceful, must be condemned because they precipitate violence. But can this assertion be logically made? Isn't this like condemning the robbed man because his possession of money precipitated the evil act of robbery? Isn't this like condemning Socrates because his unswerving commitment to truth and his philosophical delvings precipitated the misguided popular mind to make him drink the hemlock? Isn't this like condemning Jesus because His unique God-Consciousness and never-ceasing devotion to His will precipitated the evil act of crucifixion? We must come to see, as federal courts have consistently affirmed, that it is immoral to urge an individual to withdraw his efforts to gain his basic constitutional rights because the quest precipitates violence. Society must protect the robbed and punish the robber.

I had also hoped that the white moderate would reject the myth of time. I received a letter this morning from a white brother in Texas which said: "All Christians know that the colored people will receive equal rights eventually, but it is possible that you are in too great a religious hurry. It has taken Christianity almost two thousand years to accomplish what it has. The teachings of Christ take time to come to earth." All that is said here grows out of a tragic misconception of time. It is the strangely irrational notion that there is something in the very flow of time that will inevitably cure all ills. Actually time is neutral. It can be used either destructively or constructively. I am coming to feel that the people of ill will have used time much more effectively than the people of good will. We will have to repent in this generation not merely for the vitriolic words and actions of the bad people, but for the appalling silence of good people. We must come to see that human progress never rolls in on wheels of inevitability. It comes through the tireless efforts and persistent work of men willing to be coworkers with God, and without this hard work time itself becomes an ally of the forces of social stagnation. We must use time creatively, and forever realize that the time is always ripe to do right. Now is the time to make real the promise of democracy, and transform our pending national elegy into a creative psalm of brotherhood. Now is the time to lift our national policy from the quicksand of racial injustice to the solid rock of human dignity. . . .

. . . I stand in the middle of two opposing forces in the Negro community. One is a force of complacency made up of Negroes who, as a result of long years of oppression, have been so completely drained of self-respect and a sense of "somebodiness" that they have adjusted to segregation, and of a few Negroes in the middle class who, because of a degree of academic and economic security, and because at points they profit by segregation, have unconsciously become insensitive to the problems of the masses. The other force is one of bitterness and hatred, and comes perilously close to advocating violence. It is expressed in the various black-nationalist groups that are springing up over the nation, the largest and best known being Elijah Muhammad's Muslim movement. This movement is nourished by the contemporary frustration over the continued existence of racial discrimination. It is made up of people who have lost faith in America, who have absolutely repudiated Christianity, and who have concluded that the white man is an incurable "devil." I have tried to stand between these two forces, saying that we need not follow the "do-nothingism" of the complacent or the hatred and despair of the black nationalist. There is the more excellent way of love and nonviolent protest. I'm grateful to God that, through the Negro church, the dimension of nonviolence entered our struggle. If this philosophy had not emerged, I am convinced that by now many streets of the South would be flowing with floods of blood. And I am further convinced that if our white brothers dismiss as "rabble-rousers" and "outside agitators" those of us who are working through the channels of nonviolent direct action and refuse to support our nonviolent efforts, millions of Negroes, out of frustration and despair, will seek solace and security in black-nationalist ideologies, a development that will lead inevitably to a frightening racial nightmare.

Oppressed people cannot remain oppressed forever. The urge for freedom will eventually come. This is what happened to the American Negro. Something within has reminded him of his birthright of freedom; something without has reminded him that he can gain it.

Consciously and unconsciously, he has been swept in by what the Germans call the *Zeitgeist*, and with his black brothers of Africa, and his brown and yellow brothers of Asia, South America, and the Caribbean, he is moving with a sense of cosmic urgency toward the promised land of racial justice. Recognizing this vital urge that has engulfed the Negro community, one should readily understand public demonstrations. The Negro has many pent-up resentments and latent frustrations. He has to get them out. So let him march sometime; let him have his prayer pilgrimages to the city hall; understand why he must have sit-ins and freedom rides. If his repressed emotions do not come out in these nonviolent ways, they will come out in ominous expressions of violence. This is not a threat; it is a fact of history. So I have not said to my people "get rid of your discontent." But I have tried to say that this normal and healthy discontent can be channelized through the creative outlet of nonviolent direct action. Now this approach is being dismissed as extremist. I must admit that I was initially disappointed in being so categorized.

But as I continued to think about the matter I gradually gained a bit of satisfaction from being considered an extremist. Was not Jesus an extremist in love—"Love your enemies, bless them that curse you, pray for them that despitefully use you." Was not Amos an extremist for justice—"Let justice roll down like waters and righteousness like a mighty stream." Was not Paul an extremist for the gospel of Jesus Christ—"I bear in my body the marks of the Lord Jesus." Was not Martin Luther an extremist—"Here I stand; I can do none other so help me God." Was not John Bunyan an extremist—"I will stay in jail to the end of my days before I make a butchery of my conscience." Was not Abraham Lincoln an extremist—"This nation cannot survive half slave and half free." Was not Thomas Jefferson an extremist—"We hold these truths to be self-evident, that all men are created equal." So the question is not whether we will be extremist but what kind of extremist will we be. Will we be extremists for hate or will we be extremists for love? Will we be extremists for the preservation of injustice—or will we be extremists for the cause of justice? In that dramatic scene on Calvary's hill, three men were crucified. We must not forget that all three were crucified for the same crime—the crime of extremism. Two were extremists for immorality, and thusly fell below their environment. The other, Jesus Christ, was an extremist for love, truth, and goodness, and thereby rose above his environment. So, after all, maybe the South, the nation, and the world are in dire need of creative extremists. . . .

I hope the church as a whole will meet the challenge of this decisive hour. But even if the church does not come to the aid of justice, I have no despair about the future. I have no fear about the outcome of our struggle in Birmingham, even if our motives are presently misunderstood. We will reach the goal of freedom in Birmingham and all over the nation, because the goal of America is freedom. Abused and scorned though we may be, our destiny is tied up with the destiny of America. Before the pilgrims landed at Plymouth we were here. Before the pen of Jefferson etched across the pages of history the majestic words of the Declaration of Independence, we were here. For more than two centuries our fore-parents labored in this country without wages; they made cotton king, and they built the homes of their masters in the midst of brutal injustice and shameful humiliation—and yet out of a bottomless vitality they continued to thrive, and develop. If the inexpressible cruelties of slavery could not stop us, the opposition we now face will surely fail. We will win our freedom because the sacred heritage of our nation and the eternal will of God are embodied in our echoing demands.

Yours for the cause of Peace and Brotherhood,
Martin Luther King, Jr.

March on Washington "I Have a Dream" Speech, *Martin Luther King, Jr., 1963*

I am happy to join with you today in what will go down in history as the greatest demonstration for freedom in the history of our nation.

Five score years ago a great American in whose symbolic shadow we stand today signed the Emancipation Proclamation. This momentous decree was a great beacon light of hope to millions of Negro slaves who had been seared in the flames of withering injustice. It came as a joyous daybreak to end the long night of their captivity. But 100 years later the Negro still is not free. One hundred years later the life of the Negro is still badly crippled by the manacles of segregation and the chains of discrimination. One hundred years later the Negro lives on a lonely island of poverty in the midst of a vast ocean of material prosperity. One hundred years later the Negro is still languished in the corners of American society and finds himself in exile in his own land. So we've come here today to dramatize a shameful condition.

In a sense we've come to our nation's capital to cash a check. When the architects of our Republic wrote the magnificent words of the Constitution and the Declaration of Independence, they were signing a promissory note to which every American was to fall heir. This note was a promise that all men—yes, black men as well as white men—would be guaranteed the unalienable rights of life, liberty and the pursuit of happiness. It is obvious today that America has defaulted on this promissory note insofar as her citizens of color are concerned. Instead of honoring this sacred obligation, America has given the Negro people a bad check, a check which has come back marked "insufficient funds."

But we refuse to believe that the bank of justice is bankrupt. We refuse to believe that there are insufficient funds in the great vaults of opportunity of this nation. So we've come to cash this check, a check that will give us upon demand the riches of freedom and the security of justice.

We have also come to this hallowed spot to remind America of the fierce urgency of now. This is no time to engage in the luxury of cooling off or to take the tranquilizing drug of gradualism. Now is the time to make real the promises of democracy. Now is the time to rise from the dark and desolate valley of segregation to the sunlit path of racial justice. Now is the time to lift our nation from the quicksands of racial injustice to the solid rock of brotherhood.

Now is the time to make justice a reality for all of God's children. It would be fatal for the nation to overlook the urgency of the moment. This sweltering summer of the Negro's legitimate discontent will not pass until there is an invigorating autumn of freedom and equality—1963 is not an end but a beginning. Those who hope that the Negro needed to blow off steam and will now be content will have a rude awakening if the nation returns to business as usual.

There will be neither rest nor tranquility in America until the Negro is granted his citizenship rights. The whirlwinds of revolt will continue to shake the foundations of our nation until the bright day of justice emerges. And that is something that I must say to my people who stand on the worn threshold which leads into the palace of justice. In the process of gaining our rightful place we must not be guilty of wrongful deeds. Let us not seek to satisfy our thirst for freedom by drinking from the cup of bitterness and hatred.

We must forever conduct our struggle on the high plane of dignity and discipline. We must not allow our creative protests to degenerate into physical violence. Again and again we must rise to the majestic heights of meeting physical force with soul force. The marvelous new militancy which has engulfed the Negro community must not lead us to distrust all white people, for many of our white brothers, as evidenced by their presence here today, have come to realize that their destiny is tied up with our destiny.

They have come to realize that their freedom is inextricably bound to our freedom. We cannot walk alone. And as we walk we must make the pledge that we shall always march ahead. We cannot turn back. There are those who are asking the devotees of civil rights, "When will you be satisfied?" We can never be satisfied as long as the Negro is the victim of the unspeakable horrors of police brutality.

We can never be satisfied as long as our bodies, heavy with the fatigue of travel, cannot gain lodging in the motels of the highways and the hotels of the cities.

We cannot be satisfied as long as the Negro's basic mobility is from a smaller ghetto to a larger one. We can never be satisfied as long as our children are stripped of their adulthood and robbed of their dignity by signs stating "For Whites Only."

We cannot be satisfied as long as the Negro in Mississippi cannot vote and the Negro in New York believes he has nothing for which to vote.

No, no, we are not satisfied, and we will not be satisfied until justice rolls down like waters and righteousness like a mighty stream.

I am not unmindful that some of you have come here out of great trials and tribulation. Some of you have come fresh from narrow jail cells. Some of you have come from areas where your quest for freedom left you battered by the storms of persecution and staggered by the winds of police brutality. You have been the veterans of creative suffering.

Continue to work with the faith that unearned suffering is redemptive. Go back to Mississippi, go back to Alabama, go back to South Carolina, go back to Georgia, go back to Louisiana, go back to the slums and ghettos of our Northern cities, knowing that somehow this situation can and will be changed. Let us not wallow in the valley of despair.

I say to you today, my friends, though, even though we face the difficulties of today and tomorrow, I still have a dream. It is a dream deeply rooted in the American dream. I have a dream that one day this nation will rise up, live out the true meaning of its creed: "We hold these truths to be self-evident, that all men are created equal."

I have a dream that one day on the red hills of Georgia sons of former slaves and the sons of former slaveowners will be able to sit down together at the table of brotherhood. I have a dream that one day even the state of Mississippi, a state sweltering with the heat of injustice, sweltering with the heat of oppression, will be transformed into an oasis of freedom and justice.

I have a dream that my four little children will one day live in a nation where they will not be judged by the color of their skin but by the content of their character. I have a dream . . . I have a dream that one day in Alabama, with its vicious racists, with its governor having his lips dripping with the words of interposition and nullification, one day right there in Alabama little black boys and black girls will be able to join hands with little white boys and white girls as sisters and brothers.

I have a dream today . . . I have a dream that one day every valley shall be exalted, every hill and mountain shall be made low. The rough places will be made plain, and the crooked places will be made straight. And the glory of the Lord shall be revealed, and all flesh shall see it together. This is our hope. This is the faith that I go back to the South with. With this faith we will be able to hew out of the mountain of despair a stone of hope. With this faith we will be able to transform the jangling discords of our nation into a beautiful symphony of brotherhood. With this faith we will be able to work together, to pray together, to struggle together, to go to jail together, to stand up for freedom together, knowing that we will be free one day.

This will be the day when all of God's children will be able to sing with new meaning, "My country, 'tis of thee, sweet land of liberty, of thee I sing. Land where my fathers died, land of the pilgrim's pride, from every mountain side, let freedom ring." And if America is to be a great nation, this must become true. So let freedom ring from the prodigious hilltops of New Hampshire. Let freedom ring from the mighty mountains of New York. Let freedom ring from the heightening Alleghenies of Pennsylvania. Let freedom ring from the snowcapped Rockies of Colorado. Let freedom ring from the curvaceous slopes of California.

But not only that. Let freedom ring from Stone Mountain of Georgia. Let freedom ring from Lookout Mountain of Tennessee. Let freedom ring from every hill and molehill of Mississippi, from every mountainside. Let freedom ring . . .

When we allow freedom to ring—when we let it ring from every city and every hamlet, from every state and every city, we will be able to speed up that day when all of God's children, black men and white men, Jews and Gentiles, Protestants and Catholics, will be able to join hands and sing in the words of the old Negro spiritual, "Free at last, Free at last, Great God a-mighty, We are free at last."

"Great Society" Speech, *Lyndon B. Johnson, 1964*

. . . The purpose of protecting the life of our Nation and preserving the liberty of our citizens is to pursue the happiness of our people. Our success in that pursuit is the test of our success as a Nation.

For a century we labored to settle and to subdue a continent. For half a century we called upon unbounded invention and untiring industry to create an order of plenty for all of our people.

The challenge of the next half century is whether we have the wisdom to use that wealth to enrich and elevate our national life, and to advance the quality of our American civilization.

Your imagination, your initiative, and your indignation will determine whether we build a society where progress is the servant of our needs, or a society where old values and new visions are buried under unbridled growth. For in your time we have the opportunity to move not only toward the rich society and the powerful society, but upward to the Great Society.

The Great Society rests on abundance and liberty for all. It demands an end to poverty and racial injustice, to which we are totally committed in our time. But that is just the beginning.

The Great Society is a place where every child can find knowledge to enrich his mind and to enlarge his talents. It is a place where leisure is a welcome chance to build and reflect, not a feared cause of boredom and restlessness. It is a place where the city of man serves not only the needs of the body and the demands of commerce but the desire for beauty and the hunger for community.

It is a place where man can renew contact with nature. It is a place which honors creation for its own sake and for what it adds to the understanding of the race. It is a place where men are more concerned with the quality of their goals than the quantity of their goods.

But most of all, the Great Society is not a safe harbor, a resting place, a final objective, a finished work. It is a challenge constantly renewed, beckoning us toward a destiny where the meaning of our lives matches the marvelous products of our labor.

So I want to talk to you today about three places where we begin to build the Great Society—in our cities, in our countryside, and in our classrooms.

Many of you will live to see the day, perhaps fifty years from now, when there will be 400 million Americans—four-fifths of them in urban areas. In the remainder of this century urban population will double, city land will double, and we will have to build homes, highways, and facilities equal to all those built since this country was first settled. So in the next forty years we must rebuild the entire urban United States.

Aristotle said: "Men come together in cities in order to live; but they remain together in order to live the good life." It is harder and harder to live the good life in American cities today.

The catalog of ills is long: There is the decay of the centers and the despoiling of the suburbs. There is not enough housing for our people or transportation for our traffic. Open land is vanishing and old landmarks are violated.

Worst of all, expansion is eroding the precious and time-honored values of community with neighbors and communion with nature. The loss of these values breeds loneliness and boredom and indifference.

Our society will never be great until our cities are great. Today the frontier of imagination and innovation is inside those cities and not beyond their borders.

New experiments are already going on. It will be the task of your generation to make the American city a place where future generations will come, not only to live but to live the good life. . . .

A second place where we begin to build the Great Society is in our countryside. We have always prided ourselves on being not only America the strong and America the free, but America the beautiful. Today that beauty is in danger. The water we drink, the food we eat, the very air that we breathe, are threatened with pollution. Our parks are overcrowded, our seashores overburdened. Green fields and dense forests are disappearing.

A few years ago we were greatly concerned about

the "Ugly American." Today we must act to prevent an ugly America.

For once the battle is lost, once our natural splendor is destroyed, it can never be recaptured. And once man can no longer walk with beauty or wonder at nature his spirit will wither and his sustenance be wasted.

A third place to build the Great Society is in the classrooms of America. There your children's lives will be shaped. Our society will not be great until every young mind is set free to scan the farthest reaches of thought and imagination. We are still far from that goal. . . .

In many places, classrooms are overcrowded and curricula are outdated. Most of our qualified teachers are underpaid, and many of our paid teachers are unqualified. So we must give every child a place to sit and a teacher to learn from. Poverty must not be a bar to learning, and learning must offer an escape from poverty.

But more classrooms and more teachers are not enough. We must seek an educational system which grows in excellence as it grows in size. This means better training for our teachers. It means preparing youth to enjoy their hours of leisure as well as their hours of labor. It means exploring new techniques of teaching, to find new ways to stimulate the love of learning and the capacity for creation.

These are three of the central issues of the Great Society. While our government has many programs directed at those issues, I do not pretend that we have the full answer to those problems.

But I do promise this: We are going to assemble the best thought and the broadest knowledge from all over the world to find those answers for America. . . .

The solution to these problems does not rest on a massive program in Washington, nor can it rely solely on the strained resources of local authority. They require us to create new concepts of cooperation, a creative federalism, between the national capital and the leaders of local communities.

Woodrow Wilson once wrote: "Every man sent out from his university should be a man of his nation as well as a man of his time."

Within your lifetime powerful forces, already loosed, will take us toward a way of life beyond the realm of our experience, almost beyond the bounds of our imagination.

For better or for worse, your generation has been appointed by history to deal with those problems and to lead America toward a new age. You have the chance never before afforded to any people in any age. You can help build a society where the demands of morality, and the needs of the spirit, can be realized in the life of the nation.

So, will you join in the battle to give every citizen the full equality which God enjoins and the law requires, whatever his belief, or race, or the color of his skin?

Will you join in the battle to give every citizen an escape from the crushing weight of poverty?

Will you join in the battle to make it possible for all nations to live in enduring peace—as neighbors and not as mortal enemies?

Will you join in the battle to build the Great Society, to prove that our material progress is only the foundation on which we will build a richer life of mind and spirit?

There are those timid souls who say this battle cannot be won; that we are condemned to a soulless wealth. I do not agree. We have the power to shape the civilization that we want. But we need your will, your labor, your hearts, if we are to build that kind of society.

Those who came to this land sought to build more than just a new country. They sought a new world. So I have come here today to your campus to say that you can make their vision our reality. So let us from this moment begin our work so that in the future men will look back and say: It was then, after a long and weary way, that man turned the exploits of his genius to the full enrichment of his life.

Chapter 28

DECADE OF TURMOIL

Most of the decade before America's 1976 Bicentennial was marred by the politics not only of upheaval, but of deep division and internal conflict as well. Determined feminist leaders founded NOW, the National Organization for Women, as a "new movement toward true equality for all women in America, and toward a fully equal partnership of the sexes, as part of the world revolution of human rights." Even more telling in terms of fundamental change in American life, black militant demands for economic and social equality and for meaningful civil rights programs ultimately came to be pursued vigorously by national leadership, but not in time to avoid the most polarizing racial conflicts since the Civil War. Besides, violence seemed to confront Americans everywhere. Martin Luther King was assassinated in April, 1968; Senator Robert F. Kennedy was murdered two months later; and in the 1972 Presidential campaign, Alabama Governor George C. Wallace was paralyzed by a would-be assassin's bullets.

Violence on a larger scale threatened the fabric of American life, too. Mired in an undeclared yet bitterly controversial war in Vietnam that had begun with American involvement in Southeast Asia literally as far back as Dwight Eisenhower's Presidency, the nation's sense of well-being was shaken more severely perhaps than at any time in its two-hundred-year history. Eventually America would withdraw from Vietnam in what most would consider defeat, but not before angry debates over her reasons for the war as well as her conduct of the war would lead many Americans—particularly the young—cynically to question their nation's very purposes and integrity. Not before campus discontent with the war had flared into pitched battles and had found its parallel in large-scale draft dodging and desertion that further demonstrated the destructive ugliness of the Vietnamese encounter. Not before the revelations of American atrocities of My Lai were followed by tragedy at Ohio's Kent State University, where National Guardsmen fired into a group of antiwar demonstrators, killing four students, wounding more, and alarming all Americans with concern for what they were doing to themselves. Not before the pilfered Pentagon Papers had further undermined the confidence of many Americans in "the best and the brightest" of both national parties who had taken and kept us in what became America's most unwanted war, her symbol to many both of diminished world power and of moral irresponsibility.

Perhaps what astounded Americans most as they prepared for their Bicentennial was the seeming new vulnerability to public criticism and disparagement of their most highly placed leaders even as ever-expanding Executive decision-making led to fears of an emerging "Imperial Presidency." Despite his huge majorities in 1964, Lyndon B. Johnson chose not to run for reelection as President in 1968 because of widely demonstrated opposition to his war policies. And his speech on the role of the new electronic media in American life and politics, delivered immediately after he withdrew from the Presidential race, significantly pointed to broadcasting as an instrument of political activism, an interpretation not previously shared by most Americans who considered the medium essentially as an entertainment. (Earlier, of course, some leading press practitioners had themselves expressed critical concern about the larger impact on American life of the mass media, print and electronic alike, as newspaper pundit Walter Lippmann in his seminal 1922 study of "Public Opinion," and Edward R. Murrow, the most acclaimed of television newsmen, in bitterly prescient speeches late in the 1950s.) Republican Richard M. Nixon narrowly defeated Democratic Vice President Hubert H. Humphrey for the presidency in 1968, but in 1972 literally overwhelmed Democrat George S. McGovern in what was to become a virulently controversial campaign. But Nixon, who had used Vice President Spiro T. Agnew's threatening 1969 speech on the importance of television news to attack the medium for supposedly pressing upon the nation political views contrary to the Administration's, would also soon come to feel its power. Instantaneous and widespread electronic and print coverage of scandals touching on the Vice President quickly forced Agnew to resign from office, to be replaced under provisions of the never-before-used 25th Amendment to the Constitution by the appointment of Michigan Congressman Gerald R. Ford, Republican leader in the House of Representatives. And soon after that, when this nation had literally been deluged with the mass media's boldly revealing and incessant reporting of Watergate and the other scandals that suddenly disgraced his Presidency, Nixon himself felt constrained to resign when the Judiciary Committee of the House of Representatives on a bipartisan basis voted extraordinarily weighty Articles of Impeachment against the Chief Executive.

Appointed, not elected, to the second highest office of the land just months before, Gerald Ford now succeeded to the Presidency of the United States and in a brief, humble but thoroughly welcomed Inaugural Address made a first touching effort to lead a nation deeply shaken by tragedy and scandal from suspicion to faith, from despair to hope by assuring Americans that "Our long national nightmare is over." A month later, however, though his gracious explanation seemed acceptable to the nation at large, critics pilloried the new President for granting a "full, free and absolute pardon" to his predecessor. Shortly afterwards, even as some insisted that Nixon and Agnew had been unfairly hounded from office by a hostile, imperious press, Supreme Court Justice Potter Stewart, the new President's classmate at Yale Law School, argued there that America's Fourth Estate had instead "performed precisely the function it was intended to perform by those who wrote the First Amendment of our Constitution."

THE NATIONAL ORGANIZATION FOR WOMEN (NOW)
Statement of Purpose, *1966*

We, men and women, who hereby constitute ourselves as the National Organization for Women, believe that the time has come for a new movement toward true equality for all women in America, and toward a fully equal partnership of the sexes, as part of the world-wide revolution of human rights now taking place within and beyond our national borders.

The purpose of NOW is to take action to bring women into full participation in the mainstream of American society now, exercising all the privileges and responsibilities thereof in truly equal partnership with men.

We believe the time has come to move beyond the abstract argument, discussion and symposia over the status and special nature of women which has raged in America in recent years; the time has come to confront, with concrete action, the conditions that now prevent women from enjoying the equality of opportunity and freedom of choice which is their right, as individual Americans, and as human beings.

NOW is dedicated to the proposition that women, first and foremost, are human beings, who, like all other people in our society, must have the chance to develop their fullest human potential. We believe that women can achieve such equality only by accepting to the full the challenges and responsibilities they share with all other people in our society, as part of the decision-making mainstream of American political, economic and social life.

We organize to initiate or support action, nationally, or in any part of this nation, by individuals or organizations, to break through the silken curtain of prejudice and discrimination against women in government, industry, the professions, the churches, the political parties, the judiciary, the labor unions, in education, science, medicine, law, religion and every other field of importance in American society.

Enormous changes taking place in our society make it both possible and urgently necessary to advance the unfinished revolution of women toward true equality, now. With a life span lengthened to nearly seventy-five years it is no longer either necessary or possible for women to devote the greater part of their lives to child rearing; yet childbearing and rearing which continues to be a most important part of most women's lives—still is used to justify barring women from equal professional and economic participation and advance.

Today's technology has reduced most of the productive chores which women once performed in the home and in mass-production industries based upon routine unskilled labor. This same technology has virtually eliminated the quality of muscular strength as a criterion for filling most jobs, while intensifying American industry's need for creative intelligence. In view of this new industrial revolution created by automation in the mid-twentieth century, women can and must participate in old and new fields of society in full equality—or become permanent outsiders.

Despite all the talk about the status of American women in recent years, the actual position of women in the United States has declined, and is declining, to an alarming degree throughout the 1950s and '60s. Although 46.4% of all American women between the ages of eighteen and sixty-five now work outside the home, the overwhelming majority—75%—are in routine clerical, sales, or factory jobs, or they are household workers, cleaning women, hospital attendants. About two-thirds of Negro women workers are in the lowest paid service occupations. Working women are becoming increasingly—not less—concentrated on the bottom of the job ladder. As a consequence, full-time women workers today earn on the average only 60% of what men earn, and that wage gap has been increasing over the past twenty-five years in every major industry group. In 1964, of all women with a yearly income, 89% earned under $5,000 a year; half of all full-time year-round women workers earned less than $3,690; only 1.4% of full-time year-round women workers had an annual income of $10,000 or more.

Further, with higher education increasingly essential in today's society, too few women are entering and finishing college or going on to graduate or professional school. Today, women earn only one in three of the B.A.s and M.A.s granted, and one in ten of the Ph.Ds.

In all the professions considered of importance to society, and in the executive ranks of industry and government, women are losing ground. Where they are present it is only a token handful. Women comprise less than 1% of federal judges; less than 4% of all lawyers; 7% of doctors. Yet women represent 51% of the U.S. population. And, increasingly, men are replacing women in the top positions in secondary and elementary schools, in social work, and in libraries—once thought to be women's fields.

Official pronouncements of the advance in the status of women hide not only the reality of this dangerous decline, but the fact that nothing is being done to stop it. The excellent reports of the President's commission on the Status of Women and of the state commissions have not been fully implemented. Such commissions have power only to advise. They have no power to enforce their recommendations; nor have they the freedom to organize American women and men to press for action on them. The reports of these commissions have, however, created a basis upon which it is now possible to build.

Discrimination in employment on the basis of sex is now prohibited by federal law, in Title VII of the Civil Rights Act of 1964. But although nearly one-third of the cases brought before the Equal Employment Opportunity Commission during the first year dealt with sex discrimination and the proportion is increasing dramatically, the Commission has not made clear its intention to enforce the law with the same seriousness on behalf of women as of other victims of discrimination. Many of these cases were Negro women, who are the victims of the double discrimination of race and sex. Until now, too few women's organizations and official spokesmen have been willing to speak out against these dangers facing women. Too many women have been restrained by the fear of being called "feminist."

There is no civil rights movement to speak for women, as there has been for Negroes and other victims of discrimination. The National Organization for Women must therefore begin to speak.

WE BELIEVE that the power of American law, and the protection guaranteed by the U.S. Constitution to the civil rights of all individuals, must be effectively applied and enforced to isolate and remove patterns of sex discrimination, to ensure equality of opportunity in employment and education, and equality of civil and political rights and responsibilities on behalf of women, as well as for Negroes and other deprived groups.

We realize that women's problems are linked to many broader questions of social justice; their solution will require concerted action by many groups. Therefore, convinced that human rights for all are indivisible, we expect to give active support to the common cause of equal rights for all those who suffer discrimination and deprivation, and we call upon other organizations committed to such goals to support our efforts toward equality for women.

WE DO NOT ACCEPT the token appointment of a few women to high-level positions in government and industry as a substitute for a serious continuing effort to recruit and advance women according to their individual abilities. To this end, we urge American government and industry to mobilize the same resources of ingenuity and command with which they have solved problems of far greater difficulty than those now impeding the progress of women.

WE BELIEVE that this nation has a capacity at least as great as other nations to innovate new social institutions which will enable women to enjoy true equality of opportunity and responsibility in society, without conflict with their responsibilities as mothers and homemakers. In such innovations, America does not lead the Western world, but lags by decades behind many European countries. We do not accept the traditional assumption that a woman has to choose between marriage and motherhood on the one hand, and serious participation in industry or the professions on the other. We question the present expectation that all normal women will retire from job or profession for ten or fifteen years, to devote their full time to raising children, only to reenter the job market at a relatively minor level. This, in itself, is a deterrent to the aspirations of women, to their acceptance into management or professional training courses, and to the very possibility of equality of opportunity or real choice, for all but a few women. Above all, we reject the assumption that these problems are the unique responsibility of each individual woman, rather than a basic social dilemma which society must solve. True equality of opportunity and freedom of choice for women requires such practical, and possible innovations as a nationwide network of child-care centers, which will make it unnecessary for women to retire completely from society until their children are grown, and national programs to provide retraining for women who have chosen to care for their own children full-time.

WE BELIEVE that it is as essential for every girl to be educated to her full potential of human ability as it is for every boy—with the knowledge that such education is the key to effective participation in today's economy and that, for a girl as for a boy, education can only be serious where there is expectation that it will be used in society. We believe that American educators are capable of devising means of imparting such expectations to girl students. Moreover, we consider the decline in the proportion of women receiving higher and professional education to be evidence of discrimination. This discrimination may take the form of quotas against the admission of women to colleges, and professional schools; lack of encouragement by parents, counsellors and educators; denial of loans or fellowships; or the traditional or arbitrary procedures in graduate and professional training geared in terms of men, which inadvertently discriminate against women. We believe that the same serious attention must be given to high school dropouts who are girls as to boys.

WE REJECT the current assumptions that a man must carry the sole burden of supporting himself, his wife, and family, and that a woman is automatically entitled to lifelong support by a man upon her marriage, or that marriage, home and family are primarily woman's world and responsibility—hers, to dominate—his to support. We believe that a true partnership between the sexes demands a different concept of marriage, an equitable sharing of the responsibilities of home and children and of the economic burdens of their support. We believe that proper recognition should be given to the economic and social value of homemaking and child-care. To these ends, we will seek to open a reexamination of laws and mores governing marriage and divorce, for we believe that the current state of "half-equality" between the sexes discriminates against both men and women, and is the cause of much unnecessary hostility between the sexes.

WE BELIEVE that women must now exercise their political rights and responsibilities as American citizens. They must refuse to be segregated on the basis of sex into separate-and-not-equal ladies' auxiliaries in the political parties, and they must demand representation according to their numbers in the regularly constituted party committees—at local, state, and national levels—and in the informal power structure, participating fully in the selection of candidates and political decision making, and running for office themselves.

IN THE INTERESTS OF THE HUMAN DIGNITY OF WOMEN, we will protest, and endeavor to change, the false image of women now prevalent in the mass media, and in the texts, ceremonies, laws, and practices of our major social institutions. Such images perpetuate contempt for women by society and by women for themselves. We are similarly opposed to all policies and practices—in church, state, college, factory, or office—which, in the guise of protectiveness, not only deny opportunities but also foster in women self-denigration, dependence, and evasion of responsibility, undermine their confidence in their own abilities and foster contempt for women.

NOW WILL HOLD ITSELF INDEPENDENT OF ANY POLITICAL PARTY in order to mobilize the political power of all women and men intent on our goals. We will strive to ensure that no party, candidate, president, senator, governor, congressman, or any public official who betrays or ignores the principle of full equality between the sexes is elected or appointed to office. If it is necessary to mobilize the votes of men and women who believe in our cause, in order to win for women the final right to be fully free and equal human beings, we so commit ourselves.

WE BELIEVE that women will do most to create a new image of women by *acting* now, and by speaking out in behalf of their own equality, freedom, and human dignity—not in pleas for special privilege, nor in enmity toward men, who are also victims of the current, half-equality between the sexes—but in an active, self-respecting partnership with men. By so doing, women will develop confidence in their own ability to determine actively, in partnership with men, the conditions of their life, their choices, their future and their society.

"Power of the Media" Speech, *Lyndon B. Johnson, 1968*

Once again we are entering the period of national festivity which Henry Adams called the dance of democracy. At its best, that can be a time of debate and enlightenment. At its worst, it can be a period of frenzy. But always it is a time when emotion threatens to substitute for reason. Yet the basic hope of a democracy is that somehow amid all the frenzy and all the emotion that in the end reason will prevail.

Reason must prevail if democracy itself is to survive. . . .

But the real problem of informing the people is still with us, and I think I can speak with some authority about the problem of communication. I understand far better than some of my severe and perhaps intolerant critics would admit my own shortcomings as a communicator.

How does a public leader find just the right word or the right way to say no more or no less than he means to say, bearing in mind that anything he says may topple governments and may involve the lives of innocent men?

How does that leader speak the right phrase in the right way under the right conditions to suit the accuracies and contingencies of the moment when he's discussing questions of policy so that he does not stir a thousand misinterpretations and leave the wrong connotation or impression?

How does he reach the immediate audience and how does he communicate with the millions of others who are out there listening from afar? . . .

You men and women who are masters of the broadcast media I think surely must know what I am talking about. It was a long time ago a President once said, "The printing press is the most powerful weapon with which man has ever armed himself." And in our age the electronic media have added immeasurably to man's power.

You have within your hands the means to make our nation as intimate and as informed as a New England town meeting. Yet the use of broadcasting has not cleared away all the problems that we still have of communication.

In some ways, I think, sometimes it has complicated them. Because it tends to put the leader in a time capsule. It requires him often to abbreviate what he has to say. Too often it may catch a random phrase from his rather lengthy discourse and project it as the whole story.

How many men . . . in public life have watched themselves on a TV newscast and then been tempted to exclaim: "Can that really be me?"

Well, there is no denying it. You, the broadcast industry, have enormous power in your hands. You have the power to clarify. And you have the power to confuse.

Men in public life cannot remotely rival your opportunities, because day after day, night after night, hour after hour, on the hour, you shape—and the half-hour sometimes—you shape the nation's dialogue. The words that you choose, hopefully always accurate, hopefully always just, are the words that are carried out for all the people to hear.

The commentary that you provide can give the real meaning to the issues of the day or it can distort them beyond all meaning.

By your standards of what is news you can cultivate with them or you could nurture misguided passions. Your commentary carries an element of uncertainty.

Unlike the print media, television writes on the wind. There is no accumulated record which the historian can examine later with the 20-20 vision of hindsight, asking this question: How fair was he tonight? How impartial was he today? How honest was he all along?

Well, I hope the National Association of Broadcasters, with whom I have had a pleasant association for many years, will point the way to all of us in developing this kind of a record, because history is going to be asking very hard questions about our times and the period through which we are passing. And I think that we all owe it to history to complete the record.

But I did not come here this morning to sermonize in matters of fairness and judgment. No law and no set of regulations and no words of mine can improve you or dictate your daily responsibility. All I mean to do—what I'm trying to do—is to remind you where there's great power there must also be great responsibility.

This is true for broadcasters just as it's true for Presidents, and seekers for the Presidency.

What we say and what we do now will shape the kind of a world that we pass along to our children and our grandchildren. And I keep this thought constantly in my mind during the long days and the somewhat longer nights when crisis comes at home and abroad.

I took a little of your prime time last night. I wouldn't have done that except for a very prime purpose. I reported on the prospects for peace in Vietnam. I announced that the United States is taking a very important unilateral act of de-escalation which could—and I fervently pray, will—lead to mutual moves to reduce the level of violence and to de-escalate the war.

As I sat in my office last evening waiting to speak, I thought of the many times each week when television brings the war into the American home. No one can say exactly what effect those vivid scenes have on American opinion.

Historians must only guess at the effect that television would have had during earlier conflicts on the future of this nation. During the Korean War, for example, at that time when our forces were pushed back there to Pusan. Or World War II, the Battle of the Bulge, or when our men were slugging it out in Europe, or when most of our Air Force was shot down that day in June, 1942, off Australia.

But last night television was being used to carry a different message. It was a message of peace and it occurred to me that the medium may be somewhat better suited to conveying the actions of conflict than to dramatizing the words that the leaders use in trying and hoping to end the conflict.

Certainly it is more dramatic to show policemen and rioters locked in combat than to show men trying to cooperate with one another.

The face of hatred and of bigotry comes through much more clearly, no matter what its color, and the face of tolerance I seem to find is rarely newsworthy.

Progress, whether it's a man being trained for a job or millions being trained, or whether it's a child in Head Start learning to read or an older person, seventy-two, in adult education, or being cared for in Medicare, rarely makes the news, although more than twenty million of them are affected by it.

Perhaps this is because tolerance and progress are not dynamic events such as riots and conflict are events.

So peace in the new sense is a condition. War is an end. Part of your responsibility is simply to understand the consequences of that fact, the consequences of your own acts. And part of that responsibility, I think, is to try as very best we all can to draw the attention of our people to the real business of society in our system, finding and securing peace in the world, at home and abroad and for all that you have done. And that you are doing and that you will do to the end, I thank you and I commend you. . . .

Speaking as I did to the nation last night, I was moved by the very deep convictions that I entertain about the nature of the office that it's my present privilege to hold.

The office of the Presidency is the only office in this land of all the people.

Whatever may be the personal wishes or the preferences of any man who holds it, a President of all the people can afford no thought of self. At no time and in no way and for no reason can a President allow the integrity or the responsibility or the freedom of the office ever to be compromised or diluted or destroyed because when you destroy it, you destroy yourselves. And I hope and I pray by not allowing the Presidency to be involved in division and deep partisanship I shall be able to pass on to my successor a stronger office, strong enough to guard and defend all the people against all the storms that the future may bring us. . . .

You are yourselves the trustees—legally accepted trustees, legally selected trustees—of a great institution on which the freedom of our land utterly depends.

The security, the success of our country, what happens to us tomorrow rests squarely upon the media which disseminates the truth on which the decisions of democracy are made. We get a great deal of our information from you, and an informed mind is the guardian genius of democracy.

So you are the keepers of a trust and you must be just. You must guard and you must defend your media against a spirit of action, against the works of divisiveness, against bigotry, against the corrupting evils of partisanship in any guise.

For America's press as for the American Presidency, the integrity and the responsibility and the freedom—the freedom to know the truth and let the truth make us free—must never be compromised or diluted or destroyed.

The defense of our media is your responsibility. Government cannot and must not and never will, as long as I have anything to do about it, intervene in that role.

But I do want to leave this thought with you as I leave you this morning. I hope that you will give this trust your closest care. Acting as I know you can to guard not only against the obvious but to watch for the hidden, the sometimes unintentional, the often petty intrusion upon the integrity of the information by which Americans decide.

Men and women of the airways fully as much as men and women of public service have a public trust, and if liberty is to survive and to succeed that solemn trust must be faithfully kept.

I do not want and I don't think you want to wake up some morning and find America changed because we slept when we should have been awake, because we remained silent when we should have spoken up, because we went along with what was popular and fashionable and "in," rather than what was necessary and what was right.

Being faithful to our trust ought to be the prime test

of any public trustee in office or on the airways and in any society all you students of history know that a time of division is a time of danger, and in these times now we must never forget that eternal vigilance is the price of liberty.

Thank you for wanting me to come. I've enjoyed it.

"Public Opinion,"
Walter Lippmann, 1922

The world that we have to deal with politically is out of reach, out of sight, out of mind. It has to be explored, reported, and imagined. Man is no Aristotelian god contemplating all existence at one glance. He is the creature of an evolution who can just about span a sufficient portion of reality to manage his survival, and snatch what on the scale of time are but a few moments of insight and happiness. Yet this same creature has invented ways of seeing what no naked eye could see, of hearing what no ear could hear, of weighing immense masses and infinitesimal ones, of counting and separating more items than he can individually remember. He is learning to see with his mind vast portions of the world that he could never see, touch, smell, hear, or remember. Gradually he makes for himself a trustworthy picture inside his head of the world beyond his reach.

Those features of the world outside which have to do with the behavior of other human beings, insofar as that behavior crosses ours, is dependent upon us, or is interesting to us, we call roughly public affairs. The pictures inside the heads of these human beings, the pictures of themselves, of others, of their needs, purposes, and relationship, are their public opinions. Those pictures which are acted upon by groups of people, or by individuals acting in the name of groups, are Public Opinion with capital letters. And so in the chapters which follow we shall inquire first into some of the reasons why the picture inside so often misleads men in their dealings with the world outside. Under this heading we shall consider first the chief factors which limit their access to the facts. They are the artificial censorships, the limitations of social contact, the comparatively meager time available in each day for paying attention to public affairs, the distortion arising because events have to be compressed into very short messages, the difficulty of making a small vocabulary express a complicated world, and finally the fear of facing those facts which would seem to threaten the established routine of men's lives. . . .

Thus the environment with which our public opinions deal is refracted in many ways, by censorship and privacy at the source, by physical and social barriers at the other end, by scanty attention, by the poverty of language, by distraction, by unconscious constellations of feeling, by wear and tear, violence, monotony. These limitations upon our access to that environment combine with the obscurity and complexity of the facts themselves to thwart clearness and justice of perception, to substitute misleading fictions for workable ideas, and to deprive us of adequate checks upon those who consciously strive to mislead.

Each of us lives and works on a small part of the earth's surface, moves in a small circle, and of these acquaintances knows only a few intimately. Of any public event that has wide effects we see at best only a phase and an aspect. This is as true of the eminent insiders who draft treaties, make laws, and issue orders, as it is of those who have treaties framed for them, laws promulgated to them, orders given at them. Inevitably our opinions cover a bigger space, a longer reach of time, a greater number of things, than we can directly observe. They have, therefore, to be pieced together out of what others have reported and what we can imagine.

Yet even the eyewitness does not bring back a naïve picture of the scene. For experience seems to show that he himself brings something to the scene which later he takes away from it, that oftener than not what he imagines to be the account of an event is really a transfiguration of it. Few facts in consciousness seem to be merely given. Most facts in consciousness seem to be partly made. A report is the joint product of the knower and known, in which the role of the observer is always selective and usually creative. The facts we see depend on where we are placed, and the habits of our eyes. . . .

For the most part we do not first see, and then define, we define first and then see. In the great blooming, buzzing confusion of the outer world we pick out what our culture has already defined for us, and we tend to perceive that which we have picked out in the form stereotyped for us by our culture. . . .

That the manufacture of consent is capable of great refinements no one, I think, denies. The process by which public opinions arise is certainly no less intricate than it has appeared in these pages, and the opportunities for manipulation open to anyone who understands the process are plain enough.

The creation of consent is not a new art. It is a very old one which was supposed to have died out with the appearance of democracy. But it has not died out. It has, in fact, improved enormously in technique, because it is now based on analysis rather than on rule of thumb. And so, as a result of psychological research, coupled with the modern means of communication, the practice of democracy has turned a corner. A revolution is taking place, infinitely more significant than any shifting of economic power.

Within the life of the generation now in control of affairs, persuasion has become a self-conscious art and a regular organ of popular government. None of us begins to understand the consequences, but it is no daring prophecy to say that the knowledge of how to create consent will alter every political calculation and modify every political premise. Under the impact of propaganda, not necessarily in the sinister meaning of the word alone, the old constants of our thinking have become variables. It is no longer possible, for example, to believe in the original dogma of democracy; that the knowledge needed for the management of human affairs comes up spontaneously from the human heart. Where we act on that theory we expose ourselves to self-deception, and to forms of persuasion that we cannot verify. It has been demonstrated that we cannot rely upon intuition, conscience, or the accidents of casual opinion if we are to deal with the world beyond our reach.

The idea that men have to go forth and study the world in order to govern it has played a very minor part in political thought. It could figure very little, because the machinery for reporting the world in any way useful to government made comparatively little progress from the time of Aristotle to the age in which the premises of democracy were established.

Therefore, if you had asked a pioneer Democrat where the information was to come from on which the will of the people was to be based, he would have been puzzled by the question. It would have seemed a little as if you had asked him where his life or his soul came from. The will of the people, he almost assumed, exists at all times; the duty of political science was to work out the inventions of the ballot and representative government. If they were properly worked out and applied under the right conditions, such as exist in the self-contained village or the self-contained shop, the mechanism would somehow overcome the brevity of attention which Aristotle had observed, and the narrowness of its range, which the theory of a self-contained community tactily acknowledged. We have seen how even at this late date the guild socialists are transfixed by the notion that if only you can build on the right unit of voting and representation, an intricate cooperative commonwealth is possible.

Convinced that the wisdom was there if only you could find it, democrats have treated the problem of making public opinions a problem in civil liberties. "Who ever knew Truth put to the worse, in a free and open encounter?" [John Milton asked in *Areopagitica*]. Supposing that no one has ever seen it put to the worse, are we to believe then that the truth is generated by the encounter, like fire by rubbing two sticks? Behind this classic doctrine of liberty, which American democrats embodied in their Bill of Rights, there are, in fact, several different theories of the origin of truth. One is a faith that in the competition of opinions, the truest will win because there is a peculiar strength in the truth. This is probably sound if you allow the competition to extend over a sufficiently long time. When men argue in this vein they have in mind the verdict of history, and they think specifically of heretics persecuted when they lived, canonized after they were dead. Milton's question rests also on a belief that the capacity to recognize truth is inherent in all men, and that truth freely put in circulation will win acceptance. It derives no less from the experience, which has shown that men are not likely to discover truth if they cannot speak it, except under the eye of an uncomprehending policeman.

No one can possibly overestimate the practical value of these civil liberties, nor the importance of maintaining them. When they are in jeopardy, the human spirit is in jeopardy, and should there come a time when they have to be curtailed, as during a war, the suppression of thought is a risk to civilization which might prevent its recovery from the effects of war, if the hysterics, who exploit the necessity, were numerous enough to carry over into peace the taboos of war. Fortunately, the mass of men is too tolerant long to enjoy the professional inquisitors, as gradually, under the criticism of men not willing to be terrorized, they are revealed as mean-spirited creatures who nine-tenths of the time do not know what they are talking about.

But in spite of its fundamental importance, civil liberty in this sense does not guarantee public opinion in the modern world. For it always assumes, either that truth is spontaneous, or that the means of securing truth exist when there is no external interference. But when you are dealing with an invisible environment, the assumption is false. The truth about distant or complex matters is not self-evident, and the machinery for assembling information is technical and expensive. Yet political science, and especially democratic political science, has never freed itself from the original assumption of Aristotle's politics sufficiently to restate the premises, so that political thought might come to grips with the problem of how to make the invisible world visible to the citizens of a modern state.

Chicago Speech to Radio and Television News Directors Association, *Edward R. Murrow, 1958*

This just might do nobody any good. At the end of this discourse a few people may accuse this reporter of fouling his own comfortable nest, and your organization may be accused of having given hospitality to heretical and even dangerous thoughts. But the elaborate structure of networks, advertising agencies and sponsors will not be shaken or altered. It is my desire, if not my duty, to try to talk to you journeymen with some candor about what is happening to radio and television.

I have no technical advice or counsel to offer those of you who labor in this vineyard that produces words and pictures. You will forgive me for not telling you that the instruments with which you work are miraculous, that your responsibility is unprecedented or that your aspirations are frequently frustrated. It is not necessary to remind you that the fact that your voice is amplified to the degree where it reaches from one end of the country to the other does not confer upon you greater wisdom or understanding than you possessed when your voice reached only from one end of the bar to the other. All these things you know. . . .

Believing that potentially the commercial system of broadcasting as practiced in this country is the best and freest yet devised, I have decided to express my concern about what I believe to be happening to radio and television. These instruments have been good to me beyond my due. There exists in my mind no reasonable grounds for personal complaints. I have no feud, either with my employers, any sponsors, or with the professional critics of radio and television. But I am seized with an abiding fear regarding what these two instruments are doing to our society, our culture and our heritage.

Our history will be what we make it. And if there are any historians about fifty or a hundred years from now, and there should be preserved the kinescopes for one week of all three networks, they will there find recorded in black and white, or color, evidence of decadence, escapism and insulation from the realities of the world in which we live. I invite your attention to the television schedules of all networks between the hours of 8 and 11 p.m., Eastern Time. Here you will find only fleeting and spasmodic reference to the fact that this nation is in mortal danger. There are, it is true, occasional informative programs presented in that intellectual ghetto on Sunday afternoons. But during the daily peak viewing periods, television in the main insulates us from the realities of the world in which we live. If this state of affairs continues, we may alter an advertising slogan to read: LOOK NOW, PAY LATER. For surely we shall pay for using this most powerful instrument of communication to insulate the citizenry from the hard and demanding realities which must be faced if we are to survive. I mean the word *survive* literally. If there were to be a competition in indifference, or perhaps in insulation from reality, then Nero and his fiddle, Chamberlain and his umbrella, could not find a place on an early afternoon sustaining show. If Hollywood were to run out of Indians, the program schedules would be mangled beyond all recognition. Then some courageous soul with a small budget might be able to do a documentary telling what, in fact, we have done—and are still doing—to the Indians in this country. But that would be unpleasant. And we must at all costs shield the sensitive citizens from anything that is unpleasant.

I am entirely persuaded that the American public is more reasonable, restrained and more mature than most of our industry's program planners believe. Their fear of controversy is not warranted by the evidence. I have reason to know, as do many of you, that when the evidence on a controversial subject is fairly and calmly presented, the public recognizes it for what it is—an effort to illuminate rather than to agitate. . . .

Recently, network spokesmen have been disposed to complain that the professional critics of television have been "rather beastly." There have been hints that somehow competition for the advertising dollar has caused the critics of print to gang up on television and radio. This reporter has no desire to defend the critic. They have space in which to do that on their own behalf. But it remains a fact that the newspapers and magazines are the only instruments of mass communication which remain free from sustained and regular critical comment. If the network spokesmen are so anguished about what appears in print, let them come forth and engage in a little sustained and regular comment regarding newspapers and magazines. It is an ancient and sad fact that most people in network television, and radio, have an exaggerated regard for what appears in print. And there have been cases where executives have refused to make even private comment on a program for which they were responsible until they had read the reviews in print. This is hardly an exhibition of confidence.

The oldest excuse of the networks for their timidity is their youth. Their spokesmen say, "We are young; we have not developed the traditions nor acquired the experience of the older media." If they but knew it, they are building those traditions, creating those precedents every day. Each time they yield to a voice from Washington or any political pressure, each time they eliminate something that might offend some section of the community, they are creating their own body of precedent and tradition. They are, in fact, not content to be "half safe."

Nowhere is this better illustrated than by the fact that the chairman of the Federal Communications Commission publicly prods broadcasters to engage in their legal right to editorialize. Of course, to undertake an editorial policy, overt and clearly labeled, and obviously unsponsored, requires a station or a network to be responsible. Most stations today probably do not have the manpower to assume this responsibility, but the manpower could be recruited. Editorials would not be profitable; if they had a cutting edge, they might even offend. It is much easier, much less troublesome, to use the money-making machine of television and radio merely as a conduit through which to channel anything that is not libelous, obscene or defamatory. In that way one has the illusion of power without responsibility.

So far as radio—that most satisfying and rewarding instrument—is concerned, the diagnosis of its difficulties is rather easy. And obviously I speak only of news and information. In order to progress, it need only go backward. To the time when singing commercials were not allowed on news reports, when there was no middle commercial in a fifteen minute news report, when radio was rather proud, alert and fast. I recently asked a network official, "Why this great rash of five-minute news reports (including three commercials) on weekends?" He replied, "Because that seems to be the only thing we can sell." . . .

One of the basic troubles with radio and television news is that both instruments have grown up as an incompatible combination of show business, advertising and news. Each of the three is a rather bizarre and demanding profession. And when you get all three under one roof, the dust never settles. The top management of the networks, with a few notable exceptions, has been trained in advertising, research, sales or show business. But by the nature of the corporate structure, they also make the final and crucial decisions having to do with news and public affairs. Frequently they have neither the time nor the competence to do this. It is not easy for the same small group of men to decide whether to buy a new station for millions of dollars, build a new building, alter the rate card, buy a new Western, sell a soap opera, decide what defensive line to take in connection with the latest Congressional inquiry, how much money to spend on promoting a new program, what additions or deletions should be made in the existing covey or clutch of vice-presidents, and at the same time—frequently on the same long day—to give mature, thoughtful consideration to the manifold problems that confront those who are charged with the responsibility for news and public affairs.

Sometimes there is a clash between the public interest and the corporate interest. A telephone call or a letter from the proper quarter in Washington is treated rather more seriously than a communication from an irate but not politically potent viewer. It is tempting enough to give away a little air time for frequently irresponsible and unwarranted utterances in an effort to temper the wind of criticism.

Upon occasion, economics and editorial judgment are in conflict. And there is no law which says that dollars will be defeated by duty. Not so long ago the President of the United States delivered a television address to the nation. He was discoursing on the possibility or probability of war between this nation and the Soviet Union and Communist China—a reasonably compelling subject. Two networks, CBS and NBC, delayed that broadcast for an hour and fifteen minutes. If this decision was dictated by anything other than financial reasons, the networks didn't deign to explain those reasons. That hour-and-fifteen-minute delay, by the way, is about twice the time required for an ICBM to travel from the Soviet Union to major targets in the United

States. It is difficult to believe that this decision was made by men who love, respect and understand news.

So far, I have been dealing largely with the deficit side of the ledger, and the items could be expanded. But I have said, and I believe, that potentially we have in this country a free enterprise system of radio and television which is superior to any other. But to achieve its promise, it must be both free and enterprising. There is no suggestion here that networks or individual stations should operate as philanthropies. But I can find nothing in the Bill of Rights or the Communications Act which says that they must increase their net profits each year, lest the Republic collapse. I do not suggest that news and information should be subsidized by foundations or private subscriptions. I am aware that the networks have expended, and are expending, very considerable sums of money on public affairs programs from which they cannot hope to receive any financial reward. I have had the privilege at CBS of presiding over a considerable number of such programs. I testify, and am able to stand here and say, that I have never had a program turned down by my superiors because of the money it would cost.

But we all know that you cannot reach the potential maximum audience in marginal time with a sustaining program. This is so because so many stations on the network—any network—will decline to carry it. Every licensee who applies for a grant to operate in the public interest, convenience and necessity makes certain promises as to what he will do in terms of program content. Many recipients of licenses have, in blunt language, welshed on those promises. The money-making machine somehow blunts their memories. The only remedy for this is closer inspection and punitive action by the F.C.C. But in the view of many this would come perilously close to supervision of program content by a federal agency.

So it seems that we cannot rely on philanthropic support or foundation subsidies; we cannot follow the "sustaining route"—the networks cannot pay all the freight—and the F.C.C. cannot or will not discipline those who abuse the facilities that belong to the public. What, then, is the answer? Do we merely stay in our comfortable nests, concluding that the obligation of those instruments has been discharged when we work at the job of informing the public for a minimum of time? Or do we believe that the preservation of the Republic is a seven-day-a-week job, demanding more awareness, better skills and more perseverance than we have yet contemplated.

I am frightened by the imbalance, the constant striving to reach the largest possible audience for everything; by the absence of a sustained study of the state of the nation. Heywood Broun once said, "No body politic is healthy until it begins to itch." I would like television to produce some itching pills, rather than this endless outpouring of tranquilizers. It can be done. Maybe it won't be, but it could. Let us not shoot the wrong piano player. Do not be deluded into believing that the titular heads of the networks control what appears on their networks. They all have better taste. All are responsible to stockholders, and in my experience all are honorable men. But they must schedule what they can sell in the public market.

And this brings us to the nub of the question. In one sense it rather revolves around the phrase heard frequently along Madison Avenue: The Corporate Image. I am not precisely sure what this phrase means, but I would imagine that it reflects a desire on the part of the corporations who pay the advertising bills to have the public imagine, or believe, that they are not merely bodies with no souls, panting in pursuit of elusive dollars. They would like us to believe that they can distinguish between the public good and the private or corporate gain. So the question is this: Are the big corporations who pay the freight for radio and television programs wise to use that time exclusively for the sale of goods and services? Is it in their own interest and that of the stockholders so to do? . . . If [they] always, invariably, reach for the largest possible audience, then this progress of insulation, of escape from reality, will continue to be massively financed, and its apologists will continue to make winsome speeches about giving the public what it wants, or "letting the public decide."

I refuse to believe that the presidents and chairmen of the boards of these big corporations want their corporate image to consist exclusively of a solemn voice in an echo chamber, or a pretty girl opening the door of a refrigerator, or a horse that talks. They want something better, and on occasion some of them have demonstrated it. But most of the men whose legal and moral responsibility it is to spend the stockholders' money for advertising are removed from the realities of the mass media by five, six, or a dozen contraceptive layers of vice-presidents, public relations counsel and advertising agencies. Their business is to sell goods, and the competition is pretty tough.

But this nation is now in competition with malignant forces of evil who are using every instrument at their command to empty the minds of their subjects and fill those minds with slogans, determination and faith in the future. If we go on as we are, we are protecting the mind of the American public from any real contact with the menacing world that squeezes in upon us. We are engaged in a great experiment to discover whether a free public opinion can devise and direct methods of managing the affairs of the nation. We may fail. But we are handicapping ourselves needlessly. . . . For if the premise upon which our pluralistic society rests, which as I understand it is that if the people are given sufficient undiluted information, they will then somehow, even after long, sober second thoughts, reach the right decision—if that premise is wrong, then not only the corporate image but the corporations are done for. . . .

It may be that the present system, with no modifications and no experiments, can survive. Perhaps the money-making machine has some kind of built-in perpetual motion, but I do not think so. To a very considerable extent the media of mass communications in a given country reflect the political, economic and social climate in which they flourish. That is the reason ours differ from the British and French, or the Russian and Chinese. We are currently wealthy, fat, comfortable and complacent. We have currently a built-in allergy to unpleasant or disturbing information. Our mass media reflect this. But unless we get up off our fat surpluses and recognize that television in the main is being used to distract, delude, amuse and insulate us, then television and those who finance it, those who look at it and those who work at it, may see a totally different picture too late.

I do not advocate that we turn television into a twenty-seven-inch wailing wall, where longhairs constantly moan about the state of our culture and our defense. But I would just like to see it reflect occasionally the hard, unyielding realities of the world in which we live. I would like to see it done inside the existing framework, and I would like to see the doing of it redound to the credit of those who finance and program it. Measure the results by Nielsen, Trendex or Silex—it doesn't matter. The main thing is to try. The responsibility can be easily placed, in spite of all the mouthings about giving the public what it wants. It rests on big business, and on big television, and it rests at the top. Responsibility is not something that can be assigned or delegated. And it promises its own reward: good business and good television.

Perhaps no one will do anything about it. I have ventured to outline it against a background of criticism that may have been too harsh only because I think of nothing better. Someone once said—I think it was Max Eastman—that "that publisher serves his advertiser best who best serves his readers." I cannot believe that radio and television, or the corporations that finance the programs, are serving well or truly their viewers or listeners, or themselves.

I began by saying that our history will be what we make it. If we go on as we are, then history will take its revenge, and retribution will not limp in catching up with us.

We are to a large extent an imitative society. If one or two or three corporations would undertake to devote just a small fraction of their advertising appropriation along the lines that I have suggested, the procedure would grow by contagion; the economic burden would be bearable, and there might ensue a most exciting adventure—exposure to ideas and the bringing of reality into the homes of the nation.

To those who say people wouldn't look; they wouldn't be interested; they're too complacent, indifferent and insulated, I can only reply: There is, in one reporter's opinion, considerable evidence against that contention.

But even if they are right, what have they got to lose? Because if they are right, and this instrument is good for nothing but to entertain, amuse and insulate, then the tube is flickering now and we will soon see that the whole struggle is lost.

This instrument can teach, it can illuminate; yes, and it can even inspire. But it can do so only to the extent that humans are determined to use it to those ends. Otherwise it is merely wires and lights in a box. There is a great and perhaps decisive battle to be fought against ignorance, intolerance and indifference. This weapon of television could be useful.

Stonewall Jackson, who knew something about the use of weapons, is reported to have said, "When war comes, you must draw the sword and throw away the scabbard." The trouble with television is that it is rusting in the scabbard during a battle for survival.

Guildhall Speech on "Television and Politics," *Edward R. Murrow, 1959*

. . . I am to try to talk to you about television and politics. Both professions involve curious contradictions, and when combined represent a dangerous mixture. Being without substantial credentials in either area, being without political affiliation or technical skill—knowing only that the long waves are short and the short waves are long—I take refuge in a remark of my fellow countryman who said: "It is better to know less than to know so much that ain't so." So much that we think we know about both television and politics ain't so. My own attitude towards politicians has ranged from sympathy to affection, although as a political reporter I have found the late Vice President Barkley's advice to be sound. He counselled: "A political reporter must be agin everybody, some." . . .

Having undertaken massive research on this subject, you will excuse me for not saying that the television camera has revolutionized politics, and that it is an all-seeing X-ray eye which will make it inevitable that the voter will sort out the charlatan from the statesman. Nor shall I remind you that in my country we have more television sets than bathtubs. For candor compels me to confess that I do not know what this fascinating statistic proves. Television has been variously described as the opiate of the people, a group of midgets in a black box, and the most powerful instrument of communication yet devised. It was to "revolutionize politics" but it hasn't. I do know of one senator who was badly beaten in the last election who is entirely convinced that the major reason for his defeat was that he so far forgot himself as to correct his wife's pronunciation during a television program. He was inundated with furious letters from female viewers, and is persuaded that they voted him out of office. The moral of this story probably is that a penalty must be paid for correcting one's wife in front of a television camera or anywhere else.

There is also the case of a politician who ran for public office four times, always assisted by his wife. Three times he won; once he was defeated. In all three victorious campaigns his wife was pregnant; the occasion when he went down to defeat, she wasn't. It would seem that no general law regarding television and politics can be formulated as a result of this experience.

Probably the single most effective use of television in politics occurred in my own country during the 1952 presidential campaign. General Eisenhower was the Republican nominee, having been selected after a bitter convention battle over Senator Taft—not because he was better qualified but because leaders of the Republican Party thought he had a better chance of winning. Richard Nixon, a relatively obscure senator from California, was the Vice-Presidential candidate. The two men were campaigning in different parts of the country when it was disclosed that a group of California citizens had raised a special fund for Senator Nixon, and it amounted to approximately eighteen thousand dollars. This disclosure created a political storm equal to that produced in your country by the Zinoviev Letter. What came to be known as the "Nixon Fund" was to be used to pay for transportation, hotel expenses, telephone tolls, Christmas cards, advertising and general publicity. When the storm broke, excited politicians of both parties took counsel. The Democrats demanded that the Republicans jettison Nixon as their candidate. Many

Republican newspapers echoed the demand. Candidate Eisenhower echoed uncertainty. Many professional Republican politicians said privately that Nixon must go or the Party would be lost. Many personal friends and political cronies urged Nixon to resign for the good of the Party. Nixon and his advisors finally decided that he should make a nation-wide television explanation. The necessary arrangements were made, and the tension and suspense mounted. Would the senator quit or try to ride out the storm? He hadn't made up his own mind until a few hours before air time. When he faced the cameras he talked from notes, made an explanation of the fund which probably would not entirely have satisfied a Royal Commission, said he didn't think he ought to quit because he wasn't a quitter, and "incidentally," said Nixon, "Pat is not a quitter." At this point the camera panned around to show Mrs. Nixon's profile. "After all," said the senator, "her name was Patricia Ryan and she was born on St. Patrick's Day, and you know the Irish never quit." Nixon admitted that he had received one gift after his election to the Senate. He spoke as follows: "It was a little cocker spaniel dog—black and white spotted—and our little girl Tricia, the six-year-old, named it Checkers. And you know, the kids love that dog, and I just want to say this right now, that regardless of what you say about it we're going to keep it." Checkers was not present in the studio.

As the clock ran out, the candidate for Vice President, with tears in his eyes and voice, was saying: "Wire and write to the Republican National Committee on whether you think I should get off, and whatever their decision is, I will abide."

The result was sensational—telegrams, telephone calls, came pouring in; Eisenhower and Nixon staged a reunion, posed for pictures with arms around each other; and said Eisenhower to Nixon: "You're my boy!" No Hollywood writer would have dared write such a script, but it worked. Without question, Nixon was saved by television, although any fair-minded observer would probably have to give some of the credit to his wife, the Irish and to Checkers. Still the fact remains that the climate of opinion could not have been changed so quickly had television not been available to transmit throughout the country this amazing performance, which caused many to weep, and only a few to laugh.

Senator Joseph R. McCarthy, of Wisconsin, could not play upon the human emotions with the same skill as his friend, Richard Nixon. The trail that he left on the face of my country will not soon fade, and there may be others who will try to follow in his footsteps. His weapon was fear. He was a politically unsophisticated man with a flair for publicity; and he was powerfully aided by the silence of timid men who feared to be the subject of his unfounded accusations. He polluted the channels of communication, and every radio and television network, every newspaper and magazine publisher who did not speak out against him contributed to his evil work and must share part of the responsibility for what he did, not only to our fellow citizens but to our self-respect. He was in a real sense the creature of the mass media. They made him. They gave nationwide circulation to his mouthings. They defended their actions on the grounds that what he said was news, when they knew he lied. His initial appearances on television were in the role of a man whose sole desire was to oust communists from government and all responsible positions. That was his announced objective. The overwhelming majority of people undoubtedly sympathized with him. It has been said repeatedly that television caused his downfall. This is not precisely true. His prolonged exposure during the so-called Army-McCarthy Hearings certainly did something to diminish his stature. He became something of a bore. But his downfall really stemmed from the fact that he broke the rules of the club, the United States Senate, when he began attacking the integrity, the loyalty of fellow senators, he was censured by that body, and was finished. The timidity of television in dealing with this man when he was spreading fear throughout the land, is not something to which this art of communication can ever point with pride, nor should it be allowed to forget it. . . .

In a free society, politics essentially involve the resolution of conflict. It is part of television's duty to define, illuminate and illustrate the nature of the conflict—to supply the voter with the raw material upon which informed opinion may be based. Thucydides said: "We both alike know that into the discussion of human affairs the question of justice arises only where the pressure of necessity is equal; that the strong take what they can, and the weak grant what they must." The true function of television in politics is to operate a market place in which ideas may compete on an equal footing. It is true that the voter may elect to purchase the second-rate, shopworn or shoddy idea. He may mistake a mobile countenance for an agile mind. He may vote for Profile rather than for Principle. An unruly lock of hair may be more effective than a disciplined mind. There is no way to guarantee that television will prevent the voter from being as wrong as he has been so often in the past. Television offers no guarantee that demagogues can be kept from political power. It merely provides them with wider and more intimate, more immediate circulation. I would suggest that the evidence so far indicates that television can retard or accelerate a trend in public opinion, but it cannot reverse it. The hope so fondly held by enthusiasts a few years ago, the hope that television would make certain that the voter would sort out the phony from the statesman, is not proved. I would doubt that under today's system of communication a Lincoln or a Jefferson could be nominated or elected. According to all reports, Jefferson had a most abrasive voice, and did not suffer fools gladly. While being interviewed on some panel program he might have told a particularly obnoxious questioner just what he thought of him, and that, of course, would have been fatal. Mr. Lincoln did not move gracefully, was not a handsome man, had a wife who was no political asset, and he was a solitary man. In our present society, he probably would have been examined at an early age by a psychiatrist, received an unfavorable report, have been told his attitude toward "togetherness" was altogether wrong, and advised to enter a trade school if he could gain admittance. On the other hand, it is conceivable that Woodrow Wilson might have won his fight for the League of Nations, and thereby changed world history, had he been able to use the tools of television and radio. He was a rather pedantic persuader, and these instruments wouldn't have changed him, but they would have given his ideas wider circulation; and the efforts of those who attempted to distort those ideas might have had less success. It is part of the brief history of television that circulation is directly related to controversy.

But it is well to bear in mind that no large section of the public demands more information or a better presentation of it. Public affairs is a form of specialization. It is *not* recreation. The public as such does not feel the call to specialize, even in its own good. On the whole, it is unenterprising—it wants its fun. By the time most people turn on the television set, the work of the day is over. There is a welcome break in drudgery. Most people, after working hours, prefer to be called away from reality, not made to face it. There is a limit upon the attention the public is willing to devote to politics. This would be true even if television fulfilled its functions to the utmost. Television by itself does not usher in the democratic millenium, and its inability to do so is not its own peculiar failure. It is due to the unwillingness of men and women, even in the highly developed democracies of Britain and the United States, to take more trouble to govern themselves better.

Both radio and television started as novelties, not as sociological or political devices. Their social importance was not at first imagined. They cost a great deal of money to develop. The pioneers in what Americans call "the industry" were businessmen and financiers, not scholars, statesmen or politicians. They still do not put public service first, for the simple reason that in my country it must pay its way. Business success has to come first.

In a competitive society, political broadcasts must compete. Generally they don't. For example, . . . in 1957, President Eisenhower and Secretary of State Dulles delivered a half-hour report on the Summit Conference. . . . They were competing with a bunch of "good guys" and "bad guys" in a Western epic called "Wells Fargo." The gun slingers had almost precisely the same audience as the word slingers.

In 1958, President Eisenhower spoke solo for a half-an-hour to a Republican gathering. A non-politico on another network—fellow named Bat Masterson, who wears a bowler hat and goes about bashing people over the head with a gold-headed cane, was viewed by more than twice the number of people who watched the president. And on the third network, a personable young singer named Patti Page attracted the attention of a few million more citizens than the president.

During the 1956 presidential campaign, the average audience for all nighttime political programs was roughly sixty percent below the average audience for regular entertainment programs. . . .

The television viewer is not fascinated by political orations. This may be due in part to the absence of meaningful controversy. The voter isn't interested. One of our most distinguished jurists—Judge Learned Hand—has remarked: "Doubtless things might become uncomfortable enough to arouse them, but, given reasonable opportunity for personal favors, and not too irksome control, they are content to abdicate their sovereignty and to be fleeced, if the shepherds will only shear them in their sleep."

It may be that television magnifies all the facets of personality, the defects along with the merits. This ability of television to magnify the components of personality is not necessarily pure gain. A man's weaknesses may be brought to light, which is all to the good. But that is not all that happens, because a public leader in the age of television must be popular as well as sincere. He must have a quality not considered essential in the past, that is, simplicity. A politician to be popular must not be too complicated. He must not appear to be too subtle. He must be accessible, must be able to avoid the difficult question without appearing to do so. . . .

Simplicity communicates itself more easily than complexity in persons: and it also does when it comes to issues. And this is part of the change brought about by television. This is by no means a boon. It surely is essential to have abstruse and complex ideas simplified, so that many can understand them. But we live in an age in which intelligence may not be able to simplify truthfully. The frontiers of knowledge have been pushed back, and the more that comes to be known, the less is understood, or perhaps I should say completely understood, even by the wisest. And since politics and television, more than ever before, have to take account of much of this abstruse and complicated knowledge, the art of self-government is not going to be perfected by the process of simplification alone. Indeed, looking ahead to the time when human destinies are to be determined by the uses or abuses of new sources of almost unlimited physical power, one may well ask if democracy will be able to develop the competence to deal with these complexities. If so, it must be through a broadening of education and a use of communications not yet realized, or perhaps even conceived.

I would suggest that the art of government in the near future, if it is to improve or indeed survive, must develop along one of two approaches: either through a society in which politics—the whole art of governing—is left exclusively to the wise, or through an intellectually improved democracy. A society of the wise does not need television. Democracy, I suggest, cannot do its work well without it.

Supposing that freedom is more important than safety, then the tyranny of the wise is only less objectionable than the tyranny of the unwise. The choice we face is between a despotism of the ruthlessly ambitious, not of the wise, and of an intelligent democracy. The function of television in either kind of state is sure to be of tremendous importance. But in a free society it might almost be called supreme.

In a totalitarian state the role of television will not be to teach or facilitate self-government. It must be the opposite. Its purpose must be to make the governed content not to govern themselves. It will be to distract, and indeed to entertain. I suggest that what we are now asking from television is precisely what the totalitarian dictators will order when their countries have as many television sets per capita as we have. For people whose standard of living is rising, and who do not feel that their poverty is a sacrifice they are paying for the future, will need to be distracted if they are to be ruled by a despot.

It is surely ironic that we in the United States and Britain who ask for so much entertainment from television—so much escapism—so much insulation from harsh reality—are not having such programs imposed upon us by tyrants. We have been making the choice freely. But we have made it without any awareness of the nature, intensity and inevitability of the contest between the democracies and totalitarianism. We have reached our present prosperity and seeming security without taking much heed. But now our societies must take on a new and more conscious development, and television must rise to a more constructive task. We must rid ourselves of our allergy to unpleasant and disturbing information.

I have acknowledged the natural limits to the performance of this task. I have admitted that television of itself cannot usher in the Utopia of freedom. I have ventured to suggest that the great drag on the growth of democracy is that people do not care to specialize in self-government, even if they know vaguely that the science of government never was as difficult as it is growing to be. Television is a tool that is not being used to finish the job of Education.

It is the duty of the politician to see to it that the controls imposed on television do not prevent it from being a medium where ideas may compete for the allegiance of the viewer. And it is the duty of those who control television to use it as a sound mirror to reflect conditions as they are. If what is reflected on the end of that tube is bigotry, poverty, discrimination or prejudice, that is good and wholesome so long as the picture be true. Where there is controversy it must be reflected. We have no alternative system so long as we are dedicated to the proposition that the voter in the polling booth is sovereign.

Television must find a little time to remind us of our inheritance, and it must find more than a little time for the dissenters, the heretics, the minority spokesmen who may be tomorrow's majority. . . .

Perhaps the most important thing to be said about television and politics is that the politicians, whoever they are, should not be permitted to control television. Let them use it; let them be as persuasive as they may be. But do not permit them to use this instrument to prevent today's minority from becoming tomorrow's majority. . . .

The relationship between television and the politician should be at arm's length; the eye of the camera should pursue the politician to the very limits of privacy and decency. When the politicians complain, as they have in several countries, that television turns their proceedings into a circus, it should be made clear that the circus was already there, and that television has merely demonstrated that not all the performers are well trained. In short, the politicians ought to leave television alone, but never at any time should television leave the politician alone, except when he seeks refuge in his home, or when he becomes so boring as to drive viewers back to radio or a good book.

I would suppose that the important thing for politicians and others who use television to remember is that the fact the voice and picture can be transmitted from one end of the country to the other does not confer upon the speaker greater wisdom, perception or effectiveness than was the case when his voice reached only from one end of the street to the other. This new instrument only gives wider circulation to the cry of "Hope!" or "Havoc!" It doesn't make either more imminent or more believable.

The information program can compete successfully for the listener's attention, but it must be good and it must be fair, and it must be fearless. Television won't save us, and probably it won't destroy us, but we should be mindful of Bernard Shaw's counsel: "We must get what we want, or we will come to want what we get."

It is a limited medium; it can amuse, entertain, and it can sell goods. It can also arouse curiosity, stimulate interest, cause the viewer to read and argue. It can stretch the horizon of his interest. But it can't reason—and is no substitute for reading. . . .

"The Importance of Television News" Speech, *Spiro T. Agnew, 1969*

Tonight I want to discuss the importance of the television news medium to the American people. No nation depends more on the intelligent judgment of its citizens. No medium has a more profound influence over public opinion. Nowhere in our system are there fewer checks on vast power. So, nowhere should there be more conscientious responsibility exercised than by the news media. The question is, Are we demanding enough of our television news presentations? And are the men of this medium demanding enough of themselves?

Monday night a week ago, President Nixon delivered the most important address of his Administration, one of the most important of our decade. His subject was Vietnam. His hope was to rally the American people to see the conflict through to a lasting and just peace in the Pacific. For 32 minutes, he reasoned with a nation that has suffered almost a third of a million casualties in the longest war in its history.

When the President completed his address—an address, incidentally, that he spent weeks in the preparation of—his words and policies were subjected to instant analysis and querulous criticism. The audience of 70 million Americans gathered to hear the President of the United States was inherited by a small band of network commentators and self-appointed analysts, the majority of whom expressed in one way or another their hostility to what he had to say.

It was obvious that their minds were made up in advance. Those who recall the fumbling and groping that followed President Johnson's dramatic disclosure of his intention not to seek another term have seen these men in a genuine state of nonpreparedness. This was not it.

One commentator twice contradicted the President's statement about the exchange of correspondence with Ho Chi Minh. Another challenged the President's abilities as a politician. A third asserted that the President was following a Pentagon line. Others, by the expression on their faces, the tone of their questions and the sarcasm of their responses, made clear their sharp disapproval. . . .

Now every American has a right to disagree with the President of the United States and to express publicly that disagreement. But the President of the United States has a right to communicate directly with the people who elected him, and the people of this country have the right to make up their own minds and form their own opinions about a Presidential address without having a President's words and thoughts characterized through the prejudices of hostile critics before they can even be digested.

When Winston Churchill rallied public opinion to stay the course against Hitler's Germany, he didn't have to contend with a gaggle of commentators raising doubts about whether he was reading public opinion right, or whether Britain had the stamina to see the war through.

When President Kennedy rallied the nation in the Cuban missile crisis, his address to the people was not chewed over by a roundtable of critics who disparaged the course of action he'd asked America to follow.

The purpose of my remarks tonight is to focus your attention on this little group of men who not only enjoy a right of instant rebuttal to every Presidential address, but, more importantly, wield a free hand in selecting, presenting and interpreting the great issues in our nation. . . .

According to studies, for millions of Americans the networks are the sole source of national and world news. In Will Rogers' observation, what you knew was what you read in the newspaper. Today for growing millions of Americans, it's what they see and hear on their television sets.

Now how is this network news determined? A small group of men, numbering perhaps no more than a dozen anchormen, commentators and executive producers. . . .

They decide what 40 to 50 million Americans will learn of the day's events in the nation and in the world.

We cannot measure this power and influence by the traditional democratic standards, for these men can create national issues overnight.

They can elevate men from obscurity to national prominence within a week. They can reward some politicians with national exposure and ignore others.

For millions of Americans the network reporter who covers a continuing issue—like the ABM or civil rights—becomes, in effect, the presiding judge in a national trial by jury.

It must be recognized that the networks have made important contributions to the national knowledge—for news, documentaries and specials. They have often used their power constructively and creatively to awaken the public conscience to critical problems. The networks made hunger and black lung disease national issues overnight. The TV networks have done what no other medium could have done in terms of dramatizing the horrors of war. The networks have tackled our most difficult social problems with a directness and an immediacy that's the gift of their medium. They focus the nation's attention on its environmental abuses—on pollution in the Great Lakes and the threatened ecology of the Everglades . . .

Nor is their power confined to the substantive. A raised eyebrow, an inflection of the voice, a caustic remark dropped in the middle of a broadcast can raise doubts in a million minds about the veracity of a public official or the wisdom of a Government policy.

One Federal Communications Commissioner considers the powers of the networks equal to that of local state and Federal Governments all combined. Certainly it represents a concentration of power over American public opinion unknown in history.

Now what do Americans know of the men who wield this power? Of the men who produce and direct the network news, the nation knows practically nothing. Of the commentators, most Americans know little other than that they reflect an urbane and assured presence seemingly well-informed on every important matter.

We do know that to a man these commentators and producers live and work in the geographical and intellectual confines of Washington, D.C., or New York City, the latter of which James Reston terms the most unrepresentative community in the entire United States.

Both communities bask in their own provincialism, their own parochialism.

We can deduce that these men read the same newspapers. They draw their political and social views from the same sources. Worse, they talk constantly to one another, thereby providing artificial reinforcement to their shared viewpoints.

Do they allow their biases to influence the selection and presentation of the news? David Brinkley states objectivity is impossible to normal human behavior. Rather, he says, we should strive for fairness.

Another anchorman on a network news show contends, and I quote: "You can't expunge all your private convictions just because you sit in a seat like this and a camera starts to stare at you. I think your program has to reflect what your basic feelings are. I'll plead guilty to that." . . .

The American people would rightly not tolerate this concentration of power in Government.

Is it not fair and relevant to question its concentration in the hands of a tiny, enclosed fraternity of privileged men elected by no one and enjoying a monopoly sanctioned and licensed by Government?

The views of the majority of this fraternity do not—and I repeat, not—represent the views of America.

That is why such a great gulf existed between how the nation received the President's address and how the networks reviewed it . . .

As with other American institutions, perhaps it is time that the networks were made more responsive to the views of the nation and more responsible to the people they serve.

Now I want to make myself perfectly clear. I'm not asking for Government censorship or any other kind of censorship. I'm asking whether a form of censorship already exists when the news that 40 million Americans receive each night is determined by a handful of men responsible only to their corporate employers and is filtered through a handful of commentators who admit to their own set of biases.

The questions I'm raising here tonight should have been raised by others long ago. They should have been raised by those Americans who have traditionally considered the preservation of freedom of speech and freedom of the press their special provinces of responsibility.

They should have been raised by those Americans who share the view of the late Justice Learned Hand that right conclusions are more likely to be gathered out of a multitude of tongues than through any kind of authoritative selection.

Advocates for the networks have claimed a First Amendment right to the same unlimited freedom held by the great newspapers of America.

But the situations are not identical. Where the *New York Times* reaches 800,000 people, NBC reaches twenty times that number on its evening news. Nor can the tremendous impact of seeing television film and hearing commentary be compared with reading the printed page.

A decade ago, before the network news acquired such dominance over public opinion, Walter Lippmann spoke to the issue. He said there's an essential and radical difference between television and printing. The three or four competing television stations control virtually all that can be received over the air by ordinary television sets. But besides the mass circulation dailies, there are weeklies, monthlies, out-of-town newspapers and books. If a man doesn't like his newspaper, he can read another from out of town or wait for a weekly news magazine. It's not ideal, but it's infinitely better than the situation in television.

There if a man doesn't like what the networks are showing, all he can do is turn them off and listen to a phonograph.

Now a virtual monopoly of a whole medium of communication is not something that democratic people should blindly ignore. And we are not going to cut off our television sets and listen to the phonograph just because the airways belong to the networks. They don't. They belong to the people . . . And in the networks' endless pursuit of controversy, we should ask: What is the end value—to enlighten or to profit? What is the end result—to inform or to confuse? How does the ongoing exploration for more action, more excitement, more drama serve our national search for internal peace and stability?

Gresham's Law seems to be operating in the network news. Bad news drives out good news. The irrational is more controversial than the rational. Concurrence can no longer compete with dissent . . .

The labor crisis settled at the negotiating table is nothing compared to the confrontation that results in a strike—or better yet, violence along the picket lines.

Normality has become the nemesis of the network news. Now the upshot of all this controversy is that a narrow and distorted picture of America often emerges from the televised news.

A single, dramatic piece of the mosaic becomes in the

minds of millions the entire picture. And the American who relies upon television for his news might conclude that the majority of American students are embittered radicals. That the majority of black Americans feel no regard for their country. That violence and lawlessness are the rule rather than the exception on the American campus.

We know that none of these conclusions is true.

Perhaps the place to start looking for a credibility gap is not in the offices of the Government in Washington but in the studios of the networks in New York.

Television may have destroyed the old stereotypes, but has it not created new ones in their places?

What has this passionate pursuit of controversy done to the politics of progress through local compromise essential to the functioning of a democratic society?

The members of Congress or the Senate who follow their principles and philosophy quietly in a spirit of compromise are unknown to many Americans, while the loudest and most extreme dissenters on every issue are known to every man in the street.

How many marches and demonstrations would we have if the marchers did not know that the ever-faithful TV cameras would be there to record their antics for the next news show?

We've heard demands that senators and congressmen and judges make known all their financial connections so that the public will know who and what influences their decisions and their votes. Strong arguments can be made for that view.

But when a single commentator or producer, night after night, determines for millions of people how much of each side of a great issue they are going to see and hear, should he not first disclose his personal views on the issue as well?

In this search for excitement and controversy, has more than equal time gone to the minority of Americans who specialize in attacking the United States—its institutions and its citizens?

Tonight I've raised questions. I've made no attempt to suggest the answers. The answers must come from the media men. They are challenged to turn their critical powers on themselves, to direct their energy, their talent and their conviction toward improving the quality and objectivity of news presentation.

They are challenged to structure their own civic ethics to relate their great responsibilities they hold.

And the people of America are challenged, too, challenged to press for responsible news presentations. The people can let the networks know that they want their news straight and objective. The people can register their complaints on bias through mail to the networks and phone calls to local stations. This is one case where the people must defend themselves; where the citizen, not the Government, must be the reformer; where the consumer can be the most effective crusader.

By way of conclusion, let me say that every elected leader in the United States depends on these men of the media. Whether what I've said to you tonight will be heard and seen at all by the nation is not my decision, it's not your decision, it's their decision.

In tomorrow's edition of *The Des Moines Register*, you'll be able to read a news story detailing what I've said tonight. Editorial comment will be reserved for the editorial page, where it belongs.

Should not the same wall of separation exist between news and comment on the nation's networks?

Now, my friends, we'd never trust such power, as I've described, over public opinion in the hands of an elected Government. It's time we questioned it in the hands of a small and unelected elite.

The great networks have dominated America's airwaves for decades. The people are entitled to a full accounting of their stewardship.

House Judiciary Committee Watergate Articles of Impeachment v. Richard M. Nixon, *1974*

Resolved, That Richard M. Nixon, President of the United States, is impeached for high crimes and misdemeanors, and that the following articles of impeachment be exhibited to the Senate. . . .

Article I. In his conduct of the office of President of the United States, Richard M. Nixon, in violation of his constitutional oath faithfully to execute the office of President of the United States and, to the best of his ability, preserve, protect, and defend the Constitution of the United States, and in violation of his constitutional duty to take care that the laws be faithfully executed, has prevented, obstructed, and impeded the administration of justice, in that:

On June 17, 1972, and prior thereto, agents of the Committee for the Re-election of the President committed unlawful entry of the headquarters of the Democratic National Committee in Washington, District of Columbia, for the purpose of securing political intelligence. Subsequent thereto, Richard M. Nixon, using the powers of his high office, engaged personally and through his subordinates and agents, in a course of conduct or plan designed to delay, impede, and obstruct the investigation of such unlawful entry; to cover up, conceal and protect those responsible; and to conceal the existence and scope of other unlawful covert activities.

The means used to implement this course of conduct or plan included one or more of the following:

(1) making or causing to be made false or misleading statements to lawfully authorized investigative officers and employees of the United States;

(2) withholding relevant and material evidence or information from lawfully authorized investigative officers and employees of the United States;

(3) approving, condoning, acquiescing in, and counseling witnesses with respect to the giving of false or misleading statements to lawfully authorized investigative officers and employees of the United States and false or misleading testimony in duly instituted judicial and congressional proceedings;

(4) interfering or endeavoring to interfere with the conduct of investigations by the Department of Justice of the United States, the Federal Bureau of Investigation, the Office of Watergate Special Prosecution Force, and Congressional Committees;

(5) approving, condoning, and acquiescing in, the surreptitious payment of substantial sums of

money for the purpose of obtaining the silence or influencing the testimony of witnesses, potential witnesses or individuals who participated in such unlawful entry and other illegal activities;

(6) endeavoring to misuse the Central Intelligence Agency, an agency of the United States;

(7) disseminating information received from officers of the Department of Justice of the United States to subjects of investigations conducted by lawfully authorized investigative officers and employees of the United States, for the purpose of aiding and assisting such subjects in their attempts to avoid criminal liability;

(8) making false or misleading public statements for the purpose of deceiving the people of the United States into believing that a thorough and complete investigation had been conducted with respect to allegations of misconduct on the part of personnel of the executive branch of the United States and personnel of the Committee for the Re-election of the President, and that there was no involvement of such personnel in such misconduct; or

(9) endeavoring to cause prospective defendants, and individuals duly tried and convicted, to expect favored treatment and consideration in return for their silence or false testimony, or rewarding individuals for their silence or false testimony.

In all of this, Richard M. Nixon has acted in a manner contrary to his trust as President and subversive of constitutional government, to the great prejudice of the cause of law and justice and to the manifest injury of the people of the United States.

Wherefore Richard M. Nixon, by such conduct, warrants impeachment and trial, and removal from office.

Article II. Using the powers of the office of President of the United States, Richard M. Nixon . . . has repeatedly engaged in conduct violating the constitutional rights of citizens, impairing the due and proper administration of justice and the conduct of lawful inquiries, or contravening the laws governing agencies of the executive branch and the purposes of these agencies.

This conduct has included one or more of the following:

(1) He has, acting personally and through his subordinates and agents, endeavored to obtain from the Internal Revenue Service, in violation of the constitutional rights of citizens, confidential information contained in income tax returns for purposes not authorized by law, and to cause, in violation of the constitutional rights of citizens, income tax audits or other income tax investigations to be initiated or conducted in a discriminatory manner.

(2) He misused the Federal Bureau of Investigation, the Secret Service, and other executive personnel, in violation or disregard of the constitutional rights of citizens, by directing or authorizing such agencies or personnel to conduct or continue electronic surveillance or other investigations for purposes unrelated to national security, the enforcement of laws, or any other lawful function of his office; he did direct, authorize, or permit the use of information obtained thereby for purposes unrelated to national security, the enforcement of laws, or any other lawful function of his office; and he did direct the concealment of certain records made by the Federal Bureau of Investigation of electronic surveillance.

(3) He has, acting personally and through his subordinates and agents, in violation or disregard of the constitutional rights of citizens, authorized and permitted to be maintained a secret investigative unit within the office of the President, financed in part with money derived from campaign contributions, which unlawfully utilized the resources of the Central Intelligence Agency, engaged in covert and unlawful activities, and attempted to prejudice the constitutional right of an accused to a fair trial.

(4) He has failed to take care that the laws were faithfully executed by failing to act when he knew

or had reason to know that his close subordinates endeavored to impede and frustrate lawful inquiries by duly constituted executive, judicial, and legislative entities concerning the unlawful entry into the headquarters of the Democratic National Committee, and the cover-up thereof, and concerning other unlawful activities, including those relating to the confirmation of Richard Kleindienst as Attorney General of the United States, the electronic surveillance of private citizens, the break-in into the offices of Dr. Lewis Fielding, and the campaign financing practices of the Committee to Re-elect the President.

(5) In disregard of the rule of law, he knowingly misused the executive power by interfering with agencies of the executive branch, including the Federal Bureau of Investigation, the Criminal Division, and the Office of Watergate Special Prosecution Force, of the Department of Justice, and the Central Intelligence Agency, in violation of his duty to take care that the laws be faithfully executed.

In all of this, Richard M. Nixon has acted in a manner contrary to his trust as President and subversive of constitutional government, to the great prejudice of the cause of law and justice and to the manifest injury of the people of the United States.

Wherefore Richard M. Nixon, by such conduct, warrants impeachment and trial, and removal from office.

Article III. In his conduct of the office of President of the United States, Richard M. Nixon, contrary to his oath faithfully to execute the office of President of the United States . . . has failed without lawful cause or excuse to produce papers and things as directed by duly authorized subpoenas issued by the Committee on the Judiciary of the House of Representatives on April 11, 1974, May 15, 1974, May 30, 1974, and June 24, 1974, and willfully disobeying such subpoenas. The subpoenaed papers and things were deemed necessary by the Committee in order to resolve by direct evidence fundamental, factual questions relating to Presidential direction, knowledge, or approval of actions demonstrated by other evidence to be substantial grounds for impeachment of the President. In refusing to produce these papers and things, Richard M. Nixon, substituting his judgment as to what materials were necessary for the inquiry, interposed the powers of the Presidency against the lawful subpoenas of the House of Representatives, thereby assuming to himself functions and judgments necessary to the exercise of the sole power of impeachment vested by the Constitution in the House of Representatives.

In all of this, Richard M. Nixon has acted in a manner contrary to his trust as President and subversive of constitutional government, to the great prejudice of the cause of law and justice, and to the manifest injury of the people of the United States.

Wherefore Richard M. Nixon, by such conduct, warrants impeachment and trial and removal from office.

Gerald R. Ford's Inaugural Address, *1974*

Mr. Chief Justice, my dear friends, my fellow Americans: The oath that I have taken is the same oath that was taken by George Washington and by every President under the Constitution.

But I assume the Presidency under extraordinary circumstances never before experienced by Americans. This is an hour of history that troubles our minds and hurts our hearts.

Therefore, I feel it is my first duty to make an unprecedented compact with my countrymen. Not an inaugural address, not a fireside chat, not a campaign speech, just a little straight talk among friends. And I intend it to be the first of many.

I am acutely aware that you have not elected me as your President by your ballots. So I ask you to confirm me as your President with your prayers. And I hope that such prayers will also be the first of many.

If you have not chosen me by secret ballot, neither have I gained office by any secret promises. I have not campaigned either for the Presidency or the Vice Presidency. I have not subscribed to any partisan platform.

I am indebted to no man and only to one woman, my dear wife.

As I begin this very difficult job, I have not sought this enormous responsibility, but I will not shirk it. Those who nominated and confirmed me as Vice President were my friends and are my friends. They were of both parties, elected by all the people and acting under the Constitution in their name.

It is only fitting then that I should pledge to them and to you that I will be the President of all the people.

Thomas Jefferson said the people are the only sure reliance for the preservation of our liberty. And down the years, Abraham Lincoln renewed this American article of faith asking is there any better way for equal hopes in the world.

I intend on next Monday to request of the Speaker of the House of Representatives and the President pro tempore of the Senate the privilege of appearing before the Congress to share with my former colleagues and with you, the American people, my views on the priority business of the nation and to solicit your views and their views.

And may I say to the Speaker and the others, if I could meet with you right after this—these remarks—I would appreciate it.

Even though this is late in an election year there is no way we can go forward except together and no way anybody can win except by serving the people's urgent needs.

We cannot stand still or slip backward. We must go forward now together.

To the peoples and the governments of all friendly nations, and I hope that could encompass the whole world, I pledge an uninterrupted and sincere search for peace. America will remain strong and united.

But its strength will remain dedicated to the safety and sanity of the entire family of man as well as to our own precious freedom.

I believe that truth is the glue that holds governments together, not only our government but civilization itself. That bond, though strained, is unbroken at home and abroad.

In all my public and private acts as your President, I

expect to follow my instincts of openness and candor with full confidence that honesty is always the best policy in the end.

My fellow Americans, our long national nightmare is over. Our Constitution works. Our great republic is a government of laws and not of men. Here, the people rule.

But there is a higher power, by whatever name we honor Him, who ordains not only righteousness but love, not only justice but mercy.

As we bind up the internal wounds of Watergate, more painful and more poisonous than those of foreign wars, let us restore the golden rule to our political process. And let brotherly love purge our hearts of suspicion and of hate.

In the beginning, I asked you to pray for me. Before closing, I ask again your prayers for Richard Nixon and for his family. May our former President who brought peace to millions find it for himself.

May God bless and comfort his wonderful wife and daughters whose love and loyalty will forever be a shining legacy to all who bear the lonely burden of the White House.

I can only guess at those burdens although I witnessed at close hand the tragedies that befell three Presidents and the lesser trials of others.

With all the strength and all the good sense I have gained from life, with all the confidence my family, my friends, and dedicated staff impart to me, and with the goodwill of countless Americans I have encountered in recent visits to forty states, I now solemnly reaffirm my promise I made to you last December 6 to uphold the Constitution, to do what is right as God gives me to see the right, and to do the very best I can for America.

God helping me, I will not let you down.

Thank you.

Potter Stewart, Associate Justice of the Supreme Court, on Freedom of the Press, Yale Law School, *1974*

. . . It was less than a decade ago—during the Vietnam years—that the people of our country began to become aware of the twin phenomena on a national scale of so-called investigative reporting and an adversary press—that is, a press adversary to the Executive Branch of the Federal Government. And only in the two short years that culminated last summer in the resignation of a President did we fully realize the enormous power that an investigative and adversary press can exert.

The public opinion polls that I have seen indicate that some Americans firmly believe that the former Vice President and former President of the United States were hounded out of office by an arrogant and irresponsible press that had outrageously usurped dictatorial power. And it seems clear that many more Americans, while appreciating and even applauding the service performed by the press in exposing official wrongdoing at the highest levels of our national government, are nonetheless deeply disturbed by what they consider to be the illegitimate power of the organized press in the political structure of our society. It is my thesis . . . that, on the contrary, the established American press in the past ten years, and particularly in the past two years, has performed precisely the function it was intended to perform by those who wrote the First Amendment of our Constitution.

Surprisingly, despite the importance of newspapers in the political and social life of our country the Supreme Court has not until very recently been called upon to delineate their constitutional role in our structure of government.

Our history is filled with struggles over the rights and prerogatives of the press, but these disputes rarely found their way to the Supreme Court. The early years of the Republic witnessed controversy over the constitutional validity of the short-lived Alien and Sedition Act, but the controversy never reached the Court. In the next half century there was nationwide turmoil over the right of the organized press to advocate the then subversive view that slavery should be abolished. In Illinois a publisher was killed for publishing abolitionist views. But none of this history made First Amendment law because the Court had earlier held that the Bill of Rights applied only against the Federal Government, not against the individual states. With the passage of the Fourteenth Amendment, the constitutional framework has modified, and by the 1920's the Court had established that the protections of the First Amendment extend against all government—federal, state, and local.

The next fifty years witnessed a great outpouring of First Amendment litigation, all of which inspired books and articles beyond number. But, with few exceptions, neither these First Amendment cases nor their commentators squarely considered the Constitution's guarantee of a Free Press. Instead, the focus was on its guarantee of free speech. The Court's decisions dealt with the rights of isolated individuals, or of unpopular minority groups, to stand up against government power representing an angry or frightened majority. The cases that came to the Court during those years involved the rights of the soapbox orator, the nonconformist pamphleteer, the religious evangelist. The Court was seldom asked to define the rights and privileges, or the responsibilities, of the organized press.

In very recent years cases involving the established press finally have begun to reach the Supreme Court, and they have presented a variety of problems, sometimes arising in complicated factual settings.

In a series of cases, the Court has been called upon to consider the limits imposed by the free press guarantee upon a state's common or statutory law of libel. As a result of those cases, a public figure cannot successfully sue a publisher for libel unless he can show that the publisher maliciously printed a damaging untruth.

The Court has also been called upon to decide whether a newspaper reporter has a First Amendment privilege to refuse to disclose his confidential sources to a grand jury. By a divided vote, the Court found no such privilege to exist in the circumstances of the cases before it.

In another noteworthy case, the Court was asked by the Justice Department to restrain publication by the

New York Times and other newspapers of the so-called Pentagon Papers. The Court declined to do so.

In yet another case, the question to be decided was whether political groups have a First Amendment or statutory right of access to the federally regulated broadcast channels of radio and television. The Court held there was no such right of access.

Last term the Court confronted a Florida statute that required newspapers to grant a "right to reply" to political candidates they had criticized. The Court unanimously held this statute to be inconsistent with the guarantees of a free press.

It seems to me that the Court's approach to all these cases has uniformly reflected its understanding that the Free Press guarantee is, in essence, a *structural* provision of the Constitution. Most of the other provisions in the Bill of Rights protect specific liberties or specific rights of individuals; freedom of speech, freedom of worship, the right to counsel, the privilege against compulsory self-incrimination, to name a few. In contrast, the Free Press Clause extends protection to an institution. The publishing business is, in short, the only organized private business that is given explicit constitutional protection.

This basic understanding is essential, I think, to avoid an elementary error of constitutional law. It is tempting to suggest that freedom of the press means only that newspaper publishers are guaranteed freedom of expression. They *are* guaranteed that freedom, to be sure, but so are we all, because of the Free Speech Clause. If the Free Press guarantee meant no more than freedom of expression, it would be a constitutional redundancy. Between 1776 and the drafting of our Constitution, many of the state constitutions contained clauses protecting freedom of the press while at the same time recognizing no general freedom of speech. By including both guarantees in the First Amendment, the Founders quite clearly recognized the distinction between the two.

It is also a mistake to suppose that the only purpose of the constitutional guarantee of a free press is to insure that a newspaper will serve as a neutral forum for debate, a "marketplace for ideas," a kind of Hyde Park corner for the community. A related theory sees the press as a neutral conduit of information between the people and their elected leaders. These theories, in my view, again give insufficient weight to the institutional autonomy of the press that it was the purpose of the Constitution to guarantee.

In setting up the three branches of the Federal Government, the Founders deliberately created an internally competitive system. As Mr. Justice Brandeis once wrote:

> The [Founders'] purpose was, not to avoid friction, but, by means of the inevitable friction incident to the distribution of the governmental powers among three departments, to save the people from autocracy.

The primary purpose of the constitutional guarantee of a free press was a similar one: to create a fourth institution outside the Government as an additional check on the three official branches. Consider the opening words of the Free Press Clause of the Massachusetts Constitution, drafted by John Adams:

> The liberty of the press is essential to the security of the state.

The relevant metaphor, I think, is the metaphor of the Fourth Estate. What Thomas Carlyle wrote about the British Government a century ago has a curiously contemporary ring:

> Burke said there were Three Estates in Parliament; but, in the Reporters' Gallery yonder, there sat a Fourth Estate more important far than they all. It is not a figure of speech or witty saying; it is a literal fact—very momentous to us in these times.

For centuries before our Revolution, the press in England had been licensed, censored, and bedeviled by prosecutions for seditious libel. The British Crown knew that a free press was not just a neutral vehicle for the balanced discussion of diverse ideas. Instead, the free press meant organized, expert scrutiny of government. The press was a conspiracy of the intellect, with the courage of numbers. This formidable check on official power was what the British Crown had feared—and what the American Founders decided to risk.

It is the constitutional understanding, I think, that provides the unifying principle underlying the Supreme Court's recent decisions dealing with the organized press.

Consider first the libel cases. Officials within the three governmental branches are, for all practical purposes, immune from libel and slander suits for statements that they make in the line of duty. This immunity, which has both constitutional and common law origins, aims to insure bold and vigorous prosecution of the public's business. The same basic reasoning applies to the press. By contrast, the Court has never suggested that the constitutional right of free *speech* gives an *individual* any immunity from liability for either libel or slander.

In the cases involving the newspaper reporters' claims that they had a constitutional privilege not to disclose their confidential news sources to a grand jury, the Court rejected the claims by a vote of five to four, or, considering Mr. Justice Powell's concurring opinion, perhaps by a vote of four and a half to four and a half. But if freedom of the press means simply freedom of speech for reporters, this question of a reporter's asserted right to withhold information would have answered itself. None of us—as individuals—has a "free speech" right to refuse to tell a grand jury the identity of someone who has given us information relevant to the grand jury's legitimate inquiry. Only if a reporter is a representative of a protected *institution* does the question become a different one. The members of the Court disagreed in answering the question, but the question did not answer itself.

The cases involving the so-called "right to access" to the press raised the issue whether the First Amendment allows government, or indeed *requires* government, to regulate the press so as to make it a genuinely fair and open "marketplace for ideas." The Court's answer was "no" to both questions. If a newspaper wants to serve as a neutral marketplace for debate, that is an objective which it is free to choose and, within limits, that choice is probably necessary to commercially successful journalism. But it is a choice that government cannot constitutionally impose.

Finally the Pentagon Papers case involved the line between secrecy and openness in the affairs of Government. The question, or at least one question, was whether that line is drawn by the Constitution itself. The Justice Department asked the Court to find in the Constitution a basis for prohibiting the publication of allegedly stolen government documents. The Court could find no such prohibition. So far as the Constitution goes, the autonomous press may publish what it knows, and may seek to learn what it can.

But this autonomy cuts both ways. The press is free to do battle against secrecy and deception in government, but the press cannot expect from the Constitution any guarantee that it will succeed. There is no constitutional right to have access to particular government information, or to require openness from the bureaucracy. The public's interest is knowing about its government is protected by the guarantee of a Free Press, but the protection is indirect. The Constitution itself is neither a Freedom of Information Act nor an Official Secrets Act.

The Constitution, in other words, establishes the contest, not its resolution. Congress may provide a resolution, at least in some instances, through carefully drawn legislation. For the rest, we must rely, as so often in our system we must, on the tug and pull of the political forces in American society.

Newspapers, television networks, and magazines have sometimes been outrageously abusive, untruthful, arrogant, and hypocritical. But it hardly follows that elimination of a strong and independent press is the way to eliminate abusiveness, untruth, arrogance, or hypocrisy from government itself.

It is quite possible to conceive of the survival of our Republic without an autonomous press. For openness and honesty in government, for an adequate flow of information between the people and their representatives, for a sufficient check on autocracy and despotism, the traditional competition between the three branches of government, supplemented by vigorous political activity, might be enough.

The press could be relegated to the status of public utility. The guarantee of free speech would presumably put some limitation on the regulation to which the press could be subjected. But if there were no guarantee of a free press, government could convert the communications media into a neutral "marketplace of ideas." Newspapers and television networks could then be required to promote contemporary government policy or current notions of social justice.

Such a constitution is possible; it might work reasonably well. But it is not the Constitution the Founders wrote. It is not the Constitution that has carried us through nearly two centuries of national life. Perhaps our liberties might survive without an independent established press. But the Founders doubted it, and, in the year 1974, I think we can all be thankful for their doubts.

Chapter 29

CONSERVATISM REVISITED

Televised presidential debates—literally the first since John F. Kennedy and Richard M. Nixon initiated such electronic face-to-face campaign confrontations in 1960—helped Georgia's former Democratic Governor Jimmy Carter defeat Gerald Ford in 1976. So did support drawn from loyal Southerners and from the vestiges of old-time New Deal strength in organized labor, with liberal groups, and among minorities. So did the peanut farmer's plainspoken, born-again-Christian appeal to Americans' moral concerns, as well as his campaign against "big government" bureaucracy, which pictured the Georgian as an "outsider" to the traditional Washington political establishment and promised simplicities as well as pieties in the conduct of American government. These were conservative themes that would be used against Jimmy Carter himself four years later, however. For as President he found it impossible to disengage even his own Administration from the harsh realities that continued unremittingly to obtrude upon the nation. Inflation, unemployment, large budget deficits, a disintegrating urban infrastructure, racial and other minority unrest, a devastating "energy crisis," and the rapid pollution of our environment were among the whole host of domestic problems whose surfacing at the time made the Carter years seem grim, indeed, unfairly identifying the serious and deeply concerned Chief Executive as a prophet of doom and the harbinger of American decline.

Nor, with one major exception, were there significant Carter successes abroad, either. Innocently, perhaps, the President had hoped that his own desire for principled and reasonable negotiations with the Soviets, in Central America, with developing nations generally, as well as in the quagmire of Middle East oil-and-power politics would result in a more harmonious international setting for his pursuit of human rights, of disarmament and of world peace. That was not to be. He had pledged in his Inaugural Address "to move toward our ultimate goal—the elimination of nuclear weapons from this earth." But progress along these lines was stalled in the Soviet Union and even in a Congress that failed to ratify a second Strategic Arms Limitations Treaty (SALT II) despite his plea that "Between nations armed with thousands of thermonuclear weapons, each one more capable of causing unimaginable destruction, there can be no more cycles of war and peace. There can only be peace."

But there was no peace when the Soviets brutally invaded Afghanistan, no succor anywhere for Jimmy Carter's personal crusade for human rights. The American President had, in fact, electrified the world for a moment with the success of his shrewd negotiation of the 1978 "Camp David Accords," which brought Egypt and Israel together for a major first step toward what might eventually be peace in the Middle East. Yet it was in that very troubled area of the world that Carter's own political fate was sealed when in 1979 the fanatical followers of the Ayatollah Khomeini stormed our Embassy in Tehran, Iran, seizing dozens of Americans and holding them hostage, to the despair of a helpless American President until the very day he left office.

Jimmy Carter's—and America's—frustration in Iran

and elsewhere around the world, along with a troubled economy, helped Republican Ronald Reagan defeat the Democratic candidate for re-election in 1980. So, too, did presidential debates staged essentially for television once again perceptibly harm an incumbent and help his challenger. Mostly, however, the former liberal movie actor turned conservative Governor of California was able to draw upon the same nostalgic yearnings for "the way we were" that had helped Carter win the Presidency earlier. Now it was Ronald Reagan's turn to "run against Washington," to reject "big government" with its giant deficits and its seemingly unending array of intractable problems and impossible challenges to a public that so much longed instead for older, simpler times.

Warm and friendly, a superb communicator who had thoroughly mastered teleprompter television, America's new medium of choice, capable so often of touching those "mystic chords of memory" that bind Americans together through their past, Reagan's appeal was to the older virtues of religion, patriotism, family, home, and hearth. He played brilliantly upon the nation's conservative reaction against a seemingly never-ending revolt in manners and morals. Though himself our first divorced President, he drew heavily upon Fundamentalists' deep concern that our moral fiber had been profoundly weakened by an astonishingly high divorce rate growing ever higher; by "humanism," but not prayer, in the schools; by permissiveness in most aspects of American life, perhaps nowhere better symbolized than by the 1973 Roe v. Wade decision in which the Supreme Court essentially legalized abortion, valuing Americans' privacy and free choice more than the "pro-life" moralism that Ronald Reagan would come ever more forcefully to advocate from the White House itself. Politically, the President benefited hugely from this rather intense backlash against modernism; unquestionably, in turn his rhetoric greatly emboldened the nation's moral crusaders, and religion began to loom so large in American political life, as a so-called "Moral Majority" attacked liberal causes and candidates, that even such a staunch Senate Republican conservative as Barry Goldwater of Arizona felt constrained to warn the single-issue religious "New Right" that it "could tear apart the very spirit of our representative system."

Yet, for most Americans the Reagan years seemed far more unifying than divisive. He was blamed for little, praised for much. And his landslide 1984 re-election—despite enthusiastic praise for New York Governor Mario Cuomo's brilliantly partisan Democratic Party "A Tale of Two Cities" rallying cry against the president, despite the Democrats' bold selection of Geraldine Ferraro as Presidential candidate Walter Mondale's running mate, and despite seemingly widespread opposition to first his covert, but then his open warlike actions against unfriendly forces in Central America—demonstrated once again not only the nation's affectionate regard for its elderly but still physically vigorous leader, but also his extraordinary ability to avoid personal responsibility for the contradictions of his Administration. Americans applauded his fervent calls for a balanced budget, but ignored his ever larger deficits. They welcomed his suggested "safety net" for the nation's needy, but protested little when he drew it ever tighter. They delighted in his dramatic and evocative words about America the strong and the proud, but never really questioned him when enemies terrorized America's outposts and massacred its Marines. They embraced his view of Russia as an "empire of evil," but accepted his trading with the Soviets, as well. They credited his innovative "Star Wars" plan as a bold, high-tech defense against nuclear war, but largely ignored its potential for escalating further the East-West race in offensive weaponry. All, perhaps, because like the buoyant, optimistic President himself, Americans wanted so much just to enjoy the material well-being most of them shared, looking to a better future without duly noting its complications, a people once again considerably more at ease with the comforts of conservatism than the challenges of liberalism. Indeed, in 1981 and again in 1985, Ronald Reagan's Inaugural words spoke boldly of the future, but their feelings were of America's past . . . appropriate for a nation about to celebrate the 200th anniversary of its still-superb instrument of governance, the Constitution of the United States. Then in 1988 his Vice President, George Bush, won the White House too, waging a particularly nasty and divisive campaign against Democrat

Michael Dukakis, all the while promising "a kinder, gentler America." Near revolutionary turmoil in Eastern Europe and in the now-divided, former Soviet Union itself did much to reduce the decades-long conflict between East and West; but by 1990 tensions in the Middle East and the Balkans threatened the world with armed conflict once again. Iraqi aggression against Kuwait resulted in a Gulf war from which an international coalition, boldly and skillfully led by President Bush, seemingly emerged triumphant, though with peace in the region remaining as elusive as ever.

Roe v. Wade, Abortion Decision: Associate Justice Harry A. Blackmun for the Supreme Court, *1973*

We forthwith acknowledge our awareness of the sensitive and emotional nature of the abortion controversy, of the vigorous opposing views, even among physicians, and of the deep and seemingly absolute convictions that the subject inspires. One's philosophy, one's experiences, one's exposure to the raw edges of human existence, one's religious training, one's attitudes toward life and family and their values, and the moral standards one establishes and seeks to observe, are all likely to influence and to color one's thinking and conclusions about abortion.

In addition, population growth, pollution, poverty, and racial overtones tend to complicate and not to simplify the problem.

Our task, of course, is to resolve the issue by constitutional measurement, free of emotion and of predilection. We seek earnestly to do this, and, because we do, we have inquired into, and in this opinion place some emphasis upon, medical and medical-legal history and what that history reveals about man's attitudes toward the abortion procedure over the centuries. We bear in mind, too, Mr. Justice Holmes' admonition in his now-vindicated dissent in *Lochner* v. *New York:*

> "[The Constitution] is made for people of fundamentally differing views, and the accident of

our finding certain opinions natural and familiar or novel and even shocking ought not to conclude our judgment upon the question whether statutes embodying them conflict with the Constitution of the United States." . . .

Jane Roe, a single woman who was residing in Dallas County, Texas, instituted this federal action in March 1970 against the District Attorney of the county. She sought a declaratory judgment that the Texas criminal abortion statutes were unconstitutional on their face, and an injunction restraining the defendant from enforcing the statutes.

Roe alleged that she was unmarried and pregnant; that she wished to terminate her pregnancy by an abortion "performed by a competent, licensed physician, under safe, clinical conditions"; that she was unable to get a "legal" abortion in Texas because her life did not appear to be threatened by the continuation of her pregnancy; and that she could not afford to travel to another jurisdiction in order to secure a legal abortion under safe conditions. She claimed that the Texas statutes were unconstitutionally vague and that they abrided her right of personal privacy, protected by the First, Fourth, Fifth, Ninth, and Fourteenth Amendments. By an amendment to her complaint Roe purported to sue "on behalf of herself and all other women" similarly situated. . . .

The principal thrust of appellant's attack on the Texas statutes is that they improperly invade a right, said to be possessed by the pregnant woman, to choose to terminate her pregnancy. Appellant would discover this right in the concept of personal "liberty" embodied in the Fourteenth Amendment's Due Process Clause; or in personal, marital, familial, and sexual privacy said to be protected by the Bill of Rights or its penumbras . . .

It perhaps is not generally appreciated that the restrictive criminal abortion laws in effect in a majority of States today are of relatively recent vintage. Those laws, generally proscribing abortion or its attempt at any time during pregnancy except when necessary to preserve the pregnant woman's life, are not of ancient or even of common-law origin. Instead, they derive from statutory changes effected, for the most part, in the latter half of the 19th century. . . .

It is thus apparent that in common law, at the time of the adoption of our Constitution, and throughout the major portion of the 19th century, abortion was viewed with less disfavor than under most American statutes currently in effect. Phrasing it another way, a woman enjoyed a substantially broader right to terminate a pregnancy than she does in most States today. At least with respect to the early stage of pregnancy, and very possibly without such a limitation, the opportunity to make this choice was present in this country well into the 19th century. Even later, the law continued for some time to treat less punitively an abortion procured in early pregnancy. . . .

The Constitution does not explicitly mention any right of privacy. In a line of decisions, however, going back perhaps as far as *Union Pacific R. Co.* v. *Botsford* (1891), the Court has recognized that a right of personal privacy, or a guarantee of certain areas or zones of privacy, does exist under the Constitution. In varying contexts, the Court or individual Justices have, indeed, found at least the roots of that right in the First Amendment; in the Fourth and Fifth Amendments; in the penumbras of the Bill of Rights; in the Ninth Amendment; or in the concept of liberty guaranteed by the first section of the Fourteenth Amendment. These decisions make it clear that only personal rights that can be deemed "fundamental" or "implicit in the concept of ordered liberty," are included in this guarantee of personal privacy. They also make it clear that the right has some extension to activities relating to marriage; procreation; contraception; family relationships; and child rearing and education.

This right of privacy, whether it be founded in the Fourteenth Amendment's concept of personal liberty and restrictions upon state action, as we feel it is, or, as the District Court determined, in the Ninth Amendment's reservation of rights to the people, is broad enough to encompass a woman's decision whether or not to terminate her pregnancy. The detriment that the State would impose upon the pregnant woman by denying this choice altogether is apparent. Specific and direct harm medically diagnosable even in early pregnancy may be involved. Maternity, or additional offspring, may force upon the woman a distressful life and future. Psychological harm may be imminent. Mental and physical health may be taxed by child care. There is also the distress, for all concerned, associated with the unwanted child, and there is the problem of bringing a child into a family already unable, psychologically and otherwise, to care for it. In other cases, as in this one, the additional difficulties and continuing stigma of unwed motherhood may be involved. All these factors the woman and her responsible physician necessarily will consider in consultation.

On the basis of elements such as these, appellant and some *amici* argue that the woman's right is absolute and that she is entitled to terminate her pregnancy at whatever time, in whatever way, and for whatever reason she alone chooses. With this we do not agree. Appellant's arguments that Texas either has no valid interest strong enough to support any limitation upon the woman's sole determination, is unpersuasive. The Court's decisions recognizing a right of privacy also acknowledge that some state regulation in areas protected by that right is appropriate. As noted above, a State may properly assert important interests in safeguarding health, in maintaining medical standards, and in protecting potential life. At some point in pregnancy, these respective interests become sufficiently compelling to sustain regulation of the factors that govern the abortion decision. The privacy right involved, therefore, cannot be said to be absolute. In fact, it is not clear to us that the claim asserted by some *amici* that one has an unlimited right to do with one's body as one pleases bears a close relationship to the right of privacy previously articulated in the Court's decisions. The Court has refused to recognize an unlimited right of this kind in the past.

We, therefore, conclude that the right of personal privacy includes the abortion decision, but that this right is not unqualified and must be considered against important state interests in regulation.

We note that those federal and state courts that have recently considered abortion law challenges have reached the same conclusion.

Although the results are divided, most of these courts have agreed that the right of privacy, however based, is broad enough to cover the abortion decisions; that the right, nonetheless, is not absolute and is subject to some limitations; and that at some point the state interests as to protection of health, medical standards, and prenatal life, become dominant. We agree with this approach. . . .

The appellee and certain *amici* argue that the fetus is a "person" within the language and meaning of the Fourteenth Amendment. In support of this, they outline at length and in detail the well-known facts of fetal development. If this suggestion of personhood is established, the appellant's case, of course, collapses, for the fetus' right to life is then guaranteed specifically by the amendment. The appellant conceded as much on reargument. On the other hand, the appellee conceded on reargument that no case could be cited that holds that a fetus is a person within the meaning of the Fourteenth Amendment.

The Constitution does not define "person" in so many words. The use of the word is such that it has application only postnatally. None indicates, with any assurance, that it has any possible prenatal application.

All this, together with our observation, *supra,* that throughout the major portion of the 19th century prevailing legal abortion practices were far freer than they are today, persuades us that the word "person," as used in the Fourteenth Amendment, does not include the unborn. . . .

Texas urges that, apart from the Fourteenth Amendment, life begins at conception and is present throughout pregnancy, and that, therefore, the State has a compelling interest in protecting that life from and after conception. We need not resolve the difficult question of when life begins. When those trained in the respective disciplines of medicine, philosophy, and theology are unable to arrive at any consensus, the judiciary, at this point in the development of man's knowledge, is not in a position to speculate as to the answer. . . .

In areas other than criminal abortion, the law has been reluctant to endorse any theory that life, as we recognize it, begins before live birth or to accord legal rights to the unborn except in narrowly defined situations and except when the rights are continent upon live birth. . . . In short, the unborn have never been recognized in the law as persons in the whole sense.

In view of all this, we do not agree that, by adopting one theory of life, Texas may override the rights of the pregnant woman that are at stake. We repeat, however, that the State does have an important and legitimate interest in preserving and protecting the health of the pregnant woman. . . .

With respect to the State's important and legitimate interest in the health of the mother, the "compelling" point, in the light of present medical knowledge, is at approximately the end of the first trimester. This is so because of the now-established medical fact, that until the end of the first trimester mortality in abortion may be less than mortality in normal childbirth. It follows that, from and after this point, a State may regulate the abortion procedure to the extent that the regulation reasonably relates to the preservation and protection of maternal health. Examples of permissible state regulation in this area are requirements as to the qualifications of the person who is to perform the abortion; as to the licensure of that person; as to the facility in which the procedure is to be performed, that is, whether it must be a hospital or may be a clinic or some other place of less-than-hospital status; as to the licensing of the facility; and the like. . . .

With respect to the State's important and legitimate interest in potential life, the "compelling" point is at viability. This is so because the fetus then presumably has the capability of meaningful life outside the mother's womb. State regulation protective of fetal life after viability thus has both logical and biological justifications. If the State is interested in protecting fetal life after viability, it may go so far as to proscribe abortion during that period, except when it is necessary to preserve the life or health of the mother.

Measured against these standards, Art. 1196 of the Texas Penal Code, in restricting legal abortions to those "procured or attempted by medical advice for the purpose of saving the life of the mother," sweeps too broadly. The statute makes no distinction between abortions performed early in pregnancy and those performed later, and its limits to a single reason, "saving" the mother's life, the legal justification for the procedure. The statute, therefore, cannot survive the constitutional attack made upon it here.

Senator Barry Goldwater on Conservatism, Religion, and Politics, *1981*

It's a wonderful feeling to be a conservative these days. When I ran for President 17 years ago I was told I was behind the times. Now everybody tells me I was ahead of my time. All I can say is that time certainly is an elusive companion.

But those reactions illustrate how far the ideological pendulum has swung in recent years. The American people have expressed their desire for a new course in our public policy in this country, a conservative course.

Being a conservative in America traditionally has meant that one holds a deep, abiding respect for the Constitution. We conservatives believe sincerely in the integrity of the Constitution. We treasure the freedoms that document protects.

We believe, as the founding fathers did, that we "are endowed by our Creator with certain unalienable rights; that among these are life, liberty and the pursuit of happiness."

And for 205 years this nation, based on those principles, has endured. Through foreign wars and civil wars, through political scandals and economic disasters, through civil disorders and Presidential assassinations, our flag has flown high. Through it all we've survived every possible attack on our freedom.

But another force could succeed in dividing our country. The specter of single-issue religious groups is growing over our land.

One of the great strengths of our political system always has been our tendency to keep religious issues in the background. By maintaining the separation of church and state, the United States has avoided the intolerance which has so divided the rest of the world with religious wars.

Throughout our 200-plus years, public policy debate has focused on political and economic issues, on which there can be compromise.

Madison saw this as the great paradox of our system: How do you control the factions without violating the people's basic freedoms?

And in a well-constructed representative Government like ours, Madison said, one of our greatest strengths is our ability to "break and control the violence of faction."

Can any of us refute the wisdom of Madison and the other framers? Can anyone look at the carnage in Iran, the bloodshed in Northern Ireland or the bombs bursting in Lebanon and yet question the dangers of injecting religious issues into the affairs of state?

There is no position on which people are so immovable as their religious beliefs. There is no more powerful ally one can claim in a debate than Jesus Christ, or God, or Allah or whatever one calls his Supreme Being.

But, like any powerful weapons, the use of God's name on one's behalf should be used sparingly.

The religious factions that are growing in our land are not using their religious clout with wisdom. They are trying to force government leaders into following their positions 100 percent.

In the past couple of years, I have seen many news items that referred to the Moral Majority, pro-life and other religious groups as "the new right," and the "new conservatism." Well, I have spent quite a number of years carrying the flag of the "old conservatism." And I can say with conviction that the religious issues of these groups have little or nothing to do with conservative or liberal politics.

The uncompromising position of these groups is a divisive element that could tear apart the very spirit of our representative system, if they gain sufficient strength.

As it is, they are diverting us away from the vital issues that our Government needs to address.

Far too much of the time of members of Congress and officials in the Executive Branch is used up dealing with special-interest groups on issues like abortion, school busing, ERA, prayer in the schools and pornography. While these are important moral issues, they are secondary right now to our national security and economic survival.

I must make it clear that I don't condemn these groups for what they believe. I happen to share many of the values emphasized by these organizations.

I'm frankly sick and tired of the political preachers across this country telling me as a citizen that if I want to be a moral person, I must believe in "A," "B," "C," and "D." Just who do they think they are? And from where do they presume to claim the right to dictate their moral beliefs to me?

And I am even more angry as a legislator who must endure the threats of every religious group who thinks it has some God-granted right to control my every roll call in the Senate.

I am warning them today: I will fight them every step of the way if they try to dictate their moral convictions to all Americans in the name of "conservatism."

This unrelenting obsession with a particular goal destroys the perspective of many decent people. They have become easy prey to manipulation and misjudgment. . . .

And the religious factions will go on imposing their will on others unless the decent people connected to them recognize that religion has no place in public policy.

They must learn to make their views known without trying to make their views the only alternatives.

The great decisions of Government cannot be dictated by the concerns of religious factions. This was true in the days of Madison, and it is just as true today.

We have succeeded for 205 years in keeping the affairs of state separate from the uncompromising idealism of religious groups and we mustn't stop now.

To retreat from that separation would violate the principles of conservatism and the values upon which the framers built this democratic republic.

Ronald Reagan's Inaugural Addresses, *1981, 1985*

1981

These United States are confronted with an economic affliction of great proportions.

We suffer from the longest and one of the worst sustained inflations in our national history. It distorts our economic decisions, penalizes thrift and crushes the struggling young and the fixed-income elderly alike. It threatens to shatter the lives of millions of our people.

Idle industries have cast workers into unemployment, human misery and personal indignity.

Those who do work are denied a fair return for their labor by a tax system which penalizes successful achievement and keeps us from maintaining full productivity.

But great as our tax burden is, it has not kept pace with public spending. For decades we have piled deficit upon deficit, mortgaging our future and our children's future for the temporary convenience of the present.

To continue this long trend is to guarantee tremendous social, cultural, political and economic upheavals.

You and I, as individuals, can, by borrowing, live beyond our means, but for only a limited period of time. Why then should we think that collectively, as a nation, we are not bound by the same limitation?

We must act today in order to preserve tomorrow. And let there be no misunderstanding—we're going to begin to act beginning today.

The economic ills we suffer have come upon us over several decades.

They will not go away in days, weeks or months, but they will go away. They will go away because we as Americans have the capacity now, as we have had in the past, to do whatever needs to be done to preserve this last and greatest bastion of freedom.

In this present crisis, government is not the solution to our problem, government is the problem.

From time to time we've been tempted to believe that society has become too complex to be managed by self-rule, that government by an elite group is superior to government for, by and of the people.

But if no one among us is capable of government himself, then who among us has the capacity to govern someone else?

All of us together—in and out of government—must bear the burden. The solutions we seek must be equitable with no one group singled out to pay a higher price.

We hear much of special interest groups. Well our concern must be for a special interest group that has been too long neglected.

It knows no sectional boundaries, or ethnic and racial divisions and it crosses political party lines. It is made up of men and women who raise our food, patrol our streets, man our mines and factories, teach our children, keep our homes and heal us when we're sick.

Professionals, industrialists, shopkeepers, clerks, cabbies and truck drivers. They are, in short, "We the people." This breed called Americans.

Well, this Administration's objective will be a healthy, vigorous, growing economy that provides equal opportunities for all Americans with no barriers born of bigotry or discrimination.

Putting America back to work means putting all Americans back to work. Ending inflation means freeing all Americans from the terror of runaway living costs.

All must share in the productive work of this "new beginning," and all must share in the bounty of a revived economy.

With the idealism and fair play which are the core of our system and our strength, we can have a strong, prosperous America at peace with itself and the world.

So as we begin, let us take inventory.

We are a nation that has a government—not the other way around. And this makes us special among the nations of the earth.

Our Government has no power except that granted it by the people. It is time to check and reverse the growth of government which shows signs of having grown beyond the consent of the governed.

It is my intention to curb the size and influence of the Federal establishment and to demand recognition of the distinction between the powers granted to the Federal Government and those reserved to the states or to the people.

All of us—all of us need to be reminded that the Federal Government did not create the states; the states created the Federal Government.

Now, so there will be no misunderstanding, it's not my intention to do away with government.

It is rather to make it work—work with us, not over us; to stand by our side, not ride on our back. Government can and must provide opportunity, not smother it; foster productivity, not stifle it.

If we look to the answer as to why for so many years we achieved so much, prospered as no other people on earth, it was because here in this land we unleashed the energy and individual genius of man to a greater extent than has ever been done before.

Freedom and the dignity of the individual have been more available and assured here than in any other place on earth. The price for this freedom at times has been high, but we have never been unwilling to pay that price.

It is no coincidence that our present troubles parallel and are proportionate to the intervention and intrusion in our lives that result from unnecessary and excessive growth of Government.

It is time for us to realize that we are too great a nation to limit ourselves to small dreams. We're not, as some would have us believe, doomed to an inevitable decline; I do not believe in a fate that will fall on us no matter what we do. I do believe in a fate that will fall on us if we do nothing.

So, with all the creative energy at our command let us begin an era of national renewal. Let us renew our determination, our courage and our strength. And let us renew our faith and our hope. We have every right to dream heroic dreams.

Your dreams, your hopes, your goals are going to be the dreams, the hopes and the goals of this Administration, so help me God.

We shall reflect the compassion that is so much a part of your makeup.

How can we love our country and not love our countrymen? And loving them reach out a hand when they fall, heal them when they're sick and provide opportunity to make them self-sufficient so they will be equal in fact and not just in theory?

Can we solve the problems confronting us? Well, the answer is an unequivocal and emphatic yes.

To paraphrase Winston Churchill, I did not take the oath I've just taken with the intention of presiding over the dissolution of the world's strongest economy.

In the days ahead I will propose removing the roadblocks that have slowed our economy and reduced productivity.

Steps will be taken aimed at restoring the balance between the various levels of government. Progress may be slow—measured in inches and feet, not miles—but we will progress.

It is time to reawaken this industrial giant, to get government back within its means and to lighten our punitive tax burden.

And these will be our first priorities, and on these principles there will be no compromise. . . .

I believe we the Americans of today are ready to act worthy of ourselves, ready to do what must be done to insure happiness and liberty for ourselves, our children and our children's children.

And as we renew ourselves here in our own land we will be seen as having greater strength throughout the world. We will again be the examplar of freedom and a beacon of hope for those who do not now have freedom.

To those neighbors and allies who share our freedom, we will strengthen our historic ties and assure them of our support and firm commitment.

We will match loyalty with loyalty. We will strive for mutually beneficial relations. We will not use our friendship to impose on their sovereignty, for our own sovereignty is not for sale.

As for the enemies of freedom, those who are potential adversaries, they will be reminded that peace is the highest aspiration of the American people. We will negotiate for it, sacrifice for it; we will not surrender for it—now or ever.

Our forbearance should never be misunderstood.

Our reluctance for conflict should not be misjudged as a failure of will.

When action is required to preserve our national security, we will act. We will maintain sufficient strength to prevail if need be, knowing that if we do so we have the best chance of never having to use that strength.

Above all we must realize that no arsenal or no weapon in the arsenals of the world is so formidable as the will and moral courage of free men and women.

It is a weapon our adversaries in today's world do not have.

It is a weapon that we as Americans do have.

Let that be understood by those who practice terrorism and prey upon their neighbors.

1985

When I took this oath four years ago, I did so in a time of economic stress. Voices were raised saying that we had to look to our past for the greatness and glory. But we, the present-day Americans, are not given to looking backward. In this blessed land, there is always a better tomorrow.

Four years ago I spoke to you of a new beginning, and we have accomplished that. But in another sense, our new beginning is a continuation of that beginning created two centuries ago when, for the first time in history, government, the people said, was not our master. It is our servant; its only power that which we, the people, allow it to have.

That system has never failed us. But for a time we failed the system. We asked for things of government that government was not equipped to give. We yielded authority to the national government that properly belonged to states or to local governments or to the people themselves. We allowed taxes and inflation to rob us of our earnings and savings and watched the great industrial machines that had made us the most productive people on earth slow down and the number of unemployed increase.

By 1980 we knew it was time to renew our faith, to strive with all our strength toward the ultimate in individual freedom consistent with an orderly society.

We believed then and now there are no limits to growth and human progress when men and women are free to follow their dreams. And we were right. And we were right to believe that. Tax rates have been reduced, inflation cut dramatically and more people are employed than ever before in our history.

We are creating a nation once again vibrant, robust and alive. But there are many mountains yet to climb. We will not rest until every American enjoys the fullness of freedom, dignity and opportunity as our birthright. It is our birthright as citizens of the great republic.

And if we meet this challenge, these will be years when Americans have restored their confidence and tradition of progress; when our values of faith, family, work and neighborhood were restated for a modern age; when our economy was finally freed from government's grip; when we made sincere efforts at meaningful arms reductions by rebuilding our defenses, our economy, and developing new technologies helped preserve peace in a troubled world; when America courageously supported the struggle for individual liberty, self-government and free enterprise throughout the world and turned the tide of history away from totalitarian darkness and into the warm sunlight of human freedom.

My fellow citizens, our nation is poised for greatness. We must do what we know is right and do it with all our might. Let history say of us, these were golden years—when the American Revolution was reborn, when freedom gained new life and America reached for her best.

Our two-party system has served us well over the years, but never better than in those times of great challenge, when we came together not as Democrats or Republicans but as Americans united in the common cause.

Two of our Founding Fathers, a Boston lawyer named Adams and a Virginia planter named Jefferson, members of that remarkable group who met in Independence Hall and dared to think they could start the world over again, left us an important lesson. They had become, in the years spent in government, bitter political rivals. In the Presidential election of 1800, then years later, when both were retired and age had softened their anger, they began to speak to each other again through letters.

A bond was re-established between those two who had helped create this government of ours.

In 1826, the 50th anniversary of the Declaration of Independence, they both died. They died on the same day, within a few hours of each other. And that day was the Fourth of July.

In one of those letters exchanged in the sunset of their lives, Jefferson wrote, "It carries me back to the times when, beset with difficulties and dangers, we were fellow laborers in the same cause, struggling for what is most valuable to man, his right to self-government. Laboring always at the same oar, with some wave ever ahead threatening to overwhelm us, and yet passing harmless we rode through the storm with heart and hand."

Well, with heart and hand, let us stand as one today: one people under God determined that our future shall be worthy of our past. As we do, we must not repeat the well-intentioned errors of our past. We must never again abuse the trust of working men and women by sending their earnings on a futile chase after the spiraling demands of a bloated Federal establishment. You elected us in 1980 to end this prescription for disaster. And I don't believe you re-elected us in 1984 to reverse course.

The heart of our efforts is one idea vindicated by 25 straight months of economic growth: freedom and incentives unleash the drive and entrepreneurial genius that are the core of human progress. We have begun to increase the rewards for work, savings and investment; reduce the increase in the cost and size of government and its interference in people's lives.

We must simplify our tax system, make it more fair and bring the rates down for all who work and earn. We must think anew and move with a new boldness so every American who seeks work can find work; so the least among us shall have an equal chance to achieve the greatest things—to be heroes who heal our sick, feed the hungry, protect peace among nations and leave this world a better place.

The time has come for a new American Emancipation, a great national drive to tear down economic barriers and liberate the spirit of enterprise in the most distressed areas of our country. My friends, together we can do this, and do it we must, so help me God.

From new freedom will spring new opportunities for growth, a more productive, fulfilled and united people and a stronger America, an America that will lead the technological revolution and also open its mind and heart and soul to the treasuries of literature, music and poetry, and the values of faith, courage and love.

A dynamic economy, with more citizens working and paying taxes, will be our strongest tool to bring down budget deficits. But an almost unbroken 50 years of deficit spending has finally brought us to a time of reckoning.

We've come to a turning point, a moment for hard decisions. I have asked the Cabinet and my staff a question and now I put the same question to you. If not us, who? And if not now, when? It must be done by all of us going forward with a program aimed at reaching a balanced budget. We can then begin reducing the national debt.

I will shortly submit a budget to the Congress aimed at freezing government program spending for the next year. Beyond this, we must take further steps to permanently control government's power to tax and spend.

We must act now to protect future generations from government's desire to spend its citizens' money and tax them into servitude when the bills come due. Let us make it unconstitutional for the Federal Government to spend more than the Federal Government takes in.

We have already started returning to the people and to state and local governments responsibilities better handled by them. Now, there is a place for the Federal Government in matters of social compassion. But our fundamental goals must be to reduce dependency and upgrade the dignity of those who are infirm or disadvantaged. And here a growing economy and support from family and community offer our best chance for a society where compassion is a way of life, where the old and infirm are cared for, the young and, yes, the unborn, protected, and the unfortunate looked after and made self-sufficient.

Now there is another area where the Federal Government can play a part. As an older American, I remember a time when people of different race, creed or ethnic origin in our land found hatred and prejudice installed in social custom and, yes, in law. There's no story more heartening in our history than the progress that we've made toward the brotherhood of man that God intended for us. Let us resolve: There will be no turning back or hesitation on the road to an America rich in dignity and abundant with opportunity for all our citizens.

Let us resolve that we, the people, will build an American opportunity society in which all of us—white and black, rich and poor, young and old—will go forward together, arm in arm. Again, let us remember that, though our heritage is one of blood lines from every corner of the earth, we are all Americans pledged to carry on this last best hope of man on earth.

And I have spoken of our domestic goals, and the limitations we should put on our national government. Now let me turn to a task that is the primary responsibility of national government—the safety and security of our people.

Today we utter no prayer more fervently than the ancient prayer for peace on earth. Yet history has shown that peace does not come, nor will our freedom be preserved, by good will alone. There are those in the world who scorn our vision of human dignity and freedom. One nation, the Soviet Union, has conducted the greatest military buildup in the history of man, building arsenals of awesome offensive weapons.

We've made progress in restoring our defense capability. But much remains to be done. There must be no wavering by us, nor any doubts by others, that America will meet her responsibilities to remain free, secure, and at peace.

There is only one way safely and legitimately to reduce the cost of national security, and this is to reduce the need for it. And this we're trying to do in negotiating with the Soviet Union. We're not just discussing limits on a further increase of nuclear weapons. We seek, instead, to reduce their number. We seek the total elimination, one day, of nuclear weapons from the face of the earth.

Now for decades we and the Soviets have lived under

the threat of mutual assured destruction; if either resorted to the use of nuclear weapons, the other could retaliate and destroy the one who had started it. Is there either logic or morality in believing that if one side threatens to kill tens of millions of our people, our only resource is to threaten killing tens of millions of theirs?

I have approached a research program to find, if we can, a security shield that will destroy nuclear missiles before they reach their target: It wouldn't kill people, it would destroy weapons. It wouldn't militarize space, it would help demilitarize the arsenals of earth. It would render nuclear weapons obsolete. We will meet with the Soviets hoping that we can agree on a way to rid the world of the threat of nuclear destruction.

We strive for peace and security, heartened by the changes all around us. Since the turn of the century, the number of democracies in the world has grown fourfold. Human freedom is on the march, and nowhere more so than in our own hemisphere. Freedom is one of the deepest and noblest aspirations of the human spirit. People worldwide hunger for the right of self-determination, for those inalienable rights that make for human dignity and progress.

Americans must remain freedom's staunchest friend, for freedom is our best ally, and it is the world's only hope to conquer poverty and preserve peace. Every blow we inflict against poverty will be a blow against its dark allies of oppression and war. Every victory for human freedom will be a victory for world peace.

So we go forward today a nation still mighty in its youth and powerful in its purpose. With our alliances strengthened, with our economy leading the world to a new age of economic expansion, we look to a future rich in possibilities. And all of this is because we worked and acted together, not as members of political parties, but as Americans.

My friends, we, we live in a world that's lit by lightning. So much is changing and will change, but so much endures and transcends time.

History is a ribbon, always unfurling; history is a journey. And as we continue on our journey we think of those who traveled before us. We stand again at the steps of this symbol of our democracy, or we would've been standing at the steps if it hadn't gotten so cold. Now, we're standing inside this symbol of our democracy, and we see and hear again the echoes of our past.

A general falls to his knees in the hard snow of Valley Forge; a lonely President paces the darkened halls and ponders his struggle to preserve the Union; the men of the Alamo call out encouragement to each other; a settler pushes west and sings a song, and the song echoes out forever and fills the unknowing air.

It is the American sound: It is hopeful, big-hearted, idealistic—daring, decent and fair. That's our heritage, that's our song. We sing it still. For all our problems, our differences, we are together as of old. We raise our voices to the God who is the author of this most tender music. And may He continue to hold us close as we fill the world with our sound—in unity, affection and love. One people under God, dedicated to the dream of freedom that He has placed in the human heart, called upon now to pass that dream on to a waiting and a hopeful world.

God bless you and may God bless America.

"A Tale of Two Cities" Keynote Address, Democratic National Convention, *Governor Mario M. Cuomo, 1984*

On behalf of the Empire State and the family of New York, I thank you for the great privilege of being allowed to address this convention.

Please allow me to skip the stories and the poetry and the temptation to deal in nice but vague rhetoric.

Let me instead use this valuable opportunity to deal with the questions that should determine this election and that are vital to the American people.

Ten days ago, President Reagan admitted that although some people in this country seemed to be doing well nowadays, others were unhappy, and even worried, about themselves, their families and their futures.

The president said he didn't understand that fear. He said, "Why, this country is a shining city on a hill."

The president is right. In many ways we *are* "a shining city on a hill."

But the hard truth is that not everyone is sharing in this city's splendor and glory.

A shining city is perhaps all the president sees from the portico of the White House and the veranda of his ranch, where everyone seems to be doing well.

But there's another part of the city, the part where some people can't pay their mortgages and most young people can't afford one, where students can't afford the education they need and middle-class parents watch the dreams they hold for their children evaporate.

In this part of the city there are more poor than ever, more families in trouble, more and more people who need help but can't find it.

Even worse: there are elderly people who tremble in the basements of the houses there.

There are people who sleep in the city's streets, in the gutter, where the glitter doesn't show.

There are ghettos where thousands of young people, without an education or a job, give their lives away to drug dealers every day.

There is despair, Mr. President, in faces you never see, in the places you never visit in your shining city.

In fact, Mr. President, this nation is more a "tale of two cities" than it is a "shining city on a hill."

Maybe if you visited more places, Mr. President, you'd understand.

Maybe if you went to Appalachia where some people still live in sheds, and to Lackawanna where thousands of unemployed steelworkers wonder why we subsidized foreign steel while we surrender their dignity to unemployment and to welfare checks; maybe if you stepped into a shelter in Chicago and talked with some of the homeless there; maybe Mr. President, if you asked a woman who'd been denied the help she needs to feed her children because you say we need the money to give a tax break to a millionaire or to build a missile we can't even afford to use—maybe then you'd understand.

Maybe, Mr. President.

But I'm afraid not.

Because, the truth is, this is how we were warned it would be.

President Reagan told us from the beginning that

he believed in a kind of social Darwinism. Survival of the fittest. "Government can't do everything," we were told. "So it should settle for taking care of the strong and hope that economic ambition and charity will do the rest. Make the rich richer and what falls from their table will be enough for the middle class and those trying to make it into the middle class."

The Republicans called it trickle-down when Hoover tried it. Now they call it supply side. It is the same shining city for those relative few who are lucky enough to live in its good neighborhoods.

But for the people who are excluded—locked out—all they can do is to stare from a distance at that city's glimmering towers.

It's an old story. As old as our history.

The difference between Democrats and the Republicans has always been measured in courage and confidence.

The Republicans believe the wagon train will not make it to the frontier unless some of our old, some of our young, and some of our weak are left behind by the side of the trail.

The strong will inherit the land!

We Democrats believe that we can make it all the way with the whole family intact.

We have, more than once.

Ever since Franklin Roosevelt lifted himself from his wheelchair to lift this nation from its knees. Wagon train after wagon train. To new frontiers of education, housing, peace. The whole family aboard. Constantly reaching out to extend and enlarge that family. Lifting them up into the wagon on the way. Blacks and Hispanics, people of every ethnic group, and Native Americans—all those struggling to build their families claim some small share of America.

For nearly fifty years we carried them to new levels of comfort, security, dignity, even affluence.

Some of us are in this room today only because this nation had that confidence.

It would be wrong to forget that.

So, we are here at this convention to remind ourselves where we come from and to claim the future for ourselves and for our children.

Today our great Democratic party, which has saved this nation from depression, from fascism, from racism, from corruption, is called upon to do it again . . . this time to save the nation from confusion and division, from the threat of eventual fiscal disaster and most of all from a fear of nuclear holocaust.

In order to succeed, we must answer our opponent's polished and appealing rhetoric with a more telling reasonableness and rationality.

We must win this case on the merits.

We must get the American public to look past the glitter, beyond the showmanship. . . . To reality, to the hard substance of things. And we will do that not so much with speeches that sound good as with speeches that are good and sound.

Not so much with speeches that bring people to their feet as with speeches that bring people to their senses.

We must make the American people hear our "tale of two cities."

We must convince them that we don't have to settle for two cities, that we can have one city, indivisible, shining for *all* its people.

We will have no chance to do that if what comes out of this convention—what is heard through the campaign—is a babel of arguing voices.

To succeed we will have to surrender small parts of our individual interests, to build a platform we can *all* stand on, at once, comfortably—proudly singing out the truth for the nation to hear, in chorus; its logic so clear and commanding that no slick commercial, no amount of geniality, no martial music will be able to muffle it.

We Democrats must unite so that the entire nation can. Surely the Republicans won't bring the nation together. Their policies divide the nation . . . into the lucky and the left-out, the royalty and the rabble.

The Republicans are willing to treat that division as victory. They would cut this nation in half, into those temporarily better off and those worse than before, and call it recovery.

We should not be embarrassed or dismayed if the process of unifying is difficult, even at times wrenching.

Unlike any other party, we embrace men and women of every color, every creed, every orientation, every economic class. In our family are gathered everyone from the abject poor of Essex County in New York, to the enlightened affluent of the gold coasts at both ends of our nation. And in between is the heart of our constituency. The middle class. The people not rich enough to be worry free but not poor enough to be on welfare. Those who work for a living because they have to. White collar and blue collar. Young professionals. Men and women in small business desperate for the capital and contracts they need to prove their worth.

We speak for the minorities who have not yet entered the main stream.

For ethnics who want to add their culture to the mosaic that is America.

For women indignant that we refuse to etch into our governmental commandants the simple rule "Thou shalt not sin against equality," a commandant so obvious it can be spelled in three letters . . . ERA.

For young people demanding an education and a future.

For senior citizens terrorized by the idea that their only security . . . their *Social* Security . . . is being threatened.

For millions of reasoning people fighting to preserve our environment from greed and stupidity. And fighting to preserve our very existence from a macho intransigence that refuses to make intelligent attempts to discuss the possibility of nuclear holocaust with our enemy; refusing because they believe we can pile missiles so high that they will pierce the clouds and the sight of them will frighten our enemies into submission.

We're proud of this diversity. Grateful we don't have to manufacture its appearance the way the Republicans will next month in Dallas, by propping up mannequin delegates on the convention floor.

But we pay a price for it.

The different people we represent have many points of view. Sometimes they compete, and then we have debates, even arguments. That's what our primaries were about.

But now the primaries are over and it is time to lock arms and move into this campaign together.

If we need any inspiration to make the effort to put aside our small differences, all we need to do is to reflect on the Republican policy of divide and cajole and how it has injured our land since 1980.

The president has asked us to judge him on whether or not he's fulfilled the promises he made four years ago.

I accept that. Just consider what he said and what he's done.

Inflation is down since 1980. But not because of the supply-side miracle promised by the president. Inflation was reduced the old-fashioned way, with a recession, the worst since 1932. More than 55,000 bankruptcies. Two years of massive unemployment, 200,000 farmers and ranchers forced off the land. More homeless than at any time since the Great Depression. More hungry, more poor—mostly women—and a nearly 200 billion dollar deficit threatening our future.

The president's deficit is a direct and dramatic repudiation of his promise to balance our budget by 1983.

That deficit is the largest in the history of this universe; more than three times larger than the deficit in President Carter's last year.

It is a deficit that, according to the president's own fiscal advisor, could grow as high as 300 billion dollars a year, stretching "as far as the eye can see."

It is a debt so large that as much as one-half of our revenue from the income tax goes to pay the interest on it each year.

It is a mortgage on our children's futures that can only be paid in pain and that could eventually bring this nation to its knees.

Don't take my word for it . . . I'm a Democrat.

Ask the Republican investment bankers on Wall Street what they think the chances are this recovery will be permanent. If they're not too embarrassed to tell you the truth, they'll say they are appalled and frightened by the president's deficit. Ask them what they think of our economy, now that it has been driven by the distorted value of the dollar back to its colonial condition—

exporting agricultural products and importing manufactured ones.

Ask those Republican investment bankers what they expect the interest rate to be a year from now. And ask them what they predict for the inflation rate then.

How important is this question of the deficit?

Think about it: What chance would the Republican candidate have have had in 1980 if he had told the American people that he intended to pay for his so-called economic recovery with bankruptcies, unemployment and the largest government debt known to humankind? Would American voters have signed the loan certificate for him on election day? Of course not! It was an election won with smoke and mirrors . . . with illusions. It is a recovery made of the same stuff.

And what about foreign policy?

They said they would make us and the whole world safer. They say they have.

By creating the largest defense budget in history, one even they now admit is excessive. By escalating to a frenzy the nuclear arms race. By incendiary rhetoric. By refusing to discuss peace with our enemies. By the loss of 279 young Americans in Lebanon in pursuit of a plan and a policy no one can find or describe.

We give monies to Latin American governments that murder nuns, and then lie about it.

We have been less than zealous in our support of the only real friend we have in the Middle East, the one democracy there, our flesh and blood ally, the state of Israel.

Our policy drifts with no real direction, other than an hysterical commitment to an arms race that leads nowhere. . . . If we're lucky. If we're not . . . could lead us to bankruptcy or war.

Of course we must have a strong defense!

Of course Democrats believe that there are times when we must stand and fight. And we have. Thousands of us have paid for freedom with our lives. But always—when we've been at our best—our best—our purposes were clear.

Now they're not. Now our allies are as confused as our enemies.

Now we have no real commitment to our friends or our ideals . . . to human rights, to the refusenicks, to Sakharov, to Bishop Tutu and the others struggling for freedom in South Africa.

We have spent more than we can afford. We have pounded our chests and made bold speeches. But we lost 279 young Americans in Lebanon and we are forced to live behind sand bags in Washington.

How can anyone believe that we are stronger, safer, or better?

That's the Republican record.

That its disastrous quality is not more fully understood by the American people is attributable, I think, to the president's amiability and the failure by some to separate the salesman from the product.

It's now up to us to make the case to America.

And to remind Americans that if they are not happy with all the president has done so far, they should consider how much worse it will be if he is left to his radical proclivities for another four years unrestrained by the need once again to come before the American people.

If July brings back Ann Gorsuch Burford . . . what can we expect of December?

Where would another four years take us?

How much larger will the deficit be?

How much deeper the cuts in programs for the struggling middle class and the poor to limit that deficit? How high the interest rates? How much more acid rain killing our forests and fouling our lakes?

What kind of Supreme Court? What kind of court and country will be fashioned by the man who believes in having government mandate people's religion and morality?

The man who believes that trees pollute the environment, that the laws against discrimination go too far. The man who threatens Social Security and Medicaid and help for the disabled.

How high will we pile the missiles?

How much deeper will be the gulf between us and our enemies?

Will we make meaner the spirit of our people?

This election will measure the record of the past four

years. But more than that, it will answer the question of what kind of people we want to be.

We Democrats *still* have a dream. We *still* believe in this nation's future.

And this is our answer—*our* credo:

We believe in *only* the government we need but we insist on all the government we need.

We believe in a government characterized by fairness and *reasonableness,* a reasonableness that goes beyond labels, that doesn't distort or promise to do what it knows it can't do.

A government strong enough to use the words "love" and "compassion" and smart enough to convert our noblest aspirations into practical realities.

We believe in encouraging the talented, but we believe that while survival of the fittest may be a good working description of the process of evolution, a government of humans should elevate itself to a higher order, one which fills the gaps left by chance or a wisdom we don't understand.

We would rather have laws written by the patron of this great city, the man called the "world's most sincere democrat"—St. Francis of Assisi—than laws written by Darwin.

We believe, as Democrats, that a society as blessed as ours, the most affluent democracy in the world's history, that can spend trillions on instruments of destruction, ought to be able to help the middle class in its struggle, ought to be able to find work for all who can do it, room at the table, shelter for the homeless, care for the elderly and infirm, hope for the destitute.

We proclaim as loudly as we can the utter insanity of nuclear proliferation and the need for a nuclear freeze, if only to affirm the simple truth that peace is better than war because life is better than death.

We believe in firm but fair law and order, in the union movement, in privacy for people, openness by government, civil rights, and human rights.

We believe in a single fundamental idea that describes better than most textbooks and any speech what a proper government should be. The idea of family. Mutuality. The sharing of benefits and burdens for the good of all. Feeling one another's pain. Sharing one another's blessings. Reasonably, honestly, fairly—without respect to race, or sex, or geography or political affiliation.

We believe we must be the family of America, recognizing that at the heart of the matter we are bound one to another, that the problems of a retired school teacher in Duluth are *our* problems. That the future of the child in Buffalo is *our* future. The struggle of a disabled man in Boston to survive, to live decently is *our* struggle. The hunger of a woman in Little Rock, *our* hunger. The failure anywhere to provide what reasonably we might, to avoid pain, is *our* failure.

For fifty years we Democrats created a better future for our children, using traditional democratic principles as a fixed beacon, giving us direction and purpose, but constantly innovating, adapting to new realities: Roosevelt's alphabet programs; Truman's NATO and the GI Bill of Rights; Kennedy's intelligent tax incentives and the Alliance for Progress; Johnson's civil rights; Carter's human rights and the nearly miraculous Camp David Peace Accord.

Democrats did it . . . and Democrats can do it again.

We can build a future that deals with our deficit.

Remember, fifty years of progress never cost us what the last four years of stagnation have. We can deal with that deficit intelligently, by shared sacrifice, with all parts of the nation's family contributing, building partnerships with the private sector, providing a sound defense without depriving ourselves of what we need to feed our children and care for our people.

We can have a future that provides for all the young of the present, by marrying common sense and compassion.

We *know* we can, because we did it for nearly fifty years before 1980.

We can do it again. If we do not forget. Forget that this entire nation has profited by these progressive principles. That they helped lift up generations to the middle class and higher: gave us a chance to work, to go to college, to raise a family, to own a house, to be secure in our old age and, before that, to reach heights that our own parents would not have dared dream of.

That struggle to live with dignity is the real story of the shining city. It's a story I didn't read in a book, or learn in a classroom. I saw it, and lived it. Like many of you.

I watched a small man with thick calluses on both hands work fifteen and sixteen hours a day. I saw him once literally bleed from the bottoms of his feet, a man who came here uneducated, alone, unable to speak the language, who taught me all I needed to know about faith and hard work by the simple eloquence of his example. I learned about our kind of democracy from my father. I learned about our obligation to each other from him and from my mother. They asked only for a chance to work and to make the world better for their children and to be protected in those moments when they would not be able to protect themselves. This nation and its government did that for them.

And that they were able to build a family and live in dignity and see one of their children go from behind their little grocery store on the other side of the tracks in South Jamaica where he was born, to occupy the highest seat in the greatest state of the greatest nation in the only world we know, is an ineffably beautiful tribute to the democratic process.

And on January 20, 1985, it will happen again. Only on a much grander scale. We will have a new president of the United States, a Democrat born not to the blood of kings but to the blood of immigrants and pioneers.

We will have America's first woman vice-president. The child of immigrants, a New Yorker, opening with one magnificent stroke, a whole new frontier for the United States.

It will happen—*if we make it happen.*

I ask you—ladies and gentlemen, brothers and sisters—for the good of all of us—for the love of this great nation, for the family of America—for the love of God. Please, make this nation remember how futures are built.

Chapter 30

THE END OF THE AMERICAN CENTURY

William Jefferson Clinton, the youthful, middle-of-the-road Democratic Governor of Arkansas, was chosen as the nation's 42nd chief executive in 1992, his opposition divided between Republican incumbent George Bush and Texas maverick billionaire Ross Perot, a highly contentious third-party candidate. Six years of intensely partisan confrontations later, Clinton would become the only elected President of the United States ever to be impeached, the victim of both his own self-inflicted wounds, and of a clearly unpopular conservative attempt at a veritable Republican coup d'état.

Even before his election, Clinton had been handicapped by an unconscionable media feeding frenzy concerning the kinds of reports and rumors about his private life that earlier American leaders had never before been forced to endure. Besides, the new President and his articulate, activist wife, Hillary Rodham Clinton, had been too quickly demeaned by bitter opponents in both parties as symbols of America's cultural and behavioral revolution stemming from the radical 1960's to permit an early record of legislative achievement. In particular, the Clintons' determined effort to reform the nation's woefully inadequate health care system was effectively scuttled, and their party was roundly defeated in the 1994 House and Senate races.

In September of that year, conservative Georgia Congressman Newt Gingrich had set forth as his party's dramatic campaign platform a ten-point Republican "Contract with America" outlining specific legislative objectives. Victorious at the polls, Gingrich was chosen Speaker of the House of Representatives, gaining consideration for his ten points in a promised first one hundred days. He won some of these battles against the Democrats, but lost others to Bill Clinton's extraordinary but clearly infuriating ability to modify and then to adopt as his own such popular Republican positions as a balanced budget, tax and welfare reform, and the control of crime in the streets. Jousting successfully with his congressional opponents on these issues, and with the American economy booming, in 1996 Clinton and Vice President Al Gore won a surprising second term against Kansas conservative Bob Dole, former Republican majority leader of the Senate, as well as, once again, independent candidate Perot.

To many it appeared that in America conservatism had indeed been revisited, but thoroughly co-opted by Bill Clinton, much to the chagrin of a core of extremist Republican legislators and their behind-the-scenes financial supporters. What these right-wing opponents cleverly foresaw, however, and based their anti-Clinton strategies upon, was the impact of sexual scandals in the President's personal life that they could force to the surface and that would be kept there month after month by an increasingly voracious and sensationalist press, both print and electronic. With the millennium fast approaching, on January 27, 1998, the President then stood before both houses of Congress, members of the Supreme Court and of his Cabinet, other dignitaries and his family and friends, and delivered perhaps his most brilliantly evocative, hopeful, and forward-looking State of the Union Address. Yet just eleven months later, despite his having effectively turned back congressional opponents at the polls, on December 19, 1998, by the thinnest of margins and by an almost strictly party vote, a Republican House of Representatives voted to impeach Democrat William Jefferson Clinton for "high crimes and misdemeanors," leaving it to a Republican Senate to convict or otherwise deal as it would with the twice popularly-elected President of the United States. He was acquitted, but not without more divisiveness.

Thus, for all of the nation's achievements in the arts and humanities, in space and cyberspace, in medicine and pure science, in the production of great wealth, even in the politics of world leadership—and despite the enormous challenges that still lay before Americans of all persuasions in such vital areas of national concern as education, Social Security, race relations, crime and its punishment, the environment, campaign finance reform, immigration, and universal health insurance—the American Century was poised to end on an unprecedented and shockingly polarized and partisan note, seemingly mired in "the politics of personal destruction." The rest is history.

Republican Contract with America, *1994*

As Republican Members of the House of Representatives and as citizens seeking to join that body we propose not just to change its policies, but even more important, to restore the bonds of trust between the people and their elected representatives.

That is why, in this era of official evasion and posturing, we offer instead a detailed agenda for national renewal, a written commitment with no fine print.

This year's election offers the chance, after four decades of one-party control, to bring to the House a new majority that will transform the way Congress works. That historic change would be the end of government that is too big, too intrusive, and too easy with the public's money. It can be the beginning of a Congress that respects the values and shares the faith of the American family.

Like Lincoln, our first Republican president, we intend to act "with firmness in the right, as God gives us to see the right." To restore accountability to Congress. To end its cycle of scandal and disgrace. To make us all proud again of the way free people govern themselves.

On the first day of the 104th Congress, the new Republican majority will immediately pass the following major reforms, aimed at restoring the faith and trust of the American people in their government:

- **FIRST,** require all laws that apply to the rest of the country also apply equally to the Congress;
- **SECOND,** select a major, independent auditing firm to conduct a comprehensive audit of Congress for waste, fraud or abuse;
- **THIRD,** cut the number of House committees, and cut committee staff by one-third;

- **FOURTH,** limit the terms of all committee chairs;
- **FIFTH,** ban the casting of proxy votes in committee;
- **SIXTH,** require committee meetings to be open to the public;
- **SEVENTH,** require a three-fifths majority vote to pass a tax increase;
- **EIGHTH,** guarantee an honest accounting of our Federal Budget by implementing zero baseline budgeting.

Thereafter, within the first 100 days of the 104th Congress, we shall bring to the House Floor the following bills, each to be given full and open debate, each to be given a clear and fair vote and each to be immediately available this day for public inspection and scrutiny.

1. The Fiscal Responsibility Act

A balanced budget/tax limitation amendment and a legislative line-item veto to restore fiscal responsibility to an out-of-control Congress, requiring them to live under the same budget constraints as families and businesses.

2. The Taking Back Our Streets Act

An anticrime package including stronger truth-in-sentencing, "good faith" exclusionary rule exemptions, effective death penalty provisions, and cuts in social spending from this summer's "crime" bill to fund prison construction and additional law enforcement to keep people secure in their neighborhoods and kids safe in their schools.

3. The Personal Responsibility Act

Discourage illegitimacy and teen pregnancy by prohibiting welfare to minor mothers and denying increased AFDC for additional children while on welfare, cut spending for welfare programs, and enact a tough two-years-and-out provision with work requirements to promote individual responsibility.

4. The Family Reinforcement Act

Child support enforcement, tax incentives for adoption, strengthening rights of parents in their children's education, stronger child pornography laws, and an elderly dependent care tax credit to reinforce the central role of families in American society.

5. The American Dream Restoration Act
A $500 per child tax credit, begin repeal of the marriage tax penalty, and creation of American Dream Savings Accounts to provide middle-class tax relief.
6. The National Security Restoration Act
No U.S. troops under U.N. command and restoration of the essential parts of our national security funding to strengthen our national defense and maintain our credibility around the world.
7. The Senior Citizens Fairness Act
Raise the Social Security earnings limit which currently forces seniors out of the work force, repeal the 1993 tax hikes on Social Security benefits and provide tax incentives for private long-term care insurance to let Older Americans keep more of what they have earned over the years.
8. The Job Creation and Wage Enhancement Act
Small business incentives, capital gains cut and indexation, neutral cost recovery, risk assessment/cost-benefit analysis, strengthening the Regulatory Flexibility Act and unfunded mandate reform to create jobs and raise worker wages.
9. The Common Sense Legal Reform Act
"Loser pays" laws, reasonable limits on punitive damages and reform of product liability laws to stem the endless tide of litigation.
10. The Citizen Legislature Act
A first-ever vote on term limits to replace career politicians with citizen legislators.

Further, we will instruct the House Budget Committee to report to the floor and we will work to enact additional budget savings, beyond the budget cuts specifically included in the legislation described above, to ensure that the Federal budget deficit will be *less* than it would have been without the enactment of these bills.

Respecting the judgment of our fellow citizens as we seek their mandate for reform, we hereby pledge our names to this Contract with America.

____________________ ________________

Name State/District

William Jefferson Clinton, State of the Union Address, *January, 1998*

THE PRESIDENT: Mr. Speaker, Mr. Vice President, members of the 105th Congress, distinguished guests, my fellow Americans . . .

For 209 years it has been the President's duty to report to you on the state of the Union. Because of the hard work and high purpose of the American people, these are good times for America. We have more than 14 million new jobs; the lowest unemployment in twenty-four years; the lowest core inflation in thirty years; incomes are rising; and we have the highest home-ownership in history. Crime has dropped for a record five years in a row. And the welfare rolls are at their lowest levels in twenty-seven years. Our leadership in the world is unrivaled. Ladies and gentlemen, the state of our Union is strong.

With barely 700 days left in the twentieth century, this is not a time to rest. It is a time to build, to build the America within reach: an America where everybody has a chance to get ahead with hard work; where every citizen can live in a safe community; where families are strong, schools are good and all young people can go to college; an America where scientists find cures for diseases from diabetes to Alzheimer's to AIDS; an America where every child can stretch a hand across a keyboard and reach every book ever written, every painting ever painted, every symphony ever composed; where government provides opportunity and citizens honor the responsibility to give something back to their communities; an America which leads the world to new heights of peace and prosperity.

This is the America we have begun to build; this is the America we can leave to our children—if we join together to finish the work at hand. Let us strengthen our nation for the twenty-first century.

Rarely have Americans lived through so much change, in so many ways, in so short a time. Quietly, but with gathering force, the ground has shifted beneath our feet as we have moved into an Information Age, a global economy, a truly new world.

For five years now we have met the challenge of these changes as Americans have at every turning point—by renewing the very idea of America; widening the circle of opportunity, deepening the meaning of our freedom, forging a more perfect union.

We have moved past the sterile debate between those who say government is the enemy and those who say government is the answer. My fellow Americans, we have found a third way. We have the smallest government in thirty-five years, but a more progressive one. We have a smaller government, but a stronger nation. We are moving steadily toward an even stronger America in the twenty-first century: an economy that offers opportunity, a society rooted in responsibility and a nation that lives as a community.

First, Americans in this chamber and across our nation have pursued a new strategy for prosperity: fiscal discipline to cut interest rates and spur growth; investments in education and skills, in science and technology and transportation, to prepare our people for the new economy; new markets for American products and American workers.

When I took office, the deficit for 1998 was projected to be $357 billion, and heading higher. This year, our deficit is projected to be $10 billion, and heading lower. For three decades, six Presidents have come before you to warn of the damage deficits pose to our nation. Tonight, I come before you to announce that the federal deficit—once so incomprehensibly large that it had eleven zeroes—will be, simply, zero. I will submit to Congress for 1999 the first balanced budget in thirty years. And if we hold fast to fiscal discipline, we may balance the budget this year—four years ahead of schedule.

You can all be proud of that, because turning a sea of red ink into black is no miracle. . . . Here's the really good news: If we maintain our resolve, we will produce balanced budgets as far as the eye can see.

We must not go back to unwise spending or untargeted tax cuts that risk reopening the deficit. . . . My plan to balance the budget next year includes both new investments and new tax cuts targeted to the needs of working families: for education, for child care, for the environment.

But whether the issue is tax cuts or spending, I ask all of you to meet this test: Approve only those priorities that can actually be accomplished without adding a dime to the deficit.

Now, if we balance the budget for next year, it is projected that we'll then have a sizeable surplus in the years that immediately follow. What should we do with this projected surplus? I have a simple four-word answer: Save Social Security first.

Tonight, I propose that we reserve 100 percent of the surplus—that's every penny of any surplus—until we have taken all the necessary measures to strengthen the Social Security system for the twenty-first century. Let us say to all Americans watching tonight—whether you're seventy or fifty, or whether you just started paying into the system—Social Security will be there when you need it. Let us make this commitment: Social Security first. Let's do that together. . . .

In an economy that honors opportunity, all Americans must be able to reap the rewards of prosperity. Because these times are good, we can afford to take one simple, sensible step to help millions of workers struggling to provide for their families: We should raise the minimum wage.

The Information Age is, first and foremost, an education age, in which education must start at birth and continue throughout a lifetime. Last year, from this podium, I said that education has to be our highest priority. I laid out a ten-point plan to move us forward and urged all of us to let politics stop at the schoolhouse door. Since then, this Congress, across party lines, and the American people have responded, in the most important year for education in a generation—expanding public school choice, opening the way to 3,000 new charter schools, working to connect every classroom in the country to the Information Superhighway, committing to expand Head Start to a million children, launching America Reads, sending literally thousands of college students into our elementary schools to make sure all our eight-year-olds can read.

Last year I proposed, and you passed, 220,000 new Pell Grant scholarships for deserving students. Student loans, already less expensive and easier to repay, now you get to deduct the interest. Families all over America now can put their savings into new tax-free education IRAs. And this year, for the first two years of college, families will get a $1,500 tax credit—a HOPE Scholarship that will cover the cost of most community college tuition. And for junior and senior year, graduate school, and job training, there is a lifetime learning credit. . . .

And because of these actions, I have something to say to every family listening to us tonight: Your children can go on to college. If you know a child from a poor family, tell her not to give up—she can go on to college. If you know a young couple struggling with bills, worried they won't be able to send their children to college, tell them not to give up—their children can go on to college. If you know somebody who's caught in a dead-end job and afraid he can't afford the classes necessary to get better jobs for the rest of his life, tell him not to give up—he can go on to college. Because of the things that have been done, we can make college as universal in the twenty-first century as high school is today. And, my friends, that will change the face and future of America.

We have opened wide the doors of the world's best system of higher education. Now we must make our public elementary and secondary schools the world's best as well—by raising standards, raising expectations, and raising accountability.

Thanks to the actions of this Congress last year, we will soon have, for the very first time, a voluntary national test based on national standards in fourth grade reading and eighth grade math. Parents have a right to know whether their children are mastering the basics. And every parent already knows the key: good teachers and small classes.

Tonight, I propose the first ever national effort to reduce class size in the early grades.

My balanced budget will help to hire 100,000 new teachers who have passed a state competency test. Now, with these teachers—listen—with these teachers, we will actually be able to reduce class size in the first, second, and third grades to an average of eighteen students a class, all across America.

If I've got the math right, more teachers teaching smaller classes requires more classrooms. So I also propose a school construction tax cut to help communities modernize or build 5,000 schools.

We must also demand greater accountability. When we promote a child from grade to grade who hasn't mastered the work, we don't do that child any favors. It is time to end social promotion in America's schools.

As we enter the twenty-first century, the global economy requires us to seek opportunity not just at home, but in all the markets of the world. We must shape this global economy, not shrink from it. In the last five years, we have led the way in opening new markets, with 240 trade agreements that remove foreign barriers to products bearing the proud stamp "Made in the USA." Today, record high exports account for fully one-third of our economic growth. I want to keep them going, because that's the way to keep America growing and to advance a safer, more stable world. . . .

I know there is opposition to more comprehensive trade agreements. I have listened carefully and I believe that the opposition is rooted in two fears: first, that our trading partners will have lower environmental and labor standards which will give them an unfair advantage in our market and do their own people no favors, even if there's more business; and, second, that if we have more trade, more of our workers will lose their jobs and have to start over. I think we should seek to advance worker and environmental standards around the world. I have made it abundantly clear that it should be a part of our trade agenda. But we cannot influence other countries' decisions if we send them a message that we're backing away from trade with them.

This year, I will send legislation to Congress, and ask other nations to join us, to fight the most intolerable labor practice of all—abusive child labor. We should also offer help and hope to those Americans temporarily left behind by the global marketplace or by the march of technology, which may have nothing to do with trade. That's why we have more than doubled funding for training dislocated workers since 1993—and if my new budget is adopted, we will triple funding. That's why we must do more, and more quickly, to help workers who lose their jobs for whatever reason.

You know, we help communities in a special way when their military base closes. We ought to help them in the same way if their factory closes. Again, I ask the Congress to continue its bipartisan work to consolidate the tangle of training programs we have today into one single G.I. Bill for Workers, a simple skills grant so people can, on their own, move quickly to new jobs, to higher incomes and brighter futures. . . . You know, whether we like it or not, in ways that are mostly positive, the world's economies are more and more interconnected and interdependent. Today, an economic crisis anywhere can affect economies everywhere. Recent months have brought serious financial problems to Thailand, Indonesia, South Korea, and beyond.

Now, why should Americans be concerned about this? First, these countries are our customers. If they sink into recession, they won't be able to buy the goods we'd like to sell them. Second, they're also our competitors. So if their currencies lose their value and go down, then the price of their goods will drop, flooding our market and others with much cheaper goods, which makes it a lot tougher for our people to compete. And, finally, they are our strategic partners. Their stability bolsters our security.

The American economy remains sound and strong, and I want to keep it that way. But because the turmoil in Asia will have an impact on all the world's economies, including ours, making that negative impact as small as possible is the right thing to do for America—and the right thing to do for a safer world.

Our policy is clear: No nation can recover if it does not reform itself. But when nations are willing to undertake serious economic reform, we should help them do it. So I call on Congress to renew America's commitment to the International Monetary Fund. And I think we should say to all the people we're trying to represent here that preparing for a far-off storm that may reach our shores is far wiser than ignoring the thunder until the clouds are just overhead.

A strong nation rests on the rock of responsibility.

A society rooted in responsibility must first promote the value of work, not welfare. We can be proud that after decades of finger-pointing and failure, together we ended the old welfare system. And we're now we replacing welfare checks with paychecks.

Last year, after a record four-year decline in welfare rolls, I challenged our nation to move 2 million more Americans off welfare by the year 2000. I'm pleased to report we have also met that goal, two full years ahead of schedule. . . . We still have a lot more to do, all of us, to make welfare reform a success—providing child care, helping families move closer to available jobs, challenging more companies to join our welfare-to-work partnership, increasing child support collections from deadbeat parents who have a duty to support their own children. I also want to thank Congress for restoring some of the benefits to immigrants who are here legally and working hard—and I hope you will finish that job this year.

We have to make it possible for all hard-working families to meet their most important responsibilities. Two years ago, we helped guarantee that Americans can keep their health insurance when they change jobs. Last year, we extended health care to up to 5 million children. This year, I challenge Congress to take the next historic steps.

One hundred sixty million of our fellow citizens are in managed care plans. These plans save money and they can improve care. But medical decisions ought to be made by medical doctors, not insurance company accountants. I urge this Congress to reach across the aisle and write into law a Consumer Bill of Rights that says this: You have the right to know all your medical options, not just the cheapest. You have the right to choose the doctor you want for the care you need. You have the right to emergency room care, wherever and whenever you need it. You have the right to keep your medical records confidential. Traditional care or managed care, every American deserves quality care.

Millions of Americans between the ages of fifty-five and sixty-five have lost their health insurance. Some are retired; some are laid off; some lose their coverage when their spouses retire. After a lifetime of work, they are left with nowhere to turn. So I ask the Congress: Let these hard-working Americans buy into the Medicare system. It won't add a dime to the deficit—but the peace of mind it will provide will be priceless.

Next, we must help parents protect their children from the gravest health threat that they face: an epidemic of teen smoking, spread by multimillion-dollar marketing campaigns. I challenge Congress: Let's pass bipartisan, comprehensive legislation that improve public health, protect our tobacco farmers, and change the way tobacco companies do business forever. Let's do what it takes to bring teen smoking down. . . .

Child care is the next frontier we must face to enable people to succeed at home and at work. . . . We've got to raise the quality of child care. We've got to make it safer. We've got to make it more affordable.

Help families to pay for child care for a million more children. Scholarships and background checks for child care workers, and a new emphasis on early learning. Tax credits for businesses that provide child care for their employees. And a larger child care tax credit for working families . . . what this means is that a family of four with an income of $35,000 and high child care costs will no longer pay a single penny of federal income tax. . . . A society rooted in responsibility must provide safe streets, safe schools, and safe neighborhoods. We pursued a strategy of more police, tougher punishment, smarter prevention, with crime-fighting partnerships with local law enforcement and citizen groups, where the rubber hits the road. I can report to you tonight that it's working. Violent crime is down, robbery is down, assault is down, burglary is down—for five years in a row, all across America. We need to finish the job of putting 100,000 more police on our streets.

Again, I ask Congress to pass a juvenile crime bill that provides more prosecutors and probation officers, to crack down on gangs and guns and drugs, and bar violent juveniles from buying guns for life. And I ask you to dramatically expand our support for after-school programs. I think every American should know that most juvenile crime is committed between the hours of 3:00 in the afternoon and 8:00 at night. We can keep so many of our children out of trouble in the first place if we give them someplace to go other than the streets, and we ought to do it.

Drug use is on the decline. . . . I ask you to join me in a ground-breaking effort to hire 1,000 new border patrol agents and to deploy the most sophisticated available new technologies to help close the door on drugs at our borders. . . .

We must exercise responsibility not just at home, but around the world. On the eve of a new century, we have the power and the duty to build a new era of peace and security. But, make no mistake about it, today's possibilities are not tomorrow's guarantees. America must stand against the poisoned appeals of extreme nationalism. We must combat an unholy axis of new threats from terrorists, international criminals and drug traffickers. These twenty-first century predators feed on technology and the free flow of information and ideas and people. And they will be all the more lethal if weapons of mass destruction fall into their hands. . . .

I ask Congress to join me in pursuing an ambitious agenda to reduce the serious threat of weapons of mass destruction. This year, four decades after it was first proposed by President Eisenhower, a comprehensive nuclear test ban is within reach. By ending nuclear testing we can help to prevent the development of new and more dangerous weapons and make it more difficult for non-nuclear states to build them. . . . We also must confront the new hazards of chemical and biological weapons, and the outlaw states, terrorists and organized criminals seeking to acquire them. Saddam Hussein has spent the better part of this decade, and much of his nation's wealth, not on providing for the Iraqi people, but on developing nuclear, chemical, and biological weapons—and the missiles to deliver them. The United Nations weapons inspectors have done a truly remarkable job, finding and destroying more of Iraq's arsenal than was destroyed during the entire Gulf War. Now Saddam Hussein wants to stop them from completing their mission.

I know I speak for everyone in this chamber, Republicans and Democrats, when I say to Saddam Hussein: You cannot defy the will of the world. And when I say to him: You have used weapons of mass destruction before; we are determined to deny you the capacity to use them again. . . .

Our founders set America on a permanent course toward "a more perfect union." To all of you I say it is a journey we can only make together—living as one community. First, we have to continue to reform our government—the instrument of our national community. Everyone knows elections have become too expensive, fueling a fundraising arms race. . . . I ask you to strengthen our democracy and pass campaign finance reform this year. . . .

Our communities are only as healthy as the air our children breathe, the water they drink, the Earth they will inherit. Last year, we put in place the toughest-ever controls on smog and soot. We moved to protect Yellowstone, the Everglades, Lake Tahoe. We expanded every community's right to know about the toxins that threaten their children. Just yesterday, our food safety plan took effect, using new science to protect consumers from dangers like E. coli and salmonella.

Tonight, I ask you to join me in launching a new Clean Water Initiative, a far-reaching effort to clean our rivers, our lakes, our coastal waters for our children.

Our overriding environmental challenge tonight is the worldwide problem of climate change, global warming, the gathering crisis that requires worldwide action. The vast majority of scientists have concluded unequivocally that if we don't reduce the emission of greenhouse gases, at some point in the next century we'll disrupt our climate and put our children and grandchildren at risk. This past December, America led the world to reach a historic agreement committing our nation to reduce greenhouse gas emissions through market forces, new technologies, energy efficiency. We have it in our power to act right here, right now. I propose $6 billion in tax cuts and research and development to encourage innovation, renewable energy, fuel-effective cars, energy-efficient homes.

Every time we have acted to heal our environment, pessimists have told us it would hurt the economy. Well, today our economy is the strongest in a generation, and our environment is the cleanest in a generation. We have always found a way to clean the environment and grow the economy at the same time. And when it comes to global warming, we'll do it again.

Finally, community means living by the defining American value—the ideal heard round the world that we are all created equal. Throughout our history, we haven't always honored that ideal and we've never fully lived up to it. Often it's easier to believe that our differences matter more than what we have in common. It may be easier, but it's wrong.

What we have to do in our day and generation to make sure that America becomes truly one nation—what do we have to do? We're becoming more and more and more diverse. Do you believe we can become one nation? The answer cannot be to dwell on our differences, but to build on our shared values. We all cherish family and faith, freedom and responsibility. We all want our children to grow up in a world where their talents are matched by their opportunities. . . .

We, in this chamber and in this government, must do all we can to address the continuing American challenge to build one America. But we'll only move forward if all our fellow citizens—including every one of you at home watching tonight—is also committed to this cause.

We must work together, learn together, live together, serve together. On the forge of common enterprise Americans of all backgrounds can hammer out a common identity. We see it today in the United States military, in the Peace Corps, in AmeriCorps. Wherever people of all races and backgrounds come together in a shared endeavor and get a fair chance, we do just fine. With shared values and meaningful opportunities and honest communication and citizen service, we can unite a diverse people in freedom and mutual respect. We are many; we must be one. . . .

And while we honor the past, let us imagine the future. Think about this—the entire store of human knowledge now doubles every five years. In the 1980s, scientists identified the gene causing cystic fibrosis—it took nine years. Last year, scientists located the gene that causes Parkinson's Disease—in only nine days. Within a decade, "gene chips" will offer a road map for prevention of illnesses throughout a lifetime. Soon we'll be able to carry all the phone calls on Mother's Day on a single strand of fiber the width of a human hair. A child born in 1998 may well live to see the twenty-second century.

Tonight, as part of our gift to the millennium, I propose a twenty-first century Research Fund for path-breaking scientific inquiry—the largest funding increase in history for the National Institutes of Health, the National Science Foundation, the National Cancer Institute.

We have already discovered genes for breast cancer and diabetes. I ask you to support this initiative so ours will be the generation that finally wins the war against cancer, and begins a revolution in our fight against all deadly diseases.

As important as all this scientific progress is, we must continue to see that science serves humanity, not the other way around. We must prevent the misuse of genetic tests to discriminate against any American. And we must ratify the ethical consensus of the scientific and religious communities, and ban the cloning of human beings.

We should enable all the world's people to explore the far reaches of cyberspace. Think of this—the first time I made a State of the Union speech to you, only a handful of physicists used the World Wide Web. Literally, just a handful of people. Now, in schools, in libraries, homes and businesses, millions and millions of Americans surf the Net every day. We must give parents the tools they need to help protect their children from inappropriate material on the Internet. But we also must make sure that we protect the exploding global commercial potential of the Internet. We can do the kinds of things that we need to do and still protect our kids. . . .

Nearly 200 years ago, a tattered flag, its broad stripes and bright stars still gleaming through the smoke of a fierce battle, moved Francis Scott Key to scribble a few words on the back of an envelope—the words that became our national anthem. Today, that Star Spangled Banner, along with the Declaration of Independence, the Constitution and the Bill of Rights, are on display just a short walk from here. They are America's treasures and we must also save them for the ages.

I ask all Americans to support our project to restore

all our treasures so that the generations of the twenty-first century can see for themselves the images and the words that are the old and continuing glory of America; an America that has continued to rise through every age, against every challenge, of people of great works and greater possibilities, who have always, always found the wisdom and strength to come together as one nation—to widen the circle of opportunity, to deepen the meaning of our freedom, to form that "more perfect union." Let that be our gift to the twenty-first century.

God bless you, and God bless the United States.

Chapter 31

AMERICA AT THE MILLENNIUM

That domestic political and judicial upheaval, as well as recession and economic distress, and finally international terrorism and war would greet them as the millennium dawned should not have surprised Americans. For the tumultuous twentieth century had surely not passed gently into the night, and the twenty-first was only proving rightful heir to its grievous troubles as well as its hopes and aspirations.

Articles of Impeachment voted by a conservative, Republican-dominated House of Representatives against liberal, two-term Democratic President Bill Clinton had ultimately been rejected by a Senate presided over by Chief Justice William Rehnquist, picturesquely costumed for never-ending television coverage as something of a Republican Lord High Executioner. Not long thereafter, however, the nation's highest judicial officer would in turn participate in a bitterly divided Supreme Court decision that would dismay Democratic Vice President Al Gore and the impressive numbers of American voters who in November 2000 had opted for him as President of the United States rather than for Republican candidate George W. Bush or for "spoiler" Green Party candidate Ralph Nader. In a five to four mid-December decision that came many strained weeks after election day itself, and that many Americans considered partisan rather than judicious, the high court set aside crucial Florida Supreme Court cases, effectively giving that state's electoral college vote and thus the long-contested Presidency to "compassionate conservative" Texas Governor Bush. Then, however much disappointed and convinced both men were that justice had not been done, to the applause of their countrymen neither Al Gore nor Connecticut Senator Joseph I. Lieberman, his handpicked Vice Presidential running mate, chose to carry the issue further. And thus the principal deed of American democracy was done . . . not at the ballot box, but in the courtroom.

Whoever had really "won" and could take most legitimate title to it, of course, now Republicans would occupy the White House, and before long—even without anything like a popular mandate at the polls—the new administration would demonstrate what a difference this made in the details as well as the thrust of governance. Not unexpectedly, with Vice President Richard B. Cheney playing an extraordinarily active role in the development and execution of conservative governmental policy—more often than not, indeed, appearing to be a surrogate or acting President despite bouts with serious heart disease that could not be kept from the press—many steps were taken to reverse Clinton administration policies and to derail earlier government actions that tended to diminish the role of America's rich and wellborn or to favor its disadvantaged.

This was particularly true in large and small matters alike relating to energy policies and the environment (with a pronounced shift from Clinton's efforts at conservation to a Bush/Cheney emphasis on the commercial exploitation of Alaskan oil reserves and America's other natural resources); to job retraining and labor safety issues; to funding Social Security and Medicare and other health care reform measures; to social issues such as "right-to-life" versus "free choice," stem cell research, race relations and the separation of church and state; to budgetary and tax policies designed to deal with an increasingly severe economic recession that plagued the new administration from its earliest days.

With a final end to the nineties' bull market, with increasing failures among more than just Internet-boom "dot com" companies, with rising unemployment figures and used-up benefits for the jobless, with deficits rather than surpluses now the order of the day, economic stimulation through tax and budget cuts loomed clearly as government's best response as far as Bush/Cheney leadership was concerned . . . but always corporate and personal tax cuts that seemed to benefit the very rich more than they did the very poor or even more than they did middle-class Americans, and budget cuts that persistently diminished much-needed aid programs for the dispossessed of the nation.

Democrats (who had gained marginal control of the Senate when Vermont Senator Jim Jeffords gave up his Republican affiliation in protest against his party's leadership tactics) continued to press for their traditional liberal policies, while Republicans who controlled the House of Representatives remained largely supportive of the administration's conservatism . . . indeed, most often even in its vanguard. How America would fare domestically in the midst of this partisan standoff remained to be seen, of course, even as appalling instances of irresponsible, but politically very highly connected "anything goes" corporate greed—as with the spectacular collapse of the Texas-based Enron Corporation—would demonstrate the continuing need for meaningful, bipartisan campaign finance reform.

In America's dealings with the world outside, her major parties were also significantly at odds with each other. To the chagrin of most of our allies abroad (as well as concerned environmentalists at home) President Bush unilaterally rejected the Kyoto Protocol on Global Warming. He spurned the Anti-Ballistic Missile Treaty with Russia as well, reverting to Ronald Reagan's idea of creating a massive shield in the sky against America's potential enemies. Generally, too, the new administration seemed early on to take a "go it alone" attitude toward foreign friends and foes alike. Many Democrats thought this the height of folly, and while reluctant to challenge the President in too many areas at the very beginning of his term of office, nevertheless feared his words and deeds as a throwback to earlier Republican isolationism.

Yet, while partisan conflict did not necessarily end at

the water's edge as much then as at times in the past, on September 11, 2001, a totally unprecedented and particularly shocking series of events suddenly changed everything, for all times, for all Americans, seeming to unify us as never before.

For terrorism and war came to America that late-summer day as an incredibly detailed, intricately planned and cruelly executed terrorist plot brought giant passenger airliners—literally captive human missiles—screaming into New York City's unsuspecting World Trade Center, destroying its two mighty towers, familiar all over the world as enduring symbols of America's strength and great wealth, and then into the Pentagon, the very heart of the nation's military command center in Washington, taking the lives of thousands of innocent civilians—men, women and children of all ages, nationalities, colors, and creeds. Terrorists had struck Americans before, but almost invariably overseas—as at our embassies in Tanzania and Kenya, and on the destroyer *Cole*—but never before so boldly or so devastatingly as here at home on 9/11.

"There is America, hit by God in one of its softest spots," terrorist mastermind Osama bin Laden would soon gloat. "Its greatest buildings were destroyed, thank God for that. There is America, full of fear from its north to its south, from its west to its east. Thank God for that."

And that we Americans everywhere now feared for our lives and for our loved ones, there was no doubt. Never before had we confronted such hatred nurtured by religious fanaticism that knew no bounds, that embraced Islam and perversely invoked its God to justify brutal and inhumane terrorism and to sanctify terrorists, granting them a place in heaven as reward for the hell they had wreaked among innocents.

"This war is fundamentally religious," claimed bin Laden. "The people of the East are Muslims. They sympathized with Muslims against the people of the West, who are Crusaders." Led by America, however, decent and thoughtful people all over the world rejected the dread notion that a war against terrorism must fundamentally be a religious war, a struggle against Islam itself. Addressing a Joint Session of Congress the week following 9/11, a determined President of the United States assured his countrymen: "The terrorists practice a fringe form of Islamic extremism that has been rejected by Muslim scholars and the vast majority of Muslim clerics—a fringe movement that perverts the peaceful teachings of Islam. The terrorists' directive commands them to kill Christians and Jews, to kill all Americans, to make no distinction among military and civilians, including women and children."

To Muslims throughout the world, George W. Bush spoke directly: "We respect your faith. It's practiced freely by many millions of Americans, and by millions more in countries that America counts as friends. Its teachings are good and peaceful, and those who commit evil in the name of Allah blaspheme the name of Allah. . . . The enemy of America is not our many Muslim friends; it is not our many Arab friends. Our enemy is a radical network of terrorists, and every government that supports them."

Immediately following the World Trade Center and Pentagon attacks, George Bush had told a prayer service at the National Cathedral in Washington: "War has been waged against us by stealth and deceit and murder. . . . This nation is peaceful, but fierce when stirred to anger. This conflict was begun on the timing and terms of others; it will end in a way and at an hour of our choosing." To which we Americans gave our Amen, enthusiastically applauded our increasingly articulate and now hugely popular new President, recognized that domestic security concerns would likely be with us for all times hereafter, and went doggedly about the demanding business of engaging and destroying our terrorist enemies.

Yet those enemies and the evil within them could not, did not, reduce America to becoming merely a machine of destruction or a vehicle for collective blame. Instead, there was an intense morality to our response, one noted and well summed up in a touching contemporary article by Elie Wiesel, the gentle naturalized-American teacher, writer, Holocaust survivor and Nobel Peace Prize laureate, who perceived, "The terrorists have chosen shame. We choose honor."

Most significantly, too, Americans chose to honor—through unending plaudits and unstinting admiration—one New Yorker in particular who seemed best to symbolize the strength and determination of America's largest city to survive the brutal attack upon its very being, its perennially contentious and highly achieving mayor, Rudy Giuliani. Indeed, in later making him its "Person of the Year 2001," perhaps *Time* magazine best revealed how brilliantly "a very human man taught us superhuman courage."

> Sixteen hours had passed since the Twin Towers crumbled and fell, and people kept telling Rudy Giuliani to get some rest. The indomitable mayor of New York City had spent the day and night holding his town together. He arrived at the World Trade Center just after the second plane hit, watched human beings drop from the sky and—when the south tower imploded—nearly got trapped inside his makeshift command center near the site. Then he led a battered platoon of city officials, reporters and civilians north through the blizzard of ash and smoke, and a detective jimmied open the door to a firehouse so the mayor could revive his government there. Giuliani took to the airwaves to calm and reassure his people, made a few hundred rapid-fire decisions about the security and rescue operations, toured hospitals to comfort the families of the missing, and made four more visits to the apocalyptic attack scene.

Nearly four months later, of course, it remained for New York's Rudy Giuliani himself to sum up the root source of the courage and energies he displayed in the grim black period after 9/11, qualities that led him to be acclaimed everywhere and dubbed "Mayor of the World." Leaving office because municipal term limits forbade him to run then for a third term, Giuliani's December 2001 farewell address was symbolically delivered at lower Manhattan's St. Paul's Chapel, where George Washington had come after his first inauguration as President of the United States, and which two centuries and more later had miraculously survived the villainies of fanatical terrorism as the neighboring World

Trade Center collapsed next to it, killing so many innocent people of many faiths and from many nations.

George W. Bush, Washington National Cathedral Prayer Service, *September 2001*

We are here in the middle hour of our grief. So many have suffered so great a loss, and today we express our nation's sorrow. We come before God to pray for the missing and the dead, and for those who loved them.

On Tuesday, our country was attacked with deliberate and massive cruelty. We have seen the images of fire and ashes and bent steel.

Now come the names, the list of casualties we are only beginning. They are the names of men and women who began their day at a desk or in an airport, busy with life. They are the names of people who faced death and in their last moments called home to say, "Be brave" and "I love you."

They are the names of passengers who defied their murderers and prevented the murder of others on the ground. They are the names of men and women who wore the uniform of the United States and died at their posts.

They are the names of rescuers—the ones whom death found running up the stairs and into the fires to help others. We will read all these names. We will linger over them and learn their stories, and many Americans will weep.

To the children and parents and spouses and families and friends of the lost, we offer the deepest sympathy of the nation. And I assure you, you are not alone.

Just three days removed from these events, Americans do not yet have the distance of history, but our responsibility to history is already clear: to answer these attacks and rid the world of evil.

War has been waged against us by stealth and deceit and murder.

This nation is peaceful, but fierce when stirred to anger. This conflict was begun on the timing and terms of others; it will end in a way and at an hour of our choosing.

Our purpose as a nation is firm, yet our wounds as a people are recent and unhealed and lead us to pray. In many of our prayers this week, there's a searching and an honesty. At St. Patrick's Cathedral in New York, on Tuesday, a woman said, "I pray to God to give us a sign that He's still here."

Others have prayed for the same, searching hospital to hospital, carrying pictures of those still missing.

God's signs are not always the ones we look for. We learn in tragedy that His purposes are not always our own, yet the prayers of private suffering, whether in our homes or in this great cathedral, are known and heard and understood.

There are prayers that help us last through the day or endure the night. There are prayers of friends and strangers that give us strength for the journey, and there are prayers that yield our will to a will greater than our own.

This world He created is of moral design. Grief and tragedy and hatred are only for a time. Goodness, remembrance and love have no end, and the Lord of life holds all who die and all who mourn.

It is said that adversity introduces us to ourselves.

This is true of a nation as well. In this trial, we have been reminded and the world has seen that our fellow Americans are generous and kind, resourceful and brave.

We see our national character in rescuers working past exhaustion, in long lines of blood donors, in thousands of citizens who have asked to work and serve in any way possible. And we have seen our national character in eloquent acts of sacrifice. Inside the World Trade Center, one man who could have saved himself stayed until the end and at the side of his quadriplegic friend. A beloved priest died giving the last rites to a firefighter. Two office workers, finding a disabled stranger, carried her down sixty-eight floors to safety.

A group of men drove through the night from Dallas to Washington to bring skin grafts for burned victims. In these acts and many others, Americans showed a deep commitment to one another and an abiding love for our country.

Today, we feel what Franklin Roosevelt called "the

warm courage of national unity." This is a unity of every faith and every background. This has joined together political parties and both houses of Congress. It is evident in services of prayer and candlelight vigils and American flags, which are displayed in pride and waved in defiance. Our unity is a kinship of grief and a steadfast resolve to prevail against our enemies. And this unity against terror is now extending across the world.

America is a nation full of good fortune, with so much to be grateful for, but we are not spared from suffering. In every generation, the world has produced enemies of human freedom. They have attacked America because we are freedom's home and defender, and the commitment of our fathers is now the calling of our time.

On this national day of prayer and remembrance, we ask almighty God to watch over our nation and grant us patience and resolve in all that is to come. We pray that He will comfort and console those who now walk in sorrow. We thank Him for each life we now must mourn, and the promise of a life to come.

As we've been assured, neither death nor life nor angels nor principalities, nor powers nor things present nor things to come nor height nor depth can separate us from God's love.

May He bless the souls of the departed. May He comfort our own. And may He always guide our country.

God bless America.

George W. Bush, Joint Session of Congress, *September 2001*

Mr. Speaker, Mr. President Pro Tempore, members of Congress, and fellow Americans:

In the normal course of events, Presidents come to this chamber to report on the state of the union. Tonight, no such report is needed. It has already been delivered by the American people.

We have seen it in the courage of passengers who rushed terrorists to save others on the ground—passengers like an exceptional man named Todd Beamer. And would you please help me to welcome his wife, Lisa Beamer, here tonight.

We have seen the state of our union in the endurance of rescuers, working past exhaustion. We have seen the unfurling of flags, the lighting of candles, the giving of blood, the saying of prayers—in English, Hebrew, and Arabic. We have seen the decency of a loving and giving people who have made the grief of strangers their own.

My fellow citizens, for the last nine days, the entire world has seen for itself the state of our union—and it is strong.

Tonight we are a country awakened to danger and called to defend freedom. Our grief has turned to anger, and anger to resolution. Whether we bring our enemies to justice, or bring justice to our enemies, justice will be done.

I thank the Congress for its leadership at such an important time. All of America was touched on the evening of the tragedy to see Republicans and Democrats joined together on the steps of this Capitol, singing "God Bless America." And you did more than sing; you acted, by delivering forty billion dollars to rebuild our communities and meet the needs of our military.

Speaker Hastert, Minority Leader Gephardt, Majority Leader Daschle and Senator Lott, I thank you for your friendship, for your leadership and for your service to our country.

And on behalf of the American people, I thank the world for its outpouring of support. America will never forget the sounds of our national anthem playing at Buckingham Palace, on the streets of Paris, and at Berlin's Brandenburg Gate.

We will not forget South Korean children gathering to pray outside our embassy in Seoul, or the prayers of sympathy offered at a mosque in Cairo. We will not forget moments of silence and days of mourning in Australia and Africa and Latin America.

Nor will we forget the citizens of eighty other nations who died with our own: dozens of Pakistanis; more than one hundred thirty Israelis; more than two hundred fifty citizens of India; men and women from El Salvador, Iran, Mexico and Japan; and hundreds of British citizens. America has no truer friend than Great Britain. Once again, we are joined together in a great cause—so honored the British prime minister has crossed an ocean to show his unity of purpose with America. Thank you for coming, friend.

On September the eleventh, enemies of freedom committed an act of war against our country. Americans have known wars—but for the past one hundred thirty-six years, they have been wars on foreign soil, except for one Sunday in 1941. Americans have known the casualties of war—but not at the center of a great city on a peaceful morning. Americans have known surprise attacks—but never before on thousands of civilians. All of this was brought upon us in a single day—and night fell on a different world, a world where freedom itself is under attack.

Americans have many questions tonight. Americans are asking: Who attacked our country? The evidence we have gathered all points to a collection of loosely affiliated terrorist organizations known as al Qaeda. They are the same murderers indicted for bombing American embassies in Tanzania and Kenya, and responsible for bombing the USS *Cole*.

Al Qaeda is to terror what the Mafia is to crime. But its goal is not making money; its goal is remaking the world—and imposing its radical beliefs on people everywhere.

The terrorists practice a fringe form of Islamic extremism that has been rejected by Muslim scholars and the vast majority of Muslim clerics—a fringe movement that perverts the peaceful teachings of Islam. The terrorists' directive commands them to kill Christians and Jews, to kill all Americans, and make no distinction among military and civilians, including women and children.

This group and its leader—a person named Osama bin Laden—are linked to many other organizations in different countries, including the Egyptian Islamic Jihad and the Islamic Movement of Uzbekistan. There are thousands of these terrorists in more than sixty countries. They are recruited from their own nations and neighborhoods and brought to camps in places like Afghanistan, where they are trained in the tactics of terror. They are sent back to their homes or sent to hide in countries around the world to plot evil and destruction.

The leadership of al Qaeda has great influence in Afghanistan and supports the Taliban regime in controlling most of that country. In Afghanistan, we see al Qaeda's vision for the world.

Afghanistan's people have been brutalized—many are starving and many have fled. Women are not allowed to attend school. You can be jailed for owning a television. Religion can be practiced only as their leaders dictate. A man can be jailed in Afghanistan if his beard is not long enough.

The United States respects the people of Afghanistan—after all, we are currently its largest source of humanitarian aid—but we condemn the Taliban regime. It is not only repressing its own people, it is threatening people everywhere by sponsoring and sheltering and supplying terrorists. By aiding and abetting murder, the Taliban regime is committing murder.

And tonight the United States of America makes the following demands on the Taliban: Deliver to United States authorities all the leaders of al Qaeda who hide in your land. Release all foreign nationals, including American citizens, you have unjustly imprisoned. Protect foreign journalists, diplomats and aid workers in your country. Close immediately and permanently every terrorist training camp in Afghanistan, and hand over every terrorist, and every person in their support structure, to appropriate authorities. Give the United States full access to terrorist training camps, so we can make sure they are no longer operating.

These demands are not open to negotiation or discussion. The Taliban must act, and act immediately. They will hand over the terrorists, or they will share in their fate.

I also want to speak tonight directly to Muslims throughout the world. We respect your faith. It's practiced freely by many millions of Americans, and by millions more in countries that America counts as friends. Its teachings are good and peaceful, and those who commit evil in the name of Allah blaspheme the name of Allah. The terrorists are traitors to their own faith, trying, in effect, to hijack Islam itself. The enemy of America is not our many Muslim friends; it is not our many Arab friends. Our enemy is a radical network of terrorists, and every government that supports them.

Our war on terror begins with al Qaeda, but it does not end there. It will not end until every terrorist group of global reach has been found, stopped and defeated.

Americans are asking: Why do they hate us? They hate what we see right here in this chamber—a democratically elected government. Their leaders are self-appointed. They hate our freedoms—our freedom of religion, our freedom of speech, our freedom to vote and assemble and disagree with each other.

They want to overthrow existing governments in many Muslim countries, such as Egypt, Saudi Arabia and Jordan. They want to drive Israel out of the Middle East. They want to drive Christians and Jews out of vast regions of Asia and Africa.

These terrorists kill not merely to end lives, but to disrupt and end a way of life. With every atrocity, they hope that America grows fearful, retreating from the world and forsaking our friends. They stand against us because we stand in their way.

We are not deceived by their pretenses to piety. We have seen their kind before. They are the heirs of all the murderous ideologies of the twentieth century. By sacrificing human life to serve their radical visions—by abandoning every value except the will to power—they follow in the path of fascism and Nazism and totalitarianism. And they will follow that path all the way to where it ends: in history's unmarked grave of discarded lies.

Americans are asking: How will we fight and win this war? We will direct every resource at our command—every means of diplomacy, every tool of intelligence, every instrument of law enforcement, every financial influence and every necessary weapon of war—to the disruption and to the defeat of the global terror network.

This war will not be like the war against Iraq a decade ago, with a decisive liberation of territory and a swift conclusion. It will not look like the air war above Kosovo two years ago, where no ground troops were used and not a single American was lost in combat.

Our response involves far more than instant retaliation and isolated strikes. Americans should not expect one battle, but a lengthy campaign, unlike any other we have ever seen. It may include dramatic strikes, visible on TV, and covert operations, secret even in success. We will starve terrorists of funding, turn them one against another, drive them from place to place, until there is no refuge or no rest. And we will pursue nations that provide aid or safe haven to terrorism. Every nation, in every region, now has a decision to make. Either you are with us or you are with the terrorists. From this day forward, any nation that continues to harbor or support terrorism will be regarded by the United States as a hostile regime.

Our nation has been put on notice: We are not immune from attack. We will take defensive measures against terrorism to protect Americans. Today, dozens of federal departments and agencies, as well as state and local governments, have responsibilities affecting homeland security. These efforts must be coordinated at the highest level. So tonight I announce the creation of a cabinet-level position reporting directly to me—the Office of Homeland Security.

And tonight I also announce a distinguished American to lead this effort, to strengthen American security: a military veteran, an effective governor, a true patriot, a trusted friend—Pennsylvania's Tom Ridge. He will lead, oversee and coordinate a comprehensive national strategy to safeguard our country against terrorism and respond to any attacks that may come.

These measures are essential. But the only way to defeat terrorism as a threat to our way of life is to stop it, eliminate it and destroy it where it grows.

Many will be involved in this effort, from FBI agents to intelligence operatives to the reservists we have called to active duty. All deserve our thanks, and all have our prayers. And tonight, a few miles from the damaged Pentagon, I have a message for our military: Be ready. I've called the armed forces to alert, and there is reason. The hour is coming when America will act, and you will make us proud.

This is not, however, just America's fight. And what is at stake is not just America's freedom. This is the world's fight. This is civilization's fight. This is the fight of all who believe in progress and pluralism, tolerance and freedom.

We ask every nation to join us. We will ask, and we will need, the help of police forces, intelligence services and banking systems around the world. The United States is grateful that many nations and many international organizations have already responded—with sympathy and with support. Nations from Latin America to Asia, to Africa, to Europe, to the Islamic world. Perhaps the NATO charter reflects best the attitude of the world: An attack on one is an attack on all.

The civilized world is rallying to America's side. They understand that, if this terror goes unpunished, their own cities, their own citizens may be next. Terror unanswered cannot only bring down buildings—it can threaten the stability of legitimate governments. And you know what? We're not going to allow it.

Americans are asking: What is expected of us? I ask you to live your lives, and hug your children. I know many citizens have fears tonight, and I ask you to be calm and resolute, even in the face of a continuing threat.

I ask you to uphold the values of America, and remember why so many have come here. We are in a fight for our principles, and our first responsibility is to live by them. No one should be singled out for unfair treatment or unkind words because of their ethnic background or religious faith.

I ask you to continue to support the victims of this tragedy with your contributions. Those who want to give can go to a central source of information, libertyunites.org, to find the names of groups providing direct help in New York, Pennsylvania and Virginia.

The thousands of FBI agents who are now at work in this investigation may need your cooperation, and I ask you to give it.

I ask for your patience with the delays and inconveniences that may accompany tighter security, and for your patience in what will be a long struggle.

I ask your continued participation and confidence in the American economy. Terrorists attacked a symbol of American prosperity. They did not touch its source.

America is successful because of the hard work and creativity and enterprise of our people. These were the true strengths of our economy before September eleventh, and they are our strengths today.

And finally, please continue praying for the victims of terror and their families, for those in uniform and for our great country. Prayer has comforted us in sorrow and will help strengthen us for the journey ahead.

Tonight I thank my fellow Americans for what you have already done and for what you will do. And ladies and gentlemen of the Congress, I thank you, their representatives, for what you have already done and for what we will do together.

Tonight we face new and sudden national challenges. We will come together to improve air safety, to dramatically expand the number of air marshals on domestic flights, and take new measures to prevent hijacking. We will come together to promote stability and keep our airlines flying, with direct assistance during this emergency.

We will come together to give law enforcement the additional tools it needs to track down terror here at home. We will come together to strengthen our intelligence capabilities to know the plans of terrorists before they act, and find them before they strike.

We will come together to take active steps that strengthen America's economy, and put our people back to work.

Tonight we welcome two leaders who embody the extraordinary spirit of all New Yorkers: Governor George Pataki, and Mayor Rudolph Giuliani. As a symbol of America's resolve, my administration will work with Congress, and these two leaders, to show the world that we will rebuild New York City.

After all that has just passed—all the lives taken and all the possibilities and hopes that died with them—it is natural to wonder if America's future is one of fear. Some speak of an age of terror. I know there are struggles ahead and dangers to face. But this country will define our times, not be defined by them. As long as the United States of America is determined and strong, this will not be an age of terror, this will be an age of liberty, here and across the world.

Great harm has been done to us. We have suffered great loss. And in our grief and anger we have found our mission and our moment. Freedom and fear are at war. The advance of human freedom—the great achievement of our time, and the great hope of every time—now depends on us. Our nation—this generation—will lift a dark threat of violence from our people and our future. We will rally the world to this cause by our efforts, by our courage. We will not tire, we will not falter and we will not fail.

It is my hope that, in the months and years ahead, life will return almost to normal. We'll go back to our lives and routines, and that is good. Even grief recedes with time and grace. But our resolve must not pass. Each of us will remember what happened that day and to whom it happened. We'll remember the moment the news came—where we were and what we were doing. Some will remember an image of a fire or a story of rescue. Some will carry memories of a face and a voice gone forever.

And I will carry this: It is the police shield of a man named George Howard, who died at the World Trade Center trying to save others. It was given to me by his mom, Arlene, as a proud memorial to her son. This is my reminder of lives that ended and a task that does not end.

I will not forget this wound to our country or those who inflicted it. I will not yield. I will not rest. I will not relent in waging this struggle for freedom and security for the American people.

The course of this conflict is not known, yet its outcome is certain. Freedom and fear, justice and cruelty have always been at war, and we know that God is not neutral between them.

Fellow citizens, we'll meet violence with patient justice—assured of the rightness of our cause and confident of the victories to come. In all that lies before us, may God grant us wisdom, and may He watch over the United States of America.

Thank you.

Rudolph Giuliani's Farewell Address, *2001*

Thank you very, very much. Thank you and good morning and thank you for coming. Very often in the past three months plus people asked me where do I get my energy? Where does it come from? Well, it's really simple: It comes from you and it comes from here. What I mean by that, my strength and energy comes entirely from the people of the city of New York and it comes from a place like this, St. Paul's Chapel. This is a house of God and it's one of the homes of our republic.

Although I have to leave you as the mayor soon I resume the much more honorable title of citizen: citizen of New York and citizen of the United States. You get to be mayors and council members and congressmen and senators and governors and even presidents for short periods of time, but you always remain a citizen. And the people of the city should understand that all of the sources of my strength absolutely endure because you have it and you have that strength and you've displayed it. . . .

Abraham Lincoln used to say that the test of your Americanism was not your family tree; the test of your Americanism was how much you believed in America. Because we're like a religion really. A secular religion. We believe in ideas and ideals. We're not one race, we're many; we're not one ethnic group, we're everyone; we're not one language, we're all of these people.

So what ties us together? We're tied together by our belief in political democracy. We're tied together by our belief in religious freedom. We're tied together by our belief in capitalism, a free economy where people make their own choices about the spending of their money. We're tied together because we respect human life. We're tied together because we respect the rule of law. Those are the group of ideas that make us Americans.

And being in this chapel is very, very appropriate. The reason I chose this chapel is not because it has wonderful Christmas decorations or whatever that thing is. The reason I chose this chapel is because this chapel is thrice-hallowed ground. This is a place of really special importance to people who have a feeling and a sense and an emotion and an understanding of patriotism. This is hallowed by the fact that it was consecrated as a house of God in 1766. That's a long time ago. And in 1789, in April of 1789, George Washington came, and after he was inaugurated as the first president of our republic, he prayed right here in this church, which makes it very sacred ground to people who feel what America is all about.

But then it was consecrated one more time, in 2001 on September eleventh. When I walked in here from the back, I looked up because every time I've walked in this church when I looked up I saw the twin towers just way, way above. This church existed for many years in the shadow of the twin towers. And on September eleventh when the twin towers were viciously attacked and came crashing to the ground in the worst attack on America, destroyed buildings all around, did damages far away as city hall all the way south in the southern part of Battery Park City and covered this whole area with debris, body parts and in many, many ways damaged buildings—this chapel remained not only not destroyed, not a single window was broken, not a single thing hurt. And I think there's some very, very special significance in that. The place where George Washington prayed when he first became President of the United States stood strong, powerful, untouched, undaunted by the attacks of these people who hate what we stand for. Because what we stand for is so much stronger than they are.

So this chapel stands for our values. And it's a very important place. And I hope you return here often to reflect on what it means to be an American and a New Yorker. . . .

. . . I think the key to our success as a city, the reason we are the most famous city in the world, and the reason why we really legitimately are the capital of the world, is really just one thing: immigration. We are an open city. We have never been afraid of people. We've never been afraid of people no matter what their color, religion, ethnic background. We're a city in which our diversity is our greatest strength.

I remember after the attack on the World Trade Center, it just came very naturally for me to say to people, do not engage in group blame. Do not go single out people who are Arab-Americans and blame the attack on the World Trade Center on them. Because the people who attacked the World Trade Center, we weren't even sure exactly who it was then. But the people who attacked the World Trade Center, obviously are vicious criminals of the worst kind. And there isn't a single group that sits out there that doesn't have among them vicious criminals of some kind. Every ethnic group, religious group, racial group has some bad, really bad people in that group.

And then the question becomes are you the kind of prejudiced, irrational human being that defines the group based on the bad people in that group, which means you are going to end up hating everybody. Or do you kind of get beyond that and see that, in fact, in every group, most people are decent people who are just trying to do the same thing that you are doing?

I think the experience of New York allows more and more people to see that than any place else. Because we keep bumping into each other all the time. And you keep bumping into people who look different than you do. I mean, you see them all over. They have different outfits and they talk different languages. And they wear different clothes. And they say different things. And that experience, if you're a person of some degree of common sense and intelligence, that experience opens you up to the feeling that, well, people are basically all the same.

And it's the greatest strength that we have, the greatest strength that we have as a city is immigration. And keeping ourselves open to people. And we shouldn't allow what has happened to us in the last three, three and a half months—we shouldn't allow what has happened to us to stop that in any way at all. We should continue to be open to people.

It doesn't mean we shouldn't have more security. It doesn't mean we should be open to people with criminal backgrounds. It doesn't mean that we shouldn't, in a very, very proper and appropriate and even tough way, screen the people who come here to make sure that we are not letting terrorists in. But it does mean that we should continue to be a city and a country that's open to new people coming here from all over the world. . . .

Our enemies insanely commit suicide to serve some irrational purpose. And they think that we are afraid—they used to think that we are afraid to die for what we believe in. And the reality is that we don't want to die. And we don't believe that it's our right to make that choice for ourselves. We think God only has that right. But the reality is that we're just a few blocks from a site in which hundreds and hundreds of men and women freely by choice gave up their life. First, to protect the lives of other people. And secondly, to preserve the dignity and honor of the United States of America while under attack.

This war will go on for some time: to find the terrorists, to eliminate terrorism, to eliminate terrorists. I don't know how long it will go on. It will go on probably for a longer time than we would like.

But I hope you realize that we have already won it. We have already won the war. It's just a matter now of finishing it. And that isn't easy. And it's going to mean more sacrifices and more lives lost. It could even mean more attacks. I don't know. But I know we won.

I know we won because I saw within hours the reaction of first, the people of New York City, then the people of the United States of America. I saw within the first hours the three firefighters who lifted the American flag up high, within hours of the attack while it was still life-threatening to be there, as it was for a long time.

They took the American flag and they lifted it up high into the sky. And that picture was shown all over the world. It was quite clear that we had already won when so many people came here from all over the country to help us and assist us. And came to this church, which is now used to give some relief and some help to all those people who are doing this very, very difficult work. And they came here from all over the country. When the people lined up along the West Side Highway for days. Day after day after day waving the American flag, holding signs saying WE LOVE YOU, giving water to the relief workers that were going down there. . . .

We are in a very holy place. And we are really on territory that is hallowed in very special ways, by the presence of George Washington and all of our brave heroes that gave their lives. Never before, I don't think, in the history of America have so many people died and then ended up saving so many people. It's an unbelievable thing that that happened.

So I really believe we shouldn't think about this site out there right beyond us right here as a site of economic development. I think we should think about it this way. We should think about how we can find the most creative minds possible who love and honor America and can express that in artistic ways that I can't, but they can. And we should think about a soaring monumental beautiful memorial that just draws millions of people here that just want to see it. And then also want to come here for reading and education and background and research.

Long after we are all gone, it's the sacrifice of our patriots and their heroism that is going to be what this place is remembered for. This is going to be a place that is remembered one hundred and one thousand years from now, like the great battlefields of Europe and of the United States. And we really have to be able to do with it what they did with Normandy or Valley Forge or Bunker Hill or Gettysburg. We have to be able to create something here that enshrines this forever and that allows people to build on it and grow from it.

And it's going to happen if we just think about it in a very narrow way. How do you replace the offices? And how do you get the jobs? There is plenty of— We can do all that. We've got to think about it from the point of view of a soaring beautiful memorial. And then if we do that right, if we do that part right, then the economic development will just happen. And millions of people will come here. And you'll have all the economic development you want. And you can do the office space in a lot of different places. And I feel very, very strongly about this. And it is something I'm not going to forget and something I'm going to continue to speak up on because I feel I owe that in a very, very personal way. Thousands of people died there. And hundreds of them died as rescue workers. They didn't have to go there. They walked in to try to pull people out. Some of them are very close friends of mine. And some of them are very close friends of people that I love and care about and are related to the people that I love and I care about. . . .

So I think we have an obligation to the people who did die to make sure of two things about which there can be absolutely no compromise: Their families need to be protected just as if they had been alive, financially and in every other way that we can help and assist their families—there should be no compromise about that, ever; and second, this place has to be sanctified. This place has to become a place in which when anybody comes here immediately they're going to feel the great power and strength and emotion of what it means to be an American. We have to do that and not worry about other things. Because this is too important a place. In their memory we have to do that. . . .

God bless New York and God bless America.

Chapter 32

THE POLITICS OF HOPE

. . . It's that fundamental belief—I am my brother's keeper, I am my sister's keeper—that makes this country work. It's what allows us to pursue our individual dreams, yet still come together as a single American family. "E pluribus unum." Out of many, one.

Yet even as we speak, there are those who are preparing to divide us, the spin masters and negative ad peddlers who embrace the politics of anything goes. Well, I say to them tonight, there's not a liberal America and a conservative America—there's the United States of America.

There's not a black America and white America and Latino America and Asian America; there's the United States of America. The pundits like to slice and dice our country into Red States and Blue States: Red States for Republicans, Blue States for Democrats. But I've got news for them, too. We worship an awesome God in the Blue States, and we don't like federal agents poking around our

> libraries in the Red States. We coach Little League in the Blue States and have gay friends in the Red States. There are patriots who opposed the war in Iraq and patriots who supported it. We are one people, all of us pledging allegiance to the stars and stripes, all of us defending the United States of America.
>
> In the end, that's what this election is about. Do we participate in a politics of cynicism or a politics of hope . . . the hope of a skinny kid with a funny name who believes that America has a place for him, too? The audacity of hope! . . . In the end, that is God's greatest gift to us, the bedrock of this nation, the belief in things not seen, the belief that there are better days ahead. I believe we can give our middle-class relief and provide working families with a road to opportunity. I believe we can provide jobs to the jobless, homes to the homeless, and reclaim young people in cities across America from violence and despair. I believe that as we stand on the crossroads of history, we can make the right choices, and meet the challenges that face us.

Thus its Keynote Speaker—a young and as yet little-known Illinois state legislator—electrified the 2004 Democratic Presidential Convention with these unifying words, clearly marking him for future higher office. Later that year, he would be elected to the United States Senate, in another four years chosen as the first African-American President of the United States of America. The "politics of hope . . . the audacity of hope," indeed! With a call for economic opportunity for all reminiscent of Franklin D. Roosevelt almost four generations earlier, Barack Hussein Obama thus spoke to the concerns of liberal Democrats bridling under the laissez-faire, lower taxes for the rich, privatize Social Security, deregulate Wall Street and the world of finance, pro-business economic and social philosophy of the Bush/Cheney Administration.

Democrats who then chose Senators John Kerry of Massachusetts and John Edwards of North Carolina as their 2004 standard bearers also rallied to a belatedly strong stand against the Administration's "preemptive war" policy in Iraq. September 11, 2001, had united most Americans in support of thoughtful defense measures against terrorism and of bringing the battle directly to those who had so viciously targeted America. But Democrats had differed importantly among themselves about the uncompromising Bush/Cheney choice of Iraq's Saddam Hussein to war against—a choice that had pointedly flouted the wishes of America's would-be allies around the world, had overestimated whatever threat Saddam did actually pose to Americans, and, perhaps most important, had largely ignored the need to focus America's limited military resources against the real al Qaeda enemy in Afghanistan.

Most Democrats, perhaps fearing to be labeled "unpatriotic," perhaps sincerely believing promises the President of the United States had made to wage war against Iraq only as a last resort and after the presence there of weapons of mass destruction had been confirmed, had supported a 2002 Congressional Resolution authorizing war—the "shock and awe" campaign that did quickly rid the world of Saddam, but led also to seemingly never-ending hostilities that boasted no exit strategy and would continue to take their toll of thousands of American lives and scores of thousands of Iraqi lives seven and even more years later . . . despite the "Mission Accomplished" declaration by George W. Bush as early as 2003.

Other Democrats had forcefully and consistently spoken out against going to war with Iraq, as Barack Obama did just before the War Resolution in October 2002:

> I stand before you as someone who is not opposed to war in all circumstances. The Civil War was one of the bloodiest in history, and yet it was only through the crucible of the sword, the sacrifice of multitudes, that we could begin to perfect this union, and drive the scourge of slavery from our soil. I don't oppose all wars.
>
> My grandfather signed up for a war the day after Pearl Harbor . . . fought in Patton's army . . . saw the dead and dying across the fields of Europe . . .

heard the stories of fellow troops who first entered Auschwitz and Treblinka . . . fought in the name of a larger freedom . . . and he did not fight in vain. I don't oppose all wars.

After September Eleventh, after witnessing the carnage and destruction, the dust and the tears, I supported this administration's pledge to hunt down and root out those who would slaughter innocents in the name of intolerance, and I would willingly take up arms myself to prevent such tragedy from happening again. I don't oppose all wars.

What I am opposed to is a dumb war. What I am opposed to is a rash war. What I am opposed to is the cynical attempt by Richard Perle and Paul Wolfowitz and other armchair, weekend warriors in this administration to shove their own ideological agendas down our throats, irrespective of the costs in lives lost and in hardships borne.

What I am opposed to is the attempt by political hacks like Karl Rove to distract us from a rise in the uninsured, a rise in the poverty rate, a drop in the median income—to distract us from corporate scandals and a stock market that has just gone through the worst month since the Great Depression. That's what I'm opposed to. A dumb war. A rash war. A war based not on reason but on passion, not on principle but on politics.

I suffer no illusions about Saddam Hussein. He is a brutal man. A ruthless man. A man who butchers his own people to secure his own power . . . He's a bad guy. The world, and the Iraqi people, would be better off without him. . . . But I also know that Saddam poses no imminent and direct threat to the United States, or to his neighbors, that the Iraqi economy is in shambles, that the Iraqi military [has] a fraction of its former strength, and that in concert with the international community he can be contained until . . . he falls away into the dustbin of history. I know that even a successful war against Iraq will require a US occupation of undetermined length, an undetermined cost, with undetermined consequences. I know that an invasion of Iraq without a clear rationale and without strong international support will only fan the flames of the Middle East, and encourage the worst, rather than the best, impulses of the Arab world, and strengthen the recruitment arm of al Qaeda. I am not opposed to all wars. I'm opposed to dumb wars. . . .

The consequences of war are dire, the sacrifices immeasurable. We may have occasion in our lifetime to once again rise up in defense of our freedom, and pay the wages of war. But we ought not . . . travel down that hellish path blindly. Nor should we allow those who would march off and pay the ultimate sacrifice, who would prove the full measure of devotion with their blood to make such an awful sacrifice in vain.

But the war came. Public opinion polls attested to its growing unpopularity, and a bipartisan blue-ribbon investigative "9/11 Commission" denied the legitimacy of connecting it to the terrorist attack on America. Yet, even though American casualties as well as mistakes in statecraft, political decisions, and on-the-ground operations in Iraq mounted, as they had in Vietnam decades before; even though confusing sectional, religious and tribal divisions in that faraway, largely unknown land seemed ever more bloody and unending; even though corruption and profiteering in America's "nation building" and reconstruction efforts surfaced again and again; even though prisoner abuse scandals in Abu Ghraib, accusations of torture, and unprecedented detention practices at Guantánamo Bay all raised questions about America's moral fiber no less than its national objectives; and even though wiretapping and other measures earlier considered illegal at home were instead increasingly authorized by executive order alone in the name of national security—still the Republican pro-war ticket prevailed quite impressively at the polls in 2004. And President Bush thought his new "political capital" sufficient to pursue even further his conservative social and economic goals at home and neoconservative efforts to aggressively "promote democracy" abroad.

Not quite, however. The President's objective of

privatizing Social Security was never achieved . . . much to the good fortune of a nation that ultimately would see the Bush/Cheney years end in a collapsing stock market, a disrupted banking system, deep recession, and a threatened depression. And the failure of an Administration that touted its managerial skills and business "know-how" to respond either efficiently or humanely in 2005 to Hurricane Katrina and its devastating aftermath in large areas of the United States undermined the President's claim to an effective "compassionate conservatism." Besides, the home-market bubble began to burst. Long boosted beyond belief by banking and loan practices fostered by an unrelieved conservative mantra of "deregulation" at all levels of government, now home values declined precipitously, with bankruptcies and foreclosures in numbers—and in fear, itself—reminiscent of the Great Depression. Production in America slackened; major industries tottered on the brink, surviving only with massive government "bailouts"; jobs disappeared; unemployment insurance claims swelled; wages that had long since been stagnant lowered still further. And in 2006 Democrats had won control of both Houses of Congress for the first time since 1994, with their leaders soon vying intensely for the party's 2008 Presidential nomination.

Not that the eight years of Bush/Cheney hadn't seen many of their objectives achieved. The war in Iraq was theirs to wage, and they did, whatever the cost in American and Iraqi lives and in American dollars and future indebtedness, whatever the damage to America's relations with allies abroad, whatever the erosion of Americans' own belief in being "the last best hope of mankind," however much Americans' civil liberties were perhaps both unnecessarily as well as necessarily compromised for the sake of national security. In addition, the Administration had undone at home much that it had *set out* to undo. Decades of efforts at environmental protections were undermined. Barriers between church and state were eroded. Labor unions were further weakened. Faith-based policies compromised science at many levels. Voting reform measures were stymied. Federal prosecutions were variously begun or ended for partisan purposes. Tax policies were restructured to favor the very rich, who got ever richer. In short, in the Bush/ Cheney years a veritable social, economic and political *counter*revolution—begun in the Reagan Presidency and aimed at the many progressive changes in American life brought about from the New Deal onward—seemed to have grown ever more intense and widespread. But ultimately only its history could serve as such "folly's antidote," in Arthur M. Schlesinger's poignant observation. Perhaps nowhere was this Republican thrust better articulated and defended than in several brilliant broadcast interviews over those years given by Dick Cheney, the uniquely powerful Vice President of the United States, considered by some as the Administration's true guiding spirit, by others, as its "evil genius." Few of these exchanges were as pointed as the lame duck Vice President's "exit" interviews with Jim Lehrer on the PBS *News Hour* and then with Bob Schieffer on CBS News' *Face the Nation* in January 2009.

It was, moreover, great political shrewdness in appointing dozens of carefully chosen conservatives to the Federal judiciary that gave the Republican leaders their most lasting legacy. For years to come, the fate of many of their initiatives would now be determined by court majorities led ideologically by their appointees to the Supreme Court of the United States—Chief Justice John G. Roberts and Associate Justice Samuel Alito—both of whom seemed well-disposed in their jurisprudence to the seminal Bush/Cheney concept of a "Unitary Executive"—one in which greater and greater powers are presumed to reside, both in war and peace, in the Office of the President of the United States, rather than in the Congress and the Judiciary as well. An important, however potentially dangerous, tool of governance, it was clearly not unknown to both Abraham Lincoln and Franklin D. Roosevelt, Barack Obama's most compelling models. And to what extent, in what manner, how persistently, and with what purpose in mind America's new President will himself embrace this singular approach to his most solemn oath to "preserve, protect and defend the Constitution of the United States" would largely compose the American story still to be told.

For with its appealing message of change and of possibility ("Yes we can!"), an extraordinary new voice had been heard in the land, one seemingly tempered as well with reason and enormous respect both for continuity and for the best of America's heritage. Inspiringly eloquent, yet cool, confident, and above all pragmatic in his every political judgment, Barack Obama had hardly entered the Senate before he declared for his party's 2008 Presidential nomination. Presumably, it was considerably more experienced Hillary Clinton's to lose. And she did, though barely, and only after a long, hard primary campaign that had importantly mobilized and energized women, African-Americans, Hispanics, and particularly young voters in an intense contest between liberal candidates who seemed usually to complement rather than to oppose one another on foreign policy and on what Democrats saw as overriding domestic issues: inadequate health care in America, a failing educational system, diminishing energy resources and a threatened environment. Besides, in defeating Clinton for the Democratic nomination, Obama had over long months honed fine his campaign skills, making unprecedentedly powerful use of new technologies—from e-mail to social networking to political blogs—that would continue to serve him well in communicating with and in mobilizing eager followers. And finally, with an unforgiving economy getting worse each month, and with a Republican White House incumbent whose public ratings had sunk to historic depths, it seemed more and more unlikely that even personally popular Republican Presidential candidate John McCain could bring four more years in power to his party, though his choice of little-known Alaska governor Sarah Palin as his running mate enabled him further to "mobilize his base," gaining support among conservative voters who would find it hard to accept an African-American as President of the United States.

Race, of course, had surfaced in Barack Obama's very bid for the Democratic Presidential nomination. How could it have been otherwise in a nation seemingly torn forever by the ravages of slavery and then of racism, torn between "the bondsman's two hundred fifty years of unrequited toil" and "the better angels of our nature"? In March 2008 in Philadelphia, where generations before Americans had met as "We the people, in order to form a more perfect union," Obama boldly faced up to race in America in a much heralded address that focused first on his long association with his own outspokenly radical former pastor, Reverend Jeremiah Wright, whose angry racial expressions had so jeopardized the young candidate, but broadened finally to the larger, more important issues that jeopardize all Americans. Even some supporters felt the candidate had not dealt adequately here with the significance of Reverend Wright. But Obama's "A More Perfect Union" speech achieved its goal. Race now became much less a campaign burden. And in November, with former rivals Senator Joe Biden as his running mate and Senator Hillary Clinton working unceasingly in his support, the man from Illinois, "Land of Lincoln," won the Presidency with handsome popular and Electoral College majorities. The curse of race in America, many thought, had been exorcized. But others questioned whether it had not merely been trumped temporarily by fear—fear of a devastated economy—and by opposition to a now seemingly endless as well as unpopular war, for both of which distraught voters held Republicans responsible.

Speech after speech had established Barack Obama as perhaps America's most gifted political orator since John F. Kennedy and, before him, Franklin Delano Roosevelt. Now, speaking to incredible throngs of true believers in Chicago's Grant Park on election night, 2008, and in his inspiring 2009 Inaugural Address, the triumphant young President illumined once again the politics of hope . . . the audacity of hope!

Vice President Cheney on PBS' *NewsHour, 2009*

JIM LEHRER: Yesterday President Bush said that he will leave Washington next week with a great sense of accomplishment. Do you feel the same way?

VICE PRESIDENT DICK CHENEY: I do.

LEHRER: Why? Explain.

CHENEY: Well, I think there are a number of areas where we've had a significant impact on events or on the course of history, if you will. The one that stands out in my mind, that I think is most important, is something that didn't happen and that's the fact that we were able to interrupt, block, defeat all further attempts by al Qaeda to launch mass-casualty attacks against the United States after 9/11. That's taken some very tough decisions by the president, some great work by a lot of folks in the intelligence services, in the military and so forth. But I look at that and the lives that were saved and the threats that were defeated as probably our greatest achievement.

LEHRER: And you feel it's actions that you took, the president took, the administration took—resulted in this happening? In other words, prevented these further attacks—there would have been further attacks had you not been there and you'd not taken action.

CHENEY: Yes, sir. I can go back—and a lot of the details are still obviously classified—but what we did in effect was, in the aftermath of 9/11, in '02, '03 time frame, when we first began to capture high-value detainees—senior members of al Qaeda like Khalid Sheikh Muhammad or Abu Zubaydah—we then were able to interrogate them and collect intelligence from them, both about the al Qaeda organization generally: how they functioned, who they were, where they came from, how they were financed. But then also to get specific intelligence on prospective attacks and allow us to go out and wrap up, capture and arrest others. And that list is very impressive.

LEHRER: And if that had not happened, you think there would have been further attacks?

CHENEY: There's no doubt in mind there would have been.

LEHRER: Serious attacks of the level like 9/11?

CHENEY: Serious attacks, well, plans, for example, to fly an airliner into the tallest building on the West Coast, plans to develop a so-called dirty device to be detonated someplace in the United States, plans to hijack aircraft that were all headed for Heathrow and then to capture them, blow them up over Heathrow. And plans to launch aircraft that they'd captured in Europe and destroy them as they came into the United States. I mean, it was a robust set of programs. There were others; other regions of the world that were involved as well as the United States. We got a wealth of information from those programs that are the source of some controversy, obviously, but we did not have a lot of information on al Qaeda on 9/11; it was very important that we develop it in the aftermath of 9/11 and we did.

LEHRER: The president has also said that he made some mistakes in the last eight years. Did you make any?

CHENEY: Well, make mistakes— I can think of places where I underestimated things. For example, talking about Iraq, the extent of which the Iraqi population had been beaten down by Saddam Hussein was greater than I anticipated. That is, we thought that the Iraqis would be able to bounce back fairly quickly once Saddam was gone or the new government established, and step up and take major responsibilities for governing Iraq, building a military and so forth and that took longer than I expected. I think that what happened in Saddam's reign as well as what happened in '91, when after the Gulf War there was an uprising in Iraq that was brutally crushed by Saddam. I think that eliminated a lot of the people that were potential leaders; if they'd stuck their heads up they'd have been chopped off. And if I were to look for one where there was a miscalculation on my part, I think I underestimated the difficulty of getting an Iraqi government stood up.

LEHRER: When you look back on that, why? How did that miscalculation come about?

CHENEY: Well, we didn't have that good of intelligence—I don't think—with respect to the sort of the state of affairs inside Iraq. A lot of that had been wiped out over the years. Saddam Hussein was so brutal, killed so many people, slaughtered so many innocents, that it had a lasting effect on Iraqi society that was greater than I expected.

LEHRER: Is it fair to say, then, that the miscalculation resulted in chaotic situation that existed immediately after for awhile and got—immediately after the invasion and all that sort of stuff?

CHENEY: I can't say that. I can't like those two particular points. What I can say is I think if we had been able to move more rapidly to stand up a government that was capable, I think we might have avoided some of that. But I don't want to blame all that on the Iraqi government; it was a difficult situation, but it was successful. We now find ourselves in a situation where, five years later, we've achieved most of the objectives that you would have set out in the spring of a '03 when we launched into Iraq. We've got the violence level down to the its lowest level since '03, we've had three national elections, a constitution written, a new government stood up, a new army recruited and trained, the Iraqis are increasingly able to take on responsibility for themselves and we've now entered into a strategic framework agreement with the new Iraqi government that will provide for the ultimate withdrawal of U.S. forces. You could not have asked for much more than that in terms of the policies that we started on in '03.

LEHRER: Mr. Vice President, getting from there to here, 4,500 Americans have died, at least a hundred thousand Iraqis have died. Has it been worth that?

CHENEY: I think so.

LEHRER: Why?

CHENEY: Because I believed at the time that what Saddam Hussein represented was, especially in the aftermath of 9/11, was a terror-sponsoring state—so designated by the State Department. He was making payments to the families of suicide bombers; he provided a safe haven and sanctuary for Abu Nidal and other terrorist operations. He had produced and used weapons of mass destruction, chemical and biological agents. He'd had a nuclear program in the past. He killed hundreds of thousands of his own people and he did have a relationship with al Qaeda. Now, we've had this debate, keeps people trying to conflate those arguments. That's not to say that Saddam was responsible for 9/11; it is to say—as George Tenet, CIA director, testified in open session in the Senate—that there was a relationship there that went back ten years. So this was a terror-sponsoring state with access to weapons of mass destruction and that's the greatest threat we faced in the aftermath of 9/11: The next time we found terrorists in the middle of one of our cities, it wouldn't be nineteen guys armed with airline tickets and box cutters—it would be terrorists armed with a biological agent or maybe even a nuclear device. So I think, given the track record of Saddam Hussein, I think we did exactly the right thing, I think the country's better off for it today. I think it's been part of the effort alongside Afghanistan to liberate 50 million people and establish a vibrant democracy in the heart of the Middle East. I think those are major, major accomplishments.

LEHRER: Speaking of Afghanistan and miscalculations, do you consider it a miscalculation to have gone into Iraq before Osama bin Laden had been found, arrested, killed? Before al Qaeda had been completely destroyed, before the Taliban had been routed in Afghanistan?

CHENEY: I don't. We had pretty well routed the Taliban and the al Qaeda and closed the training camps and captured and killed a great many of al Qaeda members as well as the Taliban when we originally went in. The situation now, obviously, is that we've got to continue to be engaged in Afghanistan. It's one of the most difficult places to work in because of the territory, the geography, the terrain, but also because it's one of the poorest countries in the world; they don't have a lot of resources. And we've now got the added problem that's totally unrelated to Iraq, that in Pakistan, next door to Afghanistan, you've got a sanctuary, for example, for some al Qaeda that are still there, as well as the Taliban and move back and forth across the border. We'll be involved there for a long time, but that doesn't mean we shouldn't have taken out Saddam Hussein. I think we were capable of doing both; I think in effect we've done both.

LEHRER: But you didn't do both simultaneously, right?

CHENEY: Well, pretty much simultaneously. I mean, there'd been—

LEHRER: Osama bin Laden's still—that's what I mean—al Qaeda's still functioning.

CHENEY: But Osama bin Laden—wherever he is, and he's in a deep hole—he does not have much impact on the organization, as best we can tell. The important thing was to go after the organization—after al Qaeda. Even if you got Osama bin Laden tomorrow, you'd still have a problem in terms of whatever residue of al Qaeda is out there. We have had a big impact on al Qaeda; this is a significantly diminished organization, I think, compared to what it was four or five years ago when we killed Abu Musab Zarqawi, the head of al Qaeda in Iraq in June of '06—major accomplishment. And over the last—I don't want to get in the classified area, obviously, but within the last year or so we've had a very significant impact on senior al Qaeda leadership.

LEHRER: One more general scope here, Mr. Vice President. What do you make of a current suggestion that you have been in fact the most powerful vice president in history, but in one of the most failed presidencies in history?

CHENEY: I don't buy that.

LEHRER: You don't buy that?

CHENEY: No, I think the argument that this is a failed presidency is just dead wrong. I think we'll hear that from some of our critics, but when I look back at what we've been able to do—we dealt with big issues. We didn't deal with school uniforms—we dealt with the fact that we brought down two of the worst regimes in the twentieth century: the Taliban in Afghanistan and Saddam Hussein in Iraq. We were forced when we arrived—shortly after we arrived—to have to deal with the global war on terror, which had not been managed properly before that. We ended up inheriting a situation that has been very challenging, but we've been very successful at it. And when you look at what we've been able to do, both in terms of our activities overseas as well as our operations that allowed us to block any further attack against the United States here at home, I think those are great successes and I think there aren't many administrations that can point to successes on that scale.

LEHRER: What about in the domestic area? What of the economy? The economic downturn is on scope or on a par with the Great Depression. Was it not a miscalculation or a failure to see that coming?

CHENEY: No, I don't think it was a miscalculation. I think we had good economic policies, especially in the early years. I think the tax packages we passed in '03, for example, produced fifty-two months—uninterrupted months of job growth. We've run into trouble recently, obviously, beginning in '08, because of the financial crisis, as well as the recession, but those are not U.S. problems alone. Those are global problems. Those are problems that have affected nations and economies all over the world; that's not something that is just a U.S. problem. As I look at it, I think we've been successful at intervening.

LEHRER: On the economy you've been successful?

CHENEY: We've been successful at intervening economically with respect to the financial crisis, in that what we did with respect to TARP by moving as aggressively as we did, that there is, in fact, positive progress. We stabilized, if you will, the financial system out there. Now, there's still a lot of work to be done yet, but the interbank lending rate's back down where it belongs; interest rates are low—all of these things are moves in the right direction. And I think if we had not intervened as aggressively as we did, the situation would be worse. But I don't think you can blame that financial crisis on George Bush; I just don't think that's a valid judgment.

LEHRER: What about—going back to the original question—about seeing this coming? Isn't that part of the stewardship of the president, of the vice president and of his administration—to see these things coming and try to prevent them from coming, rather than to act after they've happened?

CHENEY: Did you see it coming, Jim? You're an expert.

LEHRER: I'm not the president or the vice president of the United States.

CHENEY: It's a— I think we did see some elements of it, in terms of our concerns about Fannie Mae and Freddie Mac. And a couple of years ago, we went forward with proposed recommendations to Fannie Mae and Freddie Mac—couldn't get them through the Democrat-controlled Congress. That might have helped forestall what one of the key triggers was of the financial crisis. But I think no; I think some of the best financial minds in the country didn't see it coming. We saw that five key investment banks in New York are no more, or have been transformed in a major way. They're folks that deal in this area all day, every day, and they didn't foresee it coming.

LEHRER: So you don't accept any responsibility for— on the—

CHENEY: I don't think we caused the economic downturn.

LEHRER: Okay, okay. Why do you believe that the public approval, at least measured by the polls and other things, is so low—in your case, almost historically low?

CHENEY: Have you checked it recently? I don't know what it is.

LEHRER: I have, I have. The—in terms of history, polling goes on seventy years. The only vice president that's ever had a lower approval rating is Dan Quayle.

CHENEY: Mm-hmm. Well, how does that fit with the other perception—

LEHRER: My question is, why is that happening? What's your reading of that?

CHENEY: Well, I—in terms—let's talk generally about polls. We've tried very hard not to govern based on polls. That is to say, we haven't tailored our policies in order to appeal to polls. We did start out— I think one of the things that contributed to the amount of hostility that's out there in the body politic was what happened in the 2000 election, that it was as close as it was, and I think that there were some people out there who questioned the legitimacy of our administration, given the way the Florida recount ultimately turned out. I think that contributed to it. I think the decisions we've had to make on things like terrorist surveillance, like on interrogation of detainees, Patriot Act and so forth, those steps we've had to take to guard against another attack have been controversial. And have been attacked robustly by our critics and our opponents. But that's not why we came to office, Jim. We did win reelection, I think, comfortably—not a landslide, obviously. And we went out there and put what we were doing on the line in the way, historically, it's to be tested in a democracy, and we got reelected. And we have been able, I think again, to achieve those objectives we set for ourselves. Now, over time, I expect that history will judge this administration in a fairly favorable light. I served in the Ford administration. I was there and remember what it was like when Gerry Ford made a very controversial decision to pardon Richard Nixon and fell thirty points in the polls in a week. I also know that thirty years later, he was much-revered and much-respected for that decision, because he made it without regard to what it would do to him politically.

LEHRER: But, Mr. Vice President, people would say back to you: Wait a minute. You govern in the present, not about what some historian is going to say fifty years from now. The idea, in a democratic society, of having a—the disapproval of an overwhelming majority of the American people—does that work?

CHENEY: That's what elections are for, Jim. And as I say, we went out and stood for election and were reelected comfortably. But you cannot, in these circumstances especially, start worrying about the polls in terms of whether or not you're going to make these tough decisions. The easy thing to do is, well, let's not do terrorist surveillance, let's not have a robust interrogation program of these al Qaeda folks when we capture them, let's not take aggressive action to defend the nation, because then the *New York Times* will love us and we'll get editorials written about us all over the country and our numbers will go up in the polls. That's not what we came to town to do; we came to town to make those tough decisions. And I think the president of the United States is the only one who can make those kinds of decisions. This president did it; I think he did it very well. I think he's been tough and aggressive when he needed to be, and been willing to take the political heat, which is more important, in my opinion, than being loved.

LEHRER: More important than having the approval of the people who elected you?

CHENEY: Well, how do you want to go out and measure that? Do you want to go out and poll and say, "Gee, we aren't up to 70 percent yet. We'd better not make any tough decisions here"? I mean, you cannot be driven by the polls. The polls change all the time; they're easily manipulated by whoever wants to ask those poll questions; they go up; they go down. You've got to steer a more steady course than that if you're going to be president of the United States in these circumstances. And that's what we did. And you guys get to go on the tube every night and comment on it. There's a lot of debate out there about it. The public gets to decide whether or not they want to continue us in office. Obviously, we weren't up in '08, but they certainly did in '04.

LEHRER: So it doesn't trouble you at all to be leaving office next week with the overwhelming disapproval of the majority of the people, as measured by the polls? It doesn't bother you, personally?

CHENEY: I don't buy that. No, first of all—I don't buy that. And I find, when I get out and talk with people, that that's not the unanimous view, as you would have it. Things that count for me, in terms of the people I want to make certain are with us are, for example, the American military—young men and women who serve, the folks who go out and put their lives on the line to carry out the policies we've decided upon. The president and I had the opportunity, for example, last Saturday. We went down to Norfolk; we commissioned a brand-new aircraft carrier named after his father. Then we went over and spent the afternoon with about 650 Navy

SEALS. These are guys that have been in the battle in Iraq, in Afghanistan, deployed many, many times—have done all the heavy lifting in connection with our policies that we pursued in that part of the world. And they are a magnificent group of people. They also are very, very supportive of what we did. And they're the ones who went out and, as I say, put their lives on the line for the rest of us. It's not just cocktail party talk for them; this is the real world they live in. And having their respect and their approval counts for an enormous amount.

LEHRER: On a more personal level, Mr. Vice President, there's one thesis that the Dick Cheney who has been the vice president for the last eight years is a different Dick Cheney who had been a member of Congress, who had been in the previous administrations of Bush I, as well as the Ford administration—that somehow, you've changed dramatically, significantly. Is that correct?

CHENEY: Well, I'm older. I've got less hair. I don't think I've changed, in terms of sort of my basic, fundamental philosophy or personality. My family doesn't think that I've changed—although as I say, to get older. I have more grandkids now than I used to have. I think what was significant for me was 9/11. And I think it's easy, if you didn't experience that, or if you're not worried about it now, because it was seven years ago, easy to forget what that entailed or what that involved. But that was a devastating attack on the United States—killed nearly 3,000 Americans—worst attack ever on the history of—on the homeland. And when you contemplated the consequences of it—what it meant with respect to the possibility of a terrorist in the middle of our cities with a nuclear weapon, which is now the threat we're faced with—then, it seems to me, you're justified in—and obligated—to focus on that threat and do everything you can to defeat it. The president and I took an oath when we were sworn in on January of '01 to support and defend the Constitution against all enemies, foreign and domestic. And when you sit there every day and read the intelligence every morning—six days a week—and look at what we're faced with out there on a global basis, and look at the threat and the determination, if you will, of our enemies to come and kill more Americans, that's our problem, that's our job—to deal with that. We're the ones who've got to sit down every day and figure out how to cope with that, and that's what we did. And now, some people can sit and say, "Gee, Cheney changed." No, I think circumstances changed. I think the United States was no longer safe and secure behind its oceans. I think we found ourselves in a situation where, because of modern technology and the rise of Islamic fundamentalism in the Middle East, we're faced with a threat, the likes of which we've never had to deal with before.

LEHRER: So, in this same context, people say you're—you hardened, you became less willing to compromise, less interested in a bipartisan approach to things—as a result—if that happened, that came as a result of 9/11 and the new attitude that you just explained.

CHENEY: Well, I think in terms of partisanship, or lack of partisanship, that's— You know, Joe Lieberman's my favorite Democrat. Joe's a great guy and he agrees with us on these issues. I think the significant thing is that the American people need to realize and need to be aware that the threat does still exist and that we still have to continue those policies. The interesting thing to watch, now, is how President-Elect Obama is going to adjust to these concerns. He's reading the morning intelligence report, now, on a daily basis; he's finding out what the nature of the threat is out there, and they're wrestling with this question of what are they going to do with Guantánamo, what are they going to do with terrorist surveillance program or the interrogation program for high-value detainees. And it will be interesting to see how he resolves those. It would be my personal view, if they don't continue those policies, they will in fact, put the nation at risk. We'll see.

LEHRER: A specific question related to that: Lead story in the *Washington Post* this morning is about a Bush administration official, Susan Crawford, who said, on the record, that she had recommended against charging one of the detainees at Guantánamo, a native of Saudi Arabia, because he had, in fact, been tortured at Guantánamo. And she made this comment, here— This is Susan Crawford, who used to work for you, I understand, right?

CHENEY: She worked at the department when I was there, correct.

LEHRER: When you were at the Pentagon. She said, "I think someone should acknowledge that mistakes were made and that they hurt the effort," meaning the whole effort in Guantánamo and dealing with the terrorists, quote, "and take responsibility for it." End quote. Do you agree with her?

CHENEY: Well, I don't know the specifics of what she's talking about.

LEHRER: You have never heard about this Saudi Arabian.

CHENEY: I had heard about this individual before. This is Mr. Qatani, who was the twentieth hijacker. He tried to get into the United States so he could get on one of the airplanes on 9/11 and fly into the Pentagon or the World Trade Center. He was stopped by an alert customs agent in Florida, I believe. I'm also, as I recall—I read the article this morning—that she said all of the techniques that were utilized were authorized. None of them were in violation of the basic fundamental tenets that we used out there. She was, as I understand it, complaining about the way in which—well, specifically, the way in which they were administered. I don't have any way to judge that; I'm sure that the Defense Department has or will thoroughly investigate it and get to the bottom of it. They're very good at those sort of things. So it's entirely possible there was a problem in terms of how one specific prisoner was handled. I can't claim perfection. But what I can say is that in terms of what the policies of the administration were—both at the White House level and at the Defense Department—was that enhanced interrogation was okay. We had specific techniques that were approved by the Justice Department—but that we don't torture and that we would not support torture from the standpoint of policy. It was not the policy of this administration.

LEHRER: But just, for a general premise here, looking back, you don't—nothing happened that you feel was over the line or that you feel that was a miscalculation or mistake of some kind?

CHENEY: Well, in terms of the treatment of a specific individual, I can't say that. We had Abu Ghraib, for example. In that case, I believe, based on what I've seen, that that was the result of some military personnel who were improperly supervised—weren't given the right kind of guidance, weren't managed properly. As we dig in and look at hundreds of cases, we may well find a few people who were not properly treated. You know, I ran the Pentagon. I know that you can't absolutely guarantee, at all times, that everybody's doing it the way they're supposed to be doing it. I can tell you what the policy was; I can tell you that we had all the legal authorization we needed to do it, including the sign-off of the Justice Department. I can tell you it produced phenomenal results for us, and that a great many Americans are alive today because we did all that. And I think those are the important considerations.

LEHRER: And you're personally very comfortable with that?

CHENEY: I am.

LEHRER: For what happened and the reasons it happened and the end result?

CHENEY: In terms of the interrogation, generally?

LEHRER: General policy.

CHENEY: Absolutely.

Vice President Cheney on CBS' *Face the Nation*, 2009

BOB SCHIEFFER: [Y]ou and President Bush were elected in 2000, so I guess I'd ask you the question that Ronald Reagan used to ask: Are we better off now than we were eight years ago?

VICE PRESIDENT CHENEY: Well, I think we've got— I think we've done some very good things over the course of the last eight years. Defending the country against further terrorist attacks like 9/11, I think, is a major accomplishment, for example. I think we made progress on education with No Child Left Behind and prescription drug benefits for seniors, and so forth. I can point to tax policies, a series of policies and actions that were put in place that were significant progress. There's no question that the new administration and President Obama are going to have their hands full with a new set of problems, if you will, centered especially upon the economy, upon the difficulties that have developed in the financial markets over the last six months. Just as our task when we came in was ultimately to deal with the aftermath of 9/11, and we have to take on the global war on terror. So each administration has its challenges. The Obama administration certainly has theirs.

SCHIEFFER: The situation in Iraq. What do you see there now? What do you think the state of Iraq is right now?

CHENEY: I think Iraq is much better off than it was before we went in in '03 and got rid of Saddam Hussein. I think we are close to achieving most of our objectives. We've seen a significant reduction in the overall level of violence. It's lower now than virtually anytime since we've been there in the spring of '03. We've seen the elimination of one of the world's worst regimes. We've seen the Iraqis write a constitution and hold three national elections. We've now entered into a strategic framework agreement with the Iraqis that calls for ultimately the U.S. completion of the assignment and withdrawal of our forces from Iraq. All of those things I think by anybody's standard would be—excuse me—evidence of significant success. And I think we're very close to achieving what it is we set out to do five years ago when we first went into Iraq.

SCHIEFFER: When we— Back there, when we decided to go into Iraq, we told Saddam Hussein to leave or else, to either leave or we were coming in there to take him out. Did you really think that he would stand and fight?

CHENEY: We didn't know. Now you look back on it, he clearly was into self-deception in a major way. I think he totally underestimated George Bush and what we were prepared to do. He tried to sort of bluff his way through, I guess, would be the best way to describe it, and we called his bluff. He had been in the business—This is a guy who had started two wars, who had killed hundreds of thousands of people, including many of his own, with weapons of mass destruction. It was one of the most despicable regimes of the twentieth century. And he thought he could get away with continuing that. And I think he assumed that the U.S. would never go in. And he was wrong.

SCHIEFFER: Do you think on reflection that, in fact, we did have a bad plan? I mean, when you step back—people in the military were saying it would take a much larger force than we decided to go in with. And in fact, we had a force that was mobile, it was quick, we were able to get to Baghdad. But once we got there, the Iraqis just sort of faded into the civilian population. We didn't really have enough people to guard those ammo dumps that Saddam Hussein abandoned. Wouldn't it have been better, on reflection, to have had a better and a larger force?

CHENEY: Well, we could debate that forever, and we may well. I think that the original campaign was masterfully done, in terms of the small, fast-moving force, as you say, that achieved our initial objectives of taking down the regime and capturing Baghdad. It was a masterful performance. I think the thing that we underestimated—at least I underestimated—was the damage that had been done to the Iraqi population by all those years of Saddam's rule. So that there weren't any Iraqis early on who were willing to stand up and take responsibility for their own affairs. Anybody who had had that kind of get up and go in earlier years had had their head chopped off. And I think we underestimated the damage that had been done during those years of Saddam's rule, as well as what happened in '91, you may remember, when they rose up after the Gulf War, and Saddam, you know, very brutally and very aggressively put down those uprisings around the country. So I would chalk that up to miscalculation. I'm not at all sure that having had four or five hundred thousand troops there would have achieved the objective we're talking about. What we finally did—what finally sort of got us across the goal line here was the surge the president decided upon, coupled with a counterinsurgency strategy.

SCHIEFFER: But isn't that, I mean, isn't that—just underline that the original strategy was wrong? I mean, once you got enough troops in there to handle the situation, things calmed down.

CHENEY: Well, the number of troops we put in weren't that much more than we'd had there before. We added five brigades. This is, what, maybe 30,000 men. And it was up close to where we'd been at the time of the elections, when we had forces there to monitor the elections and to provide security for the Iraqis to hold elections. We never went over 200,000 troops. We were always significantly below that. And we still succeeded.

SCHIEFFER: But how do you think we got it so wrong? I mean, we thought he had weapons of mass destruction and he didn't. We thought we would be greeted with open arms and we weren't. What happened?

CHENEY: Well, I don't look at it as we got it so wrong, Bob. I think we have in fact . . .

SCHIEFFER: We got a big part of it wrong. There weren't any weapons of mass destruction.

CHENEY: Correct. The original intelligence was wrong, no question about it. But there were parts of it that were right. It wasn't 100 percent wrong. It was correct in saying he had the technology. It was correct in saying he still had the people who knew how to build weapons of mass destruction. I think it was also correct in the assessment that once sanctions came off, he would go back to doing what he had been doing before. Where it was wrong was saying he had stockpiles, and he clearly didn't. So the intelligence was flawed. But you never have perfect intelligence in this business. You have got to deal with the best you can in terms of making your decisions. The question of how we moved forward, you can debate about whether or not we had the right structure in place, for example. Was—would we have been better off with setting up a government in exile, with exiled Iraqis, and getting that organized and in place before we went in and then turning it over to them? We made the judgment that if we were going to take down the government, we had an obligation to try to restore the best kind of system we could. And that was to give them a shot at democracy.

SCHIEFFER: Do you think that perhaps you'd looked at the intelligence and saw what you wanted to see rather than make a real logical analysis of what you saw?

CHENEY: No, I don't, Bob. I think if you go back and you look at what we were receiving as intelligence from the intelligence community, going back to the very day we were sworn in— I've seen a report, for example, it was one of the very first we received, that warned about Iraqis' weapons of mass destruction program. As a matter of fact, it was written by a guy who has been one of the public critics of what we did. He was responsible for that first report. We had reporting like that all the time we were there, right up until we went into Iraq. So the— It wasn't a matter just of us looking and seeing what we wanted to see. Everybody believed that intelligence. Saddam Hussein had peddled that notion to his senior officers and officials. They all believed he had weapons of mass destruction. The intelligence services of other countries, the Clinton administration that had been there for eight years before we had, had exactly the same conclusion that we had. And we had numerous reports afterwards with all the studies that were done—the Robb-Silberman commission, the Senate Intelligence Committee—that said that there was no manipulation of the data, no pressure brought to bear on the analysis. This is what they saw, and they got part of it wrong.

SCHIEFFER: Mr. Vice President, in an interview last month with Chris Wallace over at FOX, you said that starting in 2001, the administration and in many cases you personally kept congressional leaders fully briefed on the program to monitor America's international phone calls without a warrant. You said that the Republican and Democratic leaders were unanimous when you briefed them that the programs were essential and did not require further congressional action. But the *New York Times* has noted that Senator Rockefeller wrote you a letter in 2003, reiterating concerns that he said he had expressed at those meetings that the programs raised profound issues and created concern regarding the direction the administration was taking. So were congressional leaders kept fully informed or were they not?

CHENEY: They were kept fully informed.

SCHIEFFER: Well, why would he have written that letter?

CHENEY: I have no idea. I know when—what happened was the—everybody who was in the room that day, for example, when I got the leadership down, the chairman and ranking member of the intelligence committees, including Senator Rockefeller, and asked them if we thought they should continue—if they thought we should continue the program. They said yes. Do we need to come to Congress to get authorization for it? And they said no. And he was there. He never objected or posed that in any way. Later on, when this became public, when the *New York Times* broke the story, which, frankly, I think was an outrageous decision on their part—they were asked by the president of the United States not to, on the grounds it would damage national security—then Senator Rockefeller decided he wanted to hark back to this letter. But the fact was he couldn't even find it. He had to call my office for a copy of the letter that he allegedly had written, some years before, raising some questions that he had about the program, but I always felt it was a bit of a CYA letter, that, in those crucial meetings, when we sat down to debate the program and tell them about it, in fact, everybody in the room signed up to it. Nobody objected.

SCHIEFFER: Do you feel you went too far, Mr. Vice President, in—in your surveillance?

CHENEY: Absolutely not. I think what we did was one of the great success stories of the intelligence business in the last century. I think what the National Security Agency did under General Mike Hayden, working with the CIA, at the direction of the president, was masterfully done. I think it provided crucial intelligence for us. It's one of the main reasons we've been successful in defending the country against further attacks. And I don't believe we violated anybody's civil liberties. This was all done in accordance with the president's constitutional authority, under Article II of the Constitution, as commander in chief, with the resolution that was passed by the Congress immediately after 9/11. And subsequently, we have gotten the legislative authority, signed up to last year, when we passed and modify the FISA statute.

SCHIEFFER: Do you believe that the president, in time of war, that anything he does is legal?

CHENEY: I can't say that anything he does is legal. I think we do, and we have historic precedent of taking action that you wouldn't take in peacetime but that you will take, sometimes, in wartime, in order to do the basic job that you sign up to when you take the oath of office, which is to support and defend the Constitution against all enemies, foreign and domestic. If you hark back in our history, you can look at Abraham Lincoln, who suspended the writ of habeas corpus in the middle of the Civil War.

SCHIEFFER: But nobody thinks that that was legal.

CHENEY: Well, no. Well, it certainly was, in the sense he wasn't impeached. And it was a wartime measure that he took that I think, today, history says, yes, that was probably a good thing to do. There have been other examples, Lyndon—or FDR, in World War II, when he provided for internment camps for Japanese-American citizens. Most people now look back and say that was wrong. But what we did was modest by those comparisons. And I would also emphasize that what we did, we did with the support and involvement, for example, of the Justice Department. Every single time the president reauthorized the terrorist surveillance program, which he did every thirty or forty-five days, it was only after the . . .

SCHIEFFER: But is it not true that the courts and others have now said that some of those orders that the Justice Department was putting out proved to be . . .

CHENEY: That was—that was the rules . . .

SCHIEFFER: . . . not correct?

CHENEY: . . . that we had to operate by. And the attorney general of the United States signed off on every single one of those exceptions. The president would not extend the program without the attorney general's authorization and approval on there, in terms of all of our actions. We worked—stayed close to the Office of Legal Counsel. We followed the guidance we got, which is what you're supposed to do and where you're supposed to do it. There have subsequently been some controversies that—the Supreme Court's made some decisions that didn't agree with what we did at the time. But what we did was authorized by the legal authorities that were to be the source of that kind of advice.

SCHIEFFER: Let me talk to you a little bit about torture. You have said that you do not believe that waterboarding, for example, was torture.

CHENEY: Right.

SCHIEFFER: You and members of the Cabinet sat in the White House and approved the methods of interrogation that were used by the CIA. Why would something like that reach your level, Mr. Vice President?

CHENEY: Well, because the CIA did not want to proceed without having a very clear understanding of what was authorized and what was appropriate. I'd seen situations before where the CIA would get out and undertake an assignment or a mission, and then find that the politicians would all run for the hills. Think Iran-Contra. In fact, what we had here was a situation where the CIA was being very careful and very cautious. They had prisoners like Khalid Sheikh Muhammed, who was the mastermind of 9/11, in custody. They wanted to know what kind of techniques they could use going forward and still maintain consistency with the statutes and the international agreements that we're a party to.

SCHIEFFER: Would you do it again if you had to make those same decisions again? Because a lot of people now say that some of the things that happened here may be the reason that some of our casualties happened, because people saw the publicity of these things, the kinds of things that happened at Abu Ghraib.

CHENEY: I would absolutely do it again, Bob. I think the loss of life, if there had been further mass-casualty attacks against the United States over the last seven and a half years, fully justifies it. Think of what would happen if there had been an attack and we hadn't taken any of these measures. And you'd be sitting here today, you know, grilling me, saying why didn't you guys do everything you could to stop it? Why didn't you find out what the enemy was planning to do? Why didn't you interfere with the attacks?

SCHIEFFER: So you would suggest that Barack Obama continue those things?

CHENEY: I would. If he were to seek my advice. He hasn't. But if he were to seek my advice, I would say, look, before you go out and start to make policy based on the campaign rhetoric we heard last year, what you need to do is to sit down and find out what we've done, find out how we did it, what the justification was for it, what kind of results it's produced, and then make an informed judgment about whether or not you want to keep these things. But I would hope he would avoid doing what others have done in the past, which is letting the campaign rhetoric guide his judgment in this absolutely crucial area. We were very careful. We did everything by the book. And in fact, we produced very significant results. And I would hope that for the sake of the nation, that this administration and future administrations will continue those policies.

SCHIEFFER: Guantánamo. You've said it should remain open, but for how long, Mr. Vice President?

CHENEY: Well, Guantánamo is there to hold people we believe are unlawful combatants that were captured in the war on terror, many of them members of al Qaeda. They're well treated. Their cases are reviewed annually by military commissions to see whether or not they should stay or go. We've released more than we've held. There have been hundreds that have been sent back to their home country. But the problem you've got is what do you do with prisoners that are there? Now, if you bring them on shore into the United States, they immediately fall here to certain legal rights and privileges that will create problems. And there are also—I don't know many congressional districts that are eager to have two hundred al Qaeda terrorists deposited on their soil.

"Folly's Antidote," Arthur M. Schlesinger, Jr., The Century Association, *New York Times* Op Ed *1/1/07*

Many signs point to a growing historical consciousness among the American people. I trust that this is so. It is useful to remember that history is to the nation as memory is to the individual. As persons deprived of memory become disoriented and lost, not knowing where they have been and where they are going, so a nation denied a conception of the past will be disabled in dealing with its present and its future. "The longer you look back," said Winston Churchill, "the farther you can look forward."

But all historians are prisoners of their own experience. We bring to history the preconceptions of our personalities and of our age. We cannot seize on ultimate and absolute truths. So the historian is committed to a doomed enterprise—the quest for an unattainable objectivity.

Conceptions of the past are far from stable. They are perennially revised by the urgencies of the present. When new urgencies arise in our own times and lives, the historian's spotlight shifts, probing at last into the darkness, throwing into sharp relief things that were always there but that earlier historians had carelessly excised from the collective memory. New voices ring out of the historical dark and demand to be heard.

One has only to note how in the last half century the movements for women's rights and civil rights have reformulated and renewed American history. Thus the present incessantly reinvents the past. In this sense, all history, as Benedetto Croce said, is contemporary history. It is these permutations of consciousness that make history so endlessly fascinating an intellectual adventure. "The one duty we owe to history," said Oscar Wilde, "is to rewrite it."

We are the world's dominant military power, and I believe a consciousness of history is a moral necessity for a nation possessed of overweening power. History verifies John F. Kennedy's proposition, stated in the first year of his thousand days: "We must face the fact that the United States is neither omnipotent nor omniscient—that we are only 6 percent of the world's population; that we cannot impose our will upon the other 94 percent of mankind; that we cannot right every wrong or reverse each adversity; and therefore there cannot be an American solution to every world problem."

History is the best antidote to delusions of omnipotence and omniscience. Self-knowledge is the indispensable prelude to self-control, for the nation as well as for the individual, and history should forever remind us of the limits of our passing perspectives. It should strengthen us to resist the pressure to convert momentary impulses into moral absolutes. It should lead us to acknowledge our profound and chastening frailty as human beings—to a recognition of the fact, so often and so sadly displayed, that the future outwits all our certitudes and that the possibilities of the future are more various than the human intellect is designed to conceive.

Sometimes, when I am particularly depressed, I ascribe our behavior to stupidity—the stupidity of our leadership, the stupidity of our culture. Three decades ago, we suffered defeat in an unwinnable war against tribalism, the most fanatic of political emotions, fighting against a country about which we knew nothing and in which we had no vital interests. Vietnam was hopeless enough, but to repeat the same arrogant folly thirty years later in Iraq is unforgivable. The Swedish statesman Axel Oxenstierna famously said, "Behold, my son, with how little wisdom the world is governed."

A nation informed by a vivid understanding of the ironies of history is, I believe, best equipped to manage the tragic temptations of military power. Let us not bully our way through life, but let a growing sensitivity to history temper and civilize our use of power. In the meantime, let a thousand historical flowers bloom. History is never a closed book or a final verdict. It is forever in the making. Let historians never forsake the quest for knowledge in the interests of an ideology, a religion, a race, a nation.

The great strength of history in a free society is its capacity for self-correction. This is the endless excitement of historical writing—the search to reconstruct what went before, a quest illuminated by those ever-changing prisms that continually place old questions in a new light.

History is a doomed enterprise that we happily pursue because of the thrill of the hunt, because exploring the past is such fun, because of the intellectual challenges involved, because a nation needs to know its own history. Or so we historians insist. Because in the end, a nation's history must be both the guide and the domain not so much of its historians as its citizens.

"A More Perfect Union" Speech on Race, *Senator Barack Obama, 2008*

"We the people, in order to form a more perfect union."

Two hundred and twenty-one years ago, in a hall that still stands across the street, a group of men gathered and, with these simple words, launched America's improbable experiment in democracy. Farmers and scholars; statesmen and patriots who had traveled across an ocean to escape tyranny and persecution finally made real their declaration of independence at a Philadelphia convention that lasted through the spring of 1787.

The document they produced was eventually signed but ultimately unfinished. It was stained by this nation's original sin of slavery, a question that divided the colonies and brought the convention to a stalemate until the founders chose to allow the slave trade to continue for at least twenty more years, and to leave any final resolution to future generations.

Of course, the answer to the slavery question was already embedded within our Constitution—a Constitution that had at its very core the ideal of equal citizenship under the law; a Constitution that promised its people liberty, and justice, and a union that could be and should be perfected over time.

And yet words on a parchment would not be enough to deliver slaves from bondage, or provide men and women of every color and creed their full rights and obligations as citizens of the United States. What would be needed were Americans in successive generations who were willing to do their part—through protests and struggle, on the streets and in the courts, through a civil war and civil disobedience and always at great risk—to narrow that gap between the promise of our ideals and the reality of their time.

This was one of the tasks we set forth at the beginning of this campaign—to continue the long march of those who came before us, a march for a more just, more equal, more free, more caring and more prosperous America. I chose to run for the presidency at this moment in history because I believe deeply that we cannot solve the challenges of our time unless we solve them together—unless we perfect our union by understanding that we may have different stories, but we hold common hopes; that we may not look the same and we may not have come from the same place, but we all want to move in the same direction—towards a better future for our children and our grandchildren.

This belief comes from my unyielding faith in the decency and generosity of the American people. But it also comes from my own American story.

I am the son of a black man from Kenya and a white woman from Kansas. I was raised with the help of a white grandfather, who survived a Depression to serve in Patton's Army during World War II, and a white grandmother, who worked on a bomber assembly line at Fort Leavenworth while he was overseas. I've gone to some of the best schools in America and lived in one of the world's poorest nations. I am married to a black American who carries within her the blood of slaves and slave owners—an inheritance we pass on to our two precious daughters. I have brothers, sisters, nieces, nephews, uncles and cousins, of every race and every hue, scattered across three continents, and for as long as I live, I will never forget that in no other country on Earth is my story even possible.

It's a story that hasn't made me the most conventional candidate. But it is a story that has seared into my genetic makeup the idea that this nation is more than the sum of its parts—that out of many, we are truly one.

Throughout the first year of this campaign, against all predictions to the contrary, we saw how hungry the American people were for this message of unity. Despite the temptation to view my candidacy through a purely racial lens, we won commanding victories in states with some of the whitest populations in the country. In South Carolina, where the Confederate flag still flies, we built a powerful coalition of African-Americans and white Americans.

This is not to say that race has not been an issue in the campaign. At various stages in the campaign, some commentators have deemed me either "too black" or "not black enough." We saw racial tensions bubble to the surface during the week before the South Carolina primary. The press has scoured every exit poll for the latest evidence of racial polarization, not just in terms of white and black, but black and brown as well.

And yet it has only been in the last couple of weeks that the discussion of race in this campaign has taken a particularly divisive turn.

On one end of the spectrum, we've heard the implication that my candidacy is somehow an exercise in affirmative action; that it's based solely on the desire of wide-eyed liberals to purchase racial reconciliation on the cheap. On the other end, we've heard my former pastor, Reverend Jeremiah Wright, use incendiary language to express views that have the potential not only to widen the racial divide, but views that denigrate both the greatness and the goodness of our nation; that rightly offend white and black alike.

I have already condemned, in unequivocal terms, the statements of Reverend Wright that have caused such controversy. For some, nagging questions remain. Did I know him to be an occasionally fierce critic of American domestic and foreign policy? Of course. Did I ever hear him make remarks that could be considered controversial while I sat in church? Yes. Did I strongly disagree with many of his political views? Absolutely—just as I'm sure many of you have heard remarks from your pastors, priests, or rabbis with which you strongly disagreed.

But the remarks that have caused this recent firestorm weren't simply controversial. They weren't simply a religious leader's effort to speak out against perceived injustice. Instead, they expressed a profoundly distorted view of this country—a view that sees white racism as endemic, and that elevates what is wrong with America above all that we know is right with America; a view that sees the conflicts in the Middle East as rooted primarily in the actions of stalwart allies like Israel, instead of emanating from the perverse and hateful ideologies of radical Islam.

As such, Reverend Wright's comments were not only wrong but divisive, divisive at a time when we need unity; racially charged at a time when we need to come together to solve a set of monumental problems—two wars, a terrorist threat, a falling economy, a chronic health care crisis and potentially devastating climate change; problems that are neither black or white or Latino or Asian, but rather problems that confront us all.

Given my background, my politics, and my professed values and ideals, there will no doubt be those for whom my statements of condemnation are not enough. Why associate myself with Reverend Wright in the first place? they may ask. Why not join another church? And I confess that if all that I knew of Reverend Wright were the snippets of those sermons that have run in an endless loop on the television and YouTube, or if Trinity United Church of Christ conformed to the caricatures being peddled by some commentators, there is no doubt that I would react in much the same way

But the truth is, that isn't all that I know of the man. The man I met more than twenty years ago is a man who helped introduce me to my Christian faith, a man who spoke to me about our obligations to love one another; to care for the sick and lift up the poor. He is a man who served his country as a U.S. Marine; who has studied and lectured at some of the finest universities and seminaries in the country; and who for over thirty years led a church that serves the community by doing God's work here on Earth—by housing the homeless, ministering to the needy, providing day-care services and scholarships and prison ministries, and reaching out to those suffering from HIV/AIDS.

In my first book, *Dreams from My Father*, I described the experience of my first service at Trinity:

> People began to shout, to rise from their seats and clap and cry out, a forceful wind carrying the reverend's voice up into the rafters. . . . And in that single note—hope!—I heard something else; at the foot of that cross, inside the thousands of churches across the city, I imagined the stories of ordinary black people merging with the stories of David and Goliath, Moses and Pharaoh, the Christians in the lion's den, Ezekiel's field of dry bones. Those stories—of survival, and freedom, and hope—became our story, my story; the blood that had spilled was our blood, the tears our tears; until this black church, on this bright day, seemed once more a vessel carrying the story of a people into future generations and into a larger world. Our trials and triumphs became at once unique and universal, black and more than black; in chronicling our journey, the stories and songs gave us a means to reclaim memories that we didn't need to feel shame about . . . memories that all people might study and cherish—and with which we could start to rebuild.

That has been my experience at Trinity. Like other predominantly black churches across the country, Trinity embodies the black community in its entirety—the doctor and the welfare mom, the model student and the former gangbanger. Like other black churches, Trinity's services are full of raucous laughter and sometimes bawdy humor. They are full of dancing, clapping, screaming and shouting that may seem jarring to the untrained ear. The church contains in full the kindness and cruelty, the fierce intelligence and the shocking ignorance, the struggles and successes, the love and, yes, the bitterness and bias that make up the black experience in America.

And this helps explain, perhaps, my relationship with Reverend Wright. As imperfect as he may be, he has been like family to me. He strengthened my faith, officiated my wedding, and baptized my children. Not once in my conversations with him have I heard him talk about any ethnic group in derogatory terms, or treat whites with whom he interacted with anything but courtesy and respect. He contains within him the contradictions—the good and the bad—of the community that he has served diligently for so many years.

I can no more disown him than I can disown the black community. I can no more disown him than I can my white grandmother—a woman who helped raise me, a woman who sacrificed again and again for me, a woman who loves me as much as she loves anything in this world, but a woman who once confessed her fear of black men who passed by her on the street, and who on more than one occasion has uttered racial or ethnic stereotypes that made me cringe.

These people are a part of me. And they are a part of America, this country that I love.

Some will see this as an attempt to justify or excuse comments that are simply inexcusable. I can assure you, it is not. I suppose the politically safe thing would be to move on from this episode and just hope that it fades into the woodwork. We can dismiss Reverend Wright as a crank or a demagogue, just as some have dismissed Geraldine Ferraro, in the aftermath of her recent statements, as harboring some deep-seated racial bias.

But race is an issue that I believe this nation cannot afford to ignore right now. We would be making the same mistake that Reverend Wright made in his offending sermons about America—to simplify and stereotype and amplify the negative to the point that it distorts reality.

The fact is that the comments that have been made and the issues that have surfaced over the last few weeks reflect the complexities of race in this country that we've never really worked through—a part of our union that we have yet to perfect. And if we walk away now, if we simply retreat into our respective corners, we will never be able to come together and solve challenges like health care, or education, or the need to find good jobs for every American.

Understanding this reality requires a reminder of how we arrived at this point. As William Faulkner once wrote, "The past isn't dead and buried. In fact, it isn't even past." We do not need to recite here the history of racial injustice in this country. But we do need to remind ourselves that so many of the disparities that exist in the African-American community today can be directly traced to inequalities passed on from an earlier generation that suffered under the brutal legacy of slavery and Jim Crow.

Segregated schools were, and are, inferior schools; we still haven't fixed them, fifty years after Brown v. Board of Education, and the inferior education they provided, then and now, helps explain the pervasive achievement gap between today's black and white students.

Legalized discrimination—where blacks were prevented, often through violence, from owning property, or loans were not granted to African-American business owners, or black homeowners could not access FHA mortgages, or blacks were excluded from unions, or the police force, or fire departments—meant that black families could not amass any meaningful wealth to bequeath to future generations. That history helps explain the wealth and income gap between black and white, and the concentrated pockets of poverty that persists in so many of today's urban and rural communities.

A lack of economic opportunity among black men, and the shame and frustration that came from not being able to provide for one's family, contributed to the erosion of black families—a problem that welfare policies for many years may have worsened. And the lack of basic services in so many urban black neighborhoods—parks for kids to play in, police walking the beat, regular garbage pickup and building-code enforcement—all helped create a cycle of violence, blight and neglect that continues to haunt us.

This is the reality in which Reverend Wright and other African-Americans of his generation grew up. They came of age in the late fifties and early sixties, a time when segregation was still the law of the land and opportunity was systematically constricted. What's remarkable is not how many failed in the face of discrimination, but rather how many men and women overcame the odds; how many were able to make a way out of no way for those like me who would come after them.

But for all those who scratched and clawed their way to get a piece of the American Dream, there were many who didn't make it—those who were ultimately defeated, in one way or another, by discrimination. That legacy of defeat was passed on to future generations—those young men and increasingly young women who we see standing on street corners or languishing in our prisons, without hope or prospects for the future. Even for those blacks who did make it, questions of race, and racism, continue to define their worldview in fundamental ways. For the men and women of Reverend Wright's generation, the memories of humiliation and doubt and fear have not gone away; nor have the anger and the bitterness of those years. That anger may not get expressed in public, in front of white coworkers or white friends. But it does find voice in the barbershop or around the kitchen table. At times, that anger is exploited by politicians, to gin up votes along racial lines, or to make up for a politician's own failings.

And occasionally it finds voice in the church on Sunday morning, in the pulpit and in the pews. The fact that so many people are surprised to hear that anger in some of Reverend Wright's sermons simply reminds us of the old truism that the most segregated hour in American life occurs on Sunday morning. That anger is not always productive; indeed, all too often it distracts attention from solving real problems; it keeps us from squarely facing our own complicity in our condition, and prevents the African-American community from forging the alliances it needs to bring about real change. But the anger is real; it is powerful; and to simply wish it away, to condemn it without understanding its roots only serves to widen the chasm of misunderstanding that exists between the races.

In fact, a similar anger exists within segments of the white community. Most working- and middle-class white Americans don't feel that they have been particularly privileged by their race. Their experience is the immigrant experience—as far as they're concerned, no one's handed them anything; they've built it from scratch. They've worked hard all their lives, many times only to see their jobs shipped overseas or their pension dumped after a lifetime of labor. They are anxious about their futures, and feel their dreams slipping away; in an era of stagnant wages and global competition, opportunity comes to be seen as a zero-sum game, in which your dreams come at my expense. So when they are told to bus their children to a school across town; when they hear that an African-American is getting an advantage in landing a good job or a spot in a good college because of an injustice that they themselves never committed; when they're told that their fears about crime in urban neighborhoods are somehow prejudiced, resentment builds over time.

Like the anger within the black community, these resentments aren't always expressed in polite company. But they have helped shape the political landscape for at least a generation. Anger over welfare and affirmative action helped forge the Reagan Coalition. Politicians routinely exploited fears of crime for their own electoral ends. Talk-show hosts and conservative commentators built entire careers unmasking bogus claims of racism while dismissing legitimate discussions of racial injustice and inequality as mere political correctness or reverse racism.

Just as black anger often proved counterproductive, so have these white resentments distracted attention from the real culprits of the middle-class squeeze—a corporate culture rife with inside dealing, questionable accounting practices, and short-term greed; a Washington dominated by lobbyists and special interests; economic policies that favor the few over the many. And yet, to wish away the resentments of white Americans, to label them as misguided or even racist, without recognizing they are grounded in legitimate concerns—this too widens the racial divide, and blocks the path to understanding.

This is where we are right now. It's a racial stalemate we've been stuck in for years. Contrary to the claims of some of my critics, black and white, I have never been so naive as to believe that we can get beyond our racial divisions in a single election cycle, or with a single candidacy—particularly a candidacy as imperfect as my own.

But I have asserted a firm conviction—a conviction rooted in my faith in God and my faith in the American people—that working together we can move beyond some of our old racial wounds, and that in fact we have no choice if we are to continue on the path of a more perfect union.

For the African-American community, that path means embracing the burdens of our past without becoming victims of our past. It means continuing to insist on a full measure of justice in every aspect of American life. But it also means binding our particular grievances—for better health care, and better schools, and better jobs—to the larger aspirations of all Americans—the white woman struggling to break the glass ceiling, the white man who's been laid off, the immigrant trying to feed his family. And it means taking full responsibility for our own lives—by demanding more from our fathers, and spending more time with our children, and reading to them, and teaching them that while they may face challenges and discrimination in their own lives, they must never succumb to despair or cynicism; they must always believe that they can write their own destiny.

Ironically, this quintessentially American—and yes, conservative—notion of self-help found frequent expression in Reverend Wright's sermons. But what my former pastor too often failed to understand is that embarking on a program of self-help also requires a belief that society can change.

The profound mistake of Reverend Wright's sermons is not that he spoke about racism in our society. It's that he spoke as if our society was static; as if no progress has been made; as if this country—a country that has made it possible for one of his own members to run for the highest office in the land and build a coalition of white and black, Latino and Asian, rich and poor, young and old—is still irrevocably bound to a tragic past. But what we know—what we have seen—is that America can change. That is the true genius of this nation. What we have already achieved gives us hope—the audacity to hope—for what we can and must achieve tomorrow.

In the white community, the path to a more perfect union means acknowledging that what ails the African-American community does not just exist in the minds of black people; that the legacy of discrimination and current incidents of discrimination, while less overt than in the past, are real and must be addressed. Not just with words, but with deeds—by investing in our schools and our communities; by enforcing our civil rights laws and ensuring fairness in our criminal justice system; by providing this generation with ladders of opportunity that were unavailable for previous generations. It requires all Americans to realize that your dreams do not have to come at the expense of my dreams; that investing in the health, welfare, and education of black and brown and white children will ultimately help all of America prosper.

In the end, then, what is called for is nothing more, and nothing less, than what all the world's great religions demand—that we do unto others as we would have them do unto us. Let us be our brother's keeper, Scripture tells us. Let us be our sister's keeper. Let us find that common stake we all have in one another, and let our politics reflect that spirit as well.

For we have a choice in this country. We can accept a politics that breeds division, and conflict, and cynicism. We can tackle race only as spectacle—as we did in the OJ trial—or in the wake of tragedy, as we did in the aftermath of Katrina—or as fodder for the nightly news. We can play Reverend Wright's sermons on every channel, every day, and talk about them from now until the election, and make the only question in this campaign whether or not the American people think that I somehow believe or sympathize with his most offensive words. We can pounce on some gaffe by a Hillary supporter as evidence that she's playing the race card, or we can speculate on whether white men will all flock to John McCain in the general election regardless of his policies.

We can do that.

But if we do, I can tell you that in the next election, we'll be talking about some other distraction. And then another one. And then another one. And nothing will change.

That is one option. Or, at this moment, in this election, we can come together and say, "Not this time." This time we want to talk about the crumbling schools that are stealing the future of black children and white children and Asian children and Hispanic children and Native American children. This time we want to reject the cynicism that tells us that these kids can't learn; that those kids who don't look like us are somebody else's problem. The children of America are not those kids—they are our kids, and we will not let them fall behind in a twenty-first-century economy. Not this time.

This time we want to talk about how the lines in the emergency room are filled with whites and blacks and Hispanics who do not have health care; who don't have the power on their own to overcome the special interests in Washington, but who can take them on if we do it together.

This time we want to talk about the shuttered mills that once provided a decent life for men and women of every race, and the homes for sale that once belonged to Americans from every religion, every region, every walk of life. This time we want to talk about the fact that the real problem is not that someone who doesn't look like you might take your job; it's that the corporation you work for will ship it overseas for nothing more than a profit.

This time we want to talk about the men and women of every color and creed who serve together, and fight together, and bleed together under the same proud flag. We want to talk about how to bring them home from a war that never should've been authorized and never should've been waged, and we want to talk about how we'll show our patriotism by caring for them, and their families, and giving them the benefits they have earned.

I would not be running for president if I didn't believe with all my heart that this is what the vast majority of Americans want for this country. This union may never be perfect, but generation after generation has shown that it can always be perfected. And today, whenever I find myself feeling doubtful or cynical about this possibility, what gives me the most hope is the next generation—the young people whose attitudes and beliefs and openness to change have already made history in this election.

There is one story in particular that I'd like to leave you with today—a story I told when I had the great honor of speaking on Dr. King's birthday at his home church, Ebenezer Baptist, in Atlanta.

There is a young, twenty-three-year-old white woman named Ashley Baia, who organized for our campaign in Florence, South Carolina. She had been working to organize a mostly African-American community since the beginning of this campaign, and one day she was at a roundtable discussion where everyone went around telling their story and why they were there.

And Ashley said that when she was nine years old, her mother got cancer. And because she had to miss days of work, she was let go and lost her health care. They had to file for bankruptcy, and that's when Ashley decided that she had to do something to help her mom.

She knew that food was one of their most expensive costs, and so Ashley convinced her mother that what she really liked and really wanted to eat more than anything else was mustard and relish sandwiches. Because that was the cheapest way to eat.

She did this for a year until her mom got better, and she told everyone at the roundtable that the reason she joined our campaign was so that she could help the millions of other children in the country who want and need to help their parents too.

Now Ashley might have made a different choice. Perhaps somebody told her along the way that the source of her mother's problems were blacks who were on welfare and too lazy to work, or Hispanics who were coming into the country illegally. But she didn't. She sought out allies in her fight against injustice.

Anyway, Ashley finishes her story and then goes around the room and asks everyone else why they're supporting the campaign. They all have different stories and reasons. Many bring up a specific issue. And finally they come to this elderly black man who's been sitting there quietly the entire time. And Ashley asks him why he's there. And he does not bring up a specific issue. He does not say health care or the economy. He does not say education or the war. He does not say that he was there because of Barack Obama. He simply says to everyone in the room, "I am here because of Ashley."

"I'm here because of Ashley." By itself, that single moment of recognition between that young white girl and that old black man is not enough. It is not enough to give health care to the sick, or jobs to the jobless, or education to our children.

But it is where we start. It is where our union grows stronger. And as so many generations have come to realize over the course of the two hundred and twenty-one years since a band of patriots signed that document in Philadelphia, that is where the perfection begins.

Election Night Address,
President-Elect Barack Obama, 2008

If there is anyone out there who still doubts that America is a place where all things are possible, who still wonders if the dream of our founders is alive in our time, who still questions the power of our democracy, tonight is your answer.

It's the answer told by lines that stretched around schools and churches in numbers this nation has never seen, by people who waited three hours and four hours, many for the first time in their lives, because they believed that this time must be different, that their voices could be that difference. It's the answer spoken by young and old, rich and poor, Democrat and Republican, black, white, Hispanic, Asian, Native American, gay, straight, disabled and not disabled. Americans who sent a message to the world that we have never been just a collection of individuals or a collection of red states and blue states.

We are, and always will be, the United States of America.

It's the answer that led those who've been told for so long by so many to be cynical and fearful and doubtful about what we can achieve to put their hands on the arc of history and bend it once more toward the hope of a better day.

It's been a long time coming, but tonight, because of what we did on this date in this election at this defining moment change has come to America.

. . . I was never the likeliest candidate for this office. We didn't start with much money or many endorsements. Our campaign was not hatched in the halls of Washington. It began in the backyards of Des Moines and the living rooms of Concord and the front porches of Charleston. It was built by working men and women who dug into what little savings they had to give $5 and $10 and $20 to the cause.

It grew strength from the young people who rejected the myth of their generation's apathy . . . who left their homes and their families for jobs that offered little pay and less sleep.

It drew strength from the not-so-young people who braved the bitter cold and scorching heat to knock on doors of perfect strangers, and from the millions of Americans who volunteered and organized and proved that more than two centuries later a government of the people, by the people, and for the people has not perished from the Earth.

This is your victory.

And I know you didn't do this just to win an election. And I know you didn't do it for me.

You did it because you understand the enormity of the task that lies ahead. For even as we celebrate tonight, we know the challenges that tomorrow will bring are the greatest of our lifetime—two wars, a planet in peril, the worst financial crisis in a century.

Even as we stand here tonight, we know there are brave Americans waking up in the deserts of Iraq and the mountains of Afghanistan to risk their lives for us.

There are mothers and fathers who will lie awake after the children fall asleep and wonder how they'll make the mortgage or pay their doctors' bills or save enough for their child's college education.

There's new energy to harness, new jobs to be created, new schools to build, and threats to meet, alliances to repair.

The road ahead will be long. Our climb will be steep. We may not get there in one year or even in one term. But, America, I have never been more hopeful than I am tonight that we will get there. I promise you, we as a people will get there.

There will be setbacks and false starts. There are many who won't agree with every decision or policy I make as president. And we know the government can't solve every problem.

But I will always be honest with you about the challenges we face. I will listen to you, especially when we disagree. And, above all, I will ask you to join in the work of remaking this nation, the only way it's been done in America for two hundred and twenty-one years—block by block, brick by brick, callused hand by callused hand.

What began twenty-one months ago in the depths of winter cannot end on this autumn night.

This victory alone is not the change we seek. It is only the chance for us to make that change. And that cannot happen if we go back to the way things were.

It can't happen without you, without a new spirit of service, a new spirit of sacrifice.

So let us summon a new spirit of patriotism, of responsibility, where each of us resolves to pitch in and work harder and look after not only ourselves but each other.

Let us remember that, if this financial crisis taught us anything, it's that we cannot have a thriving Wall Street while Main Street suffers.

In this country, we rise or fall as one nation, as one people. Let's resist the temptation to fall back on the same partisanship and pettiness and immaturity that have poisoned our politics for so long.

Let's remember that it was a man from this state who first carried the banner of the Republican Party to the White House, a party founded on the values of self-reliance and individual liberty and national unity.

Those are values that we all share. And while the Democratic Party has won a great victory tonight, we do so with a measure of humility and determination to heal the divides that have held back our progress.

As Lincoln said to a nation far more divided than ours, we are not enemies but friends. "Though passion may have strained, it must not break our bonds of affection."

And to those Americans whose support I have yet to

earn, I may not have won your vote tonight, but I hear your voices. I need your help. And I will be your president too.

And to all those watching tonight from beyond our shores, from parliaments and palaces, to those who are huddled around radios in the forgotten corners of the world, our stories are singular, but our destiny is shared, and a new dawn of American leadership is at hand.

To those—to those who would tear the world down: We will defeat you. To those who seek peace and security: We support you. And to all those who have wondered if America's beacon still burns as bright: Tonight we proved once more that the true strength of our nation comes not from the might of our arms or the scale of our wealth, but from the enduring power of our ideals—democracy, liberty, opportunity and unyielding hope.

That's the true genius of America: that America can change. Our union can be perfected. What we've already achieved gives us hope for what we can and must achieve tomorrow.

This election had many firsts and many stories that will be told for generations. But one that's on my mind tonight's about a woman who cast her ballot in Atlanta. She's a lot like the millions of others who stood in line to make their voice heard in this election except for one thing: Ann Nixon Cooper is one hundred and six years old.

She was born just a generation past slavery; a time when there were no cars on the road or planes in the sky; when someone like her couldn't vote for two reasons—because she was a woman and because of the color of her skin.

And tonight, I think about all that she's seen throughout her century in America—the heartache and the hope; the struggle and the progress; the times we were told that we can't, and the people who pressed on with that American creed: Yes we can.

At a time when women's voices were silenced and their hopes dismissed, she lived to see them stand up and speak out and reach for the ballot. Yes we can.

When there was despair in the dust bowl and depression across the land, she saw a nation conquer fear itself with a New Deal, new jobs, a new sense of common purpose. Yes we can.

When the bombs fell on our harbor and tyranny threatened the world, she was there to witness a generation rise to greatness and a democracy was saved. Yes we can.

She was there for the buses in Montgomery, the hoses in Birmingham, a bridge in Selma, and a preacher from Atlanta who told a people that we shall overcome. Yes we can.

A man touched down on the moon, a wall came down in Berlin, a world was connected by our own science and imagination.

And this year, in this election, she touched her finger to a screen, and cast her vote, because after one hundred and six years in America, through the best of times and the darkest of hours, she knows how America can change. Yes we can.

America, we have come so far. We have seen so much. But there is so much more to do. So tonight, let us ask ourselves—if our children should live to see the next century; if my daughters should be so lucky to live as long as Ann Nixon Cooper, what change will they see? What progress will we have made?

This is our chance to answer that call. This is our moment.

This is our time, to put our people back to work and open doors of opportunity for our kids; to restore prosperity and promote the cause of peace; to reclaim the American dream and reaffirm that fundamental truth, that, out of many, we are one; that while we breathe, we hope. And where we are met with cynicism and doubts and those who tell us that we can't, we will respond with that timeless creed that sums up the spirit of a people: Yes, we can.

Thank you. God bless you. And may God bless the United States of America.

Barack Obama's Inaugural Address, *2009*

My fellow citizens:

I stand here today humbled by the task before us, grateful for the trust you have bestowed, mindful of the sacrifices borne by our ancestors. I thank President Bush for his service to our nation, as well as the generosity and cooperation he has shown throughout this transition.

Forty-four Americans have now taken the presidential oath. The words have been spoken during rising tides of prosperity and the still waters of peace. Yet, every so often, the oath is taken amidst gathering clouds and raging storms. At these moments, America has carried on not simply because of the skill or vision of those in high office, but because We the People have remained faithful to the ideals of our forebears, and true to our founding documents.

So it has been. So it must be with this generation of Americans.

That we are in the midst of crisis is now well understood. Our nation is at war, against a far-reaching network of violence and hatred. Our economy is badly weakened, a consequence of greed and irresponsibility on the part of some, but also our collective failure to make hard choices and prepare the nation for a new age. Homes have been lost; jobs shed; businesses shuttered. Our health care is too costly; our schools fail too many; and each day brings further evidence that the ways we use energy strengthen our adversaries and threaten our planet.

These are the indicators of crisis, subject to data and statistics. Less measurable but no less profound is a sapping of confidence across our land—a nagging fear that America's decline is inevitable, and that the next generation must lower its sights.

Today I say to you that the challenges we face are real. They are serious and they are many. They will not be met easily or in a short span of time. But know this, America—they will be met.

On this day, we gather because we have chosen hope over fear, unity of purpose over conflict and discord.

On this day, we come to proclaim an end to the petty grievances and false promises, the recriminations and worn-out dogmas, that for far too long have strangled our politics.

We remain a young nation, but in the words of Scripture, the time has come to set aside childish things. The time has come to reaffirm our enduring spirit; to choose our better history; to carry forward that precious gift, that noble idea, passed on from generation to generation: the God-given promise that all are equal, all are free, and all deserve a chance to pursue their full measure of happiness.

In reaffirming the greatness of our nation, we understand that greatness is never a given. It must be earned. Our journey has never been one of shortcuts or settling for less. It has not been the path for the fainthearted—for those who prefer leisure over work, or seek only the pleasures of riches and fame. Rather, it has been the risk takers, the doers, the makers of things—some celebrated but more often men and women obscure in their labor, who have carried us up the long, rugged path towards prosperity and freedom.

For us, they packed up their few worldly possessions and traveled across oceans in search of a new life.

For us, they toiled in sweatshops and settled the West; endured the lash of the whip and plowed the hard earth.

For us, they fought and died, in places like Concord and Gettysburg; Normandy and Khe Sanh.

Time and again these men and women struggled and sacrificed and worked till their hands were raw so that we might live a better life. They saw America as bigger than the sum of our individual ambitions; greater than all the differences of birth or wealth or faction.

This is the journey we continue today. We remain the most prosperous, powerful nation on Earth. Our workers are no less productive than when this crisis began. Our minds are no less inventive, our goods and services no less needed than they were last week or last month or last year. Our capacity remains undiminished. But our time of standing pat, of protecting narrow interests and putting off unpleasant decisions—that time has surely passed. Starting today, we must pick ourselves up, dust ourselves off, and begin again the work of remaking America.

For everywhere we look, there is work to be done. The state of the economy calls for action, bold and swift, and we will act—not only to create new jobs, but to lay a new foundation for growth. We will build the roads and bridges, the electric grids and digital lines that feed our commerce and bind us together. We will restore science to its rightful place, and wield technology's wonders to raise health care's quality and lower its cost. We will harness the sun and the winds and the soil to fuel our cars and run our factories. And we will transform our schools and colleges and universities to meet the demands of a new age. All this we can do. And all this we will do.

Now, there are some who question the scale of our ambitions—who suggest that our system cannot tolerate too many big plans. Their memories are short. For they have forgotten what this country has already done; what free men and women can achieve when imagination is joined to common purpose, and necessity to courage.

What the cynics fail to understand is that the ground has shifted beneath them—that the stale political arguments that have consumed us for so long no longer apply. The question we ask today is not whether our government is too big or too small, but whether it works—whether it helps families find jobs at a decent wage, care they can afford, a retirement that is dignified. Where the answer is yes, we intend to move forward. Where the answer is no, programs will end. And those of us who manage the public's dollars will be held to account—to spend wisely, reform bad habits, and do our business in the light of day—because only then can we restore the vital trust between a people and their government.

Nor is the question before us whether the market is a force for good or ill. Its power to generate wealth and expand freedom is unmatched, but this crisis has reminded us that without a watchful eye, the market can spin out of control—and that a nation cannot prosper long when it favors only the prosperous. The success of our economy has always depended not just on the size of our Gross Domestic Product, but on the reach of our prosperity; on our ability to extend opportunity to every willing heart—not out of charity, but because it is the surest route to our common good.

As for our common defense, we reject as false the choice between our safety and our ideals. Our Founding Fathers, faced with perils we can scarcely imagine, drafted a charter to assure the rule of law and the rights of man, a charter expanded by the blood of generations. Those ideals still light the world, and we will not give them up for expedience's sake. And so to all other peoples and governments who are watching today, from the grandest capitals to the small village where my father was born: know that America is a friend of each nation and every man, woman, and child who seeks a future of peace and dignity, and that we are ready to lead once more.

Recall that earlier generations faced down fascism and communism not just with missiles and tanks, but with sturdy alliances and enduring convictions. They understood that our power alone cannot protect us, nor does it entitle us to do as we please. Instead, they knew that our power grows through its prudent use; our security emanates from the justness of our cause, the force of our example, the tempering qualities of humility and restraint.

We are the keepers of this legacy. Guided by these principles once more, we can meet those new threats that demand even greater effort—even greater cooperation and understanding between nations. We will begin to responsibly leave Iraq to its people, and forge a hard-earned peace in Afghanistan. With old friends and former foes, we will work tirelessly to lessen the nuclear threat, and roll back the specter of a warming planet. We will not apologize for our way of life, nor will we waver in its defense, and for those who seek to advance their aims by inducing terror and slaughtering innocents, we say to you now that our spirit is stronger and cannot be broken; you cannot outlast us, and we will defeat you.

For we know that our patchwork heritage is a strength, not a weakness. We are a nation of Christians and Muslims, Jews and Hindus—and nonbelievers. We are shaped by every language and culture, drawn from every end of this Earth; and because we have tasted the bitter swill of civil war and segregation, and emerged from that dark chapter stronger and more united, we cannot help but believe that the old hatreds shall someday pass; that the lines of tribe shall soon dissolve; that as the world grows smaller, our common humanity shall reveal itself; and that America must play its role in ushering in a new era of peace.

To the Muslim world, we seek a new way forward, based on mutual interest and mutual respect. To those leaders around the globe who seek to sow conflict, or blame their society's ills on the West—know that your people will judge you on what you can build, not what you destroy. To those who cling to power through corruption and deceit and the silencing of dissent, know that you are on the wrong side of history; but that we will extend a hand if you are willing to unclench your fist.

To the people of poor nations, we pledge to work alongside you to make your farms flourish and let clean waters flow; to nourish starved bodies and feed hungry minds. And to those nations like ours that enjoy relative plenty, we say we can no longer afford indifference to suffering outside our borders; nor can we consume the world's resources without regard to effect. For the world has changed, and we must change with it.

As we consider the road that unfolds before us, we remember with humble gratitude those brave Americans who, at this very hour, patrol far-off deserts and distant mountains. They have something to tell us today, just as the fallen heroes who lie in Arlington whisper through the ages. We honor them not only because they are guardians of our liberty, but because they embody the spirit of service; a willingness to find meaning in something greater than themselves. And yet, at this moment—a moment that will define a generation—it is precisely this spirit that must inhabit us all.

For as much as government can do and must do, it is ultimately the faith and determination of the American people upon which this nation relies. It is the kindness to take in a stranger when the levees break, the selflessness of workers who would rather cut their hours than see a friend lose their job which sees us through our darkest hours. It is the firefighter's courage to storm a stairway filled with smoke, but also a parent's willingness to nurture a child, that finally decides our fate.

Our challenges may be new. The instruments with

which we meet them may be new. But those values upon which our success depends—hard work and honesty, courage and fair play, tolerance and curiosity, loyalty and patriotism—these things are old. These things are true. They have been the quiet force of progress throughout our history. What is demanded then is a return to these truths. What is required of us now is a new era of responsibility—a recognition, on the part of every American, that we have duties to ourselves, our nation, and the world, duties that we do not grudgingly accept but rather seize gladly, firm in the knowledge that there is nothing so satisfying to the spirit, so defining of our character, than giving our all to a difficult task.

This is the price and the promise of citizenship.

This is the source of our confidence—the knowledge that God calls on us to shape an uncertain destiny.

This is the meaning of our liberty and our creed—why men and women and children of every race and every faith can join in celebration across this magnificent mall, and why a man whose father less than sixty years ago might not have been served at a local restaurant can now stand before you to take a most sacred oath.

So let us mark this day with remembrance, of who we are and how far we have traveled. In the year of America's birth, in the coldest of months, a small band of patriots huddled by dying campfires on the shores of an icy river. The capital was abandoned. The enemy was advancing. The snow was stained with blood. At a moment when the outcome of our revolution was most in doubt, the father of our nation ordered these words be read to the people:

"Let it be told to the future world . . . that in the depth of winter, when nothing but hope and virtue could survive . . . that the city and the country, alarmed at one common danger, came forth to meet [it]."

America, in the face of our common dangers, in this winter of our hardship, let us remember these timeless words. With hope and virtue, let us brave once more the icy currents, and endure what storms may come. Let it be said by our children's children that when we were tested we refused to let this journey end, that we did not turn back nor did we falter; and with eyes fixed on the horizon and God's grace upon us, we carried forth that great gift of freedom and delivered it safely to future generations.

Thank you. God bless you.

And God bless the United States of America.